Integrating Language Arts and Social Studies for Intermediate and Middle School Students

Integrating Language Arts and Social Studies for Intermediate and Middle School Students

Richard D. Kellough
California State University, Sacramento

John Jarolimek and Walter C. Parker
Peter H. Martorella
Gail E. Tompkins and Kenneth Hoskisson

Merrill,
an imprint of Prentice Hall

Englewood Cliffs, New Jersey   Columbus, Ohio

Library of Congress Cataloging-in-Publication Data

Integrating language arts and social studies for intermediate and
   middle school students / Richard D. Kellough . . . [et al.].
      p.   cm.
    Includes bibliographical references and index.
    ISBN 0-02-362585-6
      1. Language arts (Secondary)—United States.   2. Social sciences—
—Study and teaching (Secondary)—United States.
3. Interdisciplinary approach in education—United States.
4. Middle schools—United States.   5. Junior high schools—United
States.   I. Kellough, Richard D. (Richard Dean)
LB1631.I64   1995
373.19—dc20

                                                    95–13731

Cover art: © Manuel Morales/The Image Bank
Cover Designer: Proof Positive/Farrowlyne Associates
Editor: Bradley J. Potthoff
Photo Editor: Anne Vega
Production Manager: Deidra M. Schwartz
Project management and text design provided by Elm Street Publishing Services, Inc.

This book was set in Times Roman by Carlisle Communications, Ltd. and was printed and bound by
The Banta Company. The cover was printed by The Banta Company.

© 1996 by Prentice-Hall, Inc.
A Simon & Schuster Company
Englewood Cliffs, New Jersey 07632

Photo credits: Scott Cunningham, Merrill/Prentice Hall and Todd Yarrington, Merrill/Prentice Hall.

Printed in the United States of America.

10 9 8 7 6 5 4 3 2 1

ISBN: 0-02-362585-6

Prentice-Hall International (UK) Limited, *London*
Prentice-Hall of Australia Pty. Limited, *Sydney*
Prentice-Hall of Canada, Inc., *Toronto*
Prentice-Hall Hispanoamericana, S. A., *Mexico*
Prentice-Hall of India Private Limited, *New Delhi*
Prentice-Hall of Japan, Inc., *Toyko*
Simon & Schuster Asia Pte. Ltd., *Singapore*
Editora Prentice-Hall do Brasil, Ltda., *Rio de Janeiro*

PREFACE

To many educators, it has become quite clear that to be most effective in teaching the diversity of children in today's classrooms, they must integrate much of the learning in each discipline with the whole curriculum and make it meaningful to the lives of the children, rather than simply teach it as unrelated disciplines at the same time each day.

It is also quite clear that if we define learning as being only the accumulation of bits and pieces of information, then we already know how to teach it. The accumulation of pieces of information is at the lowest end of a wide spectrum of types of learning, however. For higher levels of thinking and for learning that is most meaningful and longest lasting, research supports the use of an integrated curriculum and instructional techniques that involve the children in social, interactive learning.

This book will facilitate your understanding of how to teach language arts and social studies in the most effective way to children in intermediate and middle school grades. Beginning with a review of important historical and recent work of cognitive psychologists, work that has led to a modern view of teaching for meaningful understanding (Chapter 1), we discuss planning and providing an effective and supportive learning environment (Chapter 2), planning and implementing curriculum and lessons appropriate to children of middle-level grades (Chapters 3 and 4), assessment of student learning (Chapter 5), and the selection and use of instructional aids and resources (Chapter 6).

As a classroom teacher, your instructional task is twofold: (1) to plan for and provide developmentally appropriate hands-on experiences, with appropriate materials and the supportive environment necessary for children's meaningful exploration and discovery; and (2) to facilitate the most meaningful and longest lasting learning possible once the child's mind has been activated by the hands-on experience. It is our hope that this book will help you learn how better to complete those tasks.

While the six chapters of Part I provide fundamentals important to all teachers of children in grades 4–9, Parts II through IV are specific to curriculum and instruction in language arts and social studies. Part II presents an integrated or "whole-language" approach to language arts based on the cognitive, psycholinguistic, and sociolinguistic theories about how children learn language, first introduced in Chapter 1. In Chapter 7, the first chapter of Part II, an instructional strategy based on these theories is developed and applied for each language mode—listening, talking, reading, and writing. Building upon the earlier presentation of Chapter 2, the focus in Chapter 8 is on how the teacher can provide a language-rich classroom to support children's learning. The emphasis of Chapter 9 is on the extension of language arts across the curriculum. Then, in the last chapter of Part II, Chapter 10, we present a collection of useful action plans and activities for teaching language arts in the intermediate and middle school grades.

Each of the first three chapters of Part III focuses on an aspect of the social studies curriculum. Continuing with the learning theory introduced in Chapter 1, Chapters 11 and 12 introduce the topics of what *social studies* is, how children learn social studies subject matter, and exactly what subject matter is encompassed by social studies. Chapter 13 furthers your understanding of scope and sequence patterns in the social studies curriculum. The authors of Chapters 14 and 15 focus on how to teach the particular social studies content and skills expected to be learned by intermediate and middle school students. The last two chapters of Part III, Chapters 16 and 17, present a collection of specific activities and units for integrating social studies into the intermediate and middle school curriculum.

Part IV presents a collection of classroom-tested instructional activities that encourage interaction and cooperation among students, that depend upon collaborative learning between students and teachers, and that, in interesting ways, integrate the disciplines of language arts and social studies and, in some instances, other disciplines as well.

The term *integrated curriculum* (or any of its synonyms) refers to both a way of teaching and a way of planning and organizing the instructional program so the discrete disciplines of subject matter are related to one another in a design that matches the developmental needs of the learners and that helps to connect their learning in ways that are meaningful to their current and past experiences. It is the antithesis of traditional, disparate, subject matter–oriented teaching and curriculum designations.

Today's interest in the development and implementation of integrated curriculum and instruction derives from (1) the successful curriculum integration enjoyed by exemplary middle-level schools, (2) the literature-based movement in reading and language arts, and (3) recent research in cognitive science and neuroscience about how children learn.

As is true for traditional curriculum and instruction, an integrated curriculum approach is not without critics, nor is it the best approach for every school, the best basis for all learning for every child, nor necessarily the manner by which every teacher should or must always plan and teach. Efforts to connect children's learning with their experiences fall at various places on a spectrum or continuum of sophistication and complexity.

The activities presented in this book, especially those in Chapter 18 and in the interdisciplinary thematic unit at the end of this book, are designed to encourage interaction and cooperation among students, to encourage collaborative learning between students and their teachers, and to integrate in interesting and meaningful ways the disciplines of language arts and social studies, and sometimes other disciplines as well. Where the use of each falls on the spectrum of integrated learning is up to you and your own special set of circumstances.

Chapters begin with advance organizers and statements of chapter intent and end with questions and activities for individual and group study and discussion.

We, its editors, authors, and other contributors, hope that you find this book useful. We value your feedback about it.

Richard D. Kellough

BRIEF CONTENTS

CONTENTS

PART II
Methods and Activities for Language Arts   172

Integrating Language Arts and Social Studies for Intermediate and Middle School Students

Integrating Student Learning: Rationale and Methods

No matter how well prepared your instructional plans, those plans will likely go untaught or only poorly taught if presented to children in a classroom that is nonsupportive and poorly managed.
—*Richard D. Kellough*

Teaching children and preparing them for the 21st century requires a shift in paradigm from what was previously believed about good instruction.
—*Randall J. Souviney*

In a well-managed classroom students know what to do, have the materials necessary to do it well, and stay on task while doing it; the classroom atmosphere is supportive, the assignments and procedures for doing those assignments are clear, the materials of instruction current, interesting, and readily available, and the classroom proceedings are businesslike.
—*Richard D. Kellough*

Unless you believe that your students can learn, they will not. Unless you believe that you can teach them, you will not. Unless your students believe that they can learn and until they want to learn, they will not.
—*Richard D. Kellough*

We have two simple, yet inclusive school rules that are posted in every classroom, and they are enforced. The rules are: respect people, respect property.
—*Barry S. Raebeck*

Children need models more than they need critics.
—*Joseph Joubert*

We are establishing a "success breeds success" scenario for all students. We gave one F out of a total of 2,600 grades in the first marking period this past year.
—*Barry S. Raebeck*

Novelty is no substitute for quality.
—*Anonymous*

In recent years, to many teachers it has become quite clear that to be most effective in teaching the diversity of children in today's classrooms, much of the learning in each discipline must be integrated with the whole curriculum and made meaningful to the lives of the children, rather than simply taught as unrelated disciplines at the same time each day.

It is also quite clear that if learning is defined as being only the accumulation of bits and pieces of information, then we already know how to teach. The accumulation of pieces of information is at the lowest end of a spectrum of types of learning, however. For higher levels of thinking and for learning that is most meaningful, recent research supports the use of an integrated curriculum and instructional techniques that involve the learners in social, interactive learning, such as cooperative learning, peer tutoring, and cross-age teaching.

THE SPECTRUM OF *INTEGRATED CURRICULUM*

When learning about *integrated curriculum,* it is easy to be confused by the plethora of terms that are used, such as *thematic instruction, multidisciplinary teaching, integrated studies, interdisciplinary curriculum, interdisciplinary thematic instruction,* and *integrated curriculum.* In essence, today, all of these terms mean the same thing. Further, because it is not always easy to tell where curriculum leaves off and instruction begins, let's assume for now that there is no difference between *curriculum* and *instruction.* We shall use the two terms interchangeably in this text.

Definition of *Integrated Curriculum*

The term *integrated curriculum* (or any of its synonyms) refers to both a way of teaching and a way of planning and organizing the instructional program so the discrete disciplines of subject matter are related to one another in a design that matches the developmental needs of the learners and that helps to connect their learning in ways that are meaningful to their current and past experiences. It is the antithesis of traditional, disparate, subject matter–oriented teaching and curriculum designations.

The concept of integrated curriculum is not new. It has surfaced and gone in and out of fashion throughout most of the history of education in this country. Efforts to integrate student learning have had varying labels, and that accounts for the plethora of terms.

Without reviewing that history in depth, the most recent popularity of the concept stems from the following:

1. Some of the National Science Foundation–supported, discovery-oriented, student-centered projects of the late 1950s, such as *Elementary School Science (ESS),* an integrated science program for grades K–6; *Man: A Course of Study (MACOS),* a hands-on, anthropology-based program for fifth graders; *Interdisciplinary Approaches to Chemistry (IAS),* for high school chemistry; and *Environmental Studies* (name later changed to *ESSENCE*), an interdisciplinary program for use at all grades, K–12, regardless of subject matter orientation.
2. The "middle school movement," which began in the 1960s.
3. The whole-language movement in language arts, which had its beginning in the 1980s.

The authors of *Teaching and Learning in the Middle Level School* state, "Historically, there has been a need to develop an integrated curriculum that would consider the unique personal needs of middle level learners as well as the serious challenges found in their surrounding world" (Allen et al., 1993, p. 149). The exemplary middle-level schools continue to work at developing a curriculum that integrates personal, social, and academic dimensions into a developmentally appropriate curriculum for young adolescents. "To integrate these dimensions into a balanced curriculum framework requires interdisciplinary topics, themes, or units from the various subject matters" (p. 202).

Today's renewed interest in the development and implementation of integrated curriculum and instruction has arisen from at least three sources: (1) the successful curriculum integration enjoyed by exemplary middle-level schools (discussed in Chapter 3) and by elementary and high schools, too, (2) the literature-based movement in reading and language arts, and (3) recent cognitive science and neuroscience research about how children learn (discussed in Chapter 1).

| LEAST INTEGRATED | | | | MOST INTEGRATED |
LEVEL 1	LEVEL 2	LEVEL 3	LEVEL 4	LEVEL 5
Subject-specific topic outline	Subject-specific thematic	Multidisciplinary thematic	Interdisciplinary thematic	Integrated thematic
No student collaboration in planning	Minimal student input	Some student input	Considerable student input in selecting themes and in planning	Maximum student and teacher collaboration
Teacher solo	Solo or teams	Solo or teams	Solo or teams	Solo or teams
Student input into decision making low		Student input into decision making high		Student input into decision making very high

As is true for traditional curriculum and instruction, an integrated curriculum approach is not without critics. As stated by Jarolimek and Foster, "Parents and teachers who find conventional schools too highly structured, too regimented, and too adult-dominated find the child-centered activities of the integrated curriculum mode attractive [but] with its apparent lack of organization, its informality, and the permissiveness allowed [and] at a time when the nation seems to be calling for more fundamental approaches to education [and because school budgets are tighter], the integrated curriculum mode faces an uncertain future" (1993, p. 149).

An integrated curriculum approach may not necessarily be the best approach for every school, nor the best basis for all learning for every child, nor necessarily the manner by which every teacher should or must always plan and teach.

Levels of Curriculum Integration

Efforts to connect children's learning with their experiences fall at various places on a spectrum or continuum, as illustrated in the accompanying table, from the least integrated instruction (level 1) to the most integrated (level 5).

I do not intend for the table to be interpreted as going from "worst case scenario" (far left) to "best case scenario" (far right), although some experts may interpret it in exactly that way. It is meant solely to show how efforts to integrate fall on a continuum of sophistication and complexity. As a generalization, for intermediate and middle school education, and for reasons that should become evident as you proceed through the chapters of this book, my personal preference is for a scenario somewhere at or between levels 3 and 4. Let me now describe each level of the continuum.

Level 1 is the traditional organization of curriculum and classroom instruction, in which teachers plan and arrange the subject-specific scope and sequence using a topic outline format. Any attempts to help students connect their learning and their experiences are up to individual classroom teachers. A fourth-grade student in a school and classroom that have subject-specific instruction at varying times of the day (reading and language arts at 8:00, mathematics at 9:00, social studies at 10:30, and so on) is likely learning in a level 1 instructional environment, especially when what is being learned in one subject has little or no connection with the content in another. The same is true of the junior high school student who moves during the school day from classroom to classroom, teacher to teacher, subject to subject, and from one topic to another. A topic in science, for example, might be "earthquakes." A related topic in social studies might be "the social consequences of natural disasters." These two topics may or may not be studied by a student at the same time.

If the same students are learning English/language arts, or social studies/history, or mathematics, or science using a thematic approach rather than a topic outline, then they are learning at **level 2** integration. At this level, themes in one discipline are not necessarily planned to correspond with themes in another or to be taught simultaneously. The difference between a topic and a theme is not always clear. But, for example, whereas "earthquakes" and "social consequences of natural disasters" are topics, "natural disasters" could be the theme or umbrella under which these two topics could fall. At this level, the students may have some input into the decision making involved in planning themes and content.

When the same students are learning two or more of their core subjects (English/language arts, social studies/history, mathematics, and science) around a common theme, such as "natural disasters," from one or more teachers, they are learning at **level 3** integration. At this level, teachers agree on a common theme, then they *separately* deal with that theme in their individual subject areas, usually at the same time during the school year. So what the student is learning from a teacher in one class is related to what the student is concurrently learning in another or several others. Students may have some input into the decision making involved in selecting and planning themes and content. This is a commonly used approach and is the minimum level of expected participation for which this book is designed.

When teachers and students collaborate on a common theme and its content, and when discipline boundaries begin to disappear as teachers teach about this common theme, either solo (as in a self-contained fourth-grade classroom) or as an interdisciplinary teaching team (several teachers working with a common group of students, such as in a school-within-a-school configuration), that is **level 4** integration. This is the level of integration at which many exemplary middle schools function (see Chapter 3).

When teachers and their students have collaborated on a common theme and its content and discipline boundaries are truly blurred during instruction, and teachers of several grade levels (e.g., grades 6, 7, and 8) and of various core and exploratory subjects teach toward student understanding of aspects of the common theme, then this is **level 5,** an integrated thematic approach. For detailed accounts of teaching at this level of integration, see Chris Stevenson and Judy F. Carr (Eds.), *Integrated Studies in the Middle Grades* (New York: Teachers College Press, 1993).

Assumptions in an Integrated Curriculum

According to Jarolimek and Foster (1993), theoretically and philosophically, the integrated curriculum mode is tied most closely to the inquiry mode. When using this mode, it is assumed that children have certain natural drives, urges, and interests and that they bring these to school with them. Rather than teaching a predetermined curriculum, the teacher explores the backgrounds and interests of the children, and out of this interaction, significant activities emerge. The activities selected should capitalize on these natural interests and inclinations. A rigid time schedule and the compartmentalizing of curriculum components are rejected because they run counter to the natural exploration of children. A rich and stimulating learning environment is essential so that children may have many opportunities to explore their interests and to learn from direct experience. The teacher serves more as a guide, adviser, and expeditor than as a director of learning. Learning takes place best in settings that encourage social interaction and cooperation—children working with each other. It provides an ideal setting for cooperative learning projects. Cross-age grouping is encouraged because children learn from each other; thus, older children can help younger ones to learn.

Major Purposes

The major purpose of the integrated curriculum mode is to teach children to become self-reliant, independent problem solvers, consistent with what is known about the nature of childhood. Thus, it involves children directly and purposefully in learning. Another of its purposes is to help the children to understand and appreciate the extent to which school learning is interrelated rather than separated into a variety of discrete subjects and skills, as is the case in the traditional curriculum. It is designed to create a high level of interest in learning that will become personalized and individualized. It seeks to construct situations in which children can learn what they want and need to know rather than what the curriculum specifies. As in inquiry, the purpose of the integrated curriculum mode is to stress the process of learning as opposed to specific subject matter and skills. Moreover, it is designed to capitalize on the social values of learning. Children are encouraged to work with others in cooperative learning endeavors.

Role of the Teacher

In the integrated curriculum mode, the teacher's role can be described as setting the stage and providing the environment within which the children can engage in learning activities in terms of their own interests, needs, capabilities, personalities, and motivations. This requires a warm and stress-free atmosphere. The teacher needs to structure and guide the explorations of the children but should do so without stifling their initiative. The teacher must be skillful and resourceful in being able to capitalize on the interests of the children and to convert such leads into appropriate and workable learning activities. Also, the teacher must be imaginative in seeing the possibilities for other school-related learnings in the activities that interest the children. The teacher must provide a carefully selected assortment of learning materials for the children to handle, to use for construction, to manipulate, to experiment with, to explore, and to puzzle over. The teacher should guide and provide. The teacher's role should be that of a catalyst to stimulate children's learning. In this environment, the teacher should also be a learner along with the children.

Role of the Learner

Here, more than in any of the other modes, we find the children centrally involved in the learning process. It is expected that they will initiate activities and that they will assume responsibility for their own learning. The exercise of *initiative* and *responsibility* is basic to the role of the learner in the integrated curriculum mode. Emphasis is on cooperation; therefore, children are expected to work harmoniously with others on cooperative learning activities and projects. They are not expected to be seated at their desks, completing assignments that have been prepared by the teacher. They will, instead, be working on a project or activity in which they are interested and will be searching for answers to questions that they themselves have raised. This necessitates a mind-set of curiosity and wonderment about the environment. Considerable intellectual and physical freedom prevails. The children may move about, ask any questions they choose, and consult whatever data sources would seem to be appropriate.

Use of Instructional Resources

The integrated curriculum mode necessitates a wide variety of assorted learning materials. These should include the conventional ones (books, films, pictures, maps, and so on) and others, such as electric motors, branding irons, a computer, science equipment, carpenters' tools, historical artifacts, construction kits, art supplies, musical instruments, and audio-visual material. Indeed, anything at all that allows children to construct, explore, and manipulate might be a legitimate learning resource. A rich and responsive environment is essential to the success of the integrated curriculum mode. Because much of the learning is self-directed, these resources will be used to satisfy learner needs rather than to respond to requirements established by the teacher.

Method of Evaluation

Evaluation of learning in the integrated curriculum mode is more difficult than in the other modes because it may bear little similarity to traditional evaluative procedures. As in all cases, evaluation must be conducted in accordance with the major purposes of the mode. Therefore, in the integrated curriculum mode, the teacher would look for such things as the extent to which the children are involving themselves in their own learning; how well they are sharing, cooperating, and assuming responsibility; how well they are able to attack and puzzle through problems as they confront them; how well they are able to use the tools of learning (i.e., reading, writing, spelling, and speaking) in solving problems and meeting their needs; the extent to which their work products show evidence of improvement; and the extent to which they are overcoming their learning deficiencies. Because these programs are highly individualized, emphasis is placed on progress in terms of prior status rather than on comparing achievement with that of classmates or with nationally derived norms.

In this first part of the book, you will review important historical and recent work of cognitive psychologists, work that has led to a modern view of teaching for meaningful understanding, and a presentation of the relevant instructional methodology. As a classroom teacher, your instructional task is twofold: (1) to plan for and provide developmentally appropriate hands-on experiences, with useful materials and the supportive environment necessary for children's meaningful exploration and discovery; and (2) to know how to facilitate the most meaningful and longest lasting learning possible once the child's mind has been activated by the hands-on experience. This book is designed to help you complete that task. Although they use examples mostly from language arts and social studies, the six chapters of Part I provide fundamentals that are important to all teachers of children in grades 4–9. ■

REFERENCES

Allen, H. A., et al. (1993). *Teaching and learning in the middle level school.* New York: Macmillan.

Jarolimek, J., & Foster, C. D., Sr. (1993). *Teaching and learning in the elementary school* (5th ed.). New York: Macmillan.

CHAPTER 1

Learning and the Intellectual Development of Children

An understanding of children—how they develop intellectually, how they think, what they think about, and how they learn and process information—is essential to being an effective classroom teacher. Much of what is known about how children learn and process information derives from cognitive research of recent years. During the next few years, many more advances in our knowledge about neurological processing are expected. Meanwhile, you must understand the complexity and ramifications of the quest.

This chapter focuses your attention on how children learn and process information. Specifically, this chapter will help you understand the following:

1. What is meant by *meaningful learning*.
2. The characteristics and developmental needs of young adolescents, children in grades 4–9.
3. How learning is constructed.
4. The contributions of learning theorists Jean Piaget, Lev Vygotsky, Robert Gagné, Jerome Bruner, and David Ausubel.
5. The importance of learning as a cyclic process.
6. The importance of using multilevel instruction.
7. The rate of cognitive development and factors that affect it.
8. The importance of learning as a cooperative and collaborative effort.
9. How conceptual understanding develops.
10. The process and benefits of learning by discovery.
11. The value of concept mapping as a cognitive tool.
12. The significance of decision making and the thought-process phases of instruction.
13. The value and variety of styles in teaching and learning.
14. The significance of the concept of learning modalities.

A. MEANINGFUL LEARNING: THE CONSTRUCTION OF UNDERSTANDING

If we define learning as only the accumulation of bits and pieces of information, then we already know how to teach. However, the accumulation of pieces of information is at the lowest end of a spectrum of types of learning. We are still learning about learning and teaching for higher forms of learning, that is, for meaningful understanding and the reflective use of that understanding. Meanwhile, for higher levels of thinking and for learning that is most meaningful, recent research supports the use of instructional strategies that help students to make connections to what is being learned, strategies such as the whole-language approach to reading and interdisciplinary thematic teaching, with a curriculum that is integrated and connected to children's life experiences.

Let's begin with a review of important historical and recent work of cognitive psychologists, work that has led to a modern view of teaching for meaningful understanding. In opposition to the traditional view that sees teaching as covering the prescribed material, this modern view stresses the importance of learning being a personal process, by which each learner builds on the personal knowledge and experiences that he or she brings to the learning experience. *Meaningful learning is learning that results when the learner makes connections between a new experience and prior knowledge and experiences that were stored in long-term memory.* For meaningful learning to occur, the concept of correct instruction, then, is to begin where the children are, with what they have experienced and know, or think they know, and correct their misconceptions while building upon and connecting their understandings and experiences.

Like the construction of a skyscraper, meaningful learning is a gradual and sometimes painstakingly slow process. As emphasized by Watson and Konicek (1990, p. 685), when compared with traditional instruction, teaching in this constructivist mode is slower, involving more discussion, debate, and re-creation of ideas. Rather than following clearly defined and previously established steps, the curriculum evolves, it depends heavily on materials, and to a great extent it is determined by the children's interests and questions. Less content is covered, fewer facts are memorized and tested for, and progress is sometimes very slow.

The methodology uses what is referred to as a *hands-on doing* (the learner is learning by doing) and *minds-on learning* (the learner is thinking about what she or he is learning and doing) approach to constructing, and often reconstructing, the child's perceptions. Hands-on learning engages the learner's mind, causing questioning. Hands-on and minds-on learning encourages students to question and then to devise ways of investigating tentative but temporarily satisfactory answers to their questions. As a classroom teacher, your instructional task, then, is essentially twofold: (1) to plan for and provide the hands-on experiences, providing the materials and the supportive environment necessary for children's meaningful exploration and discovery; and (2) to know how to facilitate the most meaningful and longest lasting learning possible once the child's mind has been activated by the hands-on experience.

B. YOUNG ADOLESCENTS

Young adolescents have been given several epithets, including "transescent," "preadolescent," "preteen," "prepubescent," "in-betweenager," and "tweenager." These are youngsters as young as 10 (those enrolled in the fifth grade), or as old as 14 (the students you will find in an eighth-grade class). Although the cognomen is, perhaps, inconsequential, some understanding of the various developmental stages associated with such a group of children is essential to tailoring an educational program and instruction to address their needs.

To be most effective at facilitating meaningful and long-lasting learning in young adolescents, you must be aware of and use what is known about children of that age. Knowing and understanding their characteristics will do much to make teaching and learning an enjoyable and rewarding experience for both you and your students. Some characteristics are common to all young adolescents regardless of their individual genetic or cultural differences. A condensation of these facts about the intellectual, physical, psychological, social, and moral and ethical development of middle school students is presented later in this section. First, let's review the research about youngsters in this fascinating phase of their development.

Transescence

Donald Eichhorn (1966) called this developmental phase *transescence* and defined it summarily as follows:

[Transescence is] the stage of development which begins before the onset of puberty and extends through the early stages of adolescence. Since puberty does not occur for all precisely at the same chronological age in human development, the transescent designation is based on the many physical, social, emotional, and intellectual changes in body chemistry that appear before the time which the body gains a practical degree of stabilization over these complex pubescent changes. (p. 3)

In 1962, Tanner reported that people are biologically maturing at an accelerated rate. For example, he notes that the "age of menarche has been getting earlier by some four months per decade in Western Europe over the period of 1830–1960" (p. 43). Eichhorn believes that students should be grouped according to developmental stages rather than the traditional chronological method. Robert J. Havighurst's developmental tasks suggest that transescence encompasses a broader range of skills and abilities than those experienced at any other maturational period before or after. Havighurst (1972) separates those tasks clearly associated with what he labels "middle childhood" from those associated with what he labels "adolescence"; however, he makes no clear distinction for the developmental tasks between middle childhood and adolescence.

Although child development studies confirm that the time near age 10 through age 14 fairly well defines the transescent in chronological terms, the issue of what these children can achieve academically is less clear. The physical and biological changes occurring in transescence may be even less a factor than their lack of sophistication in adjusting to the mental changes affecting their cognitive and affective development.

Theoretically, according to Piaget's intellectual characteristics at different stages of cognitive development, youngsters in their middle teens are developing from concrete thinkers (thinking that relies on concrete objects) to formal operational thinkers (thinking that incorporates more deductions and abstractions). Epstein (1980) argues that transescent youth have not yet reached a high enough level of "formal operational reasoning" to benefit from two or three years of curriculum that require children to perform at this level. Curricula requiring formal operational reasoning would be ineffective because of the young adolescent's inability to adjust. On the other hand, it can be argued that middle schoolers are otherwise too often faced with repetition and drill and become bored and disinterested in school (Flanders, 1987; Muther, 1987).

What do diverse developmental stages suggest about middle-level schooling, and how does diverse development relate to academic performance? First, the differences may be more a matter of degree than of kind. That is, young adolescents undergo and face the same physiological, psychological, social, and emotional development challenges common to all humans; however, these encounters are greatly magnified during the transescent years. The changes are so magnified and so diverse that giant gaps emerge between expected maturation and the child's actual ability to cope. Second, academic success may be more directly related to the affective domain (the learning domain that involves attitudes, beliefs, values, and interests) than conventional science has yet been able to show fully. Mager (1968) and Rosenshine (1980), for example, provide data that show that student attitude is directly related to learning, and that school climates directly affect student attitudes. A given environment may not directly correlate with either higher or lower achievement, but it will directly correlate with attitude. Likewise, peer acceptance has been shown to be related to academic achievement (Johnson et al., 1982). Research on learning styles and classroom climates most often concentrates on within-class groupings, not on grade-spanning organizational structures (Dunn, Beaudry, & Klavas, 1989).

From experience and research, experts have come to accept certain precepts about young adolescents. These are characteristics of young adolescents regardless of their individual genetic or cultural differences.

Characteristics of Young Adolescents

Young adolescents are egocentric. Most young people are egocentric to some degree. To egocentric youth, things are important insofar as they relate to themselves. In young children, this egocentricity is quite natural, because children find themselves in a strange yet wonderful world, filled with phenomena that are constantly affecting them. They tend to interpret the phenomena based on how they affect them personally and to use everything they learn for the express purpose of adjusting to the world in which they live, whether for better or for worse. As a teacher you can help students understand this world and adjust to it in positive ways. As children develop psychologically, emotionally, and intellectually, they overcome this egocentricity.

An important skill needed to overcome egocentricity is that of listening to others, with understanding and empathy; however, many young people, and even many adults, are not very good at listening. Teachers must help students to develop that skill. One way is to ask a student to paraphrase what another has said and then ask the first student if, in fact, that is what he or she said. If it isn't, then have the student repeat what he or she said and again ask another student to paraphrase that statement. Keep doing that until the original student's statement is correctly understood.

Young adolescents are interpretive.   Young people are constantly interpreting their environment. Very often these interpretations are incomplete or even incorrect (referred to variously in the literature as *naive theories* or misconceptions, conceptual misunderstandings, or incongruent schemata, discussed shortly). However, children will continue to arrive at interpretations that satisfy them and allow them to function adequately in their daily lives.

Learners try to attach meaning to their experiences by referring to a body of related information from past experiences and knowledge stored in long-term memory. These experiences and this knowledge are called networks or *schemata*. A schema (plural, schemata) is a mental construct by which the learner organizes his or her perceptions of the environment. Learning continues by assimilating new information into a schema and modifying or forming a new schema (a process known as *accommodation*), thus allowing the learner to function adequately.

Young people's interpretations of phenomena change with their increasing maturity. Consequently, students are engaged in a constant process of revising interpretations as they grow in ability to understand and to think abstractly. A technique called concept mapping, discussed later in this chapter, is a learning strategy useful in helping students integrate their knowledge and understandings in useful schemata (Novak, 1993).

Students come to your classroom with existing schemata about almost everything, which from an adult's point of view may not always be congruent with accepted views but, nevertheless, are valid. As a teacher, one of your more important tasks is to correct students' misconceptions. Like many adults, young people are naturally resistant to change, so changing their misconceptions and promoting correct understandings is no easy task. Even after they have had corrective instruction, students will often persist in their misconceptions. Bear in mind, however, that "whenever students are asked to think about an idea in a way that questions common sense or a widely accepted assumption, that relates new ideas to ones previously learned, or that applies an idea to the problems of living, then there is a chance that good teaching is going on" (Haberman, 1991, p. 294).

Regardless of the subject and grade level, children come to your classroom with misconceptions, and correcting their misconceptions is often a long and arduous task that demands your understanding, patience, and creative instruction. Students are much more likely to modify data from their experiences to accommodate their schemata than to change their beliefs as a result of new experiences (Watson & Konicek, 1990, p. 683). Perhaps this shouldn't be so difficult to understand. There are stories of reputable scientists, politicians, and attorneys who were tempted to modify data to support their beliefs. Stubborn persistence and remaining open to change are virtuous, although conflicting, human attributes. In the words of Brooks and Brooks (1993, p. 113):

> Students of all ages develop and refine ideas about phenomena and then tenaciously hold onto these ideas as eternal truths. Even in the face of "authoritative" intervention and "hard" data that challenge their views, students typically adhere staunchly to their original notions. Through experiences that might engender contradictions, the frameworks for these notions weaken, causing students to rethink their perspectives and form new understandings.

Young adolescents are persistent.   As implied in the preceding discussion, children are tenacious. They like to achieve their objectives and will spend remarkable time and effort at activities that are important and interesting to them. With those efforts comes a feeling of personal satisfaction and a sense of accomplishment. You must take advantage of this persistence and desire to achieve by helping children to acquire ownership of what is to be learned and by providing instruction in the form of interesting and meaningful learning activities.

Young adolescents are curious. Children are naturally curious. While a young child's world is filled with wonder and excitement, an older child's curiosity will vary, depending upon what catches his or her interest. Generally speaking, students are more interested in things that move than things that don't. They are more interested in objects that make things happen than those to which things are happening. Things that appear mysterious and magical pique their curiosity. Good instruction takes advantage of this natural curiosity. That is why, for example, the use of "magic" and discrepant events (events that cause cognitive dissonance) is so popular and successful in motivating student learning in science. In the words of Brooks and Brooks, "The line between cognitive dissonance, which can provoke a student's desire to persevere, and intrapersonal frustration, which interferes with the student's desire to resolve dissonance, is a fine one that is often difficult to recognize. To foster the development of students' abilities to organize and understand their individual worlds, teachers need to encourage students to find their own problems" (1993, p. 29).

Young adolescents are adventurous. Young people love to explore. When given an object with which to play, younger children try to take it apart and then put it together again. They love to touch and feel objects. Children are always wondering "what will happen if. . . ?" and suggesting ideas for finding out. Children are natural questioners. The words *what, why,* and *how* are common in their vocabulary. While investigating, young people work and learn best when they experience firsthand. Therefore, you should provide a wide variety of experiences that involve hands-on learning. Hands-on learning engages the learner's mind, causing questioning. You should encourage rather than discourage students' questions.

Young adolescents are energetic. Young people are energetic. They would rather not sit for a long time; for some, it is nearly impossible. They would rather do than listen, and even while listening, may move their bodies restlessly. This difficulty sitting quietly has a direct bearing on the student's attention span. As a result, teaching should promote kinesthetic learning by providing many activities that give students the opportunity to be physically active.

Young adolescents are social. Children of the middle school years are social beings. They like to be with and to be accepted by their peers. They like to work together in planning and carrying out their activities. They work very well together when given proper encouragement, when they understand the procedures, and when they are given clear direction and a worthwhile task. Each student forms a self-concept through these social interactions in school. The student will develop satisfactory self-esteem when given an opportunity to work with others, to offer ideas, and to work out peer relationships. Your teaching can help foster not only learning but also the development of each student's self-esteem by incorporating social-interaction teaching strategies, such as cooperative learning, peer tutoring, and cross-age teaching.

Young adolescents have a variety of psychological needs. Abraham Maslow (1970) presented a continuum of psychological needs ranging from the most basic—*physiological needs* (for food, clothing, and shelter) and *security needs* (for a feeling of safety)—to *social needs* (for a sense of love and belonging) and *self-esteem needs* to the highest, *self-actualization needs* (for full use of talents, capacities, and abilities and acceptance of self and others). When children are frustrated because of lack of satisfaction of one or more of these needs, their classroom behavior is affected, and their learning is stifled (Reed & Sautter, 1990). Some students become aggressive and disrupt normal classroom procedures, hoping in this way to satisfy a basic need for recognition. Others become antisocial, apathetic, and fail to participate in class activities. Perhaps psychological needs are best explained by D. S. Eitzen:

Everyone needs a dream. Without a dream, we become apathetic. Without a dream, we become fatalistic. Without a dream and the hope of attaining it, society becomes our enemy. We educators must realize that some young people act in antisocial ways because they have lost their dreams. And we must realize that we as a society are partly responsible for that loss. Teaching is a noble profession whose goal is to increase the success rate for *all* children. We must do everything we can to achieve this goal. If not, we—society, schools, teachers, and students—will all fail. (1992, p. 590)

The wise teacher is alert to any student whose basic psychological needs are not being satisfied. Perhaps it is the one who comes to school hungry. Perhaps it is the one who comes to school feeling insecure because of problems at home. Maybe it is the one who comes to school tired from having to spend each night sleeping in an automobile or from being abused by a parent, friend, or relative. Although the classroom teacher cannot solve all the ailments of society, you do have an opportunity and responsibility to make all students feel welcome, respected, and wanted, at least while in your classroom.

Historically, many teachers have found children of ages 10 to 14 particularly troublesome to teach. To further your understanding of children and your ability to work with them, let's now review the general characteristics of children of that age span.

Working with Young Adolescents

Through experience and research, experts have come to accept certain precepts about young adolescents' intellectual, physical, psychological, social, and moral and ethical development. The following list is taken from the California State Department of Education's *Caught in the Middle: Educational Reform for Young Adolescents in California Public Schools* (1987, pp. 144–148).

Intellectual development
Young adolescents tend to

1. Be egocentric; argue to convince others; exhibit independent, critical thought.
2. Be intellectually at risk; that is, they face decisions that have the potential to affect major academic values and have lifelong consequences.
3. Be intensely curious.
4. Consider academic goals a secondary priority, whereas personal-social concerns dominate their thoughts and activities.
5. Display a wide range of individual intellectual development as their minds change from the concrete-manipulatory stage to the capacity for abstract thought. This change makes possible:
   - The ability to project thought into the future, to expect, and to formulate goals.
   - Analysis of the power of a political ideology.
   - Appreciation for the elegance of mathematical logic expressed in symbols.
   - Consideration of ideas contrary to fact.
   - Insight into the nuances of poetic metaphor and musical notation.
   - Insight into the sources of previously unquestioned attitudes, behaviors, and values.
   - Interpretation of larger concepts and generalizations of traditional wisdom expressed through sayings, axioms, and aphorisms.
   - Propositional thought.
   - Reasoning with hypotheses involving two or more variables.
6. Experience the phenomenon of metacognition—that is, the ability to think about one's thinking, and to know what one knows and does not know.
7. Exhibit strong willingness to learn what they consider to be useful, and enjoy using skills to solve real-life problems.
8. Prefer active over passive learning experiences; favor interaction with peers during learning activities.

Physical development
Young adolescents tend to

1. Be concerned about their physical appearance.
2. Be physically at risk; major causes of death are homicide, suicide, accident, and leukemia.

3. Experience accelerated physical development marked by increases in weight, height, heart size, lung capacity, and muscular strength.
4. Experience biological development five years sooner than adolescents of the nineteenth century; since then, the average age of menarche has dropped from 17 to 12 years of age.
5. Experience bone growth faster than muscle development; uneven muscle/bone development results in lack of coordination and awkwardness; bones may lack protection of covering muscles and supporting tendons.
6. Experience fluctuations in basal metabolism, which at times can cause either extreme restlessness or listlessness.
7. Face responsibility for sexual behavior before full emotional and social maturity has occurred.
8. Have ravenous appetites and peculiar tastes; they may overtax their digestive system with large quantities of improper foods.
9. Lack physical health; have poor levels of endurance, strength, and flexibility; be fatter and less healthy as a group.
10. Mature at varying rates of speed. Girls are often taller than boys for the first two years of early adolescence and are ordinarily more physically developed than boys.
11. Reflect a wide range of individual differences that begin to appear in prepubertal and pubertal stages of development. Boys tend to lag behind girls at this stage, and there are marked individual differences in physical development for both boys and girls. The greatest variation in physiological development and size occurs at about age 13.
12. Show changes in body contour, including temporarily large noses, protruding ears, long arms; have posture problems.

Psychological development
Young adolescents tend to

1. Be easily offended and sensitive to criticism of personal shortcomings.
2. Be erratic and inconsistent in their behavior; anxiety and fear contrast with periods of bravado; feelings shift between superiority and inferiority.
3. Be moody, restless; often feel self-conscious and alienated; lack self-esteem; be introspective.
4. Be optimistic, hopeful.
5. Be psychologically at risk; at no other point in human development is an individual likely to meet so much diversity in relation to self and others.
6. Be searching for adult identity and acceptance even in the midst of intense peer group relationships.
7. Be searching to form a conscious sense of individual uniqueness—"Who am I?"
8. Be vulnerable to naive opinions, one-sided arguments.
9. Exaggerate simple occurrences and believe that personal problems, experiences, and feelings are unique to themselves.
10. Have an emerging sense of humor based on increased intellectual ability to see abstract relationships; appreciate the double entendre.
11. Have chemical and hormonal imbalances that often trigger emotions that are frightening and poorly understood; they may regress to more childish behavior patterns at this point.

Social development
Young adolescents tend to

1. Act out unusual or drastic behavior at times; they may be aggressive, daring, boisterous, argumentative.
2. Be confused and frightened by new school settings that are large and impersonal.
3. Be fiercely loyal to peer group values and sometimes cruel or insensitive to those outside the peer group.
4. Be impacted by the high level of mobility in society; they may become anxious and disoriented when peer group ties are broken because of family relocation.

5. Be rebellious toward parents but still strongly dependent on parental values; want to make their own choices, but the authority of the family is a critical factor in final decisions.
6. Be socially at risk; adult values are largely shaped during adolescence; negative interactions with peers, parents, and teachers may compromise ideals and commitments.
7. Challenge authority figures; test limits of acceptable behavior.
8. Experience often-traumatic conflicts because of conflicting loyalties to peer group and family.
9. Refer to peers as sources for standards and models of behavior; media heroes and heroines are also singularly important in shaping both behavior and fashion.
10. Sense the negative impact of adolescent behaviors on parents and teachers; realize the thin edge between tolerance and rejection; feelings of adult rejection can drive the adolescent into the relatively secure social environment of the peer group.
11. Strive to define sex role characteristics; search to set up positive social relationships with members of the same and opposite sex.
12. Want to know and feel that significant adults, including parents and teachers, love and accept them; need frequent affirmation.

Moral and ethical development
Young adolescents tend to

1. Ask broad, unanswerable questions about the meaning of life; they do not expect absolute answers but are turned off by trivial adult responses.
2. Be morally and ethically at risk; depend on the influences of home and church for moral and ethical development; explore the moral and ethical issues that are met in the curriculum, the media, and daily interactions with their families and peer groups.
3. Be idealistic; have a strong sense of fairness in human relationships.
4. Be reflective, introspective, and analytical about their thoughts and feelings.
5. Experience thoughts and feelings of awe and wonder related to their expanding intellectual and emotional awareness.
6. Face hard moral and ethical questions with which they are unprepared to cope.

Understanding the characteristics of young adolescents and their basic needs is the foundation for studying how they learn and think and how you can use that knowledge in your teaching.

C. INTELLECTUAL DEVELOPMENT AND HOW CHILDREN LEARN

Jean Piaget, Lev Vygotsky, Robert Gagné, Jerome Bruner, and David Ausubel are five learning theorists who have played major roles in the development of today's theory of effective instruction. (See Chapters 7 and 12 for a discussion of this work's relevance to the teaching of language arts and social studies, respectively.) Of the several psychologists whose theories of learning had an impact during the last half of the twentieth century, perhaps no other had such a wide-ranging influence on education than did Swiss psychologist Jean Piaget (1896–1980). Although Piaget began to publish his insights in the 1920s, his work was not popularized in this country until the 1960s.

Piaget's Theory of Cognitive Development

Regarding the intellectual development of the child, we now know of the importance of the richness of a child's learning experiences, especially from birth to about age 11. Maintaining that knowledge is created as children interact with their social and physical environment, Piaget postulated four stages (or periods) of cognitive development that occur in a continuing process from birth to post-adolescence (see Figure 1.1). Mental development begins with the first stage and, without skipping a stage, progresses developmentally through each succeeding stage.

Age ranges in Piaget's stages of cognitive development. Although the ages listed in Figure 1.1 indicate when the *majority* of children are likely to attain each stage of development, actually children can reach these stages at widely varying ages, depending on a number of factors, including the assessment procedures used. You must be cautious about placing much reliance on the age ranges assigned to Piaget's periods of cognitive development. For example, about 5 percent of middle school children, that is, children ages 10–14, operate at the preoperational level. Furthermore, when confronted with perplexing situations, evidence indicates that many learners, including adults, tend to revert to an earlier developmental stage.

Multilevel Instruction

As an intermediate or middle school teacher, you will likely find students in your classroom to be at different stages (and substages) of mental development. It is important to try to attend to where each child is developmentally. To do that, many teachers use multilevel instruction (known also as multitasking). Multilevel instruction occurs when different students are working at different tasks to accomplish the same objective or are working at different tasks to accomplish different objectives. When integrating student learning, multitasking is an important and useful, perhaps even necessary, strategy.

Rate of Cognitive Development and Factors That Affect It

Piaget's four stages are general descriptions of the psychological processes in cognitive development, but the rate of development varies widely among children. The rate of cognitive development is affected by the individual's maturation, which is controlled by inherited biological factors, and by the child's health, the richness of the child's experiences and social interactions, and the child's equilibration. (Equilibration, discussed shortly, is the process of mentally neutralizing the effect of cognitive disequilibrium, that is, moving from disequilibrium to equilibrium, merging new and discrepant information with established knowledge.)

Lev Vygotsky: Cooperative Learning in a Supportive Environment

A contemporary of Piaget, the Soviet psychologist Lev Vygotsky (1896–1934) studied and agreed with Piaget on most points but differed with Piaget on the importance of a child's social interactions. Vygotsky argued that learning is most effective when students cooperate with one another in a supportive learning environment under the careful guidance of a teacher. Cooperative learning, group problem solving, and cross-age tutoring are instructional strategies used today that have grown in popularity as a result of research evolving from the work of Vygotsky.

Concept Development

Equilibration is the regulator of the relation between *assimilation* (input of new information into existing schemata) and *accommodation* (development of new or modification of old schemata). *Equilibrium* is the balance between assimilation and accommodation, and the brain is always internally striving for this balance. Disequilibrium is the state of imbalance. When disequilibrium occurs, the brain is motivated to assimilate and to accommodate. With or without a teacher's guidance a learner *will* assimilate information. The task of the teacher is to facilitate the learner's continuing, accurate construction of old and new schemata. Concept mapping (discussed later) has been shown to be an excellent tool for facilitating the learner's assimilation and accommodation.

To understand conceptual development and change, Piaget developed a theory of learning that involves children in a three-phase learning cycle. The three phases are (1) an exploratory hands-on phase, (2) a concept development phase, and (3) a concept application phase. A similar learning cycle approach to science teaching was developed by Robert Karplus for the Science Curriculum Improvement Study (SCIS) program. In that approach the three stages are *exploratory,* in which students explore materials freely, leading to their own questions and tentative answers; *invention,* in which, under the guidance of the teacher, the children invent concepts and principles that help them answer their questions and reorganize their ideas; and *application,* in which the children try out their new ideas by applying them to new situations that are relevant and meaningful to them. (For a further discussion of use of the learning cycle model in a constructivist classroom, see Brooks & Brooks, 1993.)

FIGURE 1.1
Piaget's Stages of Cognitive Development

Sensorimotor Stage (Birth to Age 2)

This is the stage from birth until about age 2. At this stage, children are bound to the moment and to their immediate environment. Learning and behaviors at this stage derive from the direct interaction with stimuli that the child can see or feel. Objects that are not seen are found only by random searching. Through direct interaction the child begins to build mental concepts, associating actions and reactions, and later in the stage will begin to label people and objects and to show imagining. For example, seeing a parent preparing the child's food tells the child that he or she will soon be eating. The child, then, is developing a practical base of knowledge that forms the foundation for learning in the next stage.

Preoperational Stage (Ages 2–7)

Lasting from about ages 2 to 7, the preoperational stage is characterized by the ability to imagine and think before acting, rather than only to respond to external stimuli. This stage is called "preoperational" because the child does not use logical operations in thinking. In this stage the child is egocentric. The child's world view is subjective rather than objective. Because of egocentrism, it is difficult for the child to consider and accept another person's point of view. The child is perceptually oriented, that is, makes judgments based on how things look to him or her. The child does not think logically, and therefore does not reason by implication. Instead, an intuitive approach is used and judgments are made according to how things look to the child. At this stage, when confronted with new and discrepant information about a phenomenon, the child adjusts the new information to accommodate his or her existing beliefs about it.

Children at this stage can observe and describe variables (properties of an object or aspects of a phenomenon) but concentrate on just one variable at a time, usually a variable that stands out visually. The child cannot coordinate variables, so has difficulty realizing that an object has several properties. Consequently, it is difficult for the child to combine parts into a whole. The child can make simple classifications according to one or two properties but finds it difficult to realize that multiple classifications are possible. Also, the child can arrange objects in simple series but has trouble arranging them in a long series or inserting a new object in its proper place within a series. To the child, space is restricted to the child's neighborhood, and time is restricted to hours, days, and seasons.

The child in this stage has not yet developed the concept of conservation. This means the child does not understand that several objects can be rearranged and that the size or shape or volume of a solid or liquid can be changed, yet the number of objects and the amount of solid or liquid will be unchanged or conserved. For example, if two rows of ten objects are arranged so they take up the same area, the child will state that the two rows are the same and there are the same number of objects in each row. If the objects in one row are spread out so the row is longer, the child is likely to maintain that the longer row now has more objects in it. Similarly, if the child is shown two identical balls of clay, the child will agree that both balls contain the same amount of material. When, in full view of the child, one of the balls is stretched out into the shape of a sausage, the child is likely to say the sausage has more clay because it is larger or less clay because it is thinner. Either way, the child at this stage is "centering" his or her attention on just one particular property (here, length or thickness) to the neglect of the other properties.

In both of the preceding examples the reason for the child's thinking is that the child does not yet understand reversibility. The child's thinking cannot yet reverse itself back to the point of origin. As a result,

---

When a learner is applying a concept (the third phase), the learner is involved in a hands-on activity. During application of a concept the learner may discover new information that causes a change in his or her understanding of the concept being applied. Thus, the process of learning is cyclic.

Concept Attainment: A Continuing Cyclic Process

We can think of the learner's developing understanding of concepts (concept attainment) as being a cyclical (continuing) three-stage process. The first stage is an increasing awareness that is stimulated by the quality and richness of the child's learning environment; the second stage is disequilibrium; the third stage is reformulation of the concept, which is brought on by the learner's process of equilibration.

From neuroscience, new principles are emerging that may have profound effects on teaching and on how schools are organized. For example, as stated by Caine and Caine (1990, p. 66), "Because there can be a five-year difference in maturation between any two 'average' children, gauging achievement on the basis of chronological age is inappropriate." Research indicates brain-growth spurts for students in grades 1, 2, 5, 6, 9, and 10. If schools were organized solely on this criterion, they would be configured in grade clusters K, 1–4, 5–8, and 9–12 (Sylvester,

FIGURE 1.1 cont'd

the child does not understand that since nothing has been removed or added, the extended row of objects can be rearranged to its original length, and the clay sausage can be made back into the original ball. The child does not yet comprehend that actions and thought processes are reversible.

Not yet able to use abstract reasoning and only beginning to think conceptually, students at this stage of development learn best by manipulating objects in concrete situations rather than by abstract, verbal learning alone. For children at this stage of development, conceptual change comes very gradually.

Concrete Operations Stage (Ages 7–11)

In this stage the learner can now perform logical operations. The child can observe, judge, and evaluate in less egocentric terms than in the preoperational stage and can formulate more objective explanations. As a result, the learner knows how to solve physical problems. Because the child's thinking is still concrete and not abstract, the child is limited to problems dealing with actual concrete situations. Early in this stage the learner cannot generalize, deal with hypothetical situations, or weigh possibilities.

The child can make multiple classifications and can arrange objects in long series and place new objects in their proper place in the series. The child can begin to comprehend geographical space and historical time. The child develops the concepts of conservation according to their ease of learning: first, number of objects (age 6 or 7), then matter, length, area (age 7), weight (ages 9–12), and volume (age 11 or more), in that order. The child also develops the concept of reversibility and can now reverse the physical and mental processes when numbers of objects are rearranged or when the size and shape of matter are changed.

Later in this stage children can hypothesize and do higher-level thinking. Not yet able to use abstract reasoning and only beginning to be able to think conceptually, students at this stage of development still learn best by manipulating objects in concrete situations rather than by verbal learning alone. At this stage hands-on, active learning is most effective.

Formal Operations Stage (Age 11 and Up)

Piaget initially believed that by age 15 most adolescents reach formal operational thinking, but now it is quite clear that many high school students—and even some adults—do not yet function at this level. Essentially, students who are quick to understand abstract ideas are formal thinkers. Most middle-grade-level students are not at this stage, however. For them, *metacognition* (planning, monitoring, and evaluating one's own thinking) may be very difficult. In essence, metacognition is today's term for what Piaget referred to as *reflective abstraction,* or reflection upon one's own thinking, without which continued development cannot occur. (For further clarification of the concept of metacognition, see Braten, 1991.)

In this stage the individual's method of thinking shifts from the concrete to the more formal and abstract. The learner can now relate one abstraction to another and grows in ability to think conceptually. It is in this stage that the learner can develop hypotheses, deduce possible consequences from them, then test these hypotheses with controlled experiments in which all the variables are identical except the one being tested. When approaching a new problem, the learner begins by formulating all the possibilities and then determining which ones are substantiated through experimentation and logical analysis. After solving the problem, the learner can reflect upon or rethink the thought processes that were used.

Chall, Wittrock, & Hart, 1991). With an increasing use of the 5–8 grade span, the middle school may be an indicator of an advance in that direction. (From 1981 to 1992, the number of middle-level schools using a 5–8 grade span tripled; only about one-third of middle-level schools in 1992 used the 7–9 grade span. See Valentine et al., 1993, p. 19.)

Robert Gagné and the General Learning Hierarchy

Robert Gagné is well known for his hierarchy of learning levels. According to Gagné, learning is the establishing of a capability to do something that the learner was not capable of doing previously. Notice the emphasis on the learner "doing."

Gagné postulates a hierarchy of learning capabilities. Learning one particular capability usually depends upon having previously learned one or more simpler capabilities.

For Gagné, observable changes in behavior comprise the *only* criteria for inferring that learning has occurred. It follows, then, that the beginning, or lowest, level of a learning hierarchy would include very simple behaviors. These behaviors would form the basis for learning more complex behaviors in the next level of the hierarchy. At each higher level, learning requires that the appropriate simpler, or less complex, behaviors have been acquired in the lower learning levels.

TABLE 1.1
Gagné's Learning Hierarchy

Level 8: Problem Solving
Level 7: Principle Learning
Level 6: Concept Learning
Level 5: Multiple
          Discrimination
Level 4: Verbal
          Association
Level 3: Chaining
Level 2: Stimulus-Response
          Learning
Level 1: Signal Learning

Gagné identifies eight levels of learning in this hierarchy. Beginning with the simplest and progressing to the most complex, these levels, shown in Table 1.1, are described briefly as follows.

Signal learning. The individual learns to make a general, conditioned response to a given signal. Examples are a child's pleasure at the sight of a pet animal or the child's expression of fright at the sound of a loud noise.

Stimulus-response learning. The individual acquires a precise physical or vocal response to a discriminated stimulus. Examples include a child's initial learning of words by repeating sounds and words of adults and the training of a dog to sit.

Chaining. Sometimes called skill learning, chaining involves the linking together of two or more units of simple stimulus-response learning. Chaining is limited to physical, nonverbal sequences. Examples include winding up a toy, writing, running, and opening a door. The accuracy of the learning at this level depends on practice, prior experience, and reinforcement.

Verbal association. This is a form of chaining, but the links are verbal units. Naming an object is the simplest verbal association. In this case, the first stimulus-response link is involved in observing the object, and the second is involved in enabling the child to name the object. A more complex example of verbal chaining would be the rote memorization of the letters of the alphabet in sequence. Considered alone, these learned behaviors are not usually seen as important goals of teaching. However, viewed as a level in a hierarchy, they can be important first steps to certain higher levels of learning.

Multiple discrimination. Individual learned chains are linked to form multiple discriminations. An example of learning at this level is the identification of the names of students in a classroom, in which the learner associates each student with his or her distinctive appearance and correct name.

Concept learning. Learning a concept means learning to respond to stimuli by their abstract characteristics (such as position, shape, color, and number), as opposed to concrete physical properties. A child may learn to call a two-inch cube a "block" and to apply this name to other objects that differ from it in size and shape. Later, the child learns the concept "cube," and by so doing can identify a class of objects that differ physically in many ways (say, by material, color, texture, and size). Rather than learning concepts in a trial-and-error, accidental fashion, under the careful guidance of the teacher a child's learning is sequenced in such a way as to lead to the child's improved conceptual understanding.

Principle learning. In simplest terms, a principle (or generalization) is a chain of two or more concepts. In principle learning the individual must relate two or more concepts. An example is that families are a primary means of socialization in all cultures. Three separate concepts (families, socialization, and cultures) are linked or chained together.

Problem solving. According to Gagné, and as most learning theorists will agree, problem solving is the most sophisticated type of learning. In problem solving, the individual applies learned principles in order to achieve a goal. While achieving this goal, however, the learner becomes capable of new performances by using the new knowledge. When a problem is solved, new knowledge has been acquired, and the individual's capacity advances. The individual is now able to handle a wide class of problems similar to the one solved. What has been learned, according to Gagné, is a higher-order principle, which is the combined product of two or more lower-order principles.

Thus, when a child has acquired the capabilities and behaviors of a certain level of learning, we assume that the child has also acquired the capabilities and behaviors of all the learning levels below this level. Furthermore, if the child were having difficulty in demonstrating the capabilities and behaviors for a certain level, the teacher could simply test the child on the capabilities and behaviors of the lower levels to determine which one or ones were causing the difficulty.

Jerome Bruner and Discovery Learning

While a leading interpreter and promoter of Piaget's ideas, Bruner also made his own significant contributions on how children learn. Some of his thinking was influenced by the work of Vygotsky (Bruner, 1985). Like Piaget, Bruner maintains that each child passes through stages that are age related and biologically determined and that learning will depend primarily on the developmental level that the child has attained.

Bruner's theory also encompasses three major sequential stages that he refers to as representations. They can be thought of as ways of knowing. These are *enactive representation* (knowing that is related to movement, such as through direct experiencing or concrete activities); *ikonic representation* (knowing that is related to visual and spatial, or graphic, representations, such as films and still visuals); and *symbolic representation* (knowing that is related to reason and logic, or that depends on the use of words and abstract symbolization). They correspond to the sensorimotor, concrete operations, and formal operations stages of Piaget. While Bruner's description of what happens during these three representations corresponds to that of Piaget's stages, he differs from Piaget in his interpretation of the role language plays in intellectual development.

Piaget believes that although thought and language are related, they are different systems. He posits that the child's thinking is based on a system of inner logic that evolves as the child organizes and adapts to experiences. Bruner, however, maintains that thought is internalized language. The child translates experience into language, and then uses language as an instrument of thinking.

Bruner and Piaget differ also in their attitude toward the child's readiness for learning. Piaget concluded that the child's readiness for learning depends upon maturation and intellectual development. Bruner and some other researchers, however, believe that a child is always ready to learn a concept at some level of sophistication. Bruner states that any subject can be taught effectively in some intellectually honest form to any child in any stage of development. According to Bruner, a child can learn concepts only within the framework of whichever stage of intellectual development the child is in at the time. In teaching children, it is essential then that each child be helped to pass progressively from one stage of intellectual development to the next. Schools can do this by providing challenging but developmentally appropriate problems and opportunities for children that tempt them to forge ahead into the next stages of development. As a result, the children will acquire a higher level of understanding.

Bruner and the Act of Learning

Bruner describes the act of learning as involving three almost simultaneous processes. The first is the process of acquiring new knowledge. The second is the process of manipulating this knowledge to make it fit new tasks or situations. The third is the process of evaluating the acquisition and manipulation of this knowledge. A major objective of learning is to introduce the child at an early age to the ideas and styles that will help the child become literate. Consequently, the school curriculum should be built around major conceptual schemes, skills, and values that society considers to be important. These should be taught as early as possible in a manner that is consistent with the child's stages of development and forms of thought, then revisited many times throughout the school years to increase and deepen the learner's understanding.

Bruner has been an articulate spokesperson for discovery learning. He advocates that, whenever possible, teaching and learning should be conducted in such a matter that children are given the opportunity to discover concepts for themselves.

Benefits of Discovery Learning

Bruner cites four major benefits derived from learning by discovery. First, there is an increase in intellectual potency. By this he means that discovery learning helps students learn how to learn. It helps the learner develop skills in problem solving, enabling the learner to arrange and apply what has been learned to new situations, and thus learn new concepts.

Second, there is a shift from extrinsic to intrinsic rewards. Discovery learning shifts the motive for learning away from that of satisfying others to that of satisfying oneself—the source of motivation is intrinsic rather than extrinsic.

Third, there is an opportunity to learn the working heuristics of discovery. By heuristics Bruner means the methods in which a person is educated to find out things independently. Only through the exercise of problem solving and by the effort of discovery can the learner find out things independently. The more adept the learner becomes in the working heuristics of discovery, the more effective the decisions the learner will make in problem solving and the quicker they will be made.

Fourth, there is an aid to memory processing. Knowledge resulting from discovery learning is more easily remembered, and it is more readily recalled when needed. Bruner's work, strongly supported by recent brain research, provides a rationale for using discovery and hands-on learning activities.

Gagné and Bruner differ in their emphasis upon learning. While Gagné emphasizes primarily the product of learning (the knowledge), Bruner's emphasis is on the process of learning (the skills). While for Gagné the key question is, "*What* do you want the child to know?" for Bruner it is, "*How* do you want the child to know?" For Gagné the emphasis is on learning itself, whether by discovery, review, or practice. For Bruner the emphasis is on learning by discovery; it is the method of learning that is important.

Gagné emphasizes problem solving as the highest level of learning, with the lower learning levels prerequisite to this highest level. For Gagné, the appropriate sequence in learning (and teaching) is from these lower levels toward problem solving. The teacher begins with simple ideas, relates all of them, builds on them, and works toward the more complex levels of learning. On the other hand, Bruner *begins* with problem solving, which in turn leads to the development of necessary skills. The teacher poses a question to be solved and then uses it as a catalyst to motivate children to develop the necessary skills.

Piaget, Bruner, and Gagné also differ in their attitude toward the child's readiness for learning. As has been stated earlier, Piaget believes that readiness depends upon the child's maturation and intellectual development. Bruner believes that the child is always ready to learn a concept at some level of sophistication. Gagné, however, feels that readiness is dependent on the successful development of lower level skills and prior understandings.

David Ausubel and Meaningful Verbal Learning

David Ausubel (1963) advocates reception learning, the receipt of ideas through transmission. He agrees with other psychologists that the development of problem-solving skills is a primary objective in teaching. As does Gagné, however, he feels that effective problem solving and discovery are more likely to take place after children have learned key and supporting concepts, primarily through reception learning, that is, through direct instruction (expository teaching).

Ausubel strongly urges teachers to use learning situations and examples that are familiar to the students. This helps students to assimilate what is being learned with what they already know, making their learning more meaningful. Unlike Bruner, Ausubel believes that discovery learning is too time consuming to enable students to learn all they should know within the short time allotted to learning. Like Bruner and Gagné, he suggests that children in the primary grades should work on as many hands-on learning activities as possible, but for children beyond the primary grades, he recommends the increased use of learning by transmission, using teacher explanations, concept mapping, demonstrations, diagrams, and illustrations. Ausubel cautions against learning by rote memorization, however.

An example of learning by rote is when you memorize your social security number. One must learn by rote memorization information that is not connected to any prior knowledge. Learning by rote is easier if one can connect that which is to be memorized to some prior knowledge. Often used to bridge the gap between rote learning and meaningful learning is the strategy known as *mnemonics,* which is any strategy that will assist memory. Examples of common mnemonics include:

1. The notes on a treble staff are *FACE* for the space notes and *E*mpty *G*arbage *B*efore *D*ad *F*lips (*EGBDF*) for the line notes. The notes on the bass staff are *A*ll *C*ows *E*at *G*ranola *B*ars or *G*rizzly *B*ears *D*on't *F*ly *A*irplanes.

2. The order of the planets from the Sun are *My* *V*ery *E*ducated *M*other *J*ust *S*erved *U*s *N*ine *P*izzas (*Mercury*, *Venus*, *Earth*, *Mars*, *Jupiter*, *Saturn*, *Uranus*, *Neptune*, and *Pluto*).

3. The order of colors in the color spectrum is *ROY G. BIV,* for *r*ed, *o*range, *y*ellow, *g*reen, *b*lue, *i*ndigo, and *v*iolet.

To avoid rote memorization, Ausubel encourages teachers to make the learning meaningful and longer lasting by using advance organizers, ideas that are presented to the students before the new material and that mentally prepare students to integrate the new material into previously built cognitive structures. Most language arts and social studies textbook programs today are designed in this way.

There is no doubt that the most effective teaching occurs when students see meaning in what is being taught. A danger in expository teaching (in which the student listens to the teacher, reads, and memorizes) is the tendency to rely too heavily on spoken communication, which for many learners is highly abstract and thus unlikely to be effective. This is especially so in classrooms with students who are diverse in their language proficiency, cultural backgrounds, and skill levels.

Concept Mapping

Based on Ausubel's theory of meaningful learning, a technique called concept mapping has been found useful for helping students change their misconceptions. Simply put, concepts can be thought of as classifications that attempt to organize the world of objects and events into a smaller number of categories (see Chapter 15 for further discussion of teaching concepts in social studies). In everyday usage, the term *concept* means "idea," as when someone says, "My concept of love is not the same as yours." Concepts embody a meaning that develops in complexity with experience and learning over time. For example, the concept of love held by a fourth grader is unlikely to be as complex as that held by an adult.

A concept map typically refers to a visual or graphic representation of concepts with connections (bridges) to show their relationships. See Figure 1.2, a concept map done in an integrated language arts/social studies class showing middle school students' connections of relationships while studying concepts in fruit farming and marketing. (Concept mapping is also discussed in Chapter 15.)

The general procedure for concept mapping is to have students (1) identify important concepts in materials being studied, often by circling those concepts, (2) rank order the concepts from the most general to the most specific, and then (3) arrange the concepts on a sheet of paper, connect related ideas with lines, and define the connections between the related ideas. Concept mapping has been found to help students in their ability to organize and represent their thoughts and to connect new knowledge to their past experiences and schemata. (For further information about concept mapping, see Novak, 1990; Wolff-Michael & Bowen, 1993.)

D. THE TEACHER AS DECISION MAKER

As you undoubtedly are aware, during any school day you will make hundreds of decisions, many of which must be made instantaneously. In addition, to prepare for the teaching day you will have already made many decisions about it. During one school year a teacher makes literally thousands of decisions, many of which can and will affect the lives of children for years to come. For you this should seem an awesome responsibility, and it is.

To be an effective teacher, you must become adept at decision making and make decisions that are carefully reasoned over time as well as those that are made on the spot. To be adept in making decisions that affect the students in the most positive ways you need (1) common sense, (2) intelligence, (3) a background of theory in curriculum and instruction with extended practical experience in working with young people, and (4) the willingness to think about and to reflect upon your teaching and to continue learning all that is necessary to become an exemplary teacher.

Initially, of course, you will make errors in judgment, but you will also learn that young people are fairly resilient and that there are experts who will guide you, aid you, and help you ensure that the students are not damaged severely by your errors in judgment. You can learn from your errors. Keep in mind that the sheer number of decisions you make each day

FIGURE 1.2
Sample Concept Map
SOURCE: Reprinted with the permission of Simon & Schuster, Inc. from the Macmillan College text A RESOURCE GUIDE FOR TEACHING: K–12 by Richard D. Kellough.
Copyright ©1994 by Macmillan Publishing Company, Inc.

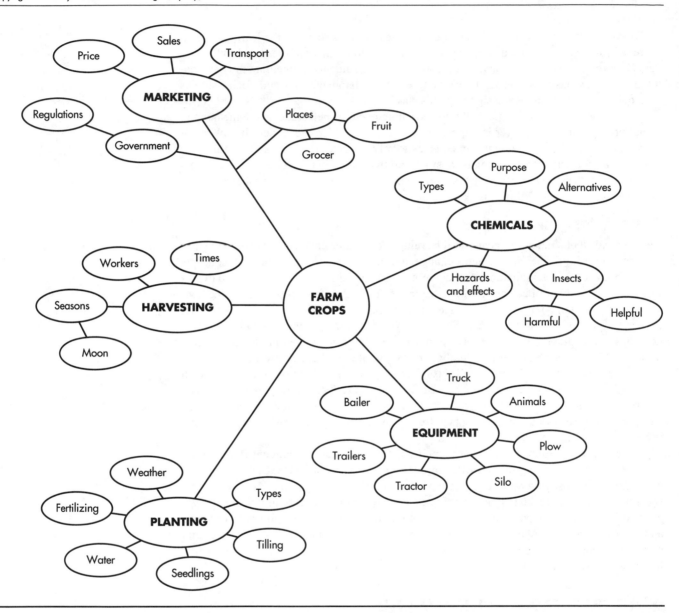

will mean that not all of them will be the best ones that could have been made had you had more time to think and better resources for planning.

Although effective teaching is based on scientific principles, good classroom teaching is as much an art as it is a science, and few rules apply to every teaching situation. In fact, decisions about the selection of content, of instructional objectives, of materials for instruction, of teaching strategies, of a teacher's response to a student's inappropriate behavior, and of techniques for the assessment of achievement in student learning are all the result of subjective judgments. Although many decisions are made at a somewhat unhurried pace when you are planning for your instruction, many others will be made intuitively on the spur of the moment. Once the school day has begun, you may lack the time for making carefully thought-out judgments. At your best, you will base decisions on your knowledge of school policies, your teaching style, pedagogical research, the curriculum, and the nature of the children in your classroom. You will also base your decisions on instinct, common sense, and reflective judgment. The better your understanding of and experience with schools, the content of the curriculum, and the students and how they develop intellectually, and the more time you devote to thinking and careful reflection, the more likely it will be that your decisions will result in the student learning that you had planned. You will reflect upon, conceptualize, and apply understandings from one teaching experience to the next. As your understandings about your classroom experiences accumulate, your teaching will become more routinized, predictable, and refined.

Decision Making and the Thought-Processing Phases of Instruction

Teaching has been defined as "the process of making and implementing decisions before, during, and after instruction—decisions that, when implemented, increase the probability of learning" (Hunter, 1994, p. 6). Instruction can be divided into four decision-making and thought-processing phases. These are the *preactive* (or planning) phase, the *interactive* (or teaching) phase, the *reflective* (analyzing and evaluating) phase, and the *projective* phase, in which your reflections upon your teaching are applied (Costa, 1991). The preactive phase consists of all those intellectual functions and decisions you will make prior to actual instruction. The interactive phase includes all the decisions made during the immediacy and spontaneity of the teaching act. As said earlier, decisions made during this phase are likely to be more intuitive, unconscious, and routine than are those made during the planning phase. The reflective phase is the time you will make to reflect on, analyze, and judge the decisions and behaviors that occurred during the interactive phase. As a result of this reflection, you will decide to use what was learned in subsequent teaching actions. At this point, you are in the projective phase, abstracting from your reflection and projecting your analysis into subsequent teaching actions.

Reflection and the Locus of Control

It is during the reflective phase that you have a choice as to whether to assume full responsibility for all instructional outcomes or for only the positive outcomes of the planned instruction while placing the blame for the negative outcomes on outside forces (parents and guardians, student peer pressure, other teachers, administrators, textbooks). Where you place responsibility for outcomes is referred to as your locus of control. It seems axiomatic that teachers who are professional and competent tend to assume full responsibility for instructional outcomes, regardless of whether those outcomes were as intended in the planning phase.

Personal Style of Teaching

Every teacher develops a personal style of teaching with which she or he feels most comfortable. This style develops from a combination of personal traits and the expertise the teacher has in methodology, subject matter, and instructional theory. The most effective teachers can vary their styles—that is, their styles are flexible enough to encompass a variety of strategies and are therefore readily adaptable to the different sorts of situations that may develop. *Teaching style is the way teachers teach, their distinctive mannerisms complemented by their choices of teaching behaviors and strategies.*

Effective teachers can modify their styles by selecting and using the strategy that is most appropriate, thus securing active student involvement and the greatest amount of student achievement. Highly effective teaching of this sort requires both expertise in a wide variety of methods and a feeling for the appropriate situation in which to use each method, as well as a command of the subject matter and an understanding of the children being taught. This may sound like a large order, but many beginning teachers become adept at this surprisingly quickly.

Thus, to be an effective teacher you should (1) develop a large repertoire of instructional strategies; (2) learn as much as you can about your students and their individual styles of learning; and (3) develop an eclectic style of teaching, one that is flexible and adaptable, that can function at many locations along the spectrum of integrated learning as introduced at the opening of Part I.

E. STYLES OF LEARNING

The most effective teachers are those who adapt their teaching styles and methods to their students, using approaches that interest the students, that are neither too easy nor too difficult, that match the students' learning styles, and that are relevant to their lives. This adaptation process is further complicated because each student is different from every other. All do not have the same interests, abilities, backgrounds, or learning styles. As a matter of fact, students not only differ from one another, but each student can change to some extent from day to day. What appeals to a student today may not have the same appeal tomorrow. Therefore, you need to consider the nature of both students in general (for example, methods appropriate for a particular fifth-grade class are unlikely to work best for most ninth graders) and each student in particular. What follows is a synopsis of what has been learned about aspects of student learning styles.

Brain Laterality

Research has shown that how a person learns is related to differences in the left and right hemispheres of the brain. This theory is sometimes referred to as *brain laterality* or *brain hemisphericity.* Verbal learning, logical and convergent thinking, and the academic cognitive processes are dominated by the left cerebral hemisphere, while affective, intuitive, spatial, emotional, divergent thinking and visual elements are dominated by the right cerebral hemisphere. Some students are oriented toward right cerebral hemisphere learning and others toward the left. This means that some students learn better through verbal interactions while others learn through visual, kinesthetic, and tactile involvement. However, "in a healthy person the two hemispheres are inextricably interactive, irrespective of whether a person is dealing with words, mathematics, music, or art" (Caine & Caine, 1990, p. 67).

Brain laterality and its implications for teaching. When integrating the disciplines and helping students connect what is being learned with real-life situations, the teacher is more likely to be teaching to both hemispheres.

Learning Modalities

Learning modality refers to the sensory portal means by which a student prefers to receive sensory reception (modality preference), or the actual way a student learns best (modality adeptness). Some students prefer learning by seeing, a visual modality; others prefer learning through instruction from others (through talk), an auditory modality; while still others prefer learning by doing and being physically involved, referred to as kinesthetic modality, and by touching objects, the tactile modality. Sometimes a student's modality preference is not that student's modality strength. While primary modality strength can be determined by observing students, it can also be mixed, and it can change as the result of experience and intellectual maturity. As one might suspect, modality integration (using several modalities at once) has been found to contribute to better achievement in student learning.

Learning modality and its implications for teaching. Because most students have neither a preference for nor a strength in auditory reception, teachers should limit their use of the lecture method of instruction, that is, of talk. Instruction that uses a singular approach, such as auditory instruction (lecturing), cheats students who learn better another way. This difference can affect student achievement. Finally, if a teacher's verbal communication conflicts with his or her nonverbal messages, students can become confused, and this too can affect their learning. (When there is a discrepancy between what the teacher says and what that teacher does, the teacher's nonverbal signal will be believed every time.)

As a general rule, students of intermediate and middle grade levels prefer to learn by touching objects, by feeling shapes and textures, by interacting with each other, and by moving things around. In contrast, sitting and listening are difficult for many of these students. Dependence on the tactile and kinesthetic modalities decreases with maturity. Some students are visual learners who can read easily and rapidly and can visualize what they are reading about.

You are advised to use strategies that integrate the modalities. Combining reception learning and cognitive mapping is an example of modality integration. When well designed, thematic units incorporate modality integration, too. In conclusion, then, when teaching a group of students of mixed learning abilities, mixed modality strengths, mixed language proficiency, and mixed cultural backgrounds, the integration of learning modalities is a must for the most successful teaching.

Learning Styles

Related to learning modality is learning style, which can be defined as independent forms of knowing and processing information. While some students are comfortable with beginning their learning of a new idea in the abstract (say, through visual or verbal symbolization), others feel the need to begin with the concrete (to learn by actually doing). Some prosper while working in groups, while others prefer to work alone. Some are quick in their studies, whereas others are slow and methodical, cautious and meticulous. Some can focus their attention on a single topic for a long time, becoming more absorbed in their study as time passes. Others are slower starters and more casual in their pursuits but are capable of shifting with ease from subject to subject. Some can study in the midst of music, noise, or movement, whereas others need quiet, solitude, and a desk or table. The point is that students vary not only in their skills at and preferences for receiving knowledge, but also in how they mentally process that information once it has been received. This latter is a person's style of learning, "a gestalt combining internal and external operations derived from the individual's neurobiology, personality, and development and reflected in learner behavior" (Keefe & Ferrell, 1990, p. 59).

Classification of Learning Styles

Although there are probably as many types of learning styles as there are individuals, most learning style classifications center around the recognition of four general types, based on the earlier work of Carl Jung (see Dunn & Dunn, 1978; Gregorc, 1985; Jung, 1923).

Anthony Gregorc (1979) classifies learning styles according to whether students prefer to begin with the concrete or the abstract and whether they prefer random or sequential ordering of information. As a result, his learning style classification has four categories:

- The *concrete sequential learner* prefers direct, hands-on experiences presented in a logical sequence.
- The *concrete random learner* prefers a more wide-open, exploratory kind of activity, such as games, role-playing, simulations, and independent study.
- The *abstract sequential learner* is skilled in decoding verbal and symbolic messages, especially when presented in logical sequence.
- The *abstract random learner* can interpret meaning from nonverbal communications and consequently does well in discussions, debates, and media presentations (adapted with permission from Heinich, Molenda, & Russell, 1993, p. 38).

Most students are better at one of the two categories of concrete learning than at either category of abstract learning.

David Kolb (1985) described two major differences in how people learn: how they perceive situations and how they process information. In their perceptions of the same new situation, some people are watchers and others are doers. It is important to note that learning style is not an indicator of intelligence, but rather an indicator of how a person learns.

More recently, Bernice McCarthy (1990, p. 32) has described the following four major learning styles.

- The *imaginative learner* perceives information concretely and processes it reflectively. Imaginative learners learn well by listening and sharing with others, integrating the ideas of others with their own experiences. Imaginative learners often have difficulty adjusting to traditional teaching, which depends less on classroom interactions and students' sharing and connecting of their prior experiences. In a traditional classroom, the imaginative learner is likely to be an at-risk student.
- The *analytic learner* perceives information abstractly and processes it reflectively. The analytic learner prefers sequential thinking, needs details, and values what experts have to offer. Analytic learners do well in traditional classrooms.
- The *common sense learner* perceives information abstractly and processes it actively. The common sense learner is pragmatic and enjoys hands-on learning. Common sense learners sometimes find school frustrating unless they can see an immediate use for what is being learned. In the traditional classroom, the common sense learner is likely to be a learner who is at risk of not completing school.

- The *dynamic learner* perceives information concretely and processes it actively. The dynamic learner also prefers hands-on learning and is excited by anything new. Dynamic learners are risk takers and are frustrated by learning if they see it as being tedious and sequential. In a traditional classroom, the dynamic learner also is likely to be an at-risk student.

With a system developed by McCarthy (called the 4MAT System), teachers employ a learning cycle of instructional strategies that reach each student's learning style. As stated by McCarthy, in the cycle, learners "sense and feel, they experience, then they watch, they reflect, then they think, they develop theories, then they try out theories, they experiment. Finally, they evaluate and synthesize what they have learned in order to apply it to their next similar experience. They get smarter. They apply experience to experiences" (1990, p. 33). And, with this process, they are likely to be using all four learning modalities. (Compare the learning cycle described here with the learning cycle concepts of Piaget and Karplus discussed earlier in this chapter; see Figure 1.1.)

Finally, in contrast to Jung's four learning styles, Howard Gardner and others have introduced seven learning styles or types of intelligences: *verbal-linguistic, logical-mathematical, intrapersonal, visual-spatial, musical-rhythmic, body-kinesthetic,* and *interpersonal* (Blythe & Gardner, 1990; Gardner, 1987; Gardner & Hatch, 1989). As implied previously, many educators believe that students who are at risk of not completing school are those who may be dominant in a cognitive learning style that is not in synch with traditional teaching methods (see, for example, Armstrong, 1988). Traditional methods are largely of McCarthy's analytic style, where information is presented in a logical, linear, sequential fashion, and of the first three Gardner types: verbal-linguistic, logical-mathematical, and intrapersonal. Consequently, to better synchronize methods of instruction with learning styles, some teachers (see Ellison, 1992) and schools (see Hoerr, 1992) have restructured the curriculum and instruction around Gardner's seven ways of knowing.

Learning style and its implications for teaching. The importance of the preceding information about learning styles is twofold:

1. Intelligence is not a fixed or static reality but can be learned, taught, and developed (Bracey, 1992; Lazear, 1992). This concept is important for your students to understand, too. When students understand that intelligence is incremental, something that is developed through use over time, they tend to be more motivated to work at learning than when they believe intelligence is a fixed entity (Resnick & Klopfer, 1989, p. 8).
2. Not all students learn and respond to learning situations in the same way. A student may learn differently according to the situation or according to the student's ethnicity, cultural background, or socioeconomic status. (For relevant discussions about students' cultural differences and learning styles, see Willis, 1993, p. 7; Gallegos, 1993.) A teacher who uses only one style of teaching for all students, or who teaches to only one or a few styles of learning, day after day, is short-changing those students who learn better another way.

A trap the teacher must avoid is to regard all students who have difficulty or who have a history of doing poorly in school as being alike. In a culture such as ours that values quantity, speed, and measurement, it is easy to make the mistake that being a slow learner is the same as being a poor learner. The perceptive teacher understands that slowness may be simply another style of learning, with potential strengths of its own. Slowness can reflect many things—caution, a desire to be thorough or a meticulous style, a great interest in the matter being studied. To ignore the slow student or to treat all students who seem slow as though they were victims of some deficiency is to risk discouraging those who have deliberately opted for slowness, thus limiting their learning opportunities.

SUMMARY

As a teacher you must acknowledge that children have different ways of receiving information and different ways of processing that information—different ways of knowing and of constructing their knowledge. These differences are unique and important, and they are what you should address in your teaching. You should try to learn as much as you can about how each student learns and processes information. But because you can never know everything about each student, the more you vary your teaching strategies and assist students in integrating their learning, the more likely you are to reach more of the students more of the time.

To be an effective teacher, you should (1) learn as much about your students and their preferred styles of learning as you can; (2) develop an eclectic style of teaching, one that is flexible and adaptable; and (3) integrate the disciplines, thereby assisting students in their conceptual understandings by helping them to make bridges or connections between what is being learned.

QUESTIONS AND ACTIVITIES FOR DISCUSSION

1. Give an example of how you would use multilevel teaching. Of what benefit is the use of multilevel teaching?

2. Explain why knowledge of teaching styles and student learning styles is important for a teacher.

3. Describe the relationship between awareness, disequilibrium, and reformulation in learning.

4. Explain why integration of the curriculum is important for learning at the intermediate and middle grade levels.

5. Explain the concept of spectrum of curriculum integration. What relevance does this concept have for you?

6. For a concept usually taught in social studies at a grade level 4–9, demonstrate specifically how you might help students bridge their learning of that concept with what is going on in their lives and with other disciplines.

7. Could the technique of concept mapping be used as an advance organizer? Explain your answer.

8. Colleen, a social studies teacher, has a class of 33 eighth graders who, during her lectures, teacher-led discussions, and recitation lessons, are restless and inattentive, creating a major problem in classroom management. At Colleen's invitation, the school psychologist tests the children for learning modality and finds that of the 33 children, 29 are predominantly kinesthetic learners. Of what use is this information to Colleen? Describe what, if anything, she should try as a result of having this information.

9. Identify a topic of a social studies lesson for a grade level of your choice, grade 4 through 9. Describe how you would teach that lesson from a behaviorist viewpoint; then describe how you would teach the same lesson from a constructivist viewpoint. Explain the differences.

10. Could you accept the view that learning is the product of creative inquiry through social interaction, with the students as active participants in that inquiry? Explain why you would or would not agree.

11. Assume that you are a junior high school teacher and that your teaching schedule includes three sections of U.S. history. Furthermore, assume that students at your school are tracked (as they are in many schools) and that one of your classes is a so-called "college prep" class with 30 students, another is a regular education class with 35 students, 2 of whom have special needs because of physical handicaps, and the third is a sheltered English class with 13 students, 9 of whom are Hispanics with limited proficiency in English (the other 4 are Southeast Asians, 2 of whom have no ability to use English). Will one lesson plan using lecture and discussion as the primary instructional strategies work for all three sections? If so, explain why. If not, explain what you will have to do and why.

12. Can you recall or invent mnemonics that would be useful in your teaching? Share them with those of your classmates.

13. Describe any prior concepts you held that changed as a result of your experiences reading this chapter. Describe the changes.

REFERENCES

Armstrong, T. (1988). Learning differences–Not disabilities. *Principal, 68* (1), 34–36.

Ausubel, D. P. (1963). *The psychology of meaningful verbal learning.* New York: Grune & Stratton.

Blythe, T., & Gardner, H. (1990). A school for all intelligences. *Educational Leadership, 47*(7), 33–37.

Bracey, G. W. (1992). Getting smart(er) in school. *Phi Delta Kappan, 73*(5), 414–416.

Braten, I. (1991). Vygotsky as precursor to metacognitive theory: I. The concept of metacognition and its roots. *Scandinavian Journal of Educational Research, 35*(3), 179–192.

Brooks, J. G., & Brooks, M. G. (1993). *In search of understanding: The case for constructivist classrooms.* Alexandria, VA: Association for Supervision and Curriculum Development.

Bruner, J. (1985). Vygotsky: A historical and conceptual perspective. In J. Wertsch (Ed.), *Culture, communication and cognition: Vygotskia perspectives.* Cambridge, England: Cambridge University Press.

Caine, R. N., & Caine, G. (1990). Understanding a brain-based approach to learning and teaching. *Educational Leadership, 48*(2), 66–70.

California State Department of Education. (1987). *Caught in the Middle: Educational reform for young adolescents in California public schools.* Sacramento, CA: Author.

Costa, A. L. (1991). *The school as a home for the mind.* Palatine, IL: Skylight Publishing.

Dunn, R., Beaudry, J. S., & Klavas, A. (1989). Survey of research on learning styles. *Educational Leadership, 47*(6), 50–58.

Dunn, R., & Dunn, K. (1978). *Teaching students through their individual learning styles.* Reston, VA: Reston Publications.

Eichhorn, D. H. (1966). *The middle school.* New York: Center for Applied Research.

Eitzen, D. S. (1992). Problem students: The sociocultural roots. *Phi Delta Kappan, 73*(8), 584–590.

Ellison, L. (1992). Using multiple intelligences to set goals. *Educational Leadership, 50*(2), 69–72.

Epstein, H. T. (1980). Brain growth and cognitive functions. In D. Steer (Ed.), *Emerging adolescent, characteristics and educational implications.* Columbus, OH: National Middle School Association.

Flanders, J. R. (1987). How much of the content in mathematics textbooks is new? *Arithmetic Teacher, 35*(1), 18–23.

Gallegos, G. (1993, Fall). Learning styles in culturally diverse classrooms. *California Catalyst, 36*–41.

Gardner, H. (1987). The theory of multiple intelligences. *Annals of Dyslexia, 37,* 19–35.

Gardner, H., & Hatch, T. (1989). Multiple intelligences go to school: Educational implications of the theory of multiple intelligence. *Educational Researcher, 18*(8), 4–9.

Gregorc, A. (1979, January). Learning and teaching styles—Potent forces behind them. *Educational Leadership, 234*–236.

Gregorc, A. (1985). *Gregorc style delineator.* Maynard, MA: Gabriel Systems.

Haberman, M. (1991). The pedagogy of poverty versus good teaching. *Phi Delta Kappan, 73*(4), 290–294.

Havighurst, R. J. (1972). *Developmental tasks and education.* New York: David McKay.

Heinich, R., Molenda, M., & Russell, J. D. (1993). *Instructional media* (4th ed.). New York: Macmillan.

Hoerr, T. R. (1992). How our school applied multiple intelligences theory. *Educational Leadership, 50*(2), 67–68.

Hunter, M. (1994). *Enhancing teaching.* New York: Macmillan.

Johnston, H. J., et al. (1982). What research says to the practitioner about peer relations in the classroom. *Middle School Journal, 13*(3), 22–26.

Jung, C. G. (1923). *Psychological types.* New York: Harcourt Brace.

Keefe, J. W., & Ferrell, B. G. (1990). Developing a defensible learning style paradigm. *Educational Leadership, 48*(2), 57–61.

Kolb, D. (1985). *The learning style inventory.* Boston: McBer & Co.

Lazear, D. G. (1992). *Teaching for multiple intelligences.* Fastback 342. Bloomington, IN: Phi Delta Kappa Educational Foundation.

Mager, R. F. (1968). *Developing attitudes toward learning.* Belmont: Fearson.

Maslow, A. H. (1970). *Motivation and personality.* New York: Harper and Row.

McCarthy, B. (1990). Using the 4MAT system to bring learning styles to schools. *Educational Leadership, 48*(2), 31–37.

Muther, C. (1987). What do we teach, and when do we teach it? *Educational Leadership, 45*(1), 77–80.

Novak, J. D. (1990). Concept maps and vee diagrams: Two metacognitive tools to facilitate meaningful learning. *Instructional Science, 19*(1), 29–52.

Novak, J. D. (1993). How do we learn our lesson? *The Science Teacher, 60*(3), 50–55.

Reed, S., & Sautter, R. C. (1990). Children of poverty: The status of 12 million young Americans. *Phi Delta Kappan, 71*(10), K1–K12.

Resnick, L. B., & Klopfer, L. E. (1989). *Toward the thinking curriculum: Current cognitive research. 1989 ASCD Yearbook.* Alexandria, VA: Association for Supervision and Curriculum Development.

Rosenshine, B. (1980). How time is spent in elementary classrooms. In C. Denham & A. Lieberman, *Time to learn.* Washington, DC: Department of Health, Education and Welfare, National Institute of Education.

Sylwester, R., Chall, J. S., Wittrock, M. C., & Hart, L. A. (1991). The educational implications of brain research. *Educational Leadership, 39*(1), 6–17.

Tanner, J. M. (1962). *Growth at adolescence* (2nd ed.). London: University of London Press.

Valentine, J. W., et al. (1993). *Leadership in middle level education.* Reston, VA: National Association of Secondary School Principals.

Watson, B., & Konicek, R. (1990). Teaching for conceptual change: Confronting students' experience. *Phi Delta Kappan, 71*(9), 680–685.

Willis, S. (1993, September). Multicultural teaching strategies. *ASCD Curriculum Update.* Alexandria, VA: Association for Supervision and Curriculum Development.

Wolf-Michael, M., & Bowen, W. (1993). The unfolding vee. *Science Scope, 16*(5), 28–32.

SUGGESTED READINGS

Banks, C. B. (1991). Harmonizing student-teacher interactions: A case for learning styles. *Synthesis, 2*(2), 1–5.

Beilin, H. (1992). Piaget's enduring contribution to developmental psychology. *Developmental Psychology, 28*(2), 191–204.

Bracey, G. W. (1991). Why can't they be like we were? *Phi Delta Kappan, 73*(2), 105–117.

Bruner, J. S. (1960). *The process of education.* Cambridge: Harvard University Press.

Bruner, J. S. (1966). *Toward a theory of instruction.* Cambridge, MA: Harvard University Press.

Bruner, J. S. (1990). *Acts of meaning.* Cambridge, MA: Harvard University Press.

Caine, R. N., & Caine, G. (1991). *Making connections: Teaching and the human brain.* Alexandria, VA: Association for Supervision and Curriculum Development.

Carns, A. W., & Carns, M. R. (1991). Teaching study skills, cognitive strategies, and metacognitive skills through self-diagnosed learning styles. *School Counselor, 38*(5), 341–346.

Cooper, J. D. (1993). *Literacy: Helping children construct meaning* (2nd ed.). Burlington, MA: Houghton Mifflin.

Cronin, J. F. (1993). Four misconceptions about authentic learning. *Educational Leadership, 50*(7), 78–80.

Curry, L. (1990). A critique of the research on learning styles. *Educational Leadership, 48*(2), 50–56.

Darling-Hammond, L. (1993). Reframing the school reform agenda. *Phi Delta Kappan, 74*(10), 753–761.

Fourgurean, J. M., et al. (1990). The link between learning style and Jungian psychological type: A finding of two bipolar preference dimensions. *Journal of Experimental Education, 58*(3), 225–237.

Fowler, C. (1990). Recognizing the role of artistic intelligence. *Music Educators Journal, 77*(1), 24–27.

Gardner, H. (1982). *Art, mind and brain.* New York: Basic Books.

Gardner, H. (1985). *Frames of mind.* New York: Basic Books.

Gardner, H. (1991). *The unschooled mind: How students think and how schools should teach.* New York: Basic Books.

Gardner, H. (1993). *Creating minds.* New York: Basic Books.

Gardner, H., & Boix-Mansilla, V. (1994). Teaching for understanding within and across the disciplines. *Educational Leadership, 51*(5), 14–18.

Grady, M. P. (1990). *Whole brain education.* Fastback 301. Bloomington, IN: Phi Delta Kappa Educational Foundation.

Jenkins, J. M. (1991). Learning styles: Recognizing individuality. *Schools in the Middle, 1*(12), 3–6.

Jones, B. F., & Fennimore, T. (1990). *The new definition of learning.* Oakbrook, IL: North Central Regional Educational Laboratory.

Keefe, J. W. (1990). Learning style: Where are we going? *Momentum, 21*(1), 44–48.

Lombardi, T. P. (1992). *Learning strategies for problem learners.* Fastback 345. Bloomington, IN: Phi Delta Kappa Educational Foundation.

Okebukola, P. A., & Olugbemiro, J. J. (1988). Cognitive preference and learning mode as determinants of meaningful learning through concept mapping. *Science Education, 72*(4), 489–500.

Perkins, D., & Blythe, T. (1994). Putting understanding up front. *Educational Leadership, 51*(5), 4–7.

Piaget, J. (1977). *The development of thought: Elaboration of cognitive structures.* New York: Viking.

Samples, B. (1992). Using learning modalities to celebrate intelligence. *Educational Leadership, 50*(2), 62–66.

Shaughnessy, M. F. (1990). Cognitive structures of the gifted: Theoretical perspectives, factor analysis, triarchic theories of intelligence, and insight issues. *Gifted Education International, 6*(3), 149–151.

Sigel, I. E., & Cocking, R. R. (1977). *Cognitive development from childhood to adolescence: A constructivist perspective.* New York: Holt, Rinehart and Winston.

Stevenson, C., & Carr, J. F. (Eds.). (1993). *Integrated studies in the middle grades.* New York: Teachers College Press.

Sylwester, R. (1993/1994). What the biology of the brain tells us about learning. *Educational Leadership, 51*(4), 46–51.

Titus, T. G., et al. (1990). Adolescent learning styles. *Journal of Research and Development in Education, 23*(3), 165–171.

Vygotsky, L. (1926). *Thought and language.* Cambridge, MA: The M.I.T. Press.

Wang, M. C., Haertel, G. D., & Walberg, H. J. (1993/1994). What helps students learn? *Educational Leadership, 51*(4), 74–79.

Yarusso, L. (1992). Constructivism vs. objectivism. *Performance and Instruction, 31*(4), 7–9.

CHAPTER 2

Planning and Implementing a Supportive Environment for Learning

No matter how well prepared your instructional plans (the topic of Chapter 4), those lessons will likely go untaught or only poorly taught if presented to children in a classroom that is nonsupportive and poorly managed. Thoughtful and thorough planning of your procedures for managing the classroom is as important a part of your preactive phase decision making as is the preparation of units and daily lessons, and that is the reason it is included here, preceding the chapter on instructional planning. And, as is true for unit and lesson planning, your management system should be planned and written by you long before you first meet your students. In this chapter you will learn how to do that. You will learn what is meant by a "supportive classroom environment," how to provide it, and how to effectively manage it for the most efficient instruction resulting in the best student achievement.

Specifically, this chapter is designed to help you understand

1. The role of the teachers' and students' perceptions in effective teaching and successful learning.
2. How to provide a supportive environment for learning.
3. How to most effectively manage the classroom.
4. The importance of getting the school year off to a good start and how to do it.
5. How to establish classroom procedures and rules of acceptable behavior.
6. How to avoid mistakes commonly made by beginning teachers.
7. How to provide a safe learning environment.

A. PERCEPTIONS

Unless you believe that your students can learn, they will not. Unless you believe that you can teach them, you will not. Unless your students believe that they can learn and until they want to learn, they will not. We all know of teachers who get the very best from their students, even from those students that many teachers find the most difficult to teach. Regardless of individual circumstances and teaching styles, successful teachers (1) know that all students can learn; (2) expect the very best from each student; (3) establish a classroom climate that is conducive to student learning, that motivates students to do their very best; and (4) effectively manage their classrooms so class time is most efficiently used, with the least amount of disturbance to the learning process.

It has long been known that the effort a student is willing to spend on a learning task is a product of two factors: (1) the degree to which the student believes he or she can successfully complete the task and achieve the rewards of that completion, and (2) the degree of value the student places on that reward. This is sometimes referred to as the expectancy × value theory (Feather, 1982). For student learning to occur, both aspects must be present—that is, the student must see meaning or value in the experience and perceive that he or she can achieve the intended outcome of the experience. A student is less likely to try to learn when he or she perceives no meaning or value in the material or feels incapable of learning it. In other words, before students *do,* they must feel they *can do,* and they must perceive the importance of doing.

Therefore, regardless of how well planned you are for the instruction, the students must have certain perceptions to support the successful implementation of those plans:

- Students must feel that the classroom environment is supportive of their efforts.
- Students must feel welcome in your classroom.
- Students must perceive the expected learning as being challenging but not impossible.
- Students must perceive the expected learning outcomes as being worth the time and effort to achieve.

This chapter provides you with strategies for setting up and managing your classroom in a way that demonstrates to students that they can learn.

B. PROVIDING A SUPPORTIVE LEARNING ENVIRONMENT

It is probably no surprise to you that teachers whose classrooms are pleasant, positive, and stimulating places to be find that their students learn and behave better than do the children of teachers whose classroom atmospheres are harsh, negative, and unchallenging. What follows now are specific suggestions for making your classroom atmosphere pleasant, positive, and stimulating, that is, ways of providing a supportive environment for the development of meaningful understandings.

Get to Know Your Students

For classes to move forward smoothly and efficiently, they should fit the students' abilities, needs, interests, and goals. To make the children's learning most meaningful and longest lasting, you must build your instruction around their interests, perceptions, and perspectives. Therefore, you need to know your students well enough to be able to provide learning activities that they will find interesting, valuable, motivating, challenging, and rewarding. Here are a number of things you can do to get to know your students as people:

- *Classroom sharing during the first week of school.* During the first week of school, many teachers take time to have each student present information about himself or herself. For instance, each child answers questions such as: "What name would you like to be called by?" "Where did you attend school last year?" "Tell us about your hobbies and other interests." You might have children share information of this sort with each other in groups of three or four while you visit each group in turn. Yet another approach is to include everyone in a game, having children answer the question on paper and then, as you read their answers, asking them to guess which student wrote each.
- *Observations of children in the classroom.* During classroom learning activities the effective teacher is constantly alert to the individual behavior (nonverbal as well as verbal) of each child in the class, noting whether the student is on task or gazing off and perhaps thinking about other things. Be cautious, however; gazing out the window does not necessarily mean that the student is not thinking about the learning task. During small-group work is a particularly good time to observe students and get to know more about each one's skills and interests.
- *Observations of students outside the classroom.* Another way to learn more about children is to observe them outside class, for example, at lunchtime, during intramural activities, on the playground, and during other school functions.

- *Conversation with students.* To learn more about your students you can spend time casually talking with individual or small groups of students during lunchtime, on the playground, and during other out-of-class activities.
- *Conferences and interviews with students.* Conferences with students, and sometimes with their parents or guardians as well, afford yet another opportunity to show that you are genuinely interested in each child as a person as well as a student. Some teachers plan a series of conferences during the first few weeks in which they interview small groups of three or four students, talking with each. Such conferences and interviews are managed by the use of open-ended questions. The teacher indicates by the questions, and by nonjudgmental and empathic responses, a genuine interest in the students.
- *Student writing.* Much can be learned about students by what they write. It is important to encourage writing in your classroom, and you will want to read everything that students write for you and to ask for clarification when needed. Journals and portfolios, discussed in later chapters, are useful for this.
- *Open-ended questionnaires.* Many teachers of students in grade 4 and up use open-ended questionnaires to learn more about them. Being careful to avoid asking questions that might infringe upon a student's right to privacy, teachers ask students to write answers to questions such as:

When at lunch with your friends, what do you usually talk about?

When you read for fun or pleasure, what do you usually read?

What are your favorite movies, videos, or TV shows?

Who are your favorite music video performers?

What do you like to do when you just hang around?

With whom do you like to hang around, and where?

What do you plan to do after you graduate from high school?

Describe your favorite hobby or non-school-related activity.

- *Cumulative record.* Held in the school office is the cumulative record for each child, containing information recorded from year to year by teachers and other school professionals. Although you must use discretion before arriving at any conclusion about information in the file, the file may afford information for getting to know a particular student better.
- *Discussions with other professionals.* To better understand a child, it is often helpful to talk with that child's other teachers or counselor to learn of their perceptions and experiences with the student. One of the advantages of schools that are divided into "villages" (discussed in Chapter 3) is that teachers with a village get to know their students better, sometimes over a period of two or three years. Talking with other teachers of the village can be enlightening when you want to better know and understand a particular child.

Learning styles.   A topic discussed in Chapter 1, learning style is included here as another important way of getting to know your students so that your instruction can be made most effective. Students who are exceptional and/or culturally different from you, in particular, may prefer to learn in ways that differ from your own preferred way of learning. As stated by Grant and Sleeter (1989), "Learning styles overlap somewhat with cultural background and gender. Although not all members of a cultural or gender group learn in the same way, patterns exist in how members of different groups tend to approach tasks. . . . [However,] rather than generalizing about your own students based on the research on group differences, it is much more useful to investigate directly your own students' learning style preferences" (pp. 12–13). For doing that, you can use the Learning Styles Record Sheet for recording five categories of data (see Figure 2.1).

After analyzing data collected on your students you may notice certain learning style patterns based on gender and ethnic background, but Grant and Sleeter emphasize that you should avoid stereotyping certain groups as learning a certain way. Instead, use the patterns you discover in your students' learning style preferences as guides for planning the lessons and selecting teaching strategies.

FIGURE 2.1
Learning Styles Record Sheet
SOURCE: Reprinted with the permission of Simon & Schuster, Inc. from the Macmillan College text TURNING ON LEARNING by Carl A. Grant and Christine E. Sleeter. Copyright ©1989 by Merrill, an imprint of Macmillan College Publishing Company, Inc.

Directions: For each student, record data you collect about the following items related to the student's preferred style of learning.

Student's name _____

		Method of Data Collection	Findings
1. Style of working:	Alone		
	With others		
2. Learning modality:	Watching		
	Reading		
	Listening		
	Discussing		
	Touching		
	Moving		
	Writing		
3. Content:	People		
	Things		
4. Need for structure:	High		
	Low		
5. Details versus generalities			

Students' experiential background.   Another way of getting to know your students is to spend time in the neighborhoods in which they live. Observe and listen, finding things that you can use as examples or as lessons to help teach concepts. Record your observations in a table (see Table 2.1).

C. CLASSROOM MANAGEMENT

Effective teaching requires a well-organized, businesslike classroom in which motivated students work diligently at their learning tasks, free from distractions and disruptions caused by inappropriate behavior. Providing such a setting for learning is called effective classroom management.

Essential for effective classroom management is the maintenance of classroom control, that is, the process of controlling student behavior in the classroom. Classroom control involves both steps for preventing inappropriate student behavior and ideas for responding to students whose behavior is inappropriate.

The control aspect of teaching is frequently the most worrisome to beginning teachers—and they have good cause to be concerned. Even experienced teachers sometimes find control difficult, particularly at the middle school and junior high school level, where students are going through rapid physiological changes, and where so many come to school with psychological baggage and have already been alienated by bad experiences in their lives.

Another part of effective classroom management is good organization and administration of activities and materials. In a well-managed classroom students know what to do, have the materials needed to do it well, and stay on task while doing it. The classroom atmosphere is supportive; the assignments and procedures for doing those assignments are clear; the materials of instruction are current, interesting, and readily available; and the classroom proceedings are businesslike. At all times, the teacher is in control, seeing that

TABLE 2.1
Sample Observation Table

Observations	Related Academic Concepts	Ideas for Using Observations
1.		
2.		
3.		
4.		
5.		
6.		
7.		

SOURCE: Carl A. Grant and Christine E. Sleeter, *Turning On Learning* (New York: Merrill, 1989), p. 19. Reprinted by permission of Macmillan Publishing Company.

students are spending their time on appropriate tasks. For your teaching to be effective you must be skilled in managing the classroom.

Effective classroom management is the process of organizing and conducting a classroom so that it maximizes student learning. To manage your classroom successfully, you need to plan your lessons thoughtfully and thoroughly; provide students with a pleasant, supportive atmosphere; instill a desire and the confidence to learn and to achieve; establish control procedures; prevent distractions and disturbances; deal quickly and quietly with distractions and disturbances that are unavoidable; and, in general, promote effective student learning. If this sounds like a tall order, don't fret: if you adhere to the guidelines set forth in this chapter, you will be successful.

What is a well-managed, effectively controlled classroom? A well-managed classroom is one where the teacher is clearly in charge and the students learn. Let's now look at how that is done.

D. PREPARATION PROVIDES CONFIDENCE AND SUCCESS

For successful classroom management, beginning the school year well may make all the difference in the world. Therefore, you should appear at your first class meeting, and every meeting thereafter, as well prepared and as confident as possible. Perhaps you will feel nervous and apprehensive, but being ready and well prepared will probably help you at least appear to be confident. Then, if you proceed in a businesslike, matter-of-fact way, the impetus of your well-prepared beginning will cause the day to proceed as desired.

FIGURE 2.2
Establishing Classroom Behavior Expectations, Routines, and Procedures

When establishing classroom behavior expectations, routines, and procedures, remember this point: the learning time needs to run efficiently (with no "dead" spots), smoothly (with routine procedures and smooth transitions between activities), and with minimum disruption. Try to state expectations for student classroom behavior in a positive manner, emphasizing procedures and desired behaviors, stressing what children *should* do rather than what they should *not* do.

As you prepare your procedures and rules for classroom behavior, you need to consider what information students need to know from the start. This should then be reviewed and rehearsed with the students several times during the first week of school, then followed consistently throughout the school year. Things that students need to know from the start include:

- *How to obtain your attention and help.* Most teachers who are effective classroom managers expect students to raise their hands until the teacher acknowledges (usually by a nod) that the student's hand has been seen. With that acknowledgment, the student should lower his or her hand. To prevent the student from becoming bored and restless while waiting, you should attend to the student as quickly as possible. Expecting students to raise their hands before speaking allows you to control the noise and confusion level and to be proactive in deciding who speaks. The latter is important if you are to manage a classroom with equality—that is, with equal attention to individuals regardless of their gender, ethnicity, proximity to the teacher, or any other personal characteristic.
- *How to enter and leave the classroom.* From the time that the class is scheduled to begin until it officially ends, teachers who are effective classroom managers expect students to be in their assigned seats or at their assigned learning stations and to be attentive to the teacher or to the learning activity.
- *How to maintain, obtain, and use materials for learning and items of personal use.* Students need to know where, when, and how to store, retrieve, and care for items such as their coats, backpacks, books, pencils, and medicines; how to get papers and materials, laboratory or shop items; and when they may use the pencil sharpener and wastebasket. Classroom control is easiest to maintain when (1) items that students need for class activities and for their personal use are neatly arranged in places that require minimum foot traffic, (2) there are established procedures that students clearly expect and understand, (3) there is the least amount of student off-task time, and (4) students do not have to line up for anything. Therefore, you will want to

---

E. CLASSROOM PROCEDURES AND RULES OF ACCEPTABLE BEHAVIOR

You undoubtedly have heard it before, and now you are going to hear it again: it is impossible to overemphasize the importance of getting the school year off to a good start, so let's begin this section by discussing how to do that.

Getting the School Year Off to a Good Beginning

Preparation before the first day of school should include the determination of your classroom procedures and expectations for the behavior of the children while they are in your classroom. These procedures and rules must seem reasonable to your students, and in enforcing them you must be consistent. Sometimes procedures and rules can cause trouble, especially if there are too many. To avoid difficulty, it is best at first to present only the minimum number of procedures and rules necessary to get off to an orderly beginning. Too many procedures and rules at the beginning will only confuse students and make the classroom atmosphere seem repressive. By establishing, explaining, and sticking to only a few, you can leave yourself some room for judgments and maneuvering. The procedures and rules should be quite specific so that students know exactly what is expected and the consequences for breaking the rules and not following procedures. (To encourage a constructive and supportive classroom environment, when responding to inappropriate behavior, we encourage you and your students to practice thinking in terms of "consequences" rather than "punishment.")

Once you have decided on your initial procedures and rules, you are ready to explain them to your students and to begin rehearsing some of the procedures on the very first day of class. You will want to do this in a positive way (see Figure 2.2). Students work best when teacher expectations are clear to them and when procedures are clearly understood and have become routine.

FIGURE 2.2   cont'd

plan the room arrangement, equipment and materials storage, preparation of equipment, materials, and transitions between activities so as to avoid needless delays and confusion. At this age level in particular, problems in classroom control will most certainly occur whenever some or all students have nothing to do, even for a brief time.

- *When they can go to the drinking fountain and the bathroom.* Normally, at this age, students should be able to take care of these matters between classes; however, sometimes they do not or, for medical reasons, can not. Reinforce the notion that they should do those things before coming into your classroom, but be flexible enough for the occasional student who has an immediate need.
- *How to behave during a class interruption.* Unfortunately, class interruptions do occur, and in some schools they occur far too often. For an important reason, the principal or some other person from the school's office may need to interrupt the class to see the teacher or a student or to make an announcement to the entire class. Students need to know what behavior is expected of them during those interruptions.
- *What to do when they are late to your class or will be leaving early.* You need to understand and reinforce school policies on early dismissals and tardiness. Routinize your own procedures so students clearly understand what they are to do if they must leave your class early (say, for a medical appointment) or when they arrive late. The procedures should be such that late-arriving and early dismissal students do not have to disturb you or the lesson in process.
- *What the consequences are for inappropriate behavior.* Most teachers who are effective classroom managers routinize their procedures for handling inappropriate behavior, ensuring that the students understand its consequences. The consequences are posted in the classroom and, when not counter to school policy, may be similar to the following five-step model (see Baron, 1992; Blendinger et al., 1993):
  1. *First offense* results in a warning to the student.
  2. *Second offense* results in the student being given a 10-minute time out in an isolation area.
  3. *Third offense* results in a 15-minute time out (in isolation).
  4. *Fourth offense* results in a phone call to the student's parents or guardian.
  5. *Fifth offense* results in the student being sent to the vice-principal's or principal's office.
- *Rules for behavior and procedures to follow during emergency drills, real or practice.* Students need to know what to do, where to go, and how to behave in emergency conditions, such as might occur because of a fire, storm, earthquake, or because of a disruptive campus intruder.

F. FIFTY COMMON TEACHER MISTAKES THAT CAUSE STUDENT MISBEHAVIOR*

Oftentimes the inappropriate behavior of students is a direct result of something that the teacher did or did not do. Following are mistakes commonly made by beginning teachers. Read and understand the relevancy of each to your teaching.

1. *Lack of or inadequate long-range planning.* Long-range, detailed planning is important for reasons discussed in the next chapter. A beginning teacher who inadequately plans ahead is heading for trouble.
2. *Sketchy daily planning.* Sketchy, inadequate daily planning is a precursor to ineffective teaching, classroom management problems, and eventual teaching failure. Sometimes, after finding a few strategies that seem to work well for them, beginning teachers' lesson planning becomes increasingly sketchy, they fall into a rut of doing pretty much the same thing day after day (too much lecture and discussion, too many videos and worksheets), and they fail to consider and plan for individual student differences. By mid-semester, they have stopped growing professionally and are experiencing an increasing number of problems with students and with parents.
3. *Emphasizing the negative.* Too many verbal warnings to students for their inappropriate behavior and too little recognition for their positive behavior do not help to establish the positive climate needed for the most effective learning to take place. Reminding students of procedures is more positive, and less repressive, than is reprimanding them when they do not follow procedures.

*Adapted from J. F. Callahan, L. H. Clark, and Richard D. Kellough, *Teaching in the Middle and Secondary Schools,* 5th ed. (Englewood Cliffs, NJ: Prentice-Hall, 1995), pp. 237–241. Copyright 1994 by Richard D. Kellough.

4. *Letting students' hands be raised too long.* Allowing students to have their hands raised too long before recognizing them and attending to their questions or responses provides them with time to fool around. Although you don't have to call on students as soon as they raise a hand, you should acknowledge them quickly, such as with a nod or a wave of your hand, so they can lower their hand and return to their work. Then get to the student as quickly as possible. These procedures should be clearly understood by the students and consistently implemented by you.

5. *Spending too much time with one student or one group while failing to monitor the entire class.* Spending too much time with any one student or a small group of students is, in effect, ignoring the rest of the class. For the best classroom management, you must continually monitor the entire classroom of students. How much time is too much? As a general rule, more than 30 seconds with any one student or small group is probably approaching too much time.

6. *Beginning a new activity before gaining student attention.* A teacher who fails to consistently insist that students follow procedures and who does not wait until all students are in compliance before starting a new activity is destined for major problems in classroom control. You must establish and maintain classroom procedures. Starting an activity before all students are in compliance is, in effect, telling the students that it is not necessary for them to follow expected procedures. You cannot afford to tell students one thing and then do another. That is poor modeling behavior. Remember, what you do has greater impact on student behavior than what you say (Williams, 1993).

7. *Too-fast pacing.* Students need time to mentally engage and understand words a teacher uses. They need time to mentally and physically disengage from one activity and engage in the next. You must remember that this always will take more time for a classroom of 30 students than it does for just one person.

8. *Voice level that is always either too loud or too soft.* A teacher's voice that is too loud day after day can become irritating to some students, as can one that cannot be heard or understood. Students will tune out a teacher they cannot understand or whose voice is too soft or too loud.

9. *Assigning a journal entry without first giving the topic careful thought.* Many teachers often begin each class meeting by assigning students the task of writing an entry in their journals. If the question or topic students are supposed to write about is ambiguous and was hurriedly prepared, without thought to how students would interpret and respond to it, students will perceive it as busywork (for example, something to do while the teacher takes attendance) and not important. Then, if they do it at all, it will be only with a great deal of disruptive commotion and much less enthusiasm than if they were writing on a topic that had meaning for them.

10. *Standing too long in one place.* When in the classroom, you must be mobile, as often said by experienced teachers, "to work the crowd."

11. *Sitting while teaching.* There is rarely time to sit while teaching. You cannot monitor the class while seated, nor can you afford to appear casual and uninterested in what students are doing.

12. *Being too serious, no fun.* No one would argue with the statement that good teaching is serious business. Students respond best, however, to teachers who obviously enjoy and have fun working with them and helping them learn.

13. *Using the same teaching strategy or combination of strategies day after day (being in a rut).* After awhile, such a teacher's classroom becomes boring to students. Because of their differences, students respond best to a variety of well-planned and meaningful classroom activities.

14. *Inadequate use of silence (wait time) after asking a subject content question.* When expected to think deeply about a question, students need time to do it. (This is discussed further in Chapter 4.)

15. *Poor or inefficient use of the overhead projector and the writing board.* A poorly prepared transparency and the ineffective use of the overhead projector and writing board say to students that you are not a competent teacher. Like a competent surgeon or automobile mechanic, a competent teacher selects and effectively uses the best professional tools available for the jobs to be done.

16. *Ineffective use of facial expressions and body language.* Your gestures and body language say more to students than do your words. For example, a teacher didn't understand why his class of seventh-grade math students would not respond to his repeated expression, "I need your attention." In one instance he used that verbal expression eight times in less than 15 minutes. Viewing his teaching that day on video helped him to understand the problem. He had been dressing very casually and standing most of the time with one hand in his pocket. At five foot eight, with a slight build and rather deadpan facial expression and nonexpressive voice, he did not have a commanding presence in the classroom. He returned to his classroom wearing a tie and using his hands, face, and voice more expressively. Rather than saying, "I need your attention," he waited in silence for the students to become attentive. It worked.

17. *Too much reliance on teacher talk for instruction and for classroom control.* Beginning teachers have a tendency to rely too much on teacher talk. Too much teacher talk is deadly. Unable to discern between the important and the unimportant verbiage, students will quickly tune the teacher out. In addition, useless verbalism, such as global praise and verbal fill-ins like "okay," causes students to pay less attention when the teacher has something to say that is truly important.

18. *Inefficient use of teacher time.* Think carefully about what you are going to be doing every minute, planning for the most efficient and therefore effective use of your time in the classroom. Consider the following example. During a lesson, Angelica, a middle school language arts teacher, is recording student contributions on a large sheet of butcher paper taped to the writing board. The tasks of soliciting student responses, acknowledging those responses, holding and manipulating a writing pen, and writing on the paper require decisions and actions that consume valuable time and can distract Angelica from her students. An effective alternative is to have a reliable student helper do the writing while Angelica handles the solicitation and acknowledgment of student responses. That way Angelica has fewer decisions and fewer actions to distract her and maintains eye contact and proximity with the children in the classroom.

19. *Talking to and interacting with only a portion of students.* When leading a class discussion, too many beginning teachers favor (by their eye contact, proximity, and verbal interaction) only 40 to 65 percent of the students, sometimes completely ignoring the others for an entire class period. Feeling ignored, those students will, in time, become disinterested and unruly. Remember to spread your interactions and to try to establish eye contact with every student at least once each minute.

20. *Not requiring students to raise their hands and to be acknowledged before responding.* You cannot be proactive and in control of your interactions with students if you allow them to shout out responses and questions whenever they feel like it. In addition, fueling their natural impulsivity is not helping them to mature intellectually.

21. *Collecting and returning homework papers before assigning students something to do.* Students will become restless and inattentive if they have nothing to do while waiting to turn in or receive papers. It is best to avoid any kind of "dead" time—time where students have nothing to do.

22. *Verbally or nonverbally interrupting students once they are on task.* Avoid doing or saying anything once students are working on a learning task or taking a test. If there is an important point you must make, write it on the board. If you want to return some papers while they are working, do it in a way and at a time when they are least likely to be distracted from their learning task.

23. *Using "Shh—" to obtain student attention or to quiet them.* When doing this, you will sound like a balloon with a slow leak. "Shh—" and the overuse of verbal fill-ins such as "okay" should be eliminated from a teacher's professional vocabulary.

24. *Overuse of verbal efforts to halt inappropriate student behavior.* Beginning teachers seem to have a tendency to rely too much on verbal interaction and not enough on nonverbal intervention techniques. To verbally reprimand a student for interrupting class activities is a use and therefore a reinforcement of that very behavior you are trying to discourage. Instead, develop indirect, silent intervention techniques.

25. *Poor body positioning in the classroom.* Always position your body so you can visually monitor the entire class.

26. *Settling for less when you should be trying for more; not getting the most from student responses to content discussion.* Don't hurry a discussion; squeeze student responses for all you can, especially when discussing a topic they are obviously interested in. Ask students for clarification or reasons for a response, ask for verification or data, have another student paraphrase what one student said, and pump students for deeper thought and meaning. Too often, a teacher will ask a question, get an abbreviated (often one-word) response from a student, and then move on to new content. Instead, follow a student response to your question with a sequence of questions to prompt and try to push student thinking to higher levels.

27. *Using threats.* One middle school teacher told her class of students that if they continued their inappropriate and disruptive talking, they would lose their break time. Have that consequence as part of the understood procedures, then don't threaten to take away their break time, do it. Follow through with procedures, but avoid threats of any kind. (It is useful, however, to remind students of procedures. Reminding students of procedures is different and more positive than is threatening them with punishment.) In addition, be very cautious about punishing the entire class for the misbehavior of only some students. Although we understand the rationale behind this tactic—to get group pressure working for you—oftentimes it backfires, and students who have been behaving well become alienated from the teacher because they feel they have been punished unfairly for the misbehavior of others. Those students (and their parents) expect the teacher to be able to handle the misbehaving students without punishing those whose behavior is appropriate; they are right.

28. *Global praise.* "Your rough drafts were really wonderful" says nothing and is simply another instance of useless verbalism. Instead, be specific, explaining what it was about their drafts that made them so wonderful.

29. *Using color but without meaning.* Use of color, such as colored pens for overhead transparencies or colored chalk for chalkboard writing, is nice but will lose its effectiveness in a very short time unless the colors have meaning. Color code everything in the classroom so students understand the meaning of the colors and their learning is facilitated.

30. *Verbally reprimanding a student from the opposite side of the classroom.* This is needless distraction of all students, plus, because of peer pressure, it simply perpetuates the "you versus them" syndrome. Reprimand when necessary, but do it quietly and privately.

31. *Interacting with only a "chosen few," rather than spreading the interactions among all students.* It is easy to fall into the habit of interacting with only a few students, especially those who are vocal and have "intelligent" contributions. However, your job is to teach all students, and to do that you must be proactive in your interactions, not reactive.

32. *Being too slow to intervene during inappropriate student behavior.* Unless you nip it in the bud, inappropriate student behavior usually gets worse, not better. It won't go away by itself. It's best to stop it quickly and resolutely. A teacher who ignores inappropriate behavior is, in effect, approving it. That approval reinforces its continuation.

33. *Not learning and using student names.* A teacher who does not know or use student names when addressing students is seen by the students as impersonal and uncaring. You will want to quickly learn student names and then use them when calling on students.

34. *Reading student papers only for correct answers and not for process and student thinking.* Reading student papers only for "correct" responses reinforces the misconception that the process of arriving at answers or solutions (thinking) and alternative solutions or answers are unimportant.

35. *Not putting time plans on the board.* Rather than yelling out how much time is left for an activity, such as a quiz or a writing or cooperative learning activity (and thereby interrupting student thinking), before the activity begins you should write on the board how much time is allowed for it. Write the time the activity is to end. If during the activity a decision is made to change that, then write the changed time on the board. Avoid distracting students once they are on task.

36. *Asking global questions that nobody will likely answer or rhetorical questions for which you do not expect a response.* Example: "Does everyone understand how that

was done?" or "Are there any questions?" or "How do you all feel about. . . ?" If you want to check for student understanding or opinions, do a spot check by asking specific questions, allowing some time to think, then calling on students. With children of this age, it is advisable to avoid rhetorical questions. Otherwise, students will not be able to tell when you expect them to think and respond.

37. *Failure to do frequent comprehension checks to see if students are understanding.* Too often, teachers simply plow through their lesson without checking for student comprehension, assuming that students are understanding everything. As a general rule, during direct instruction, do a comprehension check about once every ten minutes. Comprehension checks may be verbal, as when you ask a question, or nonverbal, as when you observe student body language and facial expressions.

38. *Use of poorly worded, ambiguous questions.* Plan your questions, write them out, answer them yourself, and try to predict whether students will understand and how they will respond to a particular question.

39. *Failure to balance interactions with students according to student gender.* Many teachers (experienced as well as beginning and female as well as male) interact more often with male than with female students. Avoid that inequity.

40. *Trying to talk over student noise.* This simply tells students that their being noisy while you are talking is okay. All that you will accomplish when trying to talk over a high student noise level is a sore throat by the end of the school day, and you will be reinforcing the unwanted behavior.

41. *Wanting to be liked by the students.* Of course, every teacher wants to be liked by the children, but for now don't worry about their liking you. Just teach. Respect will be earned as a result of your good teaching and your caring about the learning of the children. Their like for you will develop over time. Otherwise, in the beginning they may "like" you, but they will lose respect (and affection) for you later.

42. *Failure to keep students attentive to an educationally useful video or movie.* This usually happens because the teacher failed to give the students a written handout about what they are to learn from watching the audiovisual. Sometimes students need an additional focus. Furthermore, an audiovisual is exactly that—audio and visual. To reinforce the learning, add a kinesthetic aspect—in this instance, the writing. This helps to organize student learning and encourages the hands-on and minds-on learning that you want.

43. *False or stutter-start instruction.* A false or stutter start is when the teacher begins an activity, is distracted, begins again, is again distracted, tries again to start, and so on. During stutter starts, students become increasingly restless and inattentive, making the final start almost impossible for the teacher to achieve. Avoid false starts. Begin each activity clearly and decisively.

44. *Failure to give students a pleasant greeting on Monday or following a holiday or to remind them to have a pleasant weekend or holiday.* Students are likely to perceive such a teacher as uncaring or impersonal.

45. *Sounding egocentric.* Whether you are or are not egocentric, you want to avoid sounding egocentric. Sometimes egocentrism is subtle, such as when a teacher says, "What *I* am going to do now is . . ." rather than, "What *we* are going to do now is . . ." If you want to strive for group cohesiveness, that is, a sense of we-ness, then teach not as if you are the leader and your students are the followers, but rather in a manner that empowers your students in their learning.

46. *Taking too much time to give verbal directions for a new activity.* Students get impatient and restless during long verbal instructions from the teacher. It is better to give brief instructions (no more than 60 seconds should do it) and get your students started on the task. For more complicated activities, you can teach three or four students the instructions and then have them lead "workshops" with five or six students in each workshop group, thereby freeing you to monitor the progress of each group.

47. *Taking too much time for an activity.* Whether lecturing or doing group work, think carefully about how much time students can effectively pay attention. A general rule of thumb is that for most intermediate and middle school classes, when only one or two learning modalities (for example, auditory and visual) are involved, the activity should

not extend beyond about 15 minutes; when more than two senses are involved (if tactile and/or kinesthetic are added), then the activity might extend for 20 or 30 minutes.

48. *Being uptight and anxious.* Consciously or subconsciously, children are quick at detecting a teacher who is uptight and anxious, and for that teacher, events in the classroom will probably not go well. It's like a highly contagious disease. If you are uptight and anxious, your students will sense it and become the same. To prevent being uptight and anxious to the extent that it is a hindrance to good teaching and student learning, you must prepare lessons carefully, thoughtfully, and thoroughly, and then focus on their implementation. Unless there is something personal going on in your life making you anxious and uptight, you are more likely to be in control and confident in the classroom when you have lessons that are well prepared. If you have a personal problem, you will need to concentrate on ensuring that your anger, hostility, fear, or other negative emotions do not negatively affect your teaching and your interactions with the children. Regardless of what is going on in your personal life, your students will face you each day expecting to be taught.

49. *Resorting too quickly to punishment for classroom misbehavior.* Too many beginning teachers mistakenly either try to ignore inappropriate student behavior or skip steps, resorting too quickly to such punishment as taking away PATs (preferred activity time) or break time or assigning detention. In-between steps include the use of alternative activities in the classroom. Too many teachers unrealistically expect to successfully have all 30 students doing the same thing at the same time rather than having several alternative activities simultaneously occurring in the classroom (multilevel teaching). For example, a student who is being disruptive during a class discussion (perhaps the student is an immature kinesthetic learner) might behave better when given the choice of moving to a quiet reading center in the classroom or to a learning activity center to work alone or with one other student. If, after trying an alternate activity, a student continues to be disruptive, then you may have to try another alternate activity or send the student to another supervised out-of-the-classroom location arranged by you prior to the incident until you have time (after class or after school) to talk with the student about the problem.

50. *Use of negative language.* Too many beginning teachers try to control their students with negative language, such as "There should be *no* talking " or "*No* gum or candy in class or else you will get detention" (double mistake—negative language and threat) or "*No* getting out of your seats without my permission." Negative language is repressive and does not help instill a positive classroom environment. Students need to know what is expected of them, to understand classroom procedures. Therefore, to encourage a positive classroom atmosphere, you should use concise, positive language reminding students exactly what they are expected to do rather than what they are not to do.

G. PRACTICING SAFETY IN THE CLASSROOM

While all teachers must be constantly alert to potential safety hazards for their students while in the classroom and on school-sponsored excursions outside the classroom, this can be even more important when children are doing science-related activities. An unavoidable result of increased student involvement in active learning is the increased risk of injury due to the exposure to potentially harmful apparatus and materials. This fact should not deter you, however, from planning and implementing the most meaningful lessons for your children. Just be as aware as possible of potential hazardous situations, and then prepare yourself, your classroom, and your students well to prevent accidents from happening and to handle an emergency situation.

"Safety First" should be the dictum for all learning activities. Many teachers have developed and use special lessons on safety instructions in the classroom. Regardless of whether you use such a special lesson, you should remind students of the rules and procedures before beginning any lesson with a potential safety hazard.

Guidelines for Classroom Safety

Although your school district or state department of education may be able to provide specific guidelines on safety in your school, and professional magazines and journals (such as those listed in Figure 6.4 of Chapter 6) frequently have articles dealing with safety in the classroom, here are general guidelines for your consideration.

1. Post safety rules and classroom procedures in the classroom. Be sure you model them yourself, at all times. Review and rehearse the rules and procedures with students until following them becomes routine.

2. Animal pets should not be handled by students. It is probably best they not even be brought into the classroom.

3. Avoid using flammable materials and alcohol burners. Rather than alcohol burners, use lighted candles or hot plates, and do so with caution.

4. Be alert to any child who has the potential for an allergic reaction to plants, animal fur, dust, and so on.

5. Periodically inspect all electrical equipment for frayed cords. If frayed, do not use them.

6. Because of potential diseases, dead animals and decaying plant material should never be handled by children nor brought to the classroom.

7. No child should ever be left unattended or unsupervised in the classroom or while on an outing. Every child should be within sight of the teacher or another supervising adult. All activities must be carefully monitored by the teacher or other supervising adult. Students must be prohibited from doing any unauthorized activity.

8. Every classroom should be equipped with a fully charged ABC-type fire extinguisher, and you must know how to use it.

9. If your classroom is equipped with natural gas, the master control for the gas outlets should be kept turned off.

10. Heavy or otherwise dangerous items (such as glass items) should never be stored above the heads of students.

11. Maintain a neat and orderly classroom, with aisles kept clear and books, backpacks, and other personal belongings kept in designated storage areas.

12. Maintain accurate labels on all drawers, cupboards, and containers.

13. Never allow students to climb or to be in potentially dangerous body positions.

14. Avoid using extension cords; never overload an electrical circuit.

15. Plants, animals, chemicals, and apparatus that are poisonous or otherwise dangerous should never be allowed in the classroom for any reason, even if brought and intended to be used for a demonstration by the teacher or a guest speaker.

16. Sharp objects and items that could shatter when broken should not be in the classroom without teacher approval and proper supervision.

17. Students should not be permitted to overheat or to overexert themselves.

18. You and your students should know what to do in case of emergencies. Emergency procedures should be posted conspicuously in the classroom.

19. Before taking students on a field trip, solicit reliable adult help, even if only going a short distance from the school. A reasonable ratio—a rule in many schools—is one adult for every ten children.

20. A useful rule of thumb is that if you have doubts about the appropriateness of an activity for a particular group of children, then it probably is not appropriate. In any case, when in doubt discuss it with other teachers and the school principal or the principal's designee.

SUMMARY

Students are more likely to learn when they feel that the learning is important, interesting, and worth the time. In this chapter we described factors important for learning to occur. As significant as specific attempts to motivate your students is how you manage your classroom, strategies that you select, and how those strategies are implemented.

   As a classroom teacher you should not be expected to solve all the societal woes that can spill over into the classroom. But, on the other hand, as a professional you have certain responsibilities, including to thoughtfully and thoroughly prepare for your classes; to professionally manage and control your classes; to maintain a safe learning environment; and to be able to diagnose and remedy those learning difficulties, disturbances, and minor misbehaviors that are the norm for classrooms and for the age group with which you are working. If you follow the guidelines that are provided in this book, you will be well on your way to developing a teaching style and management system that, for the most part, should allow your teaching to run smoothly and effectively, without serious problems.

It is important to select the most appropriate strategies to accompany your teaching plans and compliment your management system. Chapters that follow present guidelines for doing that.

QUESTIONS AND ACTIVITIES FOR DISCUSSION

1. Identify at least four guidelines for your use of praise for a student's appropriate behavior.

2. Explain why it is important to prevent behavior problems before they occur. Describe at least five preventive steps you will take to reduce the number of management problems that you will have.

3. Too many teachers attempt to resolve problems with individual students within the regular class period. Describe two recommendations for what you can do if you have a problem with the classroom behavior of a specific student.

4. Explain the rationale for the phrase, "Catch them being good."

5. Explain why many learning psychologists (e.g., Montessori and Piaget) oppose the teacher's use of extrinsic reinforcement for managing student behavior.

6. Explain how and why your classroom management procedures and expectations might differ depending upon the nature of the students, the grade level you are teaching, and the activities in your classroom.

7. Explain why supervisors of student teachers may expect student teachers to prepare written classroom management plans.

8. Explain the difference between reprimanding a student for his or her inappropriate classroom behavior and reminding that student of classroom procedures.

9. Explain why interrupting the discussion of a topic of study to verbally reprimand a student for his or her inappropriate behavior is inappropriate teacher behavior.

10. It has been said that 90 percent of control problems in the intermediate or middle school classroom are teacher caused. Do you agree or disagree? Why?

11. Some supervisors of student teachers prefer that the student teacher never conduct a class while seated. Is it ever appropriate for a teacher to sit down while teaching? Can a teacher effectively monitor a classroom while seated?

12. In groups of four, outline a safety program that you would institute if you were members of a teaching team in a middle-level school. Ask a department chairperson or team leader in a local middle-level school to critique the program. Share the results with others in groups in your class.

13. From your current observations and fieldwork related to this teacher preparation program, clearly identify one specific example of educational practice that seems contradictory to exemplary practice or theory as presented in this chapter. Present your explanation for the discrepancy.

14. Describe any prior concepts you held that changed as a result of your experiences with this chapter. Describe the changes.

REFERENCES

Baron, E. B. (1992). *Discipline strategies for teachers*. Fastback 344. Bloomington, IN: Phi Delta Kappa Educational Foundation.

Blendinger, J., et al. (1993). *Win-win discipline*. Fastback 353. Bloomington, IN: Phi Delta Kappa Educational Foundation.

Feather, N. T. (Ed.). (1982). *Expectations and actions*. Hillsdale, NJ: Erlbaum.

Grant, C. A., & Sleeter, C. E. (1989). *Turning on learning*. New York: Merrill.

Williams, M. M. (1993). Actions speak louder than words: What students think. *Educational Leadership, 51*(3), 22–23.

SUGGESTED READINGS

Black, S. (1992). In praise of judicious praise. *Executive Editor, 14*(10), 24–27.

Chance, P. (1992). The rewards of learning. *Phi Delta Kappan, 74*(3), 200–207.

Chance, P. (1993). Sticking up for rewards. *Phi Delta Kappan, 74*(10), 787–790.

Cleary, L. M. (1990). The fragile inclination to write: Praise and criticism in the classroom. *English Journal, 79*(2), 22–28.

Froyen, L. A. (1993). *Classroom management: The reflective teacher-leader* (2nd ed.). New York: Macmillan.

Hunter, M. (1994). *Enhancing teaching.* New York: Macmillan.

Jones, F. (1987). *Positive classroom discipline.* New York: McGraw-Hill.

Kounin, J. (1977). *Discipline and group management in classrooms.* New York: Holt, Rinehart and Winston.

Merrett, R., & Wheldall, K. (1992). Teachers' use of praise and reprimands to boys and girls. *Educational Review, 44*(1), 73–79.

O'Brien, S. J. (1990). For parents particularly: Praising children—Five myths. *Childhood Education, 66*(4), 248–249.

Phillips, D. R., et al. (1994). Beans, blocks, and buttons: Developing thinking. *Educational Leadership, 51*(5), 50–53.

Tauber, R. T. (1990). Criticism and deception: The pitfalls of praise. *NASSP Bulletin, 74*(528), 95–99.

Thomas, J. (1991). You're the greatest! *Principal, 71*(1), 32–33.

Tingley, S. (1992). Negative rewards. *Educational Leadership, 50*(1), 80.

Wiske, M. S. (1994). How teaching for understanding changes the rules in the classroom. *Educational Leadership, 51*(5), 19–21.

CHAPTER 3

Planning the Curriculum

For teachers of grades 4–9, the curriculum can present a unique challenge. Unlike the curriculum in lower grades, which is usually developed for a single-grade-level teacher in a self-contained classroom, and unlike the high school curricula developed for teachers of various subjects in departmentalized classrooms, the curricula of many middle schools are developed by a common group of teachers. They collectively plan special programs for specific cohorts of children.

The backbone of an effective instructional program is the curriculum. To learn how it is developed, you must first understand how the middle school is organized—that is, how teachers are assigned to subject matter and how students are grouped for instruction.

Planning for instruction is a very large and important part of a classroom teacher's job. Responsible for planning at three levels, you will participate in long-range planning (the planning of courses for a semester or academic year and planning of units of instruction) and short-range planning (the preparation of daily lessons). Throughout your career you will be engaged almost continually in planning at each of these three levels; planning for instruction is a steady and cyclic process that involves the preactive and reflective thought-processing phases discussed in Chapter 1. The importance of mastering the process at the very beginning of your career cannot be overemphasized.

Long-range curriculum planning for grades 4–9 is the focus of this chapter. The chapter that follows prepares you for daily planning. Additional language arts–and social studies–specific discussions of curriculum are presented in Parts II and III.

Specifically, this chapter is designed to help you understand:

1. How middle schools are organized for curriculum development.
2. The components of the middle school curriculum.
3. A model for curriculum development specific to middle school education.
4. The nature and role of core curriculum.
5. The nature and role of exploratory programs.
6. The nature and role of co-curricular activities.
7. The meaning of *thematic.*
8. The meaning of *teaching unit.*
9. Procedures for preparing any type of instructional unit.
10. Procedures for developing an interdisciplinary thematic unit.

Let us begin by clarifying a few terms. A *course* is a sequence of instruction that presents to students a major division of subject matter or a discipline or integrates a couple of disciplines, such as language arts and literature, language arts and social studies, or science and mathematics. Courses are laid out for a year, a semester, a quarter, or even a few weeks, as is the case with the minicourses common to the exploratory programs found in some middle schools. A course is broken up into teaching units. A teaching (or instructional) unit is a major subdivision of a course, comprising a series of lessons of planned instruction about some central theme, topic, issue, or problem for a period of several days to several weeks. (In contrast, a *resource unit* is a general plan for a unit or a particular topic, and is designed to be used as a basis for building a teaching unit. Resource units, often found in curriculum centers and curriculum libraries, although often rich in resources, are not comprised of sequentially planned lessons, as are teaching units.) Unless they are interdisciplinary thematic units, teaching units that take much longer than three weeks tend to lose their effectiveness as recognizable units of instruction. Units are divided into lessons. A *lesson* is a subdivision of a unit, usually taught in a single class period or, on occasion, over two or three successive periods.

A. CURRICULUM DEVELOPMENT AND IMPLEMENTATION

Grade-span configurations at the school where you will be teaching (might be K–8, 5–8, 6–8, 7 and 8, 7–9, 7–12, or some other). For middle-level education, the trend is toward a 5–8 grade-level configuration, with a continuing decline in the traditional 7–9 junior high grade configuration (used with permission from Valentine et al., 1993, p. 19). Regardless of the grade-span configuration you encounter, the middle school grades are usually organized into some type of scheduling (block, modular, or flexible) that is an alternative to the traditional method of assigning students to six or seven different classes for 45 to 50 minutes each, five days a week, for the entire school year (p. 62).

Interdisciplinary Teaching and Teaching Teams

Middle-grades teachers are members of a professional team, especially those teachers of grades 5–8. Usually, two to five teachers from different subject areas work together to plan the curriculum for a common group of students each has in a classroom. Commonly, these teaching teams are made up of one teacher each from English/language arts, mathematics, science, and history/social studies. These four subject areas comprise what is called the *core curriculum*. In addition, specialty teachers may be part of the teaching team. These may include teachers of physical education, art, and music, as well as learning disabilities and at-risk specialty personnel. Because a growing number of students in grades 4–9 are identified as being at risk of not completing school, some teams may ask a school counselor or a community resource person to be a member. Because the core and specialty subjects cross different disciplines of study, these teams are commonly called *interdisciplinary teaching teams* or simply interdisciplinary teams. Valentine et al. have identified the following advantages of interdisciplinary teaming:

1. Teachers experience real collaboration within the workplace and become more satisfied professionally.
2. Students feel less isolation and, therefore, more social bonding with peers and individual teachers.
3. Teachers and students develop a strong sense of community and share a common rationale and mission for education.
4. The instructional program becomes highly coordinated across content areas in a way that encourages student creativity and critical thinking.

Many at-risk youth disengage from school during the middle grade years before physically dropping out sometime during their high school years. A Massachusetts Advocacy Center study (1986) found that as many as 50 percent of Boston's school dropouts left after grade eight, and almost 17 percent of middle school students were not promoted. These numbers become staggering when added to the number of students who drop out during high school but mentally disengage during the middle grade years, deciding not to try any more. (Other terms used for students who have mentally disengaged but who still attend school are *on-campus dropouts, disconnected youth,* and *students at risk.*)

The California State Department of Education (1986) has recommended that an increased emphasis be placed on dropout prevention at the middle and junior high school levels. Making learning more meaningful for these students at school, at home, and in life is an imperative responsibility of middle grades teachers who, for many students, are the last hope.

One method shown to be successful in making the learning meaningful for students is the use of *interdisciplinary thematic units (ITUs).* (For example, in Chapter 8, see the description of the development of a weather unit in "Planning for Instruction." A complete ITU is presented at the end of this book. Although the specifics of this approach will be presented later, for now, understand that the purpose of the thematic unit approach is to integrate the content of various subject areas by finding a common thread or theme, thereby connecting the students' learning. Students need to know that the information being learned will be practical not only in school, but in the workplace and throughout life. The essence of today's middle school concept is based on connecting *life with learning* through interdisciplinary thematic units. As explained at the opening of this part, integrated instruction, the theme of this book, is one step in that direction.

School-within-a-School

An interdisciplinary team can be thought of as a "house" or "school-within-a-school" (also called "village" or "pod"), in which each team of teachers is assigned each day to the same group of about 125 students for a common block of time. Within this block of time, teachers on the team are responsible for the many professional decisions necessary, such as how to make school meaningful to students' lives, what specific responsibilities each teacher has to fulfill each day, which guidance activities are to be implemented, what sort of special attention is needed by individual students, and how students will be grouped for instruction.

The school-within-a-school concept (used not only in many middle schools but also in some elementary schools, junior high schools, and high schools) helps students make important and meaningful connections among disciplines and provides them with peer and adult group identification that offers a significant sense of belonging . Classes for a village's teachers and students are often clustered in rooms that are close to one another, thereby increasing teacher-teacher and student-teacher communication. "Proximity of team members' classrooms can facilitate coordination of instruction, allow more flexibility in scheduling, and promote collaboration between colleagues. Classrooms scattered about the school are less likely to facilitate a cohesive learning environment" (Valentine et al., 1993, p. 53).

Common Planning Time and Lead Teachers

For an interdisciplinary team to plan a common curriculum, members must meet frequently. This is best accomplished by scheduling a shared preparation period to plan the curriculum and to discuss the progress and needs of individual students. "Common planning time is critical to the success of interdisciplinary teaming" (Valentine et al., 1993, p. 52).

Each teaching team assigns a member to be a lead teacher or teacher leader. The lead teacher organizes the planning meetings, facilitates discussions during these sessions, and acts as a liaison with other school groups and administrators to make sure the team has the necessary resources to put its plans into action. Being a lead teacher may be a responsibility rotated among team members throughout the school year, or lead teachers may be appointed by the administration or selected by team members.

Block Scheduling

To accommodate common planning time for teachers and to allow for more instructional flexibility, most middle schools use some form of block scheduling to assign students to teachers for instruction. Blocks of time ranging from 70 to 90 minutes replace the traditional class length of 45 to 60 minutes. The sample block schedule in Figure 3.1 illustrates the assignment of teachers to different classes.

FIGURE 3.1
Block Schedule
SOURCE: Reprinted with the permission of Macmillan Publishing Company from Richard D. Kellough, Noreen C. Kellough, and David L. Hough, *Middle School Teaching: Methods and Resources*, p. 77. Copyright © 1993 by Macmillan Publishing Company.

TEACHER	ADVISOR-ADVISEE	BLOCK 1		BLOCK 2		BLOCK 3		BLOCK 4	
		M W F	T TH	M W F	T TH	M W F	T TH	M W F	T TH
A	yes	Sci-6	Sci-6	Plan time	Plan time	Sci-6	Sci-6	Reading-6	Exploratory-6
B	yes	Eng-6	Eng-6	Plan time	Plan time	Eng-6	Eng-6	Reading-6	Exploratory-6
C	yes	SS-6	SS-6	Plan time	Plan time	SS-6	SS-6	Reading-6	Exploratory-6
D	yes	Mth-6	Mth-6	Plan time	Plan time	Mth-6	Mth-6	Reading-6	Exploratory-6
E	yes	Eng-7	Eng-7	Eng-7	Eng-7	Plan time	Plan time	Speech	Exploratory-6
F	yes	Sci-7	Sci-7	Sci-7	Sci-7	Plan time	Plan time	Reading-7	Exploratory-6
G	yes	SS-7	SS-7	SS-7	SS-7	Plan time	Plan time	Reading-7	Exploratory-6
H	yes	Pre Alg-7	Mth-7	Mth-7	Mth-7	Plan time	Plan time	Reading-7	Exploratory-6
I	yes	Plan time	Plan time	SS-8	SS-8	SS-8	SS-8	Reading-7	Exploratory-7
J	yes	Plan time	Plan time	Alg I-8	Pre Alg-7	Pre Alg-8	Mth-8	Mth-8	PreAlg-8
K	yes	Plan time	Plan time	Sci-8	Sci-8	Sci-8	Sci-8	Intramurals	Sci-8
L	yes	Plan time	Plan time	Eng-8	Eng-8	Eng-8	Speech	Eng-8	Eng-8
M	yes	Computer	Computer	Home Ec-8	Home Ec-8	Plan time	Plan time	Home Ec-8	Exploratory-7
N	yes					Shop-8	Shop-8	Shop-8	Exploratory-7
O	yes						Spanish-8	Exploratory-7	
P	yes	Plan time	Plan time	Art-6	Art-6	Art-7	Art-7	Art-8	Exploratory-7
Q	no						Art-8		
R	no	LD	LD	LD	LD	LD	LD	Plan time	Plan time

The sample student schedule in Figure 3.2 shows how a seventh grader might be assigned to different classes on different days.

Often, no bells are rung to signal movement from one block to the next. Instead, teachers verbally dismiss their classes. When the school building is so designed, or if the blocks are planned appropriately, students move only a short distance between classes, perhaps just across the hall or next door. Such arrangements often produce serendipitous results. For example, students may not have to carry as many books and may need to go to their lockers only twice a day between blocks. In many schools, student lockers are not used at all. Teachers can more easily supervise unstructured time and thereby have better control over the "hidden" or unplanned curriculum, as students are not roaming the halls for several minutes five or six times a day. And the reduction of bell ringing from as often as eight times a day to perhaps only two or three times a day creates less disturbance. As reported by one administrator, when village classrooms are in close proximity, there is less travel, noise, and congestion throughout a school building than in a traditional school setting (Raebeck, 1990).

B. MIDDLE SCHOOL CURRICULUM COMPONENTS

Within the framework of middle school organization lie several components that form a comprehensive program. Two terms, *curriculum* and *instruction,* combine to form the program that students experience.

FIGURE 3.2
A Seventh-Grade Student Schedule
SOURCE: Adapted from Richard D. Kellough, Noreen C. Kellough, and David L. Hough, *Middle School Teaching: Methods and Resources* (New York: Macmillan, 1993), p. 75.

Student Schedule

Name: Gibbons, Sarah   Gender: Female   Grade: 7   Counselor: Jones
Date of Birth: 5/19/79   Home Phone: 765-2098   Emergency Phone: 765-6781
Address: 1373 E. Main, Wilmington, Ohio 45177

A Week Schedule

		Mon Wed Fri	Tue Thur
7:45–8:10		Advisor-advisee	Advisor-advisee
8:10–9:35	1st Block	Social studies	Mathematics
9:35–11:35	2nd Block	English	Science
11:35–1:00	3rd Block	General music (1/2)	Art (1/2)
		P.E./Health (1/2)	P.E./Health (1/2)
1:00–2:25	4th Block	Reading	Exploratory

B Week Schedule

		Mon Wed Fri	Tue Thur
7:45–8:10		Advisor-advisee	Advisor-advisee
8:10–9:35	1st Block	Mathematics	Social studies
9:35–11:35	2nd Block	Science	English
11:35–1:00	3rd Block	Art (1/2)	General music (1/2)
		P.E./Health (1/2)	P.E./Health (1/2)
1:00–2:25	4th Block	Exploratory	Reading

Note that there are two schedules, one for "A Week" and one for "B Week." With this plan, the student's schedule alternates each week.

Curriculum is defined in various ways. Some define it as the planned learning that is presented to students. Others say that the curriculum is only that which students actually learn. Still others hold that the curriculum is all experiences students encounter, whether planned or unplanned, learned or unlearned. William Alexander, the "father of middle school education" defines curriculum as "the sum of experiences of learners which take place under the auspices of the school" (1988, p. 33).

Alexander's definition implies that many different educational experiences collectively comprise the curriculum. Four programs are identified that contribute in different ways to student learning: (1) the program of *studies* (courses offered), (2) the program of *activities* (sports, clubs, and organizations), (3) the program of *services* (transportation, lunch, nurse), and (4) the *hidden curriculum* (school climate and informal student interactions that take place before and after school, at social events, and in the halls, bathrooms, and other areas of the school that are not monitored as closely as individual classrooms).

A working definition that adheres to the middle school philosophy is one that considers curriculum as the *entire school program,* including academic course content, planned and unplanned activities, and structured and semistructured nonacademic components of schooling.

Instruction, likewise, has several definitions, some of which are not clearly distinguishable from curriculum. Where curriculum is more narrowly associated with *content,* instruction is associated with *methods*—that is, ways of conveying information or presenting content. Curriculum and instruction must go hand in hand to affect learning.

Looking at the total school program and analyzing its various component parts, or domains, you can readily see the importance of studying curriculum and instruction. In a study of middle school curricula and instruction, Hough (1989) found that student learning experiences are affected by six domains. The six domains with their components are illustrated in Figure 3.3.

FIGURE 3.3
Six Domains Affecting Middle School Curricula
SOURCE: Dr. David Hough, Associate Dean, College of Education, Southwest Missouri State University.

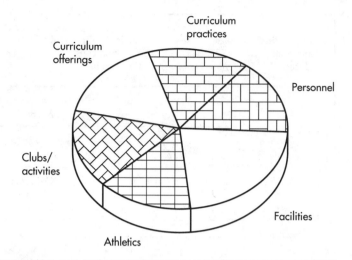

1. Domain of curriculum offerings *(content)*
   - Core subjects—usually English, science, mathematics, history/social studies
   - Specialty classes—reading, art, music, band, orchestra, typing, drama, journalism, industrial arts, home economics, foreign languages, speech, media, leadership, study skills, health, physical education, computer, and others
   - Exploratory classes—nonacademic and nongraded classes taught for a shorter time by teachers, parents, and community members and designed to provide special opportunities for students to discover learning outside the traditional classroom format
2. Domain of curriculum practices *(instruction)*
   - Cooperative learning
   - Electives
   - Learning how to learn
   - Mastery learning
   - Mini-classes and experimental projects
   - Parental involvement
   - Personal development
   - Philosophy (mission)
3. Domain of specialized personnel *(faculty and staff)*
   - Administrators
   - Art teachers
   - Coaches
   - Counselors
   - Hall monitors and security staff
   - Music teachers
   - Physical education teachers
4. Domain of *clubs and activities*
   - Assemblies
   - Cheerleading
   - Clubs (academic honors, art, audiovisual, chess, computer, drama, foreign language, Future Farmers of America, Future Teachers of America, glee, math, pep, photography, science, and others)
   - Formal dances
   - Newspaper
   - Parties
   - Student government
   - Yearbook

5. Domain of *athletics*
   - Interscholastic sports (baseball, basketball, cross country, football, golf, handball, track and field, soccer, softball, tennis, volleyball, wrestling)
   - Intramural sports (any of the preceding sports and others in which students participate for fun and experience—not competition against another school—for both girls and boys)
6. Domain of *facilities*
   - Auditorium
   - Concession stand
   - Football field
   - Gymnasium
   - Natrium
   - Nature center or trail
   - Outdoor classroom
   - Track

Although Hough's six domains do not address the so-called hidden curriculum, it is implied that various amounts and degrees of informal (unplanned) learning take place within each of the domains listed. In addition, whereas some schools include certain specialty classes as part of the core curriculum, others do not. In other words, any school's philosophy (often articulated via a mission statement) forms the underpinnings for the development of its curriculum. The middle school philosophy asserts that the needs of young adolescent youth are different from those in other stages of human development and therefore require a curriculum that attends to these needs.

Based on this principle, the various parts of the middle school curricula are grouped into three areas that combine all programs, components, and domains into a comprehensive middle school educational program. The three areas are the core curriculum, exploratories, and co-curricular activities. Following is a review of each of those three areas.

Core Curriculum

The core subjects are English, mathematics, science, and history/social studies—also referred to as the academic classes. It is in these classes that most interdisciplinary thematic units are taught. The purpose of teaching subject matter on a central theme is to avoid a departmentalized mentality that all too often communicates the wrong message to students—that learning is piecemeal and separate from one experience to another. On the contrary, the core curriculum facilitates the integration of subjects of the thematic units taught in tandem by the core teaching team. Specialty subject teachers (such as those for art, home economics, industrial arts, music, and physical education), although not part of the core, often will cooperate with the core team in developing and implementing thematic units.

Exploratory Programs

The purpose of exploratory classes is to provide a variety of experiences to help students discover areas of interest for future pursuit that perhaps will develop into a lifelong passion. Allowing middle school students opportunities to discover and explore unusual and novel topics can spawn or rekindle interests in life and school.

Exploratory classes differ from core and specialty classes in several respects. Exploratories are classes that students take to gain experience and appreciation even though they are not assigned a grade. Usually, exploratory classes are of shorter duration than the core classes, say, 30 to 45 minutes instead of 70 to 90 minutes, and might be taken only two days a week. Some exploratory programs last an entire term, but most last for two to six weeks. Sometimes students can choose 6 to 15 exploratory classes from a list of 20 or more. More common, however, is establishing an exploratory wheel, in which several classes are offered (usually 12, but ranging from 9 to 15) and each student must take each exploratory in turn.

Sometimes teachers are asked to develop exploratory classes by choosing topics of personal interest and sharing these with the students. Sometimes students are asked to list their interests and the topics they would like to study. The school then assigns a task force to find qualified personnel to design and staff the classes. Parents and community members provide a wealth of input by actually teaching exploratories, in partnership with or under the guidance of a credentialed teacher.

All students are encouraged to participate in exploratory activities, but none are penalized for not becoming proficient at a given skill or in a base of knowledge. Subject content of exploratory classes relates to areas of work and life not usually covered in core and specialty classes. These nontraditional learning experiences are therefore not associated with a specific "discipline."

Figure 3.4 lists a sampling of exploratory classes that are being implemented by middle schools throughout the United States.

Co-Curricular Activities

In traditional junior highs and comprehensive high schools, athletics, clubs, and activities are commonly labeled "extracurricular" activities. That is because they are considered separate from the academic learning of the regular school day. However, in middle schools many activities are significant components of the total educational program and are "co-curricular," rather than extracurricular. *Co-curricular* means that the activities go *with* the regular school program whether they are conducted before, during, or after school, or in some combination. The idea is to integrate these activities into the regular school program, including them as part of the total school experience, not as "add-ons" or "extras."

The co-curricular program includes student clubs, school and class activities, service organizations, and sports. Clubs can be for academic purposes, such as a math club, or they can be for fun, as a chess club. Activities can range from spirit squads and drill teams to fund raisers, pizza parties, and student government. Service organizations are often sponsored, in part, by the local business community, represented by such organizations as the Better Business Bureau, Farm Bureau, and the Kiwanis, Rotary, and Soroptomist clubs.

The following is a review of three critical co-curricular components of the middle school.

Intramural versus Interscholastic Sports

The co-curricular sports program in the middle school is achieved through *intramural* rather than *interscholastic* sports. Some middle schools try to offer both, but most experts about middle school curriculum agree that intramural programs are better suited for the needs of young adolescents.

FIGURE 3.4
Examples of Middle School Exploratory Courses

Building a house
Calligraphy
Careers and career opportunities
Conservation (including wildlife, water, plant, soil)
Cultural cooking
Fashion and design
Folk and modern dance
Home decor
Keyboarding
Library science
Map and compass
Nature study
Outdoor life (including hiking, camping, hunting, fishing, bird watching)
Photography
Politics
Recycling
Songwriting
Stars and planets (usually emphasizing our relationship with the universe)
The black hole
The tools of research
Travel (most popular title: "Planes, Trains, and Automobiles")
Water sports (including scuba diving, boating safety, and games)

In exemplary middle schools, intramural sports programs are developed to promote participation by *all* students. Emphasis is on fun, teamwork, socialization, and peer relationships in an unthreatening and relaxed environment. Evaluation is based on a student's willingness to cooperate with others and to participate, not on the student's skill or performance. A variety of intramural activities are scheduled for times before, during, or after school and may, where appropriate, be incorporated into the physical education, advisor-advisee, and exploratory classes. Through intramurals, all students can recognize and feel that they are part of a cohesive group, that they are of value as individuals, and that physical exercise is more important than skilled performance.

In many exemplary middle schools, interscholastic sports programs make every effort to include any student who chooses to participate. The focus is on participation rather than on winning. A middle school interscholastic sports committee is sometimes appointed with the responsibility to regulate all competitive sports and to design innovative ways to nurture the "athletic elite" without excluding students who are less skilled.

Study Skills

Study skills are an integral part of the learning process. The middle school student needs practical application of study skills in all content areas, but can also benefit from an intensive two- to three-week exploratory class. The optimal way to address study skills at the middle school level is to (1) provide each student with an exploratory study skills course, (2) emphasize learning techniques in each core subject content area, and (3) maintain continuous direction and adherence to study skills components throughout the school year. Study skills are also addressed in the homebase (advisor-advisee) class, demonstrating to students that the homebase teacher is interested in their personal and academic development.

In any event, study skills should not be a one-time discussion or a single unit of study in a particular class with no follow-up or integration with other classes, nor should it be the sole responsibility of each student. Middle school teachers share the responsibility for helping children learn how to learn. Giving homework assignments is *not* the same as teaching study skills.

Advisor–Advisee Program

The advisor-advisee (also called "homebase" or "homeroom") program is usually a separate class, no less than 20 minutes in length, without interruptions. All teachers are expected to participate, and it should serve as an avenue for individual and group guidance and counseling. The advisor-advisee program is intended to ensure that each student is known well by at least one adult who can give positive and constructive individual attention to that student. In fact, in many exemplary middle schools, the homebase teachers remain with the same students throughout the students' middle school years.

The homebase program should promote a student's feeling of belonging to a group and is not intended to be used for mechanical tasks. Before implementation, careful preparation of homebase teachers and parents needs to be done. The homebase program is for purposeful group activities that deal with students' social relationships and emotional development. The program should be a vehicle for dealing with affective needs and for teaching study skills, thinking skills, and decision making.

C. A MODEL FOR CURRICULUM DEVELOPMENT

Have you ever wondered how schools and teachers determine what types of learning students are to experience at school? Have you wondered why so many schools across the country have similar classes at given grade levels? Why certain subjects are always a part of the school program? How, from one school to the next, content presented to students is often quite similar? Or why some schools do not fit the norm as they experiment with kinds of learning and structure? Answers to these questions are found by looking at a prototypical model for curriculum building that combines ideals and principles of education.

Curriculum development begins with a model. Emerging from that model is content, both general and specific, that is planned to meet the needs of the learners. From that content, a set of instructional techniques is developed to implement the content. Those techniques are then set in the form of units with daily lessons.

Although many different models of curriculum development have been devised, the most widely noted and probably most frequently applied is that of Ralph W. Tyler (1949). Tyler's model of curriculum development focuses on three areas: the needs of the students, the needs of society, and the demands of the subject. From careful consideration of each of these areas, broad educational goals are derived. Those goals are then run through screens to derive specific educational programs and precise instructional objectives. The screens are recognition of an educational philosophy; consideration of the effects of groups outside of the classroom; procedures for assessment; and a mechanism for revision. Once these screens are in place, we have a prototypical model of curriculum development, composed of five components. Figure 3.5 depicts this model. Combining the curriculum-building components (or steps) with these principles allows curriculum builders to fashion a middle-level curriculum.

Notice that the model begins with the student, society, and subject needs, and then spirals outward with no sign of closure, even after the assessment and revision phase (component 5). This illustrates the unending, cyclical nature of middle school curriculum development. Continuing to expand as new ideas emerge and as needs change, the process has no outer bounds.

Basic Principles of Middle School Education Theory as Applied to the Curriculum Development Model

The following are descriptions of the basic principles of middle-level education as they are applied to the five components of curriculum development shown in Figure 3.5.

1. The *needs component*. As we all are changing individuals in an ever-changing world, middle school educators strive to educate the total child—the social, emotional, intellectual, and physical "self" that also is ever-changing. To do this, curriculum developers consider the needs of students by responding to the question, "What do we want middle school students to feel and do?" Considering the needs of society they ask, "What do we

FIGURE 3.5
Curriculum Development Model

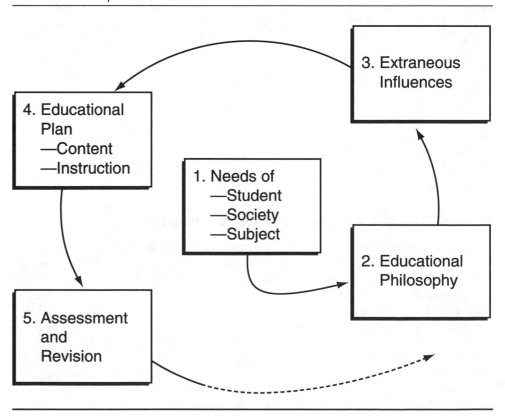

want middle school students to be and to become?" And, considering the needs of the disciplines, they respond to the question, "What should middle school students know?"

2. The *educational philosophy component.* Transescence is a developmental stage quite distinct from childhood (elementary school age) and from adolescence (high school age). Consequently, exemplary middle schools are those designed to *celebrate* this stage, not to provide a "holding ground" or transitional "waiting room" until the students' hormones have more closely reached equilibrium. To celebrate young adolescence, middle school programs and services must fit the specific needs of this developmental stage.

3. The *extraneous influences component.* Curriculum development is affected by international, national, state, and local interests, actions, and mandates. Federal legislative acts, state curriculum frameworks, district-wide and local guidelines, national reports such as "Turning Points," "A Nation At Risk," "Caught in the Middle," and publications such as *Middle School Journal, Crossroads, NASSP Bulletin, Research in Middle Level Education,* and special interest groups all affect middle school development.

4. The *educational plan component.* Included in the educational plan are the following elements:
   - *Content.* Middle schools provide opportunities for students to learn a common core of information, participate in co-curricular activities, and explore a variety of new areas.
   - *Instruction.* Middle school educators recognize the value and importance of student social interaction as a dynamic learning tool. This recognition is practiced by using interactive teaching strategies such as cooperative learning, peer tutoring, cross-age teaching, and guided practice. Structured and semistructured social activities are woven into the fabric of academic content, thereby positively influencing the "hidden" curriculum.
   - *Scope.* The depth and breadth of the educational experiences are planned so that middle school children understand the value of knowledge and how that knowledge is applied in life.
   - *Sequence.* The order in which these learning experiences take place is smoothly articulated and extends beyond the level of skill acquisition. Exemplary middle schools provide children with new learning experiences that are organized logically and that avoid redundancy, especially with the prior year's experiences.

5. The *assessment and revision component.* All curricula must be continually monitored and evaluated to find ways to improve the educational program. Evaluation of curriculum is both formative (ongoing) and summative (conclusive). Recommendations drawn from the assessment are used to make revisions to the curriculum. The spiral nature of middle school curriculum development is designed to remain responsive to modern issues; middle school curriculum development is a process without end.

D. UNIT PLANNING

Organizing the entire year's content into units makes the teaching process more manageable than when no plan or only random choices are made by a teacher. Whether or not you are teaching in a self-contained classroom, the content you intend to present to children must be organized and carefully planned well in advance. The teaching unit is a major subdivision of a course (for one course or self-contained classroom there are several or many units of instruction), and is comprised of instruction planned around a central theme, topic, issue, or problem.

The teaching unit, whether an interdisciplinary thematic unit (known also as an integrated unit), or a stand-alone, standard, subject unit, is not unlike a chapter in a book, an act or scene in a play, or a phase of work when undertaking a project such as building a house. Breaking down information or actions into component parts and then grouping the related parts makes sense out of learning and doing. The unit brings a sense of cohesiveness and structure to student learning and avoids the piecemeal approach that might otherwise unfold. You can learn to articulate lessons within, between, and among unit plans and focus on important elements while not ignoring tangential information of importance. Students remember "chunks" of information, especially when those chunks are related to specific units.

Types of Units

Although the steps for developing any type of unit are essentially the same, units can be organized in a number of ways, differentiated and described as follows.

Conventional unit. A conventional unit (known also as a standard unit) consists of a series of lessons centered on a topic, theme, major concept, or block of subject matter. In a standard unit, each lesson builds on the previous lesson by contributing additional subject matter, providing further illustrations, and supplying more practice or other added instruction, all of which are aimed at bringing about mastery of the knowledge and skills on which the unit is centered.

Integrated unit. When a conventional unit is centered on a theme, such as "railroads," then the unit may be referred to as a thematic unit. When, by design, the thematic unit integrates disciplines, such as one that combines the learning of science and mathematics or social studies and language arts, or all four of these core disciplines, then it is called an integrated (or interdisciplinary) thematic unit. It is this type of unit that is the focus of this book.

Self-instructional unit. A self-instructional unit (known also as a modular unit) is a unit of instruction that is designed for individualized or modularized self-instruction. Such a unit is designed for independent, individual study and, because it covers much less content than the units previously described, can generally be completed in a much shorter time period, frequently one class period. The unit consists of instruction, references, exercises, problems, self-correcting materials, and all other information and materials that a student needs to independently carry out the unit of work. Consequently, students can work on the units individually at their own speed, and different students can be working on different units at the same time. Students who successfully finish a modular unit can move on to another unit of work without waiting for the other students to catch up. Such units are essential ingredients of continuous-progress courses. Whether for purposes of remediation, enrichment, or make-up, self-instructional units work especially well when done at and in conjunction with a learning activity center.

Contract unit. A contract unit is an individualized unit of instruction for which a student agrees (contracts) to carry out certain activities. Some contract units have a variable-letter-grade agreement built into them. For example, specified on the contract may be information such as the following:

> To pass with a D grade, you must complete activities 1–5, and pass the posttest.
>
> For a grade of C, you must complete activities 1–5, receive at least a C on the posttest, and satisfactorily complete two optional related activities.
>
> For a grade of B, you must complete activities 1–5 plus satisfactorily complete four of the optional related activities and receive a grade of no less than B on the posttest.
>
> For a grade of A, you must complete activities 1–5 plus satisfactorily complete six of the optional activities and receive no less than a B on the posttest.

Planning and Developing Any Unit of Instruction

The steps in planning and developing a conventional unit, a contract unit, a self-instructional unit, and an interdisciplinary thematic unit are the same and are as follows:

1. *Select a suitable topic or theme.* Often these already may be laid out in your course of study or textbook or have been agreed to by members of the teaching team.
2. *Select the goals of the unit.* The goals are written as an overview or rationale, covering what the unit is about and what the students are to learn. In planning the goals, you should do the following:
   a. Become as familiar as possible with the topic and materials used.
   b. Consult curriculum documents, such as courses of study, state frameworks, and resource units, for ideas.

c. Decide the content and procedures—what the students should learn about the topic and how.

d. Write the rationale or overview, summarizing what you hope the students will learn about the topic.

e. Be sure your goals are congruent with those of the course.

3. *Select suitable specific learning objectives.*

a. Include understandings, skills, attitudes, appreciations, and ideals.

b. Be specific, avoiding vagueness and generalizations.

c. Write the objectives in behavioral terms.

d. Be as certain as possible that the objectives will contribute to the major learning described in the overview.

4. *Detail the instructional procedures.* These procedures include the subject content and the learning activities, established as a series of lessons. Proceed with the following steps in your initial planning of the instructional procedures:

a. Gather ideas for learning activities that might be suitable for the unit. Refer to curriculum documents, resource units, and other teachers as resources.

b. Check the learning activities to make sure that they will actually contribute to the learning designated in your objectives, discarding ideas that do not.

c. Make sure that the learning activities are feasible. Can you afford the time, effort, or expense? Do you have the necessary materials and equipment? If not, can they be obtained? Are the activities suited to the intellectual and maturity levels of your students?

d. Check resources available to be certain that they support the content and learning activities.

e. Decide how to introduce the unit. Provide introductory activities that
   (1) arouse student interest.
   (2) inform students what the unit is about.
   (3) help you learn about your students—their interests, abilities, and experiences and present knowledge of the topic.
   (4) provide transitions that bridge this topic with that which students have already learned.
   (5) involve the students in the planning.

f. Plan developmental activities that
   (1) sustain student interest.
   (2) provide for individual student differences.
   (3) promote the learning cited in the specific objectives.

g. Plan culminating activities that
   (1) summarize what has been learned.
   (2) bring together loose ends.
   (3) apply what has been learned to new and meaningful situations.
   (4) segue into the unit that follows.

5. *Plan for preassessment and assessment of student learning.* Preassess what students already know, or think they know. Assessment of student progress in achievement of the learning objectives (formative evaluation) should permeate the entire unit. Plan to gather information in several ways, including informal observations, observation of student performance, portfolio assessment, and paper-and-pencil assessments. Evaluation must be consistent with the specific learning objectives.

6. *Provide for the materials of instruction.* The unit cannot function without materials. Therefore, you must plan long before the unit begins for media equipment and materials, references, reading materials, reproduced materials, and community resources. Material that is not available to the students is of no help to them.

Those are six steps to follow for developing any type of unit. In addition to those six steps, there are two general points that should be made:

1. *There is no single best format for a teaching unit* that works best. Particular formats may be best for specific disciplines or topics. During your student teaching, your college or university program for teacher preparation will probably have a form that you will be expected to follow.

2. *There is no set time duration for a unit plan,* although, for specific units, curriculum guides will indicate a suggested time duration. Units may extend for a minimum of several days or, as in the case of interdisciplinary thematic units, for several weeks. However, be aware that when conventional units last more than two or three weeks, they tend to lose their identity as clearly identifiable units. The exact time duration will be dictated by several factors, including the topic or theme, the grade level, and the interests and abilities of the students.

E. INTERDISCIPLINARY THEMATIC UNITS

Whereas curriculum is the backbone of the middle school, interdisciplinary thematic units are its heart and soul. The following syllogistic formula explains why.

- *Proposition One.* To be successful, middle school programs must fit the specific needs of young adolescents.
- *Proposition Two.* Transescence is a developmental stage that embodies characteristics that are quite different from those of children of elementary age and of high school age.
- *Proposition Three.* To address the distinct needs of young adolescents, consideration must be given to the whole individual (physically, psychologically and emotionally, socially, and intellectually) and to the total educational experience, or curriculum (core, co-curricular, and exploratory).
- *Conclusion.* By recognizing the individual child and integrating the whole individual with the total curriculum, the learning experiences become meaningful to the student. Learning that is meaningful engages the student, connecting him or her with the world, thereby compelling the student to want to learn. To the student, learning is then viewed as important, meaningful, and useful.

It is probably fair to say that this syllogistic style of reasoning places more emphasis on merging student needs with specific subject-related content than do other grade-specific philosophies. This means that the primary emphasis for elementary education is on individual child development and basic skills acquisition, and the major emphasis for high school education is subject-oriented specialization. The middle school philosophy views education as a *social enterprise* in which students are challenged to discover underlying structures and meaning within interrelated subject content. This cannot be achieved through the dichotomy of "student versus subject," but rather by merging the two.

The *interdisciplinary thematic unit* is the tool used to link the learning experiences of middle school children in ways to engage them fully in the learning process. *Interdisciplinary* means that the core subjects as well as the co-curricular activities and exploratories are involved. *Thematic* means that the same topic is used to develop the teaching plan (content and instruction) for each of the different subjects in which students are enrolled. *Unit* refers to an extended teaching plan (several days to several weeks), in which a variety of goals and objectives are established that are centered around a common concept, topic, or theme.

The Meaning of *Interdisciplinary*

To comprehend how an interdisciplinary (or integrated) curriculum is fashioned and how it works, you must understand the relationships among core, co-curricular, and exploratory programs. To help in this understanding, we now review each of these middle school programs, followed by a discussion of the makings of an interdisciplinary thematic unit.

The Role of Core Curriculum

You learned that the most common core classes are English/language arts, mathematics, science, and history/social studies. However, in many middle schools, classes in art, music, physical education, and reading are also required of each student. Often, other classes are required as well—home economics, foreign languages, and industrial arts, for example. Whether "academic," "liberal," or "applied arts," all *required* courses taken by middle school children are core subjects.

The philosophical foundation of core education is that a given body of knowledge is considered essential enough for all students to share in the experience afforded by that core of knowledge. Integrating the content of core subjects by coordinating instruction around a central theme creates interdisciplinary content and methods. In many instances the choice of an interdisciplinary theme is first identified in one of the core subjects' master plans. Table 3.1 illustrates a common core of subjects articulated among grades 6, 7, and 8. In Figure 3.6, three different orientations are presented.

The Role of Exploratory Programs

Exploratories should be integrated into the interdisciplinary thematic unit. This can be done by choosing a single area of interest within the unit and either developing a special exploratory class or giving special attention to it within the framework of an existing exploratory.

For example, suppose a teaching team decides to develop a thematic unit centered around the topic of westward expansion. Let's say that the middle school had already developed an exploratory wheel of classes consisting of 12 areas of study that all students will have experienced by the end of the school year. Let's further assume that one of those classes is called "transportation," in which students learn about the history and development of various modes of travel. The team, in cooperation with the exploratory teacher (who may or may not be a member of the team), might decide to structure the westward expansion thematic unit so that it coincides with the exploratory class on transportation. The exploratory teacher then plans the class accordingly. Here is a list of options he or she might consider:

- Ask a community volunteer from a local Department of Transportation office to make a presentation or even help design the course.
- Plan intensive study of one form of transportation, for example, the wagon, stagecoach, prairie schooner, rail, automobile, horse and buggy, water, motorcycle, airplane, subway, walking, bicycling, or horseback riding; or, in a jigsaw format, have student teams study different modes.
- Study cultural or ethnic conflicts that were caused by westward expansion and resultant changes in different types of transportation.
- Retrace the Oregon Trail by examining how horse-, mule-, and ox-drawn wagons dealt with changes in weather and terrain.
- Compare different routes and modes of transportation to determine advantages and disadvantages of each.

TABLE 3.1
Sample Middle School Curriculum by Grade Level

	SIXTH GRADE	**SEVENTH GRADE**	**EIGHTH GRADE**
CORE	Language arts Social studies Mathematics Science	Language arts Social studies Mathematics Science	Language arts Social studies Mathematics Science
REQUIRED[a]	Physical education Reading Art	Physical education Reading	Physical education Computer
ELECTIVES	Band, orchestra, or vocal music	Foreign language, speech, art, band, orchestra, or vocal music	Foreign language, speech, art, band, orchestra, or vocal music
REQUIRED[b]	Exploratory Advisor-advisee	Exploratory Advisor-advisee	Exploratory Advisor-advisee
RECOMMENDED[c]	Co-curricular	Co-curricular	Co-curricular

[a] These required classes may or may not be considered part of the core.
[b] Exploratory and advisor-advisee classes are required of all students, but participation is not graded on the traditional A–F scale.
[c] Co-curricular activities are recommended as voluntary activities.

FIGURE 3.6
Comparing and Contrasting Middle School Curriculum Models

Instructions: With this figure you can compare and contrast the curriculum model (Figure 3.5) with that of three middle schools: A, B, and C. Compare the curricula of schools A, B, and C with that of Figure 3.5 by answering the following questions. Upon completion, share and discuss your results with those of your classmates.

1. Explain how schools A, B, and C differ from Figure 3.5 in terms of *core classes*.

2. Explain how schools A, B, and C differ from Figure 3.5 in *exploratories*.

3. Explain how schools A, B, and C differ from Figure 3.5 in *co-curricular programs and activities*.

4. Explain how schools A, B, and C differ from Figure 3.5 in *electives*.

5. Explain how schools A, B, and C differ from Figure 3.5 in *grade levels (vertical articulation)*.

6. Do you see any other differences between the three schools and the model curriculum of Figure 3.5? If so, explain.

| | **School A's Curriculum** | |
Sixth Grade	*Seventh Grade*	*Eighth Grade*
Advisor–advisee	Advisor–advisee	Advisor–advisee
Basic skills	*Basic skills*	*Basic skills*
Language arts	Language arts	Language arts
Mathematics	Math or pre-algebra	Math or pre-algebra
Science	Science	Science
Social studies	Social studies	Social studies
Reading	Study skills (daily or alternates with gifted)	P.E./extended basic skills or gifted
Exploratory wheel	*Exploratory wheel*	
Art	Art	
Speech/drama	Speech/drama	
Health	Health	
Journalism	Industrial arts	
General music	Home economics	

Now, using the same example, let's suppose the school had not determined the specific exploratory classes that it would be providing students, choosing, instead, to let them evolve out of specific needs that present themselves throughout the school year. In this case, the exploratory teacher has an opportunity to develop a number of different activities. For the sake of this example, let's say that the teacher chooses to develop content that focuses on cultural integration caused by the westward movement. Specific and intensive study could evolve around Native Americans and European settlers, or it could focus on the study of a single culture, incident, or individual. In this way, the exploratory teacher can augment core content and provide more in-depth study of important facets of history, art, music, literature, science, and so on than the core subject teacher may have time to provide.

FIGURE 3.6 cont'd

Exploratory electives	*Exploratory electives*	*Exploratory electives*
P.E./yearbook	Instrumental music	Instrumental music
Keyboarding	Journalism	Journalism
French	French	French
German	German	Art
Spanish	Spanish	Spanish
Study skills		Vocal music
		Speech/drama
		Health
		Industrial arts
Academic elective		
Reading plus	Reading plus	Reading plus

School B's Curriculum

Sixth Grade	*Seventh Grade*	*Eighth Grade*
Team	*Team*	*Team*
Reading	Reading	Reading
English	English	English
Mathematics	Social studies	Social studies
Social studies		
Science/health		
Enrichment	Coed/science	Mathematics
Physical education	Physical education	Physical education
	Electives	Science/skills
		Electives

School C's Curriculum

Sixth Grade	*Seventh Grade*	*Eighth Grade*
English	English	English
Science	Science	Science
Mathematics	Mathematics (pre-algebra)	Algebra
Social studies	American studies	American studies
Reading	Reading	Reading
Physical education	Physical education	Enrichment (Spanish or French)
Band, chorus, or project Earth	Band, chorus, or project Earth	Physical education
		Band, chorus, or project Earth
Exploratories	*Exploratories*	*Exploratories*
French	Spanish	Sewing
Keyboarding	Speech/drama	Business studies
Shop	Arts/crafts	Great books
Stress management	Foods	Shop

The Role of Co-Curricular Activities

All too often co-curricular activities are less a part of the interdisciplinary thematic unit than are the core and exploratories, but they are nonetheless integral components of the curriculum and must not be ignored. Again, using the theme of westward expansion, the following are examples of clubs with theme-related activities:

- Glee club: plan for students to study, sing, and play songs unique to the time. If the concept of westward expansion is not constricted by time, students could trace the underlying movement by following strands in music of that period that depict the expansion

- Social committee or student council: plan and sponsor a westward expansion party, an "old west day," or a special assembly
- Intramural sports: include games of the period
- School newspaper: print a special edition representative of the westward movement.

The co-curricular options available are limited only by the creativity of the students, teacher, and staff who plan them. Even study skills and technology classes can be included, perhaps by comparing different approaches to problem solving from one time, culture, or mode of transportation to another. Multicultural components should be an integral part of every facet of the curriculum, and the hidden curriculum is less enigmatic when teachers are aware of how students spend their free or leisure time, and plan activities (sometimes homework) that bring an air of structure into an otherwise unstructured and unsupervised situation. Such an approach is favored by John Holt in his book, *Learning All the Time* (1989).

The Meaning of *Thematic*

The underlying concept that allows for the structure and organization of specific content across disciplines is called a *theme*. Hence, a thematic unit is an instructional unit based on a common learning denominator that lends itself to integrated study—sharing a common idea within various frameworks for content, instruction, materials, and evaluation. Units of instruction can last for several days to several weeks. However, caution must be followed because teaching units that last much longer than three weeks may lose their effectiveness as recognizable units of learning. *Lessons* are subdivisions of units, usually taught in a single period or in one day.

Themes are commonly discussed in the language arts. For instance, literature might be studied thematically by grouping together stories about heroes undertaking journeys or quests; the suffering servant; people's inhumanity to other human beings, nature, or self; alienation; lost innocence; love or nature regained; and so on. In social studies the following themes might emerge: the workplace; people and the urge to create; their urge to move, explore, discover, or rule or be ruled; and the search for the unknown. In science examples might include the nurturing earth, quenching thirst, environmental disasters, the body's ecosystem, atoms and anatomies, and the forces within you. Mathematics classes might study the geometry of building a house; equations for all time; numbers with special meanings; statistical tools; or gambling odds.

Themes such as those just listed can be developed for virtually any academic or nonacademic class in the middle school, whether it is reading, physical education, art, or music, or whether it involves co-curricular, exploratory, or advisor-advisee programs. Again, the creativity of the teacher is important, and the dynamics of interactive teaching teams can produce any number of themes that are meaningful, interesting, and cohesive.

F. DEVELOPING AN INTERDISCIPLINARY THEMATIC UNIT

Of special interest to many teachers are units built around interdisciplinary themes, rather than content topics that are single-subject specific. Interdisciplinary thematic teaching helps students bridge the disciplines and connect school learning with real-life experiences. The six steps outlined earlier are essential steps for planning any type of teaching unit, including the interdisciplinary thematic (or integrated) unit. The interdisciplinary thematic unit is made of smaller subject-specific units, developed according to the preceding guidelines. (For additional guidelines, see the description in Chapter 8 of the development of a weather unit; Section B of Chapter 9, on planning thematic units with a strong language arts core; and sample units in Chapter 16 and the complete ITU at the end of the book.)

For example, in 1991, four teachers at a school in Yorktown, Virginia, decided to make connections for their ninth-grade students in their disciplines—science, algebra, geography, and English.

> Using a common planning period to collaborate, the teachers began modestly with an assignment to summarize earth science articles that strengthened students' knowledge of science as well as their writing skills. Later in the year, the teachers launched an interdisciplinary project focused on the winter Olympics in Albertville, France. In small groups, students were presented

with a problem related to one aspect of hosting the Olympics—providing transportation, food, lodging, entertainment, or security. The groups wrote proposals setting forth their solutions, drawing on what they had learned about the geography of the region and applying science knowledge and math skills. (Willis, 1992b, p. 1)

In the York School project, the English teacher taught vocabulary that students would encounter in their algebra and earth science classes. Primary responsibility for the development of interdisciplinary thematic units often depends upon the cooperation of several teachers, who, as in this example, usually represent two or more disciplines. This interdisciplinary team of teachers may meet daily during a common planning time. Careful planning of the scheduling allows for instructional blocks of time so team members have common planning time and unit lessons can, likewise, be more flexible and less constrained by time.

Some teaching teams develop one interdisciplinary thematic unit each year, semester, trimester, or quarter; that is, from one to four a year. Over time, then, the team will have developed several units for implementation. The most effective units, however, are often the most current or most meaningful to students. This means that ever-changing global, national, and local topics provide a veritable smorgasbord from which to choose, and teaching teams must constantly be aware of the changes in the world and society and the interests of students in order to update old units and develop new and exciting ones.

One teaching team's unit should not conflict with another's at the same or another grade level. If a school has two or more seventh-grade teams, for example, the teams may want to develop units on different themes and share their products. As another example, a junior high school team may want to share its units with high school teams, and, perhaps, with feeder elementary schools. Open lines of communication within, between, and among teams and schools are critical to the success of thematic teaching.

Because developing interdisciplinary thematic units is increasingly becoming an essential task for many teachers, it behooves you to learn now the process that you may be practicing later as an employed teacher (or even when student teaching). One other point needs to be made: an interdisciplinary thematic unit can be prepared and taught by one teacher, but more often these units are prepared and taught by a team of teachers. The latter instructional strategy is referred to as *interdisciplinary thematic team teaching*. Most often the team is composed of teachers from at least four areas: social studies or history, language arts or English, mathematics, and science. A thematic unit and teaching team might also consist of fewer than four areas—math and science, history and English, or social studies and language arts, for example.

Following are steps for developing an interdisciplinary thematic unit:

1. *Agree on the nature or source of origin for the interdisciplinary thematic unit.* Team members should view the interdisciplinary approach as a collective effort in which all team members (and other faculty) participate nearly equally. Discuss how the team wants students to profit from interdisciplinary instruction. Troubleshoot possible stumbling blocks.
2. *Discuss subject-specific frameworks, goals and objectives, curriculum guidelines, textbooks and supplemental materials, and units already in place for the school year.* This discussion should focus on what each teacher must teach, and it should explain the scope and sequence so all team members share an understanding of perceived constraints and limitations.
3. *Choose a topic and develop a time line.* From the information provided by each subject specialist-teacher in step 2, start listing possible topics that can be drawn from existing course outlines. Give-and-take is essential at this step, as some topics will fit certain subjects better than others. The chief goal here is to find a workable topic, that is, one that can be adapted to each subject without detracting from the educational plan already in place. This may require choosing and merging content from two or more other previously planned units. The theme is then drawn from the topic. When a team is considering a theme, it should consider these questions (Willis, 1992a, pp. 4–5):
   - Can this theme lead to a unit that is of proper duration, not too short and not too long?
   - Is it worth the time needed to create and implement it? Do we have sufficient materials and resources to supply information we might need?

- Is the theme within the realm of understanding and experience of the teachers involved? Is the theme topic one with which teachers are not already too familiar so they can share in the excitement of the learning? Will the theme be of interest to all members of the teaching team? Does it apply broadly to a wide range of subject areas?
- What is so important about this theme that it will promote future learning? Does the theme have substance and application to the real world? Does it lend itself to active learning? Will it be of interest to students? Will it motivate them to do their best? Will it fascinate students once they are into it?

4. *Set two time lines.* The first time line is for the team only and is to ensure that given dates for specific work required in developing the unit will be met by each member. The second time line is for students and teachers and shows how long the unit will be, when it will start, and in which classes.

5. *Develop the scope and sequence for content and instruction.* Follow the six steps for "Planning and Developing Any Unit of Instruction" (pages 58–59) to develop the interdisciplinary thematic unit. This should be done by each team member and also as a group during common planning time so the team members can coordinate dates and activities in logical sequence and depth. This organic process will generate ideas but also produce some anxiety. Members of the team, under the guidance of the team leader, should strive to maintain anxiety at a level conducive to learning, experimenting, and arriving at group consensus.

6. *Share goals and objectives.* Each team member should have a copy of the goals and objectives of every other member. This helps refine the unit and lesson plans and prevent unnecessary overlap and confusion.

7. *Give the unit its name.* The unit has been fashioned based on a common topic and is being held together by the theme you have chosen. Giving the theme a name and using that name lets the students know that this unit of study is integrated, important, and meaningful to school and to life.

8. *Share subject-specific units, lesson plans, print and nonprint materials.* After teachers have finalized their units, exchange them for review comments and suggestions. Keep a copy of each teacher's unit(s), and see if you could present a lesson from it for your own subject area. If you can, the plans are probably workable. If you can't, some modification may be necessary.

9. *Field-test the thematic unit.* Beginning at the time, on the date, and in the class(es) agreed-upon, present the lessons. Team members may trade classes from time to time. Team teaching may take place when two or more classes can be combined for instruction, as can be done with flexible and block scheduling. After field testing, there is, of course, one final step: assessing the thematic unit and perhaps adjusting and revising it. Team members discuss successes and failures during their common planning time and determine what needs to be changed, how, and when, to make the unit successful. Adjustments to the unit can be made along the way (by collecting data during formative assessments) and revisions made after the unit has been completed (from data collected during summative assessment).

The preceding steps are not absolutes and should be viewed only as guides. Differing compositions of teaching teams and levels of teacher experience and knowledge make strict adherence to any procedural steps less productive than group-generated plans. For instance, many teachers have found that the topic for an interdisciplinary thematic unit should be one that the team already knows well. In practice, the process that works for the team—that results in meaningful student learning and in students feeling good about themselves, about learning, and about school—is the appropriate process.

SUMMARY

In this chapter you learned about the essence of the middle school concept and the organization of the middle school curriculum—its domains and major components. You have learned how teachers' and students' schedules are organized to meet the demands of the middle school curriculum. These components are organized to include team teaching, common planning time, interdisciplinary thematic units, co-curricular activities, exploratory classes, advisor-advisee programs, intramurals, and study skills.

The middle school curriculum is predicated on the notion that children aged 10 to 14 are in a developmental stage quite distinguishable and separate from that of students of elementary school and high school age. Therefore, neither elementary nor high school curricula are appropriate for middle school children. Curriculum development should focus on the needs of the total young adolescent. This is accomplished by providing a core curriculum, co-curricular activities and programs, and exploratory classes. Developing units of instruction that integrate learning and provide a sense of meaning for the students requires coordination throughout the total curriculum, which has been defined as all the experiences students encounter while at school. Hence, learning for middle school children is a process of discovering how information, knowledge, and ideas are interrelated and making sense out of self, school, and life.

The chapter that follows will guide you through the process of developing lessons that fit the needs of the middle school student.

QUESTIONS AND ACTIVITIES FOR DISCUSSION

1. Explain why the curriculum development model is presented as a spiral shape as opposed, for example, to a line, and begins with needs.

2. Describe the five phases of curriculum development.

3. Explain why integrated units fit the middle school syllogism articulated earlier in this chapter.

4. Explain the importance of organizing instruction into units.

5. Assuming that a middle school teaching team is made up of four teachers, list three possible combinations of classes that might constitute the core curriculum. Discuss your lists with your classmates.

6. Describe several ways the interdisciplinary thematic unit differs from a standard unit.

7. Suppose that you are a key decision maker in charge of designing a three-year core curriculum for a grades 6–8 middle school. Assume that the sixth graders are to have a five-course core, seventh graders a four-course core, and eighth graders a three-course core. Which courses would you place together for each student cohort? Share and discuss your lists with your classmates.

8. Explain the difference between activities that are co-curricular and those that are extracurricular. Provide examples of each.

9. Describe the chief difference between intramural and interscholastic sports programs. Why do you suppose experts place greater importance on intramural sports programs for the middle school?

10. Examine the interdisciplinary thematic unit displayed in Chapter 18. At what level of integration (discussed at the opening of this part) do you suppose it is designed to be implemented? Why? Could it be used at another level? If so, what changes would have to be made?

11. What questions do you have about the content of this chapter? How might you find answers?

REFERENCES

Alexander, W. M. (1988). Schools in the middle: Rhetoric and reality. *Social Education, 52*(2), 107–109.

California State Department of Education. (1986). *California dropouts: A status report.* Sacramento, CA: Author.

Holt, J. (1989). *Learning all the time.* Reading, MA: Addison-Wesley.

Hough, D. L. (1989). *Middle level education in California: A survey of programs and organization.* Riverside, CA: University of California, Educational Research Cooperative.

Massachusetts Advocacy Center. (1986). *The way out: Student exclusion practices in Boston middle schools.* Boston: Author.

Raebeck, B. S. (1990). Transformation of a middle school. *Educational Leadership, 47*(7), 18–21.

Tyler, R. W. (1949). *Basic principles of curriculum and instruction.* Chicago: University of Chicago Press.

Valentine, J. W., et al. (1993). *Leadership in middle level education, volume 1.* Reston, VA: National Association of Secondary School Principals.

Willis, S. (1992a, November). Choosing a theme. *ASCD Curriculum Update,* pp. 4–5.

Willis, S. (1992b, November). Interdisciplinary learning: Movement to link disciplines gains momentum. *ASCD Curriculum Update,* p. 1.

SUGGESTED READINGS

Arnold, J. (1990). *Visions of teaching and learning: 80 exemplary middle level projects.* Columbus, OH: National Middle School Association.

Ayres, L. R. (1994). Middle school advisory programs: Findings from the field. *Middle School Journal, 25*(3), 8–14.

Barchers, S. I. (1994). *Teaching language arts: An integrated approach.* St. Paul, MN: West Publishing Co.

Beane, J. A. (1990). *A middle school curriculum: From rhetoric to reality.* Columbus, OH: National Middle School Association.

Beane, J. A. (1992). Creating an integrative curriculum: Making the connections. *NASSP Bulletin, 76*(547), 46–54.

Beane, J. A. (1993). The search for a middle school curriculum. *School Administrator, 50*(3), 8–14.

Boling, A. N. (1991). They don't like math? Well, let's do something. *Arithmetic Teacher, 38*(7), 17–19.

Boyer, M. R. (1993). The challenge of an integrated curriculum: Avoid the isolated road. *School Administrator, 50*(3), 20–21.

Brandt, R. S. (Ed.). (1988). *Content of the curriculum.* 1988 ASCD Yearbook. Alexandria, VA: Association for Supervision and Curriculum Development.

Caine, G., & Caine, R. N. (1993, Fall). The critical need for a mental model of meaningful learning. *California Catalyst,* 18–21.

Cuban, L. (1993). The lure of curricular reform and its pitiful history. *Phi Delta Kappan, 75*(2), 182–185.

Darling-Hammond, L. (1993). Reframing the school reform agenda. *Phi Delta Kappan, 74*(10), 753–761.

Dempster, F. N. (1993). Exposing our students to less should help them learn more. *Phi Delta Kappan, 74*(6), 433–437.

Elias, M. J., & Branden-Muller, L. R. (1994). Social and life skills development during the middle school years: An emerging perspective. *Middle School Journal, 25*(3), 8–14.

Ennis, C. D., et al. (1992). The role of value orientations in curricular decision making: A rationale for teachers' goals and expectations. *Research Quarterly for Exercise and Sport, 63*(1), 38–47.

Erb, T. O., & Doda, N. M. (1989). *Team organization: Promise, practices & possibilities.* Washington, DC: National Education Association.

Fogarty, R. (1991). *How to integrate the curricula.* Palatine, IL: Skylight Publishing, Inc.

Gehrke, N. J. (1991). Explorations of teachers' development of integrative curriculum. *Journal of Curriculum and Supervision, 6*(2), 107–117.

Jacobs, H. H. (1989). *Interdisciplinary curriculum: Design and implementation.* Alexandria, VA: Association for Supervision and Curriculum Development.

Jordan, C., & Smith, L. J. (1992). Planning for whole language across the curriculum (in the classroom). *Reading Teacher, 45*(6), 476–477.

Holt, J. (1989). *Learning all the time.* Reading, MA: Addison-Wesley.

Kentta, B. (1993). The challenge of an integrated curriculum: Moving with cautious velocity. *School Administrator, 50*(3), 17, 19.

Messick, R. G., & Reynolds, K. E. (1992). *Middle level curriculum.* White Plains, NY: Longman.

Parker, W. (1993). Common pitfalls in curriculum planning. *Social Studies and the Young Learner, 5*(3), 3–5.

Placek, J. (1992). Rethinking middle school physical education curriculum: An integrated, thematic approach. *Quest, 44*(3), 330–341.

Resnick, L. B., & Klopfer, L. E. (Eds.). (1989). *Toward the thinking curriculum: Current cognitive research.* 1989 ASCD Yearbook. Alexandria, VA: Association for Supervision and Curriculum Development.

Seif, E. (1993). Integrating skill development across the curriculum. *Schools in the Middle, 2*(4), 15–19.

Stevenson, C., & Carr, J. F. (1993). *Integrated studies in the middle grades.* New York: Teachers College Press.

Vars, G. F. (1987). *Interdisciplinary teaching in the middle grades: How and why.* Columbus, OH: National Middle School Association.

Wood, K. D., & Jones, J. P. (1994). Integrating collaborative learning across the curriculum. *Middle School Journal, 25*(3), 35–39.

CHAPTER 4

Daily Lesson Planning

T he emphasis in this chapter is on the importance and the details of planning daily instruction. You will be guided through the process, from selecting content for a course to preparing the specific learning outcomes expected as students learn that content. Then, from a content outline and the related and specific learning outcomes, you will learn how to prepare units and daily lessons.

Specifically, this chapter is designed to help you understand

1. Reasons for and components of careful instructional planning
2. How to plan a course of instruction
3. The meaning of *diagnostic assessment, formative assessment,* and *summative assessment.*
4. The variety of documents that provide guidance for course content selection
5. The status of the development of national curriculum standards for language arts and social studies
6. How student textbooks can be useful
7. How to use cooperation and collaboration in instructional planning
8. How to use aims, goals, and objectives
9. Instructional objectives and how to prepare them
10. How to use a response journal to assess for meaningful learning
11. Today's interest in *character education*
12. How to prepare and use questions for instruction
13. How to ensure equity in the classroom
14. Processes in instructional planning
15. How to prepare and use a course syllabus
16. How to prepare daily lessons.

Although careful planning is a critical skill for a teacher, a well-developed plan for teaching will not guarantee the success of a lesson or unit or even the overall effectiveness of a course. The lack of a well-developed plan will, however, almost certainly result in poor teaching. Like a good map, a good plan facilitates reaching the planned destination with more confidence and with fewer wrong turns.

The heart of good planning is good decision making. For every plan, you must decide what your goals and objectives are, what specific subject matter should be taught, what materials of instruction are available and appropriate, and what methods and techniques should be employed to accomplish the objectives. Making these decisions is complicated because there are so many choices. Therefore, you must be knowledgeable about the principles that undergird effective course, unit, and lesson planning. That the principles of all levels of educational planning are much the same makes mastering the necessary skills easier than you might now think.

A. REASONS FOR PLANNING

Thoughtful and thorough planning is vital if effective teaching is to occur. It helps produce well-organized classes and a purposeful classroom atmosphere, and it reduces the likelihood of problems in classroom control. A teacher who has not planned or who has underprepared will have more problems than are imaginable. While planning it is useful to keep in mind these two important teacher goals: (1) to not waste anyone's time and (2) to select strategies that keep students physically and mentally engaged on task and that ensure student learning.

Also, planning well helps guarantee that you know the subject, for in planning carefully you will more likely master the material and the methods of teaching it. You cannot know all there is to know about the subject matter, but careful planning is likely to prevent you from fumbling through half-digested, poorly understood content, making too many errors along the way. Thoughtful and thorough planning is likely to make your classes more lively, more interesting, more accurate, and more relevant and your teaching more successful. Although good planning ensures that you know the material well, have thought through the methods of instruction, and are less likely to have problems in classroom control, there are other reasons for planning thoughtfully and thoroughly.

Careful planning helps to ensure program coherence. Daily plans are an integral part of a larger plan represented by course goals and objectives. Students' learning experiences are thoughtfully planned in sequence, then orchestrated by a teacher who understands the rationale for their respective positions in the curriculum—not precluding, of course, an occasional diversion from planned activities.

Unless the subject matter you are teaching stands alone, follows nothing, and leads to nothing (which is unlikely), there are prerequisites to what you want your children to learn, and there are learning objectives that follow and build on this learning. Good planning provides a mechanism for scope (the content that is covered) and sequence (the order of the content) articulation.

The diversity of students in today's classrooms demands that you give planning considerations to individual differences—whether they be cultural experiences, different learning styles, various levels of proficiency in the use of the English language, special needs, or any other concerns.

Another reason for careful planning is to ensure program continuation. In your absence, a substitute teacher or other members of the teaching team can fill in, continuing your program.

Thorough and thoughtful planning is important for a teacher's self-assessment. After an activity, a lesson, a unit, and at the end of a semester and the school year, you will assess what was done and the effect it had on student achievement. As discussed in Chapter 1, this is the reflective phase of the thought-processing phases of instruction.

Finally, administrators expect you to plan thoroughly and thoughtfully. Your plans represent a criterion recognized and evaluated by administrators, because for those experienced in such matters, it is aphoristic that inadequate attention to planning is a precursor to incompetent teaching.

B. COMPONENTS OF PLANNING

Eight components should be considered in instructional planning:

1. *Statement of Philosophy.* This is a general statement about why the plan is important and how students will learn its content.

2. *Needs Assessment.* By its wording, the statement of philosophy should reflect an appreciation for the cultural plurality of the nation and of the school, with a corresponding perception of the needs of society and its children and of the functions served by the school. The statement of philosophy and needs of the students should be consistent with the school's mission or philosophy statement. (Every school or school district has such a statement, which usually can be found posted in the office and in classrooms and written in the student and parent handbook.)

3. *Aims, Goals, and Objectives.* The plan's stated aims, goals, and objectives should be consistent with the school's mission or philosophy statement. (The differences between these terms are discussed later in this chapter.)

4. *Sequence.* Sometimes referred to as *vertical articulation, sequence* refers to the plan's relationship to the content learning that preceded and that follows, in the kindergarten through twelfth-grade curriculum.

5. *Integration.* Sometimes referred to as *horizontal articulation, integration* refers to the plan's connection with other curriculum and co-curriculum activities across the grade level. For example, the English/language arts program may be articulated with the history/social studies program. In many schools, "writing across the curriculum" is an example of integration across grade level.

6. *Sequentially Planned Learning Activities.* This is the presentation of organized and sequential units and lessons appropriate for the subject, grade level, and age and diversity of the students.

7. *Resources Needed.* This is a listing of resources, such as books, speakers, field trips, and media materials.

8. *Assessment Strategies.* Consistent with the objectives, assessment strategies include procedures for diagnosing what students know or think they know (their misconceptions) *prior* to the instruction (diagnostic assessment or preassessment) and evaluating student achievement *during* instruction to find out what students are learning (formative assessment) and *after* instruction to find out what they have learned (summative assessment).

C. PLANNING A COURSE

When planning a course, you must decide what is to be accomplished in that time period for which students are in your classroom, whether for an academic year, a semester, or some lesser time period. To help in deciding what is to be accomplished, you will

- Probe, analyze, and translate your own convictions, knowledge, and skills into behaviors that foster the intellectual development of your students
- Review school and other public resource documents for mandates and guidelines
- Talk with colleagues and learn of common expectations.

In addition, and as discussed later in this chapter, to determine what exactly is to be accomplished and how, many teachers collaboratively plan with their students.

Documents That Provide Guidance for Content Selection

Documents produced at the national level, state department of education curriculum publications, district courses of study, and school-adopted printed and nonprinted materials are the sources you will examine. Your college or university library may be a source of such documents. Others may be borrowed from or read at local schools.

To receive accreditation (which normally occurs every three to six years), high schools are reviewed by an accreditation team. Prior to its visit, the schools prepare self-study reports in which each department reviews and updates the curriculum guides that provide descriptive information about the objectives and content of each course and program offered. In about half of the states, middle schools and junior high schools also are accredited by state or regional agencies. In other states, those schools can volunteer to be reviewed for improvement.

National Curriculum Standards

The National Council on Education Standards and Testing has recommended that national standards for subject matter content in education be developed for all core subjects—the arts, civics/social studies, English/language arts/reading, geography, history, mathematics, and science. Standards are a definition of what students should know and be able to do. For the subjects and grade level of interest to you, you will want to follow the development of national curriculum standards. For example, in 1989, the National Council of Teachers of Mathematics issued standards for mathematics for grades K–12. By 1992, more than 40 states, usually through state curriculum frameworks, were following those standards to guide what and how mathematics is taught and how student progress is assessed. (For an account of a K–12 mathematics program that does *not* follow NCTM guidelines, see Hill, 1993.) In the spring of 1994, National Standards for Arts Education were completed and approved.

As this book goes to press, several language arts and social studies projects are in various stages of development. They include the following:

- *Civics/social studies*—With grants from the U.S. Department of Education and the Pew Charitable Trust, the Center for Civic Education and the National Center for Social Studies are in the process of developing standards for civics and for social studies. The standards for social studies were expected to be completed in 1995. For information, contact the National Council for the Social Studies (NCSS), 3501 Newark Street, NW, Washington, DC 20016. Standards for civics, centered around the values and principles of the U.S. Constitution, were expected to be completed in 1995. For information, contact Center for Civic Education, 5146 Douglas Fir Road, Calabasas, CA 91302.
- *English/reading/language arts*—With an original grant from the U.S. Department of Education, standards for English are being developed jointly by the International Reading Association, the National Council of Teachers of English, and the University of Illinois Center for the Study of Reading. Although delayed because of withdrawal of USDE funding, completion of these standards is expected in 1995 or 1996. For information, contact The Center for the Study of Reading, 174 Children's Research Center, 51 Gerty Drive, Champaign, IL 61820.
- *Geography*—With a grant from the U.S. Department of Education, the Association of American Geographers, the National Council for Geographic Education, and the National Geographic Society developed standards for geography education, and were completed in 1994. For information, contact Geography Standards Project, 1600 M Street, NW, Washington, DC 20036.
- *History*—The U.S. Department of Education and the National Endowment for the Humanities provided funding to the National Center for History in the Schools to develop standards for history education, which were scheduled for completion in 1995. For information, contact National Center for History in the Schools at UCLA, 231 Moore Hall, 405 Hilgard Avenue, Los Angeles, CA 90024.

Once the new standards have been completed, they will be used by state and local school districts to revise their curriculum documents. Guided by these standards and the content of state frameworks—especially that of the larger states such as California, Florida, and Texas—publishers of student textbooks and other instructional materials will develop their new or revised printed and nonprinted instructional materials. By the year 2000, all new standards will likely be in place and having a positive effect upon student achievement in classroom learning.

Student Textbooks

Traditionally, at the intermediate and middle school level, much class time teaching language arts and social studies is devoted to use of the textbook and other printed materials. There has often been controversy surrounding the gap between what is needed in textbooks and what is found. In recent years, considerable national attention has been given to finding ways of improving the quality of student textbooks, with particular attention given to the need to develop student skills in critical thinking and higher-order problem solving.

For several reasons—the recognition of different individual learning styles of students, the increasing costs of textbooks and decreasing availability of funds, and the availability of nonprinted learning materials—textbook appearance, content, and use have changed considerably in recent years. Still, "ninety percent of all classroom activity is regulated by textbooks" (Starr, 1989, p. 106).

School districts have textbook adoption cycles (usually every five or so years), meaning books are used for several years, until the next adoption cycle. If you are a student teacher or a first-year teacher, most likely someone will tell you, "Here are the books you will be using." Starting now, you should become familiar with textbooks you may be using and how you may be using them. (Textbook value, selection, and use specific to language arts and social studies instruction are discussed in Chapters 8 and 13, respectively.)

How a textbook can be helpful to students. How can textbooks be of help? Textbooks can help students in their learning by providing

* A base for building higher-order thinking activities (inquiry discussions, problem recognition, and problem solving) that help develop critical thinking skills
* A basis for selecting subject matter that can be used for deciding content
* An organization of basic or important content with models and examples
* Information about other readings and resources to enhance the learning experiences of students
* Previously tested practice activities and suggestions for learning experiences.

Problems with reliance on a single textbook. The student textbook, however, should not be the be-all and end-all of the instructional experience. For both language arts and social studies, the textbook is only one of many teaching tools and should not be cherished as the ultimate word. Of the many methods from which you may select how you use student textbooks, the least acceptable is to show a complete dependence on a single book and require students to simply memorize content from it. That is the lowest level of learning; furthermore, it implies that you are unaware of other sources of instructional materials and have nothing more to contribute to student learning.

Another potential problem brought about by reliance upon a single textbook is that because textbook publishers prepare books for use in a larger market, that is, for national or statewide use, your state- and district-adopted textbook may not, in the minds of some members of the school community, adequately address issues of special interest and importance to your community of children and their parents or guardians. That is another reason why some teachers and schools, as well as many textbook publishers, provide supplementary printed and nonprinted materials. (At least 24 states use statewide textbook adoption review committees to review books and to then provide public school districts with lists of recommended books from which they may select books purchased with funds provided by the state.)

Another very important reason to provide supplementary reading materials is to ensure multicultural balance. A single textbook may not provide the balance needed to ensure the noncontinuance of the traditional cultural and ethnic biases that need to be corrected in our schools and in our teaching, such as linguistic bias (the use of masculine terms and pronouns); stereotyping; invisibility of women, minorities, and disabled persons on printed pages; and imbalance (the glossing over of controversial topics or complete avoidance of the discussion of reality, discrimination, and prejudice) (Sadker, Sadker, & Long, 1989). See Banks and Banks, 1989, for excellent ideas and resources on bringing multicultural balance to your curriculum.

Still another problem brought about by reliance upon a single source is that for many students the adopted textbook may just not be at the appropriate reading level (see Section A of Chapter 6). In today's heterogeneous (mixed-ability-grouping) classrooms, the reading range can vary by as much as two-thirds of the chronological age of the students in the classroom. That means that if the chronological age is 12 years (as is typical for seventh-grade students), then the reading-level range would be 8 years; that is to say, the class may have some children reading only at a preschool level while others may be reading at a level beyond high school. All teachers, not only those responsible for teaching language arts, need to know about the kinds of problem readers and share in the responsibility of seeing that those students get help in developing their reading skills.

Your attention is directed now to the following general guidelines about the use of the textbook as a learning tool.

Students can benefit from having their own textbooks, especially when the textbooks are current. Due to school budget constraints, however, the textbooks may *not* be the latest editions, and in some schools there may be only classroom sets—textbooks that students are allowed to use only while in the classroom. When that is the case, students either may not be allowed to take the books home or may only occasionally be allowed to check them out. In other classrooms there may be no textbooks at all. Maintain supplementary reading materials for student use in the classroom. School and community librarians usually are delighted to cooperate with teachers in the selection and provision of such materials.

Some students benefit from drill, practice, and reinforcement afforded by accompanying workbooks, but not all necessarily do. As a matter of fact, the traditional workbook, now nearly extinct, is being replaced by the modern technology afforded by computer software, videodiscs, and compact discs. As the costs of hardware and software programs decline, the use of programs by individual students is also becoming more common. Computers provide students with a psychologically safer learning environment. With computer programs and interactive media, the student has greater control over the pace of the instruction and can repeat instruction if necessary or ask for further clarification without fear of having to publicly ask for help.

Provide vocabulary lists to help students learn meanings of important words and phrases. Teach students how to study from their textbook, perhaps by using the SQ4R method: *survey* the chapter, ask about what was read, *read* to answer the questions, *recite* the answers, *record* important items from the chapter in a notebook, then *review* it all. Or, use the SQ3R method—*survey* the chapter, ask *questions* about what was read, *read, recite,* and *review.*

Encourage students to search other sources for content that will update that found in their textbook, especially when the book is several years old. This is especially important in social studies, above all in geography and history, where there have been so many recent developments, and, as discussed in the preceding section, it is important whenever a multicultural balance is needed.

Encourage students to be alert for errors in their books—content errors, printing errors, and discrepancies or imbalance in the treatment of minorities, women, and persons with special needs—and perhaps give students some sort of reward, such as points, when they bring an error to your attention. Encouraging students to be alert for errors in the textbook encourages critical reading, critical thinking, and healthy skepticism. For example, recently a history book is reported to have stated that the first person to lead a group through the length of the Grand Canyon was John Wesley Powell. Critically thinking students quickly made the point that perhaps Powell was only the first white person to do this. After all, evidence shows that Native Americans had traveled the length of the Grand Canyon for centuries (Reinhold, 1991).

Progressing from one cover of the textbook to the other in one school term is not necessarily an indicator of good teaching. The emphasis in instruction should be on *mastery* of content rather than simply on *coverage* of content. The textbook is one resource; to enhance their learning, students should be encouraged to use a variety of resources.

Individualize the learning for students according to their reading and learning abilities. Consider differentiated assignments in the textbook and supplementary materials. When using supplementary materials, consider using several rather than just one. Except to make life a bit simpler for the teacher, there is no advantage in having all students in the typical classroom today, with its diversity of students, doing the same assignments. When students use materials not designed to accompany their text, however, edit the materials so they relate well to your course objectives.

Encourage students to respect their books by covering and protecting them and by not making permanent marks in them. In many schools that is a rule, and at the end of the term students who have damaged or lost their books are charged a fee. In some schools students can choose whether to purchase their books, and if they do, they are probably free to mark in them.

Within the span of your professional career it is likely that you will witness and be a part of a revolution in the design of school textbooks. Already some school districts and states allow teachers in certain disciplines (where the technology is available) to choose between student textbooks as we have known them and interactive videodisc programs. For example, for elementary school science, the state of Texas allows its schools to adopt Optical Data's *Windows on Science* videodisc-based program. The program comes with a Curriculum Publishing Kit that allows teachers to design their own curriculum from the *Windows on Science* program, and users periodically receive updated data discs. Texas, followed by Utah and West Virginia, were the first states to allow schools to choose between a textbook-centered program and one that is videodisc centered for specific curriculum areas.

With the revolution in computer chip technology, it has been predicted that student textbooks may soon take on a whole new appearance. With that will come dramatic changes in the importance and use of student texts, as well as new problems for the teacher, some of which are predictable. Student "texts" may become credit-card size, increasing the chance of students losing their books. On the positive side, the classroom teacher will probably have available a variety of "textbooks" to better address the reading levels, interests, learning styles, and abilities of individual students. Distribution and maintenance of reading materials could create an even greater demand on the teacher's time. Regardless, dramatic and exciting changes have begun to transform a teaching tool that has not changed much throughout the history of education in this country. As an electronic, multimedia tool, the textbook of the twenty-first century may be "an interactive device that offers text, sound, and video" (Gifford, 1991, pp. 15–16).

D. COLLABORATIVE AND COOPERATIVE TEAM PLANNING

As you have learned, you need not do all your instructional planning from scratch, and neither do you need to do all your planning alone. Planning for teaching can be thought of as rehearsing what will be done in the classroom, both mentally and on paper (Murray, 1980). In classrooms today, which tend to be more project oriented and student and group centered than traditional classrooms, where the teacher was the primary provider of information, students more actively participate in their learning. The teacher provides some structure and assistance, but the collaborative approach requires students to inquire and interact, to generate ideas, to seriously listen and talk with one another, and to recognize that their thoughts and experiences are valuable and essential to meaningful learning.

Team Planning

As discussed in the previous chapter, many teachers plan together in teams. Planning procedures are the same as discussed earlier in this chapter, except that team members plan together or split the responsibilities and then share their individual planning, cooperatively working up a final plan. As we learned earlier, team planning works best when members of the teaching team share a common planning time.

Collaborative Teacher-Student Planning

Many teachers encourage students to participate in the planning of some phase of their learning, from planning an entire course of study or units within that course of study to planning specific learning activities within a unit of study. Such participation tends to give students a proprietary interest in the activities, thereby increasing their motivation for learning. That which students have contributed to the plan often seems more meaningful to them than what others have planned for them. And they like to see their own plans succeed. Thus, teacher-student collaboration in planning can be an effective motivational tool. (For a report on how one seventh-grade class of students designed their own course of study for an integrated unit, see Smith & Johnson, 1993.)

Preparing for the Year

While some authors believe that the first step in preparing to teach is to write the objectives, others believe that a more logical first step is to prepare a sequential topic outline, and that is the procedure followed next in this chapter. The sequential course outline might be prepared by one teacher, by a team of teachers, or collaboratively with the students. Whatever the case, from that outline, you can then prepare some of the important expected learning outcomes. Once you have decided the content and anticipated outcomes, you are ready to divide that into subdivisions or units of instruction and then prepare those units with their daily lessons (the final steps of this chapter).

Most beginning teachers are presented with the topic outlines and the instructional objectives (in the course of study or in the teacher's edition of the student textbook) with the (often unspoken) expectation that they will teach from them. And, this may be the case for you, but someone had to have written those, and that someone was one or several teachers. So, as a beginning teacher, you should know how it is done, for someday you will be concentrating on it in earnest.

A Caution about Selection and Sequencing of Content

Please be cautioned that beginning teachers sometimes have unrealistic expectations about the amount of content that a heterogeneous group of children can study, comprehend, and learn over a given period of time, especially as learning by those students is influenced by special needs and diverse cultural and language backgrounds. Reviewing school and other public documents and talking with experienced teachers in your school are very helpful in arriving at a realistic selection and sequencing of content and later developing a time frame for teaching that content. Citing the work of Duckworth (1986), Eisner (1985), and Katz (1985), Brooks and Brooks (1993) conclude,

> Constructivist teachers have discovered that the prescribed scope, sequence, and timeline often interferes with their ability to help students understand complex concepts. Rigid timelines are also at odds with research on how human beings form meaningful theories about the ways the world works, how students and teachers develop an appreciation of knowledge and understanding, and how one creates the disposition to inquire about phenomena not fully understood. Most curriculums simply pack too much information into too little time—at a significant cost to the learner (p. 29).

Once you have analyzed various curriculum documents and prepared a content outline, you are ready to prepare the anticipated learning outcomes and write the specific instructional objectives, known also as behavioral (or performance) objectives—statements that describe what the student will be able to do upon completion of the instructional experience.

E. AIMS, GOALS, AND OBJECTIVES

As a teacher, you will encounter the compound structure that reads "goals and objectives." A distinction needs to be understood. The easiest way to understand the difference between the two words *goals* and *objectives* is to look at your intent.

Goals are ideal states that you intend to reach, that is, ideals that you would like to have accomplished. Goals may be stated as teacher goals, as student goals, or, collaboratively, as course goals. Ideally, in all three, the goal should be the same. If, for example, the goal is to improve students' ability to write, it could be stated as follows:

"To help students develop their writing ability"   *Teacher or course goal*
or
"To improve my ability to write"   *Student goal*

Goals are general statements of intent, prepared early in course planning. Goals are useful when planned cooperatively with students and/or shared with students as advance mental organizers. The students then know what to expect and will begin to prepare mentally to learn that material. Whereas goals are general, the objectives based on them are specific. The value of stating learning objectives in behavioral terms and in providing advance organizers is well documented by research (Good & Brophy, 1987, p. 334). Objectives are *not* intentions. They are the actual behaviors teachers intend to cause students to display. In short, objectives are what students *do*.

The terminology used for designating the various types of objectives is not standardized. In the literature, the most general educational objectives are often called *aims;* the general objectives of schools, curricula, and courses are called *goals;* the objectives of units and lessons are called *instructional objectives.* Whereas some authors distinguish between "instructional objectives" (objectives that are *not* behavior specific) and "behavioral" or "performance objectives" (objectives that *are* behavior specific), the terms are used here interchangeably to stress the importance of writing objectives for instruction in terms that are measurable. Aims are more general than goals, goals are more general than objectives. Instructional (behavioral) objectives are quite specific.

As implied in the preceding paragraphs, goals guide the instructional methods; objectives drive student performance. Assessment (evaluation) of student achievement in learning should be an assessment of that performance. Assessment procedures that match the instructional objectives are sometimes referred to as aligned or authentic assessment (discussed in the next chapter).

Goals are general statements, usually not even complete sentences, often beginning with the infinitive "to," which identify what the teacher intends the students to learn. Objectives, stated in performance (behavioral) terms, are specific actions and should be written as complete sentences that include the verb "will" to indicate what each student is expected to be able to do as a result of the instructional experience.

While instructional goals may not always be quantifiable, that is, readily measurable, instructional objectives should be measurable. Furthermore, those objectives are, in essence, what is measured by instruments designed to authentically assess student learning.

Consider the following examples of goals and objectives.

Goals   1. To learn about the physical geography of North America.
            2. To provide reading opportunities for students.

Objectives 1. On a map, the student will identify specific mountain ranges of
             North America.
            2. The student will read two books, three short stories, and five newspaper articles at home, within a two-month period. The student will maintain a daily written log of these activities.

F. INSTRUCTIONAL OBJECTIVES AND THEIR RELATIONSHIP TO INSTRUCTION AND ASSESSMENT

As implied before, one purpose for writing objectives in specific, behavioral terms is to be able to assess with precision whether the instruction has resulted in the desired behavior. In many school districts the educational goals are established as competencies that the students are expected to achieve. This is known variously as *competency-based, performance-based,* or *outcome-based education.* (For informative articles about outcome-based education, see the March 1994 issue of *Educational Leadership.*) These goals are then divided into specific performance objectives, sometimes referred to as *goal indicators.* When students perform the competencies called for by these objectives, their education is considered successful. Expecting students to achieve one set of competencies before moving on to the next set is called *mastery learning.* The success of school curricula, teacher performance, and student achievement may each be assessed according to these criteria.

Assessment is not difficult when the desired performance is overt, that is, when it can be observed directly. Each of the two sample objectives of the preceding section is an example of an overt objective. Assessment is more difficult when the desired behavior is covert, that is, when it is not directly observable. Although certainly no less important, behaviors that call for "appreciation," "discovery," or "understanding," for example, are not directly observable because they occur within a person, and so are covert. Since covert behavior cannot be observed directly, the only way to tell whether the objective has been achieved is to observe behavior that may be indicative of that achievement. The objective, then, must be written in overt language, and evaluators can only assume or trust that the observed behavior is, in fact, indicative of the expected learning outcome.

Behaviorism and Constructivism: Are They Compatible?

While behaviorists (and behaviorism) assume a definition of learning that deals only with changes in observable (overt) behavior, constructivists (and cognitivism), as discussed in Chapter 1, hold that learning entails the construction or reshaping of mental schemata and that mental processes mediate learning, and so are concerned with both overt and covert behaviors (Perkins & Blythe, 1994).

Furthermore, when assessing whether an objective has been achieved, the assessment device must be consistent with the desired learning outcome; otherwise the assessment is invalid. When the measuring device and the learning objective are compatible, the assessment is referred to as being authentic. For example, a person's competency to teach fifth-grade children is most reliably measured by directly observing that person *doing* that very thing—teaching fifth-grade students. That is authentic assessment. Using a standardized paper-and-pencil test to determine a person's ability to teach fifth graders is not. (Assessment is the topic of the next chapter.)

Does this mean that you must be one or the other, a behaviorist or a constructivist? Probably not. For now, the point is that when writing instructional objectives, you should write most or all of your minimal competency expectations in overt terms (the topic of the next section). On the other hand, you cannot be expected to foresee all learning that will occur or to translate all that is learned into behavioral terms. We agree with those who argue that any effort to write all learning objectives in behavioral terms, in effect, neglects the individual learner; such an approach does not allow for diversity among learners. Learning that is most meaningful to children is not so neatly and easily predicted and isolated. Rather than teaching one objective at a time, much of the time your teaching will be directed toward the simultaneous learning of multiple objectives, understandings, and appreciations. When you assess for learning, however, assessment is easier and more accurate when objectives are assessed one at a time.

G. PREPARING INSTRUCTIONAL OBJECTIVES

When preparing instructional objectives you must ask yourself: "How is the student to demonstrate that the objective has been reached?" The objective must include an action that demonstrates that the objective has been achieved. That portion of the objective is sometimes referred to as the *terminal behavior,* or the *anticipated measurable performance,* and is important in an outcome-based educational (OBE) program.

Four Key Components to Writing Objectives

When completely written, an instructional objective has four key components. To aid in your understanding and remembering, you can refer to them as the ABCDs of writing behavioral objectives.

One of the components is the *audience*—that is, the student for whom the objective is intended. To address this audience, sometimes teachers begin their objectives with the phrase "The student will be able to . . ." or personalize the objective as "You will be able to. . . ."

The second key component is the expected *behavior.* The expected behavior (or performance) should be written with action verbs that are measurable so it is directly observable that an objective has been reached. As discussed in the previous section, some verbs de-

FIGURE 4.1
Verbs to Avoid when Writing Objectives

appreciate	familiarize	learn
believe	grasp	like
comprehend	indicate	realize
enjoy	know	understand

scribe covert behaviors that are vague, ambiguous, and not clearly measurable, such as appreciate, believe, comprehend, enjoy, know, learn, like, and understand (see Figure 4.1). These are to be avoided.

The third ingredient is the *conditions*—the setting in which the behavior will be demonstrated by the student and observed by the teacher. For the first sample objective discussed earlier, the conditions are "On a map." For the second sample objective beginning, "The student will read . . .," the conditions are "at home, within a two-month period."

The fourth ingredient, not always included in objectives written by teachers, is the *degree of expected performance.* This is the ingredient that allows for the assessment of student learning. When mastery learning is expected (achievement of 85 to 100 percent), the level of expected performance is usually omitted because it is understood. (In teaching for mastery learning, the performance-level expectation is 100 percent. In reality, however, the performance level will most likely be between 85 and 95 percent, particularly when working with a group of students rather than an individual student. The 5 to 15 percent difference allows for human error, as can occur with written and oral communication.)

Performance level is used to assess student achievement and, sometimes, the effectiveness of the teaching. Student grades might be based on performance levels; evaluation of teacher effectiveness might be based on the level of student performance. In recent years, there has been a rekindling of interest in performance-based (or outcome-based, or competency-based) assessment. Now, using Figure 4.2, try your skill at recognizing objectives that are measurable.

H. CLASSIFICATION OF LEARNING OBJECTIVES

Three domains for classifying learning objectives are useful for planning and assessing student learning. These are

- *Cognitive domain.* This is the domain of learning that involves mental operations, from the lowest level of simple recall of information to high-level and complex evaluative processes.

FIGURE 4.2
Recognizing Objectives That Are Measurable

Assess your ability to recognize objectives that are measurable by placing an X before each of the following that is a student-centered behavioral objective, that is, a learning objective that is clearly measurable. Although audience, conditions, and performance levels may not be stated, ask yourself, "As written, is it a student-centered and measurable objective?" After checking your answers, discuss any problems with your classmates and instructor.

_____   1. To develop an appreciation for literature.

_____   2. To identify from a list words that are homographs.

_____   3. To provide meaningful experiences for the children.

_____   4. To recognize antonym pairs.

_____   5. To boot up the program on the computer.

_____   6. To analyze and compare patterns of data on specific quartile maps.

_____   7. To develop skills in inquiry.

_____   8. To identify which of the four major events was most relevant as a cause of the Civil War.

_____   9. To use maps and graphs to identify the major areas of world petroleum production and consumption.

_____   10. To know the causes for the diminishing ozone layer.

Answer key: 2, 4, 5, 6, 8, 9.
Items 1, 3, 7, and 10 are inadequate because of their ambiguity. Item 3 is not even a student learning objective; it is a teacher goal. "To develop" and "to know" can have too many interpretations.
    Although the conditions are not given, items 2, 4, 5, 6, 8, and 9 are clearly measurable. The teacher would have no difficulty recognizing when a learner had reached those objectives.

- *Affective domain.* This domain of learning involves feelings, attitudes, and values, from lower levels of acquisition to the highest level of internalization and action.
- *Psychomotor domain.* This is the domain of learning that involves simple manipulation of materials on up to the higher level of communication of ideas, and finally, the highest level of creative performance.

Schools attempt to provide learning experiences designed to meet the needs of the total child. Specifically, five areas of developmental needs are identified: (1) intellectual, (2) physical, (3) psychological, (4) social, and (5) moral and ethical. You should include learning objectives that address each of these developmental needs. While intellectual needs fall primarily within the cognitive domain and physical needs within the psychomotor domain, the others are mostly affective. Too many teachers direct their attention solely to cognitive needs, assuming that psychomotor and affective needs will take care of themselves. Effective teachers direct their planning and sequence their teaching so students are guided from the lowest to highest levels of operation within and across each of the three domains.

The following discussion of the three developmental hierarchies will guide your understanding of how to address each of the five areas of needs. Notice the illustrative verbs within each hierarchy of each domain. These verbs will help you fashion your behavioral objectives for the lesson plans you will soon be developing.

Cognitive Domain Hierarchies

In a taxonomy of objectives that is widely accepted, Benjamin Bloom and his associates (1984) arranged cognitive objectives into classifications according to the complexity of the skills and abilities embodied in them. The resulting taxonomy portrays a ladder ranging from the simplest to the most complex intellectual processes. Rather than an orderly progression from simple to complex mental operations as illustrated by Bloom's taxonomy, other researchers prefer an identification of cognitive abilities that ranges from simple information storage and retrieval, through a higher level of discrimination and concept attainment, to the highest cognitive ability to recognize and solve problems (Gagné, Briggs, & Wager, 1988). Regardless of the domain and within each, prerequisite to a student's ability to function at one level of the hierarchy is the student's ability to function at the preceding level or levels. In other words, when a student is functioning at the third level of the cognitive domain, then that student is automatically also functioning at the first and second levels.

The six major categories (or levels) in Bloom's taxonomy of cognitive objectives are

1. *Knowledge*—recognizing and recalling information
2. *Comprehension*—understanding the meaning of information
3. *Application*—using information
4. *Analysis*—ability to dissect information into component parts and see relationships
5. *Synthesis*—putting components together to form new ideas
6. *Evaluation*—judging the worth of an idea, notion, theory, thesis, proposition, information, or opinion.

Although space does not allow elaboration here, Bloom's taxonomy includes various subcategories within each of these six major categories. It is less important that an objective be absolutely classified than that you are cognizant of hierarchies of levels of thinking and doing and understand the importance of attending to student cognitive development and intellectual behavior from lower to higher levels of operation in all three domains.

A discussion of each of Bloom's six categories follows.

Knowledge.   The basic element in Bloom's taxonomy concerns the acquisition of knowledge—that is, the ability to recognize and recall information. Although this is the lowest level of the six categories, the information to be learned may not itself be of a low level. In fact, the information may be extremely complex. Bloom includes at this level knowledge of principles, generalizations, theories, structures, and methodology, as well as knowledge of facts and ways of dealing with facts.

Action verbs appropriate for this category include *choose, complete, define, describe, identify, indicate, list, locate, match, name, outline, recall, recognize, select,* and *state.* (Note that some verbs may be appropriately used at more than one cognitive level.)

The following are examples of objectives at this cognitive level. Note especially the verb used in each example.

- From memory, the student will define *homonym* and give one example of a homonym.
- The student will recall at least two factors that are considered to be causes of the Civil War.

The remaining five categories of Bloom's taxonomy of the cognitive domain deal with the *use* of knowledge. They encompass the educational objectives aimed at developing cognitive skills and abilities, including comprehension, application, analysis, synthesis, and evaluation of knowledge. The last three—analysis, synthesis, and evaluation—are referred to as higher-order thinking skills.

Comprehension. Comprehension includes the ability to translate or explain knowledge, to interpret that knowledge, and to extrapolate from it to address new situations.

Action verbs appropriate for this category include *change, classify, convert, defend, derive, describe, estimate, expand, explain, generalize, infer, interpret, paraphrase, predict, recognize, summarize,* and *translate.*

Examples of objectives in this category are

- From a list of 20 words, the student will recognize those that have multiple meanings.
- The student will summarize factors that caused the Civil War.

Application. Once students understand information, they should be able to apply it. This is the category of operation above comprehension.

Action verbs include *apply, compute, demonstrate, develop, discover, discuss, modify, operate, participate, perform, plan, predict, relate, show, solve,* and *use.*

Examples of objectives in this category are

- In complete sentences, the student will demonstrate the different meanings of a selected homograph.
- The student will discuss the issue of slavery and its causal relationship to the Civil War.

Analysis. This category includes objectives that require students to use the skills of analysis.

Action verbs appropriate for this category include *analyze, break down, categorize, classify, compare, contrast, debate, deduce, diagram, differentiate, discriminate, identify, illustrate, infer, outline, relate, separate,* and *subdivide.*

Examples of objectives in this category include

- From a list of 20 homonyms, the student will differentiate which are homophones, which are homographs, and which are homographic homophones.
- The student will analyze and compare the economies of the North and South both before and after the Civil War.

Synthesis. This category includes objectives that involve such skills as designing a plan, proposing a set of operations, and deriving a series of abstract relations.

Action verbs appropriate for this category include *arrange, categorize, classify, combine, compile, constitute, create, design, develop, devise, document, explain, formulate, generate, modify, organize, originate, plan, produce, rearrange, reconstruct, revise, rewrite, summarize, synthesize, tell, transmit,* and *write.*

Examples of objectives in this category are

- The student will create and maintain his or her own homonym book.
- The student will create a plan that uses our knowledge of the causes of the Civil War for solving one of today's social problems.

Evaluation. The highest cognitive category of Bloom's taxonomy is evaluation. This includes offering opinions and making value judgments.

Action verbs appropriate for this category include *appraise, argue, assess, compare, conclude, consider, contrast, criticize, decide, discriminate, evaluate, explain, interpret, judge, justify, rank, rate, relate, standardize, support,* and *validate.*

Examples of objectives in this category are

- The student will read and critique other students' homonym books for the correctness of their entries.
- The student will assess a plan presented by another student that uses our knowledge of the causes of the Civil War to solve one of today's social problems.

Affective Domain Hierarchies

Krathwohl, Bloom, and Masia (1964) developed a taxonomy for the affective domain. The following are their major levels (or categories), from least internalized to most internalized:

1. *Receiving.* Being aware of the affective stimulus and beginning to have favorable feelings toward it.
2. *Responding.* Taking an interest in the stimulus and viewing it favorably.
3. *Valuing.* Showing a tentative belief in the value of the affective stimulus and becoming committed to it.
4. *Organizing.* Organizing values into a system of dominant and supporting values.
5. *Internalizing values.* Making beliefs and behavior consistent—a way of life.

The following paragraphs more fully describe the types of objectives that fit the categories of the affective domain. Although there is considerable overlap from one category to another, they do provide a basis by which to judge the quality of objectives and the nature of learning within this domain.

Receiving. At this level, which is the least internalized, the student exhibits willingness to give attention to particular phenomena or stimuli, and the teacher is able to arouse, sustain, and direct that attention.

Action verbs appropriate for this category include *ask, choose, describe, differentiate, distinguish, hold, identify, locate, name, point to, recall, recognize, reply, select,* and *use.*

Examples of objectives in this category are

- The student pays close attention to the directions for enrichment activities.
- The student listens attentively to the ideas of others.
- The student demonstrates sensitivity to the concerns of others.

Responding. Students respond to the stimulus they have received. They may do so because of some external pressure, or they may do so voluntarily because they find it interesting or because responding gives them satisfaction.

Action verbs appropriate for this category include *answer, applaud, approve, assist, comply, command, discuss, greet, help, label, perform, play, practice, present, read, recite, report, select, spend (leisure time in), tell,* and *write.*

Examples of objectives at this level are

- The student reads for enrichment.
- The student discusses what others have said.
- The student willingly cooperates with others during group activities.

Valuing. Objectives at the valuing level have to do with students' beliefs, attitudes, and appreciations. The simplest objectives concern a student's acceptance of beliefs and values. Higher objectives concern a student's learning to prefer certain values and finally becoming committed to them.

Action verbs appropriate for this level include *argue, assist, complete, describe, differentiate, explain, follow, form, initiate, invite, join, justify, propose, protest, read, report, select, share, study, support,* and *work.*

Examples of objectives in this category include

- The student protests against racial discrimination.
- The student supports actions against gender discrimination.
- The student argues in favor of or against women's right to have an abortion.

Organizing. This fourth level in the affective domain concerns the building of a personal value system. At this level the student is conceptualizing values and arranging them in a value system that recognizes priorities and the relative importance of various values faced in life.

Action verbs appropriate for this level include *adhere, alter, arrange, balance, combine, compare, defend, define, discuss, explain, form, generalize, identify, integrate, modify, order, organize, prepare, relate,* and *synthesize.*

Examples of objectives at this level are

- The student forms judgments concerning proper behavior in the classroom, school, and community.
- The student forms and adheres to a personal standard of work ethic.
- The student defends the important values of his or her own culture.

Personal value system. This is the last and highest level within the affective domain. At this level the student's behaviors are consistent with his or her beliefs.

Action verbs appropriate for this level include *act, complete, display, influence, listen, modify, perform, practice, propose, qualify, question, revise, serve, solve,* and *verify.*

Examples of objectives appropriate for this level are

- The student behaves according to a well-defined and ethical code of behavior.
- The student is accurate in his or her verbal communication.
- The student works independently and diligently.

Psychomotor Domain Hierarchies

Whereas classification within the cognitive and affective domains is generally agreed upon, there is less agreement on classification within the psychomotor domain. Originally, the goal of this domain was simply that of developing and categorizing proficiency in skills, particularly those dealing with gross and fine muscle control. Today's classification of that domain, as presented here, also includes higher creative and inventive behaviors, thus coordinating skills and knowledge from all three domains. Consequently, the objectives are arranged in a hierarchy from simple gross locomotor control to the most creative and complex, requiring originality and fine locomotor control—for example, from simply threading a needle to designing and making a piece of clothing.

Harrow (1977) developed the following taxonomy of the psychomotor domain. Included are sample objectives as well as a list of possible action verbs for each level of the psychomotor domain. The levels are

1. *Movement.* This involves gross motor coordination.
    Action verbs appropriate for this level include *adjust, carry, clean, locate, obtain* and *walk.*
    A sample objective for this level is
    - The student correctly grasps and carries the globe to the workstation.

2. *Manipulating.* This level involves fine motor coordination.

Action verbs appropriate for this level include *assemble, build, calibrate, connect,* and *thread.*

A sample objective for this level is

- The student will correctly calculate distances on a map.

3. *Communicating.* This level involves the communication of ideas and feelings.

Action verbs appropriate for this level include *analyze, ask, describe, draw, explain,* and *write.*

A sample objective for this level is

- The student will describe his or her feelings after reading the poem.

4. *Creating.* This is the highest level of this and all domains and represents the student's coordination of thinking, learning, and behaving in all three domains.

Action verbs appropriate for this level include *create, design,* and *invent.*

Sample objectives for this level are

- From his or her own data collecting and calculations, the student will design a more time-efficient and learning-effective way of moving people from one place to another on the school campus.
- Through the processes of prewriting, drafting, revising, sharing, and editing, the student will write a myth and, with the help of classmates, create a videotape of a dramatic presentation of the myth.

I. USING THE TAXONOMIES

Theoretically, as noted earlier, the taxonomies are so constructed that students achieve each lower level before being ready to move to the next higher level. But because categories and behaviors overlap, as they should, this theory does not always hold in practice. The taxonomies are important in that they emphasize the various levels to which instruction must aspire. For learning to be worthwhile, you must formulate and teach objectives from the higher levels of the taxonomies as well as from the lower ones. Student thinking and behaving must be moved from the lowest to the highest levels. When all is said and done, it is, perhaps, the highest level of the psychomotor domain (creating) that we are striving for, especially when teaching the language arts.

In using the taxonomies, remember that the point is to formulate the best objectives for the job to be done. The taxonomies provide the mechanism for ensuring that you do not spend a disproportionate amount of time on facts and other learning that is relatively trivial. Writing objectives is essential to the preparation of good items for the assessment of student learning. Clearly communicating your behavioral expectations to students and then specifically assessing student learning against those expectations makes the teaching most efficient and effective, and it makes the assessment of the learning closer to authentic. This does not mean that you will *always* write behavioral objectives for everything taught, nor will you always be able to accurately measure what students have learned. Learning that is meaningful to students is not as easily compartmentalized as the taxonomies of educational objectives would imply. As said by Caine and Caine, "The bottom line is that thoughts and feelings are inextricably interconnected—we 'think' with our feelings and 'feel' with our thoughts" (1993, p. 19).

Using a Response Journal to Assess for Meaningful Learning

In learning that is most important and that has the most meaning to students, the domains are inextricably interconnected. Consequently, when assessing for student learning, you must look for those connections. One way of doing that is to have students maintain a journal in which they reflect on and respond to their learning using the following five categories, adapted with permission from Fersh (1993, pp. 23–24):

1. *"I never knew that."* In this category, student responses are primarily to factual information, new knowledge, and bits and pieces of raw information, often expected to be memorized, regardless of how meaningful to students it might be. Because this is only fragmented knowledge and merely scratches the surface of meaningful learning, it must

not be the end-all of student learning. Learning that is truly meaningful goes beyond the "I never knew that" category, expands upon the bits and pieces, and connects them, allowing the learner to make sense out of what he or she is learning. Learning that does not extend beyond the "I never knew that" category is dysfunctional.

2. *"I never thought of that."* Here, student responses reveal an additional way of perceiving. Their responses may include elements of "I never knew that" but also contain higher-level thinking as a result of their reflection on that knowledge.

3. *"I never felt that."* In this category, student responses are connected to the affective domain, eliciting more of an emotional response than a cognitive one. Learning that is truly meaningful is much more than intellectual understanding; it includes a "felt" meaning (Caine & Caine, 1993).

4. *"I never appreciated that."* Responses in this category reflect a sense of recognition that one's own life can be enriched by what others have created or done, or that something already known can be valued from an additional perspective.

5. *"I never realized that."* In this category, student responses indicate an awareness of overall patterns and dynamic ways in which behavior is holistic, establishing meaningful and potentially useful connections among knowledge, values, and purposes.

Character Education

Related especially to the affective domain, although not exclusive of the cognitive and psychomotor domains, is a resurgence in national interest in the development of students' values (Massey, 1993), especially honesty, kindness, respect, and responsibility—what is called character education. For example, Wynne and Ryan (1993) state that "transmitting character, academics, and discipline—essentially, 'traditional' moral values—to pupils is a vital educational responsibility" (p. 3). Thus, if one agrees with that interpretation, the teaching of moral values is the transmission of character, academics, and discipline and clearly implies learning that transcends the three domains of learning presented in this chapter.

Whether defined as ethics, citizenship, moral values, or personal development, character education has long been part of public education in this country (Burrett & Rusnak, 1993, p. 10). Today, stimulated by a perceived need to reduce student antisocial behaviors (such as drug abuse and violence) and to produce more respectful and responsible citizens, with a primary focus on the affective domain, many schools and districts are developing curricula in character education and instruction in conflict resolution, with the ultimate goal of "developing mature adults capable of responsible citizenship and moral action" (Burrett & Rusnak, 1993, p. 15). Some specific techniques are to sensitize students to value issues through role-playing and creative drama, have students take the opposite point of view in discussions, promote higher-order thinking about value issues through appropriate questioning techniques, arrange action-oriented projects, use parents and community members to assist in projects, highlight examples of class and individual cooperation in serving the school and community, and make student service projects visible in the school and community (p. 29).

J. QUESTIONING TECHNIQUES

Properly following the discussion of instructional objectives is this discussion of an instructional strategy fundamental to teaching—the use of questioning. You will use questioning for so many purposes that you must be skilled in its use to teach most effectively.

Purposes for Using Questioning

You will adapt the type and form of each question that you ask to the purpose for which it is asked. The purposes that questions can serve can be separated into five categories. These are

1. *To politely give instructions.* For example, "Lucy, would you please turn out the lights so we can show the slides?" Teachers sometimes use rhetorical questions to regain student attention and maintain classroom control—for example, "José, would you please attend to your work?"

2. *To review and remind students of classroom procedures.* For example, if students continue to talk without first raising their hands and being recognized by you, you can stop the lesson and ask, "Class, I think we need to review the procedure for answering my questions. What is the procedure that we agreed upon for talking?"

3. *To gather information.* For example, "How many of you have finished the exercise?" Or, to find out whether a student knows something, such as, "Carol, can you please tell us the difference between a synonym and antonym?"

4. *To discover student interests or experiences.* For example, "How many of you have already been to the state legislature?"

5. *To guide student thinking and learning.* It is this category of questioning that is the focus of our attention now. Questions in this category are used to
   - Clarify a student response
   - Develop appreciation
   - Develop student thinking
   - Diagnose learning difficulty
   - Emphasize major points
   - Encourage students
   - Establish rapport
   - Evaluate learning
   - Give practice in expression
   - Help students in their own metacognition
   - Help students interpret materials
   - Help students organize materials
   - Probe deeper into a student's thinking
   - Provide drill and practice
   - Provide review
   - Show agreement or disagreement
   - Show relationships, such as cause and effect.

Types of Cognitive Questions

Before going further let us define, describe, and provide examples of each of the types of cognitive questions that you will use in teaching. Then, in the section that follows, we will focus your attention on the levels of cognitive questions.

Clarifying question. The clarifying question is used to gain more information from a student to help the teacher better understand a student's ideas, feelings, and thought processes. Oftentimes, asking the child to elaborate on an initial response will cause the student to think deeper, restructure his or her thinking, and while doing so, discover a fallacy in the original response. One example of a clarifying question is: "What I hear you saying is that you would rather work alone than in your group. Is that correct?" Research has shown a strong positive correlation between student learning and development of metacognitive skills and the teacher's use of questions that ask students for clarification (Costa, 1991). In addition, by seeking clarification, the teacher is likely to be demonstrating an interest in the student and her or his thinking.

Convergent thinking question. Convergent thinking questions (also called "narrow" questions) are low-order thinking questions that have a singular answer (such as recall questions, discussed and exemplified in the next section). Examples of convergent questions are "How would you classify the word spelled c-l-o-s-e, as a homophone or homograph?" "What is the name of the first battle of the Civil War?"

Cueing question. If you ask a question to which, after sufficient wait time (2 to 9 seconds), no students respond, or if their inadequate responses indicate they need more information, then you can ask a question that cues the response you are seeking. In essence, you are going backward in your questioning sequence to cue the students. For example, if, as a set induction to a lesson on the study of prefixes, a teacher asks her students, "How many legs do crayfish, lobsters, and shrimp have?" and there is no accurate response, then she might cue the answer with the following information and question: "The class to which those animals belong is class Decapoda. Does that give you a clue about the number of legs they have?"

Divergent thinking question. Divergent thinking questions (also known as "broad," "reflective," or "thought" questions) are open ended, high-order thinking questions requiring analysis, synthesis, or evaluation that force students to think creatively, to leave the comfortable confines of the known and reach out into the unknown. An example of a question that requires divergent thinking is "What measures could be taken to improve the effectiveness of crime prevention in our city?"

Evaluative question. Some types of questions, whether convergent or divergent, require students to place a value on something. These are referred to as evaluative questions. If the teacher and the students all agree on certain premises, then the evaluative question would also be a convergent question. If original assumptions differ, then the response to the evaluative question would be more subjective, and therefore that evaluative question would be divergent. An example of an evaluative question is "Should the United States allow clear cutting in its national forests?"

Focus question. This is any question designed to focus student thinking. For example, the question of the preceding paragraph is a focus question when the teacher is attempting to focus student attention on the economic issues involved in clear cutting.

Probing question. Similar to a clarifying question, the probing question requires student thinking to go beyond superficial "first-answer" or single-word responses. Examples of probing questions are "Why, Sean, do you think that every citizen has the right to say what he or she believes?" or "Could you give us an example?"

Levels of Cognitive Questions and Student Thinking

Questions posed by you are cues to your students to the level of thinking expected of them, ranging from the lowest level of mental operation, requiring simple recall of knowledge (convergent thinking), to the highest, requiring divergent thought and application of that thought. It is important that you (1) are aware of the levels of thinking, (2) understand the importance of attending to student thinking from low to higher levels of operation, and (3) understand that what may be a matter of simple recall of information for one student may require a higher-order mental activity for another.

You should structure and sequence your questions in a way that is designed to guide students to higher levels of thinking. Three levels of questioning and thinking have been identified by various authors (see, for example, Costa, 1989, 1991; Eisner, 1979). You should recognize the similarity between these three levels of questions and the six levels of thinking from Bloom's taxonomy of cognitive objectives. For your daily use of questioning it is just as useful but more practical to think and behave in terms of these three levels, rather than of six.

1. *Lowest level (the data input phase): gathering and recalling information.* At this level questions are designed to solicit from students concepts, information, feelings, or experiences that were gained in the past and stored in memory. Sample key words and desired behaviors are *complete, count, define, describe, identify, list, match, name, observe, recall, recite, select.*
2. *Intermediate level (the data processing phase): processing information.* At this level questions are designed to draw relationships of cause and effect, to synthesize, analyze, summarize, compare, contrast, or classify data. Sample key words and desired behaviors are *analyze, classify, compare, contrast, distinguish, explain, group, infer, make an analogy, organize, plan, synthesize.*
3. *Highest level (the data output phase): applying and evaluating in new situations.* Questions at this level encourage students to think intuitively, creatively, and hypothetically; to use their imaginations; to expose a value system; or to make a judgment.

Sample key words and desired behaviors are *apply a principle, build a model, evaluate, extrapolate, forecast, generalize, hypothesize, imagine, judge, predict, speculate.*

You should use the type of question best suited for the purpose, use a variety of different levels of questions, and structure questions to move student thinking to higher levels. When their teachers use higher-level questions, students tend to score higher on tests of critical thinking and on standardized tests of achievement (Newton, 1978; Redfield & Rousseau, 1981).

Developing your skill in the use of questioning needs your attention to detail and practice. The following guidelines will provide that detail.

Guidelines for Using Questioning

As is emphasized many times in several ways throughout this book, your goals are to help your students learn how to solve problems, to make decisions and value judgments, to think creatively and critically, and to feel good about themselves and their learning rather than simply to fill their minds with bits and pieces of information. How you construe your questions and carry out your questioning strategy is important to the realization of these goals.

Preparing questions. When preparing questions, consider the following:

1. Cognitive questions should be planned, thoughtfully worded, and written into your lesson plan. Thoughtful preparation of questions helps to ensure that they are clear, specific, and not ambiguous, that the vocabulary is appropriate, and that each question matches its purpose. Incorporate questions into your lessons as instructional devices, welcomed pauses, attention grabbers, and checks for student comprehension. Thoughtful teachers even plan questions that they intend to ask specific students.
2. Match questions with their purposes. Carefully planning questions allows them to be sequenced and worded to match the levels of cognitive thinking expected of students.

Demonstrate to students how to develop their thinking skills. To demonstrate, you must use terminology that is specific and that provides students with examples of experiences consonant with the meanings of the cognitive words. You should demonstrate this every day so students learn the cognitive terminology (Costa, 1991, p. 110). As stated by Brooks and Brooks (1993), "framing tasks around cognitive activities such as analysis, interpretation, and prediction—and explicitly using those terms with students—fosters the construction of new understandings" (p. 105). Here are three examples:

Instead of	*Say*
"How else might it be done?"	"How could you *apply . . . ?*"
"Are you going to get quiet?"	"If we are going to hear what Joan has to say, what do you need to do?"
"How do you know that is so?"	"What evidence do you have?"

Implementing questions. Careful preparation of questions is one part of skill in questioning; implementation is the other part. Here are guidelines for effective implementation:

1. Avoid bombarding students with too much teacher talk. Sometimes teachers talk too much. This could be especially true for teachers who are nervous, as are many during initial weeks of their student teaching. Knowledge of the guidelines presented here will help you avoid that syndrome. Remind yourself to be quiet after you ask a question that you have carefully formulated. Sometimes, due to lack of confidence or preparation, the teacher asks a question, then, with a slight change in wording, asks it again, or asks several questions, one after another. That is too much verbiage, and "shotgun" questioning only confuses students while allowing too little time for them to think.
2. After asking a question, provide students with adequate time to think. Knowing the subject better than the students know it and having given prior thought to it, too many

teachers fail to allow students sufficient time to think after asking a question. Plus, by the time they have reached middle school (or sooner), students have learned how to play the "game"—that is, they know that if they remain silent long enough, the teacher will probably answer his or her own question. After asking a well-worded question, you should remain quiet for awhile, allowing students time to think and to respond. And, if you wait long enough, they usually will.

After asking a question, how long should you wait before you do something? You should wait at least 2 seconds, and as long as 9. Stop reading now, and look at your watch or a clock to get a feeling for how long 2 seconds is. Then, observe how long 9 seconds is. Did 9 seconds seem a long time? Because most of us are not used to silence in the classroom, 2 seconds of silence can seem quite long, while 9 seconds may seem an eternity. If for some reason students have not responded after a period of 2 to 9 seconds of wait time, then you can ask the same question again using the same words, pause for several seconds, then, if you still haven't received a response, call on a student, then another, if necessary, after sufficient wait time. Soon you will get a response that can be built upon. Never answer your own question! (For a further discussion of the importance of wait time in a constructivist classroom, see Brooks and Brooks (1993), pp. 114–115).

3. Practice calling on all students, not just the bright or the slow, not just the boys or the girls, not only those in the front of the room, but all of them. To do this takes concentrated effort on your part, but it is important.

4. Give the same amount of wait time (think time) to all students. This, too, will require concentrated effort on your part but is also important. A teacher who waits for less time when calling on a slow student or students of one gender is showing prejudice or a lack of confidence in certain students, both of which are detrimental to striving to establish for all students a positive, equal, and safe environment for classroom learning. Show confidence in all students, and never discriminate by expecting less or more from some than from others.

5. When you ask questions, don't let students randomly shout out their answers; instead, require them to raise their hands and be called on before they respond. Establish that procedure and stick with it. This helps to ensure that you equally distribute your interactions with the students and that girls are not interacted with less because boys tend to be more obstreperous. Even at the college level, male students tend to be more vociferous than female students and, when allowed by the instructor, tend to outtalk and to interrupt their female peers. Every teacher has the responsibility to guarantee a nonbiased and equal distribution of interaction time in the classroom.

6. Use strong praise sparingly. Use of strong praise is sometimes appropriate, especially when working with students who are different or asking questions of simple, low-level recall. But when you want students to think divergently and creatively, you should be stingy with your use of strong praise of student responses. Strong praise from a teacher tends to terminate divergent and creative thinking.

One of your goals is to help students find intrinsic sources of motivation, that is, an inner drive that causes them to want to learn. Use of strong praise tends to build conformity, causing students to depend on outside forces (the giver of praise) for their worth, rather than on themselves. An example of strong praise is when a teacher responds to a student answer with, "That's right! Very good." On the other hand, passive acceptance responses, such as, "Okay, that seems to be one possibility," keep the door open for further thinking, particularly for higher level, divergent thinking.

Another example of a passive acceptance response is one used in brainstorming sessions: "After asking the question and giving you time to think about it, I will hear your ideas and record them on the board." Only after all student responses have been heard and recorded does the class begin its consideration of each. In the classroom, that kind of nonjudgmental acceptance of all ideas will generate a great deal of expression of high-level thought. (For further discussion of research findings about the use of praise and rewards in teaching, see Joyce & Showers, 1988; Lepper & Green, 1978.)

7. Encourage students to ask questions about content and process. There is no such thing as a "dumb" question. Sometimes students, like everyone else, ask questions that could

just as easily have been looked up. Those questions can consume precious class time. For a teacher, this can be frustrating. A teacher's initial reaction might be to quickly and mistakenly assume that the student is too lazy to look up an answer and to respond with sarcasm. In such instances, you are advised to think before responding and to respond kindly and professionally, although in the busy life of a classroom teacher, that may not always be easy. Be assured that there is a reason for the student's question. Perhaps the student is signaling a need for recognition.

In large schools, it is easy for a student to feel alone and insignificant sometimes (although this seems less the case in schools that use a school-within-a-school plan), and a student's making an effort to interact with you can be a positive sign. So carefully gauge your responses to those efforts. If a student question is really off track, off the wall, out of order, and out of context with the content of the lesson, consider this possible response: "That is an interesting question (or comment) and I would like to talk more with you about it. Could we meet at lunchtime, or before or after school?"

Student questions can and should be used as springboards for further questions, discussions, and investigations. Students should be encouraged to ask questions that challenge the textbook, the process, or another person's statements, and they should be encouraged to seek the facts or evidence behind a statement.

8. Being able to ask questions may be more important than having right answers. Knowledge is derived from asking questions. Being able to recognize problems and to formulate questions is a skill and the key to problem-solving and critical thinking skill development. Especially while teaching social studies you have a responsibility to encourage students to formulate questions and to help them word their questions in such a way that tentative answers can be sought. That is the process necessary to build a base of knowledge that can be called upon over and over to link, interpret, and explain new information in new situations (Resnick & Klopfer, 1989).

9. Questioning is the cornerstone of critical thinking and real-world problem solving. In real-world problem solving, there are usually no absolute right answers. Rather than being "correct," some answers are merely better than others. The person with a problem recognizes the problem, formulates a question about that problem (Should I buy a house or rent? Should I date this person or not? Should I take this job or not?), collects data, and arrives at a temporarily acceptable answer to the problem, while realizing that later data may dictate a review of the conclusion. For example, if an astronomer believes she has discovered a new galaxy, there is no textbook (or teacher) to which she may refer to find out if she is right. Rather, on the basis of her self-confidence in identifying problems, asking questions, collecting enough data, and arriving at a tentative conclusion based on those data, she assumes that for now her conclusion is safe.

10. Avoid bluffing when asked a question for which you do not have an answer. Nothing will cause you to lose credibility with students quicker than faking an answer. There is nothing wrong with admitting that you do not know. It helps students realize that you are human. It also helps them maintain adequate self-esteem, realizing that it's okay not to always know all the answers. What *is* important is that you know where and how to find possible answers and help students develop that same knowledge and those same skills.

Examination of the level of questions in course materials. In *Caught in the Middle,* it is reported that "of more than 61,000 questions found in teacher guides, student workbooks, and tests for nine history textbooks, more than 95 percent were devoted to factual recall" (California State Department of Education, 1987, p. 13). Using the questions in Figure 4.3, examine course materials used by a school where you might soon be teaching, and compare the results of your analysis with these data.

K. PROCESSES IN INSTRUCTIONAL PLANNING

Complete planning for instruction is an eight-step process. Some of the steps that follow have previously been addressed and are included here so you will understand where they fit in the planning process. Here are the steps and guidelines for what is referred to as the "eight-step planning process":

FIGURE 4.3
Examining Course Materials for Level of Questioning

Examine course materials for the levels of questions presented to students. Examine a student textbook (or other instructional material) for a subject and grade level you intend to teach; specifically, the questions posed for the students, probably at the ends of chapters. Also examine workbooks, examinations, instructional packages, and any other printed or electronic materials (i.e., computer software programs) used by students in the course. Share your findings with other members of your class. Include the following:

1. Materials examined (include date of publication and target students)
2. Examples of level-one (input-recall-level) questions found
3. Examples of level-two (processing-level) questions found
4. Examples of level-three (application-level) questions found
5. Approximate percentages of questions at each level:
   Level 1 = _____%   Level 2 = _____%   Level 3 = _____%
6. Did you find evidence of question-level sequencing? If so, describe it.
7. From your analysis, what can you conclude about the level of student thinking expected of students using the materials analyzed?

1. *Course and school goals.* Consider and understand your course goals and their relationship to the goals and mission of the school. Your course is not isolated but is an integral part of the total school curriculum, both vertically (in grades K–12) and horizontally (across grade levels).
2. *Expectations.* Consider topics and skills that you are "expected" to teach, such as ones that may be found in the course of study.
3. *Academic year-long calendar plan.* You must consider where you want the class of students to be months from now. So, working from your tentative topic outline and with the school calendar in hand, begin by deciding approximately how much class time should be devoted to each topic, penciling those times onto the subject outline.
4. *Course or class schedule.* This schedule becomes a part of the course syllabus that is presented to students during the first week of school. The schedule must remain flexible to allow for the unexpected, such as cancellation or interruption of a class meeting or an unpredictable extended study of a particular topic.
5. *Class meeting lessons.* Working from the course schedule, you are now ready to prepare lessons for each class meeting, keeping in mind the abilities and interests of your students while making decisions about appropriate strategies and learning experiences. Preparation of daily lessons takes considerable time and continues throughout the year and throughout your career. You will arrange and prepare instructional notes, demonstrations, discussion topics and questions, classroom exercises, appearances of guest speakers, use of audiovisual equipment and materials, field trips, and tools for assessment of student learning.

   Because what is covered in one class meeting is often determined by the accomplishments of the preceding meeting (especially if you are teaching toward mastery and/or using a constructivist approach), your lessons are never "set in stone" and, regardless of your approach, will need continual revision and evaluation.
6. *Instructional objectives.* With the finalized course or subject schedule, and as you prepare the daily lessons, you will complete your preparation of the instructional objectives. These instructional objectives are critical for accomplishment of step 7.
7. *Assessment.* This important step deals with how you will preassess student understandings and assess student achievement. Included in this component are your decisions about assignments, diagnostic tools such as tests, and the procedure by which grades will be determined. Assessment is the topic of the next chapter.
8. *Classroom management.* This final and important step in planning involves your decisions and planning for a safe and effective classroom environment so that the most efficient learning of your units and lessons will occur, and was the topic of Chapter 2.

Those are the steps in planning. They may seem overwhelming, but we will proceed step by step toward the development of your first instructional plan. First, let's consider the nature of the course syllabus.

The Course Syllabus

You probably know that a course syllabus is a written statement of information about the workings of a particular class. As a college or university student, you have seen a variety of syllabi written by professors, containing their own ideas about what general and specific logistical information is most important for students to know about a course. Even some instructors don't realize, however, that a course outline is not a course syllabus. A course outline is just one component of a syllabus.

Related to the development and use of a course syllabus are three issues: (1) *Why?* Of what value is a syllabus? What use can be made of it? What purpose does it fulfill? (2) *How?* How do I develop a course syllabus? When do I begin? Where do I start? (3) *What?* What information should be included? When should it be distributed to students? How rigidly should it be followed? Let's now consider each of those three questions.

Reasons for a course syllabus. The course syllabus is printed information about the course that is presented to students (grades 4 and up), usually on the first day or during the first week of school. It should be designed so that it

- Helps establish a rapport between students, parents (or guardians), and the teacher
- Helps students feel at ease by providing an understanding of what is expected of them
- Helps students organize, conceptualize, and synthesize their learning experiences
- Provides a reference, helping to eliminate misunderstandings and misconceptions about the nature of the class—its rules, expectations, procedures, requirements, and other policies
- Provides students with a sense of connectedness (often by allowing students to work in cooperative groups and actually participate in fashioning the syllabus)
- Serves as a plan to be followed by the teacher and the students
- Serves as a resource for members of a teaching team. Each team member should have a copy of every other member's syllabus.
- Documents what takes place in the classroom for those outside the classroom (parents or guardians, administrators, other teachers, and students).

Development of a course syllabus. Usually the course syllabus is prepared by the classroom teacher long before the first class meeting. If you maintain a syllabus template on your computer, then it is rather simple to customize it for each class of students that you teach. You may find that it is more useful if students participate in the development of the syllabus, thereby gaining a feeling of ownership of and commitment to it.

The steps shown in Figure 4.4 are suggested as a cooperative learning experience in which students spend approximately 30 minutes during an early class meeting brainstorming the content of their syllabus.

Content of a course syllabus. The course syllabus should be concise, matter-of-fact, uncomplicated, and brief—perhaps no more than two pages—and should include the following information.

1. *Descriptive information about the course.* Include the teacher's name, course title and grade level, class period, beginning and ending times, and room number.
2. *Explanation of the importance of the course.* Describe the course, cite how students will profit from it, and tell whether it is a required course, a core curriculum course, a co-curriculum course, an exploratory or elective, or some other type.
3. *Materials required.* Explain what materials—textbook, notebook, portfolio, supplementary readings—are needed. Include which are supplied by the school, which must be supplied by each student, and what materials must be brought to class each day.
4. *Statement of goals and objectives.* Include a few general goals and some specific objectives.
5. *Types of assignments that will be given.* These should be clearly explained in as much detail as possible this early in the course. State where daily assignments will be posted in the classroom (a regular place each day) and procedures for completing and turning

FIGURE 4.4

Steps for Involving Students in the Development of Their Course Syllabus

SOURCE: Richard D. Kellough, Noreen G. Kellough, and David L. Hough, *Middle School Teaching: Methods and Resources* (New York: Macmillan, 1993), p. 110. By permission of Macmillan Publishing Company.

1. Sometime during the first few days of the course, arrange students in small groups of mixed abilities to brainstorm the development of their course syllabus.
2. Instruct each group to spend five minutes listing everything they can think of that they would like to know about the course. Tell the class that a group *recorder* must be chosen to write their ideas on paper and then, when directed to do so, transfer them to the writing board or to sheets of butcher paper hung in the classroom for all to see. (You can also make a transparency sheet and pen available to each group and use an overhead transparency.) Tell them to select a group *spokesperson* who will address the class, explaining the group's list. Each group could also appoint a *materials manager,* whose job is to see that the group has the necessary materials (pen, paper, transparency, chalk), and a *task master,* whose job is to keep the group on task and to report to the teacher when each task is completed.
3. After five minutes, have the recorders prepare their lists. When using a transparency or butcher paper, the lists can be prepared simultaneously while recorders remain with their groups. If using the writing board, have recorders, one at a time, write their lists on areas of the board that you have designated for each group's list.
4. Have the spokesperson of each group explain the group's list. As this is being done, you should make a master list. If transparencies or butcher paper are being used you can ask for them as backup to the master list you have made.
5. After all spokespersons have explained their lists, ask the class collectively for additional input. "Can anyone think of anything else that should be added?"
6. Use the master list to design a course syllabus, being careful to address each question and to include items of importance that students may have omitted. However, your guidance during the preceding five steps should ensure that all bases have been covered.
7. At the next class meeting, give each student a copy of the final syllabus. Discuss its content. (Duplicate copies to distribute to colleagues, especially those on your teaching team, interested administrators, and parents and guardians at Back-to-School Night.)

---

in assignments. (Assignments are statements of *what* students will do; procedures are statements of *how* they will do it.) Parents or guardians will want to know your expectations regarding their helping their child with assignments.

6. *Assessment criteria.* Explain the assessment procedures. Will there be quizzes, tests, homework, projects, and group work? What will be their formats, coverage, and weights in the grading procedure? For group work, how will the contributions and learning of individual children be evaluated?
7. *Special information specific to the course.* Field trips? Special privileges? Class projects? Classroom procedures and rules for expected behavior should be included here.

L. THE DAILY LESSON PLAN

Effective teachers are always planning for their classes. For the long range, they plan the scope and sequence of courses and develop content for courses. Within courses they develop units, and within units they design the activities to be used and the assessments of learning to be done. They familiarize themselves with textbooks, materials, media, and innovations in their fields of interest. Yet—despite all this planning—the daily lesson plan remains pivotal to the planning process.

Assumptions about Lesson Planning

Not all teachers need elaborate written plans for every lesson. Some effective and skilled teachers need only a sketchy outline. Sometimes they may not need written plans at all. Experienced teachers who have taught the topic many times in the past may need only the presence of a class of students to stimulate a pattern of presentation that has often been successful. Beware, however, of the frequent use of old patterns that may lead to the rut of unimaginative teaching. You probably do not need to be reminded that the obsolescence of many past classroom practices has been substantiated repeatedly by researchers.

Considering the diversity among teachers, their instructional styles, their students, and what research has shown, certain assumptions can be made about lesson planning:

1. Not all teachers need elaborate written plans for all lessons.
2. Beginning teachers need to prepare detailed written lesson plans.
3. Some subject matter fields and topics require more detailed planning than do others.
4. Some experienced teachers have clearly defined goals and objectives in mind even though they have not written them into lesson plans.
5. The depth of knowledge a teacher has about a subject or topic influences the amount of planning necessary for the lessons.
6. The skill a teacher has in following a train of thought in the presence of distraction will influence the amount of detail necessary when planning activities.
7. A plan is more likely to be carefully plotted when it is written out.
8. The diversity of students within today's classroom necessitates careful and thoughtful consideration about individualizing the instruction; these considerations are best implemented when they have been thoughtfully written into lesson plans.
9. There is no particular pattern or format that all teachers need to follow when writing out plans. (Some teacher-preparation programs have agreed on certain lesson-plan formats for their student teachers; you need to know if this is the case for your program.)
10. All effective teachers have a planned pattern of instruction for every lesson, whether that plan is written out or not.

Written Lesson Plans

Well-written lesson plans have many uses. They give a teacher an agenda or outline to follow in teaching a lesson. They give a substitute teacher a basis for presenting appropriate lessons to a class. They are certainly very useful when a teacher is planning to use the same lesson again in the future. They provide the teacher with something to fall back on in case of a memory lapse, an interruption, or some other distraction, such as a call from the office or a fire drill. Above all, they provide beginners with security, because with a carefully prepared plan a beginning teacher can walk into a classroom with the confidence gained from having developed a sensible framework for that day's instruction.

Thus, as a beginning teacher, you should make considerably detailed lesson plans. Naturally, this will require a great deal of work for at least the first year or two, but the reward of knowing that you have prepared and presented effective lessons will compensate for that effort. Since most teachers plan their daily lessons only a day or two ahead, you can expect a busy first year of teaching.

Some prospective teachers are concerned about being seen using a written plan in class, thinking it may suggest that they have not mastered the subject. On the contrary, a lesson plan is a visible sign of preparation on the part of the teacher. A written lesson plan shows that thinking and planning have taken place and that the teacher has a road map to work through the lesson no matter what the distractions. Most experienced teachers agree that there is no excuse for appearing before a class without evidence of careful preparation.

A Continual Process

Experienced teachers may not require plans as detailed as those necessary for beginning teachers—after all, experienced teachers often can develop shortcuts to lesson planning without sacrificing effectiveness. Yet lesson planning is a continual process even for them (see the many sample plans of experienced teachers in Chapter 10), for there is always a need to keep materials and plans current and relevant. Because no two classes of students are ever exactly the same, today's lesson plan will probably need to be tailored to the peculiar needs of each classroom of students. Also, because the content of a course will change as new developments occur or new theories are introduced, your objectives and the objectives of the students, school, and teaching faculty will change.

For these reasons, lesson plans should be in a constant state of revision. Once the basic framework has been developed, however, the task of updating and modifying becomes minimal. If you maintain your plans on a computer, making necessary changes from time to time is even easier.

The daily lesson plan should provide a tentative outline of the class period but should always remain flexible. A carefully worked-out plan may have to be set aside because of the unpredictable, serendipitous effect of a "teachable moment" or because of unforeseen circumstances, such as a delayed school bus, an impromptu school assembly program, or a fire drill. A daily lesson planned to cover six aspects of a given topic may end with only three of the points having been considered. These occurrences are natural in a school setting, and the teacher and the plans must be flexible enough to accommodate this reality.

The Problem of Time

A lesson plan should provide enough materials and activities to consume the entire class period. Since planning is a skill that takes years of experience to master, a beginning teacher should overplan rather than run the risk of having too few activities to occupy the time the children are in the classroom. One way of ensuring that you overplan is to include alternate activities in your lesson plan, as shown in the sample lesson plan in Figure 4.5.

When a lesson plan does not provide enough activity to occupy the entire class period, a beginning teacher often loses control of the class, and behavior problems develop. Thus, it is best to prepare more than you likely can accomplish in a given class period. Students are very perceptive; they will know if you have finished the plan for the period and are attempting to bluff through the remaining minutes. If you ever do get caught short—as most teachers do at one time or another—ways to avoid embarrassment are to spend the remaining time in a review of material that has been covered that day or in the past several days, or to allow students time to begin work on a homework assignment or project.

The Daily Plan Book

At this point, a distinction needs to be made between actual lesson plans and the book of daily plans that many schools require teachers to maintain and even submit to their supervisors a week in advance. A daily plan book is most assuredly not a daily lesson plan. Rather, it is a layout sheet on which the teacher shows what lessons will be taught during the week, month, or term. Usually the book provides only a small lined box for each class period for each day of the week. These books are useful for outlining the topics, activities, and assignments projected for the week or term, and supervisors sometimes use them to check the adequacy of teachers' course plans. They can also be useful for substitute teachers, who must try to fill in for you when you are absent. But they are not daily plans. Teachers who believe that the notations in the daily plan book are lesson plans are fooling themselves. Student teachers should be wary of using these in place of authentic lesson plans.

M. CONSTRUCTING A DAILY LESSON PLAN

Each teacher should develop a personal system of lesson planning—the system that works best for that teacher. But a beginning teacher probably needs a more substantial framework from which to work. For that reason, this section provides a "preferred" lesson plan format. In addition, you will find alternative formats in this and later chapters. Nothing is sacred about any of these formats, however. Each has worked for some teachers in the past, as have the formats illustrated in Figures 4.5 and 4.6. As you review the preferred format and the others throughout the book, determine which appeals to your style of presentation and use it with your own modifications until you find or develop a better model.

Whatever the format, however, all plans should be written out in an intelligible style. There is good reason to question teachers who say they have no need for a written plan because they have their lessons planned "in their heads." The periods in a school day are many, as are the numbers of students in each class. When multiplied by the number of school days in a week, a semester, or a year, the task of keeping so many things in one's head becomes mind-boggling. Until you have considerable experience behind you, you will need to write and keep detailed daily plans for guidance and reference.

Components of a Daily Lesson Plan

As a rule, your written lesson plan should contain the following basic elements: (1) descriptive course data, (2) materials, (3) goals and objectives, (4) rationale, (5) body of the lesson plan, and (6) assessment and revision plans. These components need not be present

FIGURE 4.5
Sample Lesson Plan with Alternate Activities
SOURCE: Unpublished lesson plan, courtesy of Michelle Yendrey, 1994.

LESSON PLAN

1. **Descriptive Course Data**
   Instructor: Michelle Yendrey   Course: Western Civilizations   Period: 1
   Grade level: 9   Unit: The History of Religion   Topic: Persecution of Christians

2. **Objectives**
   Upon completion of this lesson, students will be able to:
   a. Make connections between persecutions today and persecutions that occurred approximately 2,000 years ago.
   b. Describe the main teachings of Christianity and how the position of Christianity within the Roman Empire changed over time.
   c. Share ideas in a positive and productive manner.

3. **Instructional Components**
   Activity 1 (Anticipatory Set)—10 minutes
   Write on overhead: You have until 8:40 (5 minutes) to write a defense to one of the following statements (Remember, there are no right or wrong answers. Support your position to the best of your ability):
   a. The recent hate crimes in our city can be related to our current unit on the history of religion.
   b. The recent hate crimes in our city cannot be related to our current unit on the history of religion.
   Activity 2—3–5 minutes
   Students will be asked, by a show of hands, how many chose statement A and how many chose statement B. Some reasons for each will be shared orally and then all papers collected.
   Activity 3—3–5 minutes
   Return papers from previous assignment. Give students new seat assignments for the activity that follows and have them assume their new seats.
   Activity 4—15 minutes
   The students are now arranged into seven groups. Each group will write a paragraph using the concepts from certain assigned words (from their definition sheets of Section 3 of Chapter 7, "Christianity spread through the empire") to answer the essay question(s) at the end of the definition sheet. Each group will select a
   - *Task master* to keep members of the group on task.
   - *Recorder* to write things down.
   - *Spokesperson* to present the results.
   - *Timekeeper* to keep group alert so task is completed on time. In addition, some groups will have a
   - *Source master* to look up or ask about any questions that arise.
   Activity 5—15–20 minutes
   Each group's spokesperson will come to the front of the classroom and present the group's result of activity 4.
   Alternate Activity (Plan B)—5–10 minutes
   Should the activities run more quickly than anticipated, the students will take out their "Religion Comparison Sheets." Using the Chapter 2, Section 2 "Jews worshipped a single God" and Chapter 7, Section 3 definition sheets, with the teacher's direction, the students will fill in the boxes for "similar" and "different" with regard to Christianity and Judaism.
   Second Alternate Activity (Plan C)—25–30 minutes
   In the unlikely event that timing is really off, each student will be given a blank grid and assigned 10 vocabulary words from the definition sheets. Students will be directed to create a crossword puzzle using the definitions as clues and the words as answers. After 15 to 20 minutes, the crosswords will be collected and distributed to different students to solve. If not completed in class, students will finish and hand them in later along with their essays, for a few points of extra credit. Students will be required to write their names in the appropriate spaces marked, "Created By" and "Solved By."
   Activity 6—7–10 minutes
   Collect the overhead sheets and pens. Hand out the take-home essay test. Explain and take questions about exactly what is expected from the essay (this is their first take-home test).

4. **Materials and Equipment Needed**
   Overhead projector and transparency sheets (7) and transparency markers (7); 36 copies of the essay question plus directions; 36 copies of the blank grid sheets.

---

in every written lesson plan, nor must they be presented in any particular format, nor are they inclusive or exclusive. You might choose to include additional components or subsections. You may not want to spend time developing a formal rationale, although you probably should. Figure 4.6 illustrates a format that includes the six components and sample subsections of those components.

FIGURE 4.6
Sample Lesson Plan Format with Six Components
SOURCE: Reprinted with the permission of Simon & Schuster, Inc. from the Macmillan College text MIDDLE SCHOOL
TEACHING: METHODS AND RESOURCES by Richard D. Kellough, Noreen G. Kellough, and David L. Hough. Copyright
©1993 by Macmillan College Publishing Company, Inc.

1. **Descriptive Course Data**
   Teacher _____ Class _____ Date _____
   Grade level _____ Room number _____ Period _____
   Unit _____ Lesson topic _____
2. **Lesson Goals and Objectives**
   Instructional goals (general objectives):

   Specific (performance) objectives:
      Cognitive:

      Affective:

      Psychomotor:

3. **Rationale**
4. **Plan**
   Content:

   Procedure with time plan:
      Set (introduction):

      Modeling:

      Guided (coached) practice:

      Assignments:

      Closure:

5. **Materials Needed**
   Audiovisual:

   Other:

6. **Assessment and Revision**
   Assessment of learning:

   Plan for revision:

Following are descriptions of the six major components, with explanations of why each
is essential and examples.

Descriptive course data. This is the demographic and logistical information that identifies details about the class. Anyone reading this information should be able to identify when
and where the class meets, who is teaching it, and what is being taught. Although as the
teacher you know this information, someone else may not. Administrators, members of the
teaching team, and substitute teachers—and, if you are the student teacher, your university
supervisor and cooperating teacher—appreciate this information, especially when asked to
fill in for you, even if only for a few minutes. Most teachers find out which items of descriptive data are most beneficial in their situation and then develop their own identifiers.

Remember: *The mark of a well-prepared, clearly written lesson plan is the ease with
which someone else (such as another member of your teaching team or a substitute teacher)
could implement it.*

As shown in Figures 4.5 and 4.7, the descriptive data include

1. *Name of course and grade level.* These serve as headings for the plan and facilitate orderly filing of plans.

Western Civilizations	Grade 9
(self-contained)	Grade 5

2. *Name of the unit.* Inclusion of this facilitates the orderly control of the hundreds of lesson plans a teacher constructs. For example:

Western Civilizations	Grade 9	Unit: The History of Religion
(self-contained)	Grade 5	Unit: Early English Settlers in North America

3. *Topic to be considered within the unit.* This is also useful for control and identification. For example:

Western Civilizations	Grade 9	Unit: The History of Religion Topic: Persecution of Christians
(self-contained)	Grade 5	Unit: Early English Settlers in North America Topic: Early English Explorers

Goals and objectives. In a lesson plan, the instructional goals are general statements of what students will learn from that lesson. Teachers and students need to know what the lesson is designed to accomplish. In clear, understandable language, the general goal statement provides that information. From the plans illustrated in Figures 4.5 and 4.7, examples of goals are

- To make connections between persecutions today and persecutions that occurred approximately 2,000 years ago.
- To develop a better comprehension of the United States as students study about people with different backgrounds, different ideas, and different ways of life.

The objectives of the lesson are included as specific statements detailing precisely what students will be able to do as a result of the learning of the lesson. Teachers and students need to know that. Behavioral objectives provide clear statements of what learning is to occur. In addition, from clearly written behavioral objectives, assessment items can be written to measure whether students have accomplished the objectives. The type of assessment item used (discussed in the next chapter) should not only *measure for* the instructional objective but should also *be compatible with* the objective being assessed. As discussed earlier, your specific objectives might be covert, overt, or a combination of both. As illustrated in Figures 4.5 and 4.7, examples include

- The student will be able to describe the main teachings of Christianity and how the position of Christianity within the Roman Empire changed over time. (overt, cognitive)
- The student will identify some of the explorers who first traveled from England to North America, their reasons for exploring, and some of their initial contributions to the development of the colonies. (overt, cognitive)

Setting specific objectives is a crucial step in the development of any lesson plan. It is at this point that many lessons go wrong. In writing specific objectives, teachers sometimes mistakenly list what they intend to do—such as "cover the next five pages" or "do the next ten problems"—and fail to focus on just what the learning objective in these activities truly is. When you approach this step in your lesson planning, ask yourself, "What do I want my students to learn from these lessons?" Your answer to that question is your objective!

Rationale. The rationale is an explanation of why the lesson is important and why the instructional methods chosen will achieve the objectives. Parents, students, teachers, administrators, and others have the right to know why specific content is being taught and why the methods employed are being used. Teachers become reflective decision makers when they challenge themselves to think about what they are teaching, how they are teaching it, and why it must be taught. Sometimes teachers include the rationale statement in the beginning of the unit plan, but not in each daily lesson. Sometimes, as with the unit illustrated in Figure 4.7, the rationale is included within the unit introduction and goals.

Body of the lesson plan. The plan is what the lesson consists of. For reasons discussed earlier, teachers must plan their lessons carefully. The body of the lesson plan consists of the following elements:

Content. The substance of the lesson; the information to be presented, obtained, and learned. Appropriate information is selected to meet the learning objectives, the level of competence of the students, and the requirements of the course.

To make sure your lesson actually covers what it should, you should write down exactly what content you intend to cover. This material may be placed in a separate section or combined with the procedure section. The important thing is to be sure that your information is written down so you can refer to it quickly and easily when you need to. If, for instance, you are going to introduce new material using a 10 to 15-minute lecture, you will want to outline the content of that lecture. You need not have pages of notes to sift through, nor should you ever read declarative statements to your students. You should be familiar enough with the content so that an outline (in detail, if necessary) will be sufficient to carry on the lesson, as is the following content outline:

Causes of Civil War
A. Primary causes
   1. Economics
   2. Abolitionist pressure
   3. Slavery
   4. _____
B. Secondary causes
   1. North-South friction
   2. Southern economic dependence
   3. _____

If you intend to conduct the lesson using discussion, you should write out the key discussion questions. For example:

What do you think Golding had in mind when he wrote *Lord of the Flies?*
What did the conch shell represent? Why did the other boys resent Piggy?

Instruction. The procedure or procedures to be used, sometimes referred to as the *instructional components.* Appropriate instructional methods are chosen to meet the objectives, to match the students' learning styles, and to ensure that all students have an equal opportunity to learn.

This is the section in which you establish what you and your students will do during the lesson. Ordinarily, you should plan this section of your lesson as an organized entity having a beginning (an introduction or set), a middle, and an end (called the closure). This structure is not always needed, because some lessons are simply parts of units or long-term plans and merely carry on activities spelled out in those long-term plans. Still, most daily lessons need to include in their procedure

1. an *introduction,* the process used to prepare the students mentally for the lesson, sometimes referred to as the *initiating activity* (see Chapter 7)
2. *lesson development,* the detailing of activities that occur between the beginning and the end of the lesson
3. plans for *guided (or coached) practice,* ways that you intend to have students interacting in the classroom, receiving guidance or coaching from each other and from you

FIGURE 4.7
Sample Integrated Unit Plan with One Daily Lesson
SOURCE: Adapted from Richard D. Kellough and Patricia L. Roberts, *A Resource Guide for Elementary School Teaching: Planning for Competence,* 3rd ed. (New York: Macmillan, 1994), pp. 238–239. By permission of Macmillan Publishing Company.

Sample Integrated Unit

Grade _____5_____   **Topic** _Early English Settlers in North America_

Teacher _____   **Duration** _10–11 days____

Introduction to Unit

This unit can be an adventurous one. It is a multidisciplinary unit and can readily be developed into an interdisciplinary thematic unit for use by a teaching team at any grade level. As presented here, it is designed for a fifth-grade class. Specifically addressed by this unit are the students'

1. Learning about early English settlers in North America.
2. Developing skills in reading.
3. Developing skills in studying.
4. Developing skills in thinking.

These are assessed during and at completion of this unit by use of a behavioral checklist.

This unit can present sailing ships, English and Spanish sea battles, golden treasures, hearty seadogs (captains), brave women and men, stockades at riverbank settlements, and trading with the Indians for food. Bulletin boards should be designed to interest students in this exciting part of North America's history. They could feature colorful illustrations of early explorers, captured treasure from Spanish ships, maps showing routes of explorations, pictures of early settlements and their leaders, and selected focus questions to develop students' understanding of the early settlers' adjustments to their new environment.

Goals of the Unit

This unit is part of the social studies program about the development of the United States of America. Through selected learning materials, students will develop a better comprehension of the United States as they study about people with different backgrounds, different ideas, and different ways of life. In this unit the students become acquainted with the study of the early settlement of the colonies, the people who lived there, and some of the reasons that they came to North America from England. As students learn about this historical period of United States history, with the teacher's guidance, they should compare that time with present-day events, thereby developing new insights about life in the United States today.

Day 1: Topic: Early English Explorers

Objective: Given assigned reading and student discussion about how English activity first began in North America, students will identify some of the explorers who first traveled from England to North America, their reasons for exploring, and some of their initial contributions to the development of the colonies.

Materials to begin unit: An attractive bulletin board is arranged to display pictures of early English explorers with a caption such as "Why Did Settlers and Explorers Travel to North America?" Illustrations for display might include John Cabot (Italian sea captain of the *Matthew* who sailed for North America from Bristol, England, in 1497), Sir Francis Drake (first English person to sail around the world), Sir Humphrey Gilbert (who attempted to begin a colony in Newfoundland), and Sir Walter Raleigh (who started a colony on Roanoke Island). Nearby on a learning resource table are books to accommodate a variety of reading interests and levels, maps, and supplementary materials that include information about the early settling of the colonies. In the front of the classroom there is a world globe and a large pull-down map that can be marked with chalk.

Activities: Discussing and locating information.

The teacher begins (anticipatory set; transition from previous unit of study): "Yesterday some of you mentioned reasons that the leaders of France sent explorers to North America. What were

---

4. the *lesson conclusion (or closure),* the planned process of bringing the lesson to an end, thereby providing students with a sense of completeness and (through effective teaching) accomplishment and comprehension by helping them synthesize the information learned from the lesson

FIGURE 4.7 cont'd

some of the reasons you mentioned? (Discussion.) "The leaders of another country, England, also had reasons for sending explorers to North America. As we read about the early English explorers, we'll be introduced to some new words." (Teacher turns to chart and draws attention to terms under pictures illustrating the meaning of each term.)

Vocabulary (Chart 1)

Newfoundland	colony
Nova Scotia	settlement
treasure	colonist
seadog	stockade

The teacher continues: "Let's turn to the table of contents to find the chapter we need, the one entitled 'Early English in North America.' Let's skim the contents to find the page information it contains about the chapter we need." (The teacher turns again to the chart stand and displays a second chart with the headline "WE READ AT DIFFERENT SPEEDS.")

We Read at Different Speeds (Chart 2)
When we want to find out if a page or book has
information we can use, WE READ RAPIDLY.
When we want to find an answer to a question,
We Read at a Moderate Speed.
When we are studying to understand information,
We Read Slowly.

The teacher questions: "When we want to find out whether the table of contents has information we can use, what is our reading speed?" (Students respond; the chapter page number is identified; and the students locate the beginning of the chapter in their textbooks.) "Let's read silently for the first three paragraphs on page ____ to find out the name of one of England's first explorers and his reason for exploring near North America. Since we will be studying to understand information, what reading speed should we use?" (Students respond.) After the silent reading, a discussion about John Cabot begins. "In reading these paragraphs, we've seen that John Cabot wanted to find a short, northern, all-water route to Asia." (One student is asked to trace the route with a chalk mark on the globe. Another is asked to identify Cabot's reason for exploration. Still another is asked to record Cabot's reason on a strip of construction paper and to attach the strip under the illustration of Cabot on the classroom bulletin board.) Giving reasons for silent and oral reading, the teacher guides additional reading about other early English explorers. To emphasize the importance of the students' reading slowly when they are studying for information, the teacher again turns to the chart stand and reviews these study skills from a third chart, entitled "WHEN WE STUDY TO UNDERSTAND INFORMATION."

When We Study to Understand Information (Chart 3)
We concentrate.
We have a question in mind.
We look at the pictures and read captioned information.
We read maps, charts, tables, and graphs.
We discuss and review what we have learned.

The teacher brings closure to this day's lesson and unit introduction, encouraging student thinking by asking higher-order questions: "Having completed our reading today about some of the early English explorers, you know some interesting information about them. Why do you think John Cabot wanted to travel a northern route across the Atlantic Ocean? What might have changed if Cabot had found a short, all-water route to Asia? What can we say about Raleigh and how he tried to help the English acquire land in North America? What might have changed if these early attempts to start colonies had been successful?"

5. a *timetable* that serves simply as a planning and implementation guide, and
6. *assignments,* that is, what students are instructed to do as follow-up to the lesson, either as homework or as in-class work, providing students an opportunity to learn further and to practice what is being learned.

Let's now consider lesson plan elements in further detail.

Introduction to the lesson. Like any good performance, a lesson needs an effective beginning. In many respects the introduction sets the tone for the rest of the lesson by alerting the students that the business of learning is to begin. The introduction should be an attention-getter. If it is exciting, interesting, or innovative, it can create a favorable mood for the lesson. In any case, a thoughtful introduction serves as a solid indicator that you are well prepared.

Although it is difficult to develop an exciting introduction to every lesson taught each day, there are always various options to spice up the launching of a lesson. You might, for instance, begin the lesson by briefly reviewing the previous lesson, thereby helping students connect the learning. Another possibility is to review vocabulary words from previous lessons and to introduce new ones. Still another possibility is to use the key point of the day's lesson as an introduction and then again as the conclusion. Sometimes teachers begin a lesson by demonstrating a discrepant event—an event that is contrary to what one might expect. Yet another possibility is to begin the lesson with a writing activity on some controversial aspect of the ensuing lesson. Brief examples of introductions, taken from the lessons shown in Figures 4.5 and 4.7, follow:

- "You have 5 minutes to write an argument in support of or against the following statement: 'The recent hate crimes in our city can be related to what we are learning about the history of religion.' "
- With an attractive bulletin board display, a table of resources, and a world globe and a pull-down map in the front of the room, the teacher begins with a transition statement that ties in this unit (Early English Settlers in North America) with the previous unit (about early French explorers). The teacher then poses questions for discussion, makes a statement about the new unit on English Explorers, and focuses the children's attention on a chart of new terms that will be used.

And, for a two-week unit on fables (Chapter 7), the teacher initiates the first lesson by

- Reading several fables, such as The *Tortoise and the Hare,* and explaining that these are short stories that teach a moral.

In short, you can use the introduction of the lesson to review past learning, tie the new lesson to the previous lesson, introduce new material, point out the objectives of the new lesson, help students connect their learning with other disciplines or with real life, or—by showing what will be learned and why the learning is important—induce in students a mind-set favorable to the new lesson.

Lesson development. The developmental activities, which make up the bulk of the lesson plan, are the specifics by which you intend to achieve your lesson objectives. They include activities that present information, demonstrate skills, provide reinforcement of previously learned material, and provide other opportunities to develop understanding and skill. In addition, by actions and words, during lesson development the teacher models the behaviors expected of the students. Middle grade students need such modeling. By effective modeling, the teacher can exemplify the anticipated learning outcomes. Activities of this section of the lesson plan should be described in some detail so you will know exactly what it is you plan to do and, during the stress of the class, not forget details of your plan and the subject content. For this reason, you should note the answers to the questions you intend to ask and the solutions to problems you intend to have your students solve.

Lesson conclusion. Having a clear-cut closure to the lesson is as important as having a strong introduction. The closure complements the introduction. The concluding activity should summarize and bind together what has ensued in the developmental stage and should reinforce the principal points of the lesson. One way to accomplish these ends is to restate the key points of the lesson. Another is to briefly outline the major points. Still another is to repeat the major concept. No matter what the chosen way, the concluding activity is usually brief and to the point.

The timetable. To estimate the time factors in any lesson can be very difficult. A good procedure is to gauge the amount of time needed for each learning activity and note that alongside the activity and strategy in your plan, as shown in the sample lesson plans. Placing too much faith in your time estimate may be foolish—an estimate is more for your guidance in planning than for anything else. Beginning teachers frequently find that their discussions and presentations do not last as long as expected. To avoid being embarrassed by running out of material, try to make sure you have planned enough work to consume the entire class period. Another important reason for including a time plan in your lesson is to give information to students about how much time they have for a particular activity, such as a laboratory activity or cooperative learning group activity.

Materials and equipment to be used. Materials of instruction include the textbook, supplementary readings, media, and other supplies necessary to accomplish the lesson objectives. Teachers must be sure that the proper and necessary materials are available for the lesson, which takes planning. Students cannot use what they do not have available.

Assignments. When an assignment is to be given, it should be noted in your lesson plan. When to present it to the students is optional, except that it should never be yelled as an afterthought as the students are exiting the classroom at the end of the period. Whether begun and completed during class time or done out of school, assignments are best written on the writing board or in a special place on the bulletin board, on a handout, or in the course syllabus. Take extra care to be sure that assignment specifications are clear to the students. It is also important to remember that assignments and procedures are not the same thing. An assignment tells students *what* is to be done, while procedures explain *how* to do it. Although an assignment may include specific procedures, merely spelling out procedures is not the same thing as making an academic assignment. When students are given an assignment, they need to understand the reasons for doing it as well as have some notion as to ways the assignment might be done.

Many middle-level teachers give assignments to their students on a weekly basis, requiring that the students maintain an assignment schedule in their portfolios. When given on a periodic rather than daily basis, assignments should still appear in your daily lesson plans so you can remind students of them. Once assignment specifications have been given it is a good idea not to make major modifications to them, and it is especially important not to change assignment specifications several days after an assignment has been given. Last-minute changes in assignment specifications can be very frustrating to students who have already begun or completed the assignment and show little respect for those students.

Benefits of coached practice. Allowing time in class for students to begin work on homework assignments and long-term projects is highly recommended; it provides an opportunity for the teacher to give individual attention (guided or coached practice) to students. Being able to coach students is the reason for in-class time to begin assignments. Many middle-level schools have extended class periods to allow more in-class time for teachers to guide students in their homework. The benefits of coached practice include being able to (1) monitor student work so a student doesn't go too far in the wrong direction, (2) help students to reflect on their thinking, (3) assess the progress of individual students, and (4) discover or create a "teachable moment." For example, while observing and monitoring student practice, the teacher might discover a shared student misconception. The teacher could then talk about and attempt to clarify that misconception or, collaboratively with students, plan a subsequent lesson centered around exploring the misconception.

Special notes and reminders. Many teachers provide a place in their lesson plan format for special notes and reminders. Most of the time you will not need such reminders, but when you do, it helps to have them in a regular location in your lesson plan so you can refer to them quickly. In this special section you can place reminders concerning announcements to be made, school programs, makeup work for certain students, and so on. These things may not always be important, but they do need to be remembered.

Assessment and revision. You must include in your lesson plan details of how you will assess how well students are learning (formative assessment) and how well they have learned (summative assessment). Comprehension checks for formative assessment can be in the form of questions you and the students ask during the lesson. Questions you intend to ask (and possible answers) should be built into the developmental section.

For summative assessment, teachers typically use review questions at the end of a lesson (as a closure) or the beginning of the next lesson (as a review or transfer introduction), independent practice at the completion of a lesson, and tests. Again, questions for checking for comprehension should be detailed in your lesson plan.

In most lesson plan formats there is also a section reserved for the teacher to make notes or comments about the lesson. It can be particularly useful if you plan to use the lesson again at some later date.

Sample Integrated Unit with One Daily Lesson

The sample unit shown in Figure 4.7 on pages 100–101 is an integrated unit designed for fifth-grade use, but it could easily be adapted for use at other grade levels. As you examine this sample unit, you will notice the use of an abbreviated format for presenting the daily lesson, but with an extended narrative presentation of how the teacher might actually conduct the lesson.

SUMMARY

As you reviewed curriculum documents and student textbooks, you probably found most of them well organized and useful. In your comparison and analysis of courses of study and of the teacher's editions of student textbooks, you probably discovered that some are accompanied by sequentially designed resource units from which the teacher can select and build specific teaching units. A resource unit usually consists of an extensive list of objectives, a large number and variety of kinds of activities, suggested materials, and extensive bibliographies for teachers and students, from which the teacher will select those that best suit his or her needs to build an actual teaching unit.

As you also may have discovered, some courses of study contain actual teaching units that have been prepared by teachers of that particular school district. An important question often asked by beginning teachers and by student teachers is "How closely must I follow the school's curriculum guide or course of study?" That is a question that you need to have the answer to before you begin teaching. To obtain the answer, talk with teachers and administrators of your particular school.

In conclusion, your final decisions about what content to teach are guided by all of the following:

- Articles in professional journals
- Discussions with other teachers
- Local courses of study
- State curriculum documents
- The differences, interests, and abilities of your students
- Your own personal convictions, knowledge, and skills.

After discovering what you will teach comes the process of preparing the plans. Although teachers' textbook editions and other curriculum documents make the process easier, they should never substitute for your own specific planning.

Attempting to blend the best of the behaviorism and constructivism theories of learning, many teachers do not bother to try to write specific objectives for all the learning activities that are in their teaching plans. Yet it is clear that when teachers do prepare specific objectives (by writing them themselves or borrowing them from other sources) and teach toward those objectives, student learning is enhanced. Most school districts require teachers to use objectives that are specifically stated. There is no question that clearly written instructional objectives are worth the time, especially when the teacher teaches toward those objectives and evaluates students' progress and learning against them (performance-based teaching or outcome-based or criterion-referenced assessment). It is not imperative that you write all the instructional objectives that you will need. As a matter of fact, many are usually already available in textbooks and other curriculum documents.

As a teacher, you are expected to plan well and specifically that which you intend your students to learn; to convey your expectations to your students; and to assess their learning against that specificity. The danger inherent in such performance-based or criterion-referenced teaching, however, is that, because it tends toward high objectivity, it could become too objective and have negative consequences. If students are treated as objects, then the relationship between teacher and student is impersonal and counterproductive to real learning. Highly specific and impersonal teaching can discourage serendipity, creativity, and the excitement of real discovery and meaningful learning, to say nothing of its possible negative impact on the development of students' self-esteem.

Performance-based instruction works well when teaching toward mastery of basic skills, but the concept of mastery learning tends to imply that there is some foreseeable end point to learning—an obviously erroneous assumption. With performance-based instruction, the source of student motivation tends to be mostly extrinsic. Teacher expectations, grades, and societal and peer pressures are examples of extrinsic sources that drive student performance. To be an effective teacher, the challenge to you is to use performance-based criteria, but with a teaching style that encourages the development of intrinsic sources of student motivation and allows for, provides for, and encourages coincidental learning—learning that goes beyond what might be considered predictable, immediately measurable, minimal results.

Developing units of instruction that integrate student learning and provide a sense of meaning for the students requires coordination throughout the curriculum—defined here as consisting of all the planned experiences students encounter while at school. Hence, for students, learning is a process of discovering how information, knowledge, and ideas are interrelated and learning to make sense out of self, school, and life. Combining chunks of information into units and units into daily lessons helps students process and make sense out of knowledge. Having developed your first unit of instruction, you are well on your way to becoming a competent planner of instruction.

There is no single best way to organize a daily plan, no foolproof formula that will guarantee a teacher an effective lesson. With experience and the increased competence that comes from reflecting on that experience, you will develop your own style, your own methods of implementing that style, and your own formula for preparing a lesson plan. Like a map, your lesson plan charts the course, places markers along the trails, pinpoints danger areas, highlights areas of interest and importance along the way, and ultimately brings the traveler to the objective.

QUESTIONS AND ACTIVITIES FOR DISCUSSION

1. Explain the rationale for organizing instruction into units.

2. Identify and describe criteria for selecting a topic for a unit of study.

3. Explain three reasons why a student teacher and a first-year teacher need to prepare detailed lesson and unit plans.

4. Explain why you should know how to prepare detailed plans even when the textbook program you are using provides them.

5. When, if ever, during instruction can or should you divert from the written plan?

6. Explain the importance of preassessment of student learning. When do you do a preassessment? How can it be done?

7. Explain why lesson planning should be a continual process.

8. Explain some differences between ordinary unit planning and interdisciplinary thematic unit planning.

9. Explain the concept of "student-negotiated curriculum." Is it used today? Why or why not?

10. Explain the relationship of planning to the preactive and reflective thought-processing phases of instruction.

11. Explain the intent of having national standards for each subject discipline taught in public schools. Who prepares these standards? Who decides how the standards are to be implemented and student learning assessed?

12. Explain how a textbook can be helpful to a student's learning in social studies and language arts. How might reliance on a single textbook for each subject be a hindrance to student learning?

13. From your current observations and fieldwork related to this teacher preparation program, clearly identify one specific example of educational practice that seems contradictory to exemplary practice or theory as presented in this chapter. Present your explanation for the discrepancy.

14. Describe any prior concepts you held that changed as a result of your experiences with this chapter. Describe the changes.

REFERENCES

Banks, J. A., & Banks, C. A. McGee. (Eds.). (1989). *Multicultural education: Issues and perspectives.* Boston: Allyn & Bacon.

Bloom, B. S. (Ed.). (1984). *Taxonomy of educational objectives, Book I: Cognitive domain.* White Plains, NY: Longman.

Brooks, J. G., & Brooks, M. G. (1993). *In search of understanding: The case for constructivist classrooms* (Chap. 9). Alexandria, VA: Association for Supervision and Curriculum Development.

Burrett, K., & Rusnak, T. (1993). *Integrated character education.* Fastback 351. Bloomington, IN: Phi Delta Kappa Educational Foundation.

Caine, G., & Caine, R. N. (1993, Fall). The critical need for a mental model of meaningful learning. *California Catalyst,* pp. 18–21.

California State Department of Education. (1987). *Caught in the middle.* Sacramento, CA: Author.

Costa, A. L. (1989). *The enabling behaviors.* Orangeville, CA: Search Models Unlimited.

Costa, A. L. (1991). *The school as a home for the mind.* Palatine, IL: Skylight Publishing.

Duckworth, E. (1986). Teaching as research. *Harvard Educational Review, 56*(4), 481–495.

Eisner, E. (1979). *The educational imagination.* New York: Macmillan.

Eisner, E. (Ed.). (1985). Aesthetic modes of knowing. In *Learning and teaching the ways of knowing* (pp. 23–36). Chicago: University of Chicago Press.

Fersh, S. (1993). *Integrating the trans-national/cultural dimension.* Fastback 361. Bloomington, IN: Phi Delta Kappa Educational Foundation.

Gagné, R. M., Briggs, L., & Wager, W. (1988). *Principles of instructional design* (3rd ed.). New York: Holt, Rinehart and Winston.

Gifford, B. R. (1991). The textbook of the 21st century. *Syllabus, 19,* 15–16.

Good, T. L., & Brophy, J. E. (1987). *Looking in classrooms* (4th ed.). New York: Harper & Row.

Harrow, A. J. (1977). *Taxonomy of the psychomotor domain.* White Plains, NY: Longman.

Hill, D. (1993). Math's angry man. *Teacher Magazine, 5*(1), 24–28.

Joyce, B., & Showers, B. (1988). *Student achievement through staff development.* New York: Longman.

Katz, L. G. (1985). Dispositions in early childhood education. *ERIC/EECE Bulletin, 18*(2).

Krathwohl, D. R., Bloom, B. S., & Masia, B. B. (1964). *Taxonomy of educational goals, Handbook II: Affective domain.* New York: David McKay.

Lepper, M., & Green, D. (Eds.). (1978). *The hidden cost of rewards: New perspectives on the psychology of human motivation.* New York: Erlbaum.

Massey, M. (1993). Interest in character education seen growing. *ASCD Update, 35*(4), 4–5.

Murray, D. M. (1980). Writing as process: How writing finds its own meaning. In T. R. Donovan & B. W. McClelland (Eds.), *Eight approaches to teaching composition* (p. 62). Urbana, IL: National Council for Teachers of English.

Newton, B. (1978). Theoretical basis for higher cognitive questioning—An avenue to critical thinking. *Education, 98* (3), 286–290.

Perkins, D., & Blythe, T. (1994). Putting understanding up front. *Educational Leadership, 51*(5), 4–7.

Redfield, D., & Rousseau, E. (1981). A meta-analysis of experimental research on teacher questioning behavior. *Review of Educational Research, 51*(2), 237–245.

Reinhold, R. (1991, September 29). Class struggle. *The New York Times Magazine,* p. 46.

Resnick, L. B., & Klopfer, L. E. (Eds.). (1989). *Toward the thinking curriculum: Current cognitive research.* 1989 ASCD Yearbook. Alexandria, VA: Association for Supervision and Curriculum Development.

Sadker, M., Sadker, D., & Long, L. (1989). Gender and educational equality. In J. A. Banks & C. A. McGee Banks (Eds.), *Multicultural education: Issues and perspectives* (pp. 107–108). Boston: Allyn & Bacon.

Starr, J. (1989). The great textbook war. In H. Holtz, I. Marcus, J. Dougherty, J. Michaels, & R. Peduzzi (Eds.), *Education and the American dream: Conservatives, liberals and radicals debate the future of education.* Grandy, MA: Bergin and Garvey.

Wynne, E. A., & Ryan, K. (1993). *Reclaiming our schools: A handbook on teaching character, academics, and discipline.* New York: Macmillan.

SUGGESTED READINGS

Alvino, J., et al. (1990). Building better thinkers. *Learning 90, 18*(6), 40–55.

Baloche, L., & Platt, T. J. (1993). Sprouting magic beans: Exploring literature through creative questioning and cooperative learning. *Language Arts, 70*(4), 264–272.

Benito, Y. M., et al. (1993). The effect of instruction in question-answer relationships and metacognition in social studies comprehension. *Journal of Research in Reading, 16*(1), 20–29.

Bowser, J. (1993). Structuring the middle school classroom for spoken language. *English Journal, 82*(1), 38–41.

Boyer, M. R. (1993). The challenge of an integrated curriculum: Avoid the isolated road. *School Administrator, 50*(3), 20–21.

Brandt, R. S. (1992–1993). On outcome-based education: A conversation with Bill Spady. *Educational Leadership, 50*(4), 66–70.

Building a History Curriculum: Guidelines for Teaching History in School. (1988). Westlake, OH: Bradley Commission on History in Schools.

Carroll, J. H., et al. (1993). Integrated language arts instruction. *Language Arts, 70*(4), 310–315.

Criscuola, M. M. (1994). Read, discuss, reread: Insights from the Junior Great Books Program. *Educational Leadership, 51*(5), 58–61.

Dempster, F. N. (1993). Exposing our students to less should help them learn more. *Phi Delta Kappan, 74*(6), 433–437.

Eisner, E. (1993). Why standards may not improve schools. *Educational Leadership, 50*(5), 22–23.

English-Language Arts Model Curriculum Guide. (1988). Sacramento: California Department of Education.

Evans, K. M., & King, J. A. (1994). Research on OBE: What we know and don't know. *Educational Leadership, 51*(6), 12–17.

Farivar, S. (1993). Continuity and change: Planning an integrated history-social science/English-language arts unit. *Social Studies Review, 32*(2), 17–24.

Fielding, L. G., & Pearson, P. D. (1994). Reading comprehension: What works. *Educational Leadership, 51*(5), 62–68.

Gagnon, P. (Ed.). (1989). *Historical literacy.* New York: Macmillan.

Gollnick, D. M., & Chinn, P. C. (1994). *Multicultural education in a pluralistic society* (4th ed.). New York: Macmillan.

Gray, I. L., & Hymel, G. M. (Eds.). (1992). *Successful schooling for all: A primer on outcome-based education and mastery learning.* Johnson City, NY: Network for Outcome-Based Schools.

Harmin, M. (1994). *Inspiring active learning: A handbook for teachers.* Alexandria, VA: Association for Supervision and Curriculum Development.

Haynes, C. (1990). *Religion in American history: What to teach and how.* Alexandria, VA: Association for Supervision and Curriculum Development.

Lockledge, A. (1993). Math as the language and tool of social studies. *Social Studies and the Young Learner, 6*(1), 3–6.

Marcincin, L. W. (1992). Getting involved: An interdisciplinary project on homelessness. *Schools in the Middle, 1*(3), 6–10.

Martin, B. L., & Briggs, L. J. (1986). *The affective and cognitive domains.* Englewood Cliffs, NJ: Educational Technology Publications.

McGowan, T. M., et al. (1992). Using literature studies to promote elementary social studies learning. *Social Studies and the Young Learner, 5*(1), 10–13.

Nelson, J. R., & Frederick, L. (1994). Can children design curriculum? *Educational Leadership, 51*(5), 71–74.

O'Neil, J. (1993). Can national standards make a difference? *Educational Leadership, 50*(5), 4–8.

Parker, W. C. (1991). *Renewing the social studies curriculum.* Alexandria, VA: Association for Supervision and Curriculum Development.

Pollock, J. E. (1992). Blueprints for social studies. *Educational Leadership, 49*(8), 52–53.

Ravitch, D. (1993). Launching a revolution in standards and assessments. *Phi Delta Kappan, 70*(10), 767–772.

Robb, L. (1993). A cause for celebration: Reading and writing with at-risk students. *New Advocate, 6*(1), 25–40.

Schlene, V. J. (1993). Integrated curriculum and instruction: An ERIC/ChESS sample. *Social Studies and the Young Learner, 5*(3), 15–16.

Schneider, D. (1993). The search for integration in the social studies. *Momentum, 24*(3), 34–39.

Schubert, B. (1993). Literacy: What makes it real: Integrated, thematic teaching. *Social Studies Review, 32*(2), 7–16.

Singer, H., & Donlan, D. (1990). *Reading and learning from text.* Hillsdale, NJ: Lawrence Erlbaum.

Smith, M. S., et al. (1994). National curriculum standards: Are they desirable and feasible? In R. F. Elmore & S. H. Fuhrman (Eds.), *The governance of curriculum* (Chap. 2). 1994 ASCD Yearbook. Alexandria, VA: Association for Supervision and Curriculum Development.

Stevenson, C., & Carr, J. F. (Eds.). (1993). *Integrated studies in the middle grades.* New York: Teachers College Press.

Tchudi, S. (1991). *Planning and assessing the curriculum in English and language arts.* Alexandria, VA: Association for Supervision and Curriculum Development.

Towers, J. M. (1992). Outcome-based education: Another educational bandwagon? *Educational Forum, 56*(3), 291–305.

van der Meij, H. (1993). What's the title? A case study of questioning in reading. *Journal of Research in Reading, 16*(1), 46–56.

Wiggins, G. (1993). Assessment: Authenticity, context, and validity. *Phi Delta Kappan, 75*(3), 200–214.

With history—Social science for all: Access for every student. (1992). Sacramento: California Department of Education.

Young, T. A., & Marek-Schroer, M. F. (1992). Writing to learn in social studies. *Social Studies and the Young Learner, 5*(1), 14–16.

Zabaluk, B. L., & Samuels, S. J. (1988). *Readability: Its past, present, and future.* Newark, DE: International Reading Association.

CHAPTER 5

Assessment of Learning

Assessment is an integral, ongoing process within the educational scene. Curricula, buildings, materials, specific courses, teachers, supervisors, administrators, equipment—all must be periodically assessed in relation to student learning, the purpose of any school. When gaps between anticipated results and student achievement exist, efforts are made to eliminate those factors that seem to be limiting the educational output or to in some other way improve the situation. Thus, educational progress occurs.

To learn effectively, students need to know how they are doing. Similarly, to be an effective teacher, you must be informed about what each student knows, feels, and can do so that you can help the student build on her or his skills, knowledge, and attitudes. Therefore, you and your students need continuous feedback on their progress and problems in order to plan appropriate learning activities and to make adjustments to those already planned. If this feedback says that progress is slow, you can provide alternative activities; if it indicates that some or all of the students have already mastered the desired learning, you can eliminate unnecessary activities and practice for some or all of the children. In short, assessment is the key to both effective teaching and effective learning.

The importance of continuous assessment mandates that you know the principles and techniques of assessment. This chapter explains some of those and shows you how to construct and use assessment instruments and make sense from the data obtained. We define the terms related to assessment, consider what makes a good assessment instrument, relate the criteria to both standardized and nonstandardized instruments, suggest procedures to use in the construction of assessment items, point out the advantages and disadvantages of different assessment items and procedures, and explain the construction and use of alternative assessment devices.

In addition, this chapter discusses grading and reporting of student achievement, two responsibilities that can consume much of a teacher's valuable time. Grading is time-consuming and frustrating for many teachers. What should be graded? Should marks represent student growth, level of achievement in a group, effort, attitude, general behavior, or a combination? What should determine grades—homework, tests, projects, class participation and group work, or all of these? And what should be their relative weights? These are just a few of the questions that plague teachers and parents when decisions about summative assessment and grades must be made.

In too many schools, the grade progress report and final report card are about the only communication between the school and the student's home. Yet, unless the teacher and the school have clearly determined what grades represent and periodically reviewed that information with each new set of parents or guardians, these reports may create unrest and dissatisfaction on the part of parents, guardians, and students and prove to be alienating devices. The grading system and reporting scheme, then, instead of informing parents and guardians, may separate even further the home and the school, which do have a common concern—the intellectual, physical, social, and emotional development of the student.

The development of the student encompasses growth in the cognitive, affective, and psychomotor domains. Traditional, objective paper-and-pencil tests provide only a portion of the data needed to indicate student progress in those domains. Many experts today question the traditional sources of data and encourage the search for, development of, and use of alternative means to more authentically assess the students' development of thinking and higher-level learning. Although many things are not yet clear, one thing is certain: various techniques of assessment must be used to determine how the student works, what the student is learning, and what the student can produce as a result of that learning. As a teacher, you must develop a repertoire of means of assessing learner behavior and academic progress.

Grades have been a part of school for about 100 years. Although some schools are experimenting with other ways of reporting student achievement in learning, (see for example the October 1994 issue of *Educational Leadership*) grades still seem firmly entrenched—parents, students, colleges, and employers have come to expect grades as evaluations. Some critics suggest that the emphasis in schools is on getting a high grade rather than on learning, arguing that, as traditionally measured, the two do not necessarily go hand in hand. Today's emphasis is more on what the student can do as a result of learning (performance testing) than merely on what the student can recall from the experience (memory testing).

In addition, there have been complaints about subjectivity and unfair practices. As a result of these concerns, various systems of assessment and reporting have evolved and will likely continue to evolve throughout your professional career.

When teachers are aware of alternative systems, they may be able to develop assessment and reporting processes that are fair and effective for particular situations. So, after beginning with assessment, this chapter's final focus is on today's principles and practices in grading and reporting student achievement.

Specifically, this chapter will assist your understanding of

1. Various roles of the assessment component of teaching and learning
2. Using the assessment component
3. Terms used in assessment
4. The meaning of *authentic assessment*
5. The role of assessment in cooperative learning
6. Involving students in self-assessment
7. Using portfolios for assessment
8. Using checklists for assessment
9. Maintaining records of student achievement
10. Grading, marking, and reporting student achievement
11. The difference between criterion-referenced and norm-referenced measurement
12. Determining grades
13. Testing for student learning
14. Preventing and dealing with cheating
15. The meaning of *performance* and *alternative assessment*
16. Preparation of 12 different types of assessment items
17. Meeting and collaborating with parents and guardians.

A. PURPOSES OF ASSESSMENT

Assessment of achievement in student learning is designed to serve several purposes. These are

1. *To assess and improve student learning.* To assess and improve student learning is the function usually first thought of when speaking of assessment and is the topic of this chapter.
2. *To identify children's strengths and weaknesses.* Identification and assessment of children's strengths and weaknesses are necessary for two purposes: to structure and restructure the learning activities and to restructure the curriculum. Concerning the first purpose, data on student strengths and weaknesses regarding content and process skills are important in planning activities appropriate for both skill development and intellectual development. This is diagnostic assessment (also known as preassessment). For the second purpose, data on student strengths and weaknesses in content and skills are useful for making appropriate modifications to the curriculum.
3. *To assess the effectiveness of a particular instructional strategy.* It is important for you to know how well a particular strategy helped accomplish a particular goal or objective. Competent teachers continually evaluate their strategy choices, using a number of sources: student achievement as measured by assessment instruments, their own intuition, informal feedback given by the children, and informal feedback given by colleagues, such as by members of a teaching team.
4. *To assess and improve the effectiveness of curriculum programs.* Components of the curriculum are continually assessed by committees of teachers and administrators. The assessment is done while students are learning (formative assessment) and after (summative assessment).
5. *To assess and improve teaching effectiveness.* Today's exemplary middle-level teachers are education specialists and are as unique as the clientele they serve. To improve student learning, teachers are periodically evaluated on the basis of their commitment to working with students at this level, their ability to cope with children at a particular age or grade level, and their ability to show mastery of appropriate instructional techniques—techniques that are articulated throughout this text.
6. *To communicate to and involve parents and guardians in their children's learning.* Parents, communities, and school boards all share in accountability for the effectiveness of the learning of their children. Today's schools are reaching out and engaging parents, guardians, and the community in their children's education. All teachers play an important role in the process of communicating with, reaching out to, and involving parents.

B. GUIDELINES FOR ASSESSING LEARNING

Because the welfare and, indeed, the future of so many people depend on the outcomes of assessment, it is impossible to overemphasize its importance. For a learning endeavor to be successful, the learner must have answers to basic questions: Where am I going? Where am I now? How do I get where I am going? How will I know when I get there? Am I on the right track? These questions are integral to a good program of assessment. Of course, in the process of teaching and learning, the answers may be ever-changing, and the teacher must continue to assess and adjust plans as appropriate and necessary.

Principles That Guide the Assessment Program

Based on the preceding questions, the following principles guide the assessment program:

- Teachers need to know how well they are doing.
- Students need to know how well they are doing.
- Evidence and data regarding how well the teacher and students are doing should come from a variety of sources.

- Assessment is an ongoing process. The selection and implementation of plans and activities require continuous monitoring and assessment to check on progress and to change or adopt strategies to promote desired behavior.
- Self-assessment is an important component of any successful assessment program. It also involves helping children develop the skills necessary for them to assume increasingly greater ownership of their own learning.
- The program of assessment should promote teaching effectiveness and contribute to the intellectual and psychological growth of children.
- Assessment is a reciprocal process that includes assessment of teacher performance as well as student achievement.
- A teacher's responsibility is to facilitate student learning and to assess student progress, and for that, the teacher should be held accountable.

C. CLARIFICATION OF TERMS USED IN ASSESSMENT

When discussing the assessment component of teaching and learning, it is easy to be confused by the terminology. The following clarification of terms is offered to help in your reading and understanding.

Assessment and Evaluation

Although some authors distinguish between the terms *assessment* (the process of finding out what children are learning, a relatively neutral process) and *evaluation* (making sense of what was found out, a subjective process), in this text I do not. I consider the difference to be slight and the terms essentially synonymous.

Measurement and Assessment

Measurement refers to quantifiable data about specific behaviors. Tests and the statistical procedures used to analyze the results are examples. Measurement is a descriptive and objective process, that is, it is relatively free from human value judgments.

Assessment includes objective data from measurement but also other information, some of which is more subjective, such as information from anecdotal records and teacher observations and ratings of student performance. In addition to the use of objective data (data from measurement), assessment also includes arriving at value judgments made on the basis of subjective information.

An example of the use of these terms is as follows. A teacher may share the information that Sarah Jones received a score in the 90th percentile on the eighth-grade statewide achievement test in reading (a statement of measurement) but may add that "according to my assessment of her work in my language arts class, she has not been an outstanding student" (a statement of assessment).

Validity and Reliability

The degree to which a measuring instrument actually measures that which it is intended to measure is called the instrument's validity. When we ask if an instrument (such as a performance assessment instrument) has validity, key questions concerning that instrument are

- Does the instrument adequately sample the intended content?
- Does it measure the cognitive, affective, and psychomotor knowledge and skills that are important to the unit of content being tested?
- Does it sample all the instructional objectives of that unit?

The accuracy with which a technique consistently measures that which it does measure is called its reliability. If, for example, you know that you weigh 114 pounds and a scale consistently records 114 pounds when you stand on it, then that scale has reliability. However, if the same scale consistently records 100 pounds when you stand on it, we can still say the scale has reliability. This example demonstrates that an instrument can be reliable (it produces similar results when used again and again) yet not necessarily valid (in this second instance, the scale is not measuring what it is supposed to measure, so although it is reliable, it is not valid). Although a technique can be reliable but not valid, it must have reliability before it can have validity. The greater the number of test items or situations in a particular content objective, the higher the reliability. The higher the reliability, the more consistency there will be in students' scores measuring their understanding of that particular objective.

D. ASSESSING STUDENT LEARNING

There are three general approaches for assessing a student's achievement. You can assess (1) what the student *says*—for example, the quantity and quality of a student's contributions to class discussions; (2) what the student *does*—for example, the amount and quality of a student's participation in class activities; and (3) what the student *writes*—for example, homework assignments, checklists, written tests, and the student's journal entries. Although your own situation and personal philosophy will dictate the weight you give to each avenue of assessment, you should have a strong rationale if you value and weigh the three categories differently than one-third each.

Authentic Assessment

When assessing for student achievement, it is important that you use procedures that are compatible with the instructional objectives. This is referred to as "authentic assessment." Other terms used for "authentic" assessment are "accurate," "active," "aligned," "alternative," and "direct" assessment. Although "performance" assessment is sometimes used, performance assessment refers to the type of student response being assessed, whereas "authentic" assessment refers to the assessment situation. Although not all performance assessments are authentic, assessments that are authentic are most assuredly performance assessments (Meyer, 1992). In language arts, for example, "although it may seem fairly easy to develop a criterion-referenced test, administer it, and grade it, tests often measure language *skills* rather than language use. It is extremely difficult to measure students' communicative competence with a test. Tests do not measure listening and talking very well, and a test on punctuation marks, for example, does not indicate students' ability to use punctuation marks correctly in their own writing. Instead, tests typically evaluate students' ability to add punctuation marks to a set of sentences created by someone else, or to proofread and spot punctuation errors in someone else's writing. An alternative and far better approach is to examine how students use punctuation marks in their own writing" (Tompkins & Hoskisson, 1991, p. 63). An authentic assessment of punctuation, then, would be an assessment of a performance test that involves students writing and punctuating their own writing. For an authentic assessment of the student's understanding of what has been learned, you would use a performance-based assessment procedure.

Assessment: A Three-Step Process

Assessing a student's achievement is a three-step process. It involves (1) diagnostic evaluation, which is an assessment (sometimes called a preassessment) of the student's knowledge and skills *before* the new instruction; (2) formative evaluation, the assessment of learning *during* the instruction; and (3) summative evaluation, the assessment of learning *after* the instruction, ultimately represented by the student's term, semester, or year's achievement grade. Grades shown on unit tests, progress reports, deficiency notices, and six-week or quarter grades (in a semester-based program) are examples of formative evaluation reports. An end-of-the-chapter test or a unit test is summative, however, when the test represents the absolute end of the student's learning of material of that instructional unit.

Evaluating what a student says and does. When evaluating what a student says, you should (1) listen to the student's questions, responses, and interactions with others and (2) observe the student's attentiveness, involvement in class activities, and responses to challenges.

Notice that we say you should listen and observe. While listening to what the student is saying, you should also be observing the student's nonverbal behaviors. For this you can use checklists and rating scales, behavioral growth record forms, observations of the student's performance in classroom activities, and periodic conferences with the student. Figure 5.1 illustrates a sample form for recording and evaluating teacher observations of a student's verbal and nonverbal behaviors.

Please remember that, with each technique used, you must proceed from your awareness of anticipated learning outcomes (the instructional objectives), and you must evaluate a student's progress toward meeting those objectives. That is referred to as criterion-referenced assessment.

Here are guidelines to follow when evaluating a student's verbal and nonverbal behaviors in the classroom. To evaluate what a student says and does, follow these guidelines:

1. Maintain an anecdotal record book or folder, with a separate section in it for your records of each student.
2. For a specific activity, list the desirable behaviors.
3. Check the list against the specific instructional objectives.
4. Record your observations as quickly as possible following your observation. Audio or video recordings and, of course, computer software programs can help you check the accuracy of your memory, but if this is inconvenient, you should spend time during school, immediately after, or later that evening recording your observations while still fresh in your memory.
5. Record your professional judgment about the student's progress toward the desired behavior, but think it through before transferring it to a permanent record.
6. Write comments that are reminders to yourself, such as:

   "Check validity of observation by further testing."

   "Discuss observations with student's parent."

   "Discuss observations with school counselor."

   "Discuss observations with other teachers on the teaching team."

FIGURE 5.1
Evaluating and Recording Student Behaviors: Sample Form

Student _____ Course _____ School _____		
Observer _____ Date _____ Period _____		
Objective for Time Period	Desired Behavior	What Student Did, Said, or Wrote
Teacher's (observer's) comments:		

Evaluating what a student writes. When evaluating what a student writes, you can use worksheets, written homework, student journal entries, student portfolios, and tests. In many schools, portfolios, worksheets, and homework assignments are the tools usually used for the formative evaluation of each student's achievement. Tests, too, should be a part of this evaluation, but tests are also used for summative evaluation at the end of a unit, and for diagnostic purposes as well.

Your summative evaluation of a student's achievement, and any other final judgment made by you about a student, can have an impact on the emotional and intellectual development of that student. Special attention is given to this later, in the section titled, "Recording Teacher Observations and Judgments."

When evaluating what a student writes, use the following guidelines:

1. Worksheets, homework, and test items should correlate with and be compatible with specific instructional objectives.
2. Read everything a student writes. If it is important enough for the student to do, it is equally important that you give your professional attention to it.
3. Provide positive written or verbal comments about the student's work. Rather than just writing "good" on a student's paper, briefly state what it was about it that made it "good." Try to avoid negative comments. Rather than simply pointing out that the student didn't do it right, tell or show the student acceptable ways to complete the work and how to do so. For reinforcement, use positive rewards as frequently as possible.
4. Think before writing a comment on a student's paper, asking yourself how you think the student (or a parent or guardian) will interpret the comment and if that is the interpretation you intend.
5. Avoid writing negative comments or grades in student journals. Student journals are for encouraging students to write, to think about their thinking, and to record their creative thoughts. In journal writing, students should be encouraged to write about their experiences in and out of school, especially about their experiences related to what is being learned. They should be encouraged to write about their feelings about what is being learned and how they are learning it. Writing in journals gives them practice in expressing themselves in written form and in connecting their learning, and you should provide the nonthreatening freedom to do it. Comments and evaluations from teachers might discourage creative and spontaneous expression.
6. When reading student journals, talk individually with students to seek clarification of their expressions. Student journals are useful to the teacher (of any subject field) in understanding the student's thought processes and writing skills (diagnostic evaluation), and journals should *not* be graded. For grading purposes, teachers may simply record whether the student is maintaining a journal and, perhaps, a judgment about the quantity of writing in it, but no judgment of the quality.
7. When reviewing student portfolios, discuss with students individually the progress in their learning shown by the materials in their portfolio. As with student journals, the portfolio should *not* be graded or compared in any way with those of other students. Its purpose is for student self-assessment and to show progress in learning. For this to happen, students should keep in their portfolio all papers related to the course.

Regardless of avenues chosen and their relative weights given by you, you must evaluate against the instructional objectives. Any given objective may be checked by using more than one method and more than one instrument. Subjectivity, inherent in the evaluation process, may be reduced as you check for validity, comparing results of one measuring technique against those of another.

While evaluation of cognitive objectives lends itself to traditional written tests of achievement, the evaluation of affective and psychomotor domains requires the use of performance checklists based on observing student behaviors in action. As indicated in the earlier discussion, however, for cognitive learning as well, educators today are encouraging the use of assessment alternatives to traditional paper-and-pencil written testing. Alternative assessment strategies include the use of projects, portfolios, skits, papers, oral presentations, and performance tests. Advantages claimed for the use of authentic assessment include its direct (performance-based, criterion-referenced, outcome-based) measurement of what students should know and can do and its emphasis on higher-order thinking. On the other hand, disadvantages of authentic assessment include a higher cost, difficulty in making results consistent and usable, and problems with validity, reliability, and comparability.

Unfortunately, the teacher who may never see a student again after a given school year is over may never observe the effects that teacher has had on a student's values and attitudes. On the other hand, in schools where groups or teams of teachers remain with the same cohort of students throughout several years of school (often referred to as "houses" or "villages"), those teachers often do have the opportunity to observe the positive changes in their students' values and attitudes.

E. COOPERATIVE LEARNING AND ASSESSMENT

The purpose of a cooperative learning group is for the group to learn, which means that individuals within the group must learn. Group achievement in learning, then, depends on the learning of individuals within the group. Rather than competing for rewards for achievement, members of the group cooperate with each other by helping each other to learn so the group will earn a good reward. Theoretically, when small groups of students of mixed backgrounds, skills, and capabilities work together toward a common goal, their liking and respect for one another increase. As a result, there is an increase in each student's self-esteem *and* academic achievement.

When recognizing the achievement of a cooperative learning group, group as well as individual achievement is rewarded. Remembering that the emphasis must be on peer support rather than peer pressure, you must be cautious about ever giving group grades. Some teachers give bonus points to all members of the group to add to their individual scores when everyone in the group has reached preset criteria. These preset standards can be different for individuals within a group, depending on each member's ability and past performance. It is important that each member of a group feel rewarded and successful. Some teachers also give subjective grades to individual students for their role performances within the group.

For determination of students' report card grades, individual student achievement is measured later through individual test results and other data, and the final grade is based on those as well as on the student's performance in the group.

F. INVOLVING STUDENTS IN SELF-ASSESSMENT

In exemplary school programs, students' continuous self-assessment is an important component of the evaluation process. If students are to progress in their understanding of their own thinking (metacognition) and in their intellectual development, they must receive instruction and guidance in how to become more responsible for their own learning (empowered). During that process they learn to think better of themselves and of their individual capabilities. To achieve this self-understanding and improved self-esteem requires the experiences afforded by successes, along with guidance in self-understanding.

Using Portfolios

To meet these goals, teachers should provide opportunities for students to think about what they are learning, how they are learning it, and how far they have progressed. One procedure is for students to maintain portfolios of their work, periodically using rating scales or checklists to assess their own progress. The student portfolio should be well organized and contain assignment sheets, class worksheets, homework, forms for student self-evaluation and reflection on their work, and other class materials thought important by the students and teacher.

Although portfolio assessment as an alternative to traditional methods of evaluating student progress has gained momentum in recent years, setting standards is very difficult. Thus far, research on the use of portfolios for assessment indicates that validity and reliability of teacher evaluation are quite low (O'Neil, 1993, pp. 3, 8). Before using portfolios as an alternative to traditional testing, teachers must consider and clearly understand the reasons for doing it, carefully decide on portfolio content, consider parent and guardian reactions, and anticipate grading problems (Black, 1993). (For additional resources on the use of student portfolios, refer to the Suggested Readings at the end of this chapter.) General information on portfolio assessment for educators is included in two publications: *Portfolio News,* Portfolio Assessment Clearinghouse, San Dieguito High School District, 710 Encinitas Blvd., Encinitas, CA 92024; and *Portfolio Assessment Newsletter,* Northwest Evaluation Association, 5 Centerpointe Drive, Suite 100, Lake Oswego, OR 97035.

While emphasizing the criteria for evaluation, rating scales and checklists provide students with means of expressing their feelings and give the teacher still another source of input data for use in evaluation. To provide students with reinforcement and guidance to improve their learning and development, teachers meet with individual students to discuss their self-evaluations. Such conferences should provide students with understandable and achievable short-term goals, as well as help them develop and maintain adequate self-esteem.

Although almost any of the instruments used for evaluating student work can be used for student self-evaluation, in some cases it might be better to use those constructed with the student's understanding of the instrument in mind. Student self-evaluation and reflection should be done on a regular and continuing basis, so comparisons can be made by the student from one time to the next. You will need to help students learn how to analyze these comparisons. Comparisons should provide a student with information previously not recognized about his or her own progress and growth.

One of the items maintained by students in their portfolios is a series of self-evaluation checklists.

Using Checklists

Items on the student's self-evaluation checklist will vary depending on your grade level. (See Figure 5.2 for a sample generic form.) Sample checklists specific for teaching language arts and social studies are shown in Chapters 8 and 10. Checklist items can be used easily by a student to compare present with previous self-evaluations, while open-ended questions allow the student to provide additional information as well as to do some expressive writing.

To see how one teacher uses the checklist for assessment and grading, see Figure 10.6 and the related discussion in Chapter 10. Here are general guidelines for using student portfolios in your assessment of student learning:

- Contents of the portfolio should reflect your instructional aims and course objectives.
- Date everything that goes into the portfolio.
- Determine what materials should be kept in the portfolio and clearly announce when, how, and by what criteria portfolios will be reviewed by you, preferably in your course syllabus.
- Give all responsibility for maintenance of the portfolio to the students.
- Portfolios should be kept in the classroom.

G. MAINTAINING RECORDS OF STUDENT ACHIEVEMENT

You must maintain well-organized and complete records of student achievement. You may do this in a written record book or through an electronic record book (that is, a commercially developed computer software program , or one you develop yourself, perhaps by using a computer software program spreadsheet as the base). The record book should include tardies and absences as well as all records of scores on tests, homework, projects, and other assignments.

Anecdotal records (see Figure 8.13 of Chapter 8) can be maintained in alphabetical order in a separate binder with a separate section for each student. Daily interactions and

FIGURE 5.2
Student Self-Evaluation: Sample Generic Form

Student Self-Evaluation Form

(to be kept in student's portfolio)

Student: Date:

Teacher: Number:

Circle one response for each of the first six items.

1. Since my last self-evaluation my assignments have been turned in
   a. always on time.
   b. always late.
   c. sometimes late; sometimes on time.
   d.
2. Most of my classmates
   a. like me.
   b. don't like me.
   c. ignore me.
   d.
3. I think I am
   a. smart.
   b. the smartest in the class.
   c. the slowest in the class.
   d.
4. Since my last self-evaluation, I think I am
   a. doing better.
   b. doing worse.
   c. doing about the same.
   d.
5. In this class
   a. I am learning a lot.
   b. I am not learning very much.
   c. I am not learning anything.
   d.
6. In this class
   a. I am doing the best work I can.
   b. I am not doing as well as I can.
   c.
7. Describe what you have learned since your last self-evaluation that you have used outside of school. Tell how you used it. (You can refer to your previous self-evaluation.)
8. Describe anything that you have learned about yourself since you completed your last self-evaluation. (You can refer to your previous self-evaluation.)

---

events occur in the classroom that may provide informative data about a child's intellectual, emotional, and physical development. Maintaining a dated record of your observations of these interactions and events can provide important information that might otherwise be forgotten if you do not write it down. At the end of a unit and again at the conclusion of a grading term, you will want to review your records. During the course of the school year your anecdotal records (and those of other members of your teaching team) will provide important information about the intellectual, psychological, and physical development of each student and reveal whether extra attention needs to be given to individual students.

Recording Teacher Observations and Judgments

As said before, you must carefully think through any written comments that you intend to make about a student. Students can be quite sensitive to what others say about them, particularly to negative comments about them made by a teacher.

Additionally, we have seen anecdotal comments in students' permanent records that said more about the teachers who made the comments than the students. Comments that have been carelessly, hurriedly, and thoughtlessly made can be detrimental to a student's welfare and progress in school. Teacher comments must be professional, that is, they must be diagnostically useful to the continued intellectual and psychological development of the child. This is true for any comment you make or write, whether on a student's paper, on the student's permanent school record, or on a note sent home to a parent or guardian.

As an example, consider the following unprofessional comment observed in one student's permanent record. A teacher wrote, "John is lazy." Anyone could describe John as "lazy"; it is nonproductive, and it is certainly not a professional diagnosis. How many times do you suppose John needs to receive such negative descriptions of his behavior before he begins to believe that he is just that—lazy—and, as a result, act that way even more often? Written comments like that can also be damaging because they may be read by John's next teacher, who will simply perpetuate the same expectation of John. To say that John is lazy merely describes behavior as judged by the teacher who wrote the comment. More important, and more professional, would be for the teacher to try to analyze *why* John is behaving that way, then prescribe activities likely to motivate John to assume a more constructive attitude and take charge of his own learning behavior.

For students' continued intellectual and emotional development, your comments should be useful, productive, analytical, diagnostic, and prescriptive. The professional teacher makes diagnoses and prepares descriptions; a professional teacher does *not* label students as "lazy," "vulgar," "slow," "stupid," "difficult," or "dumb." The professional teacher sees the behavior of a student as being goal directed. Perhaps "lazy" John found that particular behavioral pattern won him attention. John's goal, then, was attention (don't we all need attention?), and John assumed negative, even self-destructive, behavioral patterns to reach that goal. The professional task of any teacher is to facilitate the learner's understanding (perception) of a goal and to identify positive behaviors designed to reach that goal.

What separates the professional teacher from anyone off the street is the teacher's ability to go beyond mere description of behavior. Keep that in mind always when you write comments that will be read by students, by their parents or guardians, and by other teachers.

H. GRADING AND MARKING STUDENT ACHIEVEMENT

If conditions were ideal (which they are not), and if teachers did their job perfectly well (which many of us do not), then all students would receive top marks (the ultimate in mastery learning), and there would be less of a need to talk here about grading. Mastery learning implies that some end point of learning is attainable, but there probably isn't an end point. In any case, because conditions for teaching are never ideal and we teachers are mere humans, let us continue with the topic of grading, which is undoubtedly of special interest to you, your students, their parents or guardians, school counselors, administrators, school boards, and college admissions offices.

In this chapter we have frequently used the term *achievement*. What is meant by this term? Achievement means accomplishment, but is it accomplishment of the instructional objectives as measured against preset standards, or is it simply accomplishment? Most teachers would probably choose the former, in which the teacher subjectively establishes a standard that must be met in order for a student to receive a certain grade for an assignment, a test, a quarter, a semester, or a course. Achievement, then, is decided by degrees of accomplishment.

Preset standards are usually expressed in percentages (degrees of accomplishment) needed for marks or ABC grades. If no student achieves the standard required for an A grade, for example, then no student receives an A. On the other hand, if all students meet the preset standard for the A grade, then all receive As. Determining student grades on the basis of preset standards is referred to as criterion-referenced grading.

Criterion-Referenced versus Norm-Referenced Grading

As stated in the preceding paragraph, criterion-referenced grading is grading that is based on preset standards. Norm-referenced grading, on the other hand, is based on the relative accomplishment of individuals in the group (say, one classroom of ninth-grade English students or a larger group, perhaps all students enrolled in ninth-grade English). It compares and ranks students and is commonly known as "grading on a curve." Because it encourages competition and discourages cooperative learning, norm-referenced grading is not recommended. Norm-referenced grading is educationally dysfunctional. After all, each student is an individual and should not be converted to a statistic on a frequency-distribution curve. For your own information, after several years of teaching, you can produce frequency-distribution studies of grades you have given in a course you have been teaching, but do *not* grade students on a curve. Grades for student achievement should be tied to performance levels and determined on the basis of each student's achievement toward preset standards.

In criterion-referenced grading, the aim is to communicate information about an individual student's progress in knowledge and work skills in comparison to that student's previous attainment or in the pursuit of an absolute, such as content mastery. Criterion-referenced grading is featured in continuous-progress curricula, competency-based (outcome-based) curricula, and other programs that focus on individualized education.

Criterion-referenced or competency-based grading is based on the level at which each student meets the specified objectives (standards) for the course. The objectives must be clearly stated to represent important student learning outcomes. This approach implies that effective teaching and learning result in high grades (As) for most students. In fact, when a mastery concept is used, the student must accomplish the objectives before being allowed to proceed to the next learning task. The philosophy of teachers who favor criterion-referenced procedures recognizes individual potential. Such teachers accept the challenge of finding teaching strategies to help students progress from where they are to the next designated level. Instead of wondering how Sally compares with Juanita, the comparison is between what Juanita could do yesterday and what she can do today, and how well these performances compare to the preset standard.

Most school systems use some combination of both norm-referenced and criterion-referenced data. In beginning keyboarding, for example, a certain basic speed and accuracy are established as criteria. Perhaps only the upper third of the advanced keyboarding class is to be recommended for the advanced class in computer programming. The grading for the beginning class might appropriately be criterion based, but grading for the advanced class might be norm referenced. Sometimes both kinds of information are needed. For example, a report card for a student in the eighth grade might indicate how that student is meeting certain criteria, such as an A grade for addition of fractions. Another entry might show that this mastery is expected, however, at the sixth grade. Both criterion- and norm-referenced data may be communicated to the parents or guardians and students. Appropriate procedures should be used: a criterion-referenced approach to show whether the student can accomplish the task and a norm-referenced approach to show how well that student performs compared to the larger group to which the student belongs. Sometimes, one or the other is needed; other times, both are required.

Determining Grades

Once entered onto school transcripts, grades have a significant impact on the futures of students. Determining achievement grades for student performance is serious business, for which several important and professional decisions must be made by you. Although in a few schools, and for certain classes or assignments, only marks such as "E, S, and I" or "pass/no pass" are used, for most courses taught in middle-level schools, percentages of accomplishment and ABC grades are used. To arrive at grades, consider the following guidelines:

1. At the start of the school term, explain your marking and grading policies *first to yourself* then to your students and to their parents or guardians at "Back-to-School Night," by a written explanation that is sent home, or both.
2. When converting your interpretation of a student's accomplishments to a letter grade, be as objective as possible.
3. Build your grading policy around accomplishment rather than failure, where students proceed from one accomplishment to the next. This is continuous promotion, not necessarily from one grade to the next, but within the classroom. (Some schools have

done away with grade-level designation and, in its place, use the concept of continuous promotion from the time of student entry into the school through graduation or exit.)

4. For the selection of criteria for ABC grades, select a percentage standard, such as 92 percent for an A, 85 percent for a B, 75 percent for a C, and 65 percent for a D. Cutoff percentages used are your decision, although the district, school, or program area may have established guidelines to which you are expected to adhere.

5. "Evaluation" and "grading" are *not* synonymous. As you learned earlier, evaluation implies the collection of information from a variety of sources, including measurement techniques and subjective observations. These data, then, become the basis for arriving at a final grade, which in effect is a final value judgment. Grades are one aspect of evaluation and are intended to communicate educational progress to students and to their parents or guardians. For final grades to be valid indicators of that progress, you *must* use a variety of sources of data for their determination.

6. For the determination of students' final grades, we recommend using a point system, in which things that students write, say, and do are given points (except for journals or portfolios, unless simply based on whether the student has completed one or not); then the possible point total is the factor for grade determination. For example, if 92 percent is the cutoff for an A, and 500 points are possible, then any student with 460 points or more ($500 \times .92$) has achieved an A. Likewise, for a test or any other assignment, if the value is 100 points, the cutoff for an A is 92 ($100 \times .92$). With a point system and preset standards, the teacher and students, at any time during the year, always know the current points possible and can easily calculate a student's current grade standing. That way, students always know where they stand in the course.

7. Students will be absent and will miss assignments and tests, and it is best that you decide beforehand your policy about makeup work. Your policies about late assignments and missed tests must be clearly communicated to students and to their parents or guardians. For makeup work, please consider the following.

Homework assignments. For homework assignments, my recommendation is that, after due dates have been negotiated or set, you adhere to them, giving no credit or reduced credit for work that is turned in late. Generally, experience has shown this to be a good policy to which children can and should adjust. It prepares them for the workplace (as well as for high school and college) and is a policy that is sensible for a teacher who deals with many papers each week.

For this policy to work well, however, assignment deadlines must be given to students well in advance, and not at the last minute. You must be sympathetic and understanding to individual children and their problems. There will be times when you will accept a late paper without penalty, such as when a student has been ill or has had a serious problem at home. Many children come to school with considerable excess psychological baggage, and your acceptance of a student's late paper could mean the difference between that student continuing to perform at school and to grow intellectually, or the acceleration of that student dropping out of school entirely.

Teachers must be sympathetic and understanding to children and what is happening in their world outside of school. Establishing and following classroom rules, procedures, and assignment deadlines is important. However, as a classroom teacher, you are a professional and that means when it comes to individual children you must make intelligent and professional judgments or decisions. As someone once said, there is nothing democratic about treating unequals as equals. As a professional classroom teacher, alone or collaboratively with your students, rules, procedures, and deadlines will be set, but there will be occasional individual adjustments as good sense dictates.

Tests. Sometimes students are absent when tests are given. When that happens, you have several options. Some teachers allow students to miss or discount one test per grading period. Another technique is to allow each student to substitute a written homework assignment or project for one missed test. Still another option is to give the absent student the choice of either taking a makeup test or having the next test count double. When makeup tests are given, they should be taken within a week of the regular test unless there is a compelling medical or family problem preventing it.

Some students miss a testing period because of their involvement in other school activities. In those instances, the student may be able to arrange to come into another of your class periods, on that day or the next, to take the test.

If a student is absent during performance testing, the logistics and possible diminished reliability of having to readminister the test for one student may necessitate giving the student an alternate written test.

I. TESTING FOR ACHIEVEMENT

One source of information used for determining grades is data obtained from testing for student achievement. Competent planning, preparing, administering, and scoring of tests is an important professional skill, for which you will gain valuable practical experience during your student teaching. Here are helpful guidelines that you will want to refer to while you are student teaching and again, occasionally, during your first few years as a credentialed teacher.

Purposes for Testing

Although textbook publishers' tests, test item pools, and standardized tests are available from a variety of sources, because schools are different, teachers are different, and children are different, most of the time you will be designing and preparing your tests for your purposes for your distinct group of children.

Tests can be designed for several purposes, and a variety of kinds of tests and alternate test items will keep your testing program interesting, useful, and reliable. As a university student, you are probably most experienced with testing for measuring achievement, but, when teaching in grades 4 through 9, you will use tests for other reasons as well. Other purposes for which tests are used include

- To assess and aid in curriculum development
- To help determine teaching effectiveness
- To help students develop positive attitudes, appreciations, and values
- To help students increase their understanding and retention of facts, principles, skills, and concepts
- To motivate students
- To provide diagnostic information for planning for individualization of the instruction
- To provide review and drill to enhance teaching and learning
- To serve as a source of information for students and parents.

When and How Often to Test for Achievement

It is difficult to generalize about how often to test for student achievement, but we believe that testing should be cumulative and frequent—that is, each assessment should measure the student's understanding of previously learned material as well as of the current unit of study, and testing should occur as often as once a week. Advantages of assessment that is cumulative include the review, reinforcement, and articulation of old material with the recent. The advantages of frequent assessment include a reduction in student anxiety over tests and an increase in the validity of final grades.

Test Construction

After determining the reasons for which you are designing and administering a test, you need to identify the specific instructional objectives the test is being designed to measure. (As you learned in the previous chapter, your written instructional objectives are specific so that you can write test items to measure against those objectives.) So, the first step in test construction is identification of the purpose(s) of the test. The second step is to identify the objectives to be measured, and the third step is to prepare the test items. The best time to prepare draft items is after you have prepared your instructional objectives; that is, while the objectives are fresh in your mind, which means before the lessons are taught. After a lesson has been taught, you will want to rework your first draft of the test items for that lesson to make any modifications as a result of what was taught and learned.

Administering Tests

For many students, test taking can be a time of high anxiety. To more accurately measure student achievement, you will want to take steps to reduce that anxiety. Students demonstrate test anxiety in various ways. Just before and during testing some are quiet and thoughtful, while others are noisy and disruptive. To control or reduce student anxieties, consider the following guidelines when administering tests.

Since students respond best to familiar routines, plan your program so tests are given at regular intervals (perhaps the same day each week) and administered at the same time and in the same way. In some junior high schools, days of the week for administering major tests are assigned to departments. For example, Tuesdays might be assigned for language arts testing, while Wednesdays are for social studies testing.

Avoid writing tests that are too long and that will take too much time. Sometimes beginning teachers have unreasonable expectations of students' attention spans during testing. Frequent testing with frequent sampling of student knowledge is preferred over infrequent and long tests that attempt to cover everything.

When giving paper-and-pencil tests, try to arrange the classroom so it is well ventilated, the temperature is comfortable, and the seats are well spaced. If spacing is a problem, consider using alternate forms of the test—giving students seated adjacent to one another different forms of the same test, for example, with multiple-choice answer alternatives arranged in different order.

Before test time be certain that you have a sufficient number of copies of the test. Although this may sound trite, we have known too many instances of teachers' starting testing with an insufficient number of test copies. Perhaps the test was duplicated for the teacher by someone else and a mistake was made in the number run off. However it is done, to avoid a serious problem, be sure you have sufficient copies of the test.

Before distributing the test, explain to students what they are to do when finished, such as begin a homework assignment, because not all of the students will finish at the same time. Rather than expecting students to sit quietly after finishing a test, give them something to do.

When ready to test, don't drag it out. Distribute tests quickly and efficiently. Once testing has begun, avoid interrupting the students. Important information can be written on the board or saved until all are finished with the test. During testing, remain in the room and visually monitor the students. If the test is not going to take an entire class period (and most shouldn't) and it's a major test, give it at the beginning of the period if possible, unless you are planning a test review just prior to it. Both just prior to and immediately after a major test, it's improbable that any teacher can create a high degree of student interest in a lesson.

Cheating

Cheating on tests does occur, but you can take steps to discourage it or to reduce the opportunity and pressure to cheat. Consider the following:

1. Space students or, as mentioned before, use alternate forms of the test.
2. Frequent testing and not allowing a single test to count too much reduce test anxiety and the pressure that can cause cheating and increase student learning by "stimulating greater effort and providing intermittent feedback" to the student (Walberg, 1990, p. 472).
3. Prepare test questions that are clear and not ambiguous, thereby reducing the frustration caused by a question or instructions that students do not understand.
4. As said before, avoid tests that are too long and that will take too much time. During long tests, some students get discouraged and restless, and that is when classroom management problems can occur.
5. Performance tests, by their shear nature, can cause even greater pressure on students and also provide more opportunity for cheating. When administering performance tests to an entire class, it is best to have several monitors or, if that isn't possible, to test groups of students, such as cooperative learning groups, rather than individuals. Evaluation of test performance, then, would be based on group rather than individual achievement.

6. Consider using open-text and open-notebook tests. When students can use their books and pages of notes, it not only reduces anxiety but helps them with the organization and retention of what has been learned.

If you suspect cheating *is* occurring, move to the area of the suspected student. Usually that will stop it. When you suspect cheating *has* occurred, you are faced with a dilemma. Unless your suspicion is backed by solid proof, you are advised to forget it, but keep a close watch on the student the next time to prevent cheating from happening. Your job is not to catch students being dishonest, but to prevent it. If you have absolute proof that a student has cheated, then you are obligated to proceed with school policy on student cheating, and that may call for a session with the counselor or the student and the student's parent or guardian, and perhaps an automatic F grade on the test, or even suspension.

Time Needed to Take a Test

Again, avoid giving tests that are too long and that will take too much time. Preparing and administering good tests is a skill that you will develop over time. In the meantime, it is best to test frequently and to use tests that sample student achievement rather than try for a comprehensive measure of that achievement.

Some students take more time on the same test than do others. You want to avoid giving too much time, or classroom management problems will result. On the other hand, you don't want to cut short the time needed by students who can do well but need more time to think and to write. As a guide for determining the approximate amount of time to allow students to complete a test, see Table 5.1. For example, a test made up of ten multiple-choice items, five arrangement items, and two short-explanation items should require about 30 minutes for a group of students to complete.

J. PREPARING ASSESSMENT ITEMS

Writing good assessment items is yet another professional skill, and to become proficient at it takes study, time, and practice. Because of the recognized importance of an assessment program, please approach this professional charge seriously and responsibly. Although poorly prepared items take no time at all to prepare, they will cause you more trouble than you can ever imagine. As a professional, you should take the time to study different types of assessment items that can be used and how best to write them, then practice writing them. When preparing assessment items, you should ensure that they match and sufficiently cover the instructional objectives. In addition, you should prepare each item carefully enough to be reasonably confident that it will be understood by the student in the manner that you anticipate its being understood.

Classification of Assessment Items

Assessment items can be classified as verbal (oral or written words), visual (pictures and diagrams), and manipulative or performance based (handling of materials and equipment).

TABLE 5.1
Time to Allow for Testing as Determined by the Types of Assessment Items

TYPE OF TEST ITEM	TIME NEEDED PER ITEM
matching	1 minute per matching item
multiple choice	1 minute per item
completion	1 minute per item
completion drawing	2–3 minutes
arrangement	2–3 minutes
identification	2–3 minutes
short explanation	2–3 minutes
essay and performance	10 or more minutes

Written verbal items have traditionally been most frequently used in testing. However, visual tests are useful, for example, when working with students who lack fluency in the written word or testing for the knowledge of students who have limited proficiency in English.

Performance and Alternative Assessment

Performance items and tests are useful when measuring psychomotor skill development, as is common in performance testing of locomotor skills, such as a student's ability to manipulate a compass or to carry a microscope (gross motor skill) or to focus a microscope (fine motor skill). Performance testing can also be a part of a wider testing program that includes testing for higher-level skills and knowledge, as when a student or small group of children are given the task (objective) of creating from discarded materials a habitat for an imaginary animal, and then displaying and describing their product to the rest of the class.

As mentioned earlier, educators today have a rekindled interest in performance testing as a more authentic means of assessing learning. In a program for teacher preparation, the student teaching experience is an example of performance assessment, that is, it is used to assess the teacher candidate's ability to teach. Most of us would probably agree that student teaching is a more authentic assessment of a candidate's ability to teach than is a written (paper-and-pencil test) or verbal (oral test) assessment.

Performance testing is usually more expensive than is verbal, and verbal testing is more time consuming and expensive than is written testing. Regardless, a good program of assessment will use alternate forms of assessment and not rely solely on one form (such as written) or only on one type of that form (such as multiple choice).

The type of test and items you use depend on your purpose and objectives. Carefully consider the alternatives within that framework. As noted, a good assessment program will likely include all three types of items to provide validity checks and to account for the individual differences of students. That is what writers of articles in professional journals are referring to when they talk about alternative assessment. They are encouraging the use of multiple assessment items, as opposed to the traditional heavy reliance on objective items such as multiple-choice questions.

General Guidelines for Preparing Assessment Items

In preparing assessment items, you should

1. Include several kinds of items.
2. Ensure that content coverage is complete, that is, that all objectives are being measured.
3. Ensure that each item of the test is reliable, that it measures the intended objective. One way to check item reliability is to have more than one test item measuring for the same objective.
4. Ensure that each item is clear and unambiguous.
5. Plan the item to be difficult enough for the poorly prepared student but easy enough for the student who is well prepared.
6. Maintain a bank of your assessment items, with each item coded according to its matching instructional objective and domain (cognitive, affective, or psychomotor); perhaps according to its level within the hierarchy of that particular domain; and according to whether it requires low-level recall, processing, or application. Computer software programs are available for this purpose. Ready-made test item banks are available on computer disks and accompany many programs or textbooks. If you use them, be certain that the items match your course objectives and that they are well written. Some state departments of education have made efforts to develop test banks for teachers. For example, see Willis (1990). When preparing items for your own test bank, use your best creative writing skills—prepare items that match your objectives, put them aside, think about them, then rework them. Because writing good assessment items is so time consuming, maintaining a test bank will save you valuable time.

The test you administer to your students should represent your best professional effort and so be free of spelling and grammar errors. A quickly and poorly prepared test can cause you more grief than you can imagine. One that is obviously hurriedly prepared and fraught with spelling errors will quickly be frowned upon by discerning parents or guardians and, if you are a student teacher, will certainly bring about a strong admonishment from your university supervisor. If the sloppiness continues, expect your speedy dismissal from the program.

Attaining Content Validity

To ensure that your test measures what is supposed to be measured, you can construct a table of specifications. This two-way grid indicates behavior in one dimension and content in the other (Figures 5.3a and 5.3b). In this grid, behavior relates to the three domains: cognitive, affective, and psychomotor. In Figure 5.3a, the cognitive domain, involving mental processes, is divided according to Bloom's taxonomy (Chapter 4) into six categories: (1) knowledge or simple recall, (2) comprehension, (3) application, (4) analysis, (5) synthesis (often involving an original product in oral or written form), and (6) evaluation. The specifications table of Figure 5.3a does not specify levels within the affective and psychomotor domains.

To use a table of specifications, the teacher examining objectives for the unit decides what emphasis should be given to the behavior and to the content. For instance, if vocabulary development is a concern for this sixth-grade study of Ancient Greece, then probably having 20 percent of the test be on vocabulary is appropriate, but 50 percent would be unsuitable. This planning enables the teacher to design a test to fit the situation, rather than a haphazard test that does not correspond to the content or behavior objectives.

Since knowledge questions are easy to write, tests often fail to go beyond that level even though the objectives state that the student will analyze and evaluate. The sample table of specifications for a social studies unit on Ancient Greece indicates a distribution of questions on a test. Since this test is to be an objective test and it is so difficult to write objective items to test analysis, synthesis, and affective and psychomotor behavior, this table of specifications calls for no test items in these areas. If these categories are included in the unit objectives, some other additional assessment devices must be used to test learning in these categories. The teacher could also show the objectives tested, as indicated within parentheses in Figure 5.3a. Then, a later check on inclusion of all objectives would be easy.

The alternative table shown in Figure 5.3b is preferred by some teachers. Rather than differentiating among all six of Bloom's cognitive levels, this table separates cognitive objectives into just three levels—those that require simple low-level recall of knowledge, those that require information processing, and those that require application of the new knowledge (refer to "Levels of Cognitive Questions and Student Thinking" in Chapter 4). In addition, in this table the affective and psychomotor domains are each divided into low- and high-level behaviors. A third alternative, not illustrated here, is a table of specifications that shows all levels of each of the three domains.

K. SPECIFIC GUIDELINES FOR PREPARING ITEMS FOR USE IN ASSESSMENT

The section that follows presents the advantages, disadvantages, and guidelines for use of 12 types of assessment items. When reading the advantages and disadvantages of each type, you will notice that some types are appropriate for use in direct or performance assessment, while others are not.

Arrangement Type

Description. Terms or real objects (realia) are to be arranged in a specified order.

Example. Arrange the following list of events in order of occurrence. (List of events not included here.)

Advantages. This type of item tests for knowledge of sequence and order and is good for review, for starting discussions, and for performance assessment.

Disadvantages. Scoring may be difficult, so be cautious and meticulous when using this type for grading purposes.

FIGURE 5.3A
Table of Specifications I

CONTENT	BEHAVIORS								TOTAL
Socail Studies Grade 6	Cognitive						Affective	Psychomotor	
Electromagnetism	Knowledge	Comprehension	Application	Analysis	Synthesis	Evaluation			
I. Vocabulary Development		2 (1, 2)	3 (2)						
II. Concepts		2 (3, 4)	1 (4)						
III. Applications	1 (5)	1				1 (5)			
IV. Problem solving		1 (6)							
TOTAL	1	6	4			1			12

FIGURE 5.3B
Table of Specifications II

CONTENT	BEHAVIORS							TOTAL
	Cognitive			Affective		Psychomotor		
	Input	Processing	Application	Low	High	Low	High	
I.								
II.								
III.								
IV.								
TOTAL								

Guideline for use. To enhance reliability, you may need to include instructions to students to include the rationale for their arrangement, making it a combined arrangement and short-explanation type. Allow space for explanations on an answer sheet.

Completion-Drawing Type

Description. An incomplete drawing is presented, and the student is to complete it.

Example. Connect the following items with arrow lines to show the stages from introduction of a new bill until it becomes law.

Advantages. This type requires less time than is required for a complete drawing, as may be required in an essay item. Scoring is relatively easy.

Disadvantages. Care needs to be exercised in the instructions so students do not misinterpret the expectation.

Guidelines for use. Use occasionally for diversion, but take care in preparing. This type can be instructive when assessing for student thinking. Consider making the item a combined completion-drawing, short-explanation type by having students include their rationales for their drawings. Be sure to allow space for their explanations.

Completion-Statement Type

Description. An incomplete sentence is presented, and the student is to complete it by filling in the blank space(s).

Example 1. A group of words that have a special meaning, such as "a skeleton in the closet," is called a(n) _____.

Example 2. To test their hypotheses, social scientists conduct _____.

Advantages. This type is easy to devise, to take, and to score.

Disadvantages. When using this type, there is a tendency to emphasize rote memory. It is difficult to write this type of item to measure for higher levels of cognition. You must be alert for a correct response different from the expected. For example, although the teacher's key has "experiments" as the correct answer for Example 2, a student might answer the question with "investigations," "tests," or some other response that is equally correct.

Guideline for use. Use occasionally for review or for preassessment of student knowledge. Unless you can write quality items that extend student thinking beyond mere recall, you are advised to avoid using the type for grading. In all instances, avoid copying items verbatim from the student book. As with all types, be sure to provide adequate space for students' answers.

Correction Type

Description. Similar to the completion type, except that sentences or paragraphs are complete but with italicized or underlined words that can be changed to make the sentence correct.

Example. The work of the TVA was started by building *sand castles*. A *sand castle* is a wall built across a *kid* to stop its flow. The *sand castle* holds back the *football* so the *kids* do not overflow their *backpacks* and cause *tears*.

Advantages. Writing this type for the purpose of preassessment of student knowledge or for review can be fun for the teacher. Students may enjoy this type for the tension relief afforded by the incorrect absurdities. Can be useful for introducing words with multiple meanings.

Disadvantages. Like the completion type, the correction type tends to measure for low-level recall and rote memory. The underlined incorrect items could be so whimsical that they might cause more classroom disturbance than you want.

Guidelines for use. Use occasionally for diversion and discussion. Try to write items that measure for higher-level cognition. Consider making it a combined correction, short-explanation type. Be sure to allow space for student explanations.

Essay Type

Description. A question or problem is presented, and the student is to compose a response in the form of sustained prose, using the student's own words, phrases, and ideas, within the limits of the question or problem.

Example 1. In the story just read, does the author elaborate upon the setting in great detail or barely sketch it? Explain your response.

Example 2. Name the factors considered to be causes of the Civil War and describe why each was a cause.

Advantages. Measures higher mental processes, such as ability to synthesize material and to express ideas in clear and precise written language. Especially useful in integrated thematic teaching. Provides practice in written expression.

Disadvantages. Essay items require a good deal of time to read and to score. They tend to provide an unreliable sampling of achievement and are vulnerable to teacher subjectivity and unreliable scoring. Furthermore, they tend to punish the student who writes slowly and laboriously, who has limited proficiency in the written language, but who may have achieved as well as a student who writes faster and is more proficient in the language. Essay items tend to favor students who have fluency with words but whose achievement may not necessarily be better. In addition, unless the students have been given instruction in their meaning and in how to respond to them, the teacher should not assume that all students understand key directive verbs, such as *explain* in the first example.

Guidelines for use:

1. When preparing an essay-only test, many questions, each requiring a relatively short prose response (see "Short-Explanation Type"), are preferable to a smaller number of questions requiring long prose responses. Briefer answers tend to be more precise, and many items provide a more reliable sampling of student achievement. When preparing short prose response-type questions, be sure to avoid using words verbatim from the student textbook.
2. Allow students adequate test time for a full response.
3. Different qualities of achievement are more likely comparable when all students must answer the same questions, as opposed to selecting those they answer from a list.
4. After preparing essay items, make a tentative scoring key, deciding the key ideas you expect students to identify and how many points will be allotted to each.
5. Students should be informed about the relative test value of each essay item. Point values, if different for each item, can be listed in the margin next to each item.
6. When reading student essay responses, read all student answers one item at a time. While doing that, make notes to yourself, then read all the answers again, scoring each student's paper for that item. Repeat the process for the next item. While scoring essay responses, keep in mind the nature of the objective being measured, which may or may not include handwriting, grammar, spelling, and neatness.
7. To nullify the "halo effect," some teachers have students write a number code rather than their names on essay papers. That way, the teacher is unaware of whose paper is being read. If you do this, use caution not to misplace or confuse the identification codes.
8. While they have some understanding of a concept, many students are not yet facile with written expression, so you must remember to be patient, tolerant, positive, and helpful. Mark papers with positive and constructive comments, showing students how they could have explained or responded better.
9. Prior to using this type of test item, give instruction and practice to students in responding to key directive verbs that will be used (see Jenkinson, 1988, for example):

Compare asks for an analysis of similarity and difference, but with a greater emphasis on similarities or likenesses.

Contrast asks more for differences than for similarities.

Criticize asks for the good and bad aspects of an idea or situation.

Define asks the student to express clearly and concisely the meaning of a term, as in the dictionary or in the student's own words.

Diagram asks the student to put quantities or numerical values into the form of a chart, graph, or drawing.

Discuss asks the student to explain or argue, presenting various sides of events, ideas, or situations.

Enumerate means to count or list one after another, which is different than "explain briefly" or "tell in a few words."

Evaluate means to express worth, value, and judgment.

Explain means to describe, with emphasis on cause and effect.

Illustrate means to describe by means of examples, figures, pictures, or diagrams.

Interpret means to describe or explain a given fact, theory, principle, or doctrine in a specific context.

Justify asks the student to show reasons, with an emphasis on correct, positive, and advantageous aspects.

List means just that, to simply name items in a category or to include them in a list, without much description.

Outline means to give a short summary with headings and subheadings.

Prove means to present materials as witnesses, proof, and evidence.

Relate means to tell how specified things are connected or brought into some kind of relationship.

Summarize asks the student to recapitulate the main points without examples or illustrations.

Trace asks the student to follow a history or series of events step by step by going backward over the evidence.

Grouping Type

Description. Several items are presented, and the student is to select and group those that are related in some way.

Example 1. Separate the following words into two groups; place those that are homonyms in group A and those that are not in group B.

Example 2. Read each of the following statements, then circle those that imply prejudice.

Advantages. This type of item tests knowledge of grouping and can be used to measure for higher levels of cognition and to stimulate discussion. As in Example 2, it can be similar to a multiple-choice item.

Disadvantage. Remain alert for the student who has an alternative but valid rationale for grouping.

Guideline for use. To allow for an alternative correct response, consider making the item a combination grouping and short-explanation type, being certain to allow adequate space for student explanations.

Identification Type

Description. Unknown specimens are to be identified by name or some other criterion.

Example 1. Using the ten-volume *Our Own Encyclopedia* displayed on the table, identify the number of the volume in which you would find information about The People's Republic of China.

Example 2. Identify by name and use each of the research tools on the table.

Advantages. Verbalization (the use of abstract symbolization) is less significant, as the student is working with real objects. This item should measure higher-level learning than simple recall. It can also be written to measure procedural understanding (as in the first example), such as by asking for identification of steps in booting up a computer program. This is another useful type for authentic assessment.

Disadvantages. To be fair, specimens used should be equally familiar or unfamiliar to all students. Adequate materials must be provided.

Guidelines for use. If photographs, drawings, photocopies, and recordings are used, they must be clear and not confusing to students.

Matching Type

Description. Match related items from a list of numbered items to a list of lettered choices, or in some way connect those items that are the same or are related. Or, to eliminate the paper-and-pencil aspect and make the item more direct, use instructions such as, "Using the items from the table, pair up those that are most alike."

Example 1. In the blank space next to each cause in Column A put the letter from Column B of the result (or effect) that best matches each cause.

A (cause)

_____1. Automobiles were mass produced at low cost.

_____2. Workers needed to live close to their place of employment.

_____3. (etc.)

B (effect)

A. Immigrant workers came in large numbers.

B. People with average incomes purchased their own automobiles.

C. (etc.)

D. (etc.)

Example 2. Match items in Column A (stem column) to those of Column B (answer column) by drawing lines between the matched pairs.

Column A	*Column B*
ann/enn	conquer
auto	large
min	self
vic/vinc	small
(etc.)	year
	(etc.)

Advantages. Can measure ability to judge relationships and to differentiate between similar ideas, facts, definitions, and concepts. Easy to score. Can test a broad range of content. Reduces guessing, especially if one group contains more items than the other. Interesting to students. Adaptable for performance assessment.

Disadvantages. Not easily adapted to measuring for higher cognition. Because all parts must be homogeneous, it is possible that clues will be given, thus reducing item validity. A student might have a legitimate rationale for an "incorrect" response.

Guidelines for use. The number of items in the answer column should exceed the number in the stem column. The number of items to be matched should not exceed 12. Matching sets should have high homogeneity, that is, items in both columns (or groups) should be of the same general category. If answers can be used more than once, the directions should so state. Be prepared for the student who can legitimately defend an "incorrect" response.

Multiple-Choice Type

Description. Similar to the completion item in that statements are presented, sometimes in incomplete form, along with several options. Requires recognition or even higher cognitive processes, rather than mere recall.

Example 1. Using the map shown above, if you were to go from where you are now (marked on the map) to New York City, what direction must you travel?

a. East

b. West

c. North

d. South

Example 2. Which one of the following is a pair of antonyms?

a. loud—soft

b. halt—finish

c. absolve—vindicate

d. procure—purchase

Advantages. Items can be answered and scored quickly. A wide range of content and higher levels of cognition can be tested in a relatively short time. Excellent for all testing purposes—motivation, review, and assessment of learning.

Disadvantages. Unfortunately, because multiple-choice items are relatively easy to write, there is a tendency to write items measuring only for low levels of cognition. Multiple-choice items are excellent for major testing, but it takes time to write quality questions that measure higher levels of learning.

Guidelines for use:

1. If the item is in the form of an incomplete statement, it should be meaningful in itself and imply a direct question rather than merely lead into a collection of unrelated true and false statements.
2. Use a level of language that is easy enough for even the poorest readers to understand, and avoid unnecessary wordiness.
3. If there is much variation in the length of alternatives, arrange the alternatives in order from shortest to longest.
4. Consistent alphabetical arrangement of single-word alternatives is recommended.
5. Incorrect responses (distracters) should be plausible and related to the same concept as the correct alternative. Although an occasional humorous distracter helps to relieve test anxiety, they should be avoided. They offer no measuring value.
6. Alternatives should be uniformly arranged throughout the test and listed in vertical (column) form rather than in horizontal (paragraph) form.
7. Every item should be grammatically consistent; for example, if the stem is in the form of an incomplete sentence, it should be possible to complete the sentence by attaching any of the alternatives to it.
8. It is not necessary to maintain a fixed number of alternatives for every item, but the use of less than three is not recommended. The use of four or five reduces chance responses and guessing, thereby increasing reliability for the item.
9. The item should be expressed in positive form. A negative form presents a psychological disadvantage to students. Negative items are those that ask what is *not* characteristic of something or what is the *least* useful. Discard the item if you cannot express it in positive terminology.
10. Responses such as "all of these" or "none of these" should be used only when they will contribute more than another plausible distracter. Care must be taken that such responses answer or complete the item. "All of the above" is a poorer alternative than "none of the above" because items that use it as a correct response need to have four or five correct answers; also, if it is the right answer, knowledge of any two of the distracters will cue it.
11. There must be only one correct or best response. This is easier said than done (refer to guideline 19).
12. The stem must mean the same thing to every student.
13. Measuring for understanding of definitions is better tested by furnishing the name or word and requiring choice between alternative definitions than by presenting the definition and requiring choice between alternative words.
14. The stem should state a single and specific point.
15. The stem must not clue the correct alternative. Consider, for example, "A four-sided figure whose opposite sides are parallel is called _____. a. an octagon b. a parallelogram c. a trapezoid d. a triangle" The use of the word *parallel* clues the answer.
16. Avoid using alternatives that include absolute terms such as *never* and *always*.
17. Multiple-choice items need not be entirely verbal. Consider the use of realia, charts, diagrams, and other visuals. They will make the test more interesting, especially to students with low verbal abilities or limited proficiency in English and, consequently, make the assessment more authentic.
18. Once you have composed a multiple-choice test, tally the position of answers to be sure they are evenly distributed to avoid the common psychological mistake (when there are four alternatives) of having the correct alternative in the third position.

19. Consider providing space between test items for students to include their rationales for their response selections, thus making the test a combination multiple-choice and short-explanation item type. This provides for the student who can rationalize an alternative that you had not considered plausible. It also provides for the measurement of higher levels of cognition and encourages student writing.

20. While scoring, on a blank copy of the test, tally the incorrect responses for each item. Analyze these to discover potential errors in your scoring key. If, for example, many students select "b" for an item and your key says "a" is the correct answer, you may have made a mistake in your scoring key or in teaching the lesson.

Performance Type

Description. Provided with certain conditions or materials, the student solves a problem or accomplishes some other action.

Example 1. Create your own writing system using hieroglyphics.

Example 2. Write a retelling of your favorite fable on the computer and create a diorama to go along with it.

Advantages. Performance test item types come closer to direct measurement (authentic assessment) of certain expected outcomes than do most other types, although other types of questions can be prepared as performance-type items.

Disadvantages. The item can be difficult and time consuming to administer to a group of students. Scoring may tend to be subjective. It could be difficult to give make-up tests to students who were absent.

Guidelines for use. Use your creativity to design and use performance tests, as they tend to measure the most important objectives. To reduce subjectivity in scoring, prepare distinct scoring guidelines, as was discussed in the section on scoring essay-type questions. To set up a performance test situation you should

1. Specify the performance objective.
2. Specify the test situation or conditions.
3. Establish the criteria (scoring rubric) for judging the excellence of the process and/or product.
4. Make a checklist by which to score the performance or product. (This checklist is simply a listing of the criteria you established in step 3. It would be impossible to use a rating scale; ordinarily, a rating scale makes scoring too complicated.)
5. Prepare directions in writing, outlining the situation, with instructions for the students to follow.

   For example, this is a checklist for map work:

   Check each item if the map comes up to standard in this particular category.

   _____ 1. Accuracy.
   _____ 2. Neatness.
   _____ 3. Attention to details.

   And here is a sample rubric for assessing a student's skill in listening.

   A. Strong listener: characteristics
      Responds immediately to oral directions
      Focuses on speaker
      Maintains appropriate attention span
      Listens to what others are saying
      Is interactive

   B. Capable listener: characteristics
      Follows oral directions

Usually attentive to speaker and to discussions
Listens to others without interrupting
C. Developing listener: characteristics
Has difficulty following directions
Relies on repetition
Often inattentive
Short attention span
Often interrupts the speaker

Short-Explanation Type

Description. The short-explanation question is an essay type but requires a shorter answer.

Example 1. Briefly explain in a paragraph how you would end the story.

Example 2. Identify and explain two significant characteristics shared by Presidents Abraham Lincoln and John F.Kennedy.

Advantages. As in the essay type, the student's understanding is assessed, but this type takes less time for the teacher to read and to score. Several questions of this type can cover a greater amount of content than fewer essay questions. This type of question is good practice for students to learn to express themselves succinctly in writing.

Disadvantages. Some students will have difficulty expressing themselves in a limited fashion, or in writing. They need practice in doing so.

Guidelines for use. Useful for occasional reviews and quizzes and as an alternative to other types of questions. For scoring, establish a scoring rubric and follow the same guidelines as for the essay-type item.

True-False Type

Description. Students judge whether a statement is accurate or not.

Example 1. According to the newspaper article we read in class this week, the percentage of the population under age 10 is increasing. T or F?

Example 2. A suffix is any bound morpheme added to the end of a root word. T or F?

Advantages. Many items can be answered in a relatively short time, making broad content coverage possible. Scoring is quick and simple. True-false items are good for starting discussions, for review, and for diagnostic evaluation (preassessment).

Disadvantages. It is sometimes difficult to write true-false items that are purely true or false without qualifying them in such a way that clues the answer. Much of the content that most easily lends itself to this type of test item is trivial. Students have a 50 percent chance of guessing the correct answer, thus giving this item type poor validity and poor reliability. Scoring and grading give no clue as to why the student missed an item. The disadvantages of true-false items far outweigh the advantages; pure true-false items should *never* be used for arriving at grades. For grading purposes, you may use modified true-false items, where space is provided between items for students to write in explanations, thus making the item a combined true-false, short-explanation type.

Guidelines for preparing true-false items:
1. First write the statement as a true statement, then make it false by changing a word or phrase.
2. Avoid using negative statements since they tend to confuse students.

3. A true-false statement should include only one idea.

4. Use close to an equal number of true and false items.

5. Avoid specific determiners, which may clue that the statement is false—for example, "always," "all," or "none."

6. Avoid words that may clue that the statement is true, such as "often," "probably," and "sometimes."

7. Avoid words that may have different meanings for different students.

8. Avoid using verbatim language from the student textbook.

9. Avoid trick items.

10. To avoid "wrong" answers caused by variations in thinking, students should be encouraged to write in their rationale for selecting true or false. As stated earlier, for grading purposes, you may use modified true-false items, where space is provided between items for students to write in their explanations, thus making the item a combined true-false, short-explanation type. Another form of modified true-false item is the use of "sometimes-always-never," where a third alternative, "sometimes," is introduced to reduce the chance of guessing a correct answer.

L. REPORTING STUDENT ACHIEVEMENT

One of your major responsibilities as a classroom teacher is to report student progress in achievement to parents or guardians. In some schools the reporting is of student progress and effort as well as achievement. Reporting is done in at least two and sometimes three ways, described as follows.

The Grade Report

Every six to nine weeks a grade report (report card) is issued (from four to six times a year, depending on the school district). This grade report represents an achievement grade (formative evaluation), and the second or third one of the semester is also the semester grade. For courses that are only one semester long, it is also the final grade (summative evaluation). In essence, the first and sometimes second reports are progress notices, with the semester grade being the one that is transferred to the student's transcript of records. In some schools the traditional report card is marked and sent home either with the student or by mail. In many schools, reporting is done by computer printouts, often sent by mail directly to the student's home address. (In some schools, as an effort to involve them, parents or guardians are expected to come to the school on a given day and pick up the grade report.) Computer printouts might list all the subjects or courses taken by the student while enrolled at the school.

Whichever reporting form is used, you must separate your assessment of a student's social behaviors (classroom conduct) from that of the student's academic achievement. Academic achievement (or accomplishment) is represented by a letter (sometimes a number) grade (A through E or F; or E, S, and U; or 1 to 5; and sometimes with minuses and pluses), and social behavior by a "satisfactory" or an "unsatisfactory" or by more specific items, sometimes supplemented by the teacher's written or computer-generated comments. In some instances there is a location on the reporting form for the teacher to check whether basic grade-level standards have been met in language arts, mathematics, science, and social studies. See Figure 5.4.

Direct Contact with Parents

Although not always obligatory, some teachers contact parents or guardians by telephone, especially when a student has shown a sudden turn either for the worse or for the better in academic achievement or in classroom behavior. That initiative by the teacher is usually welcomed by parents and can lead to private and productive conferences with the teacher. A telephone conversation saves valuable time for both the teacher and the parent.

Another way of contacting parents is by letter. Contacting a parent by letter gives you time to think, to make clear your thoughts and concerns to that parent, and to invite the parent to respond at the parent's convenience by letter, by phone, or by arranging to have a conference with you.

FIGURE 5.4
Sample Progress Report

Progress Report Form

STUDENT'S NAME: _____ GRADE: _____ YEAR: _____

TEACHER: _____ SCHOOL: _____

SYMBOLS: ACHIEVEMENT AND EFFORT
A = Outstanding
B = Good
C = Satisfactory
D = Unsatisfactory
F = Failing

HONORS STUDENT: 1st Qtr. ☐   2nd Qtr. ☐   3rd Qtr. ☐   4th Qtr. ☐

SUBJECTS	1st Quarter	2nd Quarter	3rd Quarter	4th Quarter
Reading				
Mathematics				
Language				
Social Studies				
Spelling				
Science				

Citizenship				
Physical Education				
Handwriting				
Art				
Music				

O = Outstanding
G = Good
S = Satisfactory
N = Needs Improvement
U = Unsatisfactory

The Basic Grade Level Standards have been satisfactorily passed in:

Reading ☐   Mathematics ☐   Language ☐

FIRST QUARTER PROGRESS REPORT COMMENTS: _____
_____
_____
_____

SECOND QUARTER PROGRESS REPORT COMMENTS: _____
_____
_____
_____

THIRD QUARTER PROGRESS REPORT COMMENTS: _____
_____
_____
_____

FOURTH QUARTER PROGRESS REPORT COMMENTS: _____
_____
_____
_____

ASSIGNMENT FOR NEXT YEAR: _____
_____
_____

Conferences and Meetings with Parents

You will meet many parents or guardians early in the school year during Back-to-School Night and throughout the year in individual parent conferences. For the beginning teacher, these meetings with parents can be anxious times. Here are guidelines to help you with those experiences.

Back-to-School Night is the evening early in the school year when parents can come to the school and meet their child's teachers. The parents arrive at the child's homebase and then proceed through a simulation of their son's or daughter's school day, and as a group meet each class and each teacher for a few minutes. Later, there is an "Open House," where parents may have more time to talk individually with teachers, but Open House is usually a time for the school and teachers to show off the work and progress of the students for that year. Throughout the school year there will be opportunities for you and parents to meet and to talk about the children.

At Back-to-School Night. On this evening parents are anxious to learn as much as they can about their child's new teachers. You will meet each group of parents for about ten minutes. During that brief meeting you will provide them with a copy of the course syllabus, make some straightforward remarks about yourself, then briefly discuss your expectations of the students.

Although there will be precious little time for questions from the parents, during your introduction the parents will be delighted to learn that you have your program well planned, are a taskmaster, and will communicate with them. The parents and guardians will be pleased to know that you are from the school of the three F's—firm, friendly, and fair.

Specifically, parents will expect to learn about your curriculum—goals and objectives, any long-term projects, and testing and grading procedures. They will need to know what you expect of them: Will there be homework, and if so, should they help their children with it? How can they contact you? Try to anticipate other questions. Your principal, department chair, or colleagues can be of aid in helping you anticipate and prepare for these questions. Of course, you can never prepare for the question that comes from left field. Just stay calm and don't get flustered. Ten minutes will fly by quickly, and parents will be reassured to know you are an in-control person.

As parents who have attended many back-to-school nights at the schools our children have attended, we continue to be both surprised and dismayed that so few teachers seem well prepared for the few minutes they have with the parents. Considering how often we hear about teachers wanting more involvement of parents, so few seem delighted that parents have indeed come, and so few take full advantage of this time with parents to truly celebrate their programs.

Parent-Teacher Conference. When meeting parents for conferences, you should be as specific as possible when explaining the progress of their child in your class. Help them understand, but don't saturate them with more information than they need. Resist any tendency to talk too much. Allow time for the parent to ask questions. Keep your answers succinct. Never compare one student with another or with the rest of the class. If the parent asks a question for which you do not have an answer, say you will try to find an answer and will phone the parent as quickly as you can. And do it. Have the student's portfolio and other work with you during parent conferences so you can show the parent examples of what is being discussed. Also have your grade book or a computer printout of it on hand, but be prepared to conceal from the parent the names and records of the other students.

Sometimes it is helpful to have a three-way conference, a conference with the parent, the student, and you, or a conference with the parent, the principal or counselor, and several or all of the student's teachers.

Ideas for Teacher-Parent Collaboration

When a parent asks how she or he may help in the child's learning, here are suggestions for your consideration:

- As needed, plan short family meetings after dinner, but while you are still seated at the table. Ask for a "tableside report" on what's happening in school. Ask, "How can I help?" When your child expresses a concern, emphasize ways to solve problems that occur. Help the child develop his or her problem-solving skills.
- Ask your child to share with you each day one specific thing learned that day.
- Consider having students take their portfolios home each Friday to share with their parents, having a place in the portfolio where parents or guardians sign to show they have reviewed their child's work, and then having the student return the portfolio on Monday. The form for a parent's signature could also have a column for teacher and parent comments or notes to each other, to maintain this important line of communication between parent and teacher.
- Helping students become critical thinkers is one of the aims of education and one that parents can reinforce by asking "what if" questions, thinking aloud as a model for their child's thinking development, and encouraging the child's own metacognition by asking questions such as, "How did you arrive at that conclusion?" or "How do you feel about your conclusion now?" Ask these questions about the child's everyday social interactions and topics that are important to the child; ask your child to elaborate on his or her ideas, allowing him or her to make mistakes and learn from them.
- Limit and control the child's pleasure viewing of television.
- Set up a regular schedule of reviewing with the child his or her portfolio.
- Set up a regular time each evening for a family discussion about school.
- Several books are available for parents to use at home. For example, the United States government has a variety of free or low-cost booklets available. For information, contact the Consumer Information Center, Department TH, Pueblo, CO 81109. Other useful resources are *Helping Your Child Use the Library* (item 465V); *Becoming a Nation of Readers: What Parents Can Do* (item 459V); and *Help Your Child Do Better at School* (item 412V). You also can encourage the parent to go to the neighborhood public library and ask for a librarian's help in locating helpful resources. If you and parents are interested in strategies for increasing home-school collaboration, read *Beyond the Bake Sale: An Educator's Guide to Working with Parents* (Columbia, MD: National Committee for Citizens in Education, 1985) by Anne T. Henderson, Carl Marburger, and Theodora Ooms; the special section, "Parent Involvement," in *Phi Delta Kappan* (volume 72, no. 5, January 1991); *Communicating with Parents* by Janet Chrispeels, Marcia Boruta, and Mary Daugherty (San Diego: San Diego County Office of Education, 1988); *The Evidence Continues to Grow: Parent Involvement Improves Student Achievement* (Columbia, MD: National Committee for Citizens in Education, 1987); and *Parenting for Education* by Paula Lowe and Carl Trendler (Seattle: U.S. West Education Foundation, 1989).

Dealing with an Angry Parent

If a parent or guardian is angry or hostile towards you and the school, here are guidelines for dealing with that hostility:

- Remain calm in your discussion with the parent, allowing the parent to talk out his or her hostility while you say very little. Usually, the less you say, the better off you will be. What you do say must be objective and to the point concerning the child's work in your classroom. The parent may just need to vent frustrations that have very little to do with you, the school, or even the child.
- Do *not* allow yourself to be intimidated or backed into a corner. If the parent tries to do so by attacking you personally, do not press your defense at this point. Perhaps the parent has made a point that you should take time to consider, and now is a good time to arrange for another conference with the parent for about a week later. In a follow-up conference, if agreed to by the parent, you may want to bring in a mediator, such as another member of your teaching team, an administrator, or a school counselor.
- You must *not* talk about other students; keep the conversation focused on this parent's child's progress. The parent is *not* your rival. You both share a concern for the acade-

mic and emotional well-being of the child. Use your best skills in critical thinking and problem solving, trying to focus the discussion by identifying the problem, defining it, and then arriving at some decision about how mutually to go about solving it. To this end you may need to ask for help from a third party, such as the child's school counselor. Please take that step if agreed to by the parent.

- Parents do *not* need to hear about how busy you are, or about your personal problems, or about how many other students you are dealing with on a daily basis, unless, of course, they ask. Parents expect you to be a capable professional who knows what to do and to be doing it.

SUMMARY

Since assessment is an integral factor in the teaching-learning process, you must aim to include the following in your teaching performance:

1. Use a variety of instruments to assess the learning of students that focus on their individual development. Keep students informed of their progress. Return tests promptly, review answers to all questions, and respond to inquiries about marks given.

2. Use assessment procedures continuously so as to contribute to the positive development of the individual student. Such an emphasis requires that the assessment be important to the student and related to what the student considers important. Effective assessment is helping the student know her or his competencies and achievements. It encourages further learning and the selection of appropriate tasks. The goals of assessment instruments should serve as a challenge, but they should be attainable. Goals set too high or tests that are too hard discourage students and so diminish the motivational factor. Goals set too low and questions that are too easy encourage disregard of the subject content taught and a lackadaisical approach to study.

3. Adapt the grading system of the school to your situation. Establish your own standard and grade each student in relation to it.

4. Avoid using grades as a threat or overstressing them for motivational purposes. It is legitimate to consider as tentative the grade you arrive at after consideration of the objective data that have been accumulated. Consideration of extenuating circumstances, such as sudden illness, prolonged absence for a serious matter, and so on, should then take place before marking permanent grades. Raising a borderline mark to the higher alternative in the light of classroom performance is indeed a professionally defensible decision. Almost never, though, is it prudent to award a lower grade to a student than that student has already earned on the basis of the objective data.

5. Consider your grading procedures carefully, plan them, and explain your policies to the students. The various factors to be considered in arriving at a grade and the weight accorded to such things as homework, written assignments, and oral contributions should all be explained before study is begun.

6. Involve the students, whenever feasible, in setting up criteria and establishing the relative importance of activities. Such cooperative planning is a learning experience for students and encourages self-assessment.

7. Make sure that students understand the directions on any assessments that you give. Before permitting students to begin, make sure to explain any ambiguities that result from the terminology used. Base your assessments on the material that has been taught. Your purpose in giving assessments, of course, is not to trap or confuse students but to evaluate how well they have assimilated the important aspects of learning.

8. Strive for objective and impartial assessment as you put your assessment plan into operation. Do not allow personal feelings to enter into a grade. Whether you like or dislike a student, the grade earned should reflect the student's level of achievement based on the same objective standard used for all.

9. Try to minimize arguments about grades, cheating, and teacher subjectivity by involving students in the planning, reinforcing individual student development, and provid-

ing an accepting, stimulating learning environment. Remain alert while students are taking a test. Do not occupy yourself with other tasks at your desk. Circulate, observe, and present at least a psychological deterrent to cheating by your demeanor and presence, but be sure not to distract.

10. Maintain accurate and clear records of assessment results so that you will have an adequate supply of data on which to base your judgmental decisions about achievement. Sufficient data of this sort are especially helpful when final grades are called into question or when students or parents require in-depth information.

Additional discussions of assessment specific to language arts and social studies are presented in Parts II and III.

QUESTIONS AND ACTIVITIES FOR DISCUSSION

1. Other than a paper-and-pencil test, identify three alternative assessment techniques for assessing student learning during or at completion of an integrated language arts and social studies unit.

2. Investigate various ways that intermediate and middle schools are experimenting today with assessing and reporting student achievement. Share what you find with your classmates. Analyze the pros and cons of various systems of assessing and reporting.

3. When using a point system for determining student grades for a class of students, is it educationally defensible to give a student a higher grade than that student's points call for? A lower grade? Give your rationale for your answers.

4. Explain the dangers in using true-false and completion-type items in assessing student learning in language arts and social studies and using the results for grade determination.

5. Explain the concept of "authentic assessment." Is it the same as "performance assessment"? Explain why or why not.

6. Describe any student learning activities in language arts and social studies that should *not* be graded but could be used for assessment of student learning.

7. For a specified grade level that you intend to teach, describe the items that you would use for determining grades in language arts and social studies and their relative weights. Explain your rationale for the percentage weight distribution.

8. Explain the value of and give a specific example of a performance test item that you would use in teaching language arts.

9. Explain the value of and give a specific example of a performance test item that you would use in teaching social studies.

10. From your current observations and fieldwork related to this teacher preparation program, clearly identify one specific example of educational practice that seems contradictory to exemplary practice or theory as presented in this chapter. Present your explanation for the discrepancy.

11. Describe any prior concepts you held that changed as a result of your experiences with this chapter. Describe the changes.

REFERENCES

Black, S. (1993). Portfolio assessment. *Executive Educator, 15*(1), 28–31.

Jenkinson, E. B. (1988). Practice helps with essay exams. *Phi Delta Kappan, 69*(10), 726.

Meyer, C. A. (1992). What's the difference between "authentic" and "performance" assessment? *Educational Leadership, 49*(8), 39–40.

O'Neil, J. (1993). Portfolio assessment bears the burden of popularity, *ASCD Update, 35*(8), 3, 8.

Rakow, S. J. (1992). Assessment: A driving force. *Science Scope, 15*(6), 3.

Tompkins, G. E., & Hoskisson, K. (1991). *Language arts: Content and teaching strategies.* New York: Macmillan.

Walberg, H. J. (1990). Productive teaching and instruction: Assessing the knowledge base. *Phi Delta Kappan, 71*(6), 470–478.

Willis, J. A. (1990). Learning outcome testing program: Standardized classroom testing in West Virginia through item banking, test generation, and curricular management software. *Educational Measurement: Issues and Practices, 9*(2) 11–14.

SUGGESTED READINGS

Abruscato, J. (1993). Early results and tentative implications from the Vermont Portfolio Project. *Phi Delta Kappan, 74*(6), 474–477.

Bracey, G. W. (1993). Assessing the new assessments. *Principal, 72*(3), 34–36.

Chambers, D. L. (1993). Standardized testing impedes reform. *Educational Leadership, 50*(5), 80–81.

Craig, E. (1993). Performance assessment and social studies: Making the connection. *Social Studies Review, 32*(2), 63–67.

Davis, S. J. (1994). Teaching practices that encourage or eliminate student plagiarism. *Middle School Journal, 25*(3), 55–58.

Ebel, R. L., & Frisbie, D. A. (1991). *Essentials of educational measurement* (5th ed.). Needham Heights, MA: Allyn & Bacon.

Feuer, M. J., & Fulton, K. (1993). The many faces of performance assessment. *Phi Delta Kappan, 74*(6), 478.

Goldman, J. P. (1989). Student portfolios already proven in some schools. *School Administrator, 46*(11), 11.

Grady, E. (1992). *The portfolio approach to assessment.* Fastback 341. Bloomington, IN: Phi Delta Kappa Educational Foundation.

Hansen, J. (1992). Evaluation: My portfolio shows who I am. *Quarterly of the National Writing Project and the Center for the Study of Writing and Literacy, 14*(1), 5–6, 9.

Harmon, J. L., Aschbacher, P., & Winters, L. (1992). *A practical guide to alternative assessment.* Alexandria, VA: Association for Supervision and Curriculum Development.

Kohn, A. (1991). Group grade grubbing versus cooperative learning. *Educational Leadership, 48*(5), 83–87.

Krechevsky, M. (1991). Project Spectrum: An innovative assessment alternative. *Educational Leadership, 48*(5), 43–48.

Madaus, G. F., & Tan, A. G. A. (1993). The growth of assessment. In G. Cawelti (Ed.), 1993 ASCD Yearbook. *Challenges and achievements of American education.* Alexandria, VA: Association for Supervision and Curriculum Development.

Maeroff, G. I. (1991). Assessing alternative assessment. *Phi Delta Kappan, 73*(4), 272–282.

Perrone, V. (Ed.). (1991). *Expanding student assessment.* Alexandria, VA: Association for Supervision and Curriculum Development.

Popham, W. J. (1993). Educational testing in America: What's right, what's wrong? A criterion-referenced perspective. *Educational Measurement: Issues and Practices, 12*(1), 11–14.

Schulz, E. (1993). Putting portfolios to the test. *Teacher Magazine, 5*(1), 36–41.

Simmons, J. (1990). Portfolio as large-scale assessment. *Language Arts, 67*(3), 262–268.

Simmons, R. (1994). The horse before the cart: Assessing for understanding. *Educational Leadership, 51*(5), 22–23.

Wiggins, G. (1993). Assessment: Authenticity, context, and validity. *Phi Delta Kappan, 75*(3), 200–214.

Wiggins, G. (1994). Toward better report cards. *Educational Leadership, 52*(2), 28–37.

Willis, S. (1994). The well-rounded classroom: Applying the theory of multiple intelligences. *ASCD Curriculum Update, 36*(8), 1, 5, 6, 8.

Wittrock, M. C., & Baker, E. L. (1990). *Testing and cognition.* Englewood Cliffs, NJ: Prentice-Hall.

Wolf, D. P. (1989). Portfolio assessment: Sampling student work. *Educational Leadership, 46*(7), 35–39.

Worthen, B. R. (1993). Critical issues that will determine the future of alternative assessment. *Phi Delta Kappan, 74*(6), 444–454.

CHAPTER 6

The Selection and Use of Aids and Resources

C ognitive tools are important in helping students construct their understandings. You will be delighted to know that there is a large variety of useful and effective educational materials, aids, and resources from which to draw as you plan your instructional experiences for language arts and social studies learning. On the other hand, you could also become overwhelmed by the sheer quantity of different materials available for classroom use—textbooks, pamphlets, anthologies, encyclopedias, tests, supplementary texts, paperbacks, programmed instructional systems, dictionaries, reference books, classroom periodicals, newspapers, films, records and cassettes, computer software, transparencies, realia, games, filmstrips, audio- and videotapes, slides, globes, manipulatives, CD-ROMs and videodiscs, and graphics. You could spend a lot of time reviewing, sorting, selecting, and practicing with the materials and tools for your use. Although nobody can make the job easier for you, this chapter will expedite the process by providing guidelines for the use of nonprojected and projected aids and materials and information about where to obtain additional resources. Additional information and resources specific to social studies are provided in Chapter 17.

Specifically, this chapter is designed to help in

1. Using printed instructional materials.
2. Finding sources of free and inexpensive printed and audiovisual materials.
3. Discovering the variety of professional journals and periodicals relevant to teaching language arts and social studies in grades 4–9.
4. Locating sources for additional information relevant to teaching language arts and social studies in intermediate and middle schools.
5. Understanding copyright laws for copying printed materials, video, and software programs.
6. Using the classroom chalkboard.
7. Using the classroom bulletin board.
8. Using charts, posters, and graphs.
9. Using the community as a rich instructional resource.
10. Using audiovisual aids.
11. Knowing what to do when equipment malfunctions.
12. Using the overhead projector.
13. Finding sources of overhead transparencies.
14. Using slides, filmstrips, and 16-mm films.

15. Using instructional television.
16. Using videos, videodiscs, and CD-ROMs.
17. Locating sample titles and sources of videodiscs for language arts and social studies.
18. Using computers and multimedia programs.
19. Locating sample titles and sources of software programs for language arts and social studies.

A. NONPROJECTED INSTRUCTIONAL TOOLS

Whereas projected aids are those that require electricity to project images onto screens, this first part of the chapter is about nonprojected materials—printed materials, three-dimensional objects, and flat materials on which to write or display—and about the community as a rich resource. Historically, of all the nonprojected materials for instruction, the printed textbook has had the most influence on teaching.

Printed Materials

When selecting textbooks and other printed materials, one item of concern to teachers should be the reading or readability level of the material. Sometimes the reading level is supplied by the textbook publisher. If not, you can apply selections to a readability formula or use a simpler method of merely having students read selections from the book aloud. If they can read the selections without stumbling over many of the words and can tell you the gist of what they have read, you can feel confident that the textbook is not too difficult.

Readability Formulas

To estimate the reading-grade level of a student textbook, you can use a readability formula such as the Fry technique. The procedure for the Fry technique is to

1. Determine the average number of syllables in three 100-word selections taken one from the beginning, one from the middle, and one from the ending parts of the book.
2. Determine the average number of sentences in the three 100-word selections.
3. Plot the two values on the readability graph (Figure 6.1). Their intersection will give you an approximation of the text's reading level at 50 percent to 75 percent comprehension.

Since readability formulas give only the technical reading level of a book, you will have to interpret the results by subjectively estimating the conceptual reading level of the work. To do so, consider your students' experience with the subject, the number of new ideas introduced, the abstraction of the ideas, and the author's external and internal cues. Then raise or lower the estimated level of difficulty.

To tell how well your students can read the text, use the Cloze technique or an informal reading inventory. The Cloze technique that was first described by Bormuth (1968) has since appeared in a number of versions. The procedure is as follows. From the textbook, select several typical passages so that you will have a total of 400 to 415 words. Delete every eighth word in the passage except for the words in the first and last sentences, proper names, numbers, and initialed words in sentences. It will be helpful if you eliminate 50 words. Duplicate the passages with 10 to 15 blank spaces replacing the eliminated words. Pass out these "mutilated" readings to the students. Ask them to fill in the blanks with the most appropriate words they can think of. Collect the papers. Score them by counting all the words that are the exact words in the original text and by dividing the number of actual correct responses by the number possible. McKenna suggests that you not count synonyms or verbs of different tense (1976). (Having 50 blanks makes this division easy.)

$$\text{Score} = \frac{\text{Number of correct responses}}{\text{Number possible}}$$

FIGURE 6.1
Fry Readability Graph
SOURCE: Fry Readability Chart from Edward Fry, "A Readability Formula That Saves Time." *Journal of Reading* (April 1968), 11:587. Reprinted with permission.

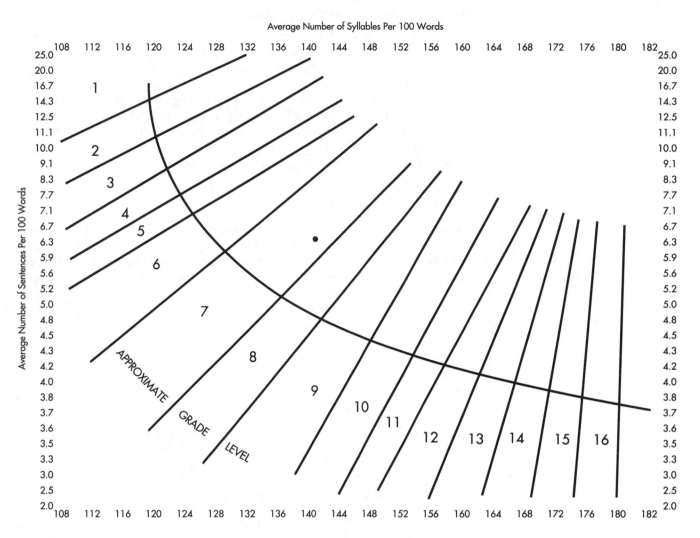

Directions:
Randomly select three 100-word passages from a book or an article. Plot average number of syllables and average number of sentences per 100 words on graph to determine the grade level of the material. Choose more passages per book if great variability is observed and conclude that the book has uneven readability. Few books will fall in gray area but when they do grade level scores are invalid.

Count proper nouns, numerals, and initializations as words. Count a syllable for each symbol. For example, "1945" is 1 word and 4 syllables and "IRA" is 1 word and 3 syllables.

Example:	**Syllables**	**Sentences**	
1st Hundred Words	124	6.6	
2nd Hundred Words	141	5.5	
3rd Hundred Words	158	6.8	
Average	141	6.3	**Readability 7th Grade** (see dot plotted on graph)

You can assume that students who score better than 50 percent can read the book quite well, students who score between 40 and 50 percent can read the book at the instructional level, and students who score below 40 percent will probably find the book difficult.

To conduct an informal silent reading inventory, ask your students to read four or five pages of the book, then give them a ten-item quiz on what they read. You can consider the text too difficult for any student who scores less than 70 percent on the quiz. Similarly, to conduct an informal oral reading inventory, have a student read a 100-word passage. The text is too difficult if the student stumbles over and misses more than 5 percent of the words (Johnson & Kress, 1965).

Multitext and Multireading Approaches

Expressing dissatisfaction with the single-textbook approach to teaching, some teachers have substituted a multitext strategy, in which they use one set of books for one topic and another set for another topic. This strategy provides some flexibility, though it really is only a series of single texts.

Other teachers, especially those using an integrated thematic approach, use a strategy that incorporates many readings for a topic during the same unit. This multireading strategy gives students a certain amount of choice in what they read. The various readings allow for differences in reading ability and interest level. By using a study guide, all the students can be directed toward specific information and concepts, but they do not all have to read the same selections.

Beginning a Resources File

Besides the student textbook and perhaps an accompanying workbook, there is a vast array of other printed materials available for use in teaching language arts and social studies, much of which is available without cost. (See sources of free and inexpensive materials that follow.) It is a good idea to immediately begin a file of printed materials and other resources that you can use in your teaching. Figure 6.2 is offered to help you begin that process.

Printed materials include books, workbooks, pamphlets, magazines, brochures, newspapers, professional journals, periodicals, and duplicated materials. When reviewing these materials, factors to be alert for are the following:

FIGURE 6.2
Beginning a Professional Materials Resource File

You should start now building your own personal file of aids and resources for teaching, a file that will continue throughout your professional career. Begin your file either on a computer data base program or on 3 × 5 file cards that are color coded by listing:

a. Name of resource
b. How to get it and when available
c. How to use it
d. Evaluative comments including grade level best suited for.

Organize the file in whatever way makes most sense to you. Cross-reference or color code your system to accommodate the following categories of aids and resources:

1. Articles from magazines, newspapers, journals, and periodicals
2. Assessment items
3. Compact disk sources
4. Computer software sources
5. Games and game sources
6. Guest speakers and other community resources
7. Manipulatives and other realia
8. Media catalogs
9. Motivational ideas
10. Multimedia program sources
11. Pictures, posters, and other stills
12. Sources of free and inexpensive items
13. Student worksheets
14. Supply catalogs
15. Thematic unit ideas
16. Unit and lesson plan ideas
17. Unit and lesson plans completed
18. Videocassette titles and sources
19. Videodisc titles and sources
20. Other or Miscellaneous.

- Appropriateness of the material in both content and reading level.
- Articles in newspapers, magazines, and periodicals related to the content that your students will be studying or the skills they will be learning.
- Assorted workbooks that emphasize thinking and problem solving rather than rote memorization. With an assortment of workbooks, you can have students working on similar but different assignments depending on their interests and abilities—an example of multilevel teaching.
- Pamphlets, brochures, and other duplicated materials that students can read for specific information and viewpoints about particular topics.
- Relatively inexpensive paperback books that would provide multiple book readings for your class and make it possible for students to read primary sources.

Sources of Free and Inexpensive Printed Materials

For free and inexpensive printed materials, look in your college, university, or public library or in the resource center at a local school district (see Figure 6.3).

Professional Journals and Periodicals for Language Arts and Social Studies Teachers of Grades 4–9

Figure 6.4 is a sample listing of the many professional periodicals and journals that can provide useful ideas for teaching language arts and social studies and information about instructional materials and how to get them. Most of these are likely to be in your university or college library. Check there for these and other titles of interest to you.

FIGURE 6.3
Resources for Free and Inexpensive Printed Materials

A Guide to Print and Nonprint Materials Available from Organizations, Industry, Governmental Agencies and Specialized Publishers. New York: Neal Schuman.

Civil Aeronautics Administration, *Sources of Free and Low-Cost Materials.* Washington, DC: U.S. Department of Commerce.

Educator's Guide to Free Materials. Randolph, WI: Educators Progress Service.

Educator's Guide to Free Teaching Aids. Randolph, WI: Educators Progress Service.

Ewing, S. *A Guide to Over One Thousand Things You Can Get for Free.* Lynn, MA: Sunnyside Publishing Company, 1984.

Free and Inexpensive Learning Materials. Nashville, TN: Division of Surveys and Field Services, George Peabody College for Teachers.

Index to Multi-Ethnic Teaching Materials and Teaching Resources. Washington, DC: National Education Association.

FIGURE 6.4
Professional Periodicals for Teachers of Intermediate and Middle School Language Arts and Social Studies

American Teacher	*Language Arts*
CBC Features	*Learning*
Childhood Education	*Middle School Journal, The*
Computing Teacher, The	*New Advocate, The*
Educational Horizons	*Phi Delta Kappan*
Educational Leadership	*Reading Teacher, The*
Educational Researcher	*Reading Today*
Elementary School Journal, The	*Social Education*
Good Apple Newspaper, The	*Social Studies, The*
History Teacher, The	*Teacher Magazine*
Horn Book, The	*Teaching K–8*
Instructor	*Teaching Political Science*
Journal of Economic Education	*Teaching Sociology*
Journal of Geography	*The WEB: Wonderfully Exciting Books*
Journal of Learning Disabilities	*Voices From the Middle*
Journal of Reading	*Writing Teacher*

The ERIC Information Network

The Educational Resources Information Center (ERIC) system, established by the United States Office of Education, is a widely used network providing access to information and research in education. While there are 16 clearinghouses providing information on specific subjects, addresses for those of particular interest for teaching language arts and social studies follow:

Elementary and Early Childhood Education. University of Illinois, College of Education, 805 W. Pennsylvania Ave., Urbana, IL 61601.

Handicapped and Gifted Children. Council for Exceptional Children, 1920 Association Drive, Reston, VA 22091.

Reading and Communication Skills. Indiana University, 2606 East 10th St., Smith Research Center, Suite 150, Bloomington, IN 47408.

Social Studies/Social Science Education. Indiana University, Social Studies Development Center, 2805 East 10th St., Bloomington, IN 47405-2373.

Tests, Measurements, and Evaluation. American Institutes for Research, Washington Research Center, 1055 Thomas Jefferson St., NW, Washington, DC 20007-3893.

Copying Printed Materials

You must know the laws about the use of copyrighted materials, printed and nonprinted. Although space here prohibits full inclusion of U.S. legal guidelines, your local school district should be able to provide a copy of current district policies for compliance with copyright laws.

When preparing to make a copy, you must find out whether the copying is permitted by law under the category of "permitted use." If not allowed under "permitted use," then you must get written permission to reproduce the material from the holder of the copyright. When using printed materials, adhere to the guidelines shown in Figure 6.5.

FIGURE 6.5

Guidelines for Copying Copyrighted Printed Materials

SOURCE: Section 107 of the 1976 Federal Omnibus Copyright Revision Act.

Permitted uses—you may make
1. Single copies of:
   - A chapter of a book
   - An article from a periodical, magazine, or newspaper
   - A short story, short essay, or short poem whether or not from a collected work
   - A chart, graph, diagram, drawing, cartoon
   - An illustration from a book, magazine, or newspaper.
2. Multiple copies for classroom use (not to exceed one copy per student in a course) of:
   - A complete poem if less than 250 words
   - An excerpt from a longer poem, but not to exceed 250 words
   - A complete article, story, or essay of less than 2,500 words
   - An excerpt from a larger printed work not to exceed 10 percent of the whole or 1,000 words
   - One chart, graph, diagram, cartoon, or picture per book or magazine issue.

Prohibited uses—you may not
1. Copy more than one work or two excerpts from a single author during one class term (semester or year).
2. Copy more than three works from a collective work or periodical volume during one class term.
3. Reproduce more than nine sets of multiple copies for distribution to students in one class term.
4. Copy to create or replace or substitute for anthologies or collective works.
5. Copy "consumable" works, e.g., workbooks, standardized tests, or answer sheets.
6. Copy the same work year after year.

B. THE WRITING BOARD

Can you imagine a classroom without a writing board? They used to be slate blackboards. Today, your classroom may have a board that is painted plywood (chalkboard), a magnetic chalkboard (plywood with a magnetic backing), or a white or colored multipurpose board on which you write with special marking pens. Multipurpose boards are important for classrooms where chalk dust would create problems—where it would aggravate allergies or interfere with computer maintenance. In addition to providing a surface upon which you can write and draw, the multipurpose board can be used as a projection screen and as a surface to which figures cut from colored transparency film will stick. It may also have a magnetic backing.

Extending the purposes of the multipurpose board is an electronic whiteboard that can transfer whatever information is written on it to a connected PC or Mac computer monitor, which in turn can save the material as a computer file. The board uses special dry-erase markers and erasers that have optically encoded sleeves that enable the device to track their position on the board. The data are then converted into a display for the computer monitor, which may then be printed, cut and pasted into other applications, sent as e-mail or a fax message, or networked to other sites. (For information, contact Microfield Graphics, Inc., 9825 SW Sunshine Court, Beaverton, OR 97005, 503-626-9393.)

Except for announcements that you place on the board, each day, each class, and even each new idea should begin with a clean board. At the end of each class, clean the board, especially if another teacher follows you in that room.

Use colored chalk (or marking pens) to highlight your "board talk." This is especially helpful for students with learning difficulties. Beginning at the top left of the board, print or write neatly and clearly, with the writing intentionally positioned to indicate content relationships—"causal, oppositional, numerical, comparative, categorical, and so on" (Hunter, 1994, p. 135).

Use the writing board to acknowledge acceptance and to record student contributions. Print instructions for an activity on the board, rather than giving them orally. At the top of the board frame you may find clips that are handy for hanging posters, maps, and charts.

Learn to write on the board without having to entirely turn your back to students or blocking their view of the board. When you have a lot of material to put on the board, do it before class, and then cover it, or better yet, put the material on transparencies and use the overhead projector rather than the board, or use both. Be careful not to write too much information. When using the writing board to complement your teacher talk, Hunter suggests that you write only key words and simple diagrams, thereby making it possible for the student's right brain hemisphere to process what is seen, while the left hemisphere processes the elaboration provided by your words (p. 133).

C. VISUAL DISPLAYS

Visual displays include bulletin boards, charts, graphs, flip charts, magnetic boards, realia (real objects), pictures, and posters. As a new or visiting member of a faculty, one of your first tasks is to find out what visual materials are available for your use and where they are kept. Here are guidelines for their use.

The Classroom Bulletin Board

Bulletin boards are found in nearly every classroom; although sometimes poorly used or not used at all, they can be relatively inexpensively transformed into attractive and valuable instructional tools. When preparing a bulletin board, it is important to be sure that the board display reflects gender and ethnic equity. Read the following suggestions for ideas for the effective use of the classroom bulletin board.

Making a CASE for bulletin boards. How can you effectively use a classroom bulletin board? Your classroom bulletin board will be most effective if you consider your "CASE" (adapted with permission from Kellough & Roberts, 1994, pp. 394–396):

C: for colorful constructions and captions

A: for attractive arrangement

S: for simple and student prepared

E: for enrichment and extensions of learning.

C: *Colorful constructions and captions.* Take time to plan the colors you select for your board and, whenever possible, include different materials for the letters and for the background of the board. For letter variety, consider patterns on bright cloth such as denim, felt, and corduroy. Search for special letters: they might be magnetic or ceramic, or precut letters of different sizes. Or make unique letters by cutting them from magazines, newspapers, posters, or stencils or by printing the letters with rubber stamps, sponges, or vegetable prints. You may print out the shapes of letters by dabbing colors on ABC shapes with sponges, rubber stamps, or vegetable slices that leave an imprint.

For the background of your board and the borders, consider gift-wrapping paper, wallpaper samples, shelf paper, remnants of fabric—flowers, polka dots, plaids, solids, or checks. Corrugated cardboard makes sturdy borders: cut out scallops for the shape of a picket fence, or make jagged points for an icicle effect. Other colorful borders can be made with wide braid, wide rickrack, or a contrasting fabric or paper. Constructions for the board may be simple ones made of yarn, ribbon, braid, cardboard pointers, maps, scrolls, banners, pennants, wheels that turn, cardboard doors that open, shuttered windows to peek through, or flaps that pull down or up and can be peered under or over.

If you need more bulletin board space, prepare large, lightweight screens from the cardboard sides of a tall refrigerator carton, available from an appliance store. One creative teacher asked for, and received without charge, several empty gallon ice-cream containers from a local ice-cream shop. The teacher then stacked five of the containers on top of one another, fastened them together with wide masking tape, painted them, and prepared her own bulletin board "totem pole" for display in the corner of the classroom. On that circular display space, the students placed their items about a current unit of study.

A: *Attractive arrangement.* Use your imagination to make the board attractive. Is your arrangement interesting? Did you use texture? Did you consider the shapes of the items selected? Are the colors attractive? Does your caption draw student attention?

S: *Simple and student prepared.* The bulletin board should be simple, emphasizing one main idea, concept, topic, or theme, and captions should be short and concise.

Are your students interested in preparing the bulletin board for your classroom? Plan class meeting time to discuss this with them. They have great ideas.

- They can help plan. Why not let them diagram their ideas and share them with each other?
- They can discuss. Is there a more meaningful way to begin to discuss their perceptions, the internal criteria that each student brings to class, or the different values that each student may have?
- They can arrange materials. Why not let them discover the concepts of balance and symmetry?
- They can construct and contribute. Will they feel they are more actively involved and are really participating if it is *their* bulletin board?
- When the bulletin board is finished, your students can get further involved by (1) reviewing the board during a class meeting, (2) discussing the materials used, and (3) discussing the information their bulletin board is emphasizing.

Additional class projects may be planned during this meeting. For instance, do the students want a bulletin board group or committee for their class? Do they want a permanent committee or one in which the membership changes from month to month? Or do they prefer that existing cooperative learning groups assume bulletin board responsibility, with periodic rotation of that responsibility? Do they want to meet on a regular basis? Can they work quietly and not disturb other students who may still be completing their other learning tasks? Should they prepare the board, or should the committee ask everyone to contribute ideas and items for the weekly or monthly bulletin board? Does the committee want to keep a register, guest book, or guest file of students who contribute to the board? Should there be an honorary list of bulletin board illustrators? Should the authors of selected captions sign their names beneath each caption? Do they want to keep a file binder of all of the different diagrams of proposed bulletin boards? At each class meeting, should they discuss the proposed diagrams with the entire class? Should they ask the class to evaluate which idea would be an appropriate one for a particular study topic? What other records do they want to keep? Should there be a bulletin board medal or a classroom award?

E. Enrichment and extensions of learning. Illustrations on the bulletin board can accent learning topics; verbs can vitalize the captions; phrases can punctuate a student's thoughts; and alliteration can announce anything you wish on the board. Following are some examples.

Animals can accent! Pandas, panthers, and parrots can help present punctuation symbols; a giant octopus can show students eight rules to remember, eight things to remember when preparing a book report, or eight activities to complete when academic work is finished early; a student can fish for anything—math facts, correctly spelled words, or the meanings of science words; a bear character helps students to "bear down" on errors of any kind; a large pair of shoes helps "stamp out" errors, incomplete work, forgotten school materials, or student misbehavior. Dinosaurs can begin a search for any topic, and pack rats can lead readers into phrases, prose, or poetry.

Verbs can vitalize! Someone or something (your choice) can "swing into" any curriculum area. Some of the verbs used often are *soar, win, buzz, rake, scurry,* and *race.*

Phrases point out! Some of the short, concise phrases used as captions may include

Roll into _____	All aboard for _____	Race into _____
Hop into _____	Peer into _____	Grow up with _____
Bone up on _____	Tune into _____	Monkey with _____
Looking good with _____	Fly high with _____	Get on track with _____

Alliteration announces! Some classroom bulletin boards show Viking ships or Voyages that guide a student to vocabulary words; Monsters Monitor Math Madness; other boards present Surprises of Spring, Fantasies of Fall, Wonders of Winter, and Safety in Summer; still other boards send messages about Library Lingo, Dictionary Dynamite, and Thesaurus Treats.

Charts, Posters, and Graphs

Charts, posters, and graphs can be used for displays just as bulletin boards are, but, as a rule, they are better suited for explaining, illustrating, clarifying, and reinforcing specific points in lessons. Charts, posters, and graphs might also be included in a bulletin board display. The previous guidelines for use of the writing board and bulletin board also apply to the use of charts, posters, and graphs. Clarity, simplicity, and attractiveness are essential considerations. (Additional information on the use of maps and globes for teaching social studies is in Chapter 14.) Here are additional suggestions for their preparation and use.

Most students enjoy making charts, posters, and graphs. Involve them in doing so, in finding information, planning how to represent it, and making the chart or poster. Have the author(s) of the chart or poster sign it, and then display it in the classroom. Students should credit their sources on the graphs and charts.

Students may need help in keeping graphs proportional, and that provides an opportunity to help students develop mathematics and thinking skills.

Students can also enjoy designing flip charts, a series of charts or posters (that may include graphs) to illustrate certain points or a series of related points. To make a large flip chart, they can use the large pads used by artists for sketching; to make mini–flip charts to use in dyads, they can use small notepads. (The use of dyads refers to a technique of pairing students to exchange oral summaries of materials they have read. See, for example, Larson & Dansereau, 1986.)

D. THE COMMUNITY AS A RESOURCE

One of the richest resources is the local community and the people and places in it. (See also Chapter 12.) You will want to build your own file of community resources—speakers, sources of free materials, and field trip locations. Your school may already have a community resource file available for your use. It may need updating, however.

A community resource file (see Figure 6.6) should contain information about possible field trip locations, community resource people who could serve as guest speakers or mentors, and local agencies that can provide information and instructional materials.

E. PROJECTED AND RECORDED INSTRUCTIONAL TOOLS

Continuing with our discussion of instructional tools available for use in teaching, the following sections focus on equipment that depends upon electricity to project light and sound and to focus images on screens. Included are projectors of various sorts, computers, CD-ROMs, sound recorders, video recorders, and laser videodisc players. The aim is *not* to teach you how to operate modern equipment, but to help you develop a philosophy for using it and to provide strategies for using these instructional tools in your teaching.

Media Equipment

Certain teaching tools that rely upon sight and sound fall into the category of media known as audiovisual aids. Included in this general category are such teaching tools as charts, models, pictures, graphs, maps, mock-ups, globes, flannel boards, writing boards, and all of the other tools previously discussed. Also included in the general category of audiovisual aids

FIGURE 6.6
Community Resources for Speakers and Field Trips

Airport	Highway patrol station
Apiary	Historical sites and monuments
Aquarium	Industrial plant
Archaeological site	Legislative session
Art gallery	Library and archive
Assembly plant	Native American reservation
Bakery	Mass transit authority
Bird and wildlife sanctuary	Military installation
Book publisher	Mines
Bookstores	Museums
Broadcasting and TV station	Newspaper plants
Building being razed	Observatory
Building under construction	Oil refinery
Canal lock	Park
Cemetery	Poetry reading
Chemical plant	Post office/package delivery
City or county planning commission	company
Courthouse	Police station
Dairy	Recycling center
Dam and flood plain	Retail stores
Dock and harbor	Sanitation department
Factory	Sawmill or lumber company
Farm	Shopping mall
Fire department	Shorelines (streams, lakes, oceans)
Fish hatchery	Telecommunications center
Flea market	Town meeting
Foreign embassy	Utility company
Forest and forest preserve	Universities and colleges
Freeway under construction	Warehouse
Gas company	Water reservoir and treatment plant
Geological sites	Wildlife parks and preserves
Health departments and hospitals	Weather bureau and storm centers
Highway construction site	Zoo

are those devices that require electricity for their operation—projectors of various sorts, computers, sound recorders, video recorders, videodisc and compact disc players, and so forth. This section is about the selection and use of tools of this second group, the ones that require electricity to project sight and sound and that focus images onto screens.

These instructional tools are aids to your teaching. It is important to remember that their role is to aid you, not to teach for you. You must still select the objectives, orchestrate the instructional plan, assess the results, and follow up the lessons. If you use audiovisual aids prudently, your teaching and students' learning will benefit.

Uses of Audiovisual Aids

The main effort of any teacher in instruction is to make the learning clear—communicate the idea, capture the content, clarify the obscure for the students. Hence, teachers almost universally rely on the spoken word as their primary medium of communication. Most of the day is filled with explanation and discourse, to the point that the teaching profession has been accused of making words more important than reality—perpetuating a culture of verbalism in the schools. Teachers use definitions, recitations, and—perhaps too often—rote memorization in quest of the goals for the day.

The learning experiences ladder.   To rely on verbalism is to rely on communication through abstract symbolization. Symbols (in this case, letters and words) may not always communicate what is intended. Audiovisual aids can serve to facilitate communication and understanding by adding dimensions to the learning, thus making the learning less abstract. To better understand this concept, which to this point has been presented entirely in one dimension (by words), let's add a dimension (a visual representation); see the Learning Experiences Ladder of Figure 6.7.

The Learning Experiences Ladder represents the range of learning experiences from most direct (bottom of ladder) to most abstract (top of ladder). When selecting learning experiences, it is important to select activities that are as direct as possible. *When students are involved in direct experiences, they are using more of their sensory input modalities (auditory, visual, tactile, kinesthetic), which leads to the most effective and longest-lasting learning.* As discussed in Chapter 1, this is hands-on/minds-on learning. This is learning at the bottom of the ladder. At the other end are abstract experiences, in which the learner is exposed only to symbolization (that is, words and numbers) requiring only one or two-senses (auditory or visual). The teacher talks while the students watch and listen. Visual and verbal symbolic experiences, although impossible to avoid when teaching, are less effective in ensuring that planned learning occurs. This is especially true with younger children, children with special needs, slower learners, learners with limited proficiency in using the English language, and intellectually immature learners. It is even true for many adult learners.

As seen from the Learning Experiences Ladder, when teaching about tide pools, the most effective mode is to take the students to a tide pool (bottom of the ladder; the most direct experience) where students can see, hear, touch, smell, and perhaps even taste (if not toxic) the tide pool. The least effective mode is for the teacher merely to talk about a tide pool (top of the ladder; the most abstract symbolic experience), which engages only one sense—the auditory sense.

Of course, for various reasons—safety, lack of resources for a field trip, location of your school—you may not be able to take the students to a tide pool. Because you cannot (and should not) always use the most direct experience, at times you must select an experience higher on the ladder, and audiovisual aids can provide the avenue for doing that. Self-discovery teaching is not always appropriate. Sometimes it is better to build upon what others have discovered and learned. Although learners do not need to "reinvent the wheel," the most effective learning engages most or all of their senses. On the Learning Experiences Ladder, these are the experiences within the bottom three rungs—the direct, simulated, and vicarious categories. Simulated and vicarious learning experiences, such as can be provided with videos and computers, can be nearly as useful as direct experiences.

Another value of direct, simulated, and vicarious experiences is that they tend to be interdisciplinary, that is, they cross subject boundaries. This makes those experiences espe-

FIGURE 6.7

The Learning Experiences Ladder

SOURCE: Reprinted with the permission of Simon & Schuster, Inc. from the Macmillan College text A RESOURCE GUIDE FOR TEACHING: K–12 by Richard D. Kellough. Copyright ©1994 by Macmillan College Publishing Company, Inc. For earlier versions of this concept, see Charles F. Hoban, Sr., et al., *Visualizing the Curriculum* (New York: Dryden, 1937), p. 39; Jerome S. Bruner, *Toward a Theory of Instruction* (Cambridge: Harvard University Press, 1966), p. 49; Edgar Dale, *Audio-Visual Methods in Teaching* (New York: Holt, Rinehart & Winston, 1969), p. 108; and Eugene C. Kim and Richard D. Kellough, *A Resource Guide for Secondary School Teaching: Planning for Competence,* 2nd ed. (New York: Macmillan, 1978), p. 136.

Verbal Experiences

Teacher talk, written words; engaging one sense; the most abstract symbolization; students are physically inactive.

Examples

1. Listening to the teacher talk about tide pools.
2. Listening to a student report on the Grand Canyon.
3. Listening to a guest speaker talk about how the state legislature functions.

Visual Experiences

Still pictures, diagrams, charts; engaging one sense; typically symbolic; students are physically inactive.

Examples

1. Viewing slides of tide pools.
2. Viewing drawings and photographs of the Grand Canyon.
3. Listening to a guest speaker talk about the state legislature as he or she shows slides of it in action.

Vicarious Experiences

Laser video-disc programs, computer programs, video programs; engaging more than one sense; students are indirectly "doing," possibly some limited physical activity.

Examples

1. Interacting with a computer program about wave action and life in tide pools.
2. Viewing and listening to a video program on the Grand Canyon.
3. Taking a field trip to observe the state legislature.

Simulated Experiences

Role-playing, experiments, simulations, mock-ups, working models; all or nearly all senses are engaged; activity often integrates disciplines and is closest to the real thing.

Examples

1. Building a working model of a tide pool.
2. Building a working model of the Grand Canyon.
3. Role-playing a session of the state legislature.

Direct Experiences

Students are actually doing what is being learned; true inquiry; all senses are engaged; activity usually integrates disciplines.

Examples

1. Visiting a tide pool.
2. Visiting the Grand Canyon.
3. Designing an elected representative body, patterned after the state legislature, to oversee the operation of the school-within-the-school program.

Abstract

Concrete

cially useful for teachers who want to help students connect the learning of one discipline with that of others and with their own life experiences. Direct, simulated, and vicarious experiences are more like real life.

General Guidelines for Using Audiovisual Aids

Like any other boon to progress, audiovisual aids must be worked with if they are to yield what is expected. The mediocre teacher who is content to get by without expending additional effort will in all likelihood remain just that, a mediocre teacher, despite the excellent quality of whatever aids he or she chances to use. Because the mediocre teacher fails to rise to the occasion and hence presents poorly, that teacher's lesson will be less effective and less impressive than it could have been. The effective teacher makes the inquiry about available audiovisual aids and expends the effort needed to implement them well for the benefit of the students. The effective teacher will capitalize on the drama made possible by the shift in interaction strategy and enhance the quest for knowledge by using vivid material. Such teaching involves four steps:

1. Selecting the proper audiovisual material
2. Preparing for using the material
3. Guiding the audiovisual activity
4. Following up the audiovisual activity

Selecting the proper audiovisual material. Care must be exercised in the selection of an audiovisual aid for use in the classroom. A poor selection of inappropriate material can turn an excellent lesson plan into a disappointing fiasco. An audiovisual aid that projects garbled sound, outdated pictures, or obscure or shaky images will not be met with a delighted response from the students. Material that is too difficult or boring, takes too long to set up, or is not suitable for students at the intermediate or middle school age level will dampen their enthusiasm.

In your selection of audiovisual materials, you should follow an inquiry routine similar to this:

1. Is the contemplated material suitable? Will it help to achieve the objective of the intended lesson? Will it present an accurate understanding of the facts in the case? Will it highlight the important points? Will it work with the equipment available at the school?
2. Is the material within the level of understanding of the students? Is it too mature? Too embarrassing? Too dated?
3. Is the material lucid in its presentation? Is it clear in its images and sounds?
4. Is the material readily available? Will it be available when needed?

The best response for most of these questions can come after a careful previewing of the material. Sometimes, because of existing conditions, this dry run is not possible. However, the best way to discover the inadequacies of catalogue descriptions of films, filmstrips, videotapes, videodiscs, computer software, and compact discs—or of the condition in which they have been left by previous users—is to try them out yourself under practice conditions.

Preparing for using the audiovisual material. To use audiovisual aids with maximum effectiveness usually will require preparation of two types: psychological and physical. From the psychological standpoint, students have to be prepped for the utilization of the material and coached on how best to profit from its presentation. You will need to set the scene, make clear the purpose of the activity, suggest points to look for, present problems to solve and, in general, clue your students about potential dangers that may mislead them.

From the physical standpoint, preparation pertaining to the machine to be used, the equipment involved, and the arrangement of the classroom furniture will have to be attended to. Sometimes, as with the writing board, preparation is minimal. All that may be necessary may be a sufficient supply of chalk and erasers, the identification of the aid, and a brief recitation concerning the use you intend to make of it. At other times, however, as when the morning or afternoon sun affects classroom visibility, you will have to check the view from each section of the classroom, as well as check the focusing dials of the apparatus for appropriate sharpness of images and the amplitude dials for clarity of sound. In the absence of preparation, bedlam can ensue. The missing chalk, the borrowing and lending of board erasers among the students, or the absence of an extension cord can spell defeat for even the best audiovisual aid. Double-checking the action readiness of the equipment to be used is vital to success.

Guiding the audiovisual activity. The purpose of audiovisual materials is not to replace teaching but to make teaching more effective. Therefore, you cannot always expect the tool to do all the work. You should, however, make it work for your purposes. You will have to highlight in advance the things that you want to be remembered most completely. You may have to enumerate the concepts that are developed or to illustrate relationships or conclusions that you wish to be drawn. You may have to prepare and distribute a study guide or a list of questions for students to respond to, to stop the presentation periodically for hints or questions, or maybe even to repeat the entire performance to ensure a more thorough grasp of particulars. Student learning via the use of audiovisual materials can be enhanced by your coached guidance before, during, and after viewing or use of the materials.

Following up the audiovisual activity. Audiovisual presentations that are allowed to stand alone squander valuable learning opportunities. Some activity and/or discussion should ensue that is pointed and directed toward closure. Such postmortems should have been a vital part of your lesson plan and preparation for the use of the material. Upon completion of the use of the aid, students should be expected to respond to the sets of questions proposed in the preview activity. Points that were fuzzily made should be clarified. Questions that were not answered should be pursued in depth. Deeper responses that go beyond the present scope of the inquiry should be noted and earmarked for further probing at some later date. Quizzes, reviews, practice, and discussions all can be used to tie loose ends together, to highlight the major concepts, to connect and clinch the essential learnings. The planned, efficient use of the aid helps create the atmosphere that audiovisual presentations are learning opportunities rather than recreational time outs.

When Equipment Malfunctions

When using audiovisual equipment, it is nearly always best to set up the equipment and have it ready to go before children arrive. That helps avoid problems in classroom management that can occur when there is a delay because the equipment was not ready. Of course, delays may be unavoidable when equipment breaks down, or if a videotape breaks.

Remember the "law" that says if anything can go wrong it will? It is particularly relevant when using equipment discussed in this section. The professional teacher is prepared for such emergencies. Effectively planning for and responding to this eventuality is a part of your system of movement management. That preparation includes consideration of the following.

When equipment malfunctions, three principles should be kept in mind: (1) You want to avoid dead time in the classroom; (2) You want to avoid causing permanent damage to equipment; (3) You want to avoid losing content continuity of a lesson. So what do you do when equipment breaks down? The answer is, *be prepared.*

If a projector bulb goes out, quickly insert another. That means that you should have an extra bulb on hand. If a tape breaks, you can temporarily splice it with cellophane tape. That means that tape should be readily available. And, if you must do a temporary splice, do it on the film or videotape that has already run through the machine, rather than on the end yet to go through, so as not to mess up the machine or the film. Then, after class or after school, be sure to notify the person in charge of the tape that a temporary splice was made, so the tape can be permanently repaired before use again.

If a fuse blows, or for some other reason you lose power, or you can see that there is going to be too much dead time before the equipment is working again, that is the time to go to an alternate lesson plan. You have probably heard the expression, "go to Plan B." It is a useful phrase and means that, without missing a beat in the lesson, you immediately and smoothly switch to an alternate learning activity. For you, the beginning teacher, it doesn't mean that you must plan *two* lessons for every one, but, when planning a lesson that utilizes audiovisual equipment, plan an alternative activity, just in case. Then you can move your students into the planned alternative activity quickly and smoothly.

F. PROJECTORS

Projection machines today are lighter, more energy efficient, and easier to operate than they were a few years ago; they have been almost "defanged." Among the most common and useful to the classroom teacher are the overhead projector, the slide projector, the filmstrip projector, and, of course, the 16-mm film projector. Because limited space in this textbook disallows the luxury of presenting the operating procedures for every model of projector that you may come across in classrooms, this presentation is limited to guidelines for their use. Since operations from one projector to the next are quite similar, learning to use them should be no major problem for you. At any school there are teachers who will gladly answer questions you may have about a specific projector.

The Overhead Projector

The overhead projector is a versatile, effective, and reliable teaching tool. Except for the bulb burning out, not much else can go wrong with an overhead projector. There is no film to break nor program to crash. And, along with a bulletin board and a writing board, nearly every classroom has one.

The overhead projector consists of a glass-topped box that contains a light source and a vertical post mounting a head that contains a lens. It projects light through objects that are transparent (see Figure 6.8). An overhead projector usually works quite well in a fully lit room. Truly portable overhead projectors that can be carried easily from place to place in their compact cases are available.

Other types of overhead projectors include rear-projection systems that allow the teacher to stand off to the side rather than between students and the screen, and overhead video projectors that use video cameras to send images that are projected by television monitors. Some schools use overhead video camera technology that focuses on an object, pages of a

FIGURE 6.8

The Overhead Projector

SOURCE: Joseph F. Callahan, Leonard H. Clark, and Richard D. Kellough, *Teaching in the Middle and Secondary Schools*, 4th ed. (New York: Macmillan Publishing Company, 1992), p. 435. Copyright © 1991 by Macmillan Publishing Company.

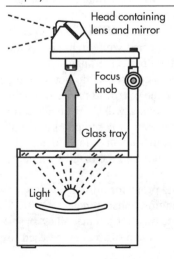

book, or a demonstration, while sending a clear image to a video monitor with a screen large enough for an entire class to clearly see.

In some respects, the overhead projector is more practical than the writing board, particularly for a beginning teacher who is nervous. Use of the overhead projector rather than the writing board can help avoid tension by decreasing the need to pace back and forth to the board. And, by using an overhead projector rather than a writing board, you can maintain both eye contact and physical proximity with students, both of which are important for maintaining classroom control.

Consider the following specific guidelines when using the overhead projector:

1. For writing using an overhead projector, ordinary felt-tip pens are not satisfactory. Select a transparency marking pen available at an office supply store. The ink of these pens is water soluble, so keep the palm of your hand from resting on the transparency or you will have ink smudges on your transparency and on your hand. Non-water-soluble pens—permanent markers—can be used, but to reuse the transparency it must be cleaned with a plastic eraser or an alcohol solvent (ditto fluid works, but, for safety, be sure there is proper ventilation). With a cleaning solvent, you can clean and dry with paper toweling or a soft rag. To highlight the writing on a transparency and to organize student learning, use pens in a variety of colors. Transparency pens tend to dry out quickly, and they are relatively expensive, so the caps must be taken on and off frequently, which is something of a nuisance when working with several colors. Practice writing on a transparency, and also practice making overlays.

2. You can use an acetate transparency roll or single sheets of flat transparencies. Flat sheets of transparency come in different colors—clear, red, blue, yellow, and green—which can be useful in making overlays.

3. Some teachers prefer to prepare an outline of a lesson in advance, on transparencies, which allows more careful preparation of the transparencies and their reuse at another time. Some teachers prefer to use an opaque material, such as 3 × 5 note cards, to block out prewritten material and then uncover it at the moment it is being discussed. For preparation of permanent transparencies, you will probably want to use "permanent marker" pens rather than those that are water soluble and easily smudged. Heavy paper frames are available for permanent transparencies; marginal notes can be written on the frames.

4. An overhead projector can show other transparent materials, such as transparent rulers and even objects that are opaque if you want to simply show a silhouette.

5. Find the best place in your classroom to place the projector. If there is no classroom projection screen, you can hang white paper or a sheet or use a white multipurpose board or a white or near-white wall.

6. Have you ever attended a presentation by someone using an overhead projector improperly? It can be frustrating to members of an audience when the image is too small, out of focus, partially off the screen, or partially blocked from view by the presenter. To use this teaching tool in a professional manner: Turn on the projector (the switch is probably on the front), place the projector so that the projected white light covers the entire screen and hits the screen at a 90-degree angle, then focus the image to be projected. Face the students while using the projector. The fact that you do not lose eye contact with your students is a major advantage of using the overhead projector rather than a writing board. What you write, as you face your students, will show up perfectly (unless out of focus or off the screen). Rather than using your finger to point to detail or pointing to the screen (thereby turning away from your students), lay a pencil directly on the transparency, with the tip of the pencil pointing to the detail being emphasized.

7. To lessen distraction, you may want to turn the overhead projector off when you want student attention to be shifted back to you or when changing transparencies.

8. Personal computers with laser printers and thermal processing (copy) machines, probably located in the teachers' workroom or in the school's main office, can be used to make permanent transparencies.

9. Calculators specifically for use on the overhead projector are available, as is a screen that fits onto the platform and is circuited to computers, so whatever is displayed on the computer monitor is also projected onto the classroom screen.
10. Tracing enlarged versions of transparent charts or drawings onto paper or onto the writing board is easily done with use of the overhead projector. The image projected onto the screen can be made smaller or larger by moving the projector closer or farther away, respectively, and then traced when you have the size you want.
11. An overhead projector or a filmstrip projector can be used as a light source (spotlight) to highlight demonstrations by you or by your students.
12. Commercial transparencies are available from a variety of school supply houses. For sources, check the catalogs available in your school office or at the audiovisual and resources centers in your school district. See Figure 6.9 for sample sources.

Slides and Filmstrips

Slides and filmstrips are variations of the same medium, and most of what can be said about the use of one is true for the other. In fact, one projector may sometimes serve both functions. Filmstrips are, in effect, a series of slides connected on a roll of film. Slides can be made into filmstrips. Relatively inexpensive technology is now available that allows you to convert slides or home movies into videocassettes. Because of their low cost and greater instructional flexibility and visual impact, videocassettes have literally replaced films and filmstrips for school use.

For teaching purposes, 35-mm slides are still quite useful and are available from school supply houses and, of course, from your own collection and from students and friends. Some schools have the equipment for making slides from computer programs.

16-Mm Films

Because they are less expensive to make and because they offer more instructional flexibility, videocassettes and videodiscs have largely replaced 16-mm films. In fact, laser videodiscs may eventually replace traditional textbooks as well. For example, in 1991, Texas became the first state to allow its schools to use state textbook funds to purchase videodisc programs as an alternative to traditional textbooks in science, and, in 1992, Utah adopted a multimedia system for teaching English as a second language. Other states will most certainly follow these precedents. Although there are still some effective and new 16-mm films available for instruction, many others are old and include dated or incorrect information. As with filmstrips, you need to view films carefully and critically before showing them to your class. Many classic films are now available on videocassette or on videodisc.

G. TELEVISION, VIDEOS, AND VIDEODISCS

Everyone knows that television, videos, and videodiscs represent a powerful medium. Their use as teaching aids, however, may present scheduling, curriculum, and physical problems that some school systems cannot adequately handle.

FIGURE 6.9
Sources of Overhead Transparencies

BJ's School Supplies, 1807 19th Street, Bakersfield, CA 93301.
Cuisenaire Co. of America, Inc., P.O. Box 5026, White Plains, NY 10602-5026.
Denoyer-Geppert Audiovisuals, 5235 Ravenswood Ave., Chicago, IL 60640.
MMI Corporation, 2950 Wyman Parkway, P.O. Box 19907, Baltimore, MD 21211.
Stasiuk Enterprises, 3150 NE 30th Ave., P.O. Box 12484, Portland, OR 97212.
3M Audio Visual, Building 225-3NE, 3M Center, St. Paul, MN 55144.
United Transparencies, P.O. Box 688, Binghamton, NY 13902.

Television

For purposes of professional discussion, television programming can be divided into three categories: instructional television, educational television, and general commercial television. Instructional television refers to programs specifically designed as classroom instruction; educational television, to programs of cable television and of public broadcasting designed to educate in general, but not aimed at classroom instruction; general commercial television programs, to the entertainment and public service programs of the television networks and local stations.

Instructional television. As just noted, television is not always used well in schools. Ideally, television should not be used for classroom instruction, but rather reserved for supplementing ordinary curricula and instruction. Nevertheless, sometimes instructional television that takes on the role of classroom instruction is necessary. Perhaps courses could not otherwise be successfully mounted, because they are beyond the capabilities of the local resources, staff, and facilities. By using television well, schools can offer students courses that otherwise would be impossible. In other school systems, to save money or bring the students in touch with master teachers, instructional television courses have been introduced as substitutes for regular courses.

The fact that a television class is taught by a master television teacher does not relieve the classroom teacher of any teaching responsibilities. He or she must plan, select, introduce, guide, and follow up, as in any other course. Otherwise, the television teaching will leave the students with learning gaps and misunderstandings. In spite of the marvels of television, students still need the personal guidance of teachers. To use instructional television properly, you should follow a procedure similar to the following:

1. Prepare for the telecast.
   a. Study the advance material. If possible, preview the telecast.
   b. Arrange the classroom.
   c. Prepare and distribute materials and supplies as needed.
   d. Discuss the lesson to be viewed. Fill in any necessary background. Teach any vocabulary necessary.
2. Guide the learning.
   a. Circulate to help students, if necessary.
   b. Observe student response. Note signs of lack of understanding or misunderstanding.
3. Follow up.
   a. Question and discuss.
   b. Reteach and clarify as necessary.
   c. Use the telecast as a springboard to new experiences involving student participation, creativity, problem solving, and critical thinking.
   d. Tie learning to past and future lessons and experiences.

General and educational television programs. Both public broadcasting stations and commercial stations offer a multitude of programs that can be used to supplement and enrich your teaching. Such programs can be excellent sources of material for use in all sorts of courses, not only, as you might surmise, for courses in the social studies.

Educational television courses, such as those given by public broadcasting stations or by colleges and universities on commercial stations, often include lectures, demonstrations, and background information usable for public school courses.

Television studios do not ordinarily adapt their schedules to those of the schools. This problem may be met in several ways. One solution is to tape programs for replay during the class period. Attention should be paid, however, to copyright laws (discussed later in this chapter). Another solution is to ask students to watch the telecast at home. This solution is fraught with problems because not everyone will be able to watch that television program. Some may not have television sets available, some may have an adult in the house who wants to watch another show at that time, and some may not have the time available to watch that show. Consequently, you should make such assignments selectively to certain individuals or committees who will report what they have seen and heard. Sometimes, when a major event is to be telecast on several networks, you might do well to ask different students to watch different channels so that they can compare the coverage. For instance, the difference in opinions of various commentators on a presidential message might be quite revealing.

Finally, television program listings can be obtained from your local commercial, educational, or cable companies or by writing directly to network stations. Addresses for the major national networks follow:

- American Broadcasting Company, Inc. (ABC), 77 West 66th Street, New York, NY 10019. (212) 458-7777.
- Arts & Entertainment Network (A&E), 235 East 45th Street, New York, NY 10017. (212) 661-4500.
- Black Entertainment Television, 1899 Ninth Street, NE, Washington, DC 20018. (202) 636-2400.
- Cable News Network—WTBS, 1050 Techwood Drive, NW, Atlanta, GA 30318. (404) 827-1896.
- Columbia Broadcasting System, Inc. (CBS-TV), 51 West 52nd Street, New York, NY 10019. (212) 975-3166.
- C-Span, 400 North Capitol Street, NW, Washington, DC 20001. (202) 737-3220.
- Discovery Channel, The, 7700 Wisconsin Avenue, Bethesda, MD 20814-3522. (301) 986-1999.
- Disney Channel, The, 4111 West Alameda Avenue, Burbank, CA 91505. (818) 569-7500.
- ESPN, ESPN Plaza, 935 Middle Street, Bristol, CN 06010. (203) 585-2000.
- Fox Broadcasting, 10201 West Pico Boulevard, Los Angeles, CA 90035. (310) 203-3553.
- Learning Channel, The, 7700 Wisconsin Avenue, Bethesda, MD 20815-3579. (301) 986-0444.
- Lifetime, 36-12 35th Avenue, Astoria, NY 11106. (718) 482-4000.
- National Broadcasting Company (NBC-TV), RCA Building, 30 Rockefeller Plaza, New York, NY 10112. (212) 664-4444.
- Public Broadcasting Service (PBS), 1320 Braddock Place, Alexandria, VA 22314. (703) 739-5068.
- Turner Broadcasting, One C&N Center, Atlanta, GA 30348-5366. (404) 827-1647.
- United Paramount Network, 5555 Melrose Avenue, MOB 1200, Los Angeles, CA 90038. (213) 956-5000.
- USA Network, 1230 Avenue of the Americas, New York, NY 10020. (212) 408-9166.
- Warner Brothers Television Network, 4000 Warner Boulevard, Building 34R, Burbank, CA 91522. (818) 954-6000.

Videos and Videodiscs

Combined with a television monitor, the VCR (videocassette recorder) is one of the most popular and frequently used pieces of audiovisual equipment in today's classroom. In a teacher survey conducted by *Instructor* "Teachers Speak Out on Technology in the Classroom," (April 1991), the videocassette recorder was reported as the most popular technology device used by teachers. Videotaped programs can do nearly everything that 16-mm films could do. In addition, the VCR combined with a video camera makes it possible to record student activities, practice, projects, and demonstrations, and your own teaching. It gives students a marvelous opportunity to self-assess as they see and hear themselves in action.

Entire course packages, as well as supplements, are now available on videocassettes or on computer programs. The schools where you student teach and where you eventually are employed may have a collection of such programs. Some teachers make their own.

Laser videodiscs and players for classroom use are reasonably priced, with an ever-increasing variety of disc topics for classroom use. There are two formats of laser videodisc: (1) freeze-frame format (CAV—constant angular velocity, or standard play) and (2) non-freeze-frame format (CLV—constant linear velocity, or extended play). Both will play on all laser disc players. Laser videodisc players are quite similar to VCRs and just as easy to operate. The discs are visual archives or data bases containing large amounts of information that can be easily retrieved, reorganized, filed, and controlled by the user with the remote control that accompanies the player. Each side of a double-sided disc stores 54,000 separate still frames of information—pictures, printed text, diagrams, films, or any combination of these. Both still and moving visuals can be stored and then selected for showing on a television monitor or programmed onto a computer disc for a special presentation. More than 2,000 videodisc titles are now available for educational use. By the time you read these words, there may be more than 3,000 titles. (See Figure 6.10 for sample titles.) Your school or district audiovisual or curriculum resource center probably has some titles already. For additional titles, refer to the latest annual edition of *Videodisc Compendium,* published and sold by Emerging Technology Consultants Inc., 2819 Hamline Avenue North, St. Paul, MN 55113. Phone (612) 639-3973, Fax (612) 639-0110.

Carefully selected programs, tapes, discs, films, and slides enhance student learning. For example, laser videodiscs offer quick and efficient accessibility to thousands of visuals, thus providing an appreciated boost to teachers of students with limited language proficiency. In social studies, for example, with the use of still-frame control, students can visually observe phenomena that previous generations of students only read about.

Resources for Videodisc Titles

Check school supply catalogs for additional titles and sources for videodiscs. Here are addresses to which you can write for information:

ABC News InterActive, 7 West 66th St., 4th Floor, New York, NY 10023.

CEL Educational Resources, 477 Madison Ave., New York: NY 10022

FIGURE 6.10
Sample Videodisc Titles and Sources for Language Arts and Social Studies

SUBJECT	TITLE	SAMPLE SOURCE
ENGLISH	*David Copperfield*	Pioneer
	Treasure Island	Pioneer
GEOGRAPHY	The Explorers: A Century	
	of Discovery	National Geographic
	Great Cities of Europe	Ztek
	Our Environment	Optilearn
	Regard for the Planet	Voyager
HISTORY	American History Videodisc,	The Laser Learning Technologies
	Divided Union, The	The Laser Learning Technologies
	Holocaust, The	Friedman & Costello Associates
	Inventors and the	
	American Revolution	Churchill Media
	Set on Freedom: The American	
	Civil Rights Movement	CEL Communications
	Struggles for Justice	Laser Learning Technologies
	Video Encyclopedia of 20th	
	Century, The	Laser Learning Technologies
LITERATURE	All Summer in a Day	Laser Learning Technologies
	Shakespeare in Conversation	Laser Learning Technologies
SOCIAL STUDIES	A Geographic Perspective on	
	American History	National Geographic
	America and the World	
	Since WW II	Pioneer
	The First Ladies	Smithsonian
	In the Holy Land	Optical Data Corporation
	Martin Luther King	Optical Data Corporation
	Video Encyclopedia of	
	the 20th Century, The	CEL Educational Resources
	Vietnam: Ten-Thousand-Day War	Pioneer

Churchill Media, 12210 Nebraska Ave., Los Angeles, CA 90025.

Coronet/MTI Film & Video, 108 Wilmot Road, 5th Floor, Deerfield, IL 60015.

Emerging Technology Consultants, Inc., 2819 Hamline Ave., North St. Paul, MN 55112.

Encyclopaedia Britannica Educational Corp., 310 S. Michigan Ave., 6th floor, Chicago, IL 60604-9839.

Friedman & Costello Assoc., 402 Hickory Hollow, Canfield, OH 44406.

IBM Corp., Multimedia Division, 4111 Northside Pkwy., Atlanta, GA 30327.

Instructional Video, P.O. Box 21, Maumee, OH 43537.

Laser Learning Technologies, 120 Lakeside Ave., Suite 240, Seattle, WA 98122-6552.

MECC, 6160 Summit Drive North, Minneapolis, MN 55430-4003.

MMI Corporation, 2950 Wyman Pkwy., P.O. Box 19907, Baltimore, MD 21211.

National Geographic Society Education Services Division, 17th & M Street, NW, Washington, DC 20036.

Optical Data Corporation, 30 Technology Dr., Warren, NJ 07059.

Optilearn, Inc., Park Ridge Dr., Suite 200, Stevens Point, WI 54481.

Pioneer Communications of America, 3255-1 Scott Blvd., Santa Clara, CA 95054.

Prentice-Hall School Group, 113 Sylvan Ave., Englewood Cliffs, NJ 07632.

Sony Corp. of America Education System Division, 10833 Valley View St., Cypress, CA 90630.

Tandy Corp./Radio Shack, 1600 One Tandy Center, Ft. Worth, TX 76102.

Videodiscovery, Inc., 1700 Westlake Ave., N, Suite 600, Seattle, WA 98109-3012.

Ztek Co., P.O. Box 1055, Louisville, KY 40201-1055.

H. COMPUTERS

As a teacher in the twenty-first century, you must understand and be able to use computers as well as you can read and write. To complete your teaching credential, your teacher education program and state teacher licensing commission probably require some level of computer competency, or will soon.

The computer can be valuable to you in several ways:

- The computer can be useful in managing instruction by obtaining information, storing and preparing test materials, maintaining attendance and grade records, and preparing programs to aid in the academic development of individual students. This category of uses of the computer is referred to as computer-managed instruction, or CMI.
- The computer can be used directly for instruction, thanks to various instructional software programs. In their analysis of research studies, Hancock and Betts (1994) report that "in some schools, computer-assisted instruction (CAI) using integrated learning systems (individualized academic tutorials) has shown impressive gains, especially in the early years and among under-achieving urban populations" (p. 25). At Benjamin Banneker Computers Elementary School (Kansas City, MO), where students are expected to spend 50 percent of their daily learning time on a computer (and where there is one classroom computer for every two students), fourth and fifth graders now test out on the Iowa Test of Basic Skills (ITBS) at grades 5.4 and 5.8, respectively. When these same fifth graders entered the program as third graders, many were more than a year behind. Today, some of those fifth graders work at a tenth-grade level (Richey, 1994).
- The computer can be used to teach about computers and to help students develop their skills in computer use.
- And, with the help of software programs about thinking, the computer can be used to help students develop their thinking skills.

Benefits of Computers

For a student, the computer is motivating, exciting, and effective as an instructional tool. Consider the following examples.

Computer programs can motivate. One teacher motivated his students to write by sending their writing work to another class electronically. That was the beginning of the *kids2kids Writing Circle,* a national electronic writing project. (For information on necessary equipment, how to participate, and how to register with the network, see Pinney, 1991.)

Computer programs can activate. In Maine, a group of students prepares maps of local land and water resources from computer analyses of satellite images of the coastline, analyzes the maps, and then advises local authorities on development. Mixing technology and environmental awareness, the students have learned that they can exercise some control over their environment and their future (Wolcott, 1991).

Computer programs can excite. Especially exciting to students are computers with telecommunications systems that connect with other students from around the world, providing an exciting format for comparing data, sharing ideas, and encouraging students to challenge each other toward better understandings of global environmental problems. As an example, many middle school classrooms have joined the World School for Adventure Learning, one goal of which is to establish and sustain a global telecommunications network of schools for ongoing, interactive environmental studies. For more information about World School, contact University of St. Thomas World School for Adventure Learning, 2115 Summit Avenue, St. Paul, MN 55105. Similarly, the National Association of Secondary School Principals has joined the Global Learning Corporation to produce World Classroom, a telecommunications network involving K–12 students and teachers in global educational activities. For further information, contact NASSP Partnerships International at 800-253-7746.

The Placement and Use of Computers in Schools

The way that you use the computer for instruction is determined by your knowledge of and skills in its use, the number of computers available, where computers are placed in the school, and the software available. Despite tight budgets, schools continue to purchase computers. Approximately 50 percent of the computers in schools are found in classrooms, and about 40 percent are in computer labs. The days of a computer in every classroom are far from having yet arrived (National School Boards Association, 1993). Here are some possible scenarios of computer placement and how classroom teachers work within each.

Scenario 1. Many schools have one or more *computer labs* to which a teacher may take an entire class or send a small group of students for computer work. For example, at Skowhegan Area Middle School (Maine), computers have been integrated into the whole curriculum. In collaboration with members of the interdisciplinary teaching teams, the manager of the school's computer lab assists students in using computers as a tool to build their knowledge—to write stories with word processors, to illustrate science diagrams with paint utilities, to create interactive reports with hypermedia and to graph data they have gathered using spreadsheets (Muir, 1994). In many school computer labs, student computers are networked to the teacher's computer so that the teacher can control and monitor the work of each student. (For a discussion on how to use cooperative learning groups on computers and a recommended list of software that works in a cooperative learning environment, see Neal, 1994.)

Scenario 2. In some schools, students can take "Computers" as an elective course. Students in your classes who are simultaneously enrolled in the computer course may be given special computer assignments that they can then share with the rest of the class.

Scenario 3. Some classrooms have one computer that is connected to a large-screen video monitor. The teacher or student works the computer, and the monitor screen can be

FIGURE 6.11

Sample Computer Software Programs

ªKey to computer brands: AP = Apple; AT = Atari; C64 = Commodore 64 or 128; Comp = Compaq; IBM = International Business Machines; TRS = Radio Shack.

TOPIC	TITLE	COMPUTERª	COMPANY
LANGUAGE ARTS	The Bank Street Writer	AP/AT/C64/IBM	Scholastic
	Story Tree	AP/C64/IBM	Scholastic
PROBLEM SOLVING	Gertrude's Puzzles	AP/C64/Comp/IBM	The Learning Co.
	The Factory	AP/AT/C64/Comp/IBM/TRS	Sunburst
SOCIAL STUDIES	The Golden Spike	AP	National Geographic

seen by the entire class. As they view the screen, students can verbally respond to and interact with what is happening on the computer.

Scenario 4. In your classroom, you may be fortunate enough to have one or more computers, a videodisc player, an overhead projector, and an LCD (liquid crystal display) projection system. Coupled with the overhead projector, the LCD projection system allows you to project onto your large wall screen (and TV monitor at the same time) any image from computer software or a videodisc. With this system, all students can see and verbally interact with the multimedia instruction.

Scenario 5. Many classrooms have one or more computers. If this is the case in your classroom, you most likely will have one or two students working at the computer while others are doing other learning activities (an example of multilevel teaching).

Computers can be an integral part of a learning activity center and an important aid in your overall effort to individualize the instruction within your classroom.

Computer and Multimedia Programs

When selecting software programs, you and your colleagues need, of course, to choose those that are compatible with your brand of computer(s) and with your instructional objectives. According to a recent study of computers in U.S. schools (National Science Teachers Association, 1994, p. 3), about half are old computers for which software is no longer made and multimedia software and computer networks are not available. As budgets permit, schools will need to replace their old computers.

Like laser videodiscs and compact discs, computer software programs are continually being developed and are too many and varied to list in this book. For a brief sampling, see Figure 6.11. (See also Chapters 8 and 17 for additional information on using computers in language arts and social studies, respectively.)

The Online Classroom*

Teachers looking to make their classrooms more student-centered, collaborative, and interactive are turning to telecommunications networks. Ranging in scale from local bulletin board systems (BBS) to the Internet, these webs of connected computers allow teachers and students from around the world to reach each other directly and gain access to quantities of information previously unimaginable.

Students using networks learn new inquiry and analytical skills in a stimulating environment and, many people believe, also gain an increased awareness of their role as world citizens. For example, Leisa Winrich, a teacher at North Middle School in Menomonee Falls, Wisconsin, connected her mathematics students to KidLink network to share local weather data with distant classes. The Menomonee Falls students compile the international data and send them back out over the network. Winrich says, "We discovered that math does help us communicate; we can grow to better understand our global neighbors and their environments by exchanging and studying numbers" (Cohen, p. 6).

*Adapted from Philip Cohen (December 1994), The online classroom, *Association for Supervision and Curriculum Development Update, 36*(10), 1, 5–6. Reprinted with permission of the Association for Supervision and Curriculum Development. Copyright © 1994 by ASCD. All rights reserved.

Many network service providers exist. Directories are available in most bookstores. Here are a few samples:

- *K12Net.* A network of bulletin board systems for teachers, students, and parents. For information, call (503) 280–5280, ext. 450.
- *I*EARN.* The International Education Resource Network, connecting students and teachers internationally with electronic mail, conferences, and travel exchanges. For information, call (914) 962–5864.
- *PBS Online's Learning Link.* A network of BBS based at local public TV stations. For information, call (703) 739–8464.
- *Global SchoolNet.* Develops collaborative electronic mail projects. For information, call (619) 475–4852.
- *International Society for Technology and Education.* Promotes use of technology in schools. For information, call (503) 346–4414.
- *TERC.* Devoted to math and science; network programs include Global Laboratory and LabNet. For information, call (617) 547–0430.
- *Classroom Connect.* A monthly teacher's guide to Internet and commercial online services. For information, call (800) 638–1639.

Selecting Computer Software

In addition to selecting software programs that are compatible with your brand of computer(s) and with your instructional objectives, you must evaluate and test them for their compatibility with your language arts or social studies objectives. Evaluation forms are usually available from the local school district or from the state department of education and from professional associations.

When reviewing computer software, you should reject any software that

- Gives an audible response to student errors. No student should be forced to advertise mistakes to the whole class.
- Rewards failure. Some programs make it more fun to fail than to succeed.
- Has sound that cannot be controlled. The teacher should be able to easily turn sound on and off.
- Has technical problems. Is the software written so that it will not crash if the user accidentally types the wrong key? Incorrect responses should lead to software-initiated help comments.
- Has uncontrolled screen advance. Advancing to the next page should be under user control, not automatically timed.
- Gives inadequate on-screen instructions. All necessary instructions to run the program must be interactively displayed on the screen (in a continuously displayed instruction window, if possible).
- Has factual errors. Information displayed must be accurate in content, spelling, and grammar.
- Contains insults, sarcasm, and derogatory remarks. Students' character should not be compromised.
- Has poor documentation. Demand a teacher's guide that compares in quality to a textbook teacher's guide or other teaching aid.
- Does not come with a backup copy. Publishers should recognize the unique vulnerability of magnetic disks and offer low-cost replacement. (Information from Souviney, 1994, p. 135; used with permission of Macmillan Publishing Company.)

The CD-ROM

Computers have three types of storage disks—the floppy disk, the hard disk, and the CD-ROM, which is an abbreviation for "compact disc—read only memory." Use of a CD-ROM disc requires a CD-ROM drive. Newer computers may have built-in CD-ROM drives, while older ones must be connected to one. As with floppy and hard disks, CD-ROMs are used for storing characters in a digital format, while images on a videodisc are stored in an analog format. The CD-ROM is capable of storing approximately 250,000 pages of text, or the equivalent of 1,520 360K floppy disks or eight 70M hard disks, and therefore is ideal for storing large amounts of information such as dictionaries, encyclopedias, and general reference works full of graphic images that you can copy and modify. Some CD-ROM discs contain information that cannot be erased, transferred to a computer, or modified in any way.

The same material is used for both CD-ROM discs and laserdiscs, but the laserdisc platter is 12 inches across, while the CD-ROM disc is just 4.5 inches across. All CD-ROM discs require the use of a computer that is connected to a CD-ROM player or has one built in. Newer CD-ROM discs include video segments, just like those of videodiscs.

Any information stored on a CD-ROM disc or a videodisc can be found and retrieved within a few seconds. CD-ROMs are available from the distributors of videodiscs. Two publications that focus on CD-ROM products are *CD-ROM Professional,* available from newsstands, and the newsletter *Children's Software Revue,* available from 520 N. Adams St., Ypsilanti, MI 48197. A comprehensive listing of multimedia educational software (i.e., titles that have either a CD-ROM or a laser videodisc component) is available from the Educational Software Institute, 4213 South 94th Street, Omaha, NE 68127 (toll-free, 1–800–955–5570).

Use of copyrighted CD-ROMs. Usually, when purchasing CD-ROMs and other multimedia software packages intended for use by schools, you pay for a license to modify and use its contents for instructional purposes. However, not all CD-ROMs include copyright permission, so always check the copyright notice on any disc you purchase and use. Whenever in doubt, don't use it until you have asked your district media specialist about copyrights or have obtained necessary permission from the original source.

Sources of Free and Inexpensive Audiovisual Materials

Check your college or university library for sources of free and inexpensive audiovisual materials, listed in Figure 6.12.

Using Copyrighted Video and Computer Programs

You must be knowledgeable about the laws on the use of videos and computer software materials that are copyrighted. Although space here prohibits full inclusion of U.S. legal guidelines, your local school district undoubtedly can provide a copy of current district policies to ensure compliance with all copyright laws. As said earlier in the discussion about the use of printed materials that are copyrighted, when preparing to make any copy you must find out whether the copying is permitted by law under the category of "permitted use." If not, then you must get written permission to reproduce the material from the holder of the copyright. Figures 6.13 and 6.14 present guidelines for the copying of videotapes and of computer software. As of this writing, there are no guidelines for fair use of films, filmstrips, and slides.

FIGURE 6.12
Resources for Free and Inexpensive Audiovisual Materials

1. Professional periodicals and journals for teachers.
2. *An Annotated Bibliography of Audiovisual Materials Related to Understanding and Teaching the Culturally Disadvantaged.* Washington, DC: National Education Association.
3. *Catalog of Audiovisual Materials: A Guide to Government Sources* (ED 198 822). Arlington, VA: ERIC Documents Reproduction Service.
4. *Catalog of Free-Loan Educational Films/Video.* St. Petersburg, FL: Modern Talking Picture Service.
5. From Educator's Progress Service, Randolph, WI:
   Educator's Guide to Free Audio and Video Materials
   Educator's Guide to Free Films
   Educator's Guide to Free Filmstrips
   Guide to Free Computer Materials

FIGURE 6.13
Copyright Law for Off-Air Videotaping
SOURCE: Reprinted with the permission of Simon & Schuster, Inc. from the Macmillan College text INSTRUCTIONAL MEDIA 4/E by Robert Heinch, Michael Molenda and James D. Russell. Copyright ©1993 by Macmillan College Publishing Company, Inc.

Permitted uses
You may
1. Request your media center or audiovisual coordinator to record a program for you if you cannot or if you lack the equipment.
2. Keep a videotaped copy of a broadcast (including cable transmission) for 45 calendar days, after which the program must be erased.
3. Use the program in class once during the first 10 school days of the 45 calendar days, and a second time if instruction needs to be reinforced.
4. Have professional staff view the program several times for evaluation purposes during the full 45-day period.
5. Make a few copies to meet legitimate needs, but these copies must be erased when the original videotape is erased.
6. Use only a part of the program if instructional needs warrant (but see the next list).
7. Enter into a licensing agreement with the copyright holder to continue use of the program.

Prohibited uses
You may *not*
1. Videotape premium cable services such as HBO without express permission.
2. Alter the original content of the program.
3. Exclude the copyright notice on the program.
4. Videorecord before a request for use—the request to record must come from an instructor.
5. Keep the program, and any copies, after 45 days.

FIGURE 6.14
Copyright Law for Use of Computer Software
SOURCE: From the December, 1980, Congressional amendment to the 1976 Copyright Act.

Permitted uses
You may
1. Make a single back-up or archival copy of the computer program.
2. Adapt the computer program to another language if the program is unavailable in the target language.
3. Add features to make better use of the computer program.

Prohibited uses
You may *not*
1. Make multiple copies.
2. Make replacement copies from an archival or back-up copy.
3. Make copies of copyrighted programs to be sold, leased, loaned, transmitted, or given away.

SUMMARY

You have learned of the variety of tools available to supplement your instruction. When used widely, these tools will help you to reach more of your students more of the time. As you know, teachers must meet the needs of a diversity of students, many of whom are linguistically and culturally different. The material presented in this chapter should be of help in doing that. The future will undoubtedly bring technological innovations that will be even more helpful—compact discs, computers, and telecommunications equipment mark only the beginning of a teaching revolution. Within the next decade, new instructional delivery systems made possible by microcomputers and multimedia workstations will likely fundamentally alter the role of the classroom teacher.

You should remain alert to developing technologies for your teaching. Laser videodiscs and CD-ROMs interfaced with computers (that is, multimedia) and telecommunications offer exciting technologies for teachers. New instructional technologies are advancing at an increasingly rapid rate. For example, in 1993, the states of California, Florida, and Texas jointly awarded a contract to a software developer and textbook publishing company to cooperate in the development of a multimedia history and social science curriculum targeted for LPE students. Called Vital Links, the program will consist of an interrelated series of videodiscs, CD-ROMs, and print materials and is planned for availability in 1995.

You and your colleagues must maintain vigilance over new developments, constantly looking for those that will not only help make student learning meaningful and interesting and your teaching effective, but be cost effective as well.

QUESTIONS AND ACTIVITIES FOR DISCUSSION

1. Explain how your effective use of the writing board can help students see relationships among verbal concepts or information.

2. In selecting student reading materials, what should you look for?

3. Where could you turn to find out more about instructional materials that might be suitable for use in your teaching?

4. Describe what you should look for when deciding whether material that you have obtained free is suitable for use in your teaching.

5. Describe ways that you could use your school neighborhood and community as a rich resource for learning.

6. Describe how the use of specific cognitive tools helps to reinforce student learning.

7. It has been said that the overhead projector can be one of the teacher's best friends. Why?

8. Describe two ways that the laser videodisc or the CD-ROM can be used in teaching integrated language arts and social studies.

9. Share with others in your class your knowledge, observations, and feelings about the use of multimedia and telecommunications for teaching. From your discussion, what more would you like to know about the use of multimedia and telecommunications for teaching integrated language arts and social studies? How might you learn more about these things?

10. Describe any prior concepts you held that changed as a result of your experiences with this chapter. Describe the changes.

REFERENCES

Bormuth, J. (1968). The Cloze readability procedure. *Elementary English, 45,* 429–436.

Hancock, V., & Betts, F. (1994). From the lagging to the leading edge. *Educational Leadership, 51*(7), 24–29.

Hunter, M. (1994). *Enhancing teaching.* New York: Macmillan.

Johnson, M. S., & Kress, R. A. (1965). *Informal reading inventories.* Newark, DE: International Reading Association.

Kellough, R. D., & Roberts, P. L. (1994). *A resource guide for elementary school teaching: Planning for competence* (3rd ed.). New York: Macmillan.

Larson, C. O., & Dansereau, D. F. (1986). Cooperative learning in dyads. *Journal of Reading, 29*(6), 516–520.

McKenna, N. (1976). Synonymic versus verbatim scoring of the Cloze procedure. *Journal of Reading, 20,* 141–143.

Muir, M. (1994). Putting computer projects at the heart of the curriculum. *Educational Leadership, 51*(7), 30–32.

National School Boards Association. (1993). Education vital signs. *The American School Board Journal, 180*(12), A22.

National Science Teachers Association. (1994, February/March). *NSTA Reports!,* 3.

Neal, J. S. (1994). The interpersonal computer. *Science Scope, 17*(4), 24–27.

Pinney, S. (1991). Long distance writing. *Instructor, 100*(8), 69–70.

Richey, E. (1994). Urban success stories. *Educational Leadership, 51*(7), 55–57.

Souviney, R. J. (1994). *Learning to teach mathematics* (2nd ed.). New York: Merrill.

Wolcott, L. (1991). The new cartographers. In Maine, students are helping map the future. *Teacher Magazine, 2*(6), 30–31.

SUGGESTED READINGS

Beardslee, E. C., & Davis, G. L. (1989). *Interactive videodisc and the teaching-learning process.* Fastback 294. Bloomington, IN: Phi Delta Kappa Educational Foundation.

Bosch, K. A. (1993). Is there a computer crisis in the classroom? *Schools in the Middle, 2*(4), 7–9.

Dalton, D. W. (1990). The effects of cooperative learning strategies on achievement and attitudes during interactive video. *Journal of Computer Based Instruction, 17*(1), 8–16.

Dockterman, D. A. (1991). A teacher's tools. *Instructor, 100*(5), 58–61.

Dyer, D. C., et al. (1991). Changes in teachers' beliefs and practices in technology-rich classrooms. *Educational Leadership, 48*(8), 45–52.

Edinger, M. (1994). Empowering young writers with technology. *Educational Leadership, 51*(7), 58–60.

Green, L. (1982). *501 ways to use the overhead projector.* Littleton, CO: Libraries Unlimited.

Hancock, M. K., & Baugh, I. W. (1991). The new kid graduates. *Computing Teacher, 18*(7), 17–19, 21.

Heinich, R., Molenda, M., & Russell, J. D. (1993). *Instructional media* (4th ed.). New York: Macmillan.

Hunter, B., et al. (1993). Technology in the classroom: Preparing students for the Information Age. *Schools in the Middle, 2*(4), 3–6.

Is It Okay for Schools to Copy Software? (1991). Washington, DC: Software Publishers Association.

Johnson, L. N., & Tulley, S. (1989). *Interactive television: Progress and potential.* Fastback 289. Bloomington, IN: Phi Delta Kappa Educational Foundation.

Kanning, R. G. (1994). What multimedia can do in our classrooms. *Educational Leadership, 51*(7), 40–44.

Kaplan, N., et al. (1992). The classroom manager. Hands-on multimedia. *Instructor, 101*(8), 105.

Kernan, M., et al. (1991). Making and using audiovisuals. *Book Report, 10*(2), 16–17, 19–21, 23, 25–35.

Malouf, D. B., et al. (1991). Integrating computer software into effective instruction. *Teaching Exceptional Children, 23*(3), 54–56.

McDermott, C., & Trimble, K. (1993, Fall). Neighborhoods as learning laboratories. *California Catalyst,* 28–34.

Mead, J., et al. (1991). Teaching with technology. *Teacher Magazine, 2*(4), 29–57.

Murray, K. T. (1994). Copyright and the educator. *Phi Delta Kappan, 75*(7), 4552–4555.

Oaks, M., & Pedras, M. J. (1992). Technology education: A catalyst for curriculum integration. *Technology Teacher, 51*(5), 11–14.

O'Neil, J. (1993). Using technology to support 'authentic learning'. *ASCD Update, 35*(8), 1, 4–5.

Roberts, N., et al. (1990). *Integrating telecommunications into education.* Englewood Cliffs, NJ: Prentice Hall.

Snider, R. C. (1992). The machine in the classroom. *Phi Delta Kappa, 74*(4), 316–323.

Taggart, L. (1994). Student autobiographies with a twist of technology. *Educational Leadership, 51*(7), 34–35.

Talab, R. S. (1989). *Copyright and instructional technologies: A guide to fair use and permissions* (2nd ed.). Washington, DC: Association for Educational Communications and Technology.

Wishnietsky, D. H. (1993). *Using computer technology to create a global classroom.* Fastback 356. Bloomington, IN: Phi Delta Kappa Educational Foundation.

II

Methods and Activities for Language Arts

The teacher's goal for language arts instruction is to help students learn to communicate effectively with others through oral and written language.

The teacher's role is twofold: to foster a wide range of language use in the classroom and to find ways to extend children's language in real-life situations.

To many educators it is clear that to be most effective in teaching the diversity of children in today's classrooms, the learning in each discipline must be integrated with the learning in other disciplines, and thus made more meaningful to the lives of the children.

For higher levels of thinking and for learning that is most meaningful, recent research supports the use of an integrated curriculum and instructional techniques for social interaction. As a classroom teacher, your instructional task is twofold: (1) to plan for and provide developmentally appropriate hands-on experiences, with useful materials and the supportive environment necessary for children's meaningful exploration and discovery; and (2) to know how to facilitate the most meaningful and longest lasting learning possible once the child's mind has been activated by the hands-on experience. In Parts II through IV, we present techniques designed to help you complete those tasks, beginning in Part II with the teaching of language arts.

The approach is an integrated or "whole language" approach, based on cognitive, psycholinguistic, and sociolinguistic theories about how children learn and how they learn language, in particular. An instructional strategy based on these theories is developed in Chapter 7 by authors Gail Tompkins and Kenneth Hoskisson, and then applied for each language mode: listening, talking, reading, and writing. In Chapter 8, Tompkins and Hoskisson focus on how the teacher can provide a language-rich classroom to support children's learning. Then, in Chapter 9, Tompkins and Hoskisson emphasize the extension of language arts across the curriculum. In the final chapter of Part II, Chapter 10, borrowing from several authors, we present a collection of genuine action plans and activities for teaching language arts in grades 4 through 9. ■

CHAPTER 7

Learning and the Language Arts

I n this chapter we present an overview of the cognitive, psycholinguistic, and sociolinguistic learning theories that provide the foundation for the language arts curriculum. Specifically, you will learn

1. How knowledge about how children learn affects the teaching of language arts.
2. How knowledge about how children learn to talk relates to the teaching strategies used in teaching language arts.
3. How knowledge about how children become literate compares with how they are taught to read and write.
4. How an instructional model for language arts programs should be developed.

Understanding how children learn and particularly how they learn language influences how we teach language arts. The instructional program should never be construed as a smorgasbord of materials and activities; instead, teachers design instruction based on what they know about how children learn. The classroom teacher's role is changing. Teachers are now viewed as decision makers, empowered with both the obligation and the responsibility to make curricular decisions. In the language arts program, these curricular decisions have an impact on the content taught and the teaching strategies employed. Our approach here incorporates cognitive, psycholinguistic, and sociolinguistic theories of learning. This approach couples the constructivist, or cognitive, theories of learning proposed by Jean Piaget and Jerome Bruner (see Chapter 1) with the psycholinguistic theories developed by Frank Smith and the sociolinguistic theories of Lev Vygotsky (also discussed in Chapter 1). *Psycholinguistics* is a discipline that combines cognitive psychology with linguistics (the study of language) to focus on the cognitive or mental aspects of language learning. *Sociolinguistics* is a similar combination of disciplines—sociology and linguistics—to emphasize the social and cultural implications of language learning.

A. HOW CHILDREN LEARN

As you will recall from Chapter 1, Jean Piaget (1896–1980) was a Swiss psychologist who developed a new theory of learning, or cognitive development, that radically changed our conceptions of child development and learning. Piaget's theoretical framework (1969) differs substantially from behavioral theories that had influenced education for decades. Piaget describes learning as the modification of students' cognitive structures as they interact with and adapt to their environment. This definition of learning requires a reexamination of the teacher's role. Instead of dispensing knowledge, teachers engage students with experiences and environments that require them to modify their cognitive structures and construct their own knowledge.

Psycholinguists view language as an example of children's cognitive development, of their ability to learn. Young children learn to talk by being immersed in a language-rich environment and without formal instruction. In a period of only three or four years, children acquire a sizable vocabulary and internalize the grammar of language. Preschoolers' oral language development provides a model of language learning that can be used in discussing how children learn to read and write.

Sociolinguists view language learning as social and as a reflection of the culture and community in which students live (Heath, 1983; Vygotsky, 1978, 1986). According to Vygotsky, language helps to organize thought, and children use language to learn as well as to communicate and share experiences with others. Understanding that children use language for social purposes allows teachers to plan instructional activities that incorporate a social component, such as having students share their writing with classmates. And, because children's language and concepts of literacy reflect their cultures and home communities, teachers must respect students' language and appreciate cultural differences in their attitudes toward learning and learning language arts in particular.

The Cognitive Structure

The *cognitive structure* is the organization of knowledge in the brain, and knowledge is organized into category systems called *schemata*. (A single category is called a *schema*.) Within the schemata are three components: categories of knowledge, the features or rules for determining what constitutes a category and what will be included in each category, and a network of interrelationships among the categories (Smith, 1975). These schemata may be compared to a conceptual filing system in which children and adults organize and store the information derived from their past experiences. Taking this analogy further, information is filed in the brain in "file folders." As children learn, they add file folders to their filing system and as they study a topic, that file folder becomes thicker.

As children learn, they invent new categories, and while each person has many similar categories, schemata are personalized according to individual experiences and interests. Some people, for example, may have only one general category, bugs, into which they lump their knowledge of ants, butterflies, spiders, and bees, while other people distinguish between insects and spiders and develop a category for each. Those who distinguish between insects and spiders also develop a set of rules based on the distinctive characteristics of these animals for classifying them into one category or the other. In addition to bug or spider categories, a network of interrelationships connects these categories to other categories. Networks, too, are individualized, depending on each person's unique knowledge and experiences. The category "spiders" might be networked as a subcategory of arachnids, and the class relationship between scorpions and spiders might be made. Other networks, such as a connection to a "poisonous animals" category or a "webs and nests" category could have been made. The networks that link categories, characteristics, and examples with other categories, characteristics, and examples are extremely complex.

As children adapt to their environment, they add new information about their experiences that requires them to enlarge existing categories or to construct new ones. According to Piaget (1969), two processes make this change possible. *Assimilation* is the cognitive process by which information from the environment is integrated into existing schemata. In contrast, *accommodation* is the cognitive process by which existing schemata are modified or new schemata are restructured to adapt to the environment. Through assimilation, children add new information to their picture of the world; through accommodation, they change their picture of the world on the basis of new information.

Learning

The mechanism for cognitive growth or learning is the process of *equilibration* (Piaget, 1975). Encountering something a child does not understand or cannot assimilate causes *disequilibrium,* or cognitive conflict. Disequilibrium typically produces confusion and agitation, feelings that impel children to seek *equilibrium,* or a comfortable balance with the environment. In other words, when confronted with new or discrepant information, children (as well as adults) are intrinsically motivated to try to make sense of it. If the child's schemata can accommodate the new information, then the disequilibrium caused by the new experience will motivate the child to learn. Equilibrium is thus regained at a higher developmental level. These are the steps of this process:

1. Equilibrium is disrupted by the introduction of new or discrepant information.
2. Disequilibrium occurs, and the dual processes of assimilation and accommodation function.
3. Equilibrium is attained at a higher developmental level.

If the new information is too difficult, however, and children cannot relate it to what they already know, they will not learn. The important implication for teachers is that new information must be puzzling, challenging, or, to use Piaget's words, "moderately novel." Information that is too easy is quickly assimilated, and information that is too difficult cannot be accommodated and will not be learned. Bybee and Sund (1982) suggest that teachers strive for an optimal mismatch between what children already know and what new information to present.

Prediction occurs as children put their schemata to use in interpreting their environment. They anticipate what will happen if they act in certain ways and predict the results of their actions. When children enter any situation, they organize their behavior according to what they can anticipate, using those schemata that would be appropriate to assimilate whatever in the environment interests them. If their schemata can assimilate all the stimuli in the situation, they relax, because they are in a comfortable state of equilibrium. If there are stimuli in the environment for which they cannot predict the results, however, they will proceed more cautiously, trying to discover the meanings of the stimuli they cannot anticipate. Children seek equilibrium, but they are always undergoing disequilibrium because they cannot assimilate discrepant stimuli without some accommodation.

More recent theories of learning emphasize social interaction. Vygotsky (1978) asserted that children learn by internalizing social relationships, and language is an important part in the learning process. Children's experiences are organized and shaped by society, but rather than merely absorbing these experiences, children negotiate and transform them as a dynamic part of the social context. They learn to talk through interactions with other people and to read and write through interactions with literate children and adults.

Implications for Learning Language Arts

Students interact with their environment and actively construct knowledge using the processes of assimilation and accommodation. Learning takes place when existing schemata must be enlarged because of assimilated information and when the schemata must be restructured to account for new experiences being acted on and accommodated.

As students engage in learning activities, they are faced with learning and discovering some new element in an otherwise known or familiar system of information. Students recognize or seek out the information embedded in a situation that makes sense and is moderately novel. By being forced to contend with the novel part of the information, students' schemata are disrupted, or put in a state of disequilibrium. Accommodation of the novel information causes a reorganization of the schemata, resulting in students having more complex schemata and being able to operate on more complex information than was previously possible.

Students learn by relating the known to the unknown as they try to make sense of what they encounter in their environment. Teachers need to tailor instruction to help students relate what they know to what they do not know. The amount of new information in a lesson should be within students' capacity to assimilate and accommodate without experiencing long periods of disequilibrium.

Vygotsky (1978) used the concept of "zone of proximal development" to explain how children learn through social interactions with adults. Adults help children in moving from their actual stage of development toward their potential, and children use language as well as experiences to learn.

In the lessons they prepare for their students, teachers can create optimal conditions for learning. When students do not have the schemata for predicting and interpreting the new information, teachers must help students relate what they know to what they do not know. Therefore, the new information must appear in a situation that makes sense and must be moderately novel; it must not be too difficult for students to accommodate to it.

Students process information or learn using one of three modes: experience, observation, and language (Smith, 1975). Imagine, for example, that a boy has just received a new two-wheel bicycle for his fifth birthday. How will he learn to ride it? Will his parents read him a book about bicycles? Will his father demonstrate how to ride the new bicycle while the boy observes? Will the boy get on his new bicycle and learn to ride it by trial and error? Of course, he will get on the new bicycle and learn to ride it by riding—through direct experience. Later, the father might demonstrate a tricky maneuver his son is having trouble mastering, or the boy may become so interested in bicycling that he will be motivated to read a book to learn more about it. Yet the learning process begins with experience for both in-school and out-of-school learning.

Experience is the most basic, concrete way of learning. According to Piaget (1969), elementary students are concrete thinkers and learn best through active involvement. The second and third learning modes, observation and language, are progressively more abstract and further removed from experience. Activities involving observation and language can be made more meaningful when used in conjunction with direct experience and real-life materials. A list of school experiences using each mode is presented in Figure 7.1.

B. HOW CHILDREN LEARN LANGUAGE

Language enables children to learn about their world, to understand it, and to control it. As they learn to talk, youngsters implicitly develop knowledge about four language systems: the phonological, syntactic, semantic, and pragmatic systems. Children develop the *phonological,* or sound, system as they learn to pronounce each of the approximately 40 English speech sounds. These individual sounds, called *phonemes,* are represented in print with diagonal lines to differentiate them from *graphemes* (letter or letter combinations). Thus, the first letter in *mother* is written *m,* while the phoneme is written /m/, and the phoneme in *soap* represented by the grapheme *oa* is written /o/.

FIGURE 7.1
Activities Using the Three Learning Modes

EXPERIENCE	OBSERVATION	LANGUAGE
interviewing	creating filmstrips	brainstorming
manipulating objects	drawing and painting	choral speaking/reading
participating in dramatic	pictures	debating
play	making diagrams,	dictating stories
participating in field	clusters, and story	discussing
trips	maps	listening to audiotapes
participating in role-play	"reading" wordless	listening to stories read
activities	picture books	aloud
using puppets	viewing films, filmstrips,	participating in
using the five senses	and videotapes	conversations
word-play activities	viewing charts, maps,	participating in readers'
writing simulated	and models	theater
journals and	viewing plays and	reading
newspapers	puppet shows	taking notes
	viewing and writing	talking
	concrete poetry	writing
	watching	
	demonstrations	
	writing class	
	collaboration stories	

The second language system is the *syntactic,* or grammar, system. The word *grammar* here means the rules governing how words are combined in sentences as opposed to the grammar of English textbooks or the correct etiquette of language. Children use the syntactic system as they combine words to form sentences and learn to comprehend and produce statements, questions, and other types of sentences during the preschool years.

Another aspect of syntax is *morphology,* the study of word forms. Children quickly learn to combine words and word parts, such as adding *-s* to *dog* to create a plural and *-ed* to *play* to indicate past tense. These words and word parts are *morphemes,* the smallest units of meaning in language. *Dog* and *play* are *free morphemes* because they convey meaning while standing alone. The endings *-s* and *-ed* are *bound morphemes* because they must be attached to free morphemes to convey meaning. Prefixes and suffixes are also bound morphemes. The prefix *un-* in *unhappy* is a bound morpheme, whereas *happy* is a free morpheme because it can stand alone as a word. In addition to combining bound morphemes with free morphemes, two or more free morphemes can be combined to form compound words. *Birthday* is an example of a compound word created by combining two free morphemes.

The third language system is the *semantic,* or meaning, system. Vocabulary and the arrangement of words in sentences are the key components of this system. As children learn to talk, they acquire a vocabulary that is continually increasing through the preschool years. It is estimated that children have a vocabulary of 5,000 words by the time they enter school, and they continue to acquire 3,000 words each year during the elementary grades. As children acquire vocabulary, they also learn how to string the words together to form English sentences; for instance, children say "The dog has a bone," never "A has dog bone the." In English, word order and the relationships among words are crucial for comprehending the message.

The fourth language system is *pragmatics,* which deals with the social and cultural aspects of language use. People use language for many different *functions,* and how they talk or write varies according to purpose and audience. Language use also varies among social classes, cultural and ethnic groups, and geographic regions. These varieties are known as *dialects.* School is one cultural community, and the language of school is *standard English.* This register is formal, the one used in grammar books, in newspapers and magazines, and by television newscasters. Other forms, including those spoken in urban ghettos, in Appalachia, and by Mexican-Americans in the Southwest, are generally classified as *nonstandard English.* These nonstandard forms of English are alternatives, in which the phonology, syntax, and semantics differ from standard English—they are neither inferior nor substandard. These forms reflect the communities of the speakers, and the speakers communicate as effectively as others who use standard English in their communities.

As children learn to talk, read, and write, they learn to control the phonological, syntactic, semantic, and pragmatic language systems. We will refer to these systems using the terminology introduced in this section. Because the terminology can be confusing, the words and their definitions are reviewed in Figure 7.2.

Stages of Language Development

Young children acquire oral language in a fairly regular and systematic way (Morrow, 1989). All children pass through the same stages, but, because of developmental differences as well as differences in social and cultural backgrounds, they do so at widely different ages (Jaggar, 1985). The ages we mention in this section are estimates, for reference only.

Birth to age one. The first real evidence that children are developing language occurs when they speak their first words. Before that time, they experiment with sounds. Typically, during the first year of life, babies vocalize a wide variety of speechlike sounds. The sounds they produce are repeated strings of consonant plus vowel syllables. Amazingly, babies' vocalizations include English sounds as well as sounds heard in German, Russian, Japanese, and other languages. The sounds not common to English gradually drop out, probably as a result of both listening to sounds in the environment and parents' reinforcement of familiar sounds, such as the eagerly awaited *ma-ma* and *da-da.* By nine months, children use a few

FIGURE 7.2
Terminology of the Four Language Systems

1. **Phonological System**

phonology	The study of the sounds in a language.
phoneme	The smallest unit of sound.
grapheme	The written representation of a sound using one or more letters.

2. **Syntactic System**

syntax or grammar	The rules governing how words are combined to form sentences.
morphology	The study of morphemes or word forms.
morpheme	The smallest unit of meaning in a language.
free morpheme	A morpheme that can stand alone as a word.
bound morpheme	A morpheme that cannot stand alone as a word and must be attached to a free morpheme.

3. **Semantic System**

semantics	The study of the meaning of a language.

4. **Pragmatic System**

pragmatics	The study of the social and cultural aspects of language.
function	The purpose for which a person uses language.
dialect	Variations in syntax and word choice due to social class, ethnic or cultural group, or geographic region.
standard English	The form of English used in textbooks and by television newscasters.
nonstandard English	Other forms of English.

familiar words such as *milk, doggie,* and *Mommy* to express whole ideas. These first words are most often nouns and invented words, and it is difficult to understand meaning without observing children's accompanying actions or gestures. For example, *ball* may mean "Look, I see a ball," "I want that ball," or "Oops, I dropped my ball, and I can't reach it."

One to two years of age. Children's vocabularies expand rapidly in this stage, and children begin putting two words together. For example, they may say *bye-bye car* and *all-gone cookie.* This language is also known as telegraphic speech, because nonessential words are omitted as they are in telegrams. Children use nouns, verbs, and adjectives—all high-information words; they usually omit low-information words—prepositions, articles, and conjunctions. Children's speech in this stage is rule governed, but it is very different from adult speech, thus offering evidence for the psycholinguists' belief that children create their own ways to represent meaning rather than simply imitate adult language.

Two to three years of age. Telegraphic speech begins to evolve into longer utterances and to sound more like adult forms of talk. Word order, the basis of syntax in English, becomes important when children begin to use utterances of three and four words. At this point, grammatical relations such as subject, verb, and object begin to appear in overt syntactic structures. The phonological, syntactic, and semantic systems are constructed as development continues to come closer and closer to the adult form of the language used in their speech communities. Children's vocabularies reach about 1,000 words by the end of their third year.

Three to four years of age. Children now use more complex sentences that include pronouns, adjectives, adverbs, possessives, and plurals. They generalize knowledge about language and then learn about exceptions, such as irregular past-tense markers. At first children use the unmarked form of irregular verbs such as *ate,* as in "I ate my cereal," that they hear in the speech of those around them. Then they perceive that past tense is marked with the *-ed* morpheme and begin to use it with practically all past tense verbs, so that they now say "I eated my cereal." Finally children realize that some verbs are regular, with the past tense marked by *-ed* (as in *talk-talked*), whereas other verbs have different past-tense forms. Then they again say "I ate my cereal." This tendency to overgeneralize the *-ed* past-tense marker of regular verbs continues in some children's speech until age five. Children's vocabularies reach about 1,500 words by the end of this year.

Four to five years of age. Children's vocabularies grow to 3,000 words, and they have acquired most of the elements of adult language. Sentences are grammatical by adult standards, and children use language for more functions. Their sentences grow in length and complexity; they develop the auxiliary systems and transformations; they develop the ability to change the word order of their sentences to express desired meanings. The initial physical and emotional context of speech with objects, people, events, and locations continues to play an important role in language development.

Five to six years of age. By age five, children's language is similar to adult language. Most grammatical rules have been mastered, and language patterns are complex. Children use language for a variety of purposes, including to entertain. They can also use language in humorous ways, and their interest in jokes and riddles usually begins at this age.

During the preschool years, parents make an important contribution to language development by expanding and extending children's talk. To the child's utterance, "Dog bark," for example, a parent might respond, "Yes, the dog is barking at the kitty," and provide information about why the dog is barking (Cazden, 1972). This interaction helps the child interpret what is happening in the environment and adds grammatical information. It is a model to learn from, not a sample to copy (Cazden, 1983). Bruner (1978) used the term *scaffold* as a metaphor to explain the value of parents' expansions and extensions of their children's language. Scaffolds are temporary launching platforms that support and encourage children's language development to more complex levels. In addition, Bruner noted that parents use these interactions to keep their children from sliding back once they have moved on to higher platforms and more complex language constructions. Teachers provide a similar type of assistance as they support students in learning language arts (Applebee & Langer, 1983).

Development in the Elementary Grades and Beyond

Although the most important period in oral language acquisition is the preschool years, children's phonological, syntactic, semantic, and pragmatic development continues in the elementary grades and beyond. They continue to acquire additional sentence patterns; their vocabularies expand tremendously; and they master the remaining sounds of English.

Phonological development. Children have mastered a large part of the phonological system by the time they come to school. A few sounds, especially in medial and final positions, however, are not acquired until after age five or six. These sounds include /v/, /th/, /ch/, /sh/, and /zh/. Even at age seven or eight, students still make some sound substitutions, especially in consonant clusters. They may, for example, substitute /w/ for /r/ or /l/, as in *cwack* for *crack* (DeStefano, 1978). When students are learning to read and write, they read words aloud the same way they say them and spell words phonetically, the same way they say them.

Syntactic development. Students acquire a variety of sentence patterns during the elementary grades. They begin to construct complex sentences and use embedding techniques to combine ideas. Whereas primary-grade students use the connector *and* to string together a series of ideas, middle- and upper-grade students learn to use dependent clauses and other connectors. A young child might say, "I have a hamster *and* he is brown *and* his name is Pumpkin *and* he likes to run on his wheel," but an older student can embed these ideas: "My brown hamster named Pumpkin likes to run on his wheel." Older students learn to use connectors such as *because, if, unless, meanwhile, in spite of,* and *nevertheless* (Loban, 1976). The constructions students learn to use in their talk also appear in their writing. Ingram (1975) found that fifth- and seventh-grade students used more complex, embedded structures in writing than in talking. This finding makes sense because when students write, they must organize their thoughts and, for efficiency, embed as much information as possible.

Students also learn more about word order in English sentences. Consider these two sentences:

Ann told Tom to leave.

Ann promised Tom to leave.

Who is going to leave? According to the Minimal Distance Principle (MDP), the noun closest to the complement verb (i.e., *to leave*) is the subject of that verb. In the first sentence, *Tom* is the person who will leave. Substitute these other verbs for *told: asked, wanted, tried, urged, commanded, implored.* In each case *Tom* is the person to leave. *Promise* is an exception to the MDP, however, so in the second sentence, it is *Ann* who will leave, not *Tom.* Chomsky (1969) found that primary-grade students overgeneralize the MDP principle and equate *promise* sentences with *tell* sentences. During the middle grades, however, students learn to distinguish the exceptions to the rule.

As students learn to read, they are introduced to the more complex syntactic forms and other conventions found in written language. One form unique to writing is the passive voice. The active voice is almost always used in talk (e.g., "Bobby broke the vase"), rather than the passive voice (e.g., "The vase was broken by Bobby").

Semantic development. Of the language systems, Lindfors (1980) says that semantic growth is the most vigorous in the elementary grades. Children's vocabulary increases rapidly, perhaps as much as 3,000 words per year. At the same time that children are learning new words, they are also learning that many words have more than one meaning. Meaning is usually based on context, or the surrounding words. The common word *run,* for instance, has more than 30 meanings listed in *The Random House Dictionary of the English Language* (Flexner, 1987), and the meaning is tied to the context in which it is used:

Will the mayor *run* for reelection?

The bus *runs* between Dallas and Houston.

The advertisement will *run* for three days.

The plane made a bombing *run.*

Will you *run* to the store and get a loaf of bread for me?

The dogs are out in the *run.*

Oh, no! I got a *run* in my new pair of pantyhose!

Primary-grade students do not have the full, adult meaning of many words; rather, they learn meanings through a process of refinement (Clark, 1971). They add "features" or layers of meaning. In the elementary grades, students use this refinement process to distinguish between pairs of words such as *ask* and *tell* to expand their range of meanings for many common words.

Pragmatic development. When children come to school they speak the language of their family and community, and at school they are introduced to standard English, which may be quite similar to or different from their own language dialect. They learn about appropriateness and to vary the language they speak or write according to form, purpose, and audience. M. A. K. Halliday (1973, 1975) has identified seven categories of language function that apply to oral and written language and even to the nonlanguage forms of communication such as gestures and pantomime. These are Halliday's seven categories:

1. Instrumental language—language to satisfy needs
2. Regulatory language—language to control the behavior of others
3. Interactional language—language to establish and maintain social relationships
4. Personal language—language to express personal opinions
5. Imaginative language—language to express imagination and creativity
6. Heuristic language—language to seek information and to find out about things
7. Informative language—language to convey information.

During the elementary grades, students learn to use oral language for a wider range of functions, and they learn written language alternatives for the oral language functions. Figure 7.3 lists some oral and written language alternatives for the seven language functions. Frank Smith (1977) has made a number of observations about how these language functions are learned and applied in school settings:

FIGURE 7.3
Language Activities Illustrating the Seven Functions of Language

FUNCTION	ORAL LANGUAGE ACTIVITY	WRITTEN LANGUAGE ACTIVITY
1. Instrumental Language	conversations commercials	notes business letters letters-to-the-editor advertisements
2. Regulatory Language	directions gestures dramatic play	directions classroom rules
3. Interactional Language	conversations sharing discussions	friendly letters pen pal letters courtesy letters dialogue journals
4. Personal Language	discussions debates show and tell sharing commercials	personal journals dialogue journals response to literature activities advertisements
5. Imaginative Language	storytelling readers' theater dramatic play role-playing	reading and writing stories and poems writing scripts simulated journals simulated newspapers
6. Heuristic Language	interviews role-playing discussions	learning logs clustering cubing researching and report writing
7. Informative Language	oral reports discussions	researching and report writing reading and writing newspapers reading and writing timelines, charts, and maps

- Language is learned in genuine communication experiences, rather than through practice activities that lack functional purposes.
- Skill in one language function does not generalize to skill in other functions.
- Language is rarely used for just one function at a time; typically, two or more language functions are involved in talking or writing.
- These language functions involve an audience—listeners for talking and readers for writing.
- Language is one communication alternative; other alternatives include gestures, drawings, pantomime, and rituals.

When children are using language functionally, they are using it for genuine communication and are interacting with others (Pinnell, 1975). These two characteristics of functional language are apparent in both oral and written language.

The teacher's role is twofold: to foster a wide range of language use in the classroom, and to find ways to extend children's language in real-life situations. Because children's ability to use one language function does not generalize to ability in other functions, it is essential that students have opportunities to use each of the seven language functions. In her study of the functions of talk in a primary-grade classroom, Pinnell (1975) found that first graders most commonly used interactional language (for social purposes) and rarely used heuristic language (to seek information) when they talked and worked in small groups. Camp (1987) studied seventh graders' language functions during science class and found that students used the same language functions—interactional and heuristic—most commonly and least commonly. These two researchers concluded that students need to experiment with all seven language functions to learn what they can accomplish with language. Some of the language functions may not occur spontaneously in students' talk and writing, and teachers need to plan genuine communication experiences that incorporate all the language functions.

The concept of language functions is relatively new, and research is currently under way that will undoubtedly affect how language arts is taught in the future. For instance, Gere and Abbott (1985) categorized students' talk in writing conferences, and Florio and Clark (1982) examined the language functions in elementary students' compositions. One drawback of much of this research is that several different frameworks are being used to categorize children's language samples, so it is difficult to compare the findings.

Implications for Learning Language Arts

How children learn to talk has important implications for how children learn language arts in school and how teachers teach language arts. These characteristics delineate the sociopsycholinguistic orientation presented in this chapter:

- Children learn to talk by being immersed in the language of their community, not by being taught talking skills in a prescribed sequential order.
- Children construct their own knowledge as they make and test hypotheses, leading to progressive refinements of their talk.
- Children learn and use language for meaningful, functional, and genuine communication purposes.
- Adults provide models and scaffolds to support children's learning.
- Parents and other caregivers expect that children will be successful in learning to talk.

Imagine how different life would be in homes with young children if adults tried to teach children to talk as they have been traditionally taught to read and write. Parents would bring workbooks and charts listing talk skills home from the hospital with the baby. Children would be kept in a quiet room, and parents would first speak to the babies only in single, one-syllable words, then in two-syllable words, and finally in short sentences. Parents would introduce consonant sounds in a particular order, and at some point they would try to use all short-vowel words in silly nonsense sentences. Ridiculous, right?

If children learn to talk so well in the short period of three or four years using a natural, immersion approach, why should teachers use an entirely different method to help children learn to read and write only a year or two later? Educators are now recognizing that the strategies parents use to help children learn to talk can be adapted for teaching language arts.

C. HOW CHILDREN BECOME LITERATE

Literacy used to mean knowing how to read, but the term has been broadened to encompass both reading and writing, so that *literacy* now means the competence "to carry out complex tasks using reading and writing related to the world of work and to life outside the school" (*Cases in Literacy,* 1989, p. 36). Educators are also identifying other literacies that they believe will be needed in the twenty-first century. Our reliance on radio and television for conveying ideas has awakened us to the importance of "oracy" (the ability to express oneself in and understand spoken language), and visual literacy is receiving a great deal of attention.

The term *literacy* is being used in different ways as well. Teachers are introducing students to computers and developing a "computer literacy." Similarly, math and science educators speak of mathematical and scientific literacies. Hirsch (1987) has called for another type of literacy, "cultural literacy," as a way to introduce children "to the major ideas and ideals from past cultures that have defined and shaped today's society." Rather than a prescription of books to read or concepts to define, however, literacy is a tool, a way to come to learn about the world and a means to participate more fully in society.

Emergent Literacy

Literacy is a process that begins well before the elementary grades and continues into adulthood, if not throughout life. It used to be that five-year-old children came to kindergarten to be "readied" for reading and writing instruction, which would formally begin in first grade. The implication was that there was a point in children's development when it was time to begin teaching them to read. For those not ready, a variety of "readiness" activities would prepare them for reading. Since the 1970s this view has been discredited by teachers' and researchers' observations (Clay, 1989). The children themselves demonstrated that they could retell stories, scribble letters, invent printlike writing, and listen to stories read aloud to them. Some children even taught themselves to read.

This new perspective on how children become literate—that is, how they learn to read and write—is known as *emergent literacy*. Studies from 1966 on have shaped the current outlook (Clay, 1967; Durkin, 1966; Holdaway, 1979; McGee & Richgels, 1989; Morrow, 1989; Taylor, 1983; Teale, 1982; Teale & Sulzby, 1989). Now, researchers are looking at literacy learning from the child's point of view. The age range has been extended to include children as young as twelve or fourteen months of age who listen to stories being read aloud, notice labels and signs in their environment, and experiment with pencils. The concept of literacy has been broadened to include the cultural and social aspects of language learning, and children's experiences with and understandings about written language—both reading and writing—are included as part of emergent literacy.

Teale and Sulzby (1989) paint a portrait of young children as literacy learners with these characteristics:

Children begin to learn to read and write very early in life.

Young children learn the functions of literacy through observing and participating in real-life settings in which reading and writing are used.

Young children's reading and writing abilities develop concurrently and interrelatedly through experiences in reading and writing.

Young children learn through active involvement with literacy materials, by constructing their understanding of reading and writing.

Teale and Sulzby describe young children as active learners who construct their own knowledge about reading and writing with the assistance of parents and other literate persons. These caregivers help by demonstrating literacy as they read and write, by supplying materials, and by structuring opportunities for children to be involved in reading and writing. The environment is positive, with children experiencing reading and writing in many facets of their everyday lives and observing others who are engaged in literacy activities.

Implications for Learning Language Arts

The way children learn about written language is remarkably similar to how they learn to talk. Children are immersed in written language as they are first in oral language. They have many opportunities to see reading and writing taking place for real purposes and to experiment with written language. Through these experiences, children actively construct their knowledge about literacy. As parents and other adults model the processes of reading and writing, they provide a scaffold for children's learning.

D. HOW CHILDREN LEARN LANGUAGE ARTS

It seems to me that the most important general goal for education in the language arts is to enable each child to communicate, as effectively as he or she can, what he or she intends and to understand, as well as he or she can, what others have communicated, intentionally or not (Brown, 1979, p. 483).

Roger Brown's statement succinctly states the goal for language arts instruction at all grade levels. The teacher's goal, then, is to help students learn to communicate effectively with others through oral and written language.

Communicative Competence

The ability to communicate effectively is known as *communicative competence* (Hymes, 1974), and it involves two components. The first component is the ability to transmit meaning through talking and writing, and the second is the ability to comprehend meaning through listening and reading. Communicative competence also involves pragmatics—students' fluency in the different registers of language as well as knowing when it is socially appropriate to use language in each register. For example, we use informal language with family members and close friends and more formal language with people we know less well or when giving a speech. Similarly, in writing we use different *registers,* or levels of formality. We write letters to close friends in a less formal register than we would use in writing a letter to the editor of the local newspaper.

The content and teaching strategies discussed in this book capitalize on students' cognitive and language abilities to help students develop communicative competence. We emphasize that teachers should provide opportunities for students to use language in situations that are meaningful, functional, and genuine. These three characteristics are important determinants in learning. Walter Loban (1979) echoes our beliefs: "The path to power over language is to use it in genuinely meaningful situations, whether we are reading, listening, writing, or speaking" (p. 485). Vygotsky (1978) concurs: "Reading and writing must be something the child needs" (p. 117); they should be "relevant to life" (p. 118).

We will discuss a variety of language activities for helping students develop communicative competence, such as:

Conducting oral interviews of community residents with special knowledge, interests, or talents

Writing a simulated journal assuming the role of a character while reading a story, autobiography, or informational book

Writing stories using the writing process and then sharing the stories with classmates and other genuine audiences

Analyzing word choice or other aspects of language in the poems they read and write

Compiling class newspapers or simulated newspapers set in the historical period being studied.

These activities exhibit the three characteristics of all worthwhile experiences with language. They use language in meaningful rather than contrived situations. They are functional, or real-life, activities. They are genuine rather than artificial activities, such as those typical of workbooks and ditto sheets, because they communicate. They are activities that provide the hands-on/minds-on learning that was discussed in Chapter 1.

The Four Language Modes with Key Concepts

Traditionally, language arts educators have defined *language arts* as the study of the four modes of language: listening, talking, reading, and writing. Thinking is sometimes referred to as the fifth language mode but, more accurately, it permeates all the language modes.

Beginning at birth, listening is children's first contact with language. Listening instruction is often neglected in intermediate and middle- grade classrooms because teachers feel that students have already learned to listen and that instructional time should be devoted to reading and writing. An alternative view of listening and listening instruction focuses on the following key concepts:

- Listening is a process of which hearing is only one part.
- Students listen for many purposes.
- Students listen differently according to their purpose.
- Students need to learn strategies for the different listening purposes.

As with listening, teachers often neglect instruction in talk during the intermediate and middle grades because they feel students already know how to talk. Students need to refine their oral language skills, however, and learn to use talk for more formal purposes. These are key concepts about talk:

- Talk is an essential part of the language arts curriculum.
- Talk is necessary for success in all academic areas.
- Talk ranges from informal conversations and discussions to more formal presentations, including oral reports and debates.
- Drama, including storytelling and role-playing, provides a valuable method of learning and powerful way of communicating.

Until recently, teachers have focused instructional time almost exclusively on reading, but now they are learning to integrate reading with writing and the other language arts. We present the integrated approach throughout this book. Key concepts about reading include the following:

- Reading and writing are interrelated strategic processes.
- Reading allows children to experience and appreciate literature.
- Reading involves both reading aloud to students and students reading independently.
- Informational books are resources for content area–related language activities (e.g., oral and written research reports).
- Proofreading is a unique type of reading that writers use when they edit their compositions.

The new emphasis on writing focuses on the writing process, and students use this process approach to draft, revise, and share their writing. Spelling and handwriting are tools that writers need to communicate effectively with their readers. The following are key concepts about writing:

- Informal writing is used as a way to learn and as prewriting.
- Writing is a process in which students cycle recursively through prewriting, drafting, revising, editing, and sharing stages.
- Students experiment with many different written language forms.
- Students learn to write stories, poems, and other forms using literature as a model.
- Spelling and handwriting are tools for writers.

The four language modes can be compared and contrasted in a variety of ways. First, oral versus written: listening and talking are oral, while reading and writing are written. Second, primary versus secondary: the oral language modes are learned informally at home before children come to school, whereas the written language modes are typically considered the school's responsibility and are taught more formally. Listening and talking are called primary language modes; reading and writing are called secondary language modes. The third way to compare the modes is receptive versus productive: two language modes, listening and reading, are receptive; talking and writing are productive. In the receptive language modes, students receive or comprehend a message orally through listening or in writing as they read. In the productive language modes, students produce a message, orally or in writing. These three sets of relationships are shown graphically in Figure 7.4.

The grouping of the four language modes is both arbitrary and artificial. This arrangement wrongly suggests that there are separate stages of development for each language mode and that children use different mental processes for listening, talking, reading, and writing (Smith, 1979). It has generally been assumed that the four language modes develop in sequence from listening to talking to reading to writing. Although listening is the first form of language to develop, with talking beginning soon after, parents and preschool teachers have recently documented children's early interest in both reading and writing (Baghban, 1984; Bissex, 1980). Also, Carol Chomsky (1971) and other researchers have observed young children experimenting with writing earlier than with reading. On the basis of reports from parents, teachers, and researchers, we can no longer assume that there is a definite sequence in learning and using the four language modes.

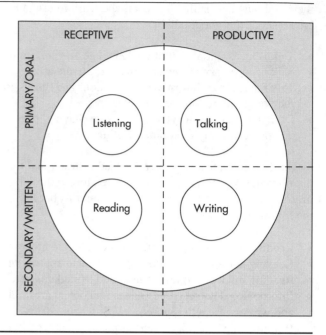

FIGURE 7.4
Relationships among the
Four Language Modes

This grouping also suggests a division among the language modes, as though they could be used separately. In reality, they are used simultaneously and reciprocally. Almost any language arts activity involves more than one language mode. For instance, in learning about stories, students use all four language modes. They begin by listening when parents and teachers read aloud to them and later by reading stories themselves. Next, they retell familiar as well as original stories. They make puppets to dramatize and role-play favorite stories. From telling stories, they move to writing stories and sharing them with classmates or other genuine audiences. The cluster in Figure 7.5 lists these and other activities for learning about stories that involve all four language modes.

Over a 13-year period, researcher Walter Loban (1976) documented the language growth and development of a group of 338 students from kindergarten through 12th grade (ages 5–18). Two purposes of his longitudinal study were to examine differences between students who used language effectively and those who did not and to identify predictable stages of language development. Three of Loban's conclusions are especially noteworthy to our discussion of the relationship among the language modes. First, Loban reported positive correlations among the four language modes. Second, he found that students with less effective oral language (listening and talking) abilities tended to have less effective written language (reading and writing) abilities. And, third, he found a strong relationship between students' oral language ability and their overall academic ability. Loban's seminal study demonstrates clear relationships among the language modes and emphasizes the need to teach oral language in the elementary school language arts curriculum.

An Instructional Model

Theories of learning and evidence about how children learn language and become literate are useful in developing a model of instruction that can be adapted to various teaching strategies in a language arts program. This model establishes a sequence of instruction for the interaction of students, teacher, and materials in an environment that promotes the assimilation and accommodation of information. Language plays a crucial role in developing concepts as information is presented and discussed. Teachers serve both as a model and a scaffold to support and extend students' learning. The six steps in the sequence of instruction follow.

1. *Initiating.* Teachers introduce the information they want students to use in learning a concept or in understanding something. The initiating step includes the teacher's initial questions, statements, and activities for stimulating interest in the lesson materials and

FIGURE 7.5
How the Language Modes Are Used in Learning about Stories

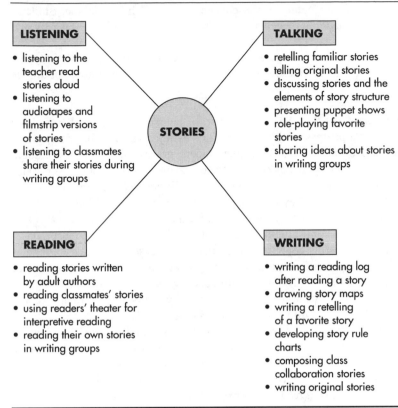

LISTENING
- listening to the teacher read stories aloud
- listening to audiotapes and filmstrip versions of stories
- listening to classmates share their stories during writing groups

TALKING
- retelling familiar stories
- telling original stories
- discussing stories and the elements of story structure
- presenting puppet shows
- role-playing favorite stories
- sharing ideas about stories in writing groups

STORIES

READING
- reading stories written by adult authors
- reading classmates' stories
- using readers' theater for interpretive reading
- reading their own stories in writing groups

WRITING
- writing a reading log after reading a story
- drawing story maps
- writing a retelling of a favorite story
- developing story rule charts
- composing class collaboration stories
- writing original stories

engaging the students' participation. The process of assimilation begins when students are stimulated to participate in the lesson, and it will continue until cognitive conflict occurs.

2. *Structuring.* In this step, teachers structure the information so that students can begin to overcome the cognitive conflict they experience in the initiating step. To overcome cognitive conflict, students begin to enlarge or restructure an existing schema to fit the information, or they begin to develop new schemata to organize the information. The information must be moderately novel and must relate in some way to what students already know. Relating new information to what students already know gives teachers greater assurance that students will be able to assimilate and accommodate it. Teachers must explore with students what information they already have in their schemata, because they can only infer students' existing schemata from what they say and do.

3. *Conceptualizing.* Teachers focus students' attention on the relationships among the pieces of information they present. In the structuring step, teachers have located and established the information; in the conceptualizing step, they try to organize and make explicit the relationships among the facts and to further the process of accommodation begun during structuring. When the accommodation process is completed, the existing schemata have been enlarged or a new schema has been developed that fits the new information. In either case, the cognitive conflict that arose in the initiating step has been eliminated.

4. *Summarizing.* Teachers review the major points of the lesson in this step. The material used in the structuring step and the relationships established during the conceptualizing step are organized and summarized for reviewing the concept. This step allows students to make any necessary adjustments in the concept or information and in the new interrelationships established within their cognitive structures. For students who did not complete the accommodation process in the conceptualizing step, summarizing presents another opportunity to accommodate the information.

5. *Generalizing.* Here teachers present information similar to that introduced in the initiating step. The same concept or information is contained in this new material. This step is a check on students' understanding of the concept presented in the lesson. Students demonstrate their understanding by generalizing from the first material to this new material.

6. *Applying.* In this step, students incorporate the concept or information in an activity that allows them to demonstrate their knowledge by using the concept in a novel or unique way.

Using the instructional model. Students do not, of course, learn in such neat little steps. Rather, learning is a process of ebb and flow in which the assimilating and accommodating processes move back and forth as the student grasps pieces of information. Students may grasp a new concept in any of the steps of the instructional model; some students may not learn it at all. Teachers will need to plan additional lessons for the students who do not learn. Whether or not they learn depends on the closeness of the fit between their schemata and the information being presented. Information that does not in some way relate to an existing schema is almost impossible to learn. Information must be just moderately novel to fit students' existing cognitive structures. Some lessons may not lend themselves readily to this six-step sequence of instruction; for certain concepts, one or more of the steps may not be appropriate, and some adjustments may be necessary.

A lesson on fables will illustrate how the teaching strategy can be used with almost any language arts concept. The application is summarized in Figure 7.6.

Fables are brief stories that teach a lesson. Our best-known fables were compiled by Aesop, a Greek slave who lived in the sixth century B.C., but many other civilizations have contributed fables as well. A number of fables have been retold for children and, recently, children's authors such as Arnold Lobel (1980) have written their own books of fables. The goal of this lesson is for students to read fables, examine how authors construct the stories, and then tell and write their own fables. The lesson is organized around the six steps of the teaching strategy we have discussed. Other activities that would be part of this two-week unit for a fourth-grade class are not included in this plan for the sake of clarity.

1. *Initiating.* The teacher reads several fables such as "The Hare and the Tortoise" and "The Lion and the Mouse" from Hague's *Aesop's Fables* (1985) and explains that these short stories that teach a moral are called fables.

2. *Structuring.* Students and teacher develop a chart listing the characteristics of fables. The list may include these characteristics:

Fables are short.

The characters are usually animals.

FIGURE 7.6
Using the Teaching Strategy

STEP	FABLES LESSON
Initiating	Read several fables and explain that fables are brief stories that teach a lesson.
Structuring	Develop a chart listing the characteristics of fables. Read one or two others and check that the chart includes all characteristics.
Conceptualizing	Have students read other fables, then choose a favorite one to retell orally, with drawings, or in writing.
Summarizing	Review the fables already read and the list of characteristics. Ask students to write a paragraph explaining fables.
Generalizing	Read other stories including some with implicitly stated morals. Have students explain why these stories are or are not fables.
Applying	Students write fables using the writing process and share their fables with other students.

The setting is usually rural and not important to the story.

Fables involve only one event.

The moral is usually stated at the end of the story.

The teacher then reads one or two other fables, and the students check that their list of the characteristics of fables is complete.

3. *Conceptualizing.* Students read other fables, and then relate a favorite fable by telling it aloud, by drawing a series of pictures, or in writing.

4. *Summarizing.* The teacher and students review the fables they have read and the list of characteristics they have developed. Then the teacher asks students to write a paragraph explaining what a fable is. Students share their explanations and compare them to the list of characteristics.

5. *Generalizing.* Students read other fables, such as Lobel's *Fables* (1980) or Lionni's *Frederick's Fables* (1985). It is important to include some fables that state the moral implicitly rather than explicitly. Students explain why these stories are or are not fables. The teacher also points out that, although these fables are based on many of the same morals that Aesop used, they were created—not retold—by Arnold Lobel and Leo Lionni.

6. *Applying.* Students write their own fables based on a moral that may be explicitly stated at the end of the story or implied in the story. Students use the writing process to draft, revise, edit, and publish their work. Later they share their fables with classmates or with students in another class who are also reading and writing fables.

SUMMARY

Language arts instruction should be based on theories and research about how children learn and how they learn language in particular. This chapter presented cognitive, psycholinguistic, and sociolinguistic theories of learning and related research to develop a paradigm for learning and teaching language arts. The paradigm includes these components:

- Children learn through immersion in their environment.
- Children actively construct their knowledge through interaction with the environment.
- Adults facilitate children's learning through modeling and providing scaffolds.
- Adults expect children to be successful in learning.

The purpose of language arts instruction is to develop children's communicative competence in the four language modes: listening, talking, reading, and writing. Based on the paradigm, language arts activities should be meaningful, functional, and genuine. Lessons may be based on a six-step instructional model.

QUESTIONS AND ACTIVITIES FOR DISCUSSION

1. Observe a language arts lesson being taught. Try to determine if the components of the language learning paradigm presented in this chapter are operationalized in the classroom. What conclusions can you draw about students' learning?

2. Observe and tape-record several students' talk. Analyze the development of their phonological, syntactic, semantic, and pragmatic language systems. If possible, compare primary grade students' language with intermediate and middle grade students' languages.

3. Observe a middle grade classroom and listen to students' oral language. Try to identify students' use of each of the seven language functions discussed in this chapter. Also, examine the writing in their writing folders to determine which of the language functions they have used.

4. Interview a language arts teacher and ask how this teacher teaches the four language arts—listening, talking, reading, and writing. Compare the teacher's comments with the information in this chapter.

5. For a specific grade level, develop a lesson plan using the teaching strategy presented in this chapter.

REFERENCES

Applebee, A. N., & Langer, J. A. (1983). Instructional scaffolding: Reading and writing and natural language activities. *Language Arts, 60,* 168–175.

Baghban, M. (1984). *Our daughter learns to read and write: A case study from birth to three.* Newark, DE: International Reading Association.

Bissex, G. L. (1980). *Gnys at wrk: A child learns to write and read.* Cambridge, MA: Harvard University Press.

Brown, R. (1979). Some priorities in language arts education. *Language Arts, 56,* 483–484.

Bruner, J. S. (1978). The role of dialogue in language acquisition. In A. Sinclair, R. J. Jarvella, & W. M. Levelt (Eds.), *The child's conception of language,* pp. 241–256. New York: Springer-Verlag.

Bybee, R. W., & Sund, R. B. (1982). *Piaget for educators* (2nd ed.). Columbus, OH: Merrill.

Camp, D. J. (1987). Language functions used by four middle grade students. Unpublished doctoral dissertation. Norman: University of Oklahoma.

Cases in literacy: An agenda for discussion. (1989). Newark, DE: International Reading Association and Urbana, IL: National Council of Teachers of English.

Cazden, C. B. (1972). *Child language and education.* New York: Holt, Rinehart and Winston.

Cazden, C. B. (1983). Adult assistance to language development: Scaffolds, models, and direct instruction. In R. P. Parker & F. A. Davis (Eds.), *Developing literacy: Young children's use of language,* pp. 3–18. Newark, DE: International Reading Association.

Chomsky, C. (1969). *The acquisition of syntax in children from 5 to 10.* Cambridge, MA: MIT Press.

Chomsky, C. (1971). Write now, read later. *Childhood Education, 47,* 296–299.

Clark, E. V. (1971). On the acquisition of the meaning of *before* and *after. Journal of Verbal Learning and Verbal Behavior, 10,* 266–275.

Clay, M. (1967). The reading behavior of five-year-old children: A research report. *New Zealand Journal of Education Studies,* 11–31.

Clay, M. (1989). Forward. In D. S. Strickland & L. M. Morrow (Eds.), *Emerging literacy: Young children learn to read and write.* Newark, DE: International Reading Association.

DeStefano, J. S. (1978). *Language, the learner and the school.* New York: Wiley.

Durkin, D. (1966). *Children who read early.* New York: Teachers College Press.

Flexner, S. B. (1987). *The Random House dictionary of the English language* (2nd ed.). New York: Random House.

Florio, S., & Clark, C. M. (1982). The functions of writing in an elementary classroom. *Research in the Teaching of English, 19,* 115–130.

Gere, A. R., & Abbott, R. D. (1985). Talking about writing: The language of writing groups. *Research in the Teaching of English, 19,* 362–381.

Hague, M. (1985). *Aesop's fables.* New York: Holt, Rinehart and Winston.

Halliday, M. A. K. (1973). *Explorations in the functions of language.* London: Edward Arnold.

Halliday, M. A. K. (1975). *Learning how to mean: Explorations in the development of language.* London: Edward Arnold.

Heath, S. B. (1983). *Ways with words: Language, life, and work in communities and classrooms.* Cambridge: Cambridge University Press.

Hirsch, E. D., Jr. (1987). *Cultural literacy: What every American needs to know.* Boston: Houghton Mifflin.

Holdaway, D. (1979). *The foundations of literacy.* New York: Scholastic.

Hymes, D. (1974). *Foundations in sociolinguistics: An ethnographic approach.* Philadelphia: University of Pennsylvania Press.

Ingram, D. (1975). If and when transformations are acquired by children. In D. P. Dato (Ed.), *Developmental psycholinguistics: Theory and applications,* pp. 99–127. Washington, DC: Georgetown University Press.

Jaggar, A. (1985). Allowing for language differences. In G. S. Pinnell (Ed.), *Discovering language with children,* pp. 25–28. Urbana, IL: National Council of Teachers of English.

Lindfors, J. W. (1980). *Children's language and learning.* Englewood Cliffs, NJ: Prentice-Hall.

Lionni, L. (1985). *Frederick's fables.* New York: Pantheon.

Loban, W. (1976). *Language development: Kindergarten through grade twelve* (Research Report No. 18). Urbana, IL: National Council of Teachers of English.

Loban, W. (1979). Relationships between language and literacy. *Language Arts, 56,* 485–486.

Lobel, A. (1980). *Fables.* New York: Harper and Row.

McGee, L. M., & Richgels, D. J. (1989). *Literacy's beginnings: Supporting young readers and writers.* Boston: Allyn and Bacon.

Morrow, L. M. (1989). *Literacy development in the early years: Helping children read and write.* Englewood Cliffs, NJ: Prentice-Hall.

Piaget, J. (1969). *The psychology of intelligence.* Paterson, NJ: Littlefield, Adams.

Piaget, J. (1975). *The development of thought: Equilibration of cognitive structures.* New York: Viking Press.

Pinnell, G. S. (1975). Language in primary classrooms. *Theory into Practice, 14,* 318–327.

Smith, F. (1975). *Comprehension and learning.* New York: Holt, Rinehart and Winston.

Smith, F. (1977). The uses of language. *Language Arts, 54,* 638–644.

Smith, F. (1979). The language arts and the learner's mind. *Language Arts, 56,* 118–125.

Taylor, D. (1983). *Family literacy: Young children learning to read and write.* Exeter, NH: Heinemann.

Teale, W. H. (1982). Toward a theory of how children learn to read and write. *Language Arts, 59,* 555–570.

Teale, W. H., & Sulzby, E. (1989). Emerging literacy: New perspectives. In D. S. Strickland & L. M. Morrow (Eds.), *Emerging literacy: Young children learn to read and write,* pp. 1–15. Newark, DE: International Reading Association.

Vygotsky, L. S. (1978). *Mind in society,.* Cambridge, MA: Harvard University Press.

Vygotsky, L. S. (1986). *Thought and language.* Cambridge, MA: MIT Press.

CHILDREN'S LITERATURE REFERENCES

Kellogg, S. (1979). *Pinkerton, behave!* New York: Dial.

Lauber, P. (1987). *Get ready for robots!* New York: Crowell.

Low, J. (1980). *Mice twice.* New York: Atheneum.

Matthews, E. (1985). *Debugging Rover.* New York: Dodd.

Metos, T. H. (1980). *Robots A_2Z.* New York: Messner.

Sendak, M. (1963). *Where the wild things are.* New York: Harper and Row.

CHAPTER 8

Teaching Language Arts

We shift the focus now from how children learn to how teachers support students while they learn. In this chapter we describe a language-rich classroom, discuss the teacher's role, and explain how to plan instruction and assess children's learning in language arts. Specifically, you will learn

1. How to arrange the classroom to facilitate students' learning.
2. What materials are needed.
3. What your role as teacher is.
4. More about how to plan units of instruction.
5. More about assessing student learning.

Language arts instruction should be based on how children learn, how they learn language, and how they become literate. More than 20 years ago, Carl Lefevre (1970) advised that language learning in school should "parallel [children's] early childhood method of learning to speak [their] native tongue—playfully, through delighted experiences of discovery—through repeated exposure to language forms and patterns, by creating imitation and manipulation, and by personal trial and error, with kindly (and not too much) correction from adults" (p. 75). Lefevre's vision is finally becoming a reality as teachers are basing instruction on cognitive, psycholinguistic, and sociolinguistic theories of learning.

A unit on mystery stories, for example, provides the type of language learning experiences that Lefevre suggests. Students begin by reading mystery stories or listening to them read aloud. Many mystery stories have been written for young students. Middle-grade students enjoy the *Encyclopedia Brown* series by Donald J. Sobol (e.g., *Encyclopedia Brown, Boy Detective*, 1963). Mystery stories have unique characteristics that students can learn to identify after reading and discussing several mysteries. A class of fourth graders developed the following list of the characteristics of mystery stories:

Mysteries have crimes or problems to solve. Some types of crimes and problems are something lost or stolen, someone killed, or someone kidnapped.

Mysteries have clues. Some examples include torn papers, footprints, fingerprints, dead bodies, and tire tracks.

Mysteries have detectives to solve the crimes or problems. (They *always* solve the crime, too!)

Detectives have unusual names, such as Encyclopedia Brown.

Detectives have something special about them, such as having a dog for an assistant or loving to eat pancakes.

Detectives have special equipment, including magnifying glasses, secret codes, knives and guns, costumes, and masks.

With this information, students are prepared to create their own stories. They write and refine their stories and then publish them as hardcover books. After reading their stories to classmates, students add their stories to the classroom library. Figure 8.1 presents the mystery story this class of fourth graders composed. The teacher and students working together composed a class story, called a *class collaboration,* which is an effective way to begin writing. After the group writing experience, students write individual stories.

A unit on mysteries provides many opportunities for students to imitate and manipulate language in a situation that is meaningful, functional, and genuine. Moreover, both the mystery stories students read and those they write can later be used for studying specific language skills. Students can, for example, examine how authors use alliteration, sentence structure, or punctuation, and they can also examine their own stories for similar conventions. Within the context of stories children read and others they write, they can examine how language is used to communicate effectively.

FIGURE 8.1
A Fourth-grade Class Collaboration Mystery Story

"EDITH, NO!"

The mud oozed around Ed Trail's boots as he beached his canoe. It was 10:00 Saturday evening as Ed made his way home through the woods from his fishing trip. He only walked a few steps when . . . SNAP . . . an old trap caught his foot and pulled him down.

As he turned over to free himself, the last thing he saw was a rock.

From the other side of the woods, Sam Baker, well-known detective, was searching for Ed at the request of his worried wife, Sally. He found the place where Ed docked his boat and followed the path from there.

A short distance up the path led Sam to where Ed Trail lay dead with a rock crushing his head.

While Sam was running to tell what had happened, he discovered a torn scarf stuck on a bush. As he observed the scarf, he discovered the initials E. T.

Sam stuck the scarf in his pocket because he knew it was a clue and went to tell Sally Trail what had happened.

Out of breath, Sam arrived at the Trails' and told Sally the horrible details. When Sam showed her the scarf, Sally got a far away look in her eyes and went upstairs. Finding this strange, Sam Baker waited outside the Trail home to see what he might find.

Meanwhile, Sally went upstairs to the room of Aunt Belle who lived with the Trails. Aunt Belle had taken care of Sally as a little girl and knew everything about Sally. Now she was crippled and in a wheel-chair.

"Well, hello dear," said Aunt Belle. "What are you doing here?" "Where are you taking me?" said Aunt Belle worriedly as Sally wheeled her to the stairs. As Sally gave the final shove Aunt Belle screamed. . . .

"EDITH, NO!"

At that moment Sam Baker knew that the initials stood for Sally Edith Trail. The S had been ripped off in her rush to leave the place of the crime.

Sam rushed in just in time to catch Aunt Belle before Sally Edith Trail sent another victim to her death.

Quickly, Sam grabbed Sally and took her to the police station.

At the station house the chief found out that Sally killed her husband to keep him from giving all his money to Aunt Belle to take care of her. Sally tried to kill Aunt Belle because she was the only one who could connect Sally with the initials E. T.

Another case wrapped up by Sam Baker.

A. THE LANGUAGE-RICH CLASSROOM

Classrooms should be authentic language environments that encourage students to listen, talk, read, and write; that is, they should be language rich (Lindfors, 1989). The physical arrangement and materials provided in the classroom play an important role in setting the stage for learning language. In the past, textbooks were the primary instructional material and students sat in desks arranged in rows facing the teacher. Now a wide variety of instructional materials are available in addition to textbooks, including trade books and newspapers. Students' desks are more often arranged in small groups, and classrooms are visually stimulating with signs, posters, charts, and other displays related to the units under study. These are components of a language-rich classroom:

- Desks arranged in groups to facilitate cooperative learning
- Classroom libraries stocked with many different kinds of reading materials
- Posted messages about the current day
- Displays of student work and projects
- A chair designated as the author's chair
- Displayed signs, labels for items, and quotations
- Posted directions for activities or use of equipment
- Materials for recording language, including pencils, pens, paper, journals, books, typewriters, computers
- Special places for reading and writing activities
- Reference materials related to literature, social studies, and science units
- A listening center and other audiovisual materials
- A puppet stage or area for presenting plays and storytelling
- Charts on which students record information (e.g., attendance or writing group charts)
- World-related print (e.g., newspapers, maps, calendars).

These components of a language-rich classroom are elaborated on in Figure 8.2.

The Physical Arrangement

No one physical arrangement best represents a language-rich classroom, but the configuration of any classroom can be modified to include many of the desirable characteristics. First, student desks or tables should be grouped to encourage students to talk, share, and work cooperatively. Separate areas are needed for reading and writing, a classroom library, a listening center, centers for materials related to content area units, and dramatic activities. At the instructional levels, kindergarten through ninth grade, some variations must occur. While fourth graders need more workstations, older students need reference centers with materials related to the units they are studying. The two diagrams in Figure 8.3 suggest ways to make the classroom design language rich.

Textbooks

Textbooks are one tool for teaching language skills. They are the most accessible resource that teachers have and, as discussed in Chapter 4, they have some benefits. They provide

- Information about language skills
- A sequence of skills for each grade level
- Models and examples
- Practice activities
- Security for beginning teachers.

There are also drawbacks, however. The textbook's format is probably its greatest drawback because it is inappropriate for many language activities. Listening, talking, reading, and writing activities involve much more than can be contained in a single textbook. Other likely weaknesses are as follows:

FIGURE 8.2
Characteristics of a Language-Rich Classroom

1. **Arrangement of desks**
   _____ Are desks arranged in groups?
   _____ Does the arrangement facilitate group interaction?
2. **Classroom library**
   _____ Are there four times as many books as there are students in the classroom?
   _____ Are picture books, informational books, poetry, and other types of trade books included?
   _____ Are magazines and newspapers included?
   _____ Were some of the books written by students?
3. **Message center**
   _____ Are schedules and announcements about the current day posted?
   _____ Are some of the messages student initiated?
4. **Display of student work**
   _____ Do all students have work displayed?
   _____ How much of the student work is less than two weeks old?
   _____ Is there an area where students can display their own work themselves?
5. **Author's chair**
   _____ Is one chair designated as the author's chair for students to use when sharing their writing?
   _____ Is the chair labeled?
6. **Signs, labels, and quotations**
   _____ Are equipment and other classroom items labeled?
   _____ Are words, phrases, and sentences posted in the classroom?
   _____ Were some of the signs, labels, and quotes written by students?
7. **Directions**
   _____ Are directions provided so that students can work independently?
   _____ Were some of the directions written by students?
8. **Materials for recording language**
   _____ Are pencils, pens, paper, journals, books, typewriters, computers, and other materials available for recording language?
   _____ Do students have to ask permission to use them?
9. **Places for reading and writing**
   _____ Are there special places for reading and writing activities?
   _____ Are they quiet and separated from other areas?
10. **Reference materials**
    _____ Are lists, clusters, pictures, charts, books, and other reference materials available for content area study?
    _____ Do students use these materials as they work on projects related to the units?
11. **Audiovisual materials**
    _____ Is a listening center available for students to use?
    _____ Are other audiovisual materials such as filmstrips, videotapes, and films, and the equipment necessary to use the materials available in the classroom?
12. **Dramatic center**
    _____ Is a puppet stage available in the classroom?
    _____ Are art materials for making puppets available?
    _____ Is an area available for presenting plays and telling stories?
    _____ Are props available?
13. **Record collection**
    _____ Are charts or sheets that call for students to record information used in the classroom?
    _____ Do students record the information themselves?
14. **World-related print**
    _____ Do students read and write newspapers, magazines, lists, maps, graphs, calendars, and other forms of world-related print?
    _____ Do students collect some of these materials?
15. **Display of student projects**
    _____ Are students' projects with accompanying written explanations and other student-made displays exhibited in the classroom?

- Little attention to listening and talking
- Excessive emphasis on grammar and usage skills
- Emphasis on rote memorization of skills rather than on effective communication
- Focus on correctness rather than on experimentation with language
- Few opportunities to individualize instruction
- Difficulty in connecting textbook activities to across-the-curriculum units.

Graves (1977) admonished us that textbooks cannot be the only instructional material for teaching language arts. Collections of trade books, tape recordings, puppets, concrete materials, notebooks, paper, and pencils are other necessary materials.

Teachers cannot assume that textbooks are equivalent to the total language arts program. To start on the first page of the language arts textbook on the first day of school and to continue page by page through the textbook fails to consider the students' language needs. Instead, we recommend that textbooks serve as only one resource for the language arts program. For example, textbooks are one resource in teaching about punctuation marks, as illustrated in Figure 8.4, which also suggests many other types of activities that involve more meaningful, functional, and genuine experiences with language.

Several elements must be carefully considered in evaluating language arts textbooks or choosing a textbook series for a school or school district. The conceptual framework of the textbook and the instructional philosophy of its authors are of primary importance. Is the textbook content centered or child centered? Textbooks should be consistent with teachers' views of language arts education and how they organize and conduct their classrooms. It is also important to consider whether a textbook incorporates the latest research on how children learn language.

The theoretical orientation is reflected in the content of the textbook, and the content is the second critical consideration. Textbooks that are based on the segmented, content-centered model typically emphasize language skills more than do textbooks based on the child-centered or whole language model. The types of listening, talking, reading, and writing activities that are included are also important. Consider, too, what other types of activities, such as grammar activities, are included and compute the percentage of space devoted to each language mode. Other considerations are whether the textbook invites students to use language in genuine ways or whether the majority of activities involve copying sentences from the textbook or filling in blanks with single letters and words. Teachers must also consider the textbook's physical features, its organization, its adaptability for special students, and its style. Figure 8.5 lists these guidelines. Some of the questions can be answered simply "yes" or "no," whereas others require a more careful and in-depth review.

Trade Books

Trade books are children's books other than textbooks, and thousands of excellent trade books are currently available for intermediate and middle-grade students. Types of trade books include picture books, wordless picture books, concept books, chapter books, poetry, biography and autobiography, and informational books.

Picture books. *Picture books* are short stories (usually about 32 pages) in which text and illustrations combine to tell the story more effectively than either could alone. The text is minimal, and the illustrations are striking. Many picture books, such as Maurice Sendak's *Where the Wild Things Are* (1963) are appropriate for young children, but some picture books, such as Thomas Locker's *The Boy Who Held Back the Sea* (1987), were written with middle-grade students in mind. Fairy tales, myths, and legends have also been retold beautifully as picture books. One example is Trina Schart Hyman's *The Sleeping Beauty* (1977). The coveted Caldecott Medal, given annually for the best illustrations in a children's book published during the preceding year, has honored many picture books.

Wordless picture books. Wordless picture books are similar to picture books but contain no text. The story is told entirely through the pictures, which makes them particularly

FIGURE 8.3
Diagrams of Classrooms

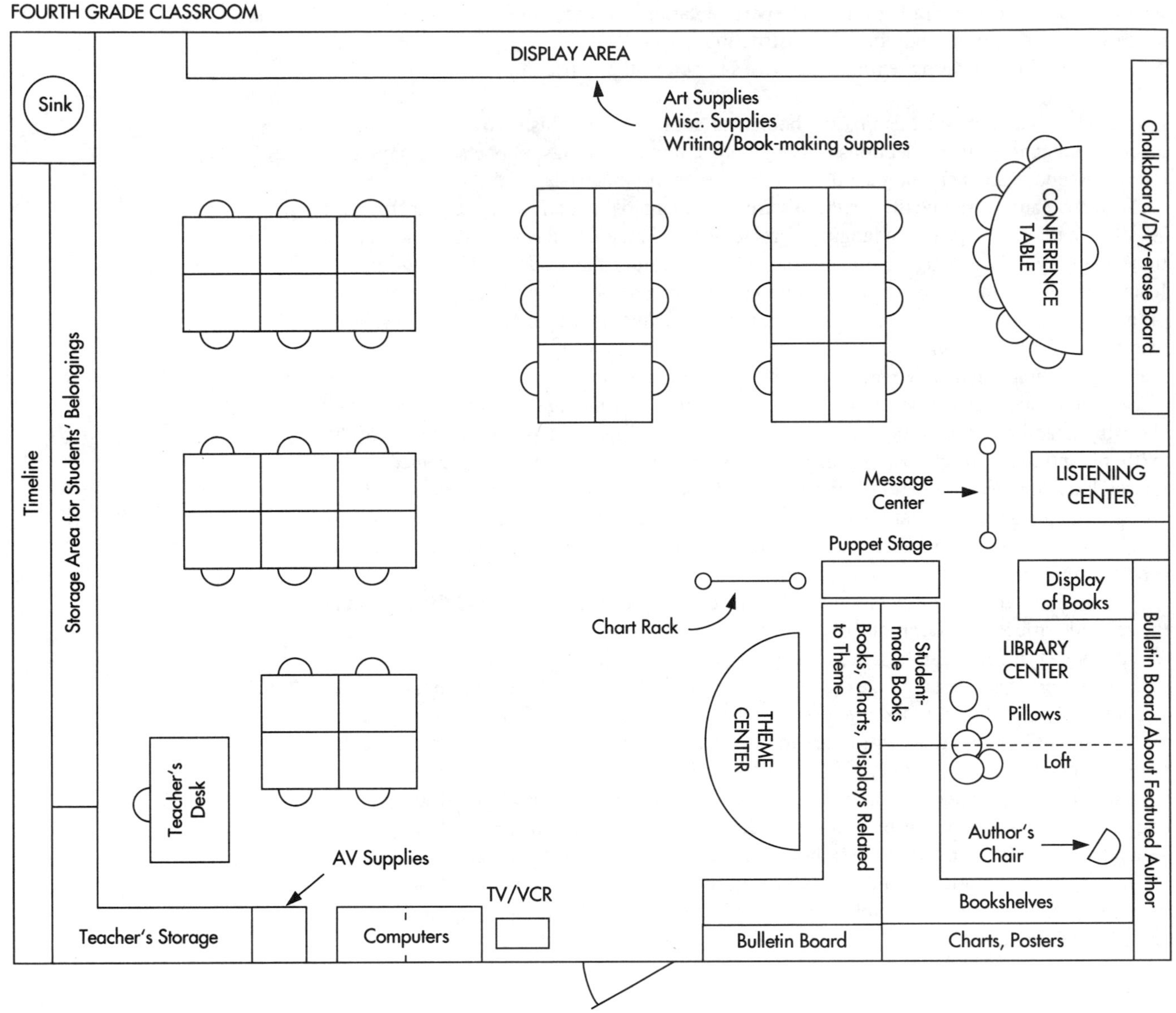

FOURTH GRADE CLASSROOM

useful for talk and writing activities. Books such as the hilarious *Frog Goes to Dinner* (Mayer, 1974) and Goodall's wordless retelling of *Little Red Riding Hood* (1988) are popular with primary and middle-grade students. Other books, such as *Anno's U.S.A.* (Anno, 1983) and *The Story of a Castle* (Goodall, 1986), appeal to middle- and upper-grade students because they can be connected to social studies or other content area units.

Concept books. *Concept books* are informational books written in the same format as picture books. A phrase or sentence of text is presented on each page with a large photograph or illustration. Gibbons's *The Post Office Book: Mail and How It Moves* (1982) is an informative description of what happens to a letter after it is mailed, and cartoonlike drawings supplement the sparse text. *My Puppy Is Born* (Cole, 1973) uses black-and-white photographs to illustrate a puppy's birth and first eight weeks of life. A very different type of concept book is Burningham's *Opposites* (1985), which presents pairs of opposites (e.g., *hard* and *soft*) illustrated on each two-page spread. ABC books might also be classified as concept books. Although many ABC books are designed for very young children, others are

FIGURE 8.3 cont'd

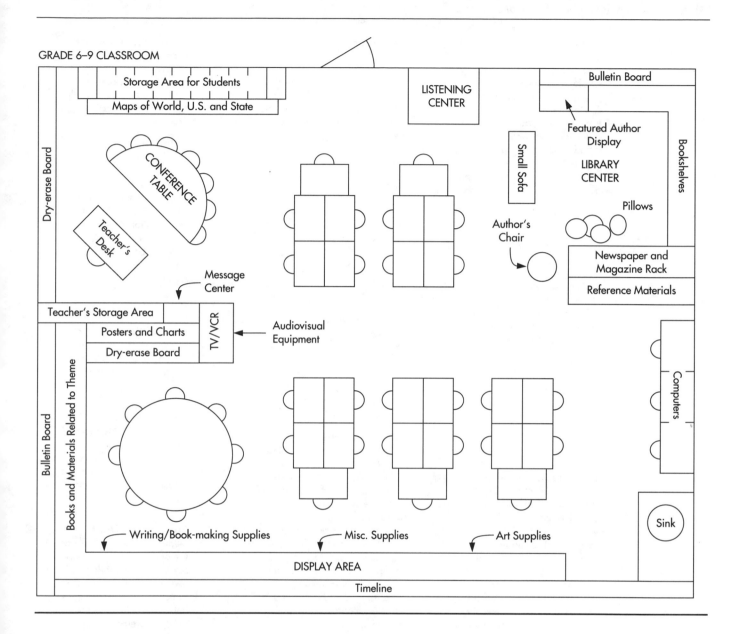

GRADE 6–9 CLASSROOM

appropriate for elementary students, such as *The National Air and Space Museum ABC* (Mayers, 1986). Crews's concept books are among the most beautiful; in *Carousel* (1982), for example, Crews combines paintings and photographs to create the sounds and sights of a carousel ride.

Informational books. *Informational books* provide information on social studies, science, math, art, music, and other topics, and many of these books are available for middle-grade students. Some are written in a story format, such as *Octopus* (Carrick, 1978), *Castle* (Macaulay, 1977), and *Sugaring Time* (Lasky, 1983) while others are written in a more traditional informational style, with a table of contents, index, and glossary. Examples of traditional informational books are *Money* (Elkin, 1983) and *The Human Body* (Caselli, 1987).

Chapter books. *Chapter books* are longer, fictional books written for students in chapter format. Most are written for middle- and upper-grade students. Chapter books for middle-grade students include Cleary's Ramona series, for example, *Ramona Quimby, Age 8* (1981), and *Bunnicula* (Howe & Howe, 1979). Upper-grade students enjoy fantasy stories,

FIGURE 8.4
Ways to Teach Students about Punctuation Marks

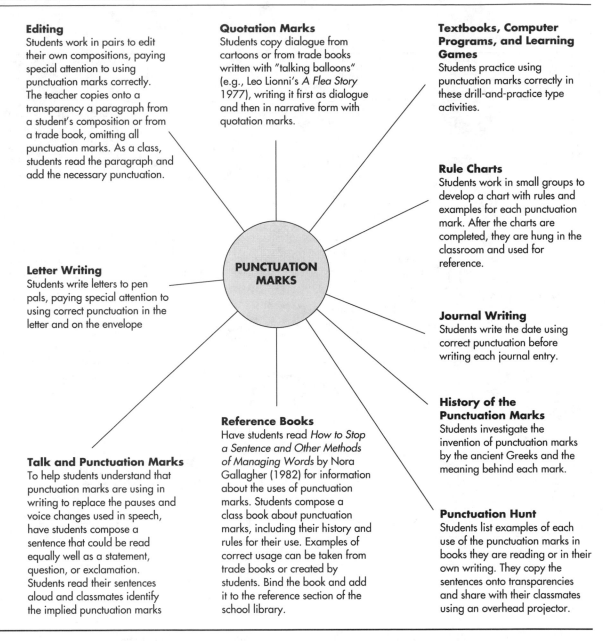

Editing
Students work in pairs to edit their own compositions, paying special attention to using punctuation marks correctly. The teacher copies onto a transparency a paragraph from a student's composition or from a trade book, omitting all punctuation marks. As a class, students read the paragraph and add the necessary punctuation.

Quotation Marks
Students copy dialogue from cartoons or from trade books written with "talking balloons" (e.g., Leo Lionni's *A Flea Story* 1977), writing it first as dialogue and then in narrative form with quotation marks.

Textbooks, Computer Programs, and Learning Games
Students practice using punctuation marks correctly in these drill-and-practice type activities.

Rule Charts
Students work in small groups to develop a chart with rules and examples for each punctuation mark. After the charts are completed, they are hung in the classroom and used for reference.

Letter Writing
Students write letters to pen pals, paying special attention to using correct punctuation in the letter and on the envelope

PUNCTUATION MARKS

Journal Writing
Students write the date using correct punctuation before writing each journal entry.

History of the Punctuation Marks
Students investigate the invention of punctuation marks by the ancient Greeks and the meaning behind each mark.

Talk and Punctuation Marks
To help students understand that punctuation marks are using in writing to replace the pauses and voice changes used in speech, have students compose a sentence that could be read equally well as a statement, question, or exclamation. Students read their sentences aloud and classmates identify the implied punctuation marks

Reference Books
Have students read *How to Stop a Sentence and Other Methods of Managing Words* by Nora Gallagher (1982) for information about the uses of punctuation marks. Students compose a class book about punctuation marks, including their history and rules for their use. Examples of correct usage can be taken from trade books or created by students. Bind the book and add it to the reference section of the school library.

Punctuation Hunt
Students list examples of each use of the punctuation marks in books they are reading or in their own writing. They copy the sentences onto transparencies and share with their classmates using an overhead projector.

and Lewis's *The Lion, the Witch and the Wardrobe* (1950) and the other books in the Chronicles of Narnia are favorites. A number of chapter books, such as *Sarah, Plain and Tall* (MacLachlan, 1985) and *The Whipping Boy* (Fleischman, 1986), have received the Newbery Medal for distinguished children's literature. In contrast to the Caldecott Medal, for outstanding illustrations, the Newbery is given for distinguished prose.

Poetry. Many delightful books of poetry for children are available today. Some are collections of poems on a single topic written by one poet, such as *Tyrannosaurus Was a Beast* (Prelutsky, 1988) about dinosaurs, and Fleischman's *Joyful Noise: Poems for Two Voices* (1988) about insects. Other collections of poetry on a single topic selected by an author or poet are Hopkins's *Good Morning to You, Valentine* (1976) and Carle's *Animals, Animals* (1989). Two excellent anthologies (collections of poems written by different poets on a variety of topics) are *The Random House Book of Poetry for Children* (Prelutsky, 1983) for younger children and *Knock at a Star: A Child's Introduction to Poetry* (Kennedy & Kennedy,

FIGURE 8.5
Guidelines for Assessing Language Arts Textbooks

Physical Features
_____ Is the textbook attractive, durable, and interesting to students?
_____ Do the size, use of margins, print style, and graphics increase the usability of the textbook?
_____ Do the illustrations enhance interest in the textbook?
_____ What supplemental materials (e.g., teacher's editions, resource books, skill handbooks, computer programs, posters, tests) are included with the textbook?

Conceptual Framework
_____ What is the theoretical orientation of the textbook?
_____ Does the textbook reflect the latest research in how language is learned?
_____ Are the instructional goals of the textbook presented clearly?
_____ How well do these goals mesh with your own views of language arts education?

Content
_____ What types of listening, talking, reading, and writing activities are included in the textbook?
_____ How much emphasis is placed on each of the four language models?
_____ How much emphasis is placed on grammar?
_____ Is quality children's literature included in the textbook?
_____ Are the language and language skill activities appropriate for the grade level at which they are presented?
_____ Are activities provided that require students to use language in genuine ways, or do most activities require students to only copy sentences from the textbook or fill in the blanks with letters and words?
_____ Are across-the-curriculum activities suggested?
_____ Does the textbook invite student involvement?
_____ Does the textbook encourage students to think critically and creatively?

Organization
_____ How is the textbook organized?
_____ Must each lesson or unit be taught in sequence?
_____ Does the scope and sequence chart provide a reasonable organization of language skills?

Adaptability
_____ Is information provided on how to adapt the textbook to meet students' individual needs?
_____ Can the textbook be adapted for gifted students?
_____ Can the textbook be adapted for learning disabled students?
_____ Can the textbook be adapted for bilingual students or students who speak nonstandard English?

Style
_____ Will students like the writing style of the textbook?
_____ Does the textbook avoid stereotypes and stereotypical language?

1982) for older children. Another format for poems is as a picture book with a line or stanza of the poem presented and illustrated on each page. This format is especially good for songs, such as Spier's *The Star-Spangled Banner* (1973), and for poems that were originally written for adults but can be made appropriate for children. Two examples are Longfellow's *Paul Revere's Ride* (Parker, 1985) and *Lewis Carroll's Jabberwocky* (Zalben, 1977).

Biographies and autobiographies. Most life-story books are chapter books, such as Hamilton's *Paul Robeson: The Life and Times of a Free Black Man* (1974), but several authors have written shorter biographies that resemble picture books. Perhaps the best-known biographer for younger children is Jean Fritz, who has written biographies of Revolutionary War figures such as *Will You Sign Here, John Hancock?* (1976). A few autobiographies have also been written for children, and one that is popular with upper-grade students is Roald Dahl's *Boy* (1984).

These books can be used in conjunction with or instead of textbooks to teach language arts or any other content area. As an illustration, Figure 8.6 presents a cluster for a unit on the American Revolution, and trade books are an important part of the unit. Students will

FIGURE 8.6
Cluster for a Unit on the American Revolution

Biography and Autobiography
Students investigate the role of historical figures in the War by reading a biography or autobiography. Books include D'Aulaires' *Benjamin Franklin* (Doubleday, 1950) and *George Washington* (Doubleday, 1936); Harold Felton's *Deborah Sampson: Soldier of the Revolution* (Dodd, 1976); Jean Fritz's *George Washington's Breakfast* (Coward, 1969), *Traitor, The Case of Benedict Arnold* (Putnam, 1981), *Where was Patrick Henry on the 29th of May?* (Coward, 1975), *Why Don't You Get a Horse, Sam Adams?* (Coward, 1974), and *Will You Sign Here, John Hancock?* (Coward, 1976); and Joseph Plumb Martin's *Yankee Doodle Boy* (Scott, 1964).

Poetry
Students read Henry Wadsworth Longfellow's *Paul Revere's Ride* (Greenwillow, 1985). Compare to Jean Fritz's *And Then What Happened, Paul Revere?* (Coward, 1973). Also, compare Revere's ride in 1775 to Jack Jouett's ride in 1781. Read *Jack Jouett's Ride* by Gail Haley (Viking, 1973).

Simulated Journals
Students keep a simulated journal as an historical figure or a common person who lived during the Revolutionary War era.

Debates
Students stage a debate between "rebels" and "royalists."

Chapter Books
Students read stories set in the Revolutionary War era, such as James and Christopher Collier's *My Brother Sam is Dead* (Four Winds, 1974) and Esther Forbes' *Johnny Tremain* (Houghton Mifflin, 1970). These books can also be read aloud.

Research Reports
Students read informational books about the period to use in preparing oral or written reports. Books include Jean Poindexter Colby's *Lexington and Concord, 1775: What Really Happened* (Hasting House, 1975); Robert Leckie's *The World Turned Upside Down: The Story of the American Revolution* (Putnam, 1973); and Bart McDowell's *The Revolutionary War: America's Fight for Freedom* (National Geographic Society, 1967).

REVOLUTIONARY WAR

Handwriting
Students copy quotes from the period, such as "Don't fire unless fired upon" (Col. John Parker); "I only regret that I have but one life to lose for my country" (Nathan Hale); and "The British are coming!" (Paul Revere).

Listening
Students listen to songs of the period including "Yankee Doodle."

Drama
Students role-play key events in the period: Paul Revere's ride, signing the Declaration of Independence, the surrender at Yorktown. Students create a puppet of an historical figure and use the puppet to give a report about the person or to stage a play.

Writing
Students write a simulated newspaper that might have been published during the Revolutionary War period.

Timelines
Students construct a timeline showing the major events leading up to the War and major battles in the war.

Spelling
Students examine spellings of the period (e.g., ye, musick) that have changed because of the nationalistic spirit of the period and Noah Webster's influence.

Art
Students view paintings depicting Revolutionary War scenes, such as Grant Wood's "The Midnight Ride of Paul Revere" and Emanuel Gottlieb Leutze's "Washington Crossing the Delaware."

read biographies and autobiographies, poems, chapter books, and informational books to learn much more about the Revolutionary War and life in those times than could ever be presented in a social studies textbook. The main drawback to using trade books is that they are not sequenced and prepackaged as textbooks are. Instead, teachers must make choices and design activities to accompany the books. Similar units incorporating trade books can be developed for almost any content area.

Every classroom should be stocked with trade books that are attractively stored in the library center. These books might be from the teacher's own collection or borrowed from the school or public library. Many of the books should relate to units of study, and these should be changed periodically. Other books for students to read independently are also included in the library center. After studying library centers in classrooms, Leslie Morrow (1989) makes the following ten recommendations:

The library center should be inviting and afford privacy.

The library center should have a physical definition with shelves, carpets, benches, sofas, or other partitions.

Five or six students should fit comfortably in the center at one time.

Two kinds of bookshelves are needed. Most of the collection should be shelved with the spines facing outward, but some books should be set so that the front covers are displayed.

Books should be shelved by category and color-coded by type.

Books written by one author or related to a theme being studied should be displayed prominently, and the displays should be changed regularly.

The floor should be covered with a rug and the area furnished with pillows, beanbag chairs, or comfortable furniture.

The center should be stocked with at least four times as many books as students in the classroom.

A variety of types of reading materials, including books, newspapers, magazines, posters, and charts, should be included in the center.

Attractive posters that encourage reading, especially if they relate to books in the library center, should be added.

Computers

As discussed in Chapter 6, computers are becoming more and more a part of school classrooms. At first, they were used primarily in mathematics, but they have great potential for all areas of the curriculum, including language arts. Robert Taylor (1980) suggests that computers have three educational applications: they can serve as tool, tutor, and tutee.

Perhaps the most valuable application of the computer in the language arts classroom is as a tool. Students can use microcomputers with word-processing programs to write stories, poems, and other writing forms (DeGroff, 1990; Dickinson, 1986; Genishi, 1988). The computer simplifies revising and editing and eliminates the tedium of recopying compositions. Several word-processing programs, such as *The Bank Street Writer* (1982), *The Writing Workshop* (1986), and *QUILL* (1983), have been developed especially for elementary students and are easy to learn to use.

Students can also use the word processor to write notes and letters to classmates and pen pals. They write these letters on the computer, revise and edit them, and then transmit them using a modem hooked up to the computer. The *QUILL* (1983) word-processing program, for instance, includes a Mailbag for exchanging messages.

A second application is as tutor—a use known as *computer assisted instruction (CAI)*. Instructional software programs are available for drill and practice, educational games, simulations, and tutorials. Programmed instruction in language skills such as letter sounds, parts of speech, and affixes is becoming increasingly available. Many of the programs resemble language arts textbook exercises except that they are presented on a monitor screen rather than in a book. Remember, though, that while students enjoy using computers, some activities are little more than electronic workbooks and are subject to the same criticisms as language arts textbooks. High-quality software programs can be useful, however, in providing individualized practice on a particular skill.

The number of software programs has grown tremendously in the past few years; some are effective, whereas others are inferior. Chomsky (1984) says the primary criterion in identifying high-quality software programs is whether they stimulate students to think about language in new and creative ways. Because of both quality and cost considerations, it is important to preview software carefully before purchasing it. Figure 8.7 offers guidelines for selecting and evaluating language arts software. Students should also help preview software programs and offer opinions and recommendations.

FIGURE 8.7
Guidelines for Selecting Language Arts Computer Software
SOURCE: Adapted from "Selecting Software for Your LD Students," by P.L. Smith and G.E. Tompkins, 1984, Academic Therapy, vol. 20 (2), 221–224. Copyright 1984 by PRO-ED, Inc. Reprinted with permission.

Computer Compatibility

Is the software program compatible with the computer students will be using?
Does the computer have sufficient memory to run the software program?
Which peripherals are needed (e.g., color monitor, printer, voice synthesizer)?

Theoretical Rationale

Is the software consistent with the philosophy of your language arts program?
Can it be integrated into your program to instruct rather than merely to entertain?

Computer Capabilities

Does the software program take advantage of the unique capabilities of the computer?
Does it provide for extensive student interaction?
Does it provide for immediate feedback?
Does it provide for dynamic text display, in which text can be built paragraph by paragraph, sentences and words can be highlighted, and text can be moved about?

Frame Display

Is the text in the software program presented in both upper- and lowercase letters?
Is between-line spacing adequate for easy reading?
Do letters resemble regular type rather than stylized lettering?
Are highlighting and other attention-getting devices overused?

Rate of Presentation

Does the student rather than the program control the rate at which text is advanced?

Readability

Is the text (especially the directions) written at students' reading level?

Graphics

Do the illustrations and animation support the instruction or serve only to gain the students' attention?

Game Format

Does the software program require students to learn or practice a skill to play the game successfully or can students simply make random choices?
Does it allow students to play against themselves and compete against their previous performances rather than against another student?

Instructions to Students

Does the program provide information on each frame of text telling students how to quit the program, get help, and see the menu?

Documentation

Does the documentation (or printed materials) accompanying the program contain information on objectives, description of the program, the target population, prerequisite language and computing skills, suggested introductory and follow-up activities, and the results of field testing and validation studies?

A third computer application is as tutee. Students can learn computer languages, such as LOGO, and how to program computers. Gifted students particularly benefit from learning computer languages as a way of extending their repertoire of communication modes.

In summarizing the promises and pitfalls of microcomputers in the language arts classroom, there are two factors restricting the usefulness of this technology. The quantity of available high-quality instructional software is still limited, and few modern computers are available in many schools. Because so few modern computers are available, students are rarely able to use them regularly. In the next few years, however, educators predict that the availability of high-quality software will improve and modern computers will be added to more classrooms.

B. THE TEACHER'S ROLE AND THEMATIC UNITS

According to Lindfors (1989), the two fundamental responsibilities of an elementary teacher are to provide a language-rich learning environment in the classroom and to support students in their use of it. It is the teacher's role to make things happen by creating a language arts program that involves students in meaningful, functional, and genuine language activities. One of the best ways to create a language arts program is through thematic units (Goodman, 1986). As discussed in Chapter 3, units may focus on literature, social studies, science, or another content area.

Planning for Instruction

As emphasized in Chapter 4, good teaching does not simply happen; it requires careful planning and a variety of activities. Activities should simulate the natural type of language learning that students experienced when they were learning to talk. As you learned in Chapters 3 and 4, when teachers plan for instruction, they go through several specific steps.

The first step is to identify units of instruction and goals and objectives. Teachers begin by identifying units in literature, social studies, science, and the other content areas they will teach. Sometimes the units are listed in state or district curriculum guides; sometimes they are provided in textbooks; and at other times, teachers choose units they believe are appropriate for their students. Examples of literature units are those that focus on *one author,* such as Tomie de Paola or Beverly Cleary; focus on *one book,* such as *Bridge to Terabithia* (Paterson, 1977); focus on a *genre,* such as mystery stories or biographies; or focus on a *theme,* such as families. Examples of social studies units are Thanksgiving, the American Revolution, and Africa.

After deciding on the unit, teachers identify the major goal or goals of the unit and the specific objectives. These can be found in curriculum guides and textbooks or can be developed by the teacher. For example, one unit that is often taught in the intermediate and middle school grades focuses on weather. The goals and objectives vary according to grade level. The goal for a unit might be for the student to gain an understanding of various types of weather and their effects on people. Objectives for students might include these:

The student will observe daily weather conditions and record information on a weather chart.

The student will explain the uses of weather measurement tools.

The student will describe the effects of different types of weather on people.

The student will explain precautions to take in case of severe weather conditions.

The second step in instruction is to collect materials to use in teaching the unit. After identifying the topic for the unit and the goals and objectives, teachers collect materials, including

- Trade books
- Magazine and newspaper articles
- Textbooks
- Maps, charts, tables
- Films, filmstrips, videotapes and videodiscs, and software programs
- Community resource persons
- Community resources
- Models, displays, equipment.

For the weather unit, teachers might collect a variety of informational books, concept books, picture books, books of poetry; the science textbook; daily newspapers with weather information and maps; charts and posters about weather; filmstrips, films, and videotapes about the weather and of children's stories set in different types of weather; and information from the National Weather Service and local television meteorologists.

Step three is to create a cluster of possibilities. As teachers collect materials related to the unit, ideas for possible activities come to mind, and they begin to list these possibilities. We recommend using a cluster format, as shown in Figure 8.8. Teachers list the activity possibilities according to the categories listed in the figure. For example, for a weather unit, teachers would consider science activities such as recording daily temperatures, experiments related to temperature and wind, examining weather instruments, and making wind socks and weather vanes. Possible art activities include making snowflakes or a fog collage (by gluing tissue paper over a scene the students had painted). Words such as *thunderstorms, clouds, evaporation, thermometer, tornado,* and *hurricane* that are related to the unit would be added in the section on Vocabulary and Spelling. As individual projects, students might keep track of the weather for a week or two, make a poster about different kinds of weather, write a book about one kind of weather, read a weather poem to the class, or research a topic related to weather. As a class project, students might write an ABC book about weather. Possible field trips to the National Weather Service or community resource persons such as a television meteorologist might be listed as community resources. Teachers would also list the trade books they had collected related to weather and relevant sections in the science textbook. The completed cluster contains more possibilities than teachers could ever use in one unit, but because of the variety, teachers can select activities for the lesson plan that best meet the needs of this particular class and the amount of time available for the unit. An example of a completed unit cluster on weather is shown in Figure 8.9.

The fourth step is to develop the lesson plan. From the cluster of possibilities, teachers choose which lessons and activities they will use within the time available for the unit, and then they write the lesson plans. Of special importance is planning an initiating activity for the first day and a culminating activity to end the unit. For the weather unit, teachers might show a film about weather to catch the students' interest. A field trip to the National Weather Service or an interview with a TV weather forecaster would be good culminating activities.

FIGURE 8.8
A Unit Cluster

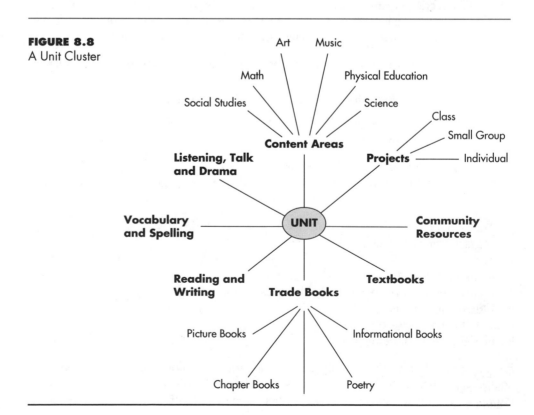

FIGURE 8.9
A Cluster for a Weather Unit

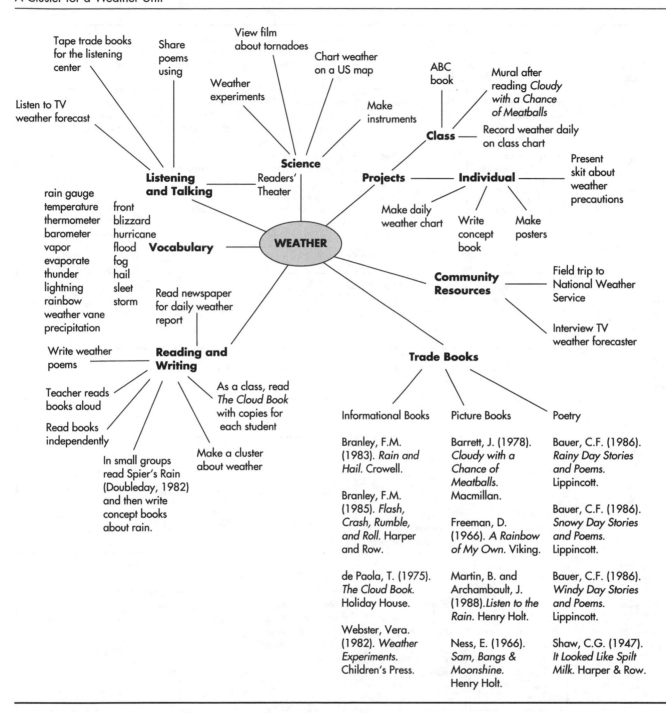

Lesson plans are usually written in time blocks. Activities for a unit may be confined to the one time block for the particular subject each day, or they can extend across areas of the curriculum. In the weather unit, for example, reading and writing activities related to the unit can be done as Language Arts, art activities as Art, and science activities as Science. Figure 8.10 presents a week-long *excerpt* from the lesson plan for the weather unit (and includes only those activities related to the weather unit). Notice that activities may occupy several time blocks each day. You will note that instead of labeling the time blocks as *Language Arts* or *Science,* in the lesson plan, they are labeled Blocks A, B, and C.

FIGURE 8.10
Excerpt from a Lesson Plan

	Monday	Tuesday	Wednesday	Thursday	Friday
8:45–9:00 Opening	Students read daily weather forecast in newspaper. Mark weather on class calendar and individual calendars. Also, add type of weather to graph.				
9:00–10:30 Block A	Finish sharing weather safety posters made last week. Choral reading: "Who Has Seen the Wind?" "I Am Flying" Make cluster on clouds.	As a class, read *The Cloud Book* (copies for each child). Write in weather log. Read aloud: *It Looked Like Spilt Milk.*	Reread *The Cloud Book.* Add to the cluster on clouds. Share more information on clouds to answer their questions. Read aloud: *Cloudy with a Chance of Meatballs.*	Review clouds cluster. Make class book on clouds. Each student makes a page. Paint mural for *Cloudy with a Chance of Meatballs.*	Share draft pages in writing group. Make revisions →
10:30–10:45 Break	Go outside to look at clouds—if it is a cloudy day.				
10:45–11:30 Math	Talk about thermometers, how to read them, and how to record temperatures ———————————————————→				
11:30–12:15 Lunch					
12:15–12:30 Independent Reading	Students read books chosen from the class collection of weather books or listen to a weather-related book at the listening center.				
12:30–1:00 Fine Arts					
1:00–2:00 Block B	Show collection of weather instruments. Discuss uses. Add words to word wall. Which can they make?	Centers 1. Examine instruments. 2. Make weather vane. 3. Make rain gauge. 4. Make wind sock.	——————————————→		View film on *Tools We Use to Measure Weather.* Make chart with notes from film.
2:00–2:15 Break					
2:15–3:00 Block C	View film on *Forecasting the Weather.* Brainstorm ideas from film. Write in weather log. Talk about interviewing TV weather forecaster.	Write class invitation (review letter format). Discuss interview. Begin list of topics for interview questions.	Develop list of questions. Students each choose a question to ask. Write questions on cards.	Rehearse interview. Read aloud *I Forecast the Weather.*	The interview
3:00–3:15 Cleanup					

Step five is to make plans for assessing learning. The time to decide how to assess students' learning in the unit is during the planning stage, not after the unit has been completed. One way to plan for assessment and grading is to develop a unit checklist identifying the assignments students will complete in class during the unit and how they will be graded. Students receive a copy of the checklist at the beginning of the unit and keep it in their unit folder. Then, as they complete the assignments, they can check them off, and it is easy for

FIGURE 8.11

An Assessment Checklist for a Unit on Weather

	Weather Unit	
Name _____	Beginning Date _____	
	Ending Date _____	
	Student's Check	Teacher's Check
1. Keep a daily weather calendar.	☐	☐
2. Make a weather instrument and write about it in your Weather Log.	☐	☐
3. Do a weather experiment and write about it in your Weather Log.	☐	☐
4. Read *The Cloud Book* and write it in your Weather Log.	☐	☐
5. Write a page for our book about clouds.	☐	☐
6. Make a weather safety poster and share it.	☐	☐
7. Read two weather books and write about them in your Weather Log.	☐	☐
8. Read *Rain* and write a poem about rain.	☐	☐
9. Do a weather project. Tell about it.	☐	☐

the teacher to make periodic checks. At the end of the unit, the teacher collects the unit folders and grades the work. A "Weather Unit Checklist" is presented in Figure 8.11. Nine assignments are included on the checklist; students put a check in the left-hand column when they complete each assignment, and the teacher adds the grade in the right-hand column. The assignments take the place of traditional worksheets and will be completed in class—they are not homework assignments. Some assignments will be graded as "done" or "not done," and others will be graded for quality.

Facilitating Student Learning

Teachers play many roles while they facilitate students' learning. They instruct, guide, model, assess, support, encourage, respond, insist upon, and explain, to name only a few of the roles. Cazden (1983) categorizes these roles as *scaffolds, models,* and *instruction.*

Just as parents provide support for their children as they learn to talk, teachers also provide temporary supports as students are listening, talking, reading, and writing. For example, teachers serve as guides or coaches as they encourage students who are preparing a puppet show or writing reports. They respond to and reflect on students' writing as any interested audience would. Through these roles, teachers provide a "scaffold" or framework to support students when they tackle complex learning tasks (Applebee & Langer, 1983; Bruner, 1978; Cazden, 1980). As students learn, the need for this scaffolding diminishes, but when they tackle a new concept, the need for support returns. Teachers must continue to be responsive to students' growing competencies to provide this assistance. It is important, too, that teachers appreciate the power of their interactions with students and how they can support students' learning.

In everything they do, teachers are models for students. If you watch children play school at home, you will appreciate just how well children internalize what the teacher models. Teachers model language learning and ways to use language; for instance, they model ways of talking, and how children respond to and interact with classmates often reflects what the teacher has modeled in his or her talk. Teachers model literacy when they read and write along with their classes. When they check a dictionary for the spelling or meaning of a word they are unsure of, they model its use more powerfully than any assignment could.

Teachers also model language learning in more direct ways. When teachers first introduce a new concept, they should model it for students. When teachers introduce the diamante or haiku poetic form, for example, the teacher explains the form and shares several sample poems. Then students compose a poem as a class with the teacher before writing their own poems, and writing the poem as a class is modeling. It is important to point out that the model the teacher supplies is one example to learn from, not a sample to copy (Cazden, 1983). Similarly, teachers first model a writing group conference with a small group of students before students break into groups to share their writing. Modeling is as important in school learning as it was in young children's learning to talk. Students are learning how to "do school" and how to use language in new ways.

Almost everything a teacher does might be called "teaching," and certainly teachers are teaching as they informally support and nurture students' learning and as they model. Another type of teaching is direct teaching, when teachers plan and teach a formal lesson. The instructional model in Chapter 7 is designed for this type of direct teaching, when teachers are helping students learn a new concept or review one that was previously introduced. This instructional model can be used to teach the whole class or small groups of students, and it can be adapted to teach concepts, strategies, and skills related to the four language arts.

Another important component of the teacher's role, as presented in Chapter 5, is to assess student progress, either informally or formally. Teachers assess informally to guide students, to clarify misunderstandings, to monitor progress, and to know when to tear down the scaffold. They also assess students more formally to judge whether they have learned a particular concept and to assign grades. To keep track of 22, 26, or 30 students in a classroom, teachers need a variety of record-keeping techniques.

Resources for Teachers

Teachers are always interested in learning more about how to teach. As you begin teaching, you will want to learn as much as possible about how to teach language arts. Most schools provide inservice or staff development programs, some of which will be devoted to language arts instruction. Two organizations dedicated to improving the quality of instruction in reading and the other language arts are the National Council of Teachers of English (NCTE) and the International Reading Association (IRA). As an undergraduate student preparing for teaching, you will find that these organizations can help you keep in touch with new ideas in the field. Both organizations publish journals of interest to preservice and classroom teachers with articles suggesting innovative teaching practices, reports of significant research studies, reviews of recently published books of children's literature, techniques for using computers in the classroom, and reviews of professional books and classroom materials. Journals for elementary teachers are *Language Arts,* published by NCTE, and *The Reading Teacher,* published by IRA. The two organizations also publish other journals for high school language arts and reading teachers, college faculty, and researchers. Figure 6.4 (Chapter 6) lists these and other periodicals of interest to teachers. Most of these journals and magazines invite readers to share their classroom-tested ideas by submitting manuscripts; information for authors appears in each publication that invites unsolicited manuscripts.

NCTE and IRA also organize yearly national conferences, which are held in major cities around the United States on a rotating basis. At these conferences, teachers can listen to presentations by well-known authorities in language arts and by children's authors and illustrators, as well as by other classroom teachers who have developed innovative programs in their classrooms. Teachers can also meet in special-interest groups to share ideas and concerns. Commercial publishers also display textbooks and other instructional materials at the conferences. In addition, these two organizations have state and local affiliate groups that teachers can join. The affiliates also publish journals and organize conferences. The local groups enable teachers to meet other teachers with similar interests and concerns.

Teachers can also learn more about teaching writing by participation in workshops sponsored by affiliate groups of the National Writing Project (NWP). The NWP began as the

Bay Area Writing Project at the University of California at Berkeley in 1974. It was conceived by James Gray and a group of English teachers who wanted to improve the quality of writing instruction in elementary and secondary schools. The NWP has spread to more than 150 affiliate groups located in almost every state and in Canada, Europe, and Asia; for example, the Gateway Writing Project serves the St. Louis area, the Capital Writing Project serves the Washington, D.C., area, and the Oklahoma Writing Project serves the state of Oklahoma. Inservice workshops are scheduled in school districts near each affiliate group. One principle on which the NWP is based is that the best teacher of other teachers is a teacher, and teachers who have been trained by the affiliate groups give presentations at the inservice workshops.

Each NWP affiliate group recruits experienced teachers who have a special interest and/or expertise in teaching writing to participate in special summer training institutes. These teachers then serve as teacher/consultants and make presentations at the inservice workshops. Many NWP affiliate groups also sponsor other workshops and study tours, young author conferences and workshops for student writers, and teacher-as-researcher projects that have direct classroom applications. For additional information about the National Writing Project or for the location of the NWP affiliate group nearest you, contact the National Writing Project, School of Education, University of California, Berkeley, CA 94720.

C. ASSESSING STUDENTS' PROGRESS IN LANGUAGE ARTS LEARNING

Assessing students' progress in the language arts is a difficult task. Although it may seem fairly easy to develop a criterion-referenced test, administer it, and grade it, tests often measure language *skills* rather than language *use*. It is extremely difficult to measure students' communicative competence with a test. Tests do not measure listening and talking very well, and a test on punctuation marks, for example, does not indicate students' ability to use punctuation marks correctly in their own writing. Instead, tests typically evaluate students' ability to add punctuation marks to a set of sentences created by someone else, or to proofread and spot punctuation errors in someone else's writing. An alternative and far better approach is to examine how students use punctuation marks in their own writing.

Assessment must be viewed as an integral part of the language arts curriculum (Goodman, et. al., 1989). We suggest seven alternative approaches to documenting children's language development and assessing students' progress. They are classroom observations, anecdotal records, conferences, checklists, interviews, language samples, and across-the-curriculum applications (Baskwill & Whitman, 1988). Information from these approaches together provides a more complete and more personal assessment picture or "portfolio" (Flood & Lapp, 1989). These approaches help teachers get to know students better and to better interpret student learning.

Classroom Observations

Instead of relying on tests, we suggest that teachers become *kid watchers,* a term that Goodman (1978) coined and defined as "direct and informal observation of students." To be an effective kid watcher, teachers must understand how children develop language and understand the role of errors in language learning. In Chapter 7 we described language development as a natural, hypothesis-testing process. Children often make miscues or "errors" as they learn to talk (Goodman & Burke, 1972). They may, for instance, say "keeped" or "goodest" when they are learning rules for forming past tense or superlatives. Instead of errors, however, these words are clues to language development. Children's sentence structure, spelling, and other "errors" provide equally valuable clues to their written language development. Teachers use kid watching spontaneously when they interact with children and are attentive to their behavior and comments. Other observation times should be planned, however, during which the teacher focuses on particular children and makes anecdotal notes about a child's use of language. Students' behavior during testing situations often does not reflect their actual ability to communicate using the language modes.

Anecdotal Records

While teachers kid-watch, they make anecdotal records noting students' performance in listening, talking, reading, and writing activities, as well as questions students ask and concepts and skills they indicate confusion about. These records document students' growth and pinpoint problem areas that need direct instruction from the teacher. A year-long collection of records provides a comprehensive picture of a student's language development. Instead of recording random samples, teachers should choose events that are characteristic of each student. An excerpt from a fifth-grade teacher's anecdotal records about one student's progress during a unit on the American Revolution appears in Figure 8.12.

Several organizational schemes are possible, and teachers should use the format that is most comfortable for them. Some teachers make a card file with dividers for each child and write anecdotes on notecards. They feel comfortable jotting notes on these small cards or even carrying around a set of cards in their pockets. Other teachers divide a spiral-bound notebook into sections for each child and write anecdotes in the notebook, which they keep on their desks. A third technique is to write anecdotes on small sheets of paper and clip the sheets into the student's assessment folder.

Conferences

Teachers often hold short, informal conferences to talk with students about their work or to help them solve a problem related to what they are studying. Most often these conferences concern students' reading or writing activities, but they could be held with the actors in a play or the students working in a small group to create an advertisement or commercial. Conferences can be held at students' desks while the teacher moves around the classroom, at the teacher's desk, or at a special conference table. These are some occasions for and types of conferences:

FIGURE 8.12
Excerpt from an Anecdotal Record

American Revolution Unit—Simulated Journals and Biographies

March 5	Matthew selected Ben Franklin as historical figure for American Revolution projects.
March 11	Matthew fascinated with information he has found about B. F. Brought several sources from home. Is completing B F.'s lifeline with many details.
March 18	Simulated journal. Four entries in four days! Interesting how he picked up language style of the period in his journal. Volunteers to share daily. I think he enjoys the oral sharing more than the writing.
March 25	Nine simulated journal entries, all illustrated. High level of enthusiasm.
March 29	Conferenced about cluster for B. F. biography. Well developed with five rays, many details. Matthew will work on "contributions" ray. He recognized it as the least-developed one.
April 2	Three chapters of biography drafted. Talked about "working titles" for chapters and choosing more interesting titles after writing that reflect the content of the chapters.
April 7	Drafting conference. Matthew has completed all five chapters. He and Dustin are competitive, both writing on B. F. They are reading each other's chapters and checking the accuracy of information.
April 12	Writing group. Matthew confused Declaration of Independence with the Constitution. Chapters longer and more complete since drafting conference. Compared with autobiography project, writing is more sophisticated. Longer, too. Reading is influencing writing style—e.g., "Luckily for Ben." He is still somewhat defensive about accepting suggestions except from me. He will make 3 revisions—agreed in writing group.
April 15	Revisions: (1) eliminated "he" (substitute), (2) re-sequenced Chapter 3 (move), and (3) added sentences in Chapter 5 (add).
April 19	Proofread with Dustin. Working hard.
April 23	Editing conference—no major problems. Discussed use of commas within sentences, capitalizing proper nouns. Matthew and Dustin more task-oriented on this project; I see more motivation and commitment.
April 29	Final copy of biography completed and shared with class.

- *On-the-spot conferences.* Teachers visit briefly with students at their desks to monitor some aspect of the student's work or to check on progress. These conferences are brief; the teacher may spend less than a minute at the student's desk before moving away.
- *Prereading or prewriting conferences.* The teacher and student make plans for reading or writing at the conference. At a prereading conference, they may talk about information related to the book, difficult concepts or vocabulary words related to the reading, or the reading log the student will keep. At a prewriting conference, they may discuss possible writing topics, how to narrow a broad topic, or how to gather and organize information before writing.
- *Revising conferences.* A small group of students and the teacher meet together to get specific suggestions about revising their compositions. These conferences offer student writers an audience to provide feedback on how well they have communicated.
- *Book discussion conferences.* A student (or small group of students) and the teacher meet to discuss the book they have read. They may share entries from their reading logs, discuss the author's use of plot or characters, compare the story to others they have read, or make plans to extend their reading by doing a project.
- *Editing conferences.* In these individual or small-group conferences, the teacher reviews students' proofread compositions and helps them correct spelling, punctuation, capitalization, and other mechanical errors.
- *Instructional "minilesson" conferences.* In these conferences, teachers meet with individual students to provide special instruction on one or two skills (e.g., capitalizing proper nouns, using commas in a series) that are particularly troublesome for certain students.
- *Assessment conferences.* In assessment conferences, the teacher meets with students after they complete an assignment or project to talk about their growth as readers or writers and their plans for the next assignment. Teachers ask students to reflect on their competencies and to set goals.

The teacher's role at conferences is to be listener and guide. Teachers can learn a great deal about students and their learning if they listen as students talk about their reading, writing, or other activities. When students explain a problem they are having, the teacher is often able to decide on a way to work through it. Graves (1983) suggests that teachers balance the amount of their talk with the student's talk during the conference and, at the end, reflect on what the student has taught them, what responsibilities the student can take, and whether the student understands what to do next.

Checklists

Teachers can use checklists during specific observations or to track students' progress on particular skills. For example, when students participate in writing conferences in which they read their compositions to small groups of classmates and ask for suggestions for improving their writing, teachers can check that students participate fully in the group, share their writing with classmates, gracefully accept suggestions about improving their writing, and make substantive changes in their writing based on some of their classmates' suggestions. Students can even help develop the checklists so they understand what types of behavior are expected of them.

Four checklists appear in Figure 8.13. The first is a "Weekly Reading–Writing Activity Sheet" that students in intermediate and middle school grades might complete each week to monitor their reading and writing activities. Notice that students are directed to write a letter to the teacher on the back of the sheet, reflecting on their work during that week. Next is a "Response to Literature Checklist" that either the teacher or the student might use to keep track of the response activities the student chooses to participate in after reading. The third checklist is an "Independent Reading Record" that students keep as they read. Students list the title and author of each book they read, the dates on which they read the book, the date of their conference with the teacher, the type of response activity, and when the student shared the response activity with the class. Fourth is a "Fables Unit Checklist" for use by fourth graders as they complete activities in their fables unit. This checklist is clipped inside a unit folder, and as students complete each assignment, they check the box

FIGURE 8.13
Four Sample Assessment Checklists

Weekly Reading–Writing Activity Sheet			
Name _____		Week _____	
Read independently	M T W Th F	Wrote in a journal	M T W Th F
Read in a guided reading group	M T W Th F	Wrote in a reading log	M T W Th F
Did a response activity	M T W Th F	Did a prewriting activity	M T W Th F
Listened to the teacher read aloud	M T W Th F	Wrote a rough draft	M T W Th F
Read during USSR time	M T W Th F	Went to a writing group	M T W Th F
Read to an adult	M T W Th F	Made revisions	M T W Th F
Read to other children	M T W Th F	Edited my own writing	M T W Th F
Read at the listening center	M T W Th F	Edited for a classmate	M T W Th F
Had a reading conference	M T W Th F	Had a writing conference	M T W Th F
Shared my reading with classmates	M T W Th F	Shared my writing with classmates	M T W Th F
Other		Other	
New words read this week		Spelling words needed this week	
Titles of books read		Titles of writings	
Write a letter to me on the back, thinking about the week and your reading and writing.			

in the right-hand column. At the end of the unit, the folder with the checklist and all student materials is submitted to the teacher.

Interviews

Teachers can interview or talk with students about language to try to understand their perceptions and to clarify misunderstandings. Teachers can ask factual questions about language and language skills, but more valuable questions are metacognitive, focusing on how the students use language. Questions such as "Do you listen the same way to something that compares one thing to another (such as alligators and crocodiles) as you do to something that has a lot of descriptive words (such as what a swamp looks like)? Why or why not?" or "What do you do when you're writing and don't know how to spell a word? What else can you do?" These questions probe students' awareness of language processes and strategies for comprehending and producing language.

FIGURE 8.13 cont'd

Response to Literature Checklist	
Name _____	Grading Period 1 2 3 4
book jacket	point of view
book seller	portrait of character
cartoons	posters
character cluster	puppets
commercial or ad	quotable quotes
crossword puzzle	read other books
diorama	reading logs
dramatization	scripts
dress as character	simulated journals
exhibit	simulated letter
filmstrip	story rewrites
interview	travel brochure
letter to author	versions
map or diagram	5 Ws cluster
mobile	Win, Lose, or Draw
movie roll	word charts
mural	
newspaper article	
oral reading	
plot diagram	
poem	

Language Samples

Teachers can collect students' oral and written language samples to use in assessing their progress. Oral language samples can be tape recorded, and written language samples can be kept in folders. The teacher can compare samples from the first month of the school year to more recent samples to identify areas of growth, as well as areas that need instruction. When language samples are to be graded, students should be allowed to choose those to be assessed from the samples that have been collected.

Across-the-Curriculum Applications

A final approach to assessing students' progress in language arts is to examine how well students have applied their knowledge about listening, talking, reading, and writing to other areas of the curriculum. In fact, these applications are probably the best indicator of students'

FIGURE 8.13 cont'd

Independent Reading Record				

Name _____ Grading Period 1 2 3 4

Title/Author	Dates Read	Conference	Response	Sharing

Fables Unit Checklist

Name _____

1. I read *Fables* by Arnold Lobel.   ☐

2. I wrote about 10 fables in my reading log.   ☐

3. I did a project   ☐
    ☐ a story map
    ☐ puppets to retell a fable
    ☐ a mobile
    ☐ _____

4. I helped write our class fable.   ☐

5. I wrote a fable using the writing process of   ☐
    ☐ prewriting
    ☐ drafting
    ☐ revising
    ☐ editing
    ☐ sharing

---

learning. As an example, students may score 100% on weekly spelling tests but continue to spell the same words incorrectly in science learning logs and research reports in social studies.

To assess students' language development systematically with alternative techniques, teachers should use at least three different evaluation approaches. Approaching an evaluation through at least three different viewpoints is called *triangulation*. In addition to tests, teachers can use these techniques: kid watching, anecdotal records, checklists, interviewing, tape recording students' talk, writing samples, and across-the-curriculum applications. Using a variety of approaches enables teachers to be much more accurate in charting and assessing students' language growth.

SUMMARY

This chapter focuses on how teachers teach language arts. As Lefevre suggests, teachers need to provide opportunities for discovery; an example is a unit on mystery stories. The classroom environment is important in teaching, and classrooms should be language rich, with a variety of literacy materials available. Through application of the characteristics of a literate environment and arrangement of the classroom, teachers can promote this language-rich setting.

Teachers facilitate students' learning in three ways: they provide scaffolds, models, and instruction. We have seen how teachers develop units, facilitate students' learning, and assess learning as exemplified in a weather unit.

Tests are only one way to assess students' learning; other ways are classroom observations, anecdotal records, conferences, checklists, interviews, language samples, and across-the-curriculum applications.

QUESTIONS AND ACTIVITIES FOR DISCUSSION

1. Visit a classroom and note which characteristics of a language-rich classroom it exemplifies. What might the teacher change in the classroom to incorporate other characteristics?

2. Examine several language arts textbooks for the grade level at which you teach or expect to teach, using the guidelines in Figure 8.5. Evaluate the textbooks and consider how they should be used in teaching language arts.

3. Preview language arts software programs using the guidelines in Figure 8.7. Three highly rated programs you may want to preview are *Story Tree* (1984), *M-ss-ng l-nks: Young People's Literature* (1983), and *Jabbertalky* (1983). Also examine word-processing programs such as *The writing workshop* (1986) and *QUILL* (1983).

4. Choose a topic and develop a unit cluster like those illustrated in Figures 8.8 and 8.9.

5. Review at least six of the journals and magazines listed in Figure 6.4. Summarize your review of each publication on an index card and include the following information:

> Title, mailing address, and sponsoring organization of the publication
>
> Number of issues published each year
>
> Cost of yearly subscription
>
> Types of articles in each issue
>
> Assessment of the journal and its value for elementary teachers

6. Interview a teacher and ask about the kinds of assessment he or she uses.

7. Read Kitagawa's article (1989) about classroom observations of individual students, then make your own day-long observation of an intermediate or middle grade student.Hooper, M. (1985).

REFERENCES

Anno, M. (1983). *Anno's U.S.A.* New York: Philomel.

Applebee, A. N., & Langer, J. A. (1983). Instructional scaffolding: Reading and writing and natural language activities. *Language Arts, 60,* 168–175.

The Bank Street writer (1982). [Computer program]. San Rafael, CA: Broderbund Software.

Baskwill, J., & Whitman, P. (1988). *Evaluation: Whole language, whole child.* New York: Scholastic.

Bruner, J. (1978). The role of dialogue in language acquisition. In A. Sinclair, R. J. Jarvelle, & W. J. M. Levelt (Eds.), *The child's concept of language.* New York: Springer-Verlag.

Burningham, J. (1985). *Opposites.* New York: Crown Books.

Carle, E. (1989). *Animals, animals.* New York: Philomel.

Carrick, C. (1978). *Octopus.* New York: Clarion Books.

Caselli, G. (1987). *The human body.* New York: Grosset & Dunlap.

Cazden, C. B. (1980). Peekaboo as an instructional model: Discourse development at home and at school. *Papers and Reports of Child Language Development, 17,* 1–29.

Cazden, C. B. (1983). Adult assistance to language development: Scaffolds, models, and direct instruction. In R. P. Parker & F. A. Davis (Eds.), *Developing literacy: Young children's use of language,* pp. 3–18. Newark, DE: International Reading Association.

Chomsky, C. (1984). Finding the best language arts software. *Classroom Computer Learning, 4,* 61–63.

Cleary, B. (1981). *Ramona Quimby, Age 8.* New York: Morrow.

Cole, J. (1973). *My puppy is born.* New York: Morrow.

Crews, D. (1982). *Carousel.* New York: Greenwillow.

Dahl, R. (1984). *Boy.* New York: Farrar, Straus & Giroux.

DeGroff, L. (1990). Is there a place for computers in whole language classrooms? *The Reading Teacher, 43,* 568–572.

Dickinson, D. K. (1986). Cooperation, collaboration, and a computer: Integrating a computer into a first-second grade writing program. *Research in the Teaching of English, 20,* 357–378.

Elkin, B. (1983). *Money.* Chicago: Children's Press.

Fleischman, P. (1988). *Joyful noise: Poems for two voices.* New York: Harper and Row.

Fleischman, S. (1986). *The whipping boy.* New York: Greenwillow.

Flood, J., & Lapp, D. (1989). Reporting reading progress: A comparison portfolio for parents. *The Reading Teacher, 42,* 508–514.

Fritz, J. (1976). *Will you sign here, John Hancock?* New York: Coward-McCann.

Genishi, C. (1988). Kindergartners and computers: A case study of six children. *The Elementary School Journal, 89,* 185–201.

Gibbons, G. (1982). *The post office book: Mail and how it moves.* New York: Harper and Row.

Goodall, J. S. (1986). *The story of a castle.* New York: Macmillan.

Goodall, J. S. (1988). *Little red riding hood.* New York: Macmillan.

Goodman, K. (1986). *What's whole in whole language?* Portsmouth, NH: Heinemann.

Goodman, K. S., Goodman, Y. M., & Hood, W. J. (Eds.). (1989). *The whole language evaluation book.* Portsmouth, NH: Heinemann.

Goodman, Y. M. (1978). Kid watching: An alternative to testing. *National Elementary Principals Journal, 57,* 41–45.

Goodman, Y. M., & Burke, C. L. (1972). *The reading miscue inventory manual.* New York: Richard C. Owen.

Graves, D. H. (1977). Research update: Language arts textbooks: A writing process evaluation. *Language Arts, 54,* 817–823.

Graves, D. H. (1983). *Writing: Teachers and children at work.* Portsmouth, NH: Heinemann.

Hamilton, V. (1974). *Paul Robeson: The life and times of a free black man.* New York: Harper and Row.

Hopkins, L. B. (1976). *Good morning to you, valentine.* New York: Harcourt Brace Jovanovich.

Howe, D., & Howe, J. (1979). *Bunnicula.* New York: Atheneum.

Hyman, T. S. (1977). *The sleeping beauty.* Boston: Little, Brown.

Jabbertalky: The programmable word game (1983). [Computer program]. Sunnyvale, CA: Automated Simulations.

Kennedy, X. J., & Kennedy, D. M. (1982). *Knock at a star: A child's introduction to poetry.* Boston: Little, Brown.

Kitagawa, M. M. (1989). Observing Carlos: One day of language use in school. In G. S. Pinnell & M. L. Matlin (Eds.), *Teachers and research: Language learning in the classroom,* pp. 3–7. Newark, DE: International Reading Association.

Lasky, K. (1983). *Sugaring time.* New York: Macmillan.

Lefevre, C. A. (1970). *Linguistics, English, and the language arts.* Boston: Allyn and Bacon.

Lewis, C. S. (1950). *The lion, the witch, and the wardrobe.* New York: Macmillan.

Lindfors, J. W. (1989). The classroom: A good environment for language learning. In P. Rigg & V. G. Allen. (Eds.), *When they don't all speak English: Integrating the ESL student into the regular classroom,* pp. 39–54. Urbana, IL: National Council of Teachers of English.

Locker, T. (1987). *The boy who held back the sea.* New York: Dial.

Macaulay, D. (1977). *Castle.* Boston: Houghton Mifflin.

MacLachlan, P. (1985). *Sarah, plain and tall.* New York: Harper and Row.

Mayer, M. (1974). *Frog goes to dinner.* New York: Dial.

Mayers, F. C. (1986). *The National Air and Space Museum ABC.* New York: Abrams.

M-ss-ng l-nks: Young people's literature (1983). [Computer program]. Pleasantville, NY: Sunburst Communications.

Morrow, L. M. (1989). Designing the classroom to promote literacy development. In D. S. Strickland & L. M. Morrow (Eds.), *Emerging literacy: Young children learn to read and write.* Newark, DE: International Reading Association.

Parker, N. W. (1985). *Paul Revere's Ride.* New York: Greenwillow.

Paterson, K. (1977). *Bridge to Terabithia.* New York: Crowell.

Prelutsky, J. (1983). *The Random House book of poetry for children.* New York: Random House.

Prelutsky, J. (1988). *Tyrannosaurus was a beast.* New York: Greenwillow.

QUILL (1983). [Computer program]. Lexington, MA: DC Heath.

Sendak, M. (1963). *Where the wild things are.* New York: Harper and Row.

Sobol, D. J. (1963). *Encyclopedia Brown, boy detective.* New York: E. P. Dutton.

Spier, P. (1973). *The star-spangled banner.* New York: Doubleday.

Story tree (1984). [Computer program]. New York: Scholastic.

Taylor, R. (1980). *Computers in the schools: Tool, tutor, and tutee.* New York: Teachers College Press.

The writing workshop (1986). [Computer program]. St. Louis: Milliken.

Zalben, J. B. (1977). *Lewis Carroll's Jabberwocky.* New York: Warne.

CHILDREN'S LITERATURE REFERENCES

Hooper, M. (1985). *Seven eggs.* New York: Harper and Row.

Lobel, A. (1970). *Frog and toad are friends.* New York: Harper and Row.

Lobel, A. (1972). *Frog and toad together.* New York: Harper and Row.

Lobel, A. (1976). *Frog and toad all year.* New York: Harper and Row.

Lobel, A. (1979). *Days with frog and toad.* New York: Harper and Row.

Sharmat, M. W. (1974). *Nate the great goes undercover.* New York: Coward-McCann.

SUGGESTED READINGS

Barber, B. (1982). Creating BYTES of language. *Language Arts, 59,* 472–475.

Hall, N. (1987). *The emergence of literacy.* Portsmouth, NH: Heinemann.

Phenix, J., & Hannan, E. (1984). Word processing in the grade one classroom. *Language Arts, 61,* 804–812.

Smith, N. J. (1985). The word processing approach to language experience. *The Reading Teacher, 38,* 556–559.

Smith, P. L., & Tompkins, G. E. (1984). Selecting software for your LD students. *Academic Therapy, 20,* 221–224.

CHAPTER 9

Extending Language Arts across the Curriculum

This chapter extends the teaching of language arts from language arts class across the curriculum into literature, social studies, and other content areas. Specifically, you will learn

1. Which language arts activities can be integrated across the curriculum.
2. What a language arts across-the-curriculum thematic unit is.
3. More about how to plan thematic units of instruction.

Students listen, talk, read, and write across the curriculum every day in classrooms, but greater learning and excitement about learning are not always the outcomes. The language arts across-the-curriculum movement, a new way of developing curriculum, focuses on using language to learn. This approach works best when the curriculum is organized into thematic units. Social studies, science, language arts, and other content areas are integrated into units that focus on broad themes, such as communication, explorers, mystery stories, the oceans, or Dr. Seuss's stories. Instead of reading content area textbooks and answering the questions at the end of each chapter, teachers and students are actively involved in researching to find answers and responding to what they learn.

Gamberg and her colleagues (1988) describe theme study as "the core of what children do in school" (p. 10). At their elementary school in Halifax, Nova Scotia, students participate in large-scale themes; one focuses on houses. Students at different grade levels studied different aspects, but all students focused on houses. One class of primary students, for example, studied homes around the world; a class of middle-grade students investigated how homes have changed through history; and a class of upper-grade students learned about building a house. Based on experiences teaching thematic units, teachers list these characteristics:

- The unit involves in-depth study.
- The topic is of interest to students.
- The topic is broad enough that it can be divided into subtopics.
- The topic lends itself to comparing and contrasting ideas.
- The unit includes opportunities for investigation and use of concrete materials and other resources.
- The unit allows for cross-disciplinary activities.
- The unit encourages students to use community resources.

Teachers work together to plan the units and to integrate content area study, language arts, and skills so that students are involved in meaningful, functional, and genuine learning activities. Theme studies are successful with all children because they help them become responsible, independent learners who cooperate with classmates at the same time that they become self-disciplined. One of the most important outcomes is that students gain self-confidence and self-esteem as they become successful and motivated to learn and apply what they are learning.

Language is a powerful learning tool, and reading, writing, listening, and talk activities are valuable ways to learn in all content areas. When students use language in meaningful ways in content area study, they learn the content information better and develop language competencies, and critical thinking skills are activated. Through listening, talking, reading, and writing activities, students develop their own knowledge of the subject. Thaiss (1986) identifies three benefits students gain from studying across the curriculum:

1. Students understand and remember better when they use listening, talking, reading, and writing to explore what they are learning.
2. Students' language learning is reinforced when they listen, talk, read, and write about what they are learning.
3. Students learn best through active involvement, collaborative projects, and interaction with classmates, the teacher, and the world.

A. LEARNING THROUGH LANGUAGE

Halliday (1980) described three components of the language arts curriculum: learning language, learning through language, and learning about language. The first component, learning language, might seem to be language arts teachers' primary responsibility. Certainly, students do need to develop communicative competence in listening, talking, reading, and writing, and instruction in each of the four language modes is essential. The third component, learning about language, involves "coming to understand the nature and function of language itself" (Halliday, 1980, p. 16). Students develop intuitive knowledge about language and its forms and purposes while they use the four language modes, and through vocabulary, spelling, and grammar instruction, their knowledge is made more explicit. But language learning does not occur in isolation, and the second component is just as important.

Learning through language is described as "how we use language to build up a picture of the world in which we live" (Halliday, 1980, p. 13). It involves using language to learn in content areas across the curriculum. Students learn content area material through language at the same time they are learning, applying, and refining language through content area study. The language arts activities that we have discussed throughout this text are applied through literature and content area study. Rather than learn about listening for the sake of listening, students learn about it so they can listen more effectively to learn math or science. Similarly, they learn to read and write for content area study.

Learning Science through Language

In learning about science, students participate in a wide variety of language activities (Hansen et al., 1985). They listen to information presented in filmstrips and videotapes, information presented by the teacher, and information read aloud. They use informal writing strategies to take notes and organize information. Clusters, note-taking/note-making sheets, learning logs, and lab reports are four forms that recording may take. Students read concept books, informational books, reference books, and magazine articles as a part of research projects and share what they are learning through oral reports, debates, written reports, "All about . . ." books, posters, charts, and diagrams. Interviewing can also be used in science; students can interview a scientist or other knowledgeable person and then share what they have learned by writing a newspaper article or other report.

~ *From the Teacher* ~

Process: Science and Writing

"Doing a science project is one of the best ways I know to practice the writing process."
   Brian Bennett, Fifth-Sixth Grade Teacher,
   Heaton Elementary School

PROCEDURE

Beginning in September, my students conduct science experiments and record the results in lab reports. One of the things I stress is to keep accurate records of what is happening. We began with a unit on air and then went to units on water, the human body, plants, and machines. In each unit, my students use the scientific method; after conducting ten or more experiments in each unit, they can apply this approach to their own experiments.

In January, we begin to talk about science fair projects to present at our science fair in April. Students brainstorm a list of things that interest them, and their science fair projects develop from these ideas. This year some students chose to explore which brand of paper towels absorbs the most water, how to recycle paper, and behavioristic training of animals. Most students work in small groups, and the whole class is involved in each project because of our sharing sessions, which function much like the Author's Chair. I try to keep most of the project work at school, but it is necessary to involve parents in some projects.

Using the scientific method, students identify the problem and write a hypothesis and research question. Next, they assemble the materials and conduct the experiment. They collect data using a chart and then interpret the data. This is probably the toughest part for them. We spend a lot of time talking about what the data show. Then they write the reports for their displays and put them together. It takes two months or more to complete the projects.

ASSESSMENT

I keep a notebook on each student with entries about his or her work on the project. When I review my entries, it is easy to see who is having difficulty. Then I talk with students, one at a time or in small groups if several students are having the same problem, to get them back on track. There are always a few students that I must work with closely. I also use a checklist that includes each of the components of the experiment and the pieces of information that must be included in the display. I give students this checklist when they begin, and they check off each step as they complete it. Then I assign points and give a grade for the project.

REFLECTIONS

My students use the writing process in creating their science fair projects. At each step of the process, students share their work with their classmates. We all sit in a circle, and students take turns talking about their projects and reading the drafts of problems, research questions, and other parts of their reports. Other students ask questions and give compliments and suggestions. This sharing also helps me keep tabs on each student's work. Science fair projects take a lot of time and hard work for the students and for me, but I think it's worth it because my students really apply the scientific method and learn how science affects their daily lives.

SCIENCE PROJECT CHECKLIST

STEPS	POINTS
1. Identify a problem.	10 _____
2. Write a hypothesis.	15 _____
3. Collect the materials and make a list of them.	5 _____
4. Write a research question.	15 _____
5. Conduct the experiment.	10 _____
6. Collect the data on a chart.	5 _____
7. Interpret the data.	15 _____
8. Report the conclusion.	10 _____
9. Prepare the display.	15 _____
TOTAL	_____

Comments

In a unit about plants, for example, students might be involved in the following types of activities. Listening activities might involve these:

- Listen to the teacher share poems about plants with the class.
- Listen to the teacher read informational books about plants.
- Listen to films, videotapes, and filmstrips about plants.
- Listen to a botanist or gardener talk about plants.

FIGURE 9.1
Two Writing Activities from a Fourth-Grade Plants Unit

MY EXPERIMENT ON PLANTS

My Question
Will plants grow without light?

My Prediction
No, plants cannot grow without light because if plants didn't have light the water wouldn't soak in and they wouldn't live because too much water would be on top of the plant.

My Log
April 9
I planted my seeds in a row and watered them after it. My seeds' color is brown.
They are about half an inch long. Their texture is very smooth.
They are an oval shape. They are bean seeds.
April 11
Mine has been in the dark for 2 days and nothing has changed.
April 14
My plants have grown half an inch tall in the dark. It really surprises me.
April 15
My plants are 4 inches tall (20 cm) according to what I can see.
April 16
My plants have grown 1 inch more.
April 17
Mine have grown 2 more inches longer in length.
April 21
Mine have grown 5 more inches and are now 12 inches tall.
April 22
Mine have grown half an inch. I planted another one and can't water it.
April 23
Mine have grown one inch taller. The other is growing too, even without water.
April 24
Mine are now 15 inches tall. My unwatered plant is 4 inches tall.
April 25
Mine have grown 2 more inches and the other 1 inch.
April 29
My plants are dying out after they've grown a lot.
May 1
My plants are dying and they smell terrible.

Talk activities include these possibilities:

- Participate in discussions about plants.
- Talk about the plant experiments they are conducting.
- Ask a botanist or gardener questions about plants.
- Give oral reports about plants.
- Retell or dramatize a plant story, such as *The Giving Tree* (Silverstein, 1964).

Reading activities would include these:

- Read concept books and informational books about plants.
- Read seed packets and planting guides.
- Read maps showing where different kinds of plants live.
- Read aloud poems about a plant.
- Read a classmate's hardbound book about plants.
- Share learning log entries and freewrites about plants.

These are writing activities that might be part of a science unit on plants:

FIGURE 9.1 cont'd

May 2
My plants have died and they look terrible.
May 6
My plants have been dying since a while ago. I have taken good care of them.
May 7
My plants have died and we will talk about them on Monday.
May 8
My plants have died and there's not even a root left.

My Conclusion

Now I know that the plants grew so tall because they were reaching for sunlight. They died because they were in the dark.
   —Aaron

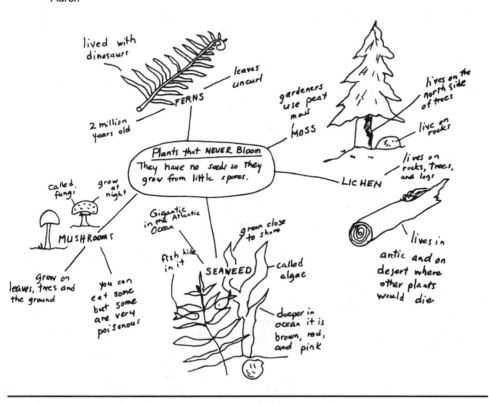

- Brainstorm a list of plant-related words.
- Make a cluster about plants, flowers, trees, or some other topic.
- Freewrite or write in a learning log about plants.
- Cube *plant, tree,* or another word related to the unit.
- Make a poster comparing deciduous and evergreen trees.
- Write a letter inviting a botanist to be interviewed.
- Record a seed's growth in a learning log.
- Make plant or ecology posters.
- Write invitations to a tree-planting ceremony.
- Write an "All about . . ." book.
- Write an ABC book about plants.
- Conduct a science experiment about plants and write a lab report.
- Research and write a report about plants.
- Write poems about plants.

Figure 9.1 shows two writing samples fourth graders wrote as part of a unit on plants. One sample is a lab report about a science experiment; the other is a cluster about nonflowering plants based on *Plants That Never Ever Bloom* (Heller, 1984). It would not be possible to list all the listening, talking, reading, and writing activities that can be related to a unit on plants, but these examples suggest the range of activities teachers should consider when planning instruction. Most importantly, our listing illustrates that the language modes are the vehicles through which students learn about plants.

Learning Social Studies through Language

Like science, social studies lends itself to language activities. To study history, geography, political science, or another of the social studies, children read picture books, concept books, informational books, reference books, magazines, and newspapers. They talk and write informally about their learning, and they talk and write to organize their learning and to share it through reports, poems, stories, and other activities. Upper-grade students who are studying the American Revolution, for instance, might be involved in these language–social studies activities. For listening:

- Listen to the teacher read aloud books about the American Revolution
- Listen to songs of the period
- View and listen to films, filmstrips, and videotapes
- Listen to classmates share their writing.

Students might participate in these talk activities:

- Discuss issues of the American Revolution
- Dramatize events from the period
- Give oral reports
- Debate in the role of a Tory or a Patriot
- Pretend to be someone from the period and be interviewed by their classmates.

They might read from among these possibilities:

- Fritz's biographies of Revolutionary personalities, such as *Why Don't You Get a Horse, Sam Adams?* (1974)
- Informational books about the American Revolution
- Chapter books set in Revolutionary War days
- Poems such as "Paul Revere's Ride"
- Maps, charts, and diagrams about the Revolutionary War
- Classmates' stories, reports, and other writings.

Writing activities might include these:

- Keeping a simulated journal as Paul Revere, Betsy Ross, or another personality from the period
- Keeping a learning log with lists of words, clusters, and note-taking/note-making pages
- Making a KWL chart listing what they know about the American Revolution, what they want to learn, and finally, what they have learned
- Writing poems about the American Revolution
- Researching and writing a report about life in the 1700s
- Writing a simulated newspaper that might have been published during the American Revolution
- Writing a biography of an American Revolutionary War personality.

An excerpt from a fifth grader's biography of Benjamin Franklin is presented in Figure 9.2. In this biography, entitled "The Life of the Great Inventor," Matthew writes four chapters focusing on Ben's childhood, his experiments with electricity, *Poor Richard's Almanack,* and Franklin's role in the Revolutionary War period. Matthew read Aliki's *The Many Lives of Benjamin Franklin* (1988), d'Aulaires' *Benjamin Franklin* (1950), and Jean Fritz's *What's the Big Idea, Ben Franklin* (1976) to gather information about Franklin. He then developed a lifeline showing key events and accomplishments. With this background of information,

FIGURE 9.2

An Excerpt from a Fifth Grader's Biography of Ben Franklin

Chapter 1: In Which a Genius Is Born

In 1706 a young genius was born. His name was Benjamin Franklin. At the time the streets of Boston, Massachusetts were still being named. Luckily, the street Ben lived on had already been named Milk Street. Ben had 17 brothers and sisters. When Ben was 9 or 10, he bought a whistle with all his money. That was the last time he spent his money unwisely. That whistle drove his family crazy.

When Ben was 12, he made a swimming machine. He got two boards and cut a hole in the middle of them. When he tested out his invention, he raced his friend Tom. Ben beat him by 10 yards.

At the age of 12, Ben's father wanted him to become a candle maker, but Ben wanted to be a sailor. Ben's father talked him into being an apprentice for his brother James. James was a printer. Back then you had to work until you were 21 if you were an apprentice.

Ben got tired of reading the same old thing from the newspaper every single day. So he wrote letters to James about things so James would put them in the newspaper. He didn't want James to know it was him so he signed it Widow Dogood. Everytime a letter came, everybody got excited. His letters made newspapers sell faster. When James found out what Ben did, he got angry and didn't let Ben give him things to put in the newspaper.

Chapter 2: Ben Discovers Electricity

On a day in 1748 it was on the front cover of the newspaper that a man had died trying to prove electricity was in lightning. The man died instantly when lightning hit the tower the man was in. The newspaper said there was machinery in the tower. So Ben figured that there was electricity in lightning. He wanted to know for sure so he got a handkerchief, 6 sticks, wire, string, and a key. He made a kite. He took the 6 sticks and used 4 of them to made a diamond. He took 2 sticks and used them for a cross for the center of the diamond. Then he used the handkerchief to wrap around the diamond. After that he tied a wire to the end of it. Then he tied some string to the end of the wire. After that he slid a key to about the center of the wire. He waited until a storm came with lightning. Then he flew the kite and lightning hit the top of the kite. A streak of electricity zoomed down the wire, but then it hit the string. When it hit Ben it was not so great but it still gave him a great shock. After he found out that electricity was in lightning he made up the lightning rod. Then he got a lot of people to become witnesses. Then he did it again and that's how we have electricity now.

—Matthew

Matthew chose topics for each chapter and used the writing process to cluster his ideas, write rough drafts of each chapter, revise the chapters in writing groups, edit to identify and correct mechanical errors and, finally, to publish his biography in a hardbound book. His finished book included a title page, table of contents, four chapters, a bibliography, and an "All about the Author" page. A unit on the American Revolution with activities such as these can be extended to include the times allocated for both language arts and social studies.

Learning Literature through Language

Literature units that focus on a single book, an author, a collection of books by the same author, a theme, or a genre can be developed the same way. Rather than just read and discuss the books, students can participate in a variety of reading, writing, talking, and listening activities (Hancock & Hill, 1987; Moss, 1984; Somers & Worthington, 1979). For a unit on Van Allsburg's fantasy picture books, middle-grade students might be involved in these listening activities:

- Listening to the teacher read aloud some of Van Allsburg's books
- Listening to other books at the listening center
- Listening to classmates share ideas about the books
- Listening to classmates share their writings in response to the books.

Talk activities might include these:

- Discussing the books
- Telling stories based on the illustrations in *The Mysteries of Harris Burdick* (1984)

- Retelling a familiar story from an unusual viewpoint, as Van Allsburg did in *Two Bad Ants* (1988)
- Dramatizing one of Van Allsburg's stories.

Students might do these reading activities:

- Read Van Allsburg's books independently.
- Read *Jumanji* (1981) as guided or shared reading.
- Read other fantasies, such as *The Lion, the Witch, and the Wardrobe* (Lewis, 1950) to compare to Van Allsburg's books.
- Examine a collection of ABC books to compare to *The Z Was Zapped* (1987).
- Read books about magic, after reading *The Garden of Abdul Gasazi* (1979).
- Share students' writing about Van Allsburg's books.

Students may participate in these writing activities:

- Keeping a reading log
- Clustering the beginning-middle-end of one of Van Allsburg's books
- Writing a letter to Van Allsburg
- Cubing Van Allsburg
- Writing a sequel to *Jumanji* (1981)
- Writing an ABC book similar to *The Z Was Zapped* (1987)
- Writing plans for a trip around the world, after reading *Ben's Dream* (1982)
- Writing directions for playing a game or researching a favorite game, after reading *Jumanji* (1981)
- Making posters about the four seasons, after reading *The Stranger* (1986)
- Writing stories to accompany the illustrations in *The Mysteries of Harris Burdick* (1984)
- Writing in response to the question "Is there a Santa Claus?", after reading *The Polar Express* (1985)
- Making posters, charts, or murals about the books.

These listening, talking, reading, and writing activities illustrate some of the possible ways literature can be extended. In a fourth-grade class, students wrote letters to Van Allsburg; one student's letter appears in Figure 9.3. As students read Van Allsburg's books, they might choose to learn more about magic, games, the seasons, ABC books, holidays, fantasies, or point of view. Students can make choices and pursue activities that interest them and involve using language to learn. Some students wrote sequels to *Jumanji;* one story is also shown in Figure 9.3.

Learning Other Content Areas through Language

Listening, talking, reading, and writing can be connected to math and other content areas as well. Two language activities for use in math class, for example, are keeping learning logs and writing story problems. Students can keep learning logs in which during the last five minutes of class they write about what they are learning (Salem, 1982; Schubert, 1987). They can write about what they have learned during that class, the steps in solving a problem, definitions of mathematical terms, and things that confuse them. Writing in learning logs has several advantages over class discussion. All students participate simultaneously in writing, and teachers can review written responses more carefully than oral ones. Also, students use mathematical vocabulary and become more precise and complete in their answers.

Students can write story problems in which they apply the mathematical concepts they have been learning. In the process of writing the problems, students consider what information to include and how to phrase the question. Audience is especially important in writing story problems, because if students do not write clearly and completely, classmates may not be able to solve the problem. In a sixth-grade class, students clipped advertisements from the local newspaper to use in writing story problems. One student used an ad for aspirin: the 72-count package was on sale for $2.99 and the 125-count package for $4.66; from this information, she composed the following problem:

Sarah went to the drugstore to buy some aspirin. She found a bottle of 125 aspirin for $4.66 and a bottle of 72 aspirin for $2.99. Which one should she buy to get the most for her money? (Answer: the bottle of 125)

To learn more about incorporating language in math class, see Richards's (1990) article in *Language Arts,* in which she describes how she uses language activities to introduce math themes, investigate math concepts, and conclude the unit. Some of the writing activities her students use are summaries, definitions, reports, freewrites, notes, lists, evaluations, predictions, arguments, and explanations. One of Richards's students sums up the value of language in math class this way: "Language helps our maths [sic] by being able to write, use words, use symbols, being able to read and listen . . . It helps explain things" (p. 14).

Students use many of the same listening, talking, reading, and writing activities in other content areas. They use informal writing strategies to take notes and organize what they are learning, and they share their learning through oral and written reports, role-playing, and other activities.

B. THEMATIC UNITS

Teachers must plan to consciously involve students in a variety of activities to facilitate learning and higher-level critical and application thinking. It is too easy to assign textbook readings and consider that content area study. Students read the textbook, discuss it (talking and listening), and write the answers to the questions at the end of the chapters. They are using the four language arts, but not as effectively as they might. A better method is to treat the textbook as one of a variety of resources for teaching a thematic unit.

Planning Thematic Units

To plan thematic units, teachers think about the types of materials and activities they want to incorporate. The cluster in Figure 9.4 illustrates 12 possible resources for developing a thematic unit, whether it focuses on social studies (e.g., California gold rush, explorers, American Revolution), science (hibernation, machines, weather), health (parts of the body, drugs, nutrition), geography (continents, the Mississippi River), literature (mystery stories, fables, myths, Halloween stories) or an author (Beverly Cleary, Tomie de Paola, Katharine Paterson).

Content area (or author) information.   Here you consider what students will learn in the unit and develop objectives. You also decide how to present the information, using reading, writing, listening, talking, and audiovisual materials. For literature units, you would include information about authors and illustrators here as well.

Stories.   Teachers locate picture books and chapter books to use in connection with the unit. Some stories will be read aloud to students (or tape recorded for the listening center), some will be read independently, and others students will read together as shared or guided reading. Investigating the topic in a library card catalog will suggest picture books and chapter books as well as other books by the same author. Textbooks sometimes list supplemental reading, another source for stories. The stories you find will be used for a variety of purposes, including these:

- To read aloud to students
- For students to read independently
- To use for shared or guided reading
- To use in teaching elements of story structure
- To use as models or patterns for storywriting.

Books should be placed in the classroom library or in a special area for theme-related materials.

Listening center.   Select tapes to accompany stories or informational books or create your own tapes so that absent students can catch up on a book you are reading aloud day by day

Pioneer Intermediate School
P.O. Box 127
Noble, OK 73068
February 22

Mr. Chris Van Allsburg
114 Lorimer Avenue
Providence, RI 02906

Dear Chris,

I really like all of your books. But I wanted to know why there is a dog like Spuds MacKenzie in every book. Also, I'd like to know why almost every woman in your books looks the same.

Are you Harris Burdick or is the story true about him? I kind of believe you. But if it was true, it would probably be on Unsolved Mysteries. By the way, I think you ought to be the host. All right, I guess that's enough of Unsolved Mysteries.

Now let's get back to your books. I've been studying your writing. I have a folder full about you and your books. So does my class. My friend and I are doing a sequel to your book *Jumanji*. We're also tracing Ben's trip in *Ben's Dream* around the world on a big map in our classroom. My favorite book is *Two Bad Ants*.

My name is Annie. I'm ten years old. I've got two bratty sisters and one dog. It's the pits. I wanted to write to you to tell you all of this. Please write back.

Your friend,

Annie Picek

RETURN TO JUMANJI

The next day on the way home from school Walter asked Peter if he would like to play a game that he had found in the park. Peter started to act weird and said, "Ah, well, ah . . . I got homework. Ah . . . I'm really tired . . . maybe, another time . . ." and he ran home as fast as he could.

At Walter and Daniel's house, Daniel opened the big long box and saw the directions and said, "Oh, how stupid—directions. Don't they have a game without directions?" "I don't know," said Walter.

Daniel rolled the dice and started to play. Move 10 spaces. Volcano eruption. Suddenly there was the loudest noise and then all of a sudden lava started filling the room. Daniel said, "Ah . . . Walter, I don't think, ah . . . I want to play this game, ah . . . any more."

"Oh, come on ya big baby. This is exciting!" said Walter. "Let's keep on playing and see what happens next."

Daniel agreed and Walter rolled the dice and moved two spaces. Laughing season. Move one space back. Suddenly Walter started laughing. He was laughing so hard his face turned red and fell out of his chair and landed in the lava. Daniel's chair fell over too and he was in it. They just could not stop laughing.

Daniel could hardly roll the dice. He rolled an 8. Dog and cat thunderstorm. Move 2 spaces back. All of a sudden dogs and cats started falling from the sky. A dog fell on Walter's head and a cat fell on Daniel's head. They stopped laughing. There were the strangest noises of meows and bow-wows. A dog got caught on the ceiling and his ears were dangling in Walter's face. The room sounded like a circus with all the meows and bow-wows of course.

Walter rolled the dice. He rolled a 9. Earthquake attack. Move 8 spaces back. The walls started shaking. Pictures fell from the mantle. Pans and pots fell from the kitchen cupboard. The table started shaking. The game fell but then Walter got it in his hands and put it back on the table.

Daniel rolled the dice. He rolled a 7. Music season. Move 5 spaces back. All of a sudden music started playing really loud. It was so loud they couldn't hear themselves think.

Walter rolled the dice. He rolled a 3. Flowers attack. Move 1 space back. Suddenly flowers started growing everywhere. A flower grew under Walter's chair. He went up to the sky. A flower grew under Daniel's chair and he went up to the sky too. Walter jumped out of his chair and landed in the lava. He said, "Im leaving." Daniel followed him. They walked out the door and closed it. Walter said, "I don't want to play this game anymore."

At 5:00 when Walter and Daniel's mom and dad got home they nearly fainted. The family moved far away from that house. But when Walter got old he got married and had two sons named Bradley and Ben. One day when Bradley and Ben were walking home from school, Bradley saw a house and tried the door. It was open. They walked in and music was blaring in their ears and dogs fell from the sky. They tried to run out but they slipped in the lava and fell down. The door closed and they never came out.

—Lori, grade 4

FIGURE 9.4
Possible Resources for Developing a Thematic Unit

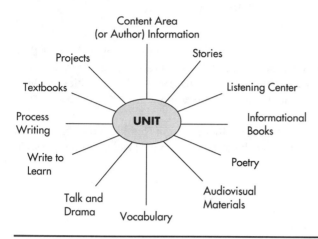

or to provide additional reading experiences for students who listen to a tape when they read or reread a story or informational book.

Informational books, magazines, newspapers, and reference books. Collect informational books, magazines, newspaper articles, and reference books. Add these to the classroom library or put them in a special area for materials related to the theme. You can also use these materials to teach students about expository text structure patterns, how to use an index and table of contents, as models or patterns for student writing, and to provide information for reports or other process writing projects.

Poetry. Locate books of poetry or individual poems that are appropriate to the unit theme to share with students. Also plan poetry writing activities using a variety of poetic forms.

Audiovisual materials. Plan the films, videotapes, filmstrips, charts, timelines, maps, models, posters, and other displays you will use in connection with the thematic unit. You can display some of these, and students can make others as they learn the content area material during the unit. Four excellent resources for locating audiovisual materials (cassette tapes, filmstrips, films, and videotapes) of children's books and authors who write for children are:

Listening Library, Inc., One Park Avenue, Old Greenwich, CT 06870

Random House Media, Department 520, 400 Hahn Road, Westminster, MD 21157

Spoken Arts, Dept. B, 310 North Avenue, New Rochelle, NY 10801

Weston Woods, Weston, CT 06883

Vocabulary. Select words related to the theme and from stories and informational books. Hang a vocabulary chart in the classroom and invite students to add new words as they encounter them. Have students write the words in their learning log. After students learn the words, they can serve as spelling words.

Talk and drama. Students can use talk and drama to learn and to demonstrate their learning (Erickson, 1988; Nelson, 1988; San Jose, 1988). These are possible activities:

- Giving oral reports
- Interviewing someone with special expertise on the theme
- Participating in a debate related to the theme
- Role-playing an event or a personality

- Participating in a readers' theater presentation of a story or poem
- Telling or retelling a story, biography, or event
- Using a puppet show to tell a story, biography, or event
- Writing and performing a skit or play.

Write to learn. Students use brainstorming, clustering, freewriting, and cubing as they take notes, list vocabulary words, write questions, make observations, clarify their thinking, and write reactions to what they are learning (Tompkins, 1990). Plan activities in which students will keep learning logs, simulated journals, or reading logs.

Process writing. At least one activity during the thematic unit should involve students in the writing process to draft, revise, edit, and share their writing. These are some possible process writing activities:

Biographies	Essays
Newspaper articles	Stories
Collaborative reports	Advertisements
Poems	Myths and legends
ABC books	"All about . . ." books
Letters	Concept books
Individual reports	Cartoons
Scripts	Posters

Textbooks. You can teach themes without textbooks; however, when information is available in a literature or content area textbook, you should consider it. Upper-grade students, in particular, can read and discuss the textbook or use it as a reference for concepts, vocabulary, and directions for further study.

Projects. Teachers plan whole class, small group, and individual projects related to the unit. Students usually complete one project independently and present their project to the class at the end of the unit. Projects should involve listening, talking, reading, and writing, as well as art, music, drama, cooking, or other activities. Figure 9.5 lists possible activities for unit projects that can be adapted for various thematic units.

Teachers brainstorm ideas for thematic units and then develop clusters of possible activities. The goal in developing unit plans is to consider a wide variety of resources that integrate listening, talking, reading, and writing with the content of the unit (Pappas, Kiefer & Levstik, 1990). We will discuss three sample thematic units for intermediate-grade students, and three for middle school students. These units integrate the four language modes with literature, social studies, and science and utilize many of the resources outlined in Figure 9.4.

Intermediate-Grade Units (Grades 4–6)

The three intermediate-grade units appear in Figure 9.6. One unit focuses on Fables (a literature unit), one on Insects (a science unit), and one on Beverly Cleary (an author unit). These unit plans suggest eight or more types of resources for teachers to choose among in developing lesson plans.

Literature unit: Fables. Fables are short stories that teach a lesson, and a number of collections of Aesop's fables as well as contemporary fables have been written for children. As shown in Figure 9.6, this unit provides reading, writing, and talk activities while students learn about this traditional form of literature. Teachers may choose from among the list of picture book versions of fables for shared or guided reading or independent reading activities. (Several of the books are available in paperback, so class sets can be purchased.) After students read fables, they write their reactions in reading logs or make clusters of the beginnings, middles, and ends of the fables. Another option is for students to make posters of the morals that have become popular sayings. Students can also retell fables orally, using puppets, or in writing.

FIGURE 9.5
Activities for Unit Projects

give an oral report
compose a rap or song
create a photo display
write and perform a readers' theater presentation, skit, or play
write a poem
construct a mobile
make puppets and present a puppet show
present an advertisement
create a mobile
make a map
cube a theme
make a diorama
write a simulated journal
create a cluster
make a chart or poster
read a book and keep a reading log
write an "All About _____" or concept book
write a simulated newspaper
write a simulated letter
write an essay arguing one viewpoint
write an ABC book
create a word search
write a report
write to a business or other organization to request information
write to an author
make a lifeline or timeline
design a book jacket
plan and present a debate
create a collage on the theme
build a model using modeling clay, blocks, or other materials
interview with someone knowledgeable about the theme
dress up as a personality related to the unit
create a filmstrip, handroll movie, or videotape
draw or paint a mural

Students can compare versions of the same fable. For instance, a number of versions of "The Tortoise and the Hare" are currently available as picture books. Students can divide into small groups to read the stories and compare how authors elaborated the beginning, middle, or end in the different versions. Students can also compare the traditional fables to modern ones, such as those of Lobel, and report their findings on a Venn diagram.

After reading and retelling fables, students can write their own fables; their first fables might be written as a class or in small groups. After this experience, students can choose a moral and write their own fables using the writing process. Some students may write traditional fables using animals as characters, and others may use well-known people, classmates, or family members as characters.

FIGURE 9.6
Clusters for Three Intermediate-Grade Units

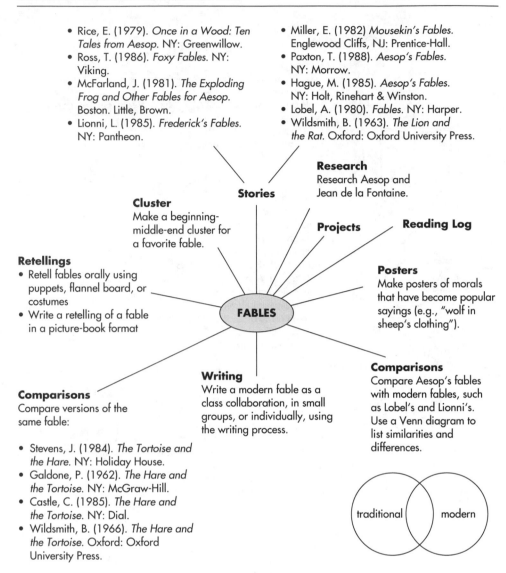

Students who become interested in these traditional stories might research Aesop or de La Fontaine, two great authors of fables. Other projects are also possible: students might make mobiles of a favorite fable, paint a mural, update and rewrite a fable with modern characters, or any of the other project possibilities listed in Figure 9.5.

Science unit: Insects. In this unit, listening, talking, reading, and writing activities extend students' learning about insects, as shown in Figure 9.6. Students read informational books about insects, use choral reading to enjoy *Joyful Noise: Poems for Two Voices* (Fleischman, 1988), and listen to a chapter book, *The Cricket in Times Square* (Selden, 1960), read aloud. Reading is a valuable way for intermediate-grade students to learn about science. They connect reading and writing by keeping a learning log in which they reflect on the book being read aloud and record scientific information from informational books and teacher presentations.

Each student chooses an insect to study in depth, and then students write a class report, with each one reporting on the insect he or she studied. They can also make charts to illustrate the life cycles or body parts of insects. As individual projects, students might make insect collections or choose one of the activities listed in Figure 9.5. Other possible activities

FIGURE 9.6 cont'd

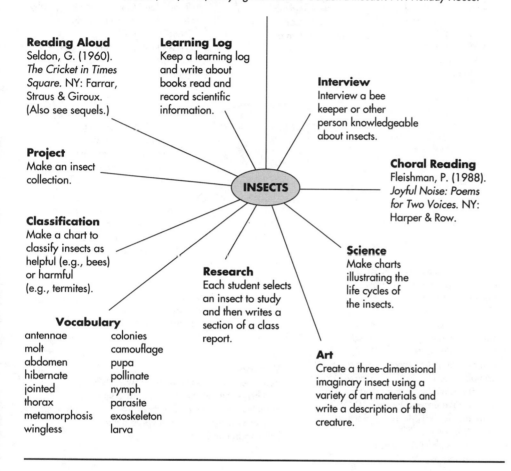

Informational Books
- Cole, J. (1984). *An Insect's Body*. NY: Morrow.
- Hutchins, R.E. (1978). *A Look at Ants*. NY: Dodd.
- Pringle, L. (1971). *Cockroaches: Here, There and Everywhere*. NY: Harper & Row.
- Oxford Scientific Films. (1980). *Dragonflies*. NY: Putnam.
- Oxford Scientific Films. (1977). *The Butterfly Cycle*. NY: Putnam.
- Conklin, G. (1978). *Praying Mantis: The Garden Dinosaur*. NY: Holiday House.

Reading Aloud
Seldon, G. (1960). *The Cricket in Times Square*. NY: Farrar, Straus & Giroux. (Also see sequels.)

Learning Log
Keep a learning log and write about books read and record scientific information.

Interview
Interview a bee keeper or other person knowledgeable about insects.

Project
Make an insect collection.

Choral Reading
Fleishman, P. (1988). *Joyful Noise: Poems for Two Voices*. NY: Harper & Row.

INSECTS

Classification
Make a chart to classify insects as helpful (e.g., bees) or harmful (e.g., termites).

Science
Make charts illustrating the life cycles of the insects.

Research
Each student selects an insect to study and then writes a section of a class report.

Vocabulary

antennae	colonies
molt	camouflage
abdomen	pupa
hibernate	pollinate
jointed	nymph
thorax	parasite
metamorphosis	exoskeleton
wingless	larva

Art
Create a three-dimensional imaginary insect using a variety of art materials and write a description of the creature.

include making a chart to classify insects as helpful or harmful, or creating imaginary insects and writing about them.

Author unit: Beverly Cleary. Beverly Cleary is a popular children's author and a good choice for a unit because she has written many books, most of which are available in paperback. This unit cluster also appears in Figure 9.6. Teachers may want to begin the unit by reading one of Cleary's Ramona books aloud. *Ramona the Pest* (1968) is a favorite of intermediate-grade students; this book introduces students to the Quimby family. Then students choose one or more of Cleary's books to read independently or as guided reading with the teacher. Students may also listen to Cleary's stories at a listening center or view filmstrips or videotapes of some books. They keep a reading log and respond to each Cleary book that they read. After reading, students can prepare a project related to the book they read, role-play a favorite episode from a story, or create an advertisement or commercial to "sell" their book.

Other activities include reading *Dear Mr. Henshaw* (1983) and inviting students to write to a favorite author (after making a class list of things to remember when writing to authors). Or, students can write about family life in Cleary's books or about their own lives. They

FIGURE 9.6 cont'd
Clusters for Three Intermediate-Grade Units

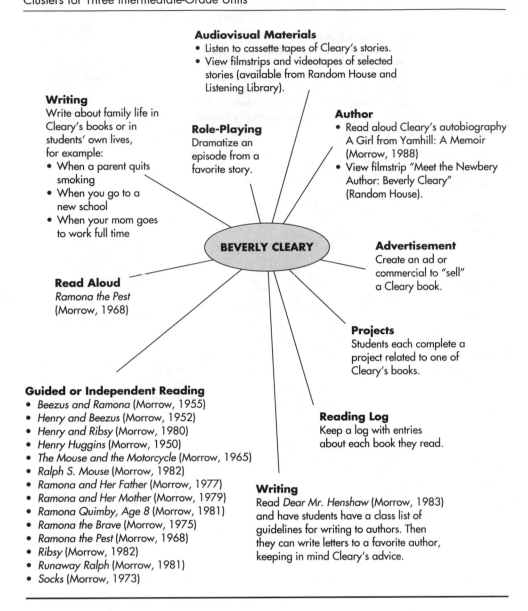

might compare events in their own lives to events in Ramona's life; possible parallels are her father's quitting smoking, her mother's going to work full time, and her moving to a new school. If students want to learn more about this author, teachers may read aloud Cleary's autobiography, *A Girl from Yamhill: A Memoir* (1988) or show a filmstrip about her.

Middle School Units

Three units designed for students in grades six, seven, eight, and nine are presented in Figure 9.7. The first is a literature unit focusing on *Anne Frank: The Diary of a Young Girl*. Connected to this modern classic is a study of the Holocaust. The second cluster is a social studies unit on the Middle Ages, and the third is a biography unit featuring Martin Luther King, Jr., and other famous Black Americans.

Literature unit: *Anne Frank: The Diary of a Young Girl.* Anne Frank's autobiographical diary is a modern classic that many eighth graders read (Figure 9.7). For young adults to understand the book's complex historical and psychological implications, they

FIGURE 9.7
Clusters for Three Middle School Units

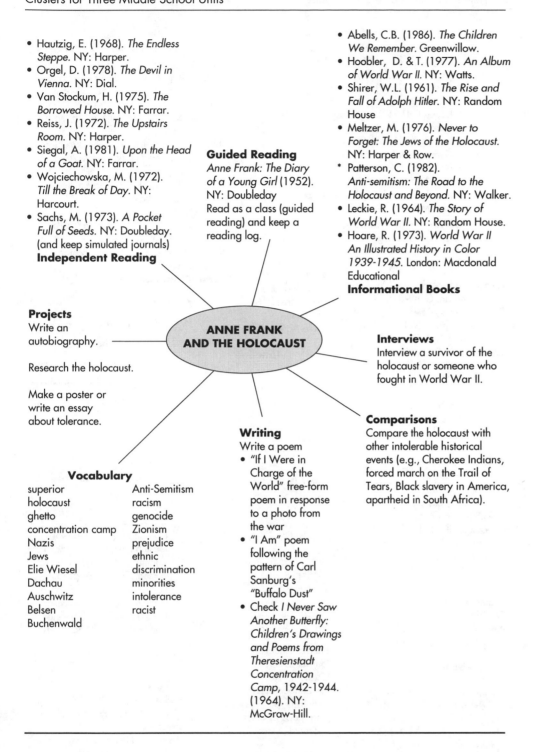

- Hautzig, E. (1968). *The Endless Steppe*. NY: Harper.
- Orgel, D. (1978). *The Devil in Vienna*. NY: Dial.
- Van Stockum, H. (1975). *The Borrowed House*. NY: Farrar.
- Reiss, J. (1972). *The Upstairs Room*. NY: Harper.
- Siegal, A. (1981). *Upon the Head of a Goat*. NY: Farrar.
- Wojciechowska, M. (1972). *Till the Break of Day*. NY: Harcourt.
- Sachs, M. (1973). *A Pocket Full of Seeds*. NY: Doubleday. (and keep simulated journals)

Independent Reading

Guided Reading
Anne Frank: The Diary of a Young Girl (1952). NY: Doubleday
Read as a class (guided reading) and keep a reading log.

- Abells, C.B. (1986). *The Children We Remember*. Greenwillow.
- Hoobler, D. & T. (1977). *An Album of World War II*. NY: Watts.
- Shirer, W.L. (1961). *The Rise and Fall of Adolph Hitler*. NY: Random House
- Meltzer, M. (1976). *Never to Forget: The Jews of the Holocaust*. NY: Harper & Row.
- * Patterson, C. (1982). *Anti-semitism: The Road to the Holocaust and Beyond*. NY: Walker.
- Leckie, R. (1964). *The Story of World War II*. NY: Random House.
- Hoare, R. (1973). *World War II An Illustrated History in Color 1939-1945*. London: Macdonald Educational

Informational Books

Projects
Write an autobiography.

Research the holocaust.

Make a poster or write an essay about tolerance.

ANNE FRANK AND THE HOLOCAUST

Interviews
Interview a survivor of the holocaust or someone who fought in World War II.

Comparisons
Compare the holocaust with other intolerable historical events (e.g., Cherokee Indians, forced march on the Trail of Tears, Black slavery in America, apartheid in South Africa).

Vocabulary

superior	Anti-Semitism
holocaust	racism
ghetto	genocide
concentration camp	Zionism
Nazis	prejudice
Jews	ethnic
Elie Wiesel	discrimination
Dachau	minorities
Auschwitz	intolerance
Belsen	racist
Buchenwald	

Writing
Write a poem
- "If I Were in Charge of the World" free-form poem in response to a photo from the war
- "I Am" poem following the pattern of Carl Sanburg's "Buffalo Dust"
- Check *I Never Saw Another Butterfly: Children's Drawings and Poems from Theresienstadt Concentration Camp, 1942-1944*. (1964). NY: McGraw-Hill.

need a background of experiences related to World War II. At the center of the unit is *Anne Frank: The Diary of a Young Girl* (Frank, 1952) which students read together as a class (shared and guided reading). Students keep a reading log to reflect on and respond to their reading. Students can also read informational books to gain more understanding of World War II and the Holocaust and read other stories with Jewish characters set during the war. Two highly recommended books are *Upon the Head of a Goat* (Siegal, 1981), the story of the Davidowitz family of Hungary, who are sent to the Auschwitz concentration camp; and *The Borrowed House* (Van Stockum, 1975), the story of 12-year-old Janna, who lives with

FIGURE 9.7 cont'd
Clusters for Three Middle School Units

- McGovern, A. (1988). *Robin Hood of Sherwood Forest.* NY: Scholastic.
- De Angeli, M. (1989). *The Door in the Wall.* NY: Doubleday.
- Grey, E.J. (1942). *Adam of the Road.* NY: Viking.
- Eager, E. (1954). *Half Magic.* NY: Harcourt, Brace Jovanovich.
- Babbitt, N. (1969). *The Search for Delicious.* NY: Farrar, Straus & Giroux.
- Bulla, C.R. (1956). *The Sword in the Tree.* NY: Harper & Row.
- Fleischman, S. (1987). *The Whipping Boy.* Mahwah, NJ: Troll.

Guided or Independent Reading

Reading Aloud
McCaughrean, G. (1984). *The Canterbury Tales.* Chicago: Rand McNally.
Sutcliff, R. (1981). *The Chronicles of Robin Hood.* NY: Oxford Univ. Press.
Pyle, H. (1952). *The Merry Adventures of Robin Hood.* NY: Grosset & Dunlap.

Comparisons
- Compare life in villages and in manors or castles.
- Make a chart or a book similar to J.S. Goodall's (1983) *Above and Below Stairs.* NY: Atheneum

Examine Middle English and French loan words

Vocabulary

apothecary	melee
baliff	mercenary
feudalism	Moors
fief	tithe
fresco	troubadour
guild	vassal
heretic	villain
journeyman	yeoman
manor	Black Death
	Crusades

Research
Research and make a class book on the Middle Ages

Timeline

MIDDLE AGES

- Goodall, J.S. (1986). *The Story of a Castle.* NY: Macmillan.
- Miquel, P. (1980). *The Days of Knights and Castles.* Morristown, NJ: Silver Burdett.
- Glubok, S. (1969). *Knights in Armor.* NY: Harper & Row.
- Black, I. (1963). *Castle, Abbey and Town: How People Lived in the Middle Ages.* NY: Holiday House.
- Sancha, S. (1983). *The Luttrell Village: Country Life in the Middle Ages.* NY: Crowell.
- Unstead, R. (1973). *Living in a Castle.* Reading, MA: Addison-Wesley.
- Macauley, D. (1977). *Castle.* Boston: Houghton Mifflin.

Informational Books

Projects
ABC book
dress doll in costume
create castle or village
make a tapestry
coat of arms
mural

Charts Maps, and Drawings

Medieval Feast
Plan and hold a medieval feast in the classroom. Each student role-plays a medieval person. Check Brandenburg, A. (1983). *A Medieval Feast.* NY: Crowell and Cosman, M.P. (1981). *Medieval Holidays and Festivals.* NY: Scribner.

Simulated Journals
Keep a simulated journal as Charlemagne, William the Conqueror, a lord, lady, fief, vassal, king, pope or other historical person.

Fairy Tales
Hodges, M. (1984). *Saint George and the Dragon,* Boston: Little, Brown.
Mayer, M. (1978). *Beauty and the Beast.* NY: Macmillan.
Hyman, T.S. (1977). *The Sleeping Beauty.* Boston: Little, Brown.

FIGURE 9.7 cont'd
Clusters for Three Middle School Units

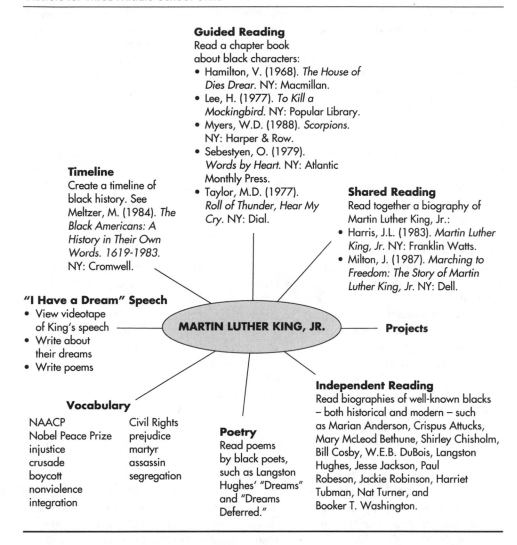

Guided Reading
Read a chapter book
about black characters:
• Hamilton, V. (1968). *The House of Dies Drear*. NY: Macmillan.
• Lee, H. (1977). *To Kill a Mockingbird*. NY: Popular Library.
• Myers, W.D. (1988). *Scorpions*. NY: Harper & Row.
• Sebestyen, O. (1979). *Words by Heart*. NY: Atlantic Monthly Press.
• Taylor, M.D. (1977). *Roll of Thunder, Hear My Cry*. NY: Dial.

Timeline
Create a timeline of black history. See Meltzer, M. (1984). *The Black Americans: A History in Their Own Words. 1619-1983*. NY: Cromwell.

Shared Reading
Read together a biography of Martin Luther King, Jr.:
• Harris, J.L. (1983). *Martin Luther King, Jr.* NY: Franklin Watts.
• Milton, J. (1987). *Marching to Freedom: The Story of Martin Luther King, Jr.* NY: Dell.

"I Have a Dream" Speech
• View videotape of King's speech
• Write about their dreams
• Write poems

MARTIN LUTHER KING, JR.

Projects

Vocabulary

NAACP	Civil Rights
Nobel Peace Prize	prejudice
injustice	martyr
crusade	assassin
boycott	segregation
nonviolence	
integration	

Poetry
Read poems by black poets, such as Langston Hughes' "Dreams" and "Dreams Deferred."

Independent Reading
Read biographies of well-known blacks – both historical and modern – such as Marian Anderson, Crispus Attucks, Mary McLeod Bethune, Shirley Chisholm, Bill Cosby, W.E.B. DuBois, Langston Hughes, Jesse Jackson, Paul Robeson, Jackie Robinson, Harriet Tubman, Nat Turner, and Booker T. Washington.

her family in a rented Dutch house and finds a Jewish Dutch boy hiding in the attic. Students might want to keep a simulated journal as they read these stories independently so they can more fully walk in these people's footsteps.

Students learn a variety of words through their reading, including *ghetto, concentration camp, intolerance, genocide,* and *anti-Semitism.* These words are added to a list hanging in the classroom, and students write them in their unit folders. Some of the words can also be used as spelling words, and students are encouraged to use the words when they write informally in their reading logs and simulated journals.

Poetry provides a good outlet for students' emotions during this unit; they can write "If I Were in Charge of the World" poems and "I Am" poems as if they were Anne Frank, Adolf Hitler, or other personalities from the war. They can also model the form of Sandburg's poem "Buffalo Dust" and write about the concentration camps or after the Nazis have gone and what is remembered. They can write a free-form poem in response to a stark black-and-white photo of the war. Students will also be interested in examining *I Never Saw Another Butterfly* (1964), a collection of poems and drawings made by children in the Theresienstadt Concentration Camp.

Other possible activities related to this unit include inviting a concentration camp survivor to visit the classroom to be interviewed or to interview other persons who remember the war. Students can also investigate other intolerant events in history (e.g., the Cherokee

Indians' forced march on the Trail of Tears, slavery in America, apartheid in South Africa) and compare them to the Holocaust.

Students also develop a project related to the unit; they may choose from the list of projects in Figure 9.5, or they may write an autobiography (perhaps in diary format), research the Holocaust and prepare an oral or written report, or make a poster or write an essay about tolerance.

Reading *Anne Frank: The Diary of a Young Girl* in isolation is difficult because the students are unfamiliar with the events of World War II and the Holocaust. Connecting history with literature in this unit makes the literature more meaningful, and students have a variety of opportunities to respond to what they are learning through listening, talking, reading, and writing.

Social studies unit: The middle ages. In a unit on the Middle Ages, teachers integrate reading, writing, listening, and speaking with history, as shown in Figure 9.7. Students use informational books to learn about the historical era, then use what they are learning for a variety of purposes. They can keep a simulated journal as a well-known person of the period, such as Charlemagne or William the Conqueror, or they may become an unrecorded personality—a lord, a lady, knight, vassal, pope, or troubadour.

Students add information to a class timeline that circles around the classroom or they can make their own using several sheets of computer paper. At the beginning of the unit, the teacher sets the limits of the time period (i.e., 1066–1485) and other key dates, then students add other dates as they read and learn more about the period.

Individual students or small groups can draw maps of the countries during the Middle Ages with an overlay of the modern countries, and they can make maps of the Crusades. They can make other types of charts, such as diagrams of castles, cathedrals, and villages, and they can also make drawings of costumes, modes of transportation, weapons, and other items related to the era. Students can also compare life in villages and in manors and castles and report the differences they find on a chart or by making a book similar to Goodall's *Above and Below Stairs* (1983).

As students research the Middle Ages, they each choose a topic for in-depth study, then write a report to share what they have learned. These reports are collected to form a larger class book on the Middle Ages.

Some novels written for these students are set in the Middle Ages, and students can read these stories independently or class sets can be purchased (e.g., *Robin Hood of Sherwood Forest* [McGovern, 1968] for directed reading). There are also some fairy tales set in the period, such as *Saint George and the Dragon* (Hodges, 1984) and *The Pied Piper of Hamelin* (Mayer, 1987), that students can read to retell or rewrite. Some stories set in the Middle Ages can be shared when read aloud by the teacher.

Word study activities can also be related to the unit. Words should be chosen from the informational books and stories students are reading; possible words are listed in the cluster in Figure 9.7. Another related activity is to study the history of English, particularly the Middle English period, and learn what French words were added to English during that time. Many of the vocabulary words show the impact the Norman kings had on English.

Students independently read the chapters and take notes using a cluster. Students each prepare a project to apply what they are learning in the unit. They choose projects, which may come from the list in Figure 9.5, in consultation with the teacher. Other possible projects are creating a castle or village, making a small tapestry, creating a coat of arms, dressing a doll in a medieval costume, or painting a mural.

As the culminating activity for the unit, students can plan and hold a medieval feast. Each student assumes the role of a medieval person, dresses in clothing of the era, and shares something (e.g., a poem, a simulated journal entry, a song, a reading, a piece of art, a skit) as that person. Students should plan food that might have been served and use music and typical activities of the time. Students can share their projects during the feast. For more information about medieval feasts and festivals, check *A Medieval Feast* (Aliki, 1983) and *Medieval Holidays and Festivals* (Cosman, 1981).

Biography unit: Martin Luther King, Jr. In this unit, students learn about a great Black American, Martin Luther King, Jr., at the same time that they learn about Black history in general and about biographies. The cluster for the unit appears in Figure 9.7. The unit begins with shared reading (or reading aloud) of a book about Martin Luther King, Jr., and learning about his life. Students view a videotape of King's "I Have a Dream" speech and write about their own dreams; they can share Hughes's poems "Dreams" and "Dreams Deferred" along with poems by other Black poets. Students apply vocabulary words that are introduced in their own reading.

Students might choose another prominent Black—historical or modern—such as Harriet Tubman, Mary McLeod Bethune, or Jesse Jackson—for independent reading and report on that person's contribution to America. Together students might develop a timeline of Black history and share it with an elementary school as part of Martin Luther King's birthday celebration or during Black History Month (in February).

Students might read chapter books by Black authors or with Black main characters under the teacher's direction, or the teacher can read one aloud. Two books listed in the cluster are *Roll of Thunder, Hear My Cry* (Taylor, 1977) and *Words by Heart* (Sebestyen, 1979). Students keep a reading log to reflect on their reading.

Developing Lesson Plans

From these unit clusters, teachers choose the activities they plan to use and develop lesson plans. They can plan special activities to initiate or conclude the unit. The plans may be part of content area classes or language arts class, or they may extend throughout the school day. There are always difficult choices to make in selecting and sequencing activities for the unit. Rarely can teachers include all the activities outlined in a unit cluster; instead, they must choose activities that are most appropriate for their students within the time and material constraints imposed on them. Teachers often identify so many possible activities and projects that students could spend six, nine, or even twelve weeks on a unit, which is simply not possible, given the great number of units that must be taught during the school year. Limited supplies of trade books, models, films, and other materials also have an impact on teachers' planning.

Planning for Assessment

After developing the lesson plans, teachers need to consider how to assess students' work during the unit. They can identify particular activities and projects that students will complete during the unit. Some activities will be assessed simply as completed or not completed; others might be assessed according to the level of quality displayed. Some activities require individual work, and others involve small group and class work. Activities should represent all four language modes: listening, talking, reading, and writing. Both informal writing activities, such as learning logs or freewrites, and process writing activities should be included.

One way to organize the assessment plan is to develop a checklist identifying the activities that will be assessed or graded. Checklists can be distributed to students at the beginning of the unit so they will understand what is expected of them. Teachers who use checklists have found that their students become more responsible in completing assignments. An assessment checklist for a middle-school unit on insects is shown in Figure 9.8. Students receive this checklist at the beginning of the unit and keep it in their unit notebooks or file folders. Students check off each of the nine activities after completing it. At the end of the unit, the teacher collects and assesses students' work on each activity.

FIGURE 9.8
Assessment Checklist for a Middle-Grade Science Unit

INSECT UNIT CHECKLIST

Name _____

_____ 1. Keep a learning log.

_____ 2. Read five informational books about insects and write about them in your learning log.

_____ 3. Help your group to make an insect life-cycle chart.

_____ 4. Construct an imaginary insect and write a description of it. (Make sure your insect has the characteristics of an insect.)

_____ 5. Listen to *The Cricket in Times Square* and write or draw in a reading log about each chapter.

_____ 6. Do a choral reading with a friend from *Joyful Noise*.

_____ 7. Make a page for our class ABC book on insects. Your page? _____

_____ 8. Study spelling words from our insect unit word wall.

_____ 9. Learn more about insects and do a project to share your learning. What is your project? _____

SUMMARY

Language arts can be integrated into thematic units for across-the-curriculum study. Integration of listening, talking, reading, and writing into science, social studies, literature, and other areas of the curriculum enhances students' learning of the content area as well as their language abilities.

Teachers plan thematic units by considering their available resources and the types of activities that would enhance content area learning. Then teachers develop clusters, outlining possible resources and activities, and write lesson plans from the clusters.

QUESTIONS AND ACTIVITIES FOR DISCUSSION

1. Plan a thematic unit using a cluster. Choose a grade level and develop a literature, social studies, science, biography, or author unit.

2. Plan a thematic unit for literature or author study using the procedure in this chapter.

3. Examine a content area textbook and find ways to expand one of the chapters or units beyond the textbook.

4. Choose a grade level that you teach or hope to teach and identify the thematic units you will teach throughout the school year.

5. Make a collection of poems you could use for teaching three different thematic units.

REFERENCES

Aliki. (1983). *A medieval feast.* New York: Crowell.

Cleary, B. (1968). *Ramona the pest.* New York: Morrow.

Cleary, B. (1983). *Dear Mr. Henshaw.* New York: Morrow.

Cleary, B. (1988). *A girl from Yamhill: A memoir.* New York: Morrow.

Cosman, M. P. (1981). *Medieval holidays and festivals.* New York: Scribner.

Erickson, K. L. (1988). Building castles in the classroom. *Language Arts, 65,* 14–19.

Fleischman, P. (1988). *Joyful noise: Poems for two voices.* New York: Harper and Row.

Frank, A. (1952). *Anne Frank: The diary of a young girl.* New York: Doubleday.

Fritz, J. (1974). *Why don't you get a horse, Sam Adams?* New York: Coward.

Gamberg, R., Kwak, W., Hutchings, M., Altheim, J., & Edwards, G. (1988). *Learning and loving it: Theme studies in the classroom.* Portsmouth, NH: Heinemann.

Goodall, J. S. (1983). *Above and below stairs.* New York: Atheneum.

Halliday, M. A. K. (1980). Three aspects of children's language development: Learning language, learning through language, learning about language. In Y. M. Goodman, M. M. Haussler, & D. S. Strickland (Eds.), *Oral and written language development research: Impact on the schools,* pp. 7–19. (Proceedings from the 1979 and 1980 IMPACT Conferences sponsored by the International Reading Association and the National Council of Teachers of English.) Urbana, IL: National Council of Teachers of English.

Hancock, J., & Hill, S. (1987). *Literature-based reading programs at work.* Portsmouth, NH: Heinemann.

Hansen, J., Newkirk, T., & Graves, D. (Eds.). (1985). *Breaking ground: Teachers relate reading and writing in the elementary school.* Portsmouth, NH: Heinemann.

Heller, R. (1984). *Plants that never ever bloom.* New York: Grosset & Dunlap.

Hodges, M. (1984). *Saint George and the dragon.* Boston: Little, Brown.

I never saw another butterfly: Children's drawings and poems from Theresienstadt Concentration Camp, 1942–1944, (1964). New York: McGraw-Hill.

Lewis, C. S. (1950). *The lion, the witch, and the wardrobe.* New York: Macmillan.

Mayer, M. (1987). *The pied piper of Hamelin.* New York: Macmillan.

McGovern, A. (1968). *Robin Hood of Sherwood Forest.* New York: Scholastic Books.

Moss, J. F. (1984). *Focus units in literature: A handbook for elementary school teachers.* Urbana, IL: NCTE.

Nelson, P. A. (1988). Drama, doorway to the past. *Language Arts, 65,* 20–25.

Pappas, C. C., Kiefer, B. Z., & Levstik, L. S. (1990). *An integrated language perspective in the elementary school: Theory into action.* New York: Longman.

Richards, L. (1990). "Measuring things in words": Language for learning mathematics. *Language Arts, 67,* 14–25.

Salem, J. (1982). Using writing in teaching mathematics. In M. Barr, P. D'Arcy, & M. K. Healy (Eds.), *What's going on? Language/learning episodes in British and American classrooms, grades 4–13,* pp. 123–134. Montclair, NJ: Boynton/Cook.

San Jose, C. (1988). Story drama in the content areas. *Language Arts, 65,* 26–33.

Schubert, B. (1987). Mathematics journals: Fourth grade. In T. Fulwiler (Ed.), *The journal book,* pp. 348–358. Portsmouth, NH: Boynton/Cook.

Sebestyen, O. (1979). *Words by heart.* New York: Atlantic Monthly Press.

Selden, G. (1960). *The cricket in Times Square.* New York: Farrar, Straus & Giroux.

Siegal, A. (1981). *Upon the head of a goat: A childhood in Hungary, 1939–1944.* New York: Farrar, Straus & Giroux.

Silverstein, S. (1964). *The giving tree.* New York: Harper and Row.

Somers, A. B., & Worthington, J. E. (1979). *Response guides for teaching children's books.* Urbana, IL: National Council of Teachers of English.

Taylor, M. D. (1977). *Roll of thunder, hear my cry.* New York: Dial.

Thaiss, C. (1986). *Language across the curriculum in the elementary grades.* Urbana, IL: ERIC Clearinghouse on Reading and Communication Skills and the National Council of Teachers of English.

Tompkins, G. E. (1990). *Teaching writing: Balancing process and product.* Columbus, OH: Merrill.

Van Allsburg, C. (1979). *The garden of Abdul Gasazi.* Boston: Houghton Mifflin.

Van Allsburg, C. (1981). *Jumanji.* Boston: Houghton Mifflin.

Van Allsburg, C. (1982). *Ben's dream.* Boston: Houghton Mifflin.

Van Allsburg, C. (1984). *The mysteries of Harris Burdick.* Boston: Houghton Mifflin.

Van Allsburg, C. (1985). *The polar express.* Boston: Houghton Mifflin.

Van Allsburg, C. (1986). *The stranger.* Boston: Houghton Mifflin.

Van Allsburg, C. (1987). *The Z was zapped.* Boston: Houghton Mifflin.

Van Allsburg, C. (1988). *Two bad ants.* Boston: Houghton Mifflin.

Van Stockum, H. (1975). *The borrowed house.* New York: Farrar.

CHAPTER 10

Action Plans and Activities for Language Arts

This final chapter of Part II presents a collection of ten case studies and action plans that show how teachers in grades four through eight use literature-based reading in their classrooms. An eleventh presentation highlights an assortment of language-based activities for use in grade nine.

In order of presentation, the plans and activities are

PRESENTATION 1:   Mrs. Blackburn Uses Literature in Her Fourth-Grade Reading Program

PRESENTATION 2:   Mrs. Ochs's Fourth-Grade Focus Unit on *The Sign of the Beaver*

PRESENTATION 3:   Mr. Kfoury's Fifth-Grade Literacy Block

PRESENTATION 4:   Tuesday Is Poetry Workshop Day in Ms. Cochran's Fifth-Grade Class

PRESENTATION 5:   Using a Vertebrate Animal Theme for Sixth Graders

PRESENTATION 6:   Ms. Epstein's Sixth-Grade Vertebrate Animal Theme Cycle

PRESENTATION 7:   Ms. Jacobs's Sixth-Grade Vertebrate Animal Unit

PRESENTATION 8:   "Readers at Work" in Mr. Diaz's Sixth-Grade Classroom

PRESENTATION 9:   Mr. Jurey's Seventh-Grade Students Learn about Expressionism

PRESENTATION 10: Ms. Daniel's Seventh- and Eighth-Grade Students Participate in Literature Discussion Groups

PRESENTATION 11: Activities for Teaching Ninth-Grade Language Arts

Mrs. Blackburn Uses Literature in Her Fourth-Grade Reading Program

PRESENTATION 1

In this case study presentation, Mrs. Blackburn and her students are involved in a focus unit on Chris Van Allsburg, and they are reading his fantasy picture books and exploring and extending their understandings of the stories using all four of the language arts—listening, talking, reading, and writing. Mrs. Blackburn uses a literature-based reading program because she believes that her students learn to read by reading literature and by using the four language arts as they respond to literature. She has a large collection of literature in her classroom library, including multiple copies of some of Chris Van Allsburg's books. These books form the core of Mrs. Blackburn's reading program, and students read real books independently, in small groups, and together as a class.

CHRIS VAN ALLSBURG UNIT

Mrs. Blackburn prepares to read aloud a copy of Chris Van Allsburg's newest book, *The Wretched Stone* (1991), to her fourth graders. *The Wretched Stone* is an old captain's log of an ocean voyage and the bizarre things that happened after the crew picked up a strange glowing stone when they stopped at an island to take on drinking water. Many of her students are already familiar with one or two of Van Allsburg's other books, and they anticipate that this new book will also be a gripping fantasy. Brian says, "All of Chris Van Allsburg's books are g-r-e-a-t! *Jumanji. The Polar Express.* They're so good I just can't get enough of them." Mrs. Blackburn points out, "This story is a little different; Mr. Van Allsburg wrote it as a ship captain's log." Her students nod in agreement; they, too, have written simulated journals, stepping into the role of a book character or a historical personality.

Mrs. Blackburn reads *The Wretched Stone* aloud, stopping several times to invite her students to make predictions about what they expect will happen next. When she finishes reading, her students get into a circle to talk about the book. Mrs. Blackburn begins the grand conversation by saying, "Let's talk about Mr. Van Allsburg's newest book," and Luther begins the discussion:

> LUTHER: That one's really weird.
>
> SEAN: I thought it was good even though it was weird. I liked when the crew turned into monkeys.
>
> AARON: Me, too.
>
> ELIZABETH: Why did they change into monkeys?
>
> SEAN: Well, whatever it was, they changed back.
>
> SASHA: Could that really happen?
>
> ADRIANNA: It's just pretend like in *The Polar Express* when the little boy went to see Santa Claus.
>
> TONY: It's more like *The Garden of Abdul Gasazi,* when the magician changed the dog into a duck and then back to a dog.
>
> KRISTEN: I didn't see the dog anywhere, and there's always a white dog in his books. (Mrs. Blackburn hands the book to Kristen and she looks for the picture of the dog and finally finds the dog's white tail hidden in an illustration.)

The conversation continues and, after a few minutes, Kelly, who has been sitting quietly, says, "It's a television. That's what the glowing rock is. You stop reading and you stop talking when you watch too much TV." Everyone is taken aback by her thoughtful analogy. Then Brian comments:

> BRIAN: Yeah, couch potatoes are monkeys.
>
> KARI: People didn't have TVs back then.
>
> KELLY: I know they didn't, but I still think that's his message.
>
> BRIAN: I think Kelly's right. It is confusing because they didn't have TVs then, but what else could the glowing stone be?

Mrs. Blackburn asks if her students would like to continue reading Chris Van Allsburg's books as a focus unit for the next several weeks. The students are unanimous in their agreement. They take a few minutes to plan the unit. Together Mrs. Blackburn and her students decide to spend two weeks reading and responding to Chris Van Allsburg's books. (Of course, Mrs. Blackburn had already done some planning for the focus unit, but she involves her students in the planning so that they are more interested in what they are learning and more responsible as well.) Students brainstorm a list of the activities they want to do:

- Read four of his books.
- Write about each book in a lit log.
- Make a chart to tell where the dog is in each book.

- Write to Chris Van Allsburg.
- Do a response project about one book.
- Share the project with the class.

Mrs. Blackburn adds these items to the class list:

- Use the writing process.
- Learn about Chris Van Allsburg.
- Learn about fantasies because most of Van Allsburg's books are fantasies.

Mrs. Blackburn has a class set of *Jumanji* (1981), a Caldecott Award book about two children who play an adventure game that comes to life, and several copies of each of his other books. She has borrowed copies from other teachers, and students lend a few of their own copies. Together they collect 42 copies of Van Allsburg's books in addition to the class set of *Jumanji* and place them on a special shelf in the class library.

During their two-week study, Mrs. Blackburn's students spend one hour each day reading and writing in response to Van Allsburg's books. During the first week, students spend most of the time reading; during the second week, they continue to read but spend more time writing and working on response projects. At the end of the second week, students also share their completed response projects with the class.

Over the two-week focus unit, Mrs. Blackburn teaches brief 10- to 15-minute minilessons every other day or so to share information about the author and about fantasies. She also teaches mini-lessons on alliteration (repetition of initial sounds in words) using Van Allsburg's *The Z Was Zapped* (1987) and on point of view using *Two Bad Ants* (1988).

Many students read independently and others form small groups to read and discuss his books. Mrs. Blackburn circulates around the classroom, conferencing briefly with students about their reading and reading their lit log entries. One day the class reads *Jumanji* together. Before reading, they talk about games and quickwrite, or write informally for five or ten minutes to reflect on their ideas about their favorite games. Then students read the book independently or with partners. After reading, they write an entry in their lit logs and talk about the book in a grand conversation, or discussion, sharing ideas and feelings as they did about *The Wretched Stone*. After students make their comments, Mrs. Blackburn asks if they would like to play Jumanji, and the grand conversation continues as students talk about whether or not they would want to play the game. Some students are so excited about the book that they decide to write a sequel as their response project.

At the end of the first week, the class talks about response projects and compiles a list of ways they might extend their reading. In these projects, students choose to respond to one of the books they have read through talk, drama, writing, research, art, or additional reading. These response projects that Mrs. Blackburn's students suggest are listed in Figure 10.1. Each student works on one or more response projects during the second week and shares the finished project with the class.

During the second week the students also use the writing process as they draft, revise, and edit a composition related to the focus unit. Some students write letters to Van Allsburg, some write sequels to *Jumanji,* some write about Christmas memories after reading *The Polar Express* (1985), and others write stories about an illustration from *The Mysteries of Harris Burdick* (1984).

On the last few days of the second week, students share their compositions and the response projects with the class. On the last day of the focus unit, one group of students makes a chart about where the white dog is hidden in each book, and another group graphs the frequency of the class's favorite Van Allsburg books.

Mrs. Blackburn uses checklists to track and assess students' work. She makes a checklist of the activities students will be involved in after the class plans the unit. Then she distributes a copy to each student. Students keep the checklist in their language arts folders with their lit logs and other papers related to the unit and check off each item as they complete it. At the end of the focus unit, Mrs. Blackburn collects the language arts folders and reviews all the materials in them. A copy of Mrs. Blackburn's assessment checklist for this focus unit is presented in Figure 10.2.

FIGURE 10.1
Response Projects for Chris Van Allsburg's Books

Jumanji
- Write a sequel.
- Make a game board of the game.
- Research a favorite game and make a poster to share what you learn.

The Stranger
- Make a chart about the four seasons.
- Make a cluster and write a descriptive paragraph about fall.

The Polar Express
- Write about a Christmas memory.
- Write about another holiday.
- Research Christmas customs and share what you learn in an oral report.

Two Bad Ants
- Retell a favorite story from a different point of view.
- Make ant puppets and use them to retell the story.

The Z Was Zapped
- Make an ABC book on Chris Van Allsburg.
- Write an ABC book on any topic and remember to use alliteration.
- Collect five ABC books and read and compare them.

The Garden of Abdul Gasazi
- Make a wordless picture book to retell the story.

The Mysteries of Harris Burdick
- Write a story about one of the pictures.

Ben's Dream
- Research one of the great monuments and share the information with the class.
- Construct one of the monuments.
- Trace Ben's trip on a world map.

The Wretched Stone
- Write a simulated journal from a crew member's point of view.
- Make a wretched stone.

Just a Dream
- Read a book to learn how to clean up the environment.
- Make a poster to put in the hallway to tell kids not to pollute.

Other
- Write to Chris Van Allsburg.
- Make a poster about Mr. Van Allsburg for the library center.
- Make a quilt with your favorite quotations from each book.
- Dramatize your favorite story.
- Do an art project about your favorite story.

CHILDREN'S LITERATURE REFERENCES

Van Allsburg, C. (1979). *The garden of Abdul Gasazi.* Boston: Houghton Mifflin.

Van Allsburg, C. (1981). *Jumanji.* Boston: Houghton Mifflin.

Van Allsburg, C. (1982). *Ben's dream.* Boston: Houghton Mifflin.

Van Allsburg, C. (1983). *The wreck of the zephyr.* Boston: Houghton Mifflin.

Van Allsburg, C. (1984). *The mysteries of Harris Burdick.* Boston: Houghton Mifflin.

Van Allsburg, C. (1985). *The polar express.* Boston: Houghton Mifflin.

FIGURE 10.2
Mrs. Blackburn's Assessment Checklist

Chris Van Allsburg Focus Unit Checklist

Name:_____ Week of:_____

1. Read four CVA books. _____
2. Write in lit log about the four books. _____
3. Take notes about mini-lessons in lit log. _____
4. Do a response project. _____
5. Share with the class. _____
6. Use the writing process. _____
7. Use good work habits. _____

Van Allsburg, C. (1986). *The stranger.* Boston: Houghton Mifflin.

Van Allsburg, C. (1987). *The Z was zapped.* Boston: Houghton Mifflin.

Van Allsburg, C. (1988). *Two bad ants.* Boston: Houghton Mifflin.

Van Allsburg, C. (1990). *Just a dream.* Boston: Houghton Mifflin.

Van Allsburg, C. (1991). *The wretched stone.* Boston: Houghton Mifflin.

Mrs. Ochs's Fourth-Grade Focus Unit on *The Sign of the Beaver*   PRESENTATION 2

Carol Ochs, a fourth-grade teacher at Jackson Elementary School, alternates reading workshop with core literature units that focus on one book or a collection of short stories. In this action plan, we describe how Mrs. Ochs teaches a four-week core literature unit on one of her favorite chapter books, Elizabeth George Speare's award-winning *The Sign of the Beaver* (1983), a wilderness survival story set in 1768. In the story, 12-year-old Matt spends the summer in the family's new cabin in the Maine wilderness while his father returns to Massachusetts to bring the rest of the family north to their new home. While his father is away, Matt tries bravely to survive on his own and is befriended by an Indian chief and his grandson, Attean. Matt expects his family to arrive in August, but when Matt's family doesn't arrive by fall, the Indians invite him to join the Beaver tribe and move north with them. Matt decides to continue waiting for his family, and at long last they finally arrive—but not until after the first snows of winter. Mrs. Ochs says, "I like this story so much because Matt is making the same kinds of difficult decisions about what is important in his life that my 10- and 11-year-olds are making about their own lives."

Mrs. Ochs begins planning the core literature unit by selecting the book and reading it two or three times if she can make time to do so. She thinks about her goals for the unit, the activities she would like to include, and related materials to use in teaching the unit. Then she brainstorms activities on a cluster, as shown in Figure 10.3. She includes more activities and materials than she will be able to use in the four-week unit on the cluster; however, she likes using the cluster to plan a unit because it provides options from which she can choose.

Another decision that Mrs. Ochs makes is about the perspective from which she will teach this unit. She decides to use primarily a critical perspective, but she will select activities from the other perspectives that highlight and focus on character development in her literature study, as shown in the cluster. Some of the literature study activities that she considers using include writing simulated literature journals (which she calls diaries) from Matt's or Attean's viewpoint, sorting vocabulary words according to character, drawing portraits of characters, dramatizing scenes from the story according to the characters' viewpoints, developing character maps, writing poems about the characters, making a list of opposites at the beginning and again at the end of the story, making a Venn diagram to compare and contrast the characters, and writing a sequel from one viewpoint or another.

After considering her possibilities, Mrs. Ochs develops lesson plans for the four weeks she has allotted to the unit. She plans to read *The Sign of the Beaver* aloud while students

FIGURE 10.3
Cluster for a Unit on *The Sign of the Beaver* (Speare, 1983)

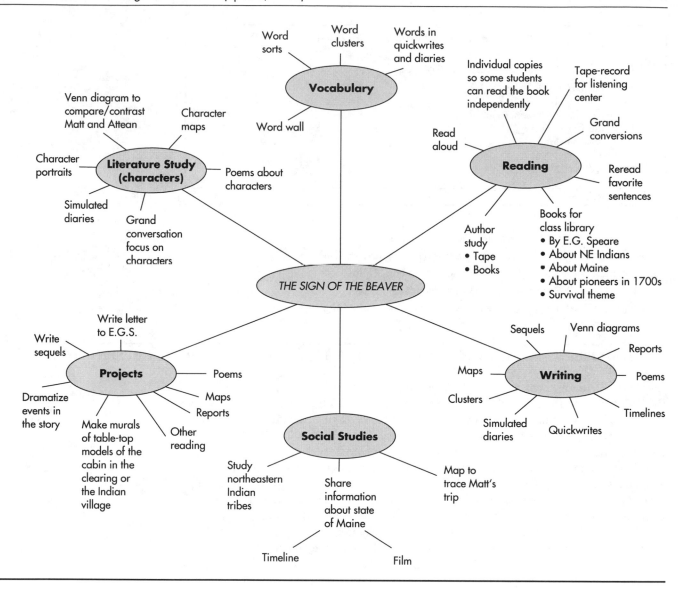

follow in their own copies of the book. She will have a word wall to list vocabulary words from each chapter, and she'll use the vocabulary in various activities. Students will write simulated diary entries from Matt's or Attean's viewpoint and participate in grand conversations after reading each chapter. They do this because Mrs. Ochs believes that students should have the opportunity to express their understanding about the book before she teaches character development. She'll also plan literature study activities on character development and allow time for projects at the end of the unit.

MRS. OCHS'S DAILY SCHEDULE

Mrs. Ochs fits core literature activities into a two-and-one-half hour language arts block time frame. This is the schedule:

8:45–9:05	Students Read Self-Selected Books Related to the Focus Unit or Theme
9:05–9:15	Students Share Simulated Diary Entries
9:15–9:45	Teacher Reads *The Sign of the Beaver* Aloud, Chapter by Chapter, as Students Follow in Their Books
9:45–10:00	Students Participate in a Grand Conversation

10:00–10:15   Students Write Simulated Diary Entries
10:15–10:30   Break
10:30–11:10   Students Participate in Activities (Vocabulary, Literature Study, Projects)
11:10–11:15   Students Reread Favorite Sentences

COMPONENTS OF THE FOCUS UNIT

The components of the focus unit are independent reading, reading the core book, grand conversations, simulated diaries, vocabulary activities, literature study, projects, and rereading. The literature study is a particularly important component because it is designed to help students acquire a more critical awareness of character. Mrs. Ochs uses activities from the other two perspectives to complement the critical perspective in her teaching.

Independent Reading

Mrs. Ochs has put together a text set of picture books, chapter books, and informational books about the New England colonies, Maine, American Indians, stories with a theme of courage, and other books written by Elizabeth George Speare. These books are related to *The Sign of the Beaver,* and they are set out on a special shelf in the library center. At the beginning of the unit, students select a book from this shelf or another book related to the core book to read independently during this period. Toward the end of the unit, students will share their books during this period.

Shared Reading with Students

Mrs. Ochs has a class set of *The Sign of the Beaver,* and she reads the book aloud, chapter by chapter, while students follow in their individual copies. Mrs. Ochs explains why she reads the book aloud: "The reading level of the book is too difficult for some of my students. By reading the book aloud, I make it accessible to everyone. I encourage those students who can read the book independently to move into a quiet corner of the classroom to read silently at their own pace." Mrs. Ochs also tape records her reading of each chapter and places the cassette tapes in the listening center so that students can "reread" the chapter or so that children who are absent can catch up.

Grand Conversations

After Mrs. Ochs finishes reading the one or two chapters for that day, the students move their chairs into a large circle for the grand conversation. During this 15-minute discussion, students first share their comments, opinions, and questions about the story. Mrs. Ochs asks that each student make at least one comment and no one may offer more than three comments until everyone has participated. Then she asks one or two questions to direct the discussion during the last few minutes to focus students' attention on the character development in the story.

Writing in Simulated Diaries

After reading each chapter, students take 15 minutes to write simulated diary entries, written either from Matt's or Attean's viewpoint. Here is one child's simulated diary entry, written from Matt's point of view:

Dear Diary,
   Yesterday Attean left. He brought me some presents though. His grandmother gave me some molasses and a pair of snowshoes. They looked great. Attean gave me his dog. I thought I ought to give him something, so I went inside and got my watch. "Here," I said to Attean and gave him the watch. I showed him how to wind it. Then we said goodbye, and he left.
   Today nothing much has happened yet. I might go hunting. The dog that Attean gave to me is a good companion. He may be scruffy, but he is a nice dog. I hope Pa gets home soon because the lake has started to freeze and food will be scarce. I set some snares and a deadfall. Tomorrow I plan to go fishing.

To begin each morning's reading activities, students share the simulated diary entries they wrote the previous day. First they share in small groups and then one student is selected from each group to share with the class. Mrs. Ochs starts with this activity because she has found it to be a good way to review the chapter read the previous day and get students ready for today's reading.

Activity Time

In the activity time, Mrs. Ochs includes three types of activities. At the beginning of the unit, the focus is on vocabulary, then on literature study activities, and during the last week of the unit, students work on projects to extend their reading.

Vocabulary activities. Mrs. Ochs hangs a large sheet of butcher paper on a wall of the classroom for a word wall. As she reads each chapter, Mrs. Ochs and her students write new and unusual words on the word wall. She tries to use different colored marking pens for each chapter to keep track of the words. For chapter one, they added these words and phrases: *reckoned, ashamed, spruce trees, haul, notch, snugly, splints, silence coiled around Matt, high time, Penobscot River, Quincy, Massachusetts, loft, puncheon table, daubed, chink in the log wall, battered, compass, you aim to leave it, aye, yourn, mite, powder horn, matchlock, ruefully,* and *johnnycake.*

Later they will use some of these words for vocabulary activities, such as word clusters, word sorts, and labels for murals and models. Students are also encouraged to use these new words in their simulated diary entries and the grand conversations. Mrs. Ochs also takes words from the word wall and weaves them into her conversation. Before long her students are listening intently, waiting to catch her use one of the word wall words.

Literature Study Activities

Mrs. Ochs and her students explore characters through a variety of activities. She begins the character study when she asks students to keep a simulated diary as though they were Matt or Attean. Other activities include a word sort in which students sort words from the word wall according to specific characters in the book, and making a list of opposites related to characters at the beginning of the book and again at the end. Students will draw portraits of the characters and work in groups to make a character cluster. As a final activity, students will make a Venn diagram to compare and contrast Matt and Attean, and one student's Venn diagram is presented in Figure 10.4.

FIGURE 10.4
A Fourth Grader's Venn Diagram to Compare Matt and Attean

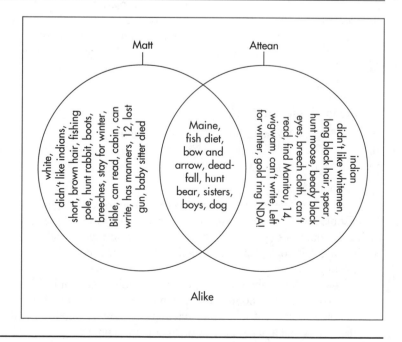

Projects

Mrs. Ochs and the students use the activity time during the last week of the unit to work on projects. Most of the students will decide to write sequels to the story, but a few choose other activities, such as researching Northeastern Indian tribes, preparing and presenting a dramatization of the story, or writing a letter to Elizabeth George Speare.

Class Read-Around

Mrs. Ochs spends the last five minutes having students reread favorite sentences from the chapter read earlier that morning. She explains, "Rereading is a great way to settle students down and end our language arts block." As students finish the activities, they return to their seats and skim through the chapter looking for a sentence special enough to share. (Some students use a pencil to mark a favorite sentence during the first reading so that they are ready to reread.) As soon as most of the class is ready, students begin taking turns rereading favorite sentences aloud. There is no set order for the rereading; rather, one student begins reading and after that student ends, there is a brief pause, and then another student reads. It is not necessary to call on students; they simply take turns and whenever there is a pause someone begins. Not every student shares every day but Mrs. Ochs asks that everyone share at least once every week. These sentences are not read in any particular order, but as students read back and forth through the chapter, they effectively review it.

MRS. OCHS'S LESSON PLAN FOR ONE WEEK

A one-week lesson plan for Mrs. Ochs's focus unit on *The Sign of the Beaver* is presented in Figure 10.5. This lesson plan is for the third week of the four-week unit. Each of the components for Mrs. Ochs's language arts block is listed, and then particular activities for this week are detailed. The students begin the language arts block each day with independent reading of self-selected books related to the core literature selection. Then in small groups they share the simulated journal entries they wrote the previous day, and one student from each group shares with the class. Then Mrs. Ochs reads aloud one or two chapters from *The Sign of the Beaver* while the students follow along in their books. On Friday of week three the class finishes reading the story. (During week four they will be involved in response activities.) After reading, students participate in a grand conversation and write in their simulated journals.

After the break, students participate in activities that focus on characters during this week. On Monday, Mrs. Ochs introduces characters and shares information about how authors reveal characters. During the week, students write about their favorite character, dramatize a scene from the story featuring a favorite character, make character clusters, do a word sort according to characters, and make a Venn diagram to compare and contrast two main characters. Students end the language arts block each day by rereading favorite sentences from the chapters read that day.

MRS. OCHS'S RECORD-KEEPING AND ASSESSMENT PROCEDURES

Mrs. Ochs develops a checklist with all the assignments students are to complete and gives copies of it to students when they begin the unit. A copy of her assessment checklist for *The Sign of the Beaver* is presented in Figure 10.6. Students keep the checklist inside their reading folders and mark off each assignment as they complete it in the column marked "Student's Check."

At the end of the unit, students turn in all written assignments in their reading folder with the assessment checklist on top. Students have already marked the checklist and written the self-assessment so they have a good idea of how well they have done in this unit. Mrs. Ochs has found that students assume more responsibility for their own work, and her grading is simplified. Teachers can grade each item using their own grading scale or they can assign points to each item (as shown in Figure 10.6). Then teachers award the points in the column marked "Teacher's Check" and total the points for a unit grade. Mrs. Ochs tries to have the total number of points equal 100 to simplify grading.

FIGURE 10.5

A One-Week Lesson Plan from a Focus Unit on *The Sign of the Beaver* (Speare, 1983)

	MONDAY	TUESDAY	WEDNESDAY	THURSDAY	FRIDAY
8:45–9:05	Independent reading of self-selected books from text.				
9:05–9:15	Students shared the simulated journal entries they wrote yesterday. Share in small groups. Then one student from each group shares with class.				
9:15–9:45 *Reading Core Book*	Chs. 17–18	Chs. 19–20	Chs. 21–22	Chs. 23–24	Ch. 25
	The Sign of the Beaver 1. Read aloud while students follow in their books. 2. Add words to word wall. 3. Have students reread silently, if time allows. • DON'T FORGET TO TAPE RECORD EACH CHAPTER!!!				
9:45–10:00	Grade conversations ──────────────────────────────▶				
10:00–10:15	Students write in simulated journals. ─────────────────▶				
10:15–10:30	BREAK				
10:30–11:00 *Activities* This week literature study on characters	• Talk about characters • Main and supporting • Four ways authors reveal characters: appearance, action, dialogue, and monologue • Quickwrite about favorite character	• Share quickwrites • Choose five words from word wall about favorite character • Divide into groups according to favorite character • Plan and rehearse skits	• Rehearse skits • Perform • In small groups, make character cluster • Prepare word sort	• Have students sort words according to character • Share word sorts and character clusters	• Venn diagram to compare Matt and Attean • Begin essay to compare/contrast characters • Review form for essay
11:00–11:15 *Read-Around.*	Students reread favorite sentences from chapters read that day.				

FIGURE 10.6

Assessment Checklist for *The Sign of the Beaver* Unit

Name: _____   Date: _____

Student's Check	Teacher's Check	
_____	_____	1. Read *The Sign of the Beaver*.
_____	_____	2. Make a map of Matt's journey in 1768. (10)
_____	_____	3. Keep a simulated diary for Matt or Attean. (20)
_____	_____	4. Do a word sort by characters. (5)
_____	_____	5. Listen to Elizabeth George Speare's taped interview and do a quickwrite about her. (5)
_____	_____	6. Draw a portrait of one of the characters. (5)
_____	_____	7. Make a character map of one of the characters. (5)
_____	_____	8. Make a Venn diagram to compare/contrast Matt or Attean to yourself. (10)
_____	_____	9. Contribute to a model or mural of the Indian village or the clearing. (15)
_____	_____	10. Write a sequel to *The Sign of the Beaver* or do another project. (20)
_____	_____	11. Write a self-assessment about your work, behavior, and effort in this unit. (5)

CHILDREN'S LITERATURE REFERENCE

Speare, E. G. (1983). *The sign of the beaver.* Boston: Houghton Mifflin.

Mr. Kfoury's Fifth-Grade Literacy Block · PRESENTATION 3

Mr. Kfoury, a fifth-grade teacher, divides his daily schedule into five time blocks: literacy block; social studies block; science block; math block; and arts block. During the literacy block he organizes reading and response activities into units or themes that focus on an author, genre, or theme, and these units usually last six to eight weeks. Each unit includes both a core literature component and a reading workshop component.

Mr. Kfoury begins most units by selecting a focus. For this unit, the focus is on courage, and he has decided to begin with a core literature component and then move to a reading workshop component. Since Mr. Kfoury has decided to begin the unit with core literature, he selects a chapter book that is central to the focus to read aloud to the whole class. Mr. Kfoury selects *Number the Stars* (Lowry, 1989), a Newbery medal story of a Christian girl's courage as she helps her Jewish friend escape from Denmark during World War II. He intends to use a reader-response perspective so students will have opportunities to respond personally to the issues presented in *Number the Stars* and the other books they read in this unit. Therefore, Mr. Kfoury makes tentative plans for some response activities that he expects all students to complete. He also prepares a list of other response activities from which students may choose. Each day Mr. Kfoury plans to read aloud one or two chapters of *Number the Stars* as students follow along in individual copies of the book. They will reread portions of the book independently, write responses in response journals, discuss their reading in grand conversations, and pursue response projects they have chosen.

Mr. Kfoury also selects additional books related to the focus for students to read in small groups. He chooses these books after reading and carefully considering many books recommended by librarians, colleagues, and students. He also has "kid-tested" them in his classroom over several years of teaching. For this unit he selects *Call It Courage* (Sperry, 1968), *Julie of the Wolves* (George, 1972), *Stone Fox* (Gardiner, 1980), *The Courage of Sarah Noble* (Dalgliesh, 1982), *Trouble River* (Byars, 1969), and *The Upstairs Room* (Reiss, 1972) for small-group reading. Several days into the unit, Mr. Kfoury gives a book talk about these books; he holds each book up, tells something about the plot, reads aloud an interesting excerpt, and arouses students' interest by raising issues or posing questions. Students sign up to read one of these books, and depending on students' interests, four, five, or six small groups, called "literacy clubs," will be formed to read and respond to the books. Mr. Kfoury meets with each group two or three times a week as they read and discuss their books. He also guides students' reading of these books and presents preparing, reading, and exploring lessons for each of the books to help students explore the book in depth. Figure 10.7 presents Mr. Kfoury's daily schedule for the core literature portion of the unit.

Mr. Kfoury uses a reading workshop approach for the second portion of his unit on courage. In this portion, students read and respond to self-selected books, conference with Mr. Kfoury about the books they are reading, attend whole-class mini-lessons to learn literacy strategies and skills, and share the books they are reading and responding to with classmates. Mr. Kfoury involves his students in collecting the reading materials they will read during reading workshop. They locate poems, stories, informational books, magazine articles, and newspaper stories about courage in the class library, school library, and local public library and arrange them together on a special shelf in the class library. Then students choose books and other reading materials from this collection to read independently.

Mr. Kfoury also meets with students individually in conferences during reading workshop. During the conferences he discusses the kinds of materials students have read (students keep a log of the titles of books, poems, and other materials they have read), listens to students read aloud a short passage to assess their use of strategies and their progress in

FIGURE 10.7
Mr. Kfoury's Schedule for Core Literature

8:30–8:45	Arrival, Lunch Count, Attendance, Independent Reading	
8:45–11:00	Literacy Block	
	8:45–9:30	Read aloud core book and response activities
	9:30–9:45	Literacy demonstrations
	9:45–10:15	Literacy club (small-group meetings, reading, and response activities)
	10:15–10:30	Recess
	10:30–11:00	Literacy club (continued)
11:00–12:00	Mathematics Block	
12:00–12:45	Lunch and Recess	
12:45–1:30	Science Block	
1:30–2:00	Arts Block: Physical education, music, art, library	
2:00–2:45	Social Studies Block	
2:45	Dismissal	

FIGURE 10.8
Mr. Kfoury's Reading Workshop Schedule

8:45–9:15	Reading Aloud to Students
9:15–9:30	Mini-lesson
9:30–9:35	Class Meeting
9:35–10:15	Self-Selected Reading, Response Activities, and Conferences
10:15–10:30	Recess
10:30–10:45	Self-Selected Reading (continued)
10:45–11:00	Student Sharing

interpreting stories and poems or learning information from informational books and magazines, reviews students' plans for response activities, and makes suggestions for future reading and projects. After each conference Mr. Kfoury writes brief notes about the student's progress, which he keeps in special folders. He meets with three or four students each day so that every two weeks he meets with each student in the class.

Each day Mr. Kfoury reads aloud to the students a variety of reading materials related to courage and teaches mini-lessons. He uses mini-lessons to introduce students to new reading strategies, provide a forum for students to share strategies they have found successful, model how to do particular response activities such as writing a simulated diary, and share strategies and activities that students can use as they prepare, read, explore, and extend a book.

Each day reading workshop ends with several students sharing the book they have been reading and their response projects with the class. Because students work individually during reading workshop, Mr. Kfoury feels that sharing is an important social activity. Figure 10.8 presents Mr. Kfoury's schedule for the reading workshop component of the unit on courage.

CHILDREN'S LITERATURE REFERENCES

Byars, B. (1969). *Trouble river.* New York: Viking.

Dagliesh, A. (1982). *The courage of Sarah Noble.* New York: Scribner.

Gardiner, J. (1980). *Stone fox.* New York: Harper & Row. Greenwillow.

George, J. (1972). *Julie of the wolves.* New York: Harper Collins.

Lowry, L. (1989). *Number the stars.* Boston: Houghton Mifflin.

Reiss, J. (1972). *The upstairs room.* New York: Harper & Row.

Sperry, A. (1968). *Call it courage.* New York: Collier.

Tuesday Is Poetry Workshop Day in Ms. Cochran's Fifth-Grade Class

At Wilson Elementary School, fifth-grade teacher Ms. Cochran is known as the poetry lady. Because she enjoys poetry and wants her students to overcome their fear of it, Ms. Cochran's students spend the first two weeks of the school year immersed in reading and writing poetry. She says, "Most poems are short visual images or word plays, and after our two-week initiation, my students find themselves as bewitched by poetry as I am." Ms. Cochran's students continue their focus on reading and writing poetry every Tuesday morning. Tuesday is the "short" day at Wilson Elementary School, when students leave one hour early so that teachers can have meetings. To further complicate matters, Ms. Cochran has several schedule changes that day including a trip to the school library for students to check out books and to a first-grade classroom for buddy-reading. Because of the weekly disruptions, Ms. Cochran and her students have decided to make Tuesday special—Poetry Workshop Day.

Ms. Cochran's classroom library is housed in plastic crates that ring the wall of the classroom. Each crate has a label—folktales, life cycle books, California books, Roald Dahl books, biographies, and so on. On one side of the room, seven crates are filled with books of poetry. Posters of favorite poems decorate the wall above the book crates. A six-foot-tall (dead) tree stands near the poetry books. This is the class poetree (Hopkins, 1987), and students hang copies of favorite poems and small response projects on the tree's branches. Ms. Cochran also has a notebook with pictures and biographical information about Shel Silverstein, Jack Prelutsky, Bryd Baylor, Eve Merriam, and other poets.

Ms. Cochran introduces her students to poetry during the first two weeks of the school year. On the first day of school, she begins by reading aloud the first chapter of *Anastasia Krupnik* (Lowry, 1979) and talking about poetry. The students make a list of rules about poetry and hang it in their classroom (Tompkins & Hoskisson, 1991). Each day her students read poems and share them with the class. She shares strategies for writing poems and introduces students to several simple formulas so that they will feel instant success as they write poems. Several days later she brings in a piece of fruit for each child and invites them to "bite in and enjoy the taste." Then she shares Eve Merriam's "How to Eat a Poem" (Dunning, Lueders, & Smith, 1966) in which the poet compares reading a poem to eating a piece of fruit, and they continue discussing poetry. Students talk about many concerns: how to choose poems, what to do when they don't understand a poem, why poems are arranged on the page as they are, how to choose words and images for poems they are writing, and so on.

THE TUESDAY POETRY WORKSHOP SCHEDULE

After the two-week focus unit on poetry, Judy plans for poetry workshop every Tuesday morning. The morning schedule is broken into two sections by the weekly library visit; the first half of the workshop focuses on reading poetry and the second half on writing poetry. Ms. Cochran's schedule is

8:30–9:00	Students Read Poems Independently
9:00–9:30	Students Share Poems They Have Read with Buddies or in Small Groups
9:30–9:45	Teacher Leads a Mini-lesson Called "A Closer Look" on Reading Poetry
9:45–10:15	Weekly Trip to Library to Check Out Books
10:15–10:30	Teacher Leads a Second Mini-lesson Called "The Poet's Craft" on Writing Poetry
10:30–11:00	Students Write Poems or Responses to Poems They Have Read
11:00–11:15	Students Share Their Writing with Classmates
11:15–11:30	Students Complete "Poetry Workshop Evaluations"

COMPONENTS OF THE TUESDAY POETRY WORKSHOP

The Tuesday Poetry Workshop includes students reading poetry, teacher-directed mini-lessons, students writing poetry, two sharing sessions, and an evaluation component.

Reading Poems Independently

Ms. Cochran's students choose books of poetry from the classroom collection to read or they read library books or books of poetry that they bring from home or have checked out from the public library. Independent reading of poems lasts for 30 minutes, and as they read, students often stick small tabs on pages to mark favorite poems to share with classmates later. Some students have favorite poets and always want to read a particular poet. Jack Prelutsky is the students' favorite; he visited the school two years ago and hasn't been forgotten. Ms. Cochran expects that her students will read at least five poems during the independent reading period and select at least two poems to share with classmates.

The mood in the classroom is different when students are reading poetry, compared to when they are reading stories and informational books. Students are mumbling as they read the poems to themselves, moving their bodies to the rhythm of the poems, and giggling in response to a humorous poem. Students also turn to classmates for help in pronouncing or understanding an unfamiliar word or phrase.

During independent reading time, Ms. Cochran circulates around the classroom, conferencing briefly with students about their reading. She uses a set of pink index cards to take notes about each student. She says, "I use pink cards for Poetry Workshop because *P* is for pink and for poetry. It's a great mnemonic device!" She takes notes about which poems and poets students are reading, their comments about their choices and interests, their developing concepts of poetry and their increasing use of poetic terminology.

Sharing Poems with Classmates

For the second 30 minutes of the Tuesday Poetry Workshop, students share favorite poems they have read with partners or in small groups. (About once every six or eight weeks, students get into a big circle and share interesting poems with the whole class to develop a strong sense of a shared community of readers.) Ms. Cochran believes in the power of sharing. She says, "Sharing is one of the most important activities in our Tuesday Poetry Workshop. Most poems aren't meant to be read silently. When students read to each other the poems they have read come to life and my students become poets."

Teaching "A Closer Look" Mini-lesson

Ms. Cochran takes 15 minutes to teach the "A Closer Look" mini-lesson that focuses on reading poetry. She explains, "My students complained that some poems were hard to understand so they gave me the idea for 'A Closer Look.' In this mini-lesson, we share poems and talk about them." Students nominate "confusing" poems or "poems too good to miss" or poems that illustrate something they've talked about in a previous mini-lesson for Ms. Cochran to use in the mini-lesson. They suggest these poems anytime during the week, and especially while they are reading and sharing poems on Tuesday morning. Then Ms. Cochran chooses several poems and while students are sharing, she quickly duplicates copies of the poems for each student and makes transparencies to use on the overhead projector.

During the mini-lesson, Ms. Cochran distributes copies of one of the poems, reads it aloud once or twice, and the student who nominated it talks about the poem, offering comments and questions. Other students share their opinions and insights, and usually the student's confusion is resolved. When necessary Ms. Cochran clarifies a point. The class repeats the procedure for each poem and spends about five minutes on each one.

During the school year, Ms. Cochran plans to focus on the following topics through the "A Closer Look" mini-lessons: rhyme, repetition, alliteration, onomatopoeia, imagery, comparisons, symbols, and wordplay. For each of these concepts, she shares poems that illustrate the concept, introduces the concept and term, and invites students to find other poems that illustrate the poetic device or technique. She also uses this mini-lesson to share information about poets and to introduce new books of poetry that she will place in the class library.

Teaching "The Poet's Craft" Mini-Lesson

Ms. Cochran leads a second 15-minute mini-lesson that focuses on writing poetry called "The Poet's Craft." She introduces poetic forms and formulas that students can use in writing poetry such as lies poems, color poems, "If I were" poems, apology poems (Koch, 1970, 1973) as well as haikus, acrostics, limericks, and free verse. She also talks about how to arrange poems on a page, how to unwrite and take out unnecessary words, and how to use capital letters and punctuation marks in poems.

For each mini-lesson, Ms. Cochran shares some poems that illustrate the strategy she wants to teach, explains the strategy, and then her class writes or revises a poem together to practice the strategy. Her students keep poetry notebooks, and Ms. Cochran asks them to take notes about the strategy she has taught at the end of the mini-lesson.

When students move into the next component of poetry workshop, writing poems, Ms. Cochran encourages them to experiment with the strategy she has taught in the mini-lesson, and many do, but they don't have to.

Writing Poems or Responses to Poems

Students spend 30 minutes writing poems or responses to poems they read earlier in the morning. Many students will continue to write, using the ideas Ms. Cochran shared in the "The Poet's Craft" mini-lesson, but others will look back through their poetry notebooks for ideas shared earlier in the year or will write poems related to their interests. Sometimes, too, students will return to a poem they read during independent reading time or a poem Ms. Cochran shared in the "A Closer Look" mini-lesson and write about these poems.

During this writing time, students share rough drafts of poems with classmates and informally get feedback about how well they are communicating. Sometimes Ms. Cochran sits in on these brief writing group meetings, and other times she is busy working with other students. Because most of the poems that students write are short, students can share their poems and get feedback quickly.

Ms. Cochran circulates around the room during this independent writing time, observing students as they work and briefly conferencing with them. She makes additional notes on her pink poetry cards, noting what students are writing, poetic devices and other techniques they are experimenting with, and poetic terminology they are using. She also notes their interest in writing poetry, the connections they make to poems they have read, and whether they go beyond rhyme to use other poetic devices.

Sharing Writing with Classmates

Students move their chairs into a large circle and spend 15 minutes sharing poems they have written and other responses to poems they have read. Students take turns sharing and after each student reads, classmates take turns offering several compliments, asking questions, or making suggestions. The sharing time is brief and only about a quarter of the class shares each week. Ms. Cochran expects that all students will share a poem or response to a poem at least once a month.

Completing "Poetry Workshop Evaluation" Sheets

Students spend the last 10 to 15 minutes of the Tuesday Poetry Workshop summarizing and evaluating their work during the workshop. Students write their evaluations on a form Ms. Cochran has developed which is shown in Figure 10.9. Ms. Cochran collects and reads these evaluation sheets and writes notes back to the students on the sheets. Then students file the sheets in the back of their poetry notebooks.

MS. COCHRAN'S LESSON PLAN FOR A TUESDAY POETRY WORKSHOP

A lesson plan for one Tuesday Poetry Workshop is presented in Figure 10.10. Students are reading, writing, and sharing poetry on this change-of-pace day. Ms. Cochran teaches two mini-lessons, one on reading poetry and one on writing poetry.

FIGURE 10.9
Tuesday Poetry Workshop Evaluation Sheet

	Summary	Evaluation
Reading Poetry		
Writing Poetry		
Sharing		

FIGURE 10.10
Tuesday Poetry Workshop Lesson Plan

	TUESDAY
8:30–9:00 *Reading*	Students choose and read poems independently.
9:00–9:30 *Sharing*	Students share poems they have read with classmates in small groups.
9:30–9:45 *Mini-lesson* "A Closer Look"	1. Choose and share a "confusing" poem 2. Choose and share a favorite poem 3. Read "Eletelephony" and introduce invented words
9:45–10:15 *Library*	Students go to the library to check out books.
10:15–10:30 *Mini-lesson* "The Poet's Craft"	1. Share odes 2. List characteristics 3. Write class poem "Ode to Raisins" • Bring raisins
10:30–11:00 *Writing*	Students write odes, other poems, or responses to poetry.
11:00–11:15 *Sharing*	Students share their writing with the class.
11:15–11:30 *Evaluation*	Students complete "Poetry Workshop Evaluation" sheets.

In the "A Closer Look" mini-lesson, Ms. Cochran shares Walter de la Mare's "Someone" (de Regniers, 1988), a two-stanza poem about sounds heard at night. Allison nominated the poem and she comments, "I liked reading this poem, but I don't think I understand it. Was it a ghost? Who is the 'someone'?" As the class talks about the poem, they talk about how many of them have heard sounds at night and that they were scared. Someone asks what *nought*, one of the words in the poem, means, and after five minutes of discussion, students decide this is a good poem to remember when they feel frightened at night and that the "someone" in the poem might be a ghost or, perhaps, just your imagination.

The second poem is Jack Prelutsky's "Louder than a Clap of Thunder!" (1984). Marty selected it and he reads it aloud with great relish. Then he explains that he chose this one because Ms. Cochran talked about comparisons last Tuesday, and he found this poem in which Prelutsky compares the noise a father makes snoring to a variety of other things. Students point out their favorite comparisons in the poem and then arrange the poem for choral reading.

The last poem Ms. Cochran shares in the mini-lesson is Laura Richards's "Eletelephony" (Prelutsky, 1983), a nonsense verse about an elephant that is tangled up with a telephone. She chose this poem because it's one of her favorites and she wants to talk about invented words. After reading the poem, the students identify the invented words and try to make up some other combinations of *elephant* and *telephone*. Ms. Cochran hangs a chart labeled "Invented Words" and writes *eletelephony* on it. One child remembers that *Bunnicula* (Howe & Howe, 1979), the title of a favorite fantasy book, is an invented word (*bunny* and *dracula*) and other children mention *brunch* (*breakfast* and *lunch*) and *smog* (*smoke* and *fog*). These students add their words to the chart, and then Ms. Cochran invites students to look for invented words in the poems they read and to pick out some to share next week.

In the second mini-lesson on "The Poet's Craft," Ms. Cochran introduces odes, poems in which the author addresses a plant, animal, or other object. She has made transparencies of four odes from *The Random House Book of Poetry for Children* (Prelutsky, 1983): Hilda Conkling's "Dandelion," Amy Lowell's "Sea Shell," Walter Brooks's "Ode to Spring," and Jack Prelutsky's "City, Oh, City!" She presents each ode on the overhead projector and reads it aloud. Together she and the students identify some of the unique characteristics of odes, and Ms. Cochran writes them on a chart that she hangs on the classroom wall.

Then Ms. Cochran passes out some raisins to each student and suggests that together as a class, they might like to write an ode to these raisins. Her students live in an agricultural area of California where raisins are grown so this idea meets with great enthusiasm. Within a minute or two, students are talking to the raisins in their hands, rehearsing lines for the class poem. Ms. Cochran takes their dictation and writes a rough draft of their poem. Students offer suggestions for revisions, and within minutes, they have written this poem:

> *Ode to a California Raisin*
> *Raisin, oh, raisin,*
> *You're nothing but a sun-dried grape.*
> *Do you remember the sunny summer days*
> *when you hung with your brothers and sisters*
> *growing plump on a grape vine?*
> *Raisin, oh, raisin,*
> *You used to be a Thompson seedless grape*
> *but in early autumn workers cut you down*
> *and laid you low in the dirt to dry out.*
> *Have you looked in the mirror lately?*
> *Raisin, oh, raisin,*
> *Now you're wrinkled, brown, and sticky*
> *turned into a nutritious, tasty snack*
> *full of ten minerals and flavor, too.*
> *Do you mind if we eat you?*
> *"Of course not," said the raisin.*

As the mini-lesson ends and students move into independent writing time, many begin to write odes to their pets, their jackets, and other personal objects.

MS. COCHRAN'S RECORD-KEEPING AND ASSESSMENT PROCEDURES

Ms. Cochran expects her students to read poems, write poems, and share their reading and writing experiences with classmates. She does not give grades for the poetry workshop, but she asks her students to summarize and evaluate their work each week. "Getting past the grades barrier has been hard," Ms. Cochran admits. "But I think I've succeeded—at least on Tuesdays." She uses the evaluation sheet presented in Figure 10.9. It took her several weeks to demonstrate to students how to summarize and evaluate their work, but now she is pleased with the work they are doing and their ability to reflect on their reading and writing experiences.

REFERENCES

Hopkins, L. B. (1987). *Pass the poetry, please!* New York: Harper Trophy.

Koch, K. (1970). *Wishes, lies, and dreams: Teaching children to write poetry.* New York: Vintage Books.

Koch, K. (1973). *Rose, where did you get that red? Teaching great poetry to children.* New York: Vintage Books.

Tompkins, G. E., & Hoskisson, K. (1991). *Language arts: Content and teaching strategies.* New York: Merrill/Macmillan.

CHILDREN'S LITERATURE REFERENCES

de Regniers, B. S. (selector). (1988). *Sing a song of popcorn: Every child's book of poems.* New York: Scholastic.

Dunning, S., Lueders. E., & Smith, H. (1966). *Reflections on a gift of watermelon pickle and other modern verse.* Glenview, IL: Scott, Foresman.

Howe, D., & Howe, J. (1979). *Bunnicula: A rabbit-tale of mystery.* New York: Atheneum.

Lowry, L. (1979). *Anastasia Krupnik.* Boston: Houghton Mifflin.

Prelutsky, J. (selector). (1983). *The Random House book of poetry for children.* New York: Random House.

Prelutsky, J. (1984). *The new kid on the block.* New York: Greenwillow.

PRESENTATION 5   ## Using a Vertebrate Animal Theme for Sixth Graders

Mr. Roberts's sixth graders are studying vertebrate animals, and he expects that they will expand their knowledge by being able to explain the characteristics of mammals, birds, reptiles, amphibians, and fish. Mr. Roberts wants his students to describe the animals' reproduction and life cycles, habitats, physical characteristics, and diet. He has live animals in the classroom including a hamster, frog, newt, salamander, and several tadpoles and fish. The science center has a collection of books about animals, magazines with information about animals, and pictures of animals. The students have learning logs in which they record their observations of the animals, summaries of books and articles they have read, and lists of theme-related words. A word wall, a large sheet of paper on which students have written over 70 words related to their study of vertebrates, hangs on one wall of the classroom.

Mr. Roberts meets with eight students at the reading table to continue reading from *Frogs, Toads, Lizards, and Salamanders* (Parker & Wright, 1991). A list of information that the students brainstormed about reptiles and amphibians before reading this book is spread out on the reading table. The list is divided into three questions: "Where do different kinds of amphibians and reptiles live?" "What do different kinds of amphibians and reptiles eat?" and "What do different kinds of amphibians and reptiles do?" The students used these three questions to guide their reading of the first portion of the book, and they wrote the answers to the questions on chart paper.

Mr. Roberts explains that students will use the reciprocal teaching procedure today to read pages 40 and 41 in *Frogs, Toads, Lizards, and Salamanders.* The students are familiar with this procedure, so Mr. Roberts calls on a volunteer to begin. Al begins by making a prediction, "I see two diagrams of the insides of a frog and a lizard. I predict we'll read about the insides of a frog and a lizard." Mr. Roberts tells Al that this is a good prediction because it uses information from the illustration. He asks Al to read the first sentence on page 40 to see if that makes any difference in his prediction. After reading, Al notes that the paragraph will probably be about the differences between amphibians and reptiles. Mr. Roberts is pleased and explains, "Al's prediction is important because it will guide the kinds of information you will look for when you read. You should read to compare how the insides of amphibians and reptiles may be alike or different."

Then all the students read the passage independently. Next, Al asks questions about the passage, "My questions are, 'How do frogs and toads breathe?' and 'We have ribs and no tail; what do frogs have?' " Students volunteer answers. Then Al continues, "My summary is that frogs and toads breathe through their skin and have no tails. Frogs and toads are different." Mr. Roberts comments that Al's summary includes some of the important information from the passage. He tells the students that one additional detail is important: that frogs and toads are cold blooded. The students brainstorm what they think this means and consult the glossary in the book. Another student continues the reciprocal teaching activity on page 41.

Next, Mr. Roberts presents a semantic feature analysis chart for amphibians and reptiles, as shown in Figure 10.11. The students work with partners to complete the analysis. They place a plus (+) to indicate that the animal has the characteristic identified on the chart and a minus (−) to indicate that it does not.

The next day students share their completed semantic feature analysis charts. Then Mr. Roberts presents a text set, a collection of informational books and magazine articles, about amphibians and reptiles. Students preview the texts, and each student selects an amphibian or reptile to investigate. As a group they brainstorm questions, such as "What does this animal eat?" on the chalkboard to guide their research. They will research and write a report about their animal using at least two of the reading materials from the text set. Later, students will gather in writing groups for feedback and suggestions on how to revise their rough drafts. Mr. Roberts will present a mini-lesson on writing bibliographic references before students prepare a final draft with a bibliography. Students will share their reports with other students and place the reports in the science center for others to read.

CHILDREN'S LITERATURE REFERENCE

Parker, M., & Wright, J. (1991). *Frogs, toads, lizards, and salamanders.* New York: Greenwillow.

FIGURE 10.11

Semantic Feature Analysis for *Frogs, Toads, Lizards, and Salamanders*
(Parker & Wright, 1991)
Code: + = yes; − = no; ? = maybe

	Amphibian	Reptile	Caudata	Salienta	Warm blooded	Cold blooded	Dry skin	Moist skin	Voiceless	Lays eggs in water	Lays eggs on land	Clawed feet
Hellbender												
California Newt												
Eastern Spadefoot Toad												
American Toad												
Bullfrog												
African Clawed Frog												
Mediterranean Gecko												
Western Skink												

PRESENTATION 6   Ms. Epstein's Sixth-Grade Vertebrate Animal Theme Cycle

Ms. Epstein is teaching a theme cycle on vertebrate animals. Her science curriculum specifies that her sixth-grade students should be able to describe the characteristics of amphibians, lizards, fish, birds, and mammals. She has several animals in her classroom including a mouse, frog, lizard, and parrot. Near the cages is a poetree (Hopkins, 1987), a tree branch potted in a large can filled with rocks, and students have hung on the tree copies of poems about the animals that they have found in books or written themselves. A veterinarian, pet store owner, and member of the humane society have visited the classroom and been interviewed by the class.

This week Ms. Epstein and eight students are reading *Frogs, Toads, Lizards, and Salamanders* (Parker & Wright, 1991). As a preparing step for reading from this book, the students each locate and share one of the poems about frogs or lizards hanging on the poetree beside the animal cages. A list of these poems appears in Figure 10.12.

Then they read several pages of the book and write responses in their learning logs using the *content response heuristic* (Brozo, 1988). Figure 10.13 presents the response heuristic, a series of questions that are used to guide reading. Today Ms. Epstein and the students discuss pages 40 and 41 of the book, which describe the similarities and differ-

FIGURE 10.12
Frog and Lizard Poems

Cambell, A. (1983). "Sally and Manda." In J. Prelutsky (Ed.), *The Random House book of poetry.* New York: Random House.

Gardner, J. (1983). "The lizard." In J. Prelutsky (Ed.) ,*The Random House book of poetry.* New York: Random House.

Hoban, R. "The tin frog." In M. Farber & M. Livingston (Eds.), *These small stones.* New York: Harper & Row.

Johnson, T. (1990). "Among the water lilies," "Lizard longing," and "Frog eggs." In T. Johnson, *I'm gonna tell Mama I want an iguana.* New York: Putnam.

Prelutsky, J. (1984). "The chameleon" and "The gallivanting gecko." In J. Prelutsky, *Zoo doings.* New York: Greenwillow.

Prelutsky, J. (1986). "Bullfrogs, bullfrogs on parade." In J. Prelutsky, *Ride a purple pelican.* New York: Morrow.

Roethke, T. (1983). "The lizard." In J. Prelutsky (Ed.), *The Random House book of poetry.* New York: Random House.

Wilbur, R. (1984). "What is the opposite of a prince?" in Z. Sutherland & M. Livingston (Eds.), *The Scott Foresman anthology of children's poetry.* Glenview, IL: Scott Foresman.

Yolen, J. (1986). "Song of the spring peeper." In J. Yolen, *Ring of Earth.* San Diego: Harcourt Brace Jovanovich.

FIGURE 10.13
Response Heuristic for Informational Books
SOURCE: Adapted with permission from W. Brozo, "Applying the Reader Response Heuristic to Expository Text," *Journal of Reading, 32* (1988): p. 140–145.

1. What was most interesting or exciting word, phrase, sentence, or picture in the text? What idea, detail, issue, or concept did you feel most strongly about?
2. What are your feelings about this idea, detail, issure, or concept? Why do you feel this way?
3. What connections can you make between your own experiences and the ideas, details, issues, and concepts in the text?
4. What places in the text made you think of something you have experiences or seen or know about? Why?

ences between amphibians and lizards. For the exploring step, they discuss these differences by reading from their learning logs and making comments. Ms. Epstein begins the discussion by saying, "Who will share the word or sentence you thought was most interesting?" Students read entries from their learning logs and respond to each other's entries. Ted says, "I like the part where toads have warty skins. But I don't get how they breathe through their skin."

Next, the students brainstorm words and phrases that reflect what they know and feel about amphibians and lizards. Ms. Epstein urges them to select words and phrases from their learning logs, from comments made in the group discussion, and from the book they are reading. They brainstorm a list of words and phrases on the chalkboard and compose two poems as a further exploring step activity:

> *Lizards*
> *dry and cold*
> *slip away as fast as the eye can blink*
> *long legs and graceful bodies*
> *But we'll never know*
> *eggs on land*
> *sounds so grand*
> *but not caviar*

> *Amphibians*
> *ribit, ribit at the pond*
> *moist and warm*
> *no ribs*
> *just belly we guess*
> *eggs in jelly*
> *under the water*
> *how do they hatch?*

Later, for an extending step activity, the students demonstrate their knowledge of the characteristics of various vertebrate animals by writing animal stories incorporating the factual information they have been learning in their descriptions of setting and character. Students will consider three or four activities to extend their study of reptiles and amphibians and other vertebrate animals and decide to study "The Frog Prince" fairy tale by reading several versions of this brothers Grimm story including *The Frog King* (Grimm & Grimm, 1989), *The Frog Prince* (Grimm & Grimm, 1989), *Frog Prince* (Berenzy, 1989), and *The Frog Prince Continued* (Scieszka, 1991). They will compare these versions to a version that Ms. Epstein found in a 1945 edition of *Grimm's Fairy Tales* (Lucas, Crane, & Edwardes).

REFERENCES

Brozo, W. (1988). Applying the reader response heuristic to expository text. *Journal of Reading, 32,* 140–145.

Hopkins, L. (1987). *Pass the poetry, please!* New York: Harper & Row.

CHILDREN'S LITERATURE REFERENCES

Berenzy, A. (1989) Frog Prince. New York: Henry Holt.

Grimm, J., & Grimm, W. (1989). *The frog king and other tales of the Brothers Grimm.* New York: Signet Classics.

Grimm, J., & Grimm, W. (1989). *The frog prince.* New York: North-South.

Lucas, E., Crane, L., & Edwardes, M. (Trans.) (1945). "The frog prince." In *Grimm's fairy tales* (pp. 85–89). New York: Grosset & Dunlap.

Parker, N., & Wright, J. (1991). *Frogs, toads, lizards, and salamanders.* New York: Greenwillow.

Scieszka, J. (1991). *The frog prince continued.* New York: Viking.

PRESENTATION 7   ## Ms. Jacobs's Sixth-Grade Vertebrate Animal Unit

Ms. Jacobs's sixth graders are studying vertebrate animals. According to the science curriculum, she is responsible for teaching reptile, amphibian, bird, fish, and mammal classes. One objective of this theme cycle is for students to compare and contrast members of these classes according to reproductive cycles, habitats, diet, and internal systems. She has several animals in her classroom including tadpoles, newts, and mice that her students will observe during the unit.

A group of eight students is researching the life cycles of frogs. As one activity they have been observing tadpoles and recording information from their observations in their learning logs. They have also been reading *Frogs, Toads, Lizards, and Salamanders* (Parker & Wright, 1991) to gain more information about frogs and lizards. Today Ms. Jacobs begins the lesson by explaining that students will be learning about an organization or structure that authors use to present information called the compare-contrast organization. As a preparing step activity, the students discuss what they know about this kind of organization, and Ms. Jacobs presents the compare-contrast organizer shown in Figure 10.14. Ms. Jacobs prepared this organizer using the information presented on pages 40 and 41 of *Frogs, Toads, Lizards, and Salamanders.* She explains that this is a visual overview of the likenesses and differences between amphibians and lizards. She talks about the organizer, stressing both its content (features distinguishing amphibians and lizards) and how compare-contrast structures work. Students notice that amphibians and lizards are compared systematically on several features such as the type of blood, type of lungs, place where eggs are laid, and moisture of skin.

Next, students compose a paragraph about the similarities and differences between frogs and lizards using the information presented in the compare-contrast organizer. Ms. Jacobs stresses that they need to include words such as *alike, different, similarities, differences, can be compared,* and *in contrast* in their compositions.

The next day the students read their paragraphs aloud. The group gives compliments, asks clarifying questions, and discusses possible revisions. Then students read pages 40 and

FIGURE 10.14
Organizer for Pages 40 and 41 from *Frogs, Toads, Lizards, and Salamanders*
(Parker & Wright, 1991)

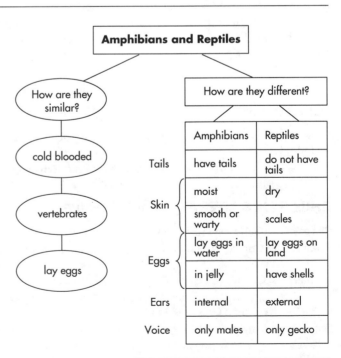

41 of *Frogs, Toads, Lizards, and Salamanders*. After reading, the students discuss the content presented on these pages and the author's use of the compare-contrast structure. As an exploring activity, they compare and contrast the paragraph they composed to the author's text. They note that the author used few of the clue words that signal a compare-contrast structure. Many students decide that their compositions were easier to read because they had more clearly signaled how frogs and lizards were alike and different. The students also discuss how readers could look for a compare-contrast structure while reading. Ms. Jacobs ends the lesson by presenting and describing a skeleton organizer for a compare-contrast structure, shown in Figure 10.15. She explains, "This is a skeleton organizer that you can use whenever you want to write a composition comparing and contrasting two things. You can also use this organizer to record information when you are reading a paragraph that compares and contrasts something."

The next day Mrs. Jacobs introduces two new books about amphibians and reptiles: *Never Kiss an Alligator!* (Bare, 1989) and *Look at Skin, Shell, and Scale* (Pluckrose, 1989). She tells the students that these books have some portions that are written in a compare-contrast structure. She reminds them that noting these structures is an important way to learn new information. Then students divide into two groups. As an extending activity, they will read one of the two books and prepare to teach the students in the other group some new information they learned, using the compare-contrast organizer for their presentations.

As another extending activity, students later will use what they have learned about vertebrate animals to compose an alphabet book following the "A is for _____," "B is for_____," "C is for _____" formula. They will read *The Yucky Reptile Alphabet Book* (Pallota, 1986) and *The Frog Alphabet Book* (Pallota, 1990) and use these as models for their book.

CHILDREN'S LITERATURE REFERENCES

Bare, C. (1989). *Never kiss an alligator!* New York: Dutton.

Pallota, J. (1986). *The yucky reptile alphabet book.* Watertown, MA: Ivory Tower.

Pallota, J. (1990). *The frog alphabet book.* Watertown, MA: Charlesbridge.

Parker, N., & Wright, J. (1990). *Frogs, toads, lizards, and salamanders.* New York: Greenwillow.

Pluckrose, H. (1989). *Look at skin, shell, and scale.* New York: Franklin Watts.

FIGURE 10.15
Skeleton Compare–Contrast Organizer

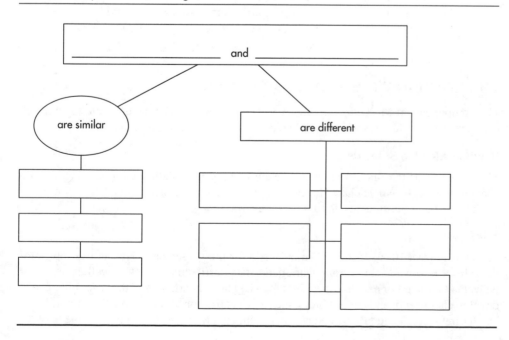

| PRESENTATION 8 | "Readers at Work" in Mr. Diaz's Sixth-Grade Classroom |

Mr. Diaz has a sign hanging on the outside of his classroom door at Deer Creek Elementary School saying "Readers at Work," and his sixth graders are really readers. For six weeks of every quarter, Mr. Diaz's students participate in a reading workshop cycle, and each student in the classroom is reading a different book. (During the other three weeks, they read core literature books in small groups or as a class.) Mr. Diaz says, "The hardest thing for me to accept was that children learn to read by reading. It's just that simple, but I kept thinking that there must be more to it than that." He has read many of the books that his students are reading, and his students often read and pass favorite books from classmate to classmate so usually there are several people in the classroom who are familiar with just about any book a student might be reading. After several months of reading workshop, Mr. Diaz remembers that it finally dawned on him that it is not really important whether or not he has read the book that a student is reading. What really matters, he concluded, was that the student is reading and enjoying it.

During the six-week reading workshop cycles, students read two, three, or more self-selected books. They talk about the books they have read with classmates and with Mr. Diaz in conferences, share the books with their classmates in sharing sessions, and extend their reading through response projects.

Mr. Diaz's classroom library is stocked with hundreds of books that he has collected. Most of the books are paperbacks that he has ordered from book clubs over the past four or five years, many with free points earned from his students' personal book club purchases. Others are gift books that students have presented to the class library on their birthdays, and others are on loan from the school library and the local public library. Students also bring some of their own books to share with classmates. Students take turns serving as the class librarian and keeping the library area orderly.

MR. DIAZ'S DAILY SCHEDULE FOR READING WORKSHOP

Mr. Diaz's class spends two-and-a-half hours each morning in reading workshop. The schedule is

8:45–9:15	Teacher Reads Aloud to Students
9:15–9:30	Teacher Gives a Mini-Lesson
9:30–10:15	Students Read Self-Selected Books
10:15–10:30	Break
10:30–11:00	Students Participate in Response Activities
11:00–11:15	Students Share Books They Are Reading or Response Projects with the Class

THE READING WORKSHOP COMPONENTS

The components in Mr. Diaz's reading workshop approach are reading aloud to students, mini-lessons, reading of self-selected books, response activities, and sharing.

Reading Aloud to Students

Mr. Diaz spends the first 30 minutes of each reading workshop session reading aloud a chapter book to the whole class. He reads one or two chapters each day and then, for the remainder of the time, students discuss the chapter(s) in a grand conversation.

Mini-Lessons

Mr. Diaz holds a 10- to 15-minute mini-lesson for the whole class. He chooses topics for these brief lessons on skills from district and state curriculum guides as well as on things he wants to teach. For example, he might focus on how a particular author uses dialogue to develop character or a reading strategy such as visualization, or talk about the author's craft by sharing a poem and talking about alliteration. He often uses excerpts from the book he is reading aloud as examples for the mini-lesson. It is important to note that Mr. Diaz integrates reading with the other language arts and teaches reading, writing, and language skills and strategies in these mini-lessons.

Students Read Self-Selected Books

Mr. Diaz says, "Reading time is sacred. I never sacrifice a minute of it. The best thing I can do is to give time for my students to read during class; therefore, I save 45 minutes every day." During the first 10 minutes of this 45-minute period, Mr. Diaz reads a book, magazine, or newspaper that he brings to class. Then during the remainder of the period, he circulates while his students continue to read, and the students do read for the entire period.

Mr. Diaz has organized students' desks into five groups, and students choose where they sit. He visits with each student in one group each day so that he can meet with every student in the class every week. Mr. Diaz squats down beside students and asks, "What are you reading?" in a hushed voice. Students tell him the name of the book, the author, and explain a little about the book and why they like it. Sometimes they softly read a brief excerpt aloud to prove a point or share a favorite episode. Mr. Diaz carries a clipboard with checklists for each student with him as he visits with students and makes notes about each student's reading.

At first, Mr. Diaz's students had trouble selecting books to read. He taught students the five-finger strategy for choosing a book at the appropriate reading level. (Students open a book to the middle and read the page, raising a finger for each unfamiliar word. If students raise all five fingers, the book may be too difficult and students should consider choosing something else.) He also helped them become more aware of the books available to choose from through book talks he gave about books in the class library. Sometimes he'd suggest that students read another book in the same genre or another book written by a favorite author. At other times he suggested that a student might like to read a book he had already read aloud to the class. He found this problem resolved itself once students started reading and sharing their books with classmates.

Mr. Diaz says that he believes in this approach and that it can meet every student's reading needs, even Seth's, who was reading at a second-grade level at the beginning of the school year. The first book he read was *Chicken Little* (Kellogg, 1985); by April he was reading *Tales of a Fourth Grade Nothing* (Blume, 1972).

Response Activities

During this response activity time, students write in buddy journals about the book they are currently reading, they meet in small groups with the teacher to talk about the books they are reading, and they work on response projects about the self-selected book they have read.

Buddy journals. After reading, students write in buddy journals (spiral notebooks) twice a week and they share their journals with another student or the teacher. They must write to the teacher once every two weeks. Two buddy journal entries are shown in Figure 10.16. The first is Lisa's letter to Mr. Diaz about *Stone Fox* (Gardiner, 1980), and the second is a classmate's letter to Lisa about *The Borrowers Afloat* (Norton, 1959). In these journal entries, students use the friendly letter form and underline the titles of books. At the beginning of the school year, Mr. Diaz modeled how to write these friendly letters in a mini-lesson, and he continues to model the form and content in the letters he writes back to students. After writing, students put their journals on another student's desk or the teacher's desk. Then students and the teacher write responses and return the journals.

Small-group conferences. While most of the students are writing in their buddy journals, Mr. Diaz meets with small groups of five or six students to talk about their reading. Students sign up on a list on the chalkboard when they finish reading and are ready to meet in a conference. Students have each read a different book so Mr. Diaz asks questions that are generic enough to be appropriate for almost any book. Each student introduces his or her book to the group, and then the group talks about story events, characters, theme, genre, or authors. The session ends with each student reading a favorite excerpt to the group. The purpose of these small-group conferences is for students to have an opportunity to share what they are reading and their personal responses, to talk about the literary elements in stories, and to make connections among books.

FIGURE 10.16
Two Buddy Journal Entries

1-10

Dear Mr. Diaz,

<u>Stone Fox</u> is one of the saddest books I've ever read. It was really sad when he carried him across the finish line. It was also one of the best books I've ever read. I liked the way she would use similies and keep you in suspence. I can't wait to see the movie.

> Your friend,
> Lisa

3/19
Dear Lisa,
I am reading The Borrowers Afloat. I know the name sounds dumb, but you'd like it, promise.
It's about Arriety, Pod, & Homily.
They think Humans are just for borrowing from. Read it!
> DD.

Response projects. Mr. Diaz and his students have developed a list of response projects that hangs on the classroom wall. After every three or four books, students choose one book on which to do a response activity. They choose an activity from the list, or they can think of a different activity. For example:

- Elizabeth is making a table-top diorama of the kitchen and living room from *Bunnicula: A Rabbit-tale of Mystery* (Howe & Howe, 1979).
- Aaron is constructing a gameboard after reading *Jumanji* (Van Allsburg, 1981).
- Carl is researching chocolate after reading *Charlie and the Chocolate Factory* (Dahl, 1964). He'll share what he learns in an oral report.
- Mary Catherine and three friends are writing a skit adapted from *Huge Harold* (Peet, 1961) that they will perform for the class.

Sharing. Students sit in a circle for 15 minutes or so to share books they are reading or have finished reading and response projects they have completed with their classmates. All students come to sharing except one or two who might be at a critical moment in their reading or are finishing a response project. To begin the session, Mr. Diaz asks, "Who's ready to share?" Students take turns sharing their books and response projects. As they share, Mr. Diaz makes notes on students' checklists about their sharing.

MR. DIAZ'S LESSON PLAN FOR READING WORKSHOP

A one-week lesson plan for Mr. Diaz's reading workshop is presented in Figure 10.17. This lesson plan is for the second week of the six weeks that Mr. Diaz's class will spend in reading workshop. Each of the components for Mr. Diaz's reading workshop is listed, and then particular activities for this week are detailed. Mr. Diaz is reading aloud Roald Dahl's *James and the Giant Peach* (1961), a chapter each day, and in Monday's mini-lesson he provides background information about the author. On Tuesday, Wednesday, and Thursday, he focuses on metaphors and similies, using *James and the Giant Peach* as well as the books students are reading independently for examples. On Friday, he turns his attention to punctuation and begins a review of commas that will continue into the following week. During the reading period, students read their self-selected books and he monitors their reading, visiting briefly with students in one group each day.

After the break, students write in buddy journals and discuss the books they have read in a conference with Mr. Diaz and several classmates. On Thursday, Mr. Diaz changes pace and spends the activities period talking to the whole class about response projects. Students choose a response activity and begin working independently or in small groups on their

FIGURE 10.17

A One-Week Lesson Plan from a Reading Workshop Cycle

	MONDAY	TUESDAY	WEDNESDAY	THURSDAY	FRIDAY
8:45–9:15 *Read aloud*	Ch. 5	Ch. 6	Ch. 7	Ch. 8	Ch. 9
	James and the Giant Peach				
	After reading, grand conversation in small groups each day to discuss the story.				
9:15–9:30 *Mini-Lesson*	(Continued from last week) • Share author information about Roald Dahl from author file and *Boy*	• Introduce comparison (similes and metaphors) • Use examples marked in *J&GP*	(Continued) • Ask students to locate and share samples from books they are reading	(Continued) • Make chart to hang in classroom with samples	• Review commas • In series • Day and year • City and state • Quotes • Compound sentences
9:30–10:15 *Reading*	• Students read independently in self-selected books				
	• Teacher briefly visits with students in one group each day to monitor their reading				
	• Remember to make notes on Reading Workshop Checklist				
	Group 3	Group 4	Group 5	Group 1	Group 2
10:15–10:30	BREAK				
10:30–11:00 *Response Activities*	• Students write in buddy journals			• Talk about response projects	• Add new activities to chart • Students choose response projects and begin work
	• Conferences with small groups (5–6 students) to discuss books they are reading				
11:00–11:15 *Sharing*	Students sit in a large circle to share books they have read and their response projects				

projects on Thursday or Friday. During the last 15 minutes of the reading workshop, Mr. Diaz and his students meet to share their reading (and later in the cycle they share their projects) with the class.

MR. DIAZ'S RECORD-KEEPING AND ASSESSMENT PROCEDURES

Mr. Diaz keeps records on each student and students keep their own records. Mr. Diaz says, "I've tried all kinds of record-keeping techniques, and checklists work best for me." He uses a checklist with the reading workshop components listed on it, as shown in Figure 10.18. He makes a copy of the checklist for each student and keeps them on a clipboard. Mr. Diaz carries his clipboard around during reading workshop and makes notes as he meets with students and observes them. After each reading workshop cycle, Mr. Diaz places the completed checklists in reading-writing portfolios that he keeps for each student.

Each student has a reading folder, the kind with two inside pockets. During the reading workshop cycle, students keep all records in this folder. One record is a list of the books the student has read. On a second sheet, students keep a record of the types of response activities they have done. Other records include notes from the mini-lessons and weekly contracts. A weekly contract is shown in Figure 10.19, and students keep track of their daily activities on this checklist. Students also keep their buddy journals in this folder.

CHILDREN'S LITERATURE REFERENCES

Blume, J. (1972). *Tales of a fourth-grade nothing.* New York: Dutton.

Dahl, R. (1961). *James and the giant peach.* New York: Knopf.

Dahl, R. (1964). *Charlie and the chocolate factory.* New York: Knopf.

Gardiner, J. R. (1980). *Stone fox.* New York: Harper & Row.

Howe, D., & Howe, J. (1979). *Bunnicula: A rabbit-tale of mystery.* New York: Atheneum.

Kellogg, S. (1985). *Chicken little.* New York: Mulberry.

Norton, M. (1959). *The borrowers afloat.* New York: Harcourt Brace Jovanovich.

Peet, B. (1961). *Huge Harold.* Boston: Houghton Mifflin.

Van Allsburg, C. (1979). *Jumanji.* Boston: Houghton Mifflin.

FIGURE 10.18
Weekly Reading Workshop Checklist

Name: _____ Week: _____

Mini-Lessons

Reading Self-Selected Books

Buddy Journals

Conferences

Response Projects

Sharing

FIGURE 10.19

A Weekly Contract for Reading Workshop

Weekly Reading Workshop Record					
Name: _____ Week: _____					
Book: _____					
Project: _____					
	Mon	Tues	Wed	Thurs	Fri
Mini-Lesson					
Reading					
Buddy Journal					
Conference					
Response Project					
Sharing					
0 = not done 1 = done A = absent					

Mr. Jurey's Seventh-Grade Students Learn about Expressionism   PRESENTATION 9

In Mr. Jurey's art class, seventh-grade students are studying expressionism, a style in which artists use brilliant colors and somewhat abstract or simple shapes. Mr. Jurey begins the unit by sharing prints of expressionistic art, such as Van Gogh's "The Starry Night," and reading *Meet Matisse* (Munthe, 1983). As they talk and read about expressionism, the class adds these words to their word wall: *simplicity, vibrate, space, color, sensations, impressions, forms, cut-outs, cold and hot colors, brilliant, swirling lines, geometric shapes, texture, strong feelings, melody, rhythm, bold patterns, abstract, negative and positive shapes, dark background, images, balance, personalized vision, light and dark colors, colors play with each other, colors vary,* and *dappled texture.* Students also experiment with cut-outs. They cut shapes from paper they have painted and texturized and play with colored backgrounds, much like Matisse did.

Next students look for picture books in the school library in which illustrators have used brilliant colors and simple shapes in an expressionistic style. They work in small groups to read the books and closely examine the illustrations. Today they share the books with the class and explain why the illustrations are expressionistic:

- Chris shares Lois Ehlert's *Feathers for Lunch* (1990), a rhyming story about an escaped housecat who tries to catch 12 birds but ends up only eating feathers for lunch. He explains, "Lois Ehlert's illustrations are expressionistic. You can see that they are brightly colored and grab your eye. These pictures of the cat, the birds, and the plants are built from basic shapes like circles and squares. Lois Ehlert used cut-outs. It looks like she built the pictures using white pieces of paper that she had brushed with watercolor paint. She also cut pieces of tissue paper and colored paper to vary the texture. You see the birds and the cat up close and get a very strong impression of prey and predator."
- Anna shares Vera B. Williams's Caldecott Honor Book *A Chair for My Mother* (1982), a story of a little girl, her mother, and grandmother who save their money to buy a comfortable armchair after all their furniture is lost in a fire. She explains, "These colors are really vivid, and that's why Vera B. Williams's illustrations are expressionistic. She uses lots of bright reds and blues in the pictures. Even though the colors are bright, they are soft and the feeling is warm and homey. You know the people in this family love each other. You can see that every bit of the page is colored—even behind the words—and the colorful border around each page adds to the intensity of the illustrations. These illustrations are painted; there are no cut-outs. Mr. Jurey said that Vera B. Williams probably used opaque watercolors."

- Jason shares Gerald McDermott's Caldecott Honor Book *Anansi the Spider* (1972), an African myth about how the moon came to be in the sky. He explains, "Gerald McDermott used bold African designs in this book. The spiders are simple geometric patterns—lines, circles, angles, squares, and triangles. The spiders in the foreground seem to vibrate and the designs in the background are softer and give the texture. Mr. McDermott also used very bright, intense colors. The colors and designs make me think of Africa and the hot climate there. It says in the back of the book that he only used four colors in the book—the primary colors and black. Orange and green are in some of the illustrations but they were made by mixing the primary colors and, of course, there is white. This book is interesting because the words are left white, and like in Anna's book, the illustrations cover the whole page."

- Michelle shares *Celebrations,* a collection of 16 holiday poems written by Myra Cohn Livingston and illustrated by Leonard Everett Fisher (1985). She explains, "These illustrations were painted with acrylic paint, and they have a lot of texture because they were painted on textured paper. I think the texture makes the illustrations softer, kind of like a memory. The colors are bright and what you expect for each holiday. You know, the St. Patrick's Day illustration is green and the Valentine's Day illustration is red. Usually Mr. Fisher painted one or two things to symbolize each holiday. For the Fourth of July, there are fireworks in the night sky. They remind me of the stars in Vincent Van Gogh's 'The Starry Night.' The illustrations cover the entire page and the poems are printed on top of the illustrations. I think these illustrations are expressionistic because the colors are intense and soft and the images are simple."

- Will shares Eric Carle's *The Mixed-up Chameleon* (1984), a pattern book about a chameleon who wishes he could be like other animals and, with each wish, the chameleon's appearance changes to incorporate a feature of that animal. At the end, the chameleon decides it is best to be himself. He explains, "I loved this book when I was a child and that's why I chose it. Eric Carle is the neatest illustrator, and I think his illustrations are expressionistic because they are cut-outs and they are brightly colored. The background is light and the cut-outs really stand out. On this page you can see the body, legs, and head of the chameleon turned white because he wanted to be a polar bear. And he has pink wings and webbed feet to be like a flamingo. He has a red, bushy fox's tail and orange goldfish fins. On this page he wants to run like a deer so Eric Carle added antlers. I think Eric Carle used fingerpaint and a pointed stick or something like that to make the texture interesting. The illustrations are simple and I think Eric Carle was smart to do that because the message of the book is so deep."

- Kevin shares *Chicka Chicka Boom Boom* (Martin & Archambault, 1989), an alphabet rhyme about what happens when the letters climb a coconut tree, and illustrated by Lois Ehlert. Kevin explains, "I'm sure this is an expressionistic book. These illustrations are really simple—just cut-outs of the upper- and lowercase letters and a coconut tree on a white background. The colors are more than bright; they are brilliant. You can see there is a hot-pink and orange polka-dotted border around three sides of each page. I think these illustrations look a lot like Matisse's—especially the palm leaves. There is no texture at all, but balance is important in these illustrations because, when too many letters climb the coconut tree, the trunk bends and the letters fall down. Lois Ehlert placed the shapes on the page very carefully."

Later students will apply what they have learned about expressionism as they write stories or poems and illustrate them in the expressionistic style.

CHILDREN'S LITERATURE REFERENCES

Carle, E. (1984). *The mixed-up chameleon.* New York: Crowell.

Ehlert, L. (1990). *Feathers for lunch.* San Diego: Harcourt Brace Jovanovich.

Livingston, M. C. (1985). *Celebrations.* New York: Holiday House.

Martin, B., Jr., & Archambault, J. (1989). *Chicka chicka boom boom.* New York: Simon & Schuster.

McDermott, G. (1972). *Anansi the spider: A tale from the Ashanti.* New York: Henry Holt.

Munthe, N. (1983). *Meet Matisse.* Boston: Little, Brown.

Williams, V. B. (1982). *A chair for my mother.* New York: Mulberry.

| Ms. Daniel's Seventh- and Eighth-Grade Students Participate in Literature Discussion Groups | PRESENTATION 10 |

Ms. Daniel teaches seventh- and eighth-grade reading classes at South Rock Creek School. Her students change classes every 50 minutes, so the time she spends with each group of students is very limited. After several years of trying to parcel out bits of time to teach reading skills, Ms. Daniel turned to the reading workshop approach. "I modeled my program on Nancie Atwell's *In the Middle* (1988) and I trusted my students," she explains. "I think that's the most important thing I did. I needed to know they could read on their own, and they needed to know they didn't need me to be able to interpret a book."

Ms. Daniel alternates reading books with students together as a class and having students read and discuss books in small groups. She calls these two approaches "teacher led" and "student led." When she reads books with students (teacher led), Ms. Daniel takes a more active role in asking questions and focusing students' attention on characters or another structural element, the author's craft, or stylistic devices, such as alliteration or symbolism. In contrast, when students are working in small groups (student led), Ms. Daniel wants them to be in charge of their own learning, and she refrains from directing the course of their discussions. Her perspective for reading instruction is reader response.

In this action plan, we describe Ms. Daniel's four-week student-led reading workshop plan for *Tuck Everlasting* (Babbitt, 1975). In this fantasy set in the 1880s, young Winnie Foster travels with the Tuck family, who have drunk water from a magic spring many years before and realize that the water they drank has given them everlasting life. Winnie must decide whether she will drink the water, and the Tucks must stop a sinister stranger who wants to find the magic water and sell it. Wheels and circles in the story symbolize the cycle of life and how the cycle is broken when someone drinks the magic water.

"This is what I call 'real-life reading,' " Ms. Daniel says. "My students think deeply about the question of immortality. They're glad that Winnie didn't drink the water, but at the same time, the question for most students is not whether they'd want to drink the water and live forever, but when to take the drink. Some students would wait until they were 16 so that they could drive a car, and others say that they'd wait until they were 21 so they could drink, drive, and do everything they're looking forward to doing."

MS. DANIEL'S DAILY SCHEDULE

Ms. Daniel meets with each class for 50 minutes each day, and during student-led reading workshop, students read independently, respond to their reading in reading logs, and participate in discussion groups. Ms. Daniel gives her students a great deal of responsibility. She specifies the number of days the class will spend on each book, and students in each discussion group organize themselves and set their own schedule for reading, writing, and discussing the book.

COMPONENTS OF MS. DANIEL'S READING WORKSHOP PROGRAM

The three components in Ms. Daniel's student-led reading workshop for *Tuck Everlasting* are reading the book, responding in a reading log, and participating in a discussion group.

Reading the Book

Ms. Daniel and her students jointly select most books that they read. She selects several favorably reviewed books, reads them, and gives a book talk to introduce the books. Then her students decide which one they want to read. Sometimes the class decides to read the same book, and sometimes students divide into groups to read different books. Other books that Ms. Daniel's students have read in teacher-led or student-led formats this year include Judy Blume's *Iggie's House* (1970), S. E. Hinton's *The Outsiders* (1967), and Paula Danziger's *The Cat Ate My Gymsuit* (1974).

As they read, students sit with friends and then get together in groups of seven or eight to talk about their reading. "I put them in discussion groups according to reading speed," Ms. Daniel explains, "because I want them to discuss their reading as soon as possible."

This technique works well because each group includes a range of reading abilities. All reading is done at school because Ms. Daniel acknowledges that she has no control over what they do outside of school hours.

Responding in a Reading Log

After students finish reading and before they meet in discussion groups, they write about their reading in reading logs. Ms. Daniel doesn't give any prompts; students are encouraged to write their reflections, predictions, questions, confusions, personal connections, and anything else they want to write. In some books, students write after every chapter, but for *Tuck Everlasting,* they write after reading each two, three, or four chapters because this book has 25 chapters, and each chapter averages 5 pages.

Students put notebook paper into folders for their reading logs, and they divide each page into two columns. The first column is headed "Reading Notes" and the second column "Discussion Notes." After reading, students write in the first column. After the discussion group meeting, they reflect on what they have learned, list opinions they have changed, and write other notes in the second column. A page from one student's reading log is presented in Figure 10.20.

Participating in a Discussion Group

The group decides how to divide the reading of the book, how often to meet, and what they do during their discussion group meetings. No one is assigned to be the group leader; instead, students work together collaboratively. They try to keep all group members productive, and even prompt each other, saying, "Jason, you haven't said anything in three days" or "Suzanne, what questions did you have about these three chapters? "

In their discussions, students talk about personal associations they have made with the book, make comments and ask questions about details in the book, offer predictions, share interpretations, and make comments to maintain the conversation. Students often build on each other's ideas. Sometimes they read what they have written and, at other times, their talk is more spontaneous. Ms. Daniel's students often find that vocabulary in the story is a problem. They have several strategies available when they want to know the meaning of a word. They can ask each other, guess from the context, ask the teacher, or look it up in the dictionary. If students think the word is important, they record it in their reading logs.

The discussion continues until all ideas have been shared and all questions and interpretations have been discussed. Then students decide how much to read before the next discussion group meeting and when the group will meet again. Then students disband to write in their reading logs, read the next two or three chapters, and write in their reading logs before meeting together again.

FIGURE 10.20
A Page from a Student's Reading Log

Reading Notes	Discussing Notes
Why does Winnie have to stay with them for a couple of days?	so they can explain about the water
pg. 45 What did Winnie mean when she said she had discovered the wings she wished she had?	Because she finally ran away
pg. 46 What did Tuck mean when he said they brung a real honest-to-goodness natural child?	They drank the water and Winnie didn't
pg. 48 Why did Tuck have a sad look on his face?	
Why was Tuck so happy that Winnie found out about them?	Because they had never told anyone about it

MS. DANIEL'S FOUR-WEEK LESSON PLAN

Ms. Daniel's four-week lesson plan for *Tuck Everlasting* is presented in Figure 10.21. On most days, students are participating in reading workshop and involved in reading the book independently, writing in reading logs, and meeting in discussion groups. During the final week, students spend two days watching the film version of *Tuck Everlasting* and comparing it to the book.

MS. DANIEL'S RECORD-KEEPING AND ASSESSMENT PROCEDURES

Students keep track of their reading workshop activities in their reading logs, and at the end of the book they write letters to Ms. Daniel reflecting on their work, how well they met their own goals, and what they will work on in the next reading workshop. The grades are for participation and effort. Ms. Daniel says, "I try very hard to get out of the competitive mode. I create a safe learning environment and I expect my students to do their best."

Ms. Daniel observes her students as they read, write, and participate in discussion groups, and she writes anecdotal notes about students' behavior, their enthusiasm, and the interpretations and personal connections they share. The following are excerpts from her anecdotal notes:

- Was Winnie kidnapped? Aaron answers, "Yeah, she was when you get right down to it." He asks, "Does Winnie have any brothers or sisters?" "She doesn't? She just lives with her mom, grandma, and her dad?"
- Ellen asked me what Queen Anne's Lace was. I told her what I thought it was, asked if she had looked it up—no—then I asked why she didn't look things up in the dictionary. I'm trying to encourage her.
- Pat asks for her discussion group's predictions about what the man in the yellow suit will do.
- Good discussion today. David asks, "Do you think _____?" several times.
- Darlene and Laura not reading again today. I asked Laura to PLEASE read. She and Darlene came to my desk. Laura showed me where it talked of "Black Magic." "Is this what this book is about?" "No." "It's strange, and I told my mother about this part." "No, this book is not about Black Magic." "Are you sure?" "Yes, I'm sure." "Well, it is strange." Now I know why they haven't been reading! Focused on one statement that they have been taught to avoid. They felt that they were compromising under coercion. Passive resistance.
- Erica is absent. I expect the group to be different today. Probably more people will participate. Sky asks what "willy-nilly" means. Jason looked it up and read it. Daniel read it! Then they looked up "helter skelter." This seems like a waste of time. If I were in the group I would tell them the answer and go on to the story. But is that like the teacher who gets through the entire book regardless of what the kids have learned? They are probably learning more doing it their way.
- Jason knew about "flapjacks." He's had them in restaurants—in his experience. His group didn't trust him; he looked it up, confirmed his answer, and laughed!
- Cathy is filling Erica in on what she missed yesterday. Erica gasped when Cathy told her about hitting the man in the yellow suit in the skull.
- Josh predicts what the man in the yellow suit is going to do. Talking about Tuck shooting himself. They need clarification.
- Daniel told Jeremy to shut up. Laura told Jeremy to shut up. I hate how rude they are to him, but he continues to ask his questions.
- Billy joins the discussion. He was absent so I told him to just read and try to catch up. I walked over to him because he was staring into space. His book was open to Chapter 11. I asked him if he had read that far. He said he had. I asked, "How?" He answered, "I've been reading ahead when I am here." I told him to join the discussion group.

She uses these notes to reflect on students' participation in the groups, group dynamics, and students' interpretation of the book.

FIGURE 10.21
Ms. Daniel's Four-Week Lesson Plan for *Tuck Everlasting* (Babbitt, 1975)

	MONDAY	TUESDAY	WEDNESDAY	THURSDAY	FRIDAY
WEEK 1	• Begin reading *Tuck Everlasting* • Divide class into four lit discussion groups according to reading speed	READING WORKSHOP 1. Independent reading 2. Reading logs 3. Discussion groups	→		
WEEK 2	READING WORKSHOP 1. Independent reading 2. Reading logs 3. Discussion groups	→			
WEEK 3	READING WORKSHOP 1. Independent reading 2. Reading logs 3. Discussion groups	→			
WEEK 4	READING WORKSHOP 1. Independent reading 2. Reading logs 3. Discussion groups	Show film of *Tuck Everlasting*	→	Final discussion group meeting to talk about the film and wrap things up	

REFERENCES

Atwell, N. (1988). *In the middle.* Portsmouth, NH: Heinemann.

CHILDREN'S LITERATURE REFERENCES

Babbitt, N. (1975). *Tuck everlasting.* New York: Farrar, Straus & Giroux.

Blume, J. (1970). *Iggie's house.* New York: Dell.

Danziger, P. (1974). *The cat ate my gymsuit.* New York: Delacorte.

Hinton, S. E. (1967). *The outsiders.* New York: Dell.

Activities for Teaching Ninth-Grade Language Arts   PRESENTATION 11

BROADENING LANGUAGE CONSCIOUSNESS

Whatever your motive for teaching grammar, your goal should be to try to make your students more aware of their language. This is a broader goal than that of grammar instruction; you are attempting to develop an interest in and a consciousness of language. Grammar or usage patterns are a part of this, but there are many other avenues to this destination. Children learn to make generalizations about language based on their varied linguistic experiences. If we can broaden that exposure in English classes to include an awareness of language as an event of psychological, social, and cultural complexity, we might deepen and enrich their consciousness. Such consciousness-raising exercises are in neither the literary tradition of language study nor in the tradition of grammar, rhetoric, and composition. Students, if they have been taught language essentially as tedious literary analysis of another's linguistic virtuosity or as dull grammar drills and rote memorization, may well look on language study as a chore whose goal is to apprehend what outside authorities dictate, rather than as an adventure of recovering their own intuitive knowledge. We would like to redirect them to exploring their own language on the personal, school, community, and global levels. To borrow from Robert MacNeil's account of his own childhood (1989), we want to make them "wordstruck."

Herbert Kohl describes such teaching in his *36 Children* (1967), an account of his experiences as a sixth-grade teacher in Harlem. One day in the midst of Kohl's frustration at not getting through to his class, one student shouted to another, "What's the matter, psyches, going to pieces again?" (p. 23). While the class broke up, he leapt on the word *psyches*. The students assumed it was spelled s-i-k-e-s. Kohl wrote the word on the board and told them the story of Psyche and Cupid. Not satisfied with the story, they wanted to know what happened to the history of the word. Not knowing the etymology and probably not willing to loose their interest, he asked them to think of all the English words that came from *cupid* and *psyche*.

> Leaping ahead, Alvin shouted, "You mean words change? People didn't always speak this way? Then how come the reader says there's a right way to talk and a wrong way?"
>
> "There's a right way now, and that only means that's how most people would like to talk now, and how people write now."
>
> Charles jumped out of his desk and spoke for the first time during the year.
>
> "You mean one day the way we talk—you know, with words like *cool* and *dig* and *sound*—may be all right?"
>
> "Uh huh. Language is alive, it's always changing, only sometimes it changes so slowly that we can't tell."
>
> "Mr. Kohl, can't we study the language we're talking about instead of spelling and grammar? They won't be any good when language changes anyway." (p. 24)

Kohl reports that on that day he began what he called in his plan book "vocabulary" and "an enrichment activity," but what was actually "the study of language and myth, of the origins and histories of words, of their changing uses and functions in human life." His was not a continuous lesson, but "a fixed point in each week's work," a point which sustained and deepened his students' original excitement as they became "word-hungry and concept-hungry" (p. 25).

We believe students at all grade levels and abilities can profit from such a heightened consciousness. Not all are ready to take the most abstract steps toward metacognition, metalinguistic awareness, but all can be encouraged to enter a basic level of investigation. We present the following Teaching Activities arranged in a progression from most concrete to most abstract. These activities engage students in multiple dimensions of language from etymology, dialect, idiom, and syntax to semantic context. Curiosity and openness are the surest approaches to awakening students' delight in our language. In Tabbert's (1984) answer to the question of why teach grammar, we find motive for these final suggestions about language consciousness raising: "True literacy is more than the negative virtue of not making mistakes, and it cannot be attained primarily through analyzing sentences and memorizing rules" (p. 42). These exercises aim to deepen students' "true literacy." (We present the instructional purpose and strategy of these Teaching Activities in enough detail to illustrate our aim, but with the caution that they will need more specific enumeration for classroom use.)

Language Consciousness–Raising Activities
1. Dialects on TV
2. New words of the street
3. Semantics of sex
4. Doublespeak
5. Stress signals of verbs and nouns

TEACHING ACTIVITY

11–1 Dialects on TV

Perera (1990) has reported that the surest way to gain a consciousness of the standard is to inundate a classroom with examples of variants. It makes sense that one clarifies and more fully defines the other. Each student selects five characters from television whose speech is a clear departure from that of the mainstream characters who dominate sitcoms, soap operas, and dramatic productions. When TV Cajun chef Justin Wilson says he likes the red wine because "it look more pretty" or explains "that is what I'm going to did," the regular comparative and the standard future are made more vivid for the interested listener. The array of departures thus weakens the stigma attached to any one variant examined alone. We encourage this exercise because it is so easy to collect and review the wide variety of dialectic expressions seen daily on television.

TEACHING ACTIVITY

11–2 New Words of the Street

Adolescent language provides a dynamic example of language change. Each generation coins words and idioms to secure its own separate identity and to differentiate itself from the adult world. Students identify words used by their peers that are unique to a specific activity or locale. The language of rock music, high school experiences, friendships, gyms, and other special phenomena provides rich possibilities for investigation. (Our own students have usually been more interested in the idioms of other schools, near or distant, than in their own. They learned, for example, that in one local high school "kicked to the curb" means to humiliate or put another person down; in another, ten miles away, the term is "wasted.") Students can also compare their own present speech community with those of just a few years past. Such semantic comparisons vertically through time or horizontally by community can engage students in the shifting vocabulary and connotations of their language.

TEACHING ACTIVITY

11–3 Semantics of Sex

Sociolinguists, such as Tannen (1990), analyze everyday conversation and identify profoundly different ways in which men and women communicate. Students listen to samples of everyday talk and examine the speech of males and females to discern differences of language and perception. They might tape conversations at lunch tables or at any other public place where people are talking freely, or record radio talk shows or television interviews.

Continued

Fictional characters (in print or on film) might also be used. For instance, a comparison might begin with a look at the sentences of John and Lorraine, who alternate as narrators in Zindel's *The Pigman.* Students might also gather examples of gender indicators (like suffixes -*ess* and -*ette*) and other gender-specific designations. Groups and the whole class can then discuss where these distinctions are changing, where they are appropriate and necessary, where they are offensive and detrimental.

11–4 Doublespeak

TEACHING
ACTIVITY

In 1949, George Orwell published the novel *1984,* in which he described "Newspeak," a sanitized form of language that makes heretical thoughts impossible. Language was manipulated to eradicate any thought which opposed the principles espoused by the government. In 1972, the National Council of Teachers of English (NCTE) passed two resolutions concerned with the misuse of language in public discourse and its effect on public policy. Two years later, the council established a committee, the Committee on Public Doublespeak, to enforce those resolutions actively. The committee began in that year to publish a newsletter, now called the *Quarterly Review of Doublespeak,* which lists examples of doublespeak from government, business, and academia. The committee also awards an annual Doublespeak Award for persons or groups who use public language that is "deceptive, evasive, euphemistic, confusing, or self-contradictory" and has potential for "pernicious social or political consequences." In 1975, it established the Orwell Award for Distinguished Contribution to Honesty and Clarity in Public Language. Here are four of the most common kinds of doublespeak, as articulated by William Lutz, the committee chairman:

Euphemisms, words or phrases that soften unpleasant realities, can be used to mislead or deceive, as when the phrase "unlawful or arbitrary deprivation of life" is substituted for "killing."

Jargon, the specialized language of members of a profession, becomes doublespeak when used in addressing (and in fact, confusing) nonmembers. In its annual report to stockholders, an airline explained a three-million-dollar loss due to a plane crash as "the involuntary conversion of a 727."

Bureaucratese refers to the use of a sheer volume of words or complicated syntax to overwhelm audiences. One bureaucrat, testifying before a Senate committee, stated, "It is a tricky problem to find the particular calibration in timing that would be appropriate to stem the acceleration in risk premiums created by falling incomes without prematurely absorbing the decline in the inflation-generated premiums."

Inflated language makes the ordinary seem extraordinary, as when car mechanics are called "automotive internists," or electronics companies describe black-and-white television sets as units with "non-multicolor capability." (as summarized in Dorney, 1988, p. 50, our paragraphing)

Once students are sensitized to our misuse of language in these and other ways (such as obfuscation and oversimplification), they can readily join in numerous data-gathering ventures. Examples surround them. Students gather examples of doublespeak—words, phrases, slogans, sentences—from advertising, public statements, and their private lives. (Prime their interest with examples of your own. For instance, White House spokespersons sometimes have called previous announcements not "false," but "no longer operative." The NCTE newsletter is a goldmine of detail.) The class in small or large groups compares samples and analyzes how they manipulate language to conceal or distort. The class might even wish to give its own Doublespeak Award. Humpty Dumpty rightly suggested the stakes in the use of language: power. In *Through the Looking Glass,* Carroll wrote:

"When I use a word," Humpty Dumpty said, in a rather scornful tone, "it means just what I choose it to mean—neither more nor less."

"The question is," said Alice, "whether you can make words mean so many different things."

"The question is," said Humpty Dumpty, "which is to be master—that's all."

Recognizing word manipulation will feel and *be* empowering to students. They may come to recognize the truth of C. J. Ducasse's observation: "To speak of 'mere words' is much like speaking of 'mere dynamite.' "

11–5 Stress Signals of Verbs and Nouns

Stress is not recognized as a significant feature of the English language. For the Chinese language, four different stress patterns of a syllable change the meaning of the sound symbol. In English, though at a much less obvious level, stress has importance, as looking at such words as *record* or *object* immediately illustrates. When students are asked to identify the meaning of such words, they are unable to be precise without hearing them used in a sentence. When the sentence is "We record the errors," they know "re córd" is a verb meaning to note, but if the sentence were "Play another Chuck Berry record" they would know "réc ord" refers to a round disk. With "ob ject" we have the verb to take issue with. The word "ób ject" is the noun referring to a thing. (In one-syllable words that work as nouns and verbs, such as *hit*, the success, and *hit*, to strike, such stress differences are hard to detect, but they exist.) Let students work in groups of three or four to make lists of all of the words that they can recall where the noun and verb are set apart in pronunciation by the use of stress. Let them compare their group lists and compile a class list. Collect newspaper and magazine headlines for examples of these confusions. Such confusions can have practical consequences. (The exercise not only sharpens the awareness of the importance of stress, but can be quite humorous as well.) Students could create their own ambiguous headlines. They might also gather a list of British pronunciations that are the same as American, but for stress. Students might find it interesting to note (record) some of these words and look for a stress pattern that separates the two versions of English or simply the pattern of noun and verb stress. If you have interested and able students you might ask them to investigate the age of acquisition of such awareness of stress patterns. Students might make a simple oral test for third-grade children and for adults over 30 to see if there is a difference between the two groups in their understanding of the effect of stress on verbs and nouns.

Whitworth (1991) suggests excellent tested language activities based on the text and the spirit of S. I. Hayakawa's classic *Language in Thought and Action* (1978). Whitworth divides his activities into "four traditional areas of general semantics: (1) language as a symbolic process; (2) the meaning of words in context; (3) referential [informative or factual] and emotive language; (4) relationships between language and thinking" (p. 50). He encourages teachers to allow students to "tinker with instructions" so that they can both envision more "fruitful ideas" and feel the pride and ownership in doing so. His list is arranged by progressive steps for those with "low language skills to those with complex language talents" (pp. 50–54).

Language as a Symbolic Process

1. Browse through Henry Dreyfuss's *Symbol Sourcebook: An Authoritative Guide to International Graphic Symbols* (1984). Discuss some of the unusual symbols such as hobo symbols, recreational signs, or semaphore signals. Or have students collect sporting symbols (very appropriate before the Olympics) and then have them create their own symbols for places and events around the school.

2. Describe the body language of a person engaged in a telephone conversation that you cannot hear. Speculate on the gist of the content. What kinds of human behavior are displayed? Or tape a segment of a soap opera or sitcom. With the sound turned off, have students "read" the body language; then replay the tape with the sound on to verify student guesses.

Meaning of Words in Context

1. Write a definition of *restaurant, theater,* or *cabin.* Compare the definitions to discover which attributes the group agrees upon and which are derived from personal experiences and biases.

2. Research quotes from reviewers for inaccuracies and intentional misleading statements in movie ads or on the flipside of paperbacks, especially those highly praised ones with suspicious omissions by use of ellipses. For example, one newspaper movie ad reviewer's quote—"Magnificent! . . . Made me cry!"—sounds like a winner, but the reviewer really wrote: "How can a director turn such a magnificent novel into such a

stinker of a movie? What they've done to it almost made me cry!" Once students get the idea, have them find really rotten reviews and turn them into positive statements with the use of ellipses.

3. Tape class discussions or alert students to note situations where the meaning of the words comes not through direct context but indirectly through "reading between the lines" of the context. Examples: "I know this sounds stupid, but . . . " or "This is just off the top of my head . . . " The intent of these disclaimers is often to soften criticism if it should occur.

How many of the following nonquestion questions have occurred in your classrooms: "Are we doing anything in here today?" "Is this movie any good?" "Is there extra credit in this class?" "Isn't this grammar stuff stupid?" Why are such nonquestions raised in class?

Referential (Informative/Factual) and Emotive Language

1. After a basketball game with a rival town's team, compare the local newspaper's writeup of the game with that of the newspaper from the rival town. What language variations are found in the two stories?

2. Create a computer data base of euphemisms and circumlocutions found in television commercials or political campaigns. Divide the entries into *softeners,* those which remove the harsh edge of reality, and *impressors,* fancy words for ordinary facts. Or use William Lutz's (1989) categories: euphemism, jargon, gobbledygook, and inflated language.

3. Play the old Bertrand Russell game of Conjugating the Irregular Verb (e.g., "I am fastidious; you are fussy; he is an old fuddyduddy" or the reverse: "He is broke; you are in debt; I am temporarily overextended") to show that although the basic meaning of the pivotal word remains the same, the value judgment does change. Bias often creeps into the language by our being very selective of words. The thesaurus often helps students to play the game effectively.

Relationships between Language and Thinking (Analyzing, Synthesizing, Inferring, and Evaluating)

1. Collect contradictory folk proverbs (such as "Two heads are better than one" and "Too many cooks spoil the broth" or "He who hesitates is lost" and "Look before you leap"). Can the contradictions be reconciled?

2. Using the tabloids, present a series of articles that seemingly prove a generalization (e.g., children of movie stars are wild; the rich and powerful are really miserable). Show how the generalization may be faulty.

If you are sensitive to your students and alert to the universe of language in which they operate, you will devise other innovative activities. Keep in mind Thomas's sense of a basic obligation of English teachers, "to keep language alive" and the common dicta: Seize the teachable moment.

REFERENCES

Dorney, J. M. (1988). *The plain English movement.* English Journal, 77 (3), 49–51.

Dreyfuss, H. (1984). *Symbol Sourcebook: An authoritative guide to international graphic symbols.* New York: Van Rostran Reinhold.

Hayakawa, S. I. (1978). *Language in thought and action* (4th ed.) . New York: Harcourt Brace Jovanovich.

Kohl, H. (1967). *36 Children.* New York: New American Library.

Lutz, W. (1989). *Doublespeak.* New York: Harper.

MacNeil, R. (1989). *Wordstruck: A memoir.* New York: Viking.

Perera, C. (1990). *Divergence and convergence in English: A creative tension?* Paper presented at the International Federation of Teachers of English, 5th International Congress, Auckland, NZ, August 26.

Tabbert, R. (1984). Raising the question "Why teach grammer?" *English Journal, 73* (8), 38–42.

Tannen, D. (1990). *You just don't understand: Women and men in conversation.* New York: Ballantine.

Whitworth, R. (1991). A book for all occasions: Activities for teaching general semantics. *English Journal, 80*(2), 50–54.

PART

III

Methods and Activities for Social Studies

In the social studies, what is presented by the teacher or in the textbook as public and agreed-upon knowledge or beliefs, is received by the student and given meaning in terms of his or her past experience and cognitive capabilities or structures.
—J. Torney-Turta

As we have said, to many educators it is clear that to be most effective in teaching the diversity of children in today's classrooms, the learning in each discipline must be integrated with the learning in other disciplines, and thus made more meaningful to the lives of the children.

Furthermore, for higher levels of thinking and for learning that is most meaningful, recent research supports the use of an integrated curriculum and instructional techniques for social interaction. Your instructional task is twofold: (1) to plan for and provide developmentally appropriate hands-on experiences, with useful materials and the supportive environment necessary for children's meaningful exploration and discovery; and (2) to know how to facilitate the most meaningful and longest lasting learning possible once the child's mind has been activated by the hands-on experience.

The beginning chapters of Part III (Chapters 11–13) provide a basis for your understanding of social studies and the social studies curriculum that is developmentally appropriate for children in intermediate and middle school grades. Chapters 14–17 then provide useful examples of instructional strategies that are appropriate for use with the children and will facilitate their developing understanding of social studies concepts and skills, particularly as related to other disciplines.

Specifically, in Chapter 11, author Peter Martorella provides a historical perspective for the origin and evolution of today's working definition of the social studies, a clear description of the primary goal of social studies education, and characteristics of exemplary social studies teachers. Then, in Chapter 12, building upon content presented in Part I, Martorella guides your understanding of how students learn social studies, of the disciplines included under the umbrella of social studies, and of valuable resources to compliment your social studies instruction. In Chapter 13, Martorella provides a clear description of the scope and sequence patterns in the social studies curriculum and of factors that affect that curriculum. In Chapters 14 and 15, Martorella provides guidance for the development of specific social studies skills relevant to teaching children in the intermediate and middle school grades.

Part II ends with two chapters by John Jarolimek and Walter C. Parker (Chapters 16 and 17), who provide specific recommendations and activities for integrating social studies with other disciplines in the curriculum. ■

CHAPTER 14
Fostering Citizenship
Competency: Developing
and Applying Research
and Analysis, Chronology,
and Spatial Skills.
*This chapter is adapted from
Peter H. Martorella,* Social
Studies for Elementary
School Children: Developing
Young Citizens *(New York:
Macmillan, 1994), pp.
179–216, and from Peter H.
Martorella,* Teaching Social
Studies in Middle and
Secondary Schools *(New
York: Macmillan, 1991), pp.
175–190. By permission of
Peter H. Martorella and the
Macmillan Publishing
Company.*

CHAPTER 15
Promoting Reflective
Inquiry: Developing and
Applying Concepts,
Generalizations, and
Hypotheses
*This chapter is adapted from
Peter H. Martorella,* Social
Studies for Elementary
School Children: Developing
Young Citizens *(New York:
Macmillan, 1994), pp.
143–176, and from Peter H.
Martorella,* Teaching Social
Studies in Middle and
Secondary Schools *(New
York: Macmillan, 1991), pp.
147–150. By permission of
Peter H. Martorella and the
Macmillan Publishing
Company.*

CHAPTER 16
Social Studies as the
Integrating Core: Literacy,
Literature, and Culture
*This chapter is adapted from
John Jarolimek and Walter
C. Parker,* Social Studies in
Elementary Education, *9th
ed. (New York: Macmillan,
1993), pp. 143–176. By per-
mission of John Jarolimek,
Walter C. Parker, and the
Macmillan Publishing
Company.*

CHAPTER 17
Learner Involvement
through Activities
*This chapter is adapted from
John Jarolimek and Walter
C. Parker,* Social Studies in
Elementary Education, *9th
ed. (New York: Macmillan,
1993), pp. 421–447. By per-
mission of John Jarolimek,
Walter C. Parker, and the
Macmillan Publishing
Company.*

CHAPTER 11

The Social Studies

Picture a little girl, Sarah, age 9. She is about to enter your fourth-grade class on the first day of school. You, the school, and the students will be a new experience for Sarah.

What does Sarah look like? Does she live in an urban, suburban, or rural area? Is her habitat a room, an apartment, a house, or a homeless shelter? Is English her first or second language? What type of family structure does she have—does it include one or more parents and other siblings? What knowledge does she bring with her? What are her dreams and fears? When she arrives at your classroom, will she be nourished, self-confident, and eager to learn? What will her day be like when she leaves the school at 3:00?

Sarah is Everychild. She represents the countless variables that effective teachers thoughtfully consider in providing nurturing and personalized learning experiences for millions of youngsters across our nation. She also embodies our aspirations for a better world and a society in which all children can reach their full potential. Within Everychild are the seeds of our nation's future.

One significant component of Everychild's increasingly complex needs intersects with the social studies curriculum. Everychild is a developing citizen who, we hope, someday will be a fellow voter and partner in civic activities. She also may be an elected official. If the social studies program is to help prepare children for roles such as these and others, it must provide ongoing opportunities to engage in social discourse and decision making. In the process, it must portray authentic events, people, and issues embedded in rich contextual frameworks. It also must supply Everychild with the models and analytical tools to help construct a fulfilling and contributing civic career.

This chapter will help you understand

1. The origins and evolution of the social studies.
2. Alternative definitions and a working definition of the social studies.
3. The context of citizenship education.
4. The enduring goal of the social studies curriculum.
5. Some characteristics of the exemplary social studies teacher.

A. THE ORIGINS AND EVOLUTION OF THE SOCIAL STUDIES

What are the origins of the social studies? In the early history of our nation, the social studies curriculum drew heavily on the areas of history, geography, and civics. The term *social studies,* according to Saxe (1991, 1992), became the official designator for the curriculum in the late nineteenth and early twentieth centuries. It came into use as an outgrowth of the writings of Sarah Bolton, Lady Jane Wilde, Heber Newton, and, later, Thomas Jesse Jones. Saxe (1991) noted: "From Newton and Jones we find that the initial use and sharpening of the term 'social studies' was directly tied to the utilization of social science data as a force in the improvement of human welfare" (p. 17).

Jones later served as a member of a group known as the Committee on the Social Studies. The committee, comprised of 21 members representing different social science disciplines and different levels of professional education, had been appointed by the National Education Association in 1912. Its charge was to make recommendations concerning the reorganization of the secondary curriculum.

The 1916 Report of the Committee on the Social Studies

The final report of the Committee, issued in 1916, was called by Hertzberg (1981) "probably the most influential in the history of the social studies" (p. 2). One social studies educator, Engle (1976), credited the committee's report with setting the general direction of the field from that time forward.

The 1916 report defined the social studies as "those whose subject matter relates directly to the organization and development of human society, and to man as a member of social groups" (U.S. Bureau of Education, 1916, p. 9). It also laid out the broad goals for the social studies, the cultivation of the "good citizen." In addition the report sketched some guidelines for the curriculum and touched on a variety of other issues, including the preparation of teachers and text materials.

Although the report looked to the social sciences as the primary sources of enlightenment for the preparation of the good citizen, the high ideals the report embodied clearly required a broader base of subject matter. For example, it asserted, "The social studies should cultivate a sense of membership in the 'world community,' with all the sympathies and sense of justice that this involves among the different divisions of human society" (U.S. Bureau of Education, 1916, p. 9).

Legacy of the 1916 report. Among other things, the 1916 report reflected the diversity of disciplines that individuals on the committee represented, the dominant perspective being that of history. It also reflected the emergence of the behavioral sciences and the growth of professional associations. Additionally it represented the flowering of progressivism and the apprehension of a nation on the brink of a world war (Hertzberg, 1981). The report became the touchstone for conceptions of what the social studies curriculum should be for the next seven decades, transcending the dramatic shifts in the nation and the world during that period.

The report also gave impetus to the rise, in 1921, of the first professional organization devoted to the concerns of social studies teachers, the National Council for the Social Studies (NCSS). Sixteen years later, the NCSS would publish the first professional journal for social studies teachers: *Social Education.* More than a half-century later, in 1988, it would publish a second journal, devoted to the elementary grades: *Social Studies and the Young Learner.*

A major legacy of the 1916 report is a festering debate that continues to the present, concerning both the nature of the social studies and the subject's relationship to the social sciences. The first sentence of *Defining the Social Studies,* written in 1977, captures the flavor of contemporary debates and analyses: "The field of social studies is so caught up in ambiguity, inconsistency, and contradiction that it represents a complex educational enigma. It has also defied any final definition acceptable to all factions of the field" (Barr, Barth, & Shermis, 1977, p. 1). In exasperation Barr and his colleagues concluded, "If the social studies is what the scholars in the field say it is, it is a schizophrenic bastard child" (p. 1).

The New Social Studies

During the era of the cold war, the Soviet Union, in the 1950s, ushered in the era of space exploration with its launching of *Sputnik.* It also initiated an intense and extensive re-assessment of the American educational system. If the Soviets had beaten the United States into space, conventional wisdom said, then something must be wrong with our schools and their curricula.

First, the science and mathematics, and later the foreign language curricula, came under intense scrutiny. In response the federal government sponsored a wave of reforms aimed at improving the curricula of the schools. By the mid-1960s the social studies also were drawn under the umbrella of reform. From that point forward, through the early years of the 1970s, the social studies would witness an unprecedented period of innovation in both the development of curricular materials and related teacher education efforts.

The fruits of this period became known as "the new social studies." The efforts at innovation were fueled primarily with funds from the federal government and private foundations. Ultimately commercial publishers would underwrite the final stages of development and publication of some of the curricular products. Haas (1977), who was involved directly in the evolution of the new social studies, wrote of the period, "If measured by sheer output of materials, the period 1964 to 1972 is unequaled in the history of social studies education in this country" (p. 61).

Driving the new social studies were more than 50 major projects (Fenton, 1967) and scores of minor ones touching every grade level (Haas, 1977). The projects were scattered throughout the nation in different centers. A firsthand observer of many of these projects and the director of a history project at Carnegie Mellon University, Fenton (1967, p. 4), wrote of them:

> They are organized in a variety of ways: one or two professors in a university run most of them; organizations of scholars such as the American Anthropological Association administer a few; others are run by school systems, groups of schools or universities, or independent non-profit corporations . . . some projects aim to turn out a single course for a single dicipline [sic], such as a course in tenth-grade geography; others are preparing units of material—anthropology, sociology, economics—which can fit into existing course structures; still others propose to develop entire curriculum sequences or to isolate the principles upon which curricula can be built.

Included in the new social studies were projects for the primary, intermediate, and middle grades, such as:

- Man: A Course of Study (MACOS)
- Social Science Laboratory Units
- The University of Georgia Geography Curriculum Project
- The University of Georgia Anthropology Curriculum Project
- The University of Minnesota Project Social Studies, K–12.

Many of the projects were based on the seminal ideas in a slender volume, *The Process of Education,* written by the psychologist Jerome Bruner (1960). Particularly appealing to social studies educators were Bruner's ideas concerning the structure of the disciplines and discovery modes of learning. Bruner himself was extensively involved in MACOS, a middle-grades curriculum that integrated the disciplines of anthropology and biology to help children discover the similarities in and differences between humans and animals.

Legacy of the new social studies. Despite the concerted efforts at curricular reform, the new social studies projects collectively failed to affect significantly the scope and sequence patterns of the social studies curriculum across the United States (Fancett & Hawke, 1982; Haas, 1977, 1986). By some accounts, the projects had no significant impact on teaching practices either (Shaver, Davis, & Hepburn, 1979; Superka, Hawke, & Morrissett, 1980).

How can we account for this? Lockwood (1985) suggested three basic reasons why, in his estimation, the new social studies had limited lasting effects: (a) Teachers perceived that adoption of the innovations would have required major changes in the scope and sequence of existing curricula and teaching practices, (b) the reading levels of the new social studies materials were too advanced, and (c) students lacked the intellectual capacities required to use the materials. Massialas (1992) argued that the new social studies lacked a research base and that projects failed to adequately address issues such as gender and ethnicity (see also Fenton, 1991; Rossi, 1992).

There is evidence, however, that the new social studies did have some significant sporadic effects. The new social studies, for example, gave rise to a larger role for the emerging social sciences. Similarly, although the new social studies failed to shake the dominance of the textbook as the primary instrument of instruction, it did stimulate the use of commercial and teacher-made supplementary materials. Further, it encouraged the use of media in teaching.

Although the new social studies did not loosen substantially the grip of teacher-centered approaches, it did open the door for a more active role for students and for greater consideration of their concerns in the curriculum. It also increased the use of instructional strategies that emphasized students' inquiry in the learning process, presaging later constructivist arguments for greater engagement of students in the learning process. The new social studies also helped establish the principle that affective concerns relating to significant beliefs, attitudes, and values should have a place in social studies classes.

Social Studies in the 1980s and 1990s

In contrast to the excitement of the new social studies era, the 1980s were a period of reaction and soul searching for the social studies. One author summed up the decade with the following metaphor:

> It can be argued that the 1980's must be the adolescent period for social studies as social studies educators, through their journals and in dialogue at national and regional meetings, are diligently seeking consensus on definition and purpose, as well as agreement on scope and sequence. At this point it is unclear how long the adolescent period will last for social studies. (Atwood, 1982, p. 10)

As the 1980s drew to a close, the social studies were awash with alternative scope and sequence curriculum proposals. These offered new options for social studies educators and text publishers to consider in modifying programs and materials. In Chapter 12 we examine in detail a cross section of these initiatives and the forces that gave rise to them.

As we approach the last half of the 1990s, the future is still largely uncharted for the social studies (e.g., see Finkelstein, Nielsen, & Switzer, 1993). In part this phenomenon reflects the historic economic, political, and social upheavals the world has experienced in recent years. It also represents the shifts in our society from a national to a global perspective and the emergence of new notions of what will be required of effective citizens in an increasingly interdependent and culturally diverse world.

B. ALTERNATIVE DEFINITIONS OF THE SOCIAL STUDIES

As noted, social studies educators have waged a vigorous debate over the nature of their field. From the time that the term *social studies* came into popular use, through the era of the new social studies, and into the current decade, many have attempted, unsuccessfully, to set out a definition of the field that would embrace all of the disparate views. Consider the following examples:

> The social studies are the social sciences simplified for pedagogical purposes. (Wesley, 1950, p. 34)

> Social studies is the integrated study of the social sciences and humanities to promote civic competence. (National Council for the Social Studies [NCSS], 1993, p. 3)

> The social studies are concerned exclusively with the education of citizens. In a democracy, citizenship education consists of two related but somewhat disparate parts: the first socialization, the second countersocialization. (Engle & Ochoa, 1988, p. 13)

The social studies is an integration of experience and knowledge concerning human relations for the purpose of citizenship education. (Barr et al., 1977, p. 69)

Social studies is a basic subject of the K–12 curriculum that (1) derives its goals from the nature of citizenship in a democratic society that is closely linked to other nations and peoples of the world; (2) draws its content primarily from history, the social sciences, and, in some respects, from the humanities and science; and (3) is taught in ways that reflect an awareness of the personal, social, and cultural experiences and developmental levels of learners. (Task Force on Scope and Sequence, 1984, p. 251)

Consider also one fifth grader's attempt to define the social studies:

Social studies is the hardest thing you could ever ask me to explain. I guess social studies is a class where you learn about different things that happen around the world, and do reports on stuff that happens around the world, or things like that. (Stodolsky, Salk, & Glaessner, 1991, p. 98)

None of these definitions or any others proposed have attracted a consensus. As Lybarger (1991) underscored, "One of the most remarkable aspects of the history of the social studies has been the ongoing debates over the nature, scope, and definition of the field" (p. 9).

A Working Definition of the Social Studies

As a point of reference, I use a working definition of the social studies. It is consistent with the purposes of the social studies curriculum that are advocated later in the chapter.

The social studies are:

selected information and modes of investigation from the social sciences,

selected information from any area that relates directly to an understanding of individuals, groups, and societies, and

applications of the selected information to citizenship education.

C. SOCIAL STUDIES AND CITIZENSHIP EDUCATION

Many of the definitions that have been proposed over the years, including mine, point toward the historic linkage of the social studies to *citizenship education*. To function, even nominally, all societies must engage in some form of citizenship education. Those entrusted with the formal responsibilities for the maintenance, defense, and improvement of the society depend on some degree of citizen participation so that social, political, and economic institutions can operate.

What we now regard as social studies came to be seen as the subject that would teach students about our nation's history, traditions, achievements, and aspirations. It also was to prepare them for responsibly exercising their rights and duties as citizens. Today, as in the past, we expect the social studies curriculum to continue its historic mission of preparing young people for their roles as effective citizens.

The Context of Citizenship Education

Citizenship education in our society occurs in many forms, both outside and inside the schools. Institutions external to the school, including those of the mass media, increasingly have assumed a larger role in the process. Advertisements, for example, on billboards and book covers urge students to serve their country in the military, to use condoms to prevent social epidemics, and to protect the environment. Political action groups, representing every shade of the political spectrum and fueled by tax exemptions and contributions, now loom as a major force in both the political and educational process.

Citizenship education also takes place informally through the "hidden" curriculum: the policies, mores, activities, rules, norms, and models that the school provides. Within the classroom itself, civic education has several dimensions, as Oppenheim and Torney (1974) reminded us:

Civic education does not merely consist in the transmission of a body of *knowledge*, . . . it aims at inculcating certain shared *attitudes* and values, such as a democratic outlook, political responsibility, the ideals of tolerance and social justice, respect for authority, and so on. . . . Indeed, the cognitive content of the curriculum is frequently used in order to highlight the underlying principles and ideology; thus, information about electoral systems could be utilized in order to bring out fundamental ideas about equality and majority rule. (p. 13)

D. ALTERNATIVE PERSPECTIVES ON CITIZENSHIP EDUCATION

Social studies educators generally agree that citizenship education should be the major focus of the social studies curriculum (Martorella, 1991). Beyond this general area of agreement, however, are disagreements regarding which specific purpose the curriculum should serve as a way to promote citizenship education. I characterize these different views as alternative perspectives on citizenship education.

A related debate continues over the characteristics of the ideal, or "good," citizen, who is the object of the social studies curriculum. In our discussions I use the term *effective citizen* to refer to this idealized type.

Classifying Alternative Perspectives

Barr et al. (1977) analyzed and attempted to categorize the statements of purposes related to citizenship education that various social studies educators have advanced in the twentieth century. From their investigation, the authors created three categories into which they grouped all approaches to citizenship education—social studies taught as (a) *transmission of the cultural heritage,* (b) *the social sciences,* and (c) *reflective inquiry.*

Further analyses by Engle (1977) and Nelson and Michaelis (1980) suggested two additional categories of approaches—social studies taught as (d) *informed social criticism,* and (e) *personal development.* These major perspectives on citizenship education and their respective emphases are summarized briefly in Figure 11.1.

These five perspectives certainly do not exhaust all of the possible classifications. Furthermore none of the alternative categories that have been outlined completely avoid overlap among the others. Often one category, when analyzed and discussed, appears to include all other categories of purposes. Teaching social studies as social criticism, for example, may at times include teaching for reflective inquiry.

Nevertheless it may be helpful to clarify your own view by considering some of the emphases or dominant perspectives that each statement of purpose reflects. As you do this, you may wish to borrow elements of several categories to create a new composite category of your own.

E. THE ENDURING GOAL OF THE SOCIAL STUDIES CURRICULUM: REFLECTIVE, COMPETENT, AND CONCERNED CITIZENS

Frequently arguments over the purpose of the social studies cannot be categorized easily into one of the five perspectives shown in Figure 11.1. For example, the NCSS (NCSS, 1993) has

FIGURE 11.1

Alternative Perspectives on Citizenship Education

Perspective *Social studies should be taught as:*	Description *Citizenship education should consist of:*
Transmission of the Cultural Heritage	Transmitting traditional knowledge and values as a framework for making decisions
Social Science	Mastering social science concepts, generalizations, and processes to build a knowledge base for later learning
Reflective Inquiry	Employing a process of thinking and learning in which knowledge is derived from what citizens need to know in order to make decisions and solve problems
Informed Social Criticism	Providing opportunites for an examination, critique, and revision of past traditions, existing social practices, and modes of problem solving
Personal Development	Developing a positive self-concept, and a strong sense of personal efficacy

endorsed the following view: "The primary purpose of social studies is to help young people develop the ability to make informed and reasoned decisions for the public good as citizens of a culturally diverse, democratic society in an interdependent world" (p. 3).

Similarly my position does not match neatly with any one of the five perspectives, although it draws on several of them. My perspective borrows heavily from the tradition of *reflective inquiry* as developed in the works of Dewey (1933), Engle (1977), Griffin (1992), Hullfish and Smith (1961), and Hunt and Metcalf (1968).

It also includes an emphasis on learning to be an informed and responsible social critic of society, as described by Engle and Ochoa (1988). Additionally the perspective reflects the influence of recent research in the field of cognitive psychology that addresses how individuals construct, integrate, retrieve, and apply knowledge.

The Nature of the Effective Citizen

The effective young citizens that such a perspective seeks to develop require a three-dimensional social studies program: one that emphasizes rationality, skillful behavior, and social consciousness. Further, such a program must cast citizen roles within the framework of a democratic society and its corresponding continuing needs for maintenance, nurturance, and renewal.

The young citizens who emerge from such a program, I will characterize as reflective, competent, and concerned citizens. I propose that reflection, competence, and concern, in some form, can be nurtured at all levels, from the primary through the intermediate and middle grades. Correspondingly, I argue that the basic purpose of the social studies curriculum across the grades is to develop reflective, competent, and concerned citizens.

Reflective individuals are critical thinkers who make decisions and solve problems on the basis of the best evidence available. *Competent* citizens possess a repertoire of skills to aid them in decision making and problem solving. *Concerned* citizens investigate their social world, address issues they identify as significant, exercise their rights, and carry out their responsibilities as members of a social community.

Social studies as a matter of the head, the hand, and the heart. Identify planning and curriculum that seek to develop the three dimensions of the reflective, competent, and concerned citizen by way of a simple metaphor: social studies as a matter of the head, the hand, and the heart. The head represents reflection; the hand, competencies (skills); and the heart, concern. The characteristics of the reflective, competent, and concerned citizen are summarized in Figure 11.2.

The interrelationship of the head, the hand, and the heart. Thinking, skillful action, and feeling are intertwined. No one of the three dimensions operates in isolation of the

---

FIGURE 11.2
The Reflective, Competent, and Concerned Citizen

Social Studies as a Matter of the Head: Reflection

The *reflective* citizen has knowledge of a body of concepts, facts, and generalizations concerning the organization, understanding, and development of individuals, groups, and societies. Also, the reflective citizen can engage in hypothesis formation and testing, problem solving, and decision making.

Social Studies as a Matter of the Hand: Competence

The *competent* citizen has a repertoire of skills. These include social, research and analysis, chronology, and spatial skills.

Social Studies as a Matter of the Heart: Concern

The *concerned* citizen has an awareness of his or her rights and responsibilities in a democracy, a sense of social consciousness, and a well-grounded framework for deciding what is right and what is wrong and for acting on decisions. Additionally, the concerned citizen has learned how to identify and analyze issues and to suspend judgment concerning alternative beliefs, attitudes, values, customs, and cultures.

other. The head, the hand, and the heart are interrelated and work in concert. Reflective citizens are responsive to what their heart dictates and apply their store of knowledge and competencies to make a decision and act on it.

The relationship between head, hand, and heart often is not systematic or linear. William, a fourth grader watching the news on television, may learn that thousands of workers at an auto plant have just lost their jobs, causing a rise in unemployment. As a result, he asks his mother why the layoffs occurred and what will happen to the employees. After their discussion, his level of social consciousness and concern is aroused. He begins to understand the relationship between the canned goods he took to church for a Thanksgiving basket and the potential economic consequences of losing a job.

The sequence of economic analysis, however, just as easily might have begun more dramatically as a matter of the heart. Suppose, for example, that William's mother lost her job and the family was evicted because it was unable to pay its rent.

Social studies programs should offer students a balance of activities and subject matter for growth in the three areas of reflection, competence, and concern. The relative proportions of time paid to matters of the head or the hand or the heart may vary according to the level of the grade, the abilities and needs of the students, and the current needs of society. A teacher may decide, for example, that the hand should receive more weight in the social studies curriculum in the lower grades and less in later years. Some attention to all three dimensions across the grades, however, is necessary for a balanced social studies program.

F. THE EXEMPLARY SOCIAL STUDIES TEACHER

What would a profile of an exemplary social studies teacher look like? What instructional strategies do exemplary teachers use? How do they engage students in meaningful learning?

One way to try to answer this question is to observe teachers recognized as exemplary and to note what they do. Brophy (1992) shared his observations from a detailed case study of one fifth-grade social studies teacher, who was given the pseudonym "Mrs. Lake." She organized the year's social studies curriculum around seven units, covering the period through the Civil War. Among her goals, Mrs. Lake wishes students to enjoy school, to experience success, and to apply what they learn. Within the framework of United States history, she hopes her students will acquire knowledge of conditions in the past and how our country developed.

As you read excerpts of Brophy's rich account, focus on what you regard as Mrs. Lake's exemplary characteristics.

> She wants her students to enjoy school and feel successful there, and she also wants them to understand, appreciate, and be able to apply what they are learning. . . . Instead of a text, she uses her own lecturing and storytelling as the basic source of input to her students. . . .
>
> Mrs. Lake is a talented storyteller, and much of the initial information that students receive about historical events comes in the form of dramatic readings from historical literature (i.e., children's trade books, not texts). Much of the rest comes in the form of storytelling or explanations backed by photos, artifacts, or other props. . . .
>
> Mrs. Lake begins the year by engaging [students] in developing information about their own personal histories. She has them interview their parents or other family members and collect artifacts and source materials (birth certificates, newspaper or almanac information on what was happening in the world on the day they were born, mementos marking events in their lives). . . .
>
> A time line describing and illustrating some of the salient events in U.S. history extends across most of the front wall of the classroom, above the chalkboard. Mrs. Lake refers to this time line periodically, especially when beginning and ending units, to help students keep track of where the current topic fits within the big picture. Similarly she refers to maps frequently to provide geographical orientation.
>
> In connection with her reading and storytelling, Mrs. Lake uses repetition, visual aids, and story mapping techniques to help students remember main themes. She emphasizes key ideas when telling stories and repeats them several times in review and follow-up activities. She posts key words (organized within "people," "places," and "events" columns) on a special social studies unit display as they are introduced, and they remain displayed throughout the rest of the unit. (pp. 147–149)

As Brophy (1992) acknowledged, Mrs. Lake's teaching lacks some dimensions that would be desirable. For example, there is an absence of student engagement in the analysis of social issues. At the same time, clearly her teaching reveals many exemplary qualities for other teachers to emulate.

Characteristics of Exemplary Social Studies Teachers

In analyzing Mrs. Lake's teaching, Brophy cataloged a number of her exemplary qualities and capabilities. Building on his foundation and adding items, let us consider a broader set of characteristics that I have hypothesized and organized into two broad categories: planning characteristics and instructional characteristics.

Planning Characteristics
Exemplary social studies teachers:
1. Have clearly formulated goals, objectives, and purposes.
2. Have acquired a well-grounded knowledge base related to the social studies curriculum.
3. Select subject matter and activities that will interest and challenge students and intersect with meaningful aspects of their lives.
4. Emphasize the coverage of a small number of topics and key ideas in depth, rather than a superficial coverage of many.
5. Strike a balance in the curriculum among reflection, competence, and concern.
6. Identify a variety of instructional resources.
7. Incorporate authentic ways to assess what students have learned.
8. Provide adequate time for social studies instruction.

Instructional Characteristics
Exemplary social studies teachers:

1. Relate new knowledge to students' existing social knowledge structures.
2. Engage students in the analysis of important social issues, values, and ethical concerns.
3. Present students with intriguing questions, puzzles, and anomalies as a way to engage them in investigating social data.
4. Afford students frequent opportunities to engage actively in constructing and applying social knowledge.
5. Develop skills in the context of solving problems or answering questions.
6. Emphasize relationships among ideas, people, places, and events.
7. Provide frequent opportunities for students to work cooperatively in small groups, developing ideas and engaging in social interaction.
8. Encourage students' oral and written communications relating to social data.

This is just one list of exemplary qualities; others have offered related suggestions (e.g., Engle & Ochoa, 1988; NCSS, 1988; Torney-Purta, 1991). You may wish to add other characteristics.

SUMMARY

This chapter has provided you with a working knowledge of the origins and evolution of the social studies, alternative definitions and a working definition of the social studies, the context of citizenship education, and the enduring goal of the social studies curriculum—reflective, competent, and concerned citizens. In addition, it has provided a list of some characteristics of the exemplary social studies teacher.

Chapters that follow will provide a detailed understanding of the social studies curriculum, how to teach it, and how to integrate it into the curriculum.

QUESTIONS AND ACTIVITIES FOR DISCUSSION

1. Discuss your recollections of social studies when you were in the elementary and middle grades. Are they pleasant or unpleasant?

2. Refer to the issues of the last two years of the following professional journals: *The Social Studies, Social Education,* and *Social Studies and the Young Learner.* Read from each of two journals two articles that interest you. Be prepared to discuss the essence of the articles and the reasons they interested you.

3. Select five individuals for an interview. Ask them to answer this question: What are the characteristics of a good citizen? Summarize the similarities and differences in the answers. Then state your own answer in a sentence or two.

4. Consider the various perspectives on citizenship education discussed in the chapter. Formulate your own position. State the reasons for the position that you have taken.

5. How much time should be devoted to learning social studies in the intermediate grades? The middle school grades? What is the rationale for the position you have taken?

6. Consider the list of characteristics of the exemplary social studies teacher. Would you add or delete any characteristics? Which do you consider to be the most important and why?

7. After consulting the References, locate a copy or a description of a curriculum project for the intermediate or middle school grades that was developed during the period of the "new social studies." Note which characteristics of the project you find especially appealing and which you regard as weaknesses.

8. Locate your state's guidelines for the teaching of social studies in the intermediate and middle school grades. Indicate which guidelines are specific and which are general.

9. Examine two other social studies methods texts for the intermediate and middle school grades. What does each state the purpose of the social studies curriculum should be? How does each define the social studies?

REFERENCES

Atwood, V. (1982). A historical perspective of social studies. *Journal of Thought, 17,* 7–11.

Barr, R. D., Barth, J. L., & Shermis, S. S. (1977). *Defining the social studies* (Bulletin 51). Washington, DC: National Council for the Social Studies.

Brophy, J. (1992). Fifth-grade U.S. history: How one teacher arranged to focus on key ideas in depth. *Theory and Research in Social Education, 20,* 141–155.

Bruner, J. (1960). *The process of education.* Cambridge, MA: Harvard University Press.

Dewey, J. (1933). *How we think.* Boston: D. C. Heath.

Engle, S. H. (1976). Exploring the meaning of the social studies. In P. H. Martorella (Ed.), *Social studies strategies: Theory into practice* (pp. 232–245). New York: Harper & Row.

Engle, S. H. (1977). Comments of Shirley H. Engle. In R. D. Barr, J. L. Barth, & S. S. Shermis (Eds.), *Defining the social studies.* (Bulletin 51, pp. 103–105). Washington, DC: National Council for the Social Studies.

Engle, S. H., & Ochoa, A. S. (1988). *Education for democratic citizenship: Decision making in the social studies.* New York: Teachers College Press.

Fancett, V., & Hawke, S. (1982). Instructional practices in social studies. *The current state of social studies: A report of project SPAN.* Boulder, CO: Social Science Education Consortium.

Fenton, E. (1967). *The new social studies.* New York: Holt, Rinehart & Winston.

Fenton, E. (1991). Reflections on the "new social studies." *The Social Studies, 82,* 84–90.

Finkelstein, J. M., Nielsen, L. E., & Switzer, T. (1993). Primary elementary social studies instruction: A status report. *Social Education, 57,* 64–69.

Griffin, A. F. (1992). *A philosophical approach to the subject matter preparation of teachers of history.* Dubuque, IA: Kendall/Hunt.

Haas, J. D. (1977). *The era of the new social studies.* Boulder, CO: Social Science Education Consortium.

Haas, J. D. (1986). Is the social studies curriculum impervious to change? *The Social Studies, 77,* 61–65.

Hertzberg, H. (1981). *Social studies reform: 1880–1980.* Boulder, CO: Social Science Education Consortium.

Hullfish, H. G., & Smith, P. G. (1961). *Reflective thinking: The method of education.* New York: Dodd, Mead.

Hunt, M. P., & Metcalf, L. E. (1968). *Teaching high school social studies: Problems in reflective thinking and social understanding* (2nd ed.). New York: Harper & Row.

Lockwood, A. L. (1985). A place for ethical reasoning in the social studies curriculum. *The Social Studies, 76,* 264–268.

Lybarger, M. B. (1991). The historiography of social studies: Retrospect, circumspect, and prospect. In J. P. Shaver (Ed.), *Handbook of research on social studies teaching and learning* (pp. 3–15). New York: Macmillan.

Martorella, P. H. (1991). Consensus building among social educators: A delphi study. *Theory and Research in Social Education, 19,* 83–94.

Massialas, B. G. (1992). The "new social studies"—Retrospect and prospect. *The Social Studies, 83,* 120–124.

National Council for the Social Studies (NCSS). (1988). *Social studies for early childhood and elementary school children preparing for the 21st century.* Washington, DC: Author.

National Council for the Social Studies (NCSS). (1993, January/February). *The Social Studies Professional.* Washington, DC: Author.

Nelson, J. L., & Michaelis, J. V. (1980). *Secondary social studies.* Englewood Cliffs, NJ: Prentice-Hall.

Oppenheim, A. N., & Torney, J. (1974). *The measurement of children's civic attitudes in different nations.* New York: Halstead.

Rossi, J. A. (1992). Uniformity, diversity, and the "new social studies." *The Social Studies, 83,* 41–45.

Saxe, D. W. (1991). *Social studies in schools: A history of the early years.* Albany: State University of New York Press.

Saxe, D. W. (1992). Social studies foundations. *Review of Educational Research, 62,* 259–277.

Shaver, J. P., Davis, Jr., O. L., & Hepburn, S. W. (1979). The status of social studies education: Impressions from three NSF studies. *Social Education, 39,* 150–153.

Stodolsky, S. S., Salk, S., & Glaessner, B. (1991). Student views about learning math and social studies. *American Educational Research Journal, 28,* 89–116.

Superka, D. P., Hawke, S., & Morrissett, I. (1980). The current and future status of the social studies. *Social Education, 40,* 362–369.

Task Force on Scope and Sequence. (1984). In search of a scope and sequence for social studies. *Social Education, 48,* 249–262.

Torney-Purta, J. (1991). Schema theory and cognitive psychology: Implications for social studies. *Theory and Research in Social Education, 19,* 189–210.

U.S. Bureau of Education. (1916). *Report of the committee on social studies.* Washington, DC: Government Printing Office.

Wesley, E. B. (1950). *Teaching social studies in high schools* (3rd ed.). Boston: D. C. Heath.

CHAPTER 12

The Sources of Subject Matter and Instructional Resources for the Social Studies

This chapter will help you understand

1. How students learn the social studies.
2. The disciplines included in the social studies.
3. Other sources of subject matter for the social studies.
4. How to use the school and the community as rich sources of social data.
5. Organizational resources for social studies instruction.

A. KNOWLEDGE CONSTRUCTION AND SUBJECT MATTER

Knowledge is the fabric of social studies instruction. Woven into it are the facts, generalizations, skills, hypotheses, beliefs, attitudes, values, and theories that students and teachers construct in social studies programs. The threads from which the rich and intricate patterns are spun are concepts.

During knowledge construction, students activate both cognitive and affective processes. *Cognitive* processes refer generally to how individuals confront, encode, reflect on, transform, and store information. In turn, *affective* processes relate to the beliefs, attitudes, values, and ethical positions we bring to and derive from analyses. These also shape the meanings we extract from information.

Schemata and Prior Knowledge in Social Studies Instruction

As was discussed in Chapter 1, our knowledge is organized into structures known as *schemata*. The term has been defined as a mental structure that represents a set of related information (Howard, 1987). Schemata provide the basis for comprehending, remembering, and learning information. Schema theory posits that the form and content of all new knowledge is in some way shaped by our *prior knowledge* (existing knowledge).

Our individual collections of schemata comprise the store of prior knowledge we bring to each new knowledge acquisition task. Students, for example, bring their map schemata to the study of spatial issues. They have certain expectations concerning the kinds of information a map contains and the types of questions a map can answer.

Schemata as elements of our prior knowledge are activated when our experiences elicit them. Perkins (1986) cited the example of how the date 1492 can serve as an important cognitive peg for analysis of parallel historical events. He suggested that such key dates in

American history provide a structure for placing intermediate events. In this way dates can be not merely facts but also tools for collecting and remembering information.

When our prior knowledge conflicts with new data, restructuring of schemata may occur. New schemata arise through comparisons with prior ones and through modifications that reflect our current experiences. For example, a little boy may acquire some new information relating to Indians who lived in caves. From this encounter, he then shapes a revised schema that accommodates earlier information about different Indian habitats. On the other hand, firmly embedded prior knowledge may be resistant to transformation and require skillful challenging by a teacher (Marzano et al., 1988).

The process of knowledge acquisition also transcends the disciplinary boundaries established by social scientists and other scholars. In solving a problem, a student is less likely to be concerned whether the relevant data are drawn, let us say, from the discipline of history, than whether they contribute to a solution, whatever the source. Further, disciplines themselves are in a constant state of flux, with shifting parameters.

Selecting Social Studies Subject Matter

Hunt and Metcalf (1968) argued: "Content assumes an emergent character. From the standpoint of the learner, it comes into existence as it is needed, it does not have a life independent of his own" (pp. 281–282). In identifying subject matter for the social studies curriculum, teachers must search for information that has the greatest potential for achieving their purposes and goals. The subject matter they select should enable students to construct knowledge that will be useful in their current and future roles as citizens. It should be information of real worth for successful functioning in our society.

The subject matter that fuels functional knowledge must be drawn from a number of sources, including *the social sciences,* other disciplines, and interdisciplinary areas. It also must embrace the school and the community. Together these resources constitute a vast reservoir of information for the social studies curriculum.

B. THE SOCIAL STUDIES AND THE SOCIAL SCIENCES

The academic disciplines of the social sciences are the touchstones of the social studies (Gross & Dynneson, 1991). Most social studies educators would concede that the field of social studies gains a significant portion of its identity from the disciplines of the social sciences: history, political science, geography, economics, sociology, anthropology, and psychology (see Figure 12.1). We consider history, which arguably may be regarded as a discipline from either the humanities or the social sciences or both, as one of the social sciences throughout our discussion. Among all of the social sciences, history and geography particularly have nourished the social studies curriculum throughout its history.

The *methods of inquiry* used in the social sciences, such as the formulation and testing of hypotheses, also are important sources of social studies subject matter. To function effectively in their daily lives, citizens often have need of the same skills as social scientists. For example, citizens frequently are called on to locate data or to verify information.

The social sciences share many commonalities—their use of the scientific method, focus on understanding and explaining human behavior, and systematic collection and application of data. Their methods are both quantitative and qualitative. Social scientists measure phenomena and draw inferences from observations. They also share an interest in predicting patterns of behavior, a concern for verification of information, and a desire for objectivity. Each social science discipline, however, claims special insights and characteristics that provide its distinct identification.

In the sections that follow, the nature and scope of each of the social sciences are outlined.

Geography

Geographers sometimes organize their discipline in terms of five central themes: location, place, relationships within place, movement, and region. *Location* is viewed as describing the positions of people and places on the Earth's surface in either absolute or relative terms. *Place* is seen as detailing the human or physical characteristics of places on the Earth. *Relationships within places* refers to cultural and physical relationships of human settle-

FIGURE 12.1
Contributions of the Social Sciences to the Social Studies Curriculum

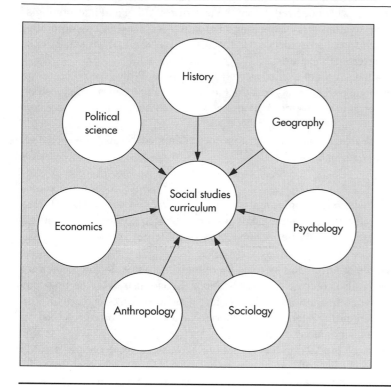

ments. The theme of *movement* describes relationships between and among places. *Regions* are viewed in terms of the ways areas may be identified, such as governmental units, language, religious or ethnic groups, and landform characteristics.

The concept of *place* is central to the discipline of geography. Geographers are concerned with the location and character of places on the Earth's surface and the factors that have shaped these places. They have an abiding interest in how the places affect the lives of those who locate there. Foremost is their interest in why people and things are located in particular places. They attempt to relate these places to events and to explain how goods, events, and people pass from place to place.

Geographers attempt to describe accurately, from many perspectives, locations on the Earth's surface. They examine, for example, what is below ground in the form of rocks and mineral deposits and what is above ground in the form of climate.

Maps and globes of all types are geographers' basic tools, as are aerial photos and remote sensing images. They also use census counts and data from surveys and fieldwork.

In addition to the ones mentioned, major concepts addressed by geographers include *population distribution, spatial interaction, environment,* and *boundaries.*

History

History includes chronicles, interpretations, syntheses, explanations, and cause-effect relationships. In essence, history is always a selective representation of reality. It is one (or more) individual's chronicles or recollections of what occurred from his or her frame of reference. Such chronicles may be oral, visual, and written, and they may relate to oneself, others, events, nations, social groups, and the like. As chroniclers, historians are concerned with constructing a coherent, accurate, and representative narrative of phenomena over time.

Although absolute objectivity—the search for truth regardless of personal preferences or objectives—is unachievable, some historians, in the tradition of Otto von Ranke, regard it as their methodological goal. Others, in the spirit of James Harvey Robinson and Carl Becker, consider such a goal to be "history without an objective" and urge historians to state explicitly the frames of reference they bring to their analyses.

Because it is impossible to record everything about any event or individual, and because all records are colored to some extent by our attitudes and frame of reference, history is also a selective *interpretation* of what occurred. Often the task of recording and interpreting an event also involves investigating and reconciling alternative accounts and incorporating documents into a pattern of verified evidence. Hence history is also a synthesis and explanation of many facts concerning the past.

Historians search for the *causes* of events, as well as the *effects*. Where the relationships between the two are ambiguous, historians construct hypotheses about causal relationships. Over time, as new evidence is uncovered, hypotheses are tested and, as a result, are supported or refuted.

In addition to the ones mentioned, major concepts addressed by historians include *change, the past, nationalism,* and *conflict.*

Economics

Economics is concerned with relationships among people that are formed to satisfy material needs. More specifically, the discipline deals with production, consumption, and exchange. The object of these three activities is some set of goods (e.g., cars) or services (e.g., lawn cutting).

Because countries often differ in their systems for organizing production, consumption, and exchange, economists also compare their applications. Economists also examine comparatively specific economic institutions within a nation, such as banks and small businesses. Similarly they examine the international patterns of exchange or currencies and how these affect economic behavior among countries.

Within the framework of production, consumption, and exchange, economists study, document, and attempt to predict patterns of human behavior. Other issues that they consider include job specialization, incentives, markets and prices, productivity, and benefits to be derived in relation to the costs incurred. Also examined is the surplus or scarcity of goods and services in relationship to people's needs and wants.

Because these issues arise at all levels and on all scales—an international conglomerate (macro level) or a local lawn cutter (micro level)—economists often examine them according to the scope of their impact. They also consider patterns of interdependence among nations and the relative levels of their imports and exports.

In addition to the ones mentioned, major concepts addressed by economists include *cost, division of labor, standard of living,* and *balance of payments.*

Political Science

The discipline of political science has its roots in philosophy and history. Works such as Plato's *Republic* and Aristotle's *Politics,* for example, are used today in college classes in both philosophy and political science. Broadly speaking, political science is concerned with an analysis of power and the processes by which individuals and groups control and manage one another. Power may be applied at the governmental level through the ballot box and political parties, but it also is exercised in many social settings. Power in some form is exercised by all individuals throughout society.

Above all, political science is concerned with the organization and governance of nations and other social units. Political scientists are interested, for example, in political interaction among institutions and the competing demands of various groups in our society as they affect governmental institutions. They analyze how different constituencies or interest groups influence and shape public policy. Such analyses include polls of public opinion and investigations of the impact of the mass media.

At the international level, political scientists are concerned with the relationships among nations, including the ways cooperation and ties develop and the ways conflicts emerge and are resolved. Political scientists trace patterns of interdependence and compare and contrast political systems. They also examine national and international legal systems and agreements between nations.

In addition to the ones mentioned, major concepts addressed by political scientists include *rules, citizenship, justice,* and *political systems.*

Anthropology

Closely aligned with the discipline of sociology is anthropology. Anthropologists, speaking broadly, say their discipline is the study of humankind. They are interested in both the biological and the environmental determinants of human behavior. Because its scope is far ranging and the discipline has a number of major subdivisions, anthropology is perhaps the most difficult subject to define.

Culture is a central concept in anthropology, much like the concept of *place* in geography. It refers to the entire way of life of a society and the shared ideas and language. Culture is unique to humans, and it is learned rather than inherited. The totality of how individuals use their genetic inheritance to adapt to and shape their environment makes up the major framework of what most anthropologists consider culture.

Cultural anthropologists are interested in how cultures change over time and how they are modified through interaction with other cultures. These scholars study cultural or subcultural groups to ascertain common patterns of behavior. They live among the groups, functioning as participant observers (recording observational data). Another group of anthropologists, *archaeologists,* unearth the past through excavations of artifacts from past generations and carbon-dating techniques. *Physical anthropologists* share many interests with natural scientists such as biologists, including the study of nonhuman primates and animal fossils.

In addition to the ones mentioned, major concepts addressed by anthropologists include *enculturation, cultural diffusion, cultural change,* and *traditions.*

Sociology

Sociology is the study of human interactions within groups. Sociologists study people in social settings, sometimes called *social systems.* They exercise wide latitude in their fields of investigation. For example, within various community settings, they examine behavior in such basic social units as the family, ethnic groupings, social classes, organizations, and clubs.

Sociologists are interested in how the basic types of institutions (e.g., social, religious, economic, political, legal) affect our daily lives. Other areas that sociologists examine include how the actions of individuals in groups, such as worker behavior in plants or teacher activities in schools, serve to preserve or change social systems.

Sociologists attempt to abstract patterns from cumulative individual studies. From the study of cases within specific social systems, such as the various families within a small community, sociologists try to derive general principles that can be applied to all similar groups.

Because the scope of sociology includes some analysis of behavior in every major institution within society, it often overlaps with the other social sciences. For example, the work of a sociologist studying the political behavior of various groups during a national election and that of a political scientist analyzing voting patterns may intersect.

In addition to the ones mentioned, major concepts addressed by sociologists include *norms, status, socialization,* and *roles.*

Psychology

A discipline with many subdivisions, psychology focuses on understanding individual mental processes and behaviors. Modern psychology derives from earlier religious and philosophical studies into the nature of humans and the reasons for their behavior. The question of whether an individual has a free will, for example, merely was shifted into a scientific arena as psychology developed.

The boundaries of psychology are often difficult to determine because its investigations often spill over into the areas of biology, medicine, and physics, as well as into the other social sciences. Psychologists study animal as well as human behavior. Like anthropologists, they are interested in both the genetic and the learned aspects of behavior. The major branches of the discipline concentrate on investigating how learning occurs, which psychologists regard as a major determinant of human behavior.

Psychology has both an applied and an experimental side. Some psychologists, such as counseling psychologists, apply knowledge directly to the solution of human problems in clinical settings, similar to a doctor-patient relationship. Other psychologists function in laboratory environments, conducting controlled experiments that may have no short-term applications to human behavior.

In addition to the ones mentioned, major concepts addressed by psychologists include *values, self, motivation,* and *learning.*

Figure 12.2 presents how a K–6 social studies curriculum can incorporate themes from each of the social science disciplines. In the example given, anthropology and sociology, which are closely related disciplines, are combined.

C. OTHER SOURCES OF SUBJECT MATTER FOR THE SOCIAL STUDIES

Besides the findings and methods of inquiry of the social sciences, the social studies curriculum has drawn and will continue to draw on many other areas for data. The social studies are concerned with the application of social knowledge to citizenship roles. Many sources of information beyond the social sciences can aid in this task.

FIGURE 12.2
A K–6 Social Studies Curriculum That Incorporates Themes from Social Science Disciplines
SOURCE: From *Looking at Me: Teacher's Manual* (pp. 15–16) by C. Cherryholmes, G. Manson, & P. H. Martorella, 1979, New York: McGraw-Hill. Copyright 1979 by McGraw-Hill. Adapted by permission.

SCOPE AND SEQUENCE	Kindergarten	Grade 1	Grade 2
Geography	Make body map. Learn left, right, up, and down.	Make body maps and simple maps of classroom.	Define *map.* Draw own route to school.
History	Study favorite holidays, how places change, sequence of events from past to present.	Study own past. How places and people change with time.	Recall facts verbally from the past, and classify them as pleasant or unpleasant.
Economics	Learn that people work and that people need special skills to do some kinds of work.	Study work of family members. Learn how people get what they need by working.	Make lists of ways students spend money. Make economic decisions.
Political Science	Begin citizenship training. Learn sources of rules and norms.	Study sources of rules and norms. Gain citizenship training through study of national symbols.	Study persons in authority and decisions they make.
Anthropology–Sociology	Learn about the family as a group and the differing norms and preferences of families. Study the grouping of people through similarities, differences.	Study family and functions, how norms are transmitted, and how people change. Group people by their cultural traits.	Study the concepts of *behavior, communication, decision making,* and *ways of learning.*
Psychology	Explore own perceptions of self and others. Learn own feelings.	Explore own and others' perceptions, feelings, and attitudes.	Study reasons for behavior. Tell about feelings of their own or others.

The arts and sciences, the humanities, the law, popular culture and music, data from students' and teachers' daily lives, the social life within the school and community, and the mass media are but a sample of the possible sources of subject matter that are outside the framework of the social sciences but that affect the human condition (see Figure 12.3). Subject matter within these areas that relates to the organization, understanding, and development of individuals, groups, and societies has considerable relevancy for the social studies curriculum.

Interdisciplinary Studies

In teaching social studies, we may draw primarily on the subject matter of a particular social science discipline, such as when we look to history for an account of the first Thanksgiving. On other occasions we may wish to use an *interdisciplinary* approach, in which several of the social sciences are tapped to explain a topic or to examine an issue. This would be the case, for example, when we used the combined insights of economists, sociologists, psychologists, anthropologists, and geographers to help explain why some areas of the United States are growing more rapidly than others.

Crafting Interdisciplinary Lessons and Activities.

Although the traditional social science disciplines are important structured sources of systematically analyzed data for students' knowledge construction, often the insightful and

FIGURE 12.2 cont'd

Grade 3	Grade 4	Grade 5	Grade 6
Explore concepts and uses of maps and globes, geography of the United States, landforms, land use in cities.	Study environments, climate types, landforms; locales in four countries.	Study North American geographic regions, waterways, and climate.	Study geography, climate, waterways of China, Nigeria, Brazil, the United Kingdom, plus an overview of the continents.
Study the concept of *history*, the history of cities, and the concept of *time lines*.	Survey the historical background of four culture groups in relation to four countries.	Study a broad, chronological overview of United States history and the history of culture groups within the United States.	Investigate the history of China, Nigeria, Brazil, and the United Kingdom.
Learn how people obtain what they need in different times and places. Learn about goods and services and economic decisions.	Learn how people in four cultures fill their needs, use resources, and make choices at minimum cost.	Study the natural resources of North America and learn about its technology and cultures. Study the workings of government and social welfare.	Study the basic concept of *economy*. Distinguish developed and underdeveloped economies.
Study the political divisions of nation, state, and city. Learn members of state and city government.	Survey forms of government in three cultures. Learn about form of government in Russia and its effects on Russian life.	Survey North American nations. Study the structure of United States government, meanings of democracy, and the struggle for equal rights.	Study a group decision-making model. Learn about majority and plurality rule. Survey government of four nations.
Investigate how people live together in families, communities, and national groups. Study the concept of interdependence.	Learn the characteristics of culture. Explore the concepts of *fairness, power, norms,* and *status.*	Study the elements of culture and the phenomenon of cultural pluralism in the United States. Study communication and decision-making models.	Study in more detail the concept of *culture*. Examine cultural clashes and culture contact. Study concept of *communication*.
Learn about cooperation, competition, conflict, and people's reasons for past actions.	Study the relationship between behavior and learning; copying, reward and punishment, trial and error.	Study the principles of learning through cultural and historical examples.	Examine beliefs about foreign peoples and cultures. Examine sources of beliefs.

FIGURE 12.3
Other Sources of the Social Studies Curriculum

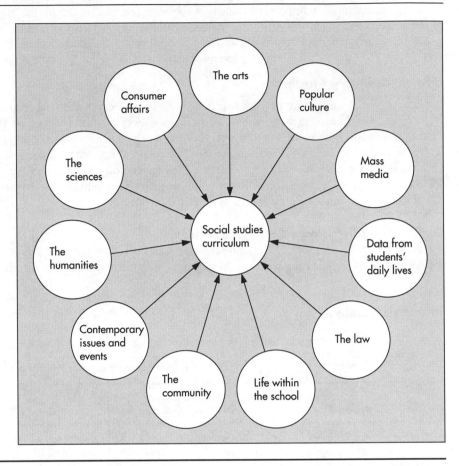

creative contributions of scholars do not fit neatly into any existing discipline. Many areas of study and many activities can be enriched through reference to subject matter drawn from several disciplines (see Sunal & Hatcher, 1986).

As an example, investigation of urgent national and international problems, which Engle and Ochoa (1988) advocated as a curricular emphasis, typically calls for interdisciplinary subject matter. Addressing such issues as poverty, the homeless, the destruction of the ozone layer, and the imbalance of resources and wealth among nations of the world also often requires the perspectives of many disciplines. More basically, individual social studies activities often can be enriched by combining the dimensions of several disciplines. Consider the lesson plan in Figure 12.4, on the causes of the Civil War. It incorporates information from economics, political science, sociology, geography, and other disciplines to engage students in a contextually rich multicultural experience.

D. THE SCHOOL AND THE COMMUNITY AS SOURCES OF SOCIAL DATA

Apart from the use of texts and disciplinary perspectives, students also need to be guided in systematically using their schools and communities as laboratories for social data (Gillis, 1991). To this end, they require assignments and activities that encourage them to view data from their daily life experiences as relevant and legitimate subject matter for analysis in the classroom. For example, a unit on crime in America might begin with students collecting objective data concerning the occurrence of crime in their own neighborhoods or communities.

The wealth of material that generally is available within every community is probably one of the least tapped resources for social studies teaching. Local organizations and busi-

FIGURE 12.4
Sample Integrated Lesson Plan
SOURCE: Borich, G. D., *Effective Teaching Methods* (1988, pp. 133–34). Reprinted by permission of the publisher.

Unit Title: United States History (Early Beginning through Reconstruction)
Lesson Title: Causes of the Civil War   Lesson 2.3

1. **Gaining Attention**
   Show the following list of wars on a transparency:
   French and Indian War   1754–1769
   Revolutionary War   1775–1781
   Civil War   1861–1865
   World War I   1914–1918
   World War II   1941–1945
   Korean War   1950–1953
   Vietnam War   1965–1975

2. **Informing the Learner of the Objective**
   Learners will be expected to know the causes of the Civil War and to show that those causes also can apply to at least one of the wars shown on the transparency.

3. **Stimulating Recall of Prerequisite Learning**
   Briefly review the causes of both the French and Indian War and the Revolutionary War as covered in Lessons 2.1 and 2.2

4. **Presenting the Stimulus Material**
   (a) Summarize major events leading to the Civil War:
   - rise of sectionalism,
   - labor-intensive economy,
   - lack of diversification.

   (b) Identify significant individuals during the Civil War and their roles:
   - Lincoln,
   - Lee,
   - Davis,
   - Grant.

   (c) Describe four general causes of war and explain which are most relevant to the Civil War:
   - economic (to profit),
   - political (to control),
   - social (to influence),
   - military (to protect).

5. **Eliciting the Desired Behavior**
   Ask the class to identify which of the four causes is most relevant to the major events leading up to the Civil War.

6. **Providing Feedback**
   Ask for student answers and indicate plausibility of the volunteered responses.

7. **Assessing the Behavior**
   Assign as homework a one-page essay assessing the relative importance of the four causes for one of the wars listed on the transparency.

---

nesses, for example, often cooperate with teachers in arranging field trips, guest speakers, information, and assistance.

Public agencies such as police and fire departments sometimes have special programs and speakers that they provide to schools. Other sources of speakers include colleges and universities, the Chamber of Commerce, and the League of Women Voters. Individuals in the community, likewise, generally are eager to offer their assistance to local schools.

Using Community Resource Persons Effectively

Typical uses of community resource persons include having individuals from different career areas report on what they do. This includes having persons work with students as mentors. Additionally it may include drawing on community members who have specialized advice concerning selected topics.

The South Carolina Department of Education (1987) has prepared a useful set of general guidelines for using resource speakers. The agency's suggestions appear in Figure 12.5.

FIGURE 12.5
Guide for Using Resource Speakers
SOURCE: From *Guide for Using Guest Speakers and Field Trips* (pp. 8–9) by South Carolina Department of Education, 1987, Columbia: Author. Copyright 1987 by South Carolina Department of Education. Courtesy of South Carolina Department of Education.

Locating Resources

Community/school contacts may be made through:

Partnership coordinator in the school district

Businesses (domestic or foreign owned)

Local Chamber of Commerce

College or university

Technical education center

Parent interest survey

Identification of students for peer teaching

Local speakers bureau

School volunteer coordinator

Clubs

Museums

Contacting Community Resources

How?

Personal contact

Phone call

Written request stating exact need

Combination of the above

Through whom?

Partnership coordinator in the school district

Public relations or community relations executive (business)

Survey information (parents)

Local Chamber of Commerce

Preparing Students

Please remember: The purpose is to enrich and enhance, not to teach the unit!

Let the students help with preparations whenever possible. A feeling of responsibility helps ensure interest.

Students will profit from understanding of some kind of expected measurable results. They should know what will be expected from them prior to the visit. The results may take the form of one or more of the following:

Quiz

Puzzle or "Treasure Hunt"

Identification List

Report or summary

Problem solving

Model or project

Interview results

Letter

Secure materials and biographical information from the speaker in advance. These materials may include:

Posters or brochures

Background of speaker

History of the company

Photographs

Audiovisual aids to be shown in advance

A number of practical suggestions for integrating resource speakers into the regular social studies curriculum are available (Monti, 1988). Lamm (1989) prepared her class for a speaker's visit by involving it in a related activity prior to the speaker's arrival. The speaker was a children's services worker from a local social service agency who was to serve the class as a resource on the problem of child abuse.

The day before the speaker arrived, the teacher gave each member of the class a card that contained one piece of information concerning a case of an abused child. Students were asked to seek out and form a group with other class members who had related information on the same child. Once each group was formed, students were to discuss what they believed would be an appropriate remedy to the case of abuse.

The following day the speaker arrived. She spent the session comparing the group's recommendations with what the services bureau typically would do in cases similar to the ones the students considered. A follow-up discussion brought out the key issues involved in child abuse cases and detailed the scope of the problem nationally and locally.

Fieldwork in the Community

In addition to bringing the community to the school to enrich lessons, students can be taken into the field to observe or to collect data. Armstrong and Savage (1976) observed that the community can function as a laboratory for students that generates a "higher degree of personal commitment and enthusiasm for social studies than can be anticipated when books, films, and other stimulators of reality are used" (p. 164). Some examples of community sites for field visits are:

Hospitals	Television studios
Observatories	Waterfronts
Historic sites	Military bases
Farms	Archaeological excavations
Museums	Post offices
Construction sites	Fire stations
Factories	Newspapers

Social scientists refer to the process of gathering information on site directly, rather than secondhand through texts and other such materials, as *fieldwork*. Fieldwork often is used to collect data, to generate or test hypotheses in problem solving, and to provide clear examples of concepts.

A trip to the field does not of itself imply fieldwork or even a meaningful activity. During fieldwork, students act on what they observe or experience by relating their experiences in the field to other information they have studied or are studying and then reflecting on the connections. Fieldwork should be a pleasant change-of-pace activity for students, not merely a diversion. It is important that a trip to the field be an integral part of the school's instructional program.

Often it may be appropriate to have individual students or small groups working in the field, either during or after school hours. When an entire class is to be engaged in fieldwork during normal school hours, a great deal of teacher planning is involved to ensure a successful and productive experience.

The planning process may be viewed in three stages—before the trip, during the trip, and following the trip—as the following guidelines suggest.

Before the Trip

1. Establish clear and specific objectives for the trip. Plan to share these with the students either before or after the trip, as appropriate to your instructional strategy.
2. View the trip as a means, rather than as an end. Consider such issues as how time will be used and how variety in experiences will be provided.
3. Familiarize yourself with the major features of the site you will visit. Identify those features of the visit that will interest students and reflect *action* (people doing things).
4. Make a list of those features of the site you plan to discuss and emphasize during the trip. Then make notes on the types of comments and questions you plan to raise concerning them.
5. If possible, obtain pictures, written information, slides, and the like to introduce the site to be visited. In preparing for the visit, focus on special features you wish students to notice.
6. If appropriate, provide students with a sheet of points to consider and data to collect during the visit. If students are to engage in an activity, be sure to indicate what they are expected to do and not to do.
7. Develop a checklist of all procedural, administrative details that need to be arranged, such as confirmation of visitation date, bus plans, parental permissions, provisions for meals or snacks (if any), rest room facilities, safety precautions (if necessary), and special student dress (if needed).
8. Organize a simple file system for collecting all forms or funds required from students and parents.

During the Trip

9. Focus students' attention on those features of the trip that are most important. Have them observe and record, where appropriate, answers to such questions as:
   What things did I see?
   What people did I see, and what were they doing?
   How did _____ get done? Which people were involved? What materials were used?

10. Where possible, engage students in some activity during the visit. Where this is not possible, raise related questions, as well as provide relevant information.
11. Take pictures or slides or make a videotape to use in discussing important aspects of the trip during the follow-up.
12. Make brief notes on what seemed to interest and bore students and on the more important questions that were asked. Note those points you would like to call attention to during the follow-up discussion.

Following the Trip

13. Ask students to offer their open-ended impressions of what they learned from the trip and what they enjoyed most from it and why.
14. Review your notes from the trip and discuss important points, referring to the data students collected.
15. Review (or identify) the objectives for the trip and relate the experiences to previous learning.
16. Engage the students in additional related follow-up activities.
17. While the procedural and substantive features of the trip are still fresh in your mind, construct a file card of notes, similar to the one shown in Figure 12.6, for future reference.

Collecting Oral Histories

A data collection project that lends itself well to individual and small group fieldwork is recording oral histories (Mehaffy, 1984; Mehaffy, Sitton, & Davis, 1979). An *oral history* may be defined as any firsthand account of an event. Although the emphasis in oral histories is on the spoken word, they may include both audio and video data.

As fieldwork, recording oral histories provides students with a sense of personal engagement in a stream of events (Totten, 1989). The activity also helps tie specific events and the larger sweep of history to a real person who was affected by them (Mehaffy, 1984). Further, when the narrator is a local person, the history may help tie the local community into the national history being examined in the classroom.

FIGURE 12.6
Sample Field Trip Data Sheet

Field Trip Data Sheet

Theme or Objectives of Trip:	How a modern factory works; assembly-line procedure; demonstration of computer components
Place:	Widgit Computer Works
Address:	1000 Futura Boulevard Silicon Valley, CA 10000
Telephone number:	100/999–1000
Contact Person:	Steve Jobs
Grade Levels for Which Trip is Appropriate:	4–9
Summary of Main Features of Trip and General Comments:	Students are shown a videotape of all the plant's operations (20 minutes). Tour of all facilities covers the parts that are used in constructing microcomputers, as well as the assembly operations. Students are allowed to ask all workers questions during the tour. At the end of the tour students are allowed to work at assembled microcomputers for as long as they wish. Tour itself, without any questions, probably takes an hour. The company provided snacks for the students.
Overall Rating of Trip:	One of the best we have ever taken!
Suggestions for Future Visits by Other Classes:	It would be helpful to students to have a general discussion before the trip concerning their perceptions and stereotypes of factories.

Procedures for Collecting Oral Histories. Numerous collections of rich oral histories already exist across the United States, covering a wide array of topics and individuals (see Totten, 1989; Zimmerman, 1981). One of the more extensive collections can be found at the John F. Kennedy Library at the University of Massachusetts in Boston. The Southern Oral History Program at the University of North Carolina at Chapel Hill is an example of a more limited collection. In fieldwork, however, the emphasis is on students collecting their own data through actually *recording* oral histories.

Foci for oral histories include events, issues, recollections of individuals, periods, places, and biographies. Each focus requires different types of questions to bring out relevant data. Zimmerman (1981), for example, recommended detailed questioning procedures for collecting oral biographies that included items such as:

- What have been the major accomplishments in your life?
- What have been the biggest problems, mistakes, or adversities in your life?

For a class project to determine why people came to America, Taba and Elkins (1950) gave students with ethnically diverse backgrounds a basic set of questions to use in interviewing their relatives. The set could be adapted easily for application to a variety of oral history projects. The students were to investigate:

1. Who came and from what country.
2. Why they came.
3. Where they went.
4. What worries they had.
5. What they found here.
6. What kinds of work they found.
7. What adjustments they had to make.

Totten (1989) suggested that a teacher introduce students to the procedures involved in recording oral histories by having them observe the teacher conduct one in class. He also recommended that prior to the recording, students be involved in developing the set of questions to be asked.

Conducting Surveys and Interviews

Closely related to oral histories are *surveys* and *interviews*. These techniques allow students to transform the school and community into a laboratory for gathering social data. Surveys and interviews can help answer such questions as What do the third-grade students in our school think about the new social studies textbooks? and How do people in my neighborhood feel about the idea of raising taxes to build a new public swimming pool? In the case of many questions, the only conclusive way to obtain an answer is to conduct surveys and interviews.

Figure 12.7 offers an excerpt of an interview that a student, Tim, conducted with a police officer in his community. The purpose was to learn more about why individuals became police officers and what their job entailed. Prior to the interview, Tim determined what his objectives were and then wrote out the questions he would use. His teacher helped refine them and suggested procedures for how he might go about arranging the interview. Tim then called the police department, indicated his objective, and set up an appointment for the interview. The actual interview took only 10 to 15 minutes and, with the officer's permission, was recorded at the police station for sharing with the class.

E. ORGANIZATIONAL RESOURCES FOR SOCIAL STUDIES INSTRUCTION

Beyond community resources, a number of agencies can help keep teachers abreast of new developments, issues, and trends within the field of social studies, as well as provide subject matter information.

FIGURE 12.7
Student's Interview

Tim:	My first question is, "Why did you want to be a policeman?"
Police Officer:	Why did I want to be a policeman? Well, I wanted to be a policeman because I thought I could help people.
Tim:	Why did you decide to live and work in Upper Dublin?
Police Officer:	Well, I don't live here. But the reason I decided to work here was I thought it would be a great opportunity for someone who wanted to be a policeman. I think it is a fine township.
Tim:	What would you be if you weren't a policeman?
Police Officer:	I really have no idea.
Tim:	Did you ever have another job?
Police Officer:	Oh, yes, I had another job. I was a mailman; before that I was in the army.
Tim:	Do you like the job of a policeman?
Police Officer:	Do I like the job? Yes, I do like the job.
Tim:	What improvements do you think could be made in Upper Dublin?
Police Officer:	As far as the Police Department goes, you mean?
Tim:	Well, I mean not just about your job, but other things.
Police Officer:	Well, I don't know. I think that's up to the taxpayers and the commissioners. I think they're doing a pretty good job, don't you?
Tim:	I don't know.
Police Officer:	Don't you really?
Tim:	Well, I never really studied it.
Police Officer:	Well, sure there are improvements that could be made, but I think they're doing the best they can.
Tim:	Do you think policemen have good enough equipment?
Police Officer:	I think it's going to get better. I think we're trying. I think it's probably not as good as it could be, but it's getting better all the time. It's eventually going to get to the point where everything is OK. Yes.
Tim:	How many people commit murder a year?
Police Officer:	I really don't know. In this township, not too many. In other places, a lot more.
Tim:	About how many robberies are there a year?
Police Officer:	We have quite a few burglaries, not robberies. We have very few robberies; we have a lot of burglaries.
Tim:	What's the difference?
Police Officer:	Well, the difference is a robbery is where somebody actually holds you up with a gun. A burglery is where someone, say, breaks into your house or business or something. We have quite a few of those—in the hundreds.
Tim:	What do you think Upper Dublin would be like without police?
Police Officer:	Well, it would be like any other place without policemen, very bad.
Tim:	Are there any things that a policeman does that most people don't know about?
Police Officer:	I think there are quite a few things that people don't know about.
Tim:	What?
Police Officer:	Well, one thing—they work different shifts, which maybe some people know about but they don't really know what the job details; they don't really know what a policeman does.
	[At this point the interview is interrupted as the police officer takes and relays to a patrol car a call for assistance.]
Tim:	What do policemen do most of the day? What kind of things do they do?
Police Officer:	Most of the day, they ride around in the patrol car, observe traffic violations, check suspicious . . . [Another call interrupts the conversation.] They ride around in cars; as I say, they observe things. They try to check various things, in other words, businesses, places of business. They get calls, they answer all calls when people call them on the telephone. In other words, you just heard one here. Right? If someone's in the house, if the person doesn't want them in there, they go and they try their best to get them out of there and possibly to arrest them if they have to. Anything that they're called upon by the general public to do, they try to answer the call.
Tim:	OK, thank you.

Teachers can look especially to professional organizations that have a particular interest in the social studies. The list that follows identifies some major institutions that meet this criterion:

American Anthropological Association
1703 New Hampshire Avenue, N.W.
Washington, DC 20009

American Bar Association
750 North Lake Shore Drive
Chicago, IL 60611

American Economic Association
1313 21st Avenue South, Suite 809
Nashville, TN 37212

American Historical Association
400 A Street, S.E.
Washington, DC 20003

American Political Science Association
1527 New Hampshire Avenue, N.W.
Washington, DC 20036

American Psychological Association
1200 17th Street, N.W.
Washington, DC 20036

American Sociological Association
1722 N Street, N.W.
Washington, DC 20036

Association of American Geographers
1700 Sixteenth Street, N.W.
Washington, DC 20009

Educational Resources Information Center (ERIC)
Clearinghouse for Social Studies/Social Science Education
Indiana University
2805 East 10th Street
Bloomington, IN 47408-2698

Joint Council on Economic Education
432 Park Avenue South
New York, NY 10016

National Council for Geographic Education
Department of Geography and Regional Planning
Indiana University of Pennsylvania
Indiana, PA 15705

National Council for the Social Studies
3501 Newark Street, N.W.
Washington, DC 20016

Organization of American Historians
112 North Bryan Street
Bloomington, IN 47408

The preceding organizations produce a number of materials, including guidelines and policy statements, such as the ones that are referenced throughout this text. Many also sponsor annual regional and national conferences for teachers of social studies on a range of issues in the field. Some of the organizations also publish newsletters and periodicals for teachers.

In addition to these national organizations, affiliate units within many of the states provide similar services. Regional social studies organizations cover several states. The national organizations listed can provide information on affiliates.

Professional Journals

A number of specialized professional periodicals are available for social studies teachers. Some of the periodicals are sponsored by the organizations cited. (See Figure 6.4 of Chapter 6.)

SUMMARY

This chapter has reviewed how students learn the social studies, described the disciplines included in and other sources of subject matter for the social studies, and described how to use the school and community as sources of social data. In addition it has presented a listing of organizational resources for social studies instruction.

Chapters that follow will provide further detailed understanding of the social studies curriculum, how to teach it, and how to integrate it into the curriculum.

QUESTIONS AND ACTIVITIES FOR DISCUSSION

1. Which of the social sciences do you think should receive the most emphasis in the intermediate grades? The middle school grades? Give reasons for your answers.

2. In your local community, make a list of the community resources that a social studies teacher could draw on. Compare your list with those of others in the group.

3. Refer to Figure 12.2, which illustrates how themes from each of the social sciences can be incorporated into the curriculum at each grade level. Discuss what additional themes you think it would be appropriate to include.

4. Consult the *International Encyclopedia of the Social Sciences* (17 vols.) (New York: Macmillan, 1968). Summarize the definition provided for each of the social sciences.

5. Besides those listed in the chapter, develop a list of ten additional concepts related to each of the social sciences.

REFERENCES

Armstrong, D. A., & Savage, Jr., T. V. (1976). A framework for utilizing the community for social learning in grades 4 to 6. *Social Education, 40,* 164–167.

Engle, S. H., & Ochoa, A. S. (1988). *Education for democratic citizenship: Decision making in the social studies.* New York: Teachers College Press.

Gillis, C. (1991). *The community as classroom.* New York: Boynton/Cook.

Gross, R. E., & Dynneson, T. (Eds.). (1991). *Social science perspectives on citizenship education.* New York: Teachers College Press.

Howard, R. W. (1987). *Concepts and schemata: An introduction.* Philadelphia: Cassell.

Hunt, M. P., & Metcalf, L. E. (1968). *Teaching high school social studies: Problems in reflective thinking and social understanding* (2nd ed.). New York: Harper & Row.

Lamm, L. (1989). *Facilitating learning through the effective use of resource persons in the classroom.* Unpublished manuscript, North Carolina State University, Department of Curriculum and Instruction, Raleigh.

Marzano, R. J., Brandt, R. S., Hughes, C. S., Jones, B. F., Presseisen, B. Z., Rankin, S. C., & Suhor, C. (1988). *Dimensions of thinking: A framework for curriculum and instruction.* Alexandria, VA: Association for Supervision and Curriculum Development.

Mehaffy, G. L. (1984). Oral history in elementary classrooms. *Social Education, 48,* 470–472.

Mehaffy, G. L., Sitton, T., & Davis, Jr., O. L. (1979). *Oral history in the classroom* (How to do it series). Washington, DC: National Council for the Social Studies.

Monti, J. (1988). Guest speaker programs bring community members to school. *NASSP Bulletin, 72,* 113.

Perkins, D. N. (1986). *Knowledge as design.* Hillsdale, NJ: Lawrence Erlbaum.

South Carolina Department of Education. (1987). *Guide for using guest speakers and field trips.* Columbia, SC: Author.

Sunal, C. S., & Hatcher, B. A. (1986). *Studying history through art* (How to do it series). Washington, DC: National Council for the Social Studies.

Taba, H., & Elkins, D. (1950). *With focus on human relations.* Washington, DC: American Council on Education.

Totten, S. (1989). Using oral histories to address social issues in the classroom. *Social Education, 53,* 114–116.

Zimmerman, W. (1981). *How to tape instant oral biographies.* New York: Guarionex.

SUGGESTED READINGS

Cherryholmes, C., Manson, G., & Martorella, P. H. (1979). *Looking at me: Teacher's manual.* New York: McGraw-Hill.

Harvey, K. D. (1993). Native Americans: The next 500 years. *Social Studies and the Young Learner, 5,* 2–3 (insert).

Torney-Purta, J. (1991). Schema theory and cognitive psychology: Implications for social studies. *Theory and Research in Social Education, 19,* 189–210.

CHAPTER 13

Scope and Sequence Patterns in the Social Studies Curriculum

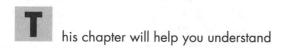 his chapter will help you understand

1. Existing and alternative social studies scope and sequence patterns.
2. The roles of basal textbooks in the social studies curriculum.
3. How to select a scope and sequence pattern.

Suppose you randomly selected ten fifth-grade classes from across the United States. What type of social studies curricula would you expect to find? What guidelines were used to shape the curricula? Who was primarily responsible for determining the curricula?

The answers to these questions are rooted in our history and constitutional framework. Because the framers of the Constitution rejected a national system of education, the matter of schools and curriculum fell to the individual states. States, in turn, often granted considerable authority in these matters to local governments. Consequently we have no national control of curriculum. Rather there exists a collection of thousands of local school districts and governing boards, each with varying degrees of autonomy over its social studies curriculum.

A. EXISTING SOCIAL STUDIES SCOPE AND SEQUENCE PATTERNS

Each state varies in the degree of control it exercises over the curriculum, including the scope and sequence patterns that local school districts may adopt. *Scope* refers to the topics included in the curriculum; *sequence* refers to the order in which they appear (see Joyce, Little, & Wronski, 1991).

Subject to general guidelines and standards for the social studies curriculum established by each state, a local school district often has considerable freedom in the development of its social studies program. Thus the potential for variety in the social studies curriculum scope and sequence patterns across the United States is great.

Although the principle of local control holds out the promise of diversity in curriculum offerings, in reality there is considerable homogeneity in the social studies programs in grades K–12 across the 50 states. Typically the pattern is as follows (Superka, Hawke, & Morrissett, 1980):

Kindergarten–Grade 1	Self, Family, School
Grade 2	Neighborhoods
Grade 3	Communities
Grade 4	State history, geographic regions
Grade 5	United States history, culture, and geography
Grade 6	World cultures, history, and geography
Grade 7	World cultures, history, and geography
Grade 8	American history
Grade 9	Civics
Grade 10	World history
Grade 11	American history
Grade 12	American government

The Curriculum Pattern in the Elementary Grades

The existing organizational pattern of the social studies curriculum in grades K–6 follows what has been characterized by Hanna (1963) as the expanding-communities curriculum pattern. This approach, which has dominated the elementary curriculum for several decades, is based on the notion that a student will be introduced during each year of school to an increasingly expanding social environment, moving from examining the self and the family in grades K–1 to the world at large in grade 6. Hanna's model also identified nine categories of basic human activities that should be addressed during each year of the social studies curriculum: expressing, producing, transporting, communicating, educating, recreating, protecting, governing, and creating (Powers, 1986).

The Curriculum Pattern in the Middle and Secondary Grades

The long-term impact of the 1916 report of the Committee on Social Studies (see Chapter 11) ironically proved to be pervasive and enduring, extending into the 1990s. Note the close similarities between the typical national pattern described in the preceding section and the following general recommendations for grades 7–12 from the 1916 report of the Committee on Social Studies:

Grades 7–9	Geography, European history, American history, civics
Grade 10	European history
Grade 11	American history
Grade 12	Problems of democracy

Contrary to the intent of the committee, its report became a paradigm of what the scope and sequence of courses in the curriculum should be. The committee itself had refrained from offering detailed outlines of courses. It believed that the selection of topics and the organization of subject matter should be determined by the needs of each community.

A further irony spawned by the report was that its recommendations often were viewed as being literal, timeless, and universal, applicable in all particulars to all generations and communities. The committee's intent, however, had been to sketch only general principles on which different schools could build their curricula in concert with the changing character of each time period, community, and group of students.

The 1916 committee constructed its recommendations in the context of a school population vastly different from the one that exists today. It saw its immediate task as planning a social studies curriculum that emphasized citizenship education for a nation in which the majority of students completed their education without entering high school. This short educational period meant that all of the essential elements in the curriculum needed to be provided before the tenth grade.

The Dominance of Traditional Scope and Sequence Patterns

Why has the dominant national scope and sequence pattern for the social studies curriculum endured so long? A major part of the answer lies, perhaps, in several interrelated factors: *tradition, accrediting agencies and professional organizations, preservice teacher education programs,* and *patterns of textbook selection and adoption.*

The weight of tradition bears down heavily on those who would challenge the conventional scope and sequence of the social studies curriculum. Parents and community members tend to encourage preservation of the status quo. Teachers themselves are often more comfortable with the known than the unknown.

Moreover, tradition influences the norms for accrediting agencies that examine the quality of our school districts across the country. It is also an important consideration for national organizations such as the National Council for the Social Studies (NCSS) and the National Council for Geographic Education (NCGE), which provide curricular guidelines for programs. These organizations represent thousands of social studies teachers across the United States and Canada.

Tradition also establishes some of the basic goals for preservice teacher education programs that seek to prepare teachers for existing conditions in schools, as well as for the future. Often in such programs the emphasis is on socialization of new teachers into the present curriculum, rather than on consideration of alternatives. Correspondingly the subject matter background of elementary and middle-grades preservice teachers frequently has been shaped to prepare them for the dominant scope and sequence pattern, rather than for the consideration and development of alternatives. This pattern of preparation also typically stresses traditional disciplines, such as history, and de-emphasizes or ignores the newer social science disciplines and interdisciplinary studies.

B. BASAL TEXTBOOKS AND THE SOCIAL STUDIES CURRICULUM

Perhaps the most significant factor in influencing the standardization of the scope and sequence pattern of the social studies curriculum is the system of selecting and adopting basal textbooks that schools employ. The impact of textbooks on perpetuating the scope and sequence of the curriculum has been profound. The best research evidence available suggests that, in social studies, basal texts are used extensively and more often than other types of curricular materials (Shaver, Davis, & Hepburn, 1979).

A basal textbook represents the major elements that the author or publisher regards as basic to provide an appropriate social studies curriculum for a particular grade or subject. Generally publishers of basal social studies texts build them around some model or notion of scope and sequence related to the grades for which the texts have been developed. Thus, adopting a basal text, in effect, means adopting the curricular pattern on which it is based.

Use of Basal Texts in the Social Studies

Teachers and schools often build on a basal text, using commercially produced and teacher-made supplementary materials, newspapers, articles, and trade books. Some teachers use no textbook at all, instead creating their own programs by following general scope and sequence guidelines. Other teachers use texts primarily as reference books. Still other teachers use a *multitext* approach, picking those units or chapters from each textbook that best meet their specific curricular needs. Textbook publishers also may offer supplementary books, such as children's literature, correlated to the basal text.

Surprisingly, perhaps, basal textbook series available from major publishers display striking similarities in the scope and sequence models they incorporate. Contrary to the canons of capitalism that we might expect to operate when major corporations are competing for large profits from widely distributed, heterogeneous customers, basal texts reflect more homogeneity than diversity. Although individual basal texts differ considerably in the types of activities, pictorial content, and specific objectives they include, in the main they reflect the dominant curricular pattern.

Mehlinger (1992, p. 149) noted: "Textbook publishers mainly reinforce the status quo. They exist to provide school customers with textbooks needed to teach the existing curriculum. Publishers rarely make money by launching ventures that deviate greatly from current practice." Typically publishers provide few alternatives for educators who wish to experiment with different curriculum configurations or even to vary the grade levels at which certain subjects (e.g., world cultures) are studied (Parker, 1991).

Selection and Adoption of Basal Textbooks

How are the textbooks that appear in elementary, middle, and secondary classrooms selected? Text adoption occurs in two basic ways. One is through local adoption, in which local districts are free to adopt any texts they wish. The other is through state adoption, in which the state in some fashion selects and prescribes the books that the local districts may use.

Currently a majority of states permit local selections of basals. However, about half use state adoption procedures: Alabama, Arkansas, California, Florida, Georgia, Hawaii, Idaho, Indiana, Kentucky, Louisiana, Mississippi, Nevada, New Mexico, North Carolina, Oklahoma, Oregon, South Carolina, Tennessee, Texas, Utah, Virginia, and West Virginia.

Texts typically are adopted for a 5- or 6-year cycle. Adoption committees at the state level often include parents, teachers, college and university faculty, civic leaders, and organizational representatives. A sample form that has been used by adoption committees to evaluate social studies texts is shown in Figure 13.1.

FIGURE 13.1

Sample Social Studies Textbook Evaluation Form

SOURCE: From Division of Instructional Materials, Department of Curriculum & Instruction, Memphis City Schools, Memphis, Tennessee. Used with permission.

ELEMENTARY
SOCIAL STUDIES
TEXTBOOK EVALUATION
FORM

DIVISION OF INSTRUCTIONAL MATERIALS & TECHNOLOGY
DEPARTMENT OF CURRICULUM & INSTRUCTION
MEMPHIS CITY SCHOOLS—MEMPHIS, TENNESSEE
copyright 1990

LIST SECTION TOTALS BELOW
A. TEXTBOOK DEVELOPMENT _____
B. PUBLISHER _____
C. COST _____
D. PHYSICAL FEATURES _____
E. ORGANIZATION _____
F. INSTRUCTIONAL FEATURES _____
G. INSTRUCTIONAL CONTENT _____
H. TEACHER'S EDITION _____
I. ANCILLARY MATERIALS _____
TOTALS—SECTIONS A–I _____

Complete one form for each textbook evaluated for each grade level or course.

Name of Textbook _____

Name of Publisher _____

Name of Series _____

Name of Committee _____ Evaluation Date _____ , 1990

RESPOND TO ALL OF THE STATEMENTS LISTED BELOW BY USING THE FOLLOWING SCALE.

N— **Not Applicable / No Information**

STRONGLY DISAGREE   0 1 2 3 4 5 6   STRONGLY AGREE
AGREE

A. TEXTBOOK DEVELOPMENT

1. There is evidence that the development team of authors, advisors, and consultants includes a wide range of people (grades 1–12 and university teachers).

2. There is evidence that the text and ancillary materials were successfully field tested. _____

3. The field-test data were used to refine and improve the text and ancillary materials. _____

4. The textbook reflects current thinking and knowledge (consider the publication date). _____

5. The textbook can be used successfully for the next six years. _____

   Textbook Development Total _____

B. PUBLISHERS

1. The publisher will provide, at no cost, sufficient professional consultants to help implement the program. _____

2. The publisher will provide, at no cost, continuous consultant services to meet school and classroom needs. _____

3. The publisher will correlate its program to the MCS's social studies objectives within a reasonable time period. _____

4. Reliable and quality service has been provided in the past by the publisher. _____

5. The consultants provided at the hearing were knowledgeable and competent. _____

   Publisher Total _____

Criticisms of Basal Textbooks

Both the process of selecting members of the textbook adoption committees, as well as the selection criteria they use and the recommendations they make, often are politically sensitive and controversial issues. A number of reviews have charged that the textbooks that emerge from the state adoption process are, among other things, bland, overburdened with factual context, overly sensitive to pressure groups, distorted, and watered down (e.g., Apple, 1992; Brophy, 1991; Nelson, 1992; People for the American Way, 1986, 1987; Sewall, 1987; Tyson-Bernstein, 1988).

Textbooks also have been charged with ignoring critical analysis of significant social issues. One social studies teacher characterized the adoption choices in her school district in

FIGURE 13.1 cont'd

C. COST
1. The cost of the textbook is comparable to the cost of other textbooks in the field. _____
2. The cost of ancillary materials is comparable to the cost of other ancillary materials in the field. _____

Cost Total ═══════

D. PHYSICAL FEATURES OF THE TEXTBOOK
1. The size and weight of the text are appropriate for the age of the student. _____
2. The type size and style are clear and appropriate for the age group. _____
3. The binding and cover are durable. _____
4. The paper quality is good. Nonglare paper is used. _____
5. The page layout is uncluttered and balanced. There is sufficient white space for easy reading. _____
6. Provisions for emphasis (heavy type, boxes, color, italics, etc.) are clear and appropriate. _____
7. The illustrations, tables, figures, graphs, charts, and maps are free from sexual and cultural bias. _____
8. The illustrations, tables, figures, graphs, charts, and maps are relevant and functional. _____
9. The cover is attractive, well designed, and appealing to students. _____

Physical Features of Textbook Total ═══════

E. ORGANIZATION OF TEXTBOOK
1. The table of contents shows a logical development of the subject. _____
2. The glossaries/appendices are clear and comprehensive. _____
3. There is uniformity in lesson format within a single text. _____
4. The unit/chapter introductions are clear and comprehensive. _____
5. The unit/chapter summaries suitably reinforce the content. _____
6. There are sufficient, relevant, and well-placed unit/chapter tests. _____
7. There are sufficient, relevant, and well-placed practice exercises. _____
8. The references, bibliographies, and resources are sufficient. _____
9. There is uniformity in development from text to text within the series. (Examine the grade level above and below your committee's grade level.) _____

Organization of Textbook Total ═══════

F. INSTRUCTIONAL FEATURES OF TEXTBOOK
1. The text is written in clear, simple, and logical terms. _____
2. Sentence structure and grammar are correct. _____
3. The style of writing improves comprehension. _____
4. The text provides sufficiently for individual differences. There are suggestions and alternative resources/activities for enrichment, as well as for remediation. _____
5. The reading level is appropriate. _____

(Instructional Features of Textbook continued on next page) _____

FIGURE 13.1 cont'd

6. Key vocabulary is made clear in context or in the glossary. _____
7. End-of-lesson questions review key ideas and vocabulary. _____
8. Atlas and gazetteer sections reinforce the lesson. _____
9. Skills are introduced, taught, and maintained throughout the text. _____
10. Skills are tied to other elementary subjects, such as reading, writing, math, etc. _____
11. The activities appeal to a wide range of student abilities and interests. _____
12. The students are sufficiently encouraged to develop skills beyond literal comprehension. _____
13. New concepts are identified in an easily distinguishable manner (boldface type, etc.). _____
14. There are opportunities for students to apply their skills in interesting, real-world situations. _____
15. There are sufficient activities for independent research and reports. _____
   Instructional Features of Textbook Total ======

G. INSTRUCTIONAL CONTENT OF TEXTBOOK
1. The objectives listed in the proposed curriculum guide under Strand I can be successfully taught using this textbook. _____
2. The objectives listed in the proposed curriculum guide under Strand II can be successfully taught using this textbook. _____
3. The objectives listed in the proposed curriculum guide under Strand III can be successfully taught using this textbook. _____
4. The objectives listed in the proposed curriculum guide under Strand IV can be successfully taught using this textbook. _____
5. The objectives listed in the proposed curriculum guide under Strand V can be successfully taught using this textbook. _____
6. The objectives listed in the proposed curriculum guide under Strand VI can be successfully taught using this textbook. _____
7. Provides thorough geographic coverage and grade-appropriate map and globe skills. _____
8. Map/globe skills are an integral part of the lesson. _____
9. Map/globe skills are reinforced in content-related activities. _____
10. Critical thinking skill development is provided at the lesson, chapter, and/or unit level. _____
11. Coverage of the content is adequate and balanced. _____
12. Sufficient examples of relationships between past and present are provided. _____
13. Covers important historical events and people. _____
14. Biographies of famous people are highlighted. _____
15. The content is actual and factual. _____
16. Historical events are clearly presented and supported by quotations and examples from firsthand accounts. _____
17. Includes all social studies disciplines (history, geography, economics, civics/government, sociology/anthropology). _____
18. Emphasizes responsibilities of citizenship in a democratic society. _____
19. Controversial issues are treated factually and objectively. _____
20. The content is free of biases and prejudices. _____
21. The content is free of sexual and cultural stereotypes. _____
22. Contributions of the sexes and various cultural groups are reflected fairly. _____
   Instructional Content of Textbook Total ======

H. TEACHER'S EDITION/RESOURCE PACKAGE
1. The teacher's edition is easy to use. _____
2. The teacher's edition is comprehensive, well organized, and contains sufficient information for even the inexperienced teacher. _____
3. Step-by-step plans are included on how to implement the student's text in the classroom. _____
4. Objectives are clearly stated. _____
5. Scope and sequence for each level are provided. _____

   (Teacher's Edition/Resource Package continued on next page)

FIGURE 13.1 cont'd

6. Sufficient, complementary assessment tools are included.   _____
7. Supplementary components are referenced in the teaching plans at the appropriate place.   _____
8. Teaching techniques are suggested that improve instructional effectiveness.   _____
9. Includes provision for reteaching skills and concepts related to objectives.   _____
10. Sufficient activities and optional strategies are provided for enrichment and remediation.   _____
11. Answers to exercises and tests are provided on the facsimiles of the student pages.   _____
12. Lists of key vocabulary are included for each unit.   _____
13. Includes a variety of strategies for teaching skills and alternative strategies for reteaching.   _____
14. The size of type is suitable.   _____
     Teacher's Edition Total   =====

I. ANCILLARY MATERIALS
1. Duplicating/blackline masters are of high quality.   _____
2. Printed and/or audiovisual materials being provided at no charge are of high quality and enhance instruction. _____
3. Quality printed and/or audiovisual materials are available at no charge to conduct independent inservice and
   to aid the individual teacher.   _____
4. Transparencies that are being provided at no charge enhance instruction.   _____
5. Software components are available to aid the individual teacher to enhance instruction, meet individual needs,
   and for remediation.   _____
   Testing and Management System
6. Tests are provided for assessment of facts, vocabulary, main ideas, and skills.   _____
7. Sufficient, relevant, and well-placed unit/chapter tests are provided.   _____
8. End-of-level tests (end-of-book) are provided.   _____
9. Placement, diagnostic, and assessment tests provided are reliable and valid.   _____
10. Reproduction rights to placement, diagnostic, and assessment tests are provided to the Memphis City Schools
    at no charge.   _____
    Workbooks
11. Workbooks are clear and well organized.   _____
12. Practice relates to previously taught skills, vocabulary, and concepts.   _____
13. Material extends understanding—not merely "busy work."   _____
14. Include a variety of activities and response formats.   _____
15. Workbooks are simple enough for independent work.   _____
16. Workbooks are appealing to a wide range of students.   _____
17. Sufficient amount of writing space is given.   _____
    Ancillary Materials Total   =====

We, the duly constituted members of the Textbook Adoption Committee, do hereby certify that the information contained in this document represents a consensus opinion that is supported by the undersigned.

1. _____
                                     (Name, School, Date)

2 _____
                                     (Name, School, Date)

3. _____
                                     (Name, School, Date)

this fashion: "Recently, we had to choose between a brain-dead textbook, with no controversy and therefore no content, and one that didn't cover all the topics in the curriculum" (Needham, 1989, p. 4).

Social studies textbooks also often have been found to be riddled with inaccuracies. In 1992, for example, the State Board of Education in Texas fined publishers $647,000 after more than 3,700 errors were discovered in U.S. history textbooks (Viadero, 1992).

Implications of State Adoption Policies

The implications of state adoption policies for the many states and the District of Columbia that do *not* have them and permit local selection are considerable. Because the costs of developing and producing major texts are considerable, publishers have been reluctant to produce more than one for each grade level. Their objective has been to design their products for the greatest possible sales. This goal involved attending carefully to the adoption criteria formulated by the states with the largest student populations among the group of nearly half having state adoption policies. The net effect of state adoption policies has been that a small minority of states have had a major impact on the textbooks that are available to all states.

However, in the wake of controversies over the nature of state adoption processes and the quality of the textbooks they provide for our classrooms, changes are occurring within the publishing industry. These changes should have major implications for the curricular choices schools have. In 1992 the *Social Studies Review* reported:

> The actual number of mass-market social studies textbooks has been gradually diminishing. Some publishers are concluding that it is no longer economic to develop and sell "one-size-fits-all" products. Educators more than ever insist on radically different themes and interpretations in their history books. Increasingly, the position of mass-market textbook publishers seems threatened, and among the headaches are the controversies that attend social studies texts. . . .
>
> The evident movement away from mass-market history textbooks surely creates opportunities for niche textbooks that seek particular audiences. The trend may benefit publishers who produce supplementary and specialized products, including collections of stories, biographies, documents, and other non-traditional source materials. CD-ROMs and video formats will undoubtedly continue to make inroads as teaching devices. ("Textbooks Today," 1992, p. 2)

State adoption processes also are undergoing changes. Utah and Texas, for example, now permit adoptions of newer technology resources such as videodiscs (see Chap. 6) in lieu of textbooks.

C. ALTERNATIVE SOCIAL STUDIES SCOPE AND SEQUENCE PATTERNS

As noted, the social studies texts found in our social studies classes mirror the dominant K–12 scope and sequence pattern that was outlined earlier. Surprisingly, although this pattern is dominant across the United States, there is no explicit national consensus among social studies educators concerning what the scope and sequence of the social studies curriculum should be. Nor is there agreement on whether it even would be desirable to adopt a single scope and sequence model for all of the nation's classrooms.

To the contrary, since the 1916 report of the Committee on Social Studies and the advent of the expanding-communities curriculum model, many social studies educators and various groups have proposed and encouraged the development of alternative patterns for organizing the curriculum (e.g., Joyce, 1972; Welton & Mallan, 1992). In recent years, states and national groups dissatisfied with the dominant pattern of the social studies have advocated detailed alternatives and have worked through the political process to implement their recommendations. We consider briefly several such alternatives, one by a *foundation* (Bradley Commission), one by a *national commission* (National Commission on Social Studies in the Schools), and several others by *national professional organizations* (NCGE/AAG and NCSS).

The Bradley Commission on History Model

In 1988 an independent foundation, the Bradley Commission on History in Schools, issued its recommendations for alternative scope and sequence guidelines. These covered all grades and emphasized the role of history in the curriculum (Bradley Commission on History in Schools, 1988). The commission included some of the same members who worked on the California model, which also places heavy emphasis on the discipline of history.

The recommendations included three alternative patterns for grades K–6 (see Figure 13.2) and four alternatives for grades 7–12.

FIGURE 13.2

Bradley Commission on History: K–6 Curriculum Model

SOURCE: From *Building a History Curriculum: Guidelines for Teaching History in Schools* (p. 18) by Bradley Commission on History in Schools, 1988, Washington, DC: Educational Excellence Network.

Pattern A

Grade	Course
K	Children of Other Lands and Times
1	Families Now and Long Ago
2	Local History: Neighborhoods and Communities
3	Urban History: How Cities Began and Grew
4	State History and Geography: Continuity and Change
5	National History and Geography: Exploration to 1865
6	World History and Geography: The Growth of Civilization

Pattern B

Grade	Course
K	Learning and Working Now and Long Ago
1	A Child's Place in Time and Space
2	People Who Make a Difference
3	Continuity and Change: Local and National History
4	A Changing State
5	United States History and Geography: Making a New Nation
6	World History and Geography: Ancient Civilizations

Pattern C

Grade	Course
K	Children's Adventures: Long Ago and Far Away
1	People Who Made America
2	Traditions, Monuments, and Celebrations
3	Inventors, Innovators, and Immigrants
4	Heroes, Folk Tales, and Legends of the World
5	Biographies and Documents in American History
6	Biographies and Documents in World History

The National Council for Geographic Education/Association of American Geographers Model

In the 1980s, at the same time that advocates for the study of history asserted its claim for supremacy in the curriculum (e.g., Ravitch & Finn, 1987), a strong base of support also developed for the systematic study of geography. As the number of geography departments across the United States decreased over the previous decade and surveys of student knowledge of geography revealed major deficiencies, there was growing national alarm over the prevalence of geographic illiteracy. It was argued, for example, that students were ill-prepared for an era of increasing global interdependence.

Providing leadership for this issue, the National Council for Geographic Education (NCGE) and the Association of American Geographers (AAG) in 1984 issued a set of scope and sequence guidelines that emphasized the study of geography, K–12 (Joint Committee on Geographic Education, 1984). The organizations recommended specific courses for

FIGURE 13.3
Summary of Recommendations for Grades K–6
SOURCE: From *Guidelines for Geographic Education* (pp. 11–16) by Joint Committee on Geographic Education, 1984, Washington, DC: Association of Geographers and National Council for Geographic Education.

Grade Level	Central Focus and Related Geographic Topics
K–2	Self in Space
	Location
	Characteristics in Place
	Homes and Schools in Different Places
	Relative Location
	Characteristics of Microenvironments
	Neighborhoods—Small Places in Larger Communities
	Location
	Environmental Changes
	Interdependence across Space
	Interaction within and between Neighborhoods
	Neighborhoods as Regions with Similarities and Differences
3–4	Community—Sharing Space with Others
	Relative Location
	Characteristics of Landscapes
	Environmental Relationships
	Interdependence and Interaction within Community
	Community as a Region
	The State, Nation, and World
	Location
	Interaction of the Human and Physical Environments
	Human Interactions within and between the State, Nation, and World
	Global Independence
	The Nature of Regions
5–6	United States, Canada, and Mexico
	Location
	Comparative Analysis of Places
	Quality of Life
	Human Interaction in the United States with Canada and Mexico
	Physical and Cultural Regions of the United States, Canada, and Mexico
	Latin America, Europe, Former Soviet Union, Middle East, Asia, and Africa
	Location
	Physical and Cultural Geographic Characteristics
	Human-Environmental Interactions
	Spatial Interrelationships
	Regions and Subregions of the World

grades 7–12, but only general guidelines for geographic topics to be addressed in the elementary school curriculum. Their general recommendations for grades K–6 are summarized in Figure 13.3. Notice the relationship of these guidelines to the current scope and sequence pattern outlined earlier.

The National Commission on Social Studies in the Schools Model

A joint project of the American Historical Association, the Organization of American Historians, the Carnegie Foundation for the Advancement of Teaching, and the NCSS, the National Commission on Social Studies in the Schools in 1989 offered its recommendations for a K–12 social studies curriculum (National Commission on Social Studies in the Schools, 1989). Its proposal avoided specifying particular subject matter for each grade level. Instead the commission's recommendations included a strong emphasis on history and geography across all the grades, as the summary of the curriculum for grades K–6 in Figure 13.4 reveals.

The National Council for the Social Studies Scope and Sequence Initiatives

As the national organization representing social studies teachers, the NCSS has searched over the years for a consensus set of scope and sequence patterns that it could adopt on behalf of its membership and recommend to schools. Early in the 1980s, the NCSS House of Delegates called for the appointment of a committee to develop a series of scope and sequence options for the K–12 curriculum in social studies. As an outgrowth, the NCSS formed a Task Force on Scope and Sequence, which completed and published its report in 1983–1984 (Task Force on Scope and Sequence, 1984).

The task force recommendations generated considerable discussion but little consensus among social studies educators. As a result of the debate, the council invited five additional sets of authors to develop further scope and sequence alternatives (Bragaw, 1986). These were reported in a special issue of *Social Education* that appeared in November/December, 1986.

FIGURE 13.4
Summary of the Curriculum for Grades K–6
SOURCE: From *Charting a Course: Social Studies for the 21st Century* (pp. 9–10) by National Commission on Social Studies in the Schools, 1989, Washington, DC: Author.

Grade	Scope
K–3	[A] sound and imaginative social studies program ought to assure that by the end of grade 3 pupils have achieved an elementary understanding of world geography—continents, major countries, and climate zones, for example—and have a familiarity through maps with their immediate environment at neighborhood, city, state, and national levels. They ought also to know a lot about the community in which they live and have an initial understanding of the civil and political traditions of the United States together with a vivid sense of the variety of human life in different continents and at different times in the past.
4–6	Three social studies courses should be taught during these grades: (a) United States history, (b) world history, and (c) geography, both physical and cultural. These courses must draw much of their content from concepts of the social sciences, especially political science, economics, and anthropology. The order in which these courses are taught is less important than that each course receives the equivalent of a full year's attention. . . . By the end of grade 6, pupils should know much factual information from the disciplines of history, geography, government, and economics and have an elementary sense of how that information relates to national and global understanding.

The National Council for the Social Studies Alternatives. In an attempt to resolve the scope and sequence issue, the NCSS, in 1988, appointed an ad hoc committee to make recommendations among the alternatives for the council's endorsement. Specifically the ad hoc committee was charged with reviewing all NCSS position statements and guidelines and other pertinent materials, including reviews of relevant research. It was to derive basic principles, criteria, and guidelines that should be reflected in any social studies curriculum scope and sequence design. Additionally the committee was to identify three scope and sequence models that most nearly met the criteria it established.

In carrying out its charge and looking to official NCSS policy statements and guidelines, the committee developed 24 general criteria for evaluating a scope and sequence model. These, shown in Figure 13.5, were used to assess the various alternative models that already had been published. The committee also recognized that, with varying degrees of modifications, a number of models could meet the criteria.

Subsequently, on recommendation of the committee, NCSS endorsed three alternative models (NCSS, 1990). In doing so, it left open the possibility that many other models might exist or could be created that met the 24 criteria. Like earlier NCSS initiatives, however, the three alternative scope and sequence models that were identified generated considerable debate but, reflecting the divisions within the field, have failed to attract a consensus.

FIGURE 13.5
Scope and Sequence Criteria
SOURCE: From *Social Studies Curriculum Planning Resources* (p. 16) by National Council for the Social Studies, 1990, Washington, DC: Author. ©National Council for the Social Studies. Reprinted with permission.

A Social Studies Scope and Sequence Should:

1. State the purpose and rationale of the program.
2. Be internally consistent with its stated purposes and rationale.
3. Designate content at every grade level, K–12.
4. Recognize that learning is cumulative.
5. Reflect a balance of local, national, and global content.
6. Reflect a balance of past, present, and future content.
7. Provide for students' understanding of the structure and function of social, economic, and political institutions.
8. Emphasize concepts and generalizations from history and the social sciences.
9. Promote the integration of skills and knowledge.
10. Promote the integration of content across subject areas.
11. Promote the use of a variety of teaching methods and instructional materials.
12. Foster active learning and social interaction.
13. Reflect a clear commitment to democratic beliefs and values.
14. Reflect a global perspective.
15. Foster the knowledge and appreciation of cultural heritage.
16. Foster the knowledge and appreciation of diversity.
17. Foster the building of self-esteem.
18. Be consistent with current research pertaining to how children learn.
19. Be consistent with current scholarships in the disciplines.
20. Incorporate thinking skills and interpersonal skills at all levels.
21. Stress the identification, understanding, and solution of local, national, and global problems.
22. Provide many opportunities for students to learn and practice the basic skills of participation, from observation to advocacy.
23. Promote the transfer of knowledge and skills to life.
24. Have the potential to challenge and excite students.

Apart from meeting the criteria established by the ad hoc committee, the three models are quite different in their designs, emphases, and complexity. Each of them is summarized here.

The Task Force Model. One of the three alternatives selected was the model recommended by the earlier 1984 Task Force on Scope and Sequence (1984, 1989): The NCSS Task Force Model. This model conforms closely to the scope and sequence pattern currently dominant (discussed earlier) across the United States. Apart from a set of basic recommendations, shown in Figure 13.6, the model also offers some optional patterns for grades 6–12.

The Themes and Questions Model. The second model that emerged from the NCSS initiative was developed by Hartoonian and Laughlin (1989). They laid out an alternative based on the assumption that specific scope and sequence decisions should be made by local curriculum committees and teachers. Although the authors did not label their approach, I characterize it as the *themes and questions model* because it spells out themes and questions that local decision makers should consider in developing the curriculum. The themes for grades K–12 are presented in Figure 13.7. The questions that are to be used to shape the K–6 curriculum are presented in Figure 13.8.

The Global Education Model. The third model, developed by Kniep (1989), also is untitled. I refer to it as the *global education model* because it emphasizes global approaches

FIGURE 13.6
NCSS Task Force Scope and Sequence Model
SOURCE: From "In search of a scope and sequence for social studies" by Task Force on Scope and Sequence, 1989, *Social Education, 53* pp. 380–382. ©National Council for the Social Studies. Reprinted with permission.

> *Kindergarten—Awareness of Self in a Social Setting*
> *Grade 1—The Individual in Primary Social Groups: Understanding School and Family Life*
> *Grade 2—Meeting Basic Needs in Nearby Social Groups: The Neighborhood*
> *Grade 3—Sharing Earth Space with Others: The Community*
> *Grade 4—Human Life in Varied Environments: The Region*
> *Grade 5—People of the Americas: The United States and Its Close Neighbors*
> *Grade 6—People and Cultures: Representative World Regions*
> *Grade 7—A Changing World of Many Nations: A Global View*
> *Grade 8—Building a Strong and Free Nation: The United States*
> *Grade 9—Systems That Make a Democratic Society Work: Law, Justice, and Economics*
> *Grade 10—Origins of Major Cultures: A World History*
> *Grade 11—The Maturing of America: United States History*
> *Grade 12—One-year course or courses to be required; selection(s) to be made from the following:*
> *Issues and Problems of Modern Society . . .*
> *Introduction to the Social Sciences . . .*
> *The Arts in Human Societies . . .*
> *International Areas Studies . . .*
> *Social Science Elective Courses . . .*
> *Supervised Experience in Community Affairs*

FIGURE 13.7

Themes and Questions Curriculum Model: Themes for Grades K–12

SOURCE: From "Designing a Social Studies Scope and Sequence for the 21st Century" by H. M. Hartoonian and M. A. Laughlin, 1989, *Social Education, 53,* p. 389. ©National Council for the Social Studies. Reprinted with permission.

Grade Levels

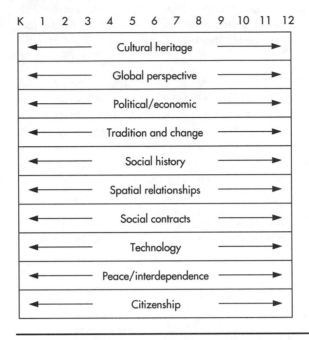

to all social studies topics. Like the themes and questions model, it encourages local decision making with respect to the actual shape of the curriculum.

Kniep proposed that the scope of the curriculum be framed around four areas of study:

- human values
- global systems
- global issues and problems
- global history

His complex model incorporates *conceptual themes, phenomenological themes,* and *persistent problem themes.* He advocates that teachers consider these themes for curriculum organization across the grades. Kniep's conceptual themes are shown in Figure 13.9. Phenomenological themes, which are more complex, include "actors and components playing major roles in the world's systems" (Kniep, 1989, p. 401) and major historical and contemporary events. The persistent problem themes, according to Kniep, address both local and global problems shown in Figure 13.10. He proposed a complex weaving of the three types of themes throughout each grade level from K–12.

FIGURE 13.8

Themes and Questions Curriculum Model: Questions for Grades K–6

SOURCE: From "Designing a Social Studies Scope and Sequence for the 21st Century" by H. M. Hartoonian and M. A. Laughlin, 1989, *Social Education, 53*, pp. 380–381. ©National Council for the Social Studies. Reprinted with permission.

Kindergarten—Awareness of Self in a Social Setting

The major thrust of the kindergarten program should be to provide socialization experiences that help children bridge their home life with the group life of the school. Teachers can expect considerable variation in the extent of kindergartners' experience in group settings. Some have been in day-care centers or preschools for two or three years. Others are entering a social environment that involves several other children for the first time. Learning about the physical and social environments of the school will thus be different for individual children. Nevertheless, they all need to begin to learn the reasons for rules as required for orderly social relationships. Awareness of self should be developed through face-to-face relationships with others in social settings. It is important at this level to provide children with success experiences to help them develop self-esteem. Some structured experiences to sensitize children to a world of many and diverse peoples and cultures need to be included.

Grade 1—The Individual in Primary Social Groups: Understanding School and Family Life

The socialization to school begun in kindergarten should be continued and extended in 1st grade. Basic concepts related to social studies content should be introduced. Children can learn the specialized roles of school personnel as an example of division of labor. Family life and structure, including variations of family structures, should be included, as well as roles of family members. Essential activities of a family in meeting basic material and psychological needs should be stressed. Variations in the way families live need to be studied: e.g., urban, rural, self-employed, single-parent family arrangements, and various housing options. Dependence of family members on one another and of the family on other families should be stressed. Children should learn that the family is the primary support group for people everywhere. The need for rules and laws should be taught as a natural extension of orderly group life. History can be presented through the study of the children's own families and the study of family life in earlier times. Learning about family life in other cultures provides opportunities for comparing ways of living. The globe should be introduced along with simple maps to promote learning of geographic concepts and relationships. It is important that the program include some study of the world beyond the neighborhood. Direct experience and hands-on activities are essential at this level, but the program should be organized around specific social studies goals and objectives rather than consisting of unstructured play activities in social settings.

Grade 2—Meeting Basic Needs in Nearby Social Groups: The Neighborhood

Meeting basic requirements of living in nearby social groups should be the central theme in 2nd grade. The program should emphasize that the neighborhood is the students' own unique place in space, and they should learn some of the ways their space interacts with the rest of the world. It is in the study of the neighborhood that students can and should learn on a firsthand basis some of the most elemental of human relationships such as sharing and caring, helping others in time of need, and living harmoniously with neighbors. The study of social functions such as education, production, consumption, communication, and transportation in a neighborhood context are appropriate as children develop an understanding and appreciation of people in groups. The need for rules and laws should be stressed and illustrated by examples from the everyday lives of children. Geographic concepts relating to direction and physical features of the landscape need to be included. A global perspective is important and can be sought through the study of a neighborhood life in another culture. Contrasting neighborhood life today with what it was in an earlier time should also be included to provide historical perspective.

(Continued)

FIGURE 13.8 cont'd

Grade 3—Sharing Earth Space with Others: The Community

The community in a global setting is the focus of study at the 3rd grade level. The local community provides an excellent laboratory for the study of social life because all aspects of social living take place there. But the concept of community should not be limited to the local area. It is essential that some attention be given to the global community. Social functions such as production, transportation, communication, distribution, and government, including their international connections, should be stressed. The concepts of dependence and interdependence can be emphasized at the local, national, and international levels. Geographic concepts and skills should be extended to include the interactions of human beings with the environment. Place location and map-reading skills must be stressed. Some emphasis should be given to the study of the history of the local community, especially relevant social history and biographies of prominent local citizens.

Grade 4—Human Life in Varied Environments: The Region

The 4th grade is the ideal level to focus on basic geographic concepts and related skills. The major emphasis in the 4th grade is the region, an area of the earth that is defined for a specific reason. Where state regulations require it, the home state may be studied as a political region. World geographic regions defined in terms of physical features, climate, agricultural production, industrial development, or economic level should be selected for study. Culture regions of the past and present may also be included. There should be some variation in the regions selected for study to illustrate the adaptability of human beings to varied environments. All the basic map- and globe-reading skills should be included in the program. History should be included in the units of study to show how places have changed over time. Economic concepts such as *resources, scarcity,* and *exchange* should be used to illustrate how regions of the world interact.

Grade 5—People of the Americas: The United States and Its Close Neighbors

The 5th grade program focuses on the development of the United States as a nation in the Western Hemisphere, with particular emphasis on developing affective attachments to those principles on which this nation was founded and that guided its development. The diverse cultural, ethnic, and racial origins of the American people should be stressed. Attention should be directed to specific individuals who have contributed to the political, social, economic, and cultural life of the nation. The inclusion of biographies of prominent American men and women of diverse ethnic origins is essential to highlight values embraced by this society. The 5th grade program should familiarize learners with the history and geography of the closest neighbor nations of the United States: Canada and Mexico.

Grade 6—People and Cultures: Representative World Regions

The focus of the 6th grade program is on selected people and cultures of the Eastern Hemisphere and Latin America. The people and cultures should be representative of (1) major geographical regions of the world; (2) levels of economic development; (3) historical development; (4) political and value systems. The interdependence of nations should be a major theme. Instruction needs to be directed toward understanding and appreciating the lifeways of other people through the development of such concepts as language, technology, institutions, and belief systems.

It is recommended that *at least* one semester of systematic study be devoted to Latin America in either the 6th *or* 7th grade. The cultural, political, and economic linkages with the United States should be emphasized. The growing importance of Latin America in international political and economic affairs should be stressed.

FIGURE 13.9

The Global Education Curriculum Model: Conceptual Themes for Grades K–12

SOURCE: From "Social Studies with a Global Education" by W. M. Kniep, 1989, *Social Education, 53,* p. 401.
©National Council for the Social Studies. Reprinted with permission.

1. **Interdependence**

   We live in a world of systems in which the actors and components interact to make up a unified, functioning whole.
   Related concepts: causation, community, government, groups, interaction systems.

2. **Change**

   The process of movement from one state of being to another is a universal aspect of the planet and is an inevitable part of life and living.
   Related concepts: adaption, cause and effect, development, evolution, growth, revolution, time.

3. **Culture**

   People create social environments and systems comprised of unique beliefs, values, traditions, language customs, technology, and institutions as a way of meeting basic human needs; these are shaped by their own physical environments and contact with other cultures.
   Related concepts: adaption, aesthetics, diversity, languages, norms, roles, values, space-time.

4. **Scarcity**

   An imbalance exists between relatively unlimited wants and limited available resources necessitating the creation of systems for deciding how resources are to be distributed.
   Related concepts: conflict, exploration, migration, opportunity, cost, policy, resources, specialization.

5. **Conflict**

   People and nations often have differing values and opposing goals resulting in disagreement, tensions, and sometimes violence, necessitating skill in coexistence, negotiation, living with ambiguity, and conflict resolution.
   Related concepts: authority, collaboration, competition, interests/positions, justice, power, rights.

D. SELECTING A SCOPE AND SEQUENCE PATTERN

For better or worse, no singular alternative scope and sequence model looms on the horizon to challenge seriously the dominant national curricular pattern outlined earlier, the one on which existing basal texts are based. Similarly no consensus has emerged regarding the issue of whether it even would be desirable to have a common pattern across all school districts, with all their diversity and disproportionate needs.

The several alternative models presented, as well as others proposed (see Downey, 1986; Engle & Ochoa, 1986; Stanley & Nelson, 1986), along with the related criteria for selecting a scope and sequence, should provide teachers and schools with some basic frameworks for decision making. Ultimately the development of reflective, competent, and concerned citizens depends less on the scope and sequence decisions that are made for the nation, states, and local school districts than on the curricula that teachers and students construct in individual classrooms.

FIGURE 13.10
The Global Education Curriculum Model: Persistent, Problem Themes, Grades K–12
SOURCE: From "Social Studies with a Global Education" by W. M. Kniep, 1989, *Social Education, 53,* p. 401.
© National Council for the Social Studies. Reprinted with permission.

Peace and Security
the arms race
East-West relations
terrorism
colonialism
democracy vs. tyranny

National/International Development
hunger and poverty
North-South relations
appropriate technology
international debt crisis

Environmental Problems
acid rain
pollution of streams
depletion of rain forests
nuclear-waste disposal
maintenance of fisheries

Human Rights
apartheid
indigenous homelands
political imprisonment
religious persecution
refugees

SUMMARY

This chapter has reviewed existing and alternative social studies scope and sequence patterns, the roles of basal textbooks in the social studies curriculum, and how to select a scope and sequence pattern.

Chapters that follow will provide further detailed understanding of how to teach the social studies and how to integrate them into the curriculum.

QUESTIONS AND ACTIVITIES FOR DISCUSSION

1. Analyze the alternative scope and sequence models discussed in the chapter and select one you find to be most appealing. Discuss what you consider to be its strengths and limitations.

2. Identify three basal social studies textbooks series for the intermediate and middle school grades. Focus on the fourth- and sixth-grade texts and the titles of unit topics in each. Compare the lists of topics for each grade level. To what extent are they similar, and how are they different?

3. Determine the adoption policies for social studies texts in either a local school district or at the state level (if applicable). Discuss what you regard as the strengths and weaknesses of the adoption policy.

REFERENCES

Apple, M. W. (1992). The text and cultural politics. *Educational Researcher, 21,* 4–11, 19.

Bradley Commission on History in Schools. (1988). *Building a history curriculum: Guidelines for teaching history in schools.* Washington, DC: Educational Excellence Network.

Bragaw, D. (1986). Scope and sequence alternatives for the future. *Social Education, 50,* 484–485.

Brophy, J. (1991). *Distinctive curriculum materials in K–6 social studies* (Elementary Subjects Center Series No. 35). East Lansing: Michigan State University, Institute for Research on Teaching, Center for the Learning and Teaching of Elementary Subjects.

Downey, M. T. (1986). Time, space, and culture. *Social Education, 50,* 490–501.

Engle, S. H., & Ochoa, A. (1986). A curriculum for democratic citizenship. *Social Education, 50,* 514–525.

Hanna, P. R. (1963). Revising the social studies: What is needed? *Social Education, 27,* 190–196.

Hartoonian, H. M., & Laughlin, M. A. (1989). Designing a social studies scope and sequence for the 21st century. *Social Education, 53,* 388–398.

Joint Committee on Geographic Education. (1984). *Guidelines for geographic education.* Washington, DC: Association of American Geographers and National Council for Geographic Education.

Joyce, B. R. (1972). *New strategies for social education.* Chicago: Science Research Associates.

Joyce, W. W., Little, T. H., & Wronski, S. P. (1991). Scope and sequence, goals, and objectives: Effects on social studies. In J. P. Shaver (Ed.), *Handbook of social studies teaching and learning* (pp. 321–331). New York: Macmillan.

Kniep, W. M. (1989). Social studies within a global education. *Social Education, 53,* 399–403.

Mehlinger, H. D. (1992). The National Commission on Social Studies in the Schools: An example of the politics of curriculum reform in the United States. *Social Education, 56,* 149–153.

National Commission on Social Studies in the Schools. (1989). *Charting a course: Social studies for the 21st century.* Washington, DC: Author.

National Council for the Social Studies (NCSS). (1990). *Social studies curriculum planning resources.* Washington, DC: Author.

Needham, N. R. (1989, March). Is there a decent textbook in your future? *NEA Today, 7,* 4–5.

Nelson, M. R. (1992). *Children's social studies* (2nd ed.). Orlando, FL: Harcourt Brace Jovanovich.

Parker, W. C. (1991). *Renewing the social studies curriculum.* Alexandria, VA: Association for Supervision and Curriculum Development.

People for the American Way. (1986). *Looking at history: A major review of U.S. history textbooks.* Washington, DC: Author.

People for the American Way. (1987). *We the people: A review of U.S. government and civics textbooks.* Washington, DC: Author.

Powers, J. B. (1986). Paul R. Hanna's scope and sequence. *Social Education, 50,* 502–512.

Ravitch, D., & Finn, C. (1987). *What do our 17-year-olds know?* New York: Harper & Row.

Sewall, G. T. (1987). *American history textbooks: An assessment of quality.* Washington DC: Educational Excellence Network.

Shaver, J. P., Davis, Jr., O. L., & Hepburn, S. W. (1979). The status of social studies education: Impressions from three NSF studies. *Social Education, 39,* 150–153.

Stanley, W. B., & Nelson, J. L. (1986). Social education for social transformation. *Social Education, 50,* 528–534.

Superka, D. P., Hawke, S., & Morrissett, I. (1980). The current and future status of the social studies. *Social Education, 40,* 362–369.

Task Force on Scope and Sequence. (1984). In search of a scope and sequence for social studies. *Social Education, 48,* 249–262.

Task Force on Scope and Sequence. (1989). In search of a scope and sequence for social studies. *Social Education, 53,* 376–387.

Textbooks today: How sensitive? How accurate? (1992, Spring). *Social Studies Review,* pp. 1–2.

Tyson-Bernstein, H. (1988). *A conspiracy of good intentions: America's textbook fiasco.* Washington, DC: Council for Basic Education.

Viadero, D. (1992, August 5). Texas assesses $860,000 in new fines for textbook errors. *Education Week,* p. 22.

Welton, D. A., & Mallan, J. T. (1992). *Children and their world: Strategies for teaching social studies* (4th ed.). Boston: Houghton-Mifflin.

Fostering Citizenship Competency: Developing and Applying Research and Analysis, Chronology, and Spatial Skills

I n this chapter you will develop your understanding of

1. The nature and extent of citizenship skills.
2. The essential skills for social studies in intermediate and middle school grades.
3. A definition of a socially competent individual.
4. Conflict resolution skills.
5. How to help your students develop research and analysis skills.
6. How to help your students develop chronology skills.
7. How to help your students develop their spatial skills.
8. How to help your students identify and use reference sources.

> During the first unit of the year, our work as a class focused on writing a book about the classroom and the school. Different activities involved surveying the school population for basic demographic information, for example, age and ethnic groups, drawing maps of the classroom, interviewing teachers, and writing autobiographies.
>
> Three weeks of the unit were spent working with maps. By the end of the year, I hope that my students will be able to interpret and use maps in meaningful ways. Rather than show them a map and teach them how to use scale and key, I decided to start our work on maps by having students construct a map of the classroom. (Wilson, 1990, p. 7)

Children, such as the students in the example above, acquire and use skills most effectively in the context of solving meaningful problems and performing tasks they regard as interesting, functional, or important. Skills facilitate knowledge construction by enabling us to locate, analyze, validate, and apply information efficiently. Effective social studies instruction encourages students to both develop and use skills. It also provides guidelines for when and why it is appropriate to employ the skills (Brophy, 1992).

A. THE NATURE OF CITIZENSHIP SKILLS

Citizens require a repertoire of competencies (skills) to function effectively in our complex society. Numerous lists of skills have been advanced for development throughout the social studies curriculum. For example, all basal social studies textbook programs provide enumerations of the various skills that are embedded in the materials. Typically such lists sequence the skills in the order they are to be taught, K–12. They also suggest the relative degrees of emphasis each type of skill should receive (Jarolimek & Parker, 1993).

Skills Lists for the Social Studies Curriculum, K–12

One such comprehensive set of skills, shown in Figure 14.1, was produced by the National Council for the Social Studies' Task Force on Scope and Sequence (Task Force on Scope and Sequence, 1989). It provides a detailed inventory of the diverse competencies that students are to develop within their social studies programs.

The list includes three major categories of skills and a number of subcategories. It also suggests the degree of emphasis that each type of skill should receive at different grade levels. This and other similar lists can serve as references for identifying skills to emphasize in planning lessons and units.

In the remainder of the chapter, we consider ways in which social studies programs across the elementary and middle grades can nurture the development and application of skills in the context of lessons and units. We focus on a sample of the skills outlined in Figure 14.1 that are organized under four categories of competencies central to effective citizenship: *social skills, research and analysis skills, chronology skills,* and *spatial skills.*

B. SOCIAL SKILLS

Whether at home, at school, on the job, or at a party, having good relationships with others, or "getting along," requires social skills. They are the glue that binds groups and society as a whole together harmoniously and productively. In whatever we hope to accomplish cooperatively with other individuals, social skills are instrumental in achieving our goals.

If our social environment is rich in positive models and experiences as we mature, we continuously acquire and integrate sets of valuable social skills. Once mastered, such skills often are applied to settings different from the ones in which they were learned. In this fashion, over time, many people manage to assimilate naturally the basic social competencies necessary to navigate successfully through life.

Socially Competent Children

We regard as *socially competent* those individuals who have acquired the necessary skills to work and communicate effectively with a variety of people in different situations. As teachers can testify, children appear at the school door for the first time with varying levels of proficiency in social skills. Social competency often is learned, at least in part, informally and naturally through family training and peer imitation. Children, for example, usually learn not to interrupt a conversation when another is speaking or how to listen as well as to talk.

One study concluded that, among other behaviors, the socially competent 6-year-old can

- get and maintain the attention of adults in socially acceptable ways
- use adults as resources in socially acceptable ways
- express both affection and hostility to adults
- both lead and follow peers, compete with them, and express both affection and hostility to them.

Conflict Resolution Skills

Arguably one of the most important skills that socially competent citizens in a democratic society have is the ability to resolve conflicts in a nonviolent and socially acceptable manner. Conflicts surround us. In all regions of our nation, children of every age and from every socioeconomic stratum are exposed to conflict in a variety of forms. Nightly on television they can view episodes of conflict between parents and among other adults, between ethnic groups or countries, among politicians, and between neighborhood gangs. The alarming national statistics on child abuse and gang deaths also suggest that many students often experience violent conflict firsthand and are themselves the victims of conflict and misplaced aggression.

Strategies for resolving conflicts. Many of children's personal conflicts deal with access to desired concrete objects (e.g., candy, toys), rather than with abstractions (e.g., different points of view). Classroom activities that encourage children to experiment with alternative ways of resolving conflicts can help prepare them to cope with the larger conflicts

FIGURE 14.1
Essential Skills for Social Studies
SOURCE: ©National Council for the Social Studies. Reprinted with permission.

Suggested strength of instructional effort:	—— Minimum or none	— Some	▬ Major	██ Intense

I. Skills related to acquiring information

A. Reading skills

1. Comprehension

K–3	4–6	7–9	10–12	Skill
▬	██	—	——	Read to get literal meaning
——	██	▬	——	Use chapter and section headings, topic sentences, and summary sentences to select main ideas
——	▬	▬	——	Differentiate main and subordinate ideas
——	▬	▬	——	Select passages that are pertinent to the topic studied
——	—	▬	██	Interpret what is read by drawing inferences
——	—	▬	—	Detect cause-and-effect relationships
——	—	▬	▬	Distinguish between the fact and opinion; recognize propaganda
				Recognize author bias
██	██	▬	—	Use picture clues and picture captions to aid comprehension
—	▬	██	██	Use literature to enrich meaning
——	▬	██	▬	Read for a variety of purposes: critically, analytically, to predict outcomes, to answer a question, to form an opinion, to skim for facts
——	—	▬	██	Read various forms of printed material: books, magazines, newspapers, directories, schedules, journals

2. Vocabulary

K–3	4–6	7–9	10–12	Skill
██	██	—	—	Use usual word attack skills: sight recognition, phonetic analysis, structural analysis
—	▬	██	—	Use context clues to gain meaning
—	▬	▬	—	Use appropriate sources to gain meaning of essential terms and vocabulary: glossary, dictionary, text, word lists
—	██	██	▬	Recognize and understand an increasing number of social studies terms

3. Rate of Reading

K–3	4–6	7–9	10–12	Skill
——	▬	▬	██	Adjust speed of reading to suit purpose
——	▬	▬	▬	Adjust rate of reading to difficulty of the material

B. Study skills

Find information

K–3	4–6	7–9	10–12	Skill
——	▬	—	—	Use various parts of a book (index, table of contents, etc.)
——	—	—	—	Use key words, letters on volumes, index, and cross references to find information
——	—	—	██	Evaluate sources of information—print, visual, electronic
——	—	▬	▬	Use appropriate source of information
——	—	▬	▬	Use the community as a resource

2. Arrange information in usable forms

K–3	4–6	7–9	10–12	Skill
——	—	▬	▬	Make outline of topic
——	—	▬	▬	Prepare summaries
——	—	▬	—	Make time lines
——	—	▬	▬	Take notes
——	—	▬	▬	Keep records
——	—	▬	▬	Use italics, marginal notes, and footnotes
██	▬	—	—	Listen for information
██	▬	—	—	Follow directions
——	—	▬	██	Write reports and research papers
——	—	▬	██	Prepare a bibliography

C. Reference and information-search skills

1. The library

K–3	4–6	7–9	10–12	Skill
——	—	▬	▬	Use card catalog to locate books
——	—	▬	▬	Use *Reader's Guide to Periodical Literature* and other indexes
——	—	—	▬	Use COMCATS (Computer Catalog Service)
——	—	—	—	Use public library telephone information service

2. Special references

K–3	4–6	7–9	10–12	Skill
——	—	—	▬	Almanacs
—	██	—	—	Encyclopedias
—	██	—	—	Dictionary
——	—	▬	—	Indexes
——	—	—	—	Government publications
——	—	—	—	Microfiche
——	—	▬	▬	Periodicals
——	—	▬	▬	News sources: newspapers, news magazines, TV, radio, videotapes, artifacts

3. Maps, globes, graphics
Use map- and globe-reading skills

K–3	4–6	7–9	10–12	Skill
——	▬	▬	—	Orient a map and note directions
—	▬	▬	—	Locate places on map and globe
——	—	▬	—	Use scale and compute distances
——	—	▬	██	Interpret map symbols and visualize what they mean

(Continued)

FIGURE 14.1 cont'd

Suggested strength of instructional effort:	——— Minimum or none	——— Some	▬▬ Major	███ Intense

Skill	K–3	4–6	7–9	10–12
Compare maps and make inferences	Minimum	Some	Major	Major
Express relative location	Minimum	Some	Major	Major
Interpret graphs	Minimum	Some	Intense	Intense
Detect bias in visual material	Minimum	Some	Intense	Intense
Interpret social and political messages of cartoons	Minimum	Some	Major	Major
Interpret history through artifacts	Minimum	Some	—	—

4. Community resources

Skill	K–3	4–6	7–9	10–12
Use sources of information in the community	Minimum	Some	Major	Major
Conduct interviews of individuals in the community	Minimum	Some	Major	Major
Use community newspapers	Minimum	Major	Major	Some

D. Technical skills unique to electronic devices

1. Computer

Skill	K–3	4–6	7–9	10–12
Operate a computer using prepared instructional or reference programs	Minimum	Some	Major	Major
Operate a computer to enter and retrieve information gathered from a variety of sources	Minimum	Some	Major	Major

2. Telephone and television information networks

Skill	K–3	4–6	7–9	10–12
Ability to access information through networks	Minimum	Some	Some	Some

II. Skills related to organizing and using information

A. Thinking skills

1. Classify information

Skill	K–3	4–6	7–9	10–12
Identify relevant factual material	Minimum	Some	Major	Major
Sense relationship between items of factual information	Minimum	Some	Major	Major
Group data in categories according to appropriate criteria	Some	Some	Major	Major
Place in proper sequence: (1) order of occurrence (2) order of importance	Minimum	Some	Major	Major
Place data in tabular form: charts, graphs, illustrations	Minimum	Some	Major	Major

2. Interpret information

Skill	K–3	4–6	7–9	10–12
State relationships between categories of information	Minimum	Some	Major	Major
Note cause-and-effect relationships	Minimum	Some	Major	Intense
Draw inferences from factual material	Minimum	Some	Major	Intense
Predict likely outcomes based on factual information	Minimum	Some	Major	Major
Recognize the value dimension of interpreting factual material	Minimum	Some	Major	Major
Recognize instances in which more than one interpretation of factual material is valid	Minimum	Some	Some	Major

3. Analyze information

Skill	K–3	4–6	7–9	10–12
Form a simple organization of key ideas related to a topic	Minimum	Some	Major	Major
Seperate a topic into major components according to appropriate criteria	Minimum	Some	Major	Major
Examine critically relationships between and among elements of a topic	Minimum	Some	Some	Major
Detect bias in data presented in various forms: graphics, tabular, visual, print	Minimum	Some	Major	Intense
Compare and contrast credibility of differing accounts of the same event	Minimum	Some	Major	Intense

4. Summarize information

Skill	K–3	4–6	7–9	10–12
Extract significant ideas from supporting, illustrative details	Minimum	Some	Major	Major
Combine critical concepts into a statement of conclusions based on information	Minimum	Some	Major	Major
Restate major ideas of a complex topic in concise form	Minimum	Some	Major	Major
Form opinion based on critical examination of relevant information	Minimum	Some	Major	Intense
State hypotheses for further study	Minimum	Some	Major	Intense

5. Synthesize information

Skill	K–3	4–6	7–9	10–12
Propose a new plan of operation, create a new	Minimum	Some	Some	Major

that reside within our society. These techniques include helping them understand the sources of disagreements and confrontations and work out constructive solutions to their own conflicts.

Approaches to teaching conflict resolution skills should communicate to children that the presence of some level of conflict is a normal, everyday occurrence in a complex, interdependent society and world. Conflicts arise when the goals of individuals or groups

FIGURE 14.1 cont'd

| Suggested strength of instructional effort: | —— Minimum or none | — Some | ▬ Major | ■ Intense |

K–3 4–6 7–9 10–12

system, or devise a futuristic scheme based on available information

Reinterpret events in terms of what *might* have happened, and show the likely effects on subsequent events

Present visually (chart, graph, diagram, model, etc.) information extracted from print

Prepare a research paper that requires a creative solution to a problem

Communicate orally and in writing

6. Evaluate information

Determine whether or not the information is pertinent to the topic

Estimate the adequacy of the information

Test the validity of the information, using such criteria as source, objectivity, technical correctness, currency

B. Decision-making skills

Identify a situation in which a dicision is required

Secure needed factual information relevant to making the decision

Recognize the values implicit in the situation and the issues that flow from them

Identify alternative courses of action and predict likely consequences of each

Make decision based on the data obtained

Take action to implement the decision

C. Metacognitive skills

Select an appropriate strategy to solve a problem

Self-monitor one's thinking process

III. Skills related to interpersonal relationships and social participation

A. Personal skills

K–3 4–6 7–9 10–12

Express personal convictions

Communicate own beliefs, feelings, and convictions

Adjust own behavior to fit the dynamics of various groups and situations

Recognize the mutual relationship between human beings in satisfying one another's needs

B. Group interaction skills

Contribute to the development of a supportive climate in groups

Participate in making rules and guidelines for group life

Serve as a leader or follower

Assist in setting goals for the group

Participate in delegating duties, organizing, planning, making decisions, and taking action in a group setting

Participate in persuading, compromising, debating, and negotiating in the resolution of conflicts and differences

C. Social and political participation skills

Keep informed on issues that affect society

Identify situations in which social action is required

Work individually or with others to decide on an appropriate course of action

Work to influence those in postitions of social power to strive for extensions of freedom, social justice, and human rights

Accept and fulfill social responsibilities associated with citizenship in a free society

---

clash. The resolution of conflict can be destructive (e.g., a fight, battle) or constructive (e.g., a compromise, treaty).

A number of practical programs, guidelines, and strategies exist for aiding teachers in addressing conflict resolution. For example, Scherer (1992) outlined ten basic negotiating skills that teachers can help children develop. These are shown in Figure 14.2. Another example of an excellent resource is Byrnes's (1987) little book, *Teacher, They*

FIGURE 14.2

Basic Negotiating Skills

SOURCE: From "Solving Conflicts—Not Just for Children" by M. Scherer, 1992, *Educational Leadership, 50,* p. 17. Copyright by ASCD. Reprinted with permission.

- Check whether you understand the other person correctly and whether he or she understands you.
- Tell the other person what you think: don't try to read another's mind or tell others what you think they think.
- Talk about needs, feelings, and interests, instead of restating opposing positions.
- Recognize negotiable conflicts and avoid nonnegotiable ones.
- Know how to tend to deal with most conflicts and recognize others' styles.
- Put yourself in the other's shoes.
- Understand how anger affects your ability to handle conflict and learn how to avoid violence even when you're angry.
- Reframe the issues; talk about them in other ways to find more common ground between yourself and the other person.
- Criticize what people say, rather than who or what they are.
- Seek win-win solutions, not compromises; find solutions where all parties get what they need, rather than solutions where all get some of what they need.

Called Me a _____! It includes items for both primary and intermediate grade children, many of which involve conflict themes.

Other activities that address conflict themes involve the use of the following, adapted from Anderson and Henner (1972):

1. *Open-ended sentences* for completion or to initiate a paragraph, such as "One reason that countries have wars is _____."
2. *Tense situations* or scenarios in which the class is given a question or premise to consider involving a conflict. Students then are asked to role-play the characters in the scene. For example, they enact an incident in which a group of youngsters unjustly accused of breaking windows tries to figure out how to make the guilty people confess.
3. *No-conflict settings* that demonstrate the positive, as well as the negative, possibilities of conflict. Students may be asked to react to scenarios similar to the following: What would football and basketball be like if there were no conflicts in the games?
4. *Fighting words* that include cases illustrating how individuals often insert into an argument provocative words they know will anger another. Students could be asked to consider words, phrases, or actions that they and others use to provoke family members or friends. They also may be asked to identify the occasions on which the words or actions might be used and the responses they produce.

Role playing, puppetry, and simulations are especially effective instructional tools for developing conflict resolution skills. Under the protection of roles or the disguise of puppets, children have an opportunity to explore and test different solutions.

C. RESEARCH AND ANALYSIS SKILLS

Research and analysis skills are interrelated and often inseparable in applications. *Research* can be viewed as the process of finding information in response to some question. It includes the identification, gathering, and recording of data. *Analysis,* however, involves the process of examining, verifying, and comparing data to arrive at some conclusion. Often such skills are labeled critical thinking skills because they incorporate elements that are essential for informed thought.

The ability to select appropriate information, record it accurately, and organize it in some accessible fashion constitutes one of the social scientist's most important collections of skills. It also is a vital competency for the effective citizen; we all, on occasion, need to have a complete and correct account of some event and to secure this information in a form that can be accessed easily.

Three subcategories of research and analysis skills that all citizens require and that we examine in more detail are *identifying and using reference sources, interpreting and comparing data,* and *processing information from pictures.*

Identifying and Using Reference Sources

One issue in using reference sources effectively is identifying just what a "reference" might be. Virtually anything or anyone may serve as a reference for a particular question or problem. For example, if we are trying to decide whether a film is worth seeing, we may either call a friend who has seen it for an opinion or locate a recent review of the film in a newspaper or magazine.

The telephone book and the Yellow Pages are examples of reference sources that most individuals have around their homes and use frequently. Similarly, when we wish to discover the meaning or correct spelling of a word, we typically consult a dictionary.

Because the range of reference materials available in their homes is often limited, students should be encouraged to go beyond them. This advancement involves learning about the nature and use of specialized reference works typically found in libraries (usually in the Reference Materials section). Where computer-based references are used, technology skills also are required.

The notion that many sources can and should be considered as appropriate reference possibilities is an important one for students to learn. Similarly, they should understand the basic criterion for judging the value of a reference work: how useful and authoritative is it for solving a problem or answering a question?

Sample reference works for social studies. A sample of the numerous reference works that both teachers and students have found to be useful in the social studies follows:

- *Album of American History.* This multivolume history of the United States is composed of pictures arranged chronologically.
- *Dictionary of American Biography.* This is a multivolume source of information on deceased Americans who have made some significant contribution to American life. Included are politicians, artists, musicians, writers, scientists, educators, and many others.
- *Dictionary of American History.* This multivolume work is arranged alphabetically and includes articles on a variety of historical topics, some famous and some not so well known.
- *Discoverers: An Encyclopedia of Explorers and Explorations.* In a single volume are included details on a number of individuals who were pioneers in their time, along with their exploits.
- *Goode's World Atlas.* This is an authoritative and comprehensive atlas of the world.
- *The Illustrated History of the World and Its People.* In 30 volumes a wealth of information is presented on the geography, people, history, arts, culture, and literature of individual countries of the world. Also covered are such topics as foods, religions, dress, holidays, festivals, customs, and educational systems of the countries, as well as many other aspects.
- *Statesman's Yearbook.* A succinct thumbnail sketch of each country is provided in one volume.
- *The Story of America: A National Geographic Picture Atlas.* An extensive collection of visual, spatial, and narrative data on each of the states.
- *The Timetables of History.* In a chronologically organized single volume, a wide variety of important dates are included, covering seven major categories of American life.
- *Worldmark Encyclopedia of the Nations.* This multivolume guide to nations is arranged alphabetically by country and provides basic information on each country's social, political, historical, economical, and geographical features.

Encyclopedias as references. To promote a well-balanced understanding of individuals or groups, teachers should alert students to the limitations of encyclopedias. Because of their attempt to be comprehensive, encyclopedias are severely constrained in the amount of space they can devote to any single topic. No matter how authoritatively and carefully any topic has been researched and written, an encyclopedia entry must omit a great deal of material. This limitation applies to both print and electronic encyclopedias.

Consider, for example, if you were asked to sum up your life in an essay that someone will use to learn about you. The restrictions are that the essay must be no more than 250

FIGURE 14.3
Sample Problem Sheet

Problem Sheet

Directions

You are to discover the identity of Country Z, a real country, described below. Use any reference sources that you wish. The ones that have been identified for you may be especially helpful. After you have discovered which country it is, list all of the references you consulted. Then tell whether each of the references helped you learn the identity of the country and in what way.

Data on Country Z

Country Z covers an area of about 900,000 square miles and has approximately 25,000,000 people. Arabic is the official language of the country. However, many people also speak French, because the country once was controlled by France.

Country Z is bordered on the north by the sea and by desert areas in other parts of the country. The nation lies north of the equator, and its coastal areas have a warm temperate climate. There are plateaus and mountains but no major lakes.

Major agricultural products include wheat, oranges, watermelons, and olives. Livestock consists of horses, cattle, sheep, goats, and camels. Country Z also has many fisheries. Two of its major exports are natural gas and oil.

Follow-up Activity

Which reference sources did you use to determine the identity?
Which sources were useful and in what way?

---

words, all of the information must be accurate and objective, the reading level must be no higher than the fourth grade, and you must include everything anyone would need to know. The reader will have no other information about you. If you feel at all uncomfortable about having to record your life's history under these limiting conditions, keep in mind that entire groups and nations are often described in encyclopedias under the same constraints.

Activities for introducing reference materials. One way to introduce reference materials in a meaningful context is to create interesting, puzzling, or intriguing questions for students that require them to use such sources. The difficulty of the questions may be varied for different age and ability groups by providing more or fewer clues. The actual reference resources to be used in answering the questions may be made available within the classroom. As alternatives, students may be given a list of helpful reference materials or just be allowed to use the school library to identify resources on their own.

Two types of activities that can be used to introduce reference materials in the context of solving interesting problems are a *problem sheet* and a *task card*.

Problem sheet. Consider the activity in Figure 14.3 for intermediate or middle school students.

The problem sheet could have contained additional information that would make the solution somewhat easier. For example, the following data can be inserted into the paragraphs of the original description to give students more clues. These additions make it easier to limit the countries that could match the description.

1. The country has approximately 20 people per square mile.
2. Life expectancy is about 62 years.
3. Approximately half of the people live in urban areas.
4. The name of the capital begins with the same letter as the name of the country.
5. The country shares a border with seven other countries.

Country Z is, in fact, Algeria, officially known as the People's Democratic Republic of Algeria. Any similar set of data that presents a puzzle or problem—whether it deals with a country, a city, an event, or an individual—can satisfy the same objective. The aim is to have students discover the functional value of reference sources through an interesting and challenging activity.

FIGURE 14.4
Sample Task Card

Task Card

Directions

The set of questions below can be answered by using the reference books identified earlier. All of these books are in the library. Find the reference book that answers each of the questions and then write the answers on a separate sheet of paper.

1. Who was the founder of the Girl Scouts of America?
2. What are some of the customs and dress of the people of Chad?
3. What are the main functions of the Federal Reserve Board?
4. How does the per-capita income of Saudi Arabia compare with that of other countries in the Middle East?
5. Locate a picture of a Model T Ford. When did it appear, and what was unusual about it?
6. What do you consider to have been the most important contribution of Charles Ives?
7. What are the major industries in Algeria?
8. What are some of the major events that happened in the year your mother (or your father) was born?
9. Locate Butte in the index for the state of Montana. What major park is southeast of it?
10. Locate and copy a recipe from a foreign country.

Task card. Even a basic set of questions listed on a card can be used to introduce reference materials in an interesting way. A task card can be used especially effectively in learning centers where young children are working independently of the teacher. The sample task card in Figure 14.4 contains a set of questions, all of which can be answered by consulting the appropriate book from the list of ten reference sources provided earlier.

Interpreting and Comparing Data

A key aspect of research and analysis is interpreting and comparing data accurately and meaningfully. This skill requires paying careful attention to what is heard, seen, felt, and even tasted or smelled. Data are encountered through all of our senses. We may process these data firsthand through personal encounters, such as attending a concert or a meeting, and also indirectly, as when we read a book that describes a person, place, or event.

Comprehensive skills programs. Comprehensive programs that promote children's reasoning abilities are available for youngsters across all ages and developmental abilities. They also cover a wide variety of skills. One such program, *Philosophy for Children,* has been developed by the Institute for the Advancement of Philosophy for Children (1987). The program includes materials for elementary, middle, and secondary grade students. Skills that the program attempts to develop include the following:

- Classifying and categorizing
- Defining terms
- Drawing inferences from premises
- Finding underlying assumptions
- Formulating causal explanations
- Searching for informal fallacies
- Predicting consequences
- Working with contradictions
- Identifying and using criteria.

Cultural filters in interpreting and comparing data. Effectively processing and interpreting data requires a recognition that each of us also filters what we experience through lenses that are shaped by our experiences and culture.

We are all familiar with the phenomenon that different individuals processing the same data often focus on different aspects and, as a result, report different accounts of what was experienced. Five people from a rural area, for example, who visit the same section of the Bowery in New York for the same length of time may come away with different accounts of what each observed. One may focus on the despair in the faces of the derelicts encountered. Another may talk about the noise and the traffic. Still another may emphasize the drab visual landscape, the scattered debris on the sidewalks and streets, and the decaying areas. A fourth may remember the melange of smells that seemed offensive but distinct. The last member may have little clear recollection of any of the above aspects, but instead vividly recall with some detail the assortment of little shops and vendors.

Each of the accounts may be a reasonably accurate report of what one person actually experienced, but they are clearly different. Further, each single observation offers only a limited view. Taken as a whole, however, the set of perspectives may present a more adequate account of the Bowery than any single report.

An activity from a social studies text provides an illustration of how students can be helped to understand cultural filters. As part of tracing the events leading up to the end of the Revolutionary War, the authors of the text *The American Nation* (Prentice-Hall, 1986, p. E8), for example, ask students to compare the views of Washington and Cornwallis concerning the Battle of Yorktown. Through the activity, the students acquire both a skill and further insights into how the long and debilitating war was viewed by both sides.

Students using the text are provided with the excerpts shown in Figure 14.5. They also are given guidelines for comparing points of view and a set of questions that includes these:

What is Cornwallis's view of the events at Yorktown?

What reason or reasons does Cornwallis give for surrendering?

What is Washington's view of the events at Yorktown?

Why did Cornwallis and Washington have different points of view?

All the different accounts of an event may be reasonably accurate reports of what each person actually experienced, but they are clearly different. Students should learn to recognize that any single account is not necessarily more accurate, representative, or factual than another. Taken as a whole, however, collective accounts may present a more complete account than any single report.

In the social studies, tasks that students are called on to perform in processing and interpreting written materials include similar considerations. In interpreting and comparing data, students must try to distinguish fact from opinion, bias from objectivity, reality from fiction, extraneous from essential information, and neutral from emotional words, as well

FIGURE 14.5
Comparing Two Points of View
SOURCE: *Teacher's Resource Guide: The American Nation* (Englewood Cliffs, NJ: Prentice-Hall, 1986), p. E8.

These two excerpts are from reports on the Battle of Yorktown. Read them carefully. Then, using the guidelines for comparing two points of view in Skill Lesson 8, answer the questions that follow.

Report of Cornwallis to the commander of British forces in America, October 19, 1781.

I have the shameful task to inform your Excellency that I have been forced to surrender the troops under my command to the combined forces of America and France. . . . [Cornwallis then describes how his outnumbered forces were surrounded and attacked by the American and French forces.]

Our numbers had been reduced by the enemy's fire, but particularly by sickness and by the fatigue of constant watching and duty. Under these circumstances, I thought it would have been inhuman to sacrifice the lives of this small body of gallant soldiers by exposing them to an assault [by the enemy] which could not fail to succeed. I therefore proposed to surrender. I enclose the terms of the surrender. I sincerely regret that better could not be obtained, but I have neglected nothing in my power to lessen the misfortune and distress of both officers and soldiers.

Report of Washington to the President of Congress, October 19, 1781.

I have the honor to inform Congress that the defeat of the British army under the command of Lord Cornwallis is most happily achieved. The tireless devotion which moved every officer and solder in the combined army on this occasion has led to this important event sooner than I had hoped. . . .

I should be lacking in gratitude if I did not mention the very able help of his Excellency the Count de Rochambeau [a French commander] and all his officers. I also feel myself indebted to the Count de Grasse [the French admiral] and the officers of the fleet under his command.

as determine the perspective of those who provide data. Students often also must reflect on what is excluded from, as well as included in, written accounts.

Interpreting and comparing written materials. In our citizen roles, we often must process and interpret information from such sources as texts and books, articles, charts, graphs, tables, and pictures. In the social studies, it is especially important that students early on begin to develop the skills to interpret and compare carefully a variety of written materials reflecting different perspectives, including those of text authors. As competent citizens, students must be able to distinguish fact from opinion, bias from objectivity, reality from fiction, and extraneous from essential information. They also must be able to differentiate neutral from emotion-laden terms and to consider what is excluded, as well as included, in written material.

The acquisition of such skills is a complex process that occurs slowly over time for children. Further, stage theorists argue that the process is related, at least in part, to the developmental level of the students (Cole & Cole, 1989). Written material, especially, often presents students with special problems in making interpretations and comparisons, frequently because they have difficulties with reading in general.

Comparing biographical accounts. All of the skills considered in the preceding section are called into play in the analysis of subject matter such as biographical accounts. Students cannot possibly avoid reading all biographies that suffer from flaws, nor should teachers try to prevent them. To attempt to shield students completely from inaccurate or distorted biographical accounts would be both undesirable and unrealistic. Doing so would cut them off from dealing with the same kind of deficiencies that abound in the mass media and everyday experiences that they encounter.

As an alternative, teachers can engage students in exercises that involve comparative analyses of biographical accounts. For example, students can be asked to read several biographical accounts of the same person and compare the discrepancies. This can be followed with discussion of questions such as these:

1. What did each of the books say about _____ with respect to the nature of his (her) childhood, important people in his (her) life, educational background, interests and aspirations, and major accomplishments?
2. What things were similar in the books you read?
3. What things were different in the books you read?
4. How would you sum up what you have learned from reading all of the books about _____'s life?

Analyzing arguments. Biographical accounts, and many other analyses of people, places, and events, often suffer from *bias, distortion,* and *faulty logic.* The ability to detect these elements in argumentation is critical to effective citizenship. Developing competency in these skills requires continuous practice and application in the context of the research and analysis of subject matter. It also involves wide exposure to bias and distortion in all its forms, including that in the mass media, arguments of respected figures and demagogues alike, and even textbooks.

Detecting bias and distortion. It is far more effective for students to encounter bias and distortion in their natural constructions, rather than in the abstracted or edited forms that typically appear in student texts. This suggests that a social studies classroom should be a forum for a wide array of materials from a diverse assortment of individuals and groups. Students also should be encouraged to share cases of bias and distortion that they encounter in materials.

If the assortment of such materials collected is rich in examples, it may evoke controversy and even possible criticism, unless the purpose for its presence is clearly established. The teacher needs to make clear at the outset and reiterate periodically that *in no way does the presence of material imply endorsement of either its content or authors and sponsors.* Similarly, it may be necessary to establish some ground rules, consistent with school policies, concerning the types of materials that must be excluded and under what circumstances (e.g., pornographic material, racial hate literature in an emotionally charged multiracial class).

Logical reasoning. Arguments that are free from bias and distortion nonetheless may be flawed in their reasoning. Helping students detect errors in reasoning requires some work with logic. This in turn demands translating assertions and arguments into some form where it can be analyzed. One such form is a *syllogism*. Syllogisms are statements arranged in the following order:

All men and women are mortal.

Catherine is a woman.

Therefore, Catherine is mortal.

Casting arguments in the form of syllogisms. Although most assertions and arguments do not appear neatly in a syllogistic form, they often can be recast with minor revisions and reorganization. Consider this hypothetical conversation between Harry and Sarah:

> *Harry:*　What are those sly Russians up to? They have just advocated more nuclear arms limitations.
> *Sarah:*　Yeah? So what's the problem with that?
> *Harry:*　You know the Russkies can never be trusted.
> *Sarah:*　You mean if they are pushing disarmament, there must be something wrong with it?
> *Harry:*　You got it.
> *Sarah:*　I see your point.

Organized as a syllogism, the argument mutually advanced by Sarah and Harry appears as follows:

If the Soviets support something, there must be something wrong with it.

The Soviets support disarmament.

There must be something wrong with disarmament.

In this case the *major premise,* the first statement in the syllogism, was inferred but never actually stated in the conversation—a frequent occurrence in discussions. When confronted with the inferred premise, Harry and Sarah likely would disavow it, since the Soviets support many things with which we would find nothing wrong, including breathing, eating, and motherhood.

If one were to accept the unstated major premise of the argument, it *would* logically follow that "there must be something wrong with disarmament." Thus, this example also illustrates how a logically *valid* argument can result from a premise that is *false*.

Testing the validity of syllogisms. One way that students can be helped to ascertain whether an argument (i.e., the conclusion follows from the major premise) is valid or invalid is through the use of circle diagrams. The one shown in Figure 14.6 diagrams the first syllogism that we presented. It demonstrates that the circle representing "Catherine" *must* be placed within the largest circle representing "mortal people," since she has been placed within the circle "men and women."

The circle diagram shown in Figure 14.7 similarly illustrates how the circles can be used to uncover *invalid* arguments. Therein, the example diagramed proceeded in this fashion: All mechanical things are made by people and computers. Airplanes are made by people and computers. They, therefore, are mechanical things. Since "airplanes" may be placed *anywhere* within the circle "things made by people and computers," it need not follow that they are one of the "mechanical things."

Interpreting and comparing charts, graphs, and tables. In our society much of the information we share with one another is communicated through charts, graphs, and tables. Each edition of a local paper carries numerous examples of each. They abound in

FIGURE 14.6
Circle Diagram Showing Argument Is Logically Valid

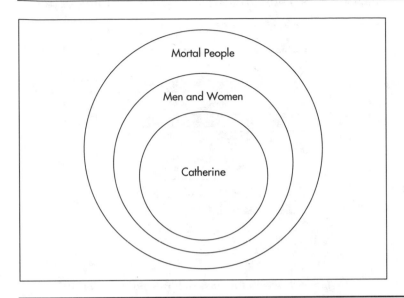

FIGURE 14.7
Circle Diagram Showing Argument Is Logically Invalid

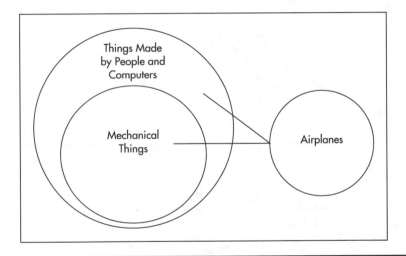

newspapers and periodicals such as the *New York Times, USA Today, Time, Newsweek,* and *U.S. News and World Report,* as well as student editions of newspapers. They also appear in televised newscasts.

Citizens, journalists, newscasters, and social scientists alike use charts, graphs, and tables to summarize information or to simplify communication. For example, if demographers wish to cut through reams of statistical data and detailed narrative to represent one dimension of population distribution, they may use a graph such as that shown in Figure 14.8. For other purposes, a table may be more appropriate (see, for example, Table 14.1).

For students, however, extracting facts, generalizations, and hypotheses from charts, graphs, and tables is frequently a difficult task. This is particularly the case when the chart, graph, or table contains many details and quantitative data.

Charts, graphs, and tables, when accompanied by probing questions and teacher-guided analysis, can serve as springboards to reflective thinking within lessons and units. For example, consider Mr. Hernandez, who wishes to have his fourth-grade students develop and test generalizations about population patterns. He initially might engage them in an analysis

FIGURE 14.8

A Graph of Population Distribution

SOURCE: From *1990 Census Profile* (p. 3) by U.S. Department of Commerce, Bureau of the Census, 1991, Washington, DC: Author.

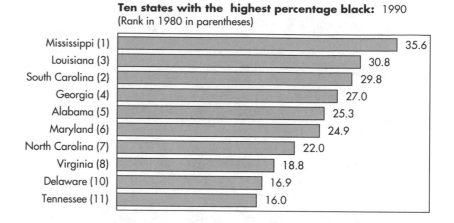

Ten states with the highest percentage black: 1990
(Rank in 1980 in parentheses)

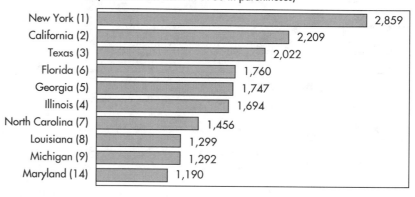

Ten states with the largest black population: 1990
(In thousands. Rank in 1980 in parentheses)

TABLE 14.1

Ten Largest American Indian Reservations (Population in Thousands), 1990

Navajo, AZ–NM–UT	143.4
Pine Ridge, NE–SD	11.2
Fort Apache, AZ	9.8
Gila River, AZ	9.1
Papago, AZ	8.5
Rosebud, SD	8.0
San Carlos, AZ	7.1
Zuni Pueblo, AZ–NM	7.1
Hopi, AZ	7.1
Blackfeet, MT	7.0

SOURCE: From *1990 Census Profile* (p. 6) by U.S. Department of Commerce, Bureau of the Census, 1991, Washington, DC: Author.

of the census data presented in Figure 14.8. Referring to a large wall map of the United States, he then could ask the class members to place red stickers on the states that had the highest percentage of black populations in the most recent census. This could be followed by an analysis of the pattern that emerged and a request for hypotheses to account for it. Students could test their hypotheses by collecting information on the states by using reference works such as almanacs.

FIGURE 14.9

Pie Chart Showing Percentages of Time Spent by a Sixth Grader during a 48-Hour Week Period

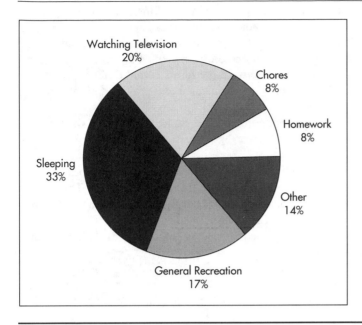

FIGURE 14.10

Percentage of Time Spent in Various Activities This Past Saturday and Sunday by Members of Our Group

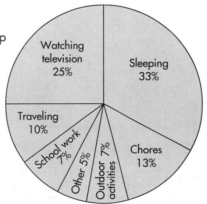

Beyond assistance in skillfully interpreting the data of others, students also need guidance in representing their own analyses in the form of charts, graphs, and tables. An example of such representations is the pie chart in Figure 14.9. They need first to gain competency in handling small, simple sets of data, rather than to be overwhelmed at the outset. Teachers can help provide natural experiences by incorporating charts, graphs, and tables into all of their lessons and current affairs discussions to help explain a point, answer a question, or frame a problem.

Children in the intermediate and middle school grades may experiment with computer tools to help them represent data in the form of charts, graphs, and tables. An example is the pie chart in Figure 14.10. It was completed by a sixth-grade student using a basic computer software graphing program called *Data Plot*.

Processing Information from Pictures

One of the most common forms of teaching materials in the social studies is pictures or pictorial print materials. Visual materials can enrich and enliven instruction. Research suggests that learning through imagery is often easier than through other forms (Somer, 1978; Wittrock, 1986; Wittrock & Goldberg, 1975).

Types of pictures. It would be impossible to categorize all of the different types of pictorial data that could be used in the social studies. Many visual materials are descriptive, such as a picture of an individual or an area. Some pictures are to be used in a set to tell a story or to represent an event, such as phases of the Battle of Gettysburg. Others have varying degrees of open-endedness, such as cartoons. These forms permit different viewers to have varied interpretations of what is being communicated and provide springboards for discussion.

Still other photos are highly expressive, portraying or arousing emotions. Examples of such pictures are shots of starving people, war-ravaged areas, and small children emoting.

Using political cartoons in instruction. Political cartoons are a visual form that can be especially effective for dramatizing an issue in social studies instruction. The cartoon shown in Figure 14.11, for example, encapsulates the rich irony that accompanies the cruel and endless tragedy of religious warfare in Lebanon.

A sample set of questions that could be used to process this and (with slight revisions) similar political cartoons is:

1. What do you see in the picture?
2. What does each of the figures and items in the picture stand for?

FIGURE 14.11
Political Cartoon
SOURCE: Tony Auth, *The Philadelphia Inquirer.*

3. What is the issue that is represented in the picture?
4. What do you think the cartoonist thought of each of the figures in the picture?
5. What would be an appropriate caption for the cartoon?

D. CHRONOLOGY SKILLS

Much of what we typically do both in our daily lives and in social studies classes involves *chronology,* some understanding of how people, places, items, and events are oriented in time. As adults, we are comfortable with related time concepts such as *a long time ago, recently, in the past,* and *infinity.* From a very young child's perspective, a basic concept of time involves understanding which items came first and which came last and a sense of what typically happens as the result of the passage of units we call hours, days, weeks, months, or years.

For middle school students, chronology competencies evolve to include an understanding of the interrelationship of events and individuals over a temporal period. They also include a sense of what is meant by a unit such as a century. Eventually, the competencies enlarge to an understanding of the abstractness and arbitrariness of all units of time, whether they be measured in nanoseconds, eons, or some new standard.

Comparative Conceptions of Time

In each society, the larger culture and various subcultures shape the ways in which individuals both conceive of time and respond to its passage. Thus, a Bostonian may come to characterize the pace of life in rural South Carolina as "slow" and that in Manhattan as "fast." On an international scale, this generalization means that diverse nations often view the past, present, and future in different terms.

On a planetary scale, different views of time also are possible. Hawking (1988), in *A Brief History of Time,* has pointed out that contemporary physicists' perspectives on time in space are quite different from those people on Earth use to guide their daily lives.

> Consider a pair of twins. Suppose that one twin goes to live on the top of a mountain while the other stays at sea level. The first twin would age faster than the second. Thus, if they meet again, one would be older than the other. In this case, the difference in ages would be very small, but it would be much larger if one of the twins went for a long trip in a spaceship at nearly the speed of light. When he returned, he would be much younger than the one who stayed on Earth. This is known as the twins paradox, but it is a paradox only if one has the idea of absolute time at the back of one's mind. In the theory of relativity there is no unique absolute time, but instead each individual has his own personal measure of time that depends on where he is and how he is moving. (p. 33)

Recording Events on Time Lines and Charts

Time lines and charts provide a simple system for listing, ordering, and comparing events over some period of time. Any unit of time may be used in a time line, ranging from a day to centuries. Similarly, any theme may be used, for instance, constitutional amendments or major advances in medicine. Time lines and charts may be organized horizontally or vertically. They appear in the form of simple sequential listings of items (time lines) or more detailed chronologies of events in their order of occurrence (time charts).

They function as a *summary* of a series of events over time or as an *exercise* that requires an individual to cognitively structure data in a meaningful pattern. To illustrate the differences in the applications, consider the simple time line shown in Figure 14.12 that *summarizes* for a reader some major events over two decades.

Alternately, entertain a task that requires you to *create* a time line. For example, place in the correct order of occurrence the following events: President Nixon's visit to China, the end of the Vietnam War, the Wright brothers' first flight, the beginning of the Civil War, the assassination of President Kennedy, the invention of xerography, and the premiere of *Gone with the Wind.* Compare your sequence with the following, arranged in ascending order:

The beginning of the Civil War

The Wright brothers' first flight

The premiere of *Gone with the Wind*

FIGURE 14.12
Simple Time Line

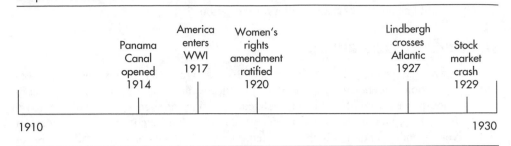

FIGURE 14.13
Simple Time Line
of Some Major
Civil War Battles

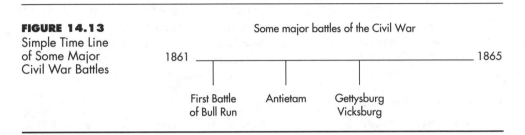

FIGURE 14.14
The Lumbee Indians: Searching for Justice, Searching for Identity
SOURCE: From *Tar Heel Junior Historian Teacher's Supplement* (p. 23) by Tar Heel Junior Historian Association, 1989,
Raleigh, NC: North Carolina Museum of History, 1989.

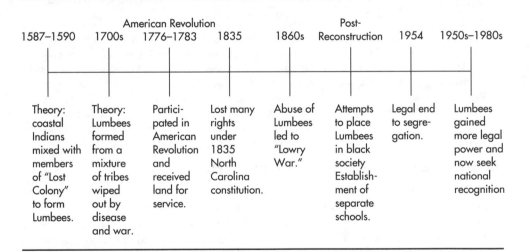

The invention of xerography

The assassination of President Kennedy

President Nixon's visit to China

The end of the Vietnam War.

Any unit of time, ranging from a day to centuries, may be used in a time line. Similarly, any context or theme may be the basis for a time line—for instance, what I did today in the order I did it. Two illustrations of time lines with differing degrees of detail are shown in Figures 14.13 and 14.14.

Time lines may be organized horizontally or vertically. They also may be three-dimensional. For instance, a clothes-hanger mobile can be used to organize drawings, pictures, artifacts, or artwork that visually symbolizes items such as forms of transportation, inventions, and changing life-styles from different time periods. Similarly, lengths of yarn and

FIGURE 14.15
Example of a Time Line Activity
SOURCE: Adapted from *Man: A Course of Study (MACOS)* by Educational Development Center, 1968, Cambridge, MA:
Author. Copyright 1968 by Educational Development Center.

Lifeline Time Line Activity

Materials List. The materials required for this activity are:

Roll of transparent tape for each group
Large box of crayons for each group
Pile of 3″ × 5″ blank cards for each group
Pile of colored construction paper for each group
Felt-tipped colored pens for each group
6′ piece of string or yarn for each child
Pair of scissors for each child
Pencil or pen for each child

Procedures. The following procedures are suggested:

Organize the children arbitrarily into groups of five in an area where they will have lots of room to spread out with their materials. A floor area may be a good place. Give directions such as these: "Each of you hold up your piece of string (or yarn) like this." (Demonstrate by stretching out your arms with one end of the string in the left hand and the other in your right.) "This is your lifeline. One end is the beginning, and the other is the end of your life. You are to put on your lifeline all of the things you can think of that have been or are important in your life. You can draw pictures of the important things or cut out things that show them." (If the children are old enough, they also may be encouraged to write on the pieces.) "After you decide on the important things and make them, put them on your lifeline with tape or in some other way. Put the *first* important thing that ever happened to you *first* on the lifeline." (And so on.) "*You may include anything you like and show it in any way you like.* Use and share any of the materials you have in your group."

Once each child is started, try to refrain from helping too much to avoid structuring children's responses. As they complete their lifelines, children should be paired off to share them, describing and explaining each event. After each pair finishes, create a new pair until each child has finished and has had an opportunity to share with at least two others. Finally, after the children hang their lifelines around the room or on lines strung up, let them move about to examine those they have not seen.

---

objects or pictures can be used. An example of this last approach for constructing a three-dimensional time line activity is presented in Figure 14.15.

Showing causal relationships with time lines and charts. Often time lines and charts can be used to illustrate *causal* relationships, as well as temporal sequences. Genealogies, like the one in Figure 14.16, are examples of such applications.

Other Chronology Activities

Some of the other ways students can be helped to grasp concepts related to time are *time visits, identification with some figure in the past,* and *developing imaginary dialogues between famous historical figures.*

Time visits require students to pick some time in the past and then to compare conditions that once existed with those in their own lives. For example, students might be asked to examine the similarities in and differences between their lives and those of children of the colonial period.

To identify with a historical character, a student must try to imagine the world of the past that the historical character experienced. Creating a make-believe diary that the character might have authored is one way of building such identification. A student might be asked to pick any special day during the period under study and to write a page in a diary telling what the day was like. The diary could record items such as what the individual would observe and record and what would seem important and interesting.

To create an imaginary dialogue between individuals, students must incorporate actual historical data and real figures from different time periods, such as George Washington and Abraham Lincoln. Through the imaginary dialogues, the students attempt to create a plausible discussion that might have taken place between the personalities. In this way they compare and contrast both different periods and individuals.

FIGURE 14.16
Genealogy of the Imperial Family
SOURCE: *Simply Japan* (Atlanta, GA: Consulate General of Japan, May 1989).

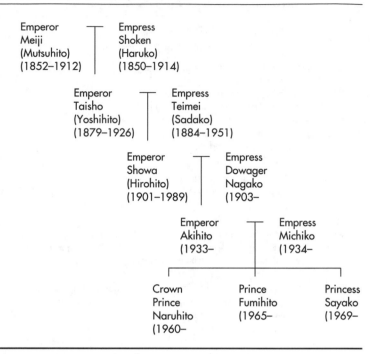

E. SPATIAL SKILLS

In an increasingly interdependent nation and world, citizens have greater need than ever before for skills that can better orient them in space. Competent citizens must be able to locate themselves and others spatially in order to travel, exchange ideas, and access artifacts. Spatial skills most often appear in social studies in the discipline of geography, but they are distributed throughout all areas of the social sciences. Identifying political boundaries, the locations of cities, landmarks, and land masses, and determining the relationship of one object in space to another are all part of spatial understanding.

The Impact of Spatial Perspectives

As citizens we also need to become aware of how our spatial perspectives and vocabularies influence many of our social, political, and economic perspectives. Whether we view something as far away, densely populated, large, hot, barren, or growing, for example, may impact on whether we decide to visit a region, seek a job there, or change our residence.

Even the language we use in describing an area can skew our perspective. Collins (no date) noted, for example, "Terms we select to describe other nations—and the present state of their social, economic, political development—influence students' perception of those nations." As an illustration, for years Africa was characterized by teachers and texts as "the dark continent," thus creating a host of negative associations. Further, unlike most other regions of the world, the continent, rather than the nations within it, was studied as a whole. This practice created the misperception of a high degree of uniformity among all Africans.

Maps and Globes as Spatial Tools

The most common ways individuals in our society use to orient themselves and to answer related spatial questions are through the application of existing maps and the creation of new ones. To a lesser extent, individuals consult globes to answer questions.

Initially maps and globes are difficult to understand when children first encounter them in the primary grades (Muir, 1985). A *globe* is a model of the Earth; *maps* are models or representations of portions of a globe. More simply stated, maps are representations of some object or place on the Earth as seen from a bird's-eye view.

FIGURE 14.17
A Robinson Projection

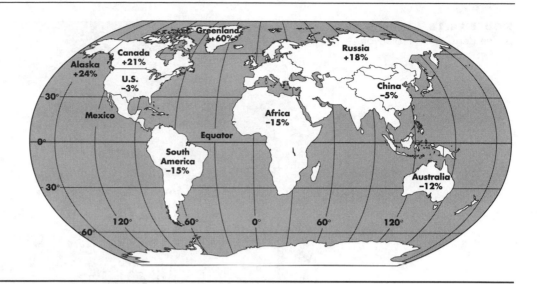

To a child, maps and globes do not look at all like what they represent. Elements such as "imaginary lines," which do not exist in reality but are clearly visible on maps and globes, are confusing. Concepts that are entwined in spatial skills, such as *boundary lines, Earth, latitude, longitude,* and *equator,* have no concrete referents in the real world. Moreover, many of the maps and globes used in classrooms contain far more information than the average elementary student can understand or use.

Map and globe distortions. Children should be sensitized to the relevant distortion and measurement issues associated with different projections. In representing regions on the Earth, maps and globes do so with varying degrees of distortion. Since the first maps, nations often have deliberately distorted, for political purposes, the maps they used. They have done this, for example, by extending or reshaping boundaries and rerouting rivers, as suits their interpretation of historical claims. Apart from those deliberate distortions, all projections of areas on the Earth's surface are functionally distorted in some ways because of the problem of translating a curved surface onto a flat one.

The National Geographical Society, in 1989, adopted the Robinson projection (see Figure 14.17) as one that produced the least distortion for most nonspecialized map applications. It is compared with the traditional Van der Grinten projection shown in Figure 14.18, which the society had used since 1922 for most of its world maps.

Notice the differences in the sizes and shapes of Greenland and the United States shown in each of the projections. Because of its location on the Earth, in seven different projections, the shape and size of Greenland will be different in each. Even in the Robinson projection shown, Greenland is still 60 percent larger than it should be. In the Van der Grinten projection, it is 554 percent larger.

Integrating Maps and Globes into All Social Studies Instruction

Jarolimek and Parker (1993, p. 174) suggested that maps can furnish eight basic types of information:

1. *Land and water forms*—continents, oceans, bays, peninsulas, islands, straits
2. *Relief features*—plains, mountains, rivers, deserts, plateaus, swamps, valleys
3. *Direction and distance*—cardinal directions, distance in miles or kilometers and relative distance, scale
4. *Social data*—population density, size of communities, location of major cities, relationship of social data to other factors
5. *Economic information*—industrial and agricultural production, soil fertility, trade factors, location of industries

FIGURE 14.18
A Van der Grinten Projection

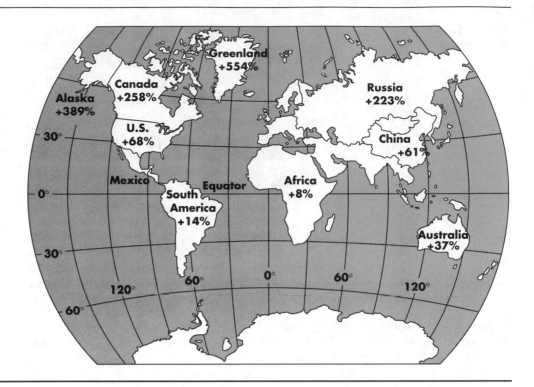

6. *Political information*—political divisions, boundaries, capitals, territorial possessions, types of government, political parties
7. *Scientific information*—locations of discoveries, ocean currents, location of mineral and ore deposits, geological formations, air movements
8. *Human factors*—cities, canals, railroads, highways, coaxial and fiber-optic cables, telephone lines, bridges, dams, nuclear power plants.

Ideally maps and globes should be an integral part of all social studies instruction. A natural and functional way to integrate the use of maps and globes into social studies is to use them to help answer questions that the teacher or the students generate while studying a subject (e.g., Why does it get colder as you travel south in Australia?)

An example of a lesson that integrates spatial, as well as research and analysis, skills is provided in Figure 14.19. The issue that the lesson centers on is, What special problems do landlocked nations face?

As they learn about people in other parts of the nation or the world, students should locate where they live on a map or a globe. Children also should discover early on that one type of map or globe can answer some spatial questions, whereas other types will be needed for different questions.

Examples of different types of maps that answer various questions are shown in Figures 14.20 and 14.21. The two maps answer questions concerning (a) the use of a scale to determine distance between two cities in a region and (b) the location of certain natural resources. Maps also can help provide answers to questions such as, Where are concentrations of minorities and ethnic groups in the United States? Where are the most promising areas to locate new major league baseball franchises? Where are the ski runs and chairlifts located at a ski resort?

Introducing Maps and Globes

Because maps and globes are the primary tools through which spatial skills are taught, it is important that children be properly introduced to them. The initial stages of instruction in map and globe usage should concentrate on those aspects for which immediate concrete referents are available. These include developing and using maps of the child's immediate environment, such as the school, classroom, and home, and the areas bordering each.

FIGURE 14.19
Lesson That Integrates Spatial Skills Development and Application
SOURCE: *Teaching Geography: A Model for Action.* (Washington, D.C.: National Geographic Society, 1988), pp. 36–37.
Copyright ©1988 National Geographic Society.

UNDERSTANDING THE DILEMMA OF LANDLOCKED NATIONS

Many of the world's independent nations are without access to the sea—they are landlocked. With some exceptions, landlocked nations are generally small, developing countries with numerous social and economic problems. This lesson plan explores the background essential to understanding the problems that landlocked nations face.

Objectives

- To define the geographic theme "location."
- To define the term "landlocked" and to identify the world's landlocked nations.
- To identify advantages and disadvantages of being landlocked in both a historical and a contemporary context.
- To research social and economic data about landlocked countries and to draw conclusions about the economic development of such countries.
- To identify the origin of problems that landlocked nations face.
- To investigate how certain countries came to be landlocked.
- To speculate on places that could become landlocked in the future.

For Discussion

- What is a landlocked nation?
- Many goods in international trade are shipped by sea for at least part of their journey. What does this mean to countries without coastlines? (Examples: Dependence on neighboring countries; delays in receiving goods; tariffs; and transportation costs.)
- Identify some countries that lost their coastlines in war.
- Using examples from current events, identify places that could become landlocked in the future.

Follow-up Activities

- Divide the class into two groups. Assign one group to report on the historical and current advantages of being landlocked. Assign the second group to report on the disadvantages. Discuss the relative merits of each viewpoint.
- Ask the class to do research on landlocked countries, using almanacs, encyclopedias, textbooks, and other resources. Display information about each country on a chart. List generalizations that can be made about landlocked nations. Point out exceptions.
- Have each student select two countries—one that is landlocked and one that is not—and use a data book or an almanac to analyze statistics about them. Suggest that students pay special attention to indicators of social and economic development, such as life expectancy, adult literacy, population growth rate, and GNP per capita. They have each student write an essay comparing the two countries.
- Have students select and read about a landlocked nation and then prepare an oral report about the country's problems. Have students include the importance of relative location to each country's problems.

In the primary grades, children begin to map the most immediately concrete objects they know—themselves—through the use of body maps. These are outlines of the children's bodies drawn on large sheets of paper.

After students have had experiences in creating body maps, they can transfer the general principle of mapping to other familiar concrete objects found in their classroom, school, home, or neighborhood (see Figure 14.22). In addition to commercially produced spatial tools, materials such as toys and blocks may be used in mapping activities for building cities and the like.

Unlike maps, globes give children a three-dimensional model of our planet. In essence, a globe is like many of the toy models of cars and dolls, with which students are already familiar. Through the use of globes, children can see the relationships between all of the land masses and bodies of water on the Earth. They also can begin to develop a sense of the relative distances between major points on the Earth. When students have access to a *relief globe,* they can even feel elevated areas of the Earth such as the Rocky Mountains.

Several useful sets of guidelines and strategies for introducing children to the use of maps and guidelines are available. Seefeldt (1989) laid out guidelines for what children require in order to make effective use of maps. She argued they must understand the following:

FIGURE 14.20
Map Showing Distance
between Two Cities

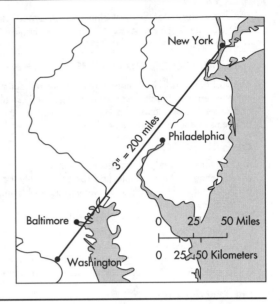

FIGURE 14.21
United States: Natural Resources
SOURCE: From SCOTT, FORESMAN SOCIAL STUDIES: CITY, TOWN AND COUNTRY, p. 43. Copyright © 1983, Scott, Foresman and Company, Glenview, Illinois. Reprinted by permission.

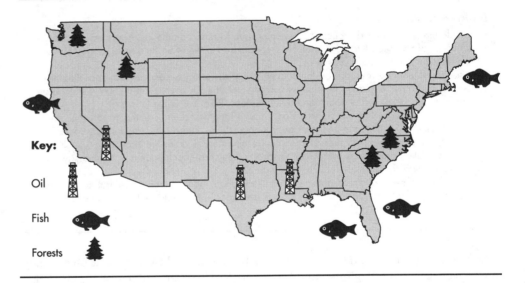

1. *Representation.* To fully understand maps, children must be able to understand that a map represents something else—a place.
2. *Symbolization.* A map, itself a symbol for a place, uses other symbols. Colors symbolize land and water, lines symbolize roads and railroad tracks, and other symbols are used for houses, churches, or schools.
3. *Perspective.* The concept that a map pictures a place as if you were looking at it from above is often difficult for young children to grasp. You must foster their understanding of a "bird's-eye view."
4. *Scale.* Maps reduce the size of an actual place. Children can be introduced to the idea that a map is like the original place, except it is much smaller. Making maps small makes it easier for people to think about the place and to hold the map. (pp. 172–173)

Bartz (1971) suggested further that maps used with children should meet the three basic criteria of *simplicity, visibility,* and *usefulness of information.* Maps for instruction with

FIGURE 14.22

Sample Map of Concrete, Familiar Objects

SOURCE: From SCOTT, FORESMAN SOCIAL STUDIES: NEIGHBORS NEAR AND FAR, p. 13. Copyright © 1983, Scott, Foresman and Company, Glenview, Illinois. Reprinted by permission.

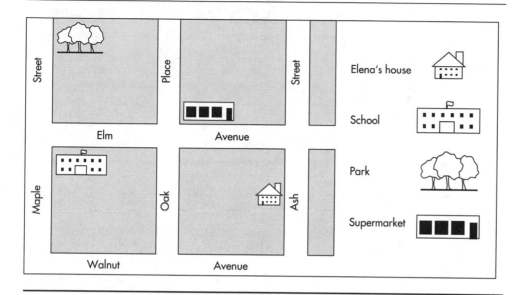

children should (a) contain only as much information as is needed, (b) be easily seen and examined, and (c) include information that children can apply in some way to their daily lives. An example of a commercial product that meets these criteria is the large vinyl-coated map that is placed on the floor and can be walked on: the *U.S. and World Floor Map* (produced by Rand McNally).

In a different vein, Louie (1993, p. 17) suggested that teachers consider using children's literature as a vehicle for furthering the development of spatial skills. She offered examples of skills and representative works of children's literature that could be used to foster the skills at different grade levels. An example for grade 4 is:

> *Skill:* Uses distance, direction, scale, and symbols. *Literature: Roxaboxen,* by Alice McLerran, illustrated by Barbara Conney (New York: Lothrop, Lee & Shepard, 1991). ISBN 0-688-07592-4.

Key Spatial Concepts

As children begin to explore different types of maps and globes, they may be introduced to other key spatial concepts. These include *place location, map symbols, scale,* and *cardinal directions.*

Place location. One of the most common uses of maps for citizens is to locate places. We often draw or consult maps to explain or determine where a place is located. Not infrequently, we supplement our maps with verbal directions about *relative* locations: "You can't miss it, it's right behind the Kmart."

In the intermediate grades, children can be given concrete experiences with *grids.* Some types of maps, such as those used for travel, frequently help us locate places by use of grids comprised of letters and numbers. The system devised for locating any place on the Earth's surface employs special grids called *parallels of latitude* (east-west lines) and *meridians of longitude* (north-south lines). These typically are found on both maps and globes and often are introduced to students as *imaginary lines.*

Children can be introduced to the grid system of locating items by making the classroom itself a living map. To do this, the teacher should organize a grid by attaching sheets of letters to two of the opposing walls and numbers to the other two at exactly 2-foot intervals.

The grid-system activity can begin as a game, with the teacher providing general directions to find coins that are hidden in different places (e.g., "The penny is somewhere in the

FIGURE 14.23
Latitude and Longitude Lines on a Globe

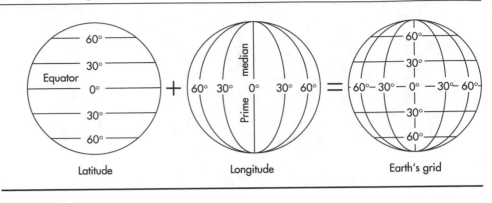

FIGURE 14.24
Map Symbols

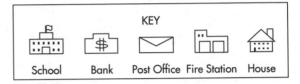

classroom"). Further clues can be more specific (e.g., "It is in front of my desk." "Look near the art center"). After the children locate the coin through these procedures, the teacher can introduce the grid system as a more efficient procedure to locate items.

To simulate lines, strings may be stretched across the floor, corresponding to each set of letters and numbers. The game then can be replayed with students covering their eyes while the teacher hides different items at various locations. The teacher proceeds to ask students to find the hidden items, this time using grid-coordinate directions (e.g., "The coin is located at B4").

Students can experiment with the grid system by themselves giving coordinates to locate other items within the classroom. As a concluding activity, the teacher can ask students whether they still could locate items by using grids if the strings were removed. The strings then are detached, and the students can test their hypothesis. At this point it is appropriate to introduce the concept of *imaginary lines* and to relate them to the longitude and latitude lines on the globe (see Figure 14.23).

Map symbols. One of the prerequisites for using any map properly is some understanding of the language used, or how to "read" a map. Map symbols can assist us in comprehending the information in a map. Also, when they are standard symbols, such as those used for railroad tracks, they enlarge children's spatial vocabulary. Once students understand the basic concept of a symbol, they can be introduced to those that commonly are used on maps, including the symbolic use of colors (e.g., blue to represent water) and boundary lines. Figure 14.24 illustrates some typical symbols used on simple maps.

Scale. The concept of scale (see Figure 14.25) is an important but complex element in map and globe communication. It requires students to understand proportional relationships between two items and to entertain notions of relative size (e.g., 150,000 square miles) and distance (e.g., 7,000 miles), which are well beyond their experience. Scale also is related closely to the concept of *symbol* in maps and globes.

Scale emerges in the primary grades in discussions of the concepts of *larger* and *smaller* and in comparisons of toys and models. In the later grades, it is represented in the use of distance scales on maps. The inches-to-miles or centimeters-to-kilometers scale commonly found on road maps is an example.

FIGURE 14.25
Scale

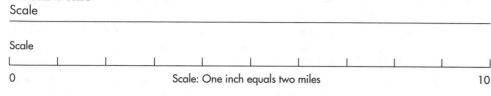

Scale

0   Scale: One inch equals two miles   10

Cardinal directions. Part of the language of spatial communications generally is the use of cardinal directions: north, south, east, and west. Cardinal directions (points of the compass) often are confusing to both students and teachers.

Teachers can use some basic strategies to help students gradually acquire these difficult concepts. These strategies include frequent use of natural landmarks and classroom locations as reference points, and scavenger-hunt games in which students follow directional clues (e.g., "Go to the north side of the school building for your next instructions").

In teaching about cardinal directions, teachers must be careful that the students do not come to regard labeled points as *absolute* cardinal points. Some students, for example, will infer, mistakenly, that north, east, west, and south are *specific points* in space, rather than directions (e.g., believe that north is "up").

Using Travel Maps

Travel maps are an effective way to engage students in spatial problem solving. A class may be asked to plan and chart a trip to a distant city. As part of the task, they may be asked to indicate routes, landmarks, cities to be visited, relative distances, and the like. Different groups may work on the same trips and then compare their itineraries.

For older children, travel maps provide an opportunity to deepen their realization that maps have real and important functional purposes. Using a collection of travel maps from different cities, states, provinces, counties, and countries is likely to heighten student interest. This strategy also increases awareness of how travel maps around the world use many of the same conventions (e.g., symbols, scale, cardinal directions). A travel map of Venice, Italy, for example, although it has foreign names, has basically the same features as a travel map of San Francisco.

Sources of travel maps. Although road maps are sold in book and map stores, they also are available free from some sources. Tourist bureaus of most states often distribute free state maps. Address an inquiry to this bureau at the address of the state capital in which you are interested. Some foreign consulates and embassies may provide road maps of the country and of each major city within the country. Addresses for writing these agencies are generally available in reference works such as *The New York Times Almanac.*

SUMMARY

This chapter has provided a description of the nature and extent of citizenship skills, outlined the essential skills for social studies in intermediate and middle school grades, defined a socially competent individual, and described conflict resolution skills. In addition, we have shown how you can help your students develop research and analysis, chronology, and spatial skills and identify and use reference sources.

Chapters that follow will provide further detailed understanding of how to teach the social studies and how to integrate them into the curriculum.

QUESTIONS AND ACTIVITIES FOR DISCUSSION

1. Locate five political cartoons. In your group, discuss how each might be used as a springboard for discussion in an intermediate or middle school class.

2. Select a topic and create a problem sheet for a fourth-grade class. Use a real country, city, or person as the subject. Also create a list of clues, similar to those in the text, that could be used to help

the students identify the subject. Try out the problem sheet with the members of the group and discuss possible modifications.

3. Select a group of five students from any grade 4–9 and complete with them the lifeline activity described in the text. Identify the grade level and briefly describe and evaluate the results of the activity. Include copies of the students' lifelines with your report.

4. Examine the chart of social studies skills provided in the chapter. Among the list of skills, which do you consider to be the most important to develop? Which skills would you add to the list, and why?

5. Identify five social studies reference works similar to the ones listed in the chapter and suitable for students in grades 4–9 to use. After each source, write a brief description of the type of material that is referenced and a sample question that the book could answer. Then create a task card, as described in the chapter, that would require the use of the references.

6. Develop a collection of different types of maps (either originals or copies) that could be used with children. To locate them, consult newspapers and periodicals, as well as reference works. For each map, list the types of questions that the map answers.

7. Examine a collection of different maps and identify the map symbols they employ. From them, construct two posters, one for grade 4 and one for grades 5–9, that include an assortment of map symbols. Alongside each symbol, place the name of the object that the symbol represents.

8. Develop a collection of different types of tables, charts, and graphs that deal with issues suitable for discussion with children in grades 4–9. To locate the materials, consult newspapers and periodicals, as well as library reference works. For each table, chart, and graph, list the types of questions it could answer. Also indicate how each item might be used as a springboard for discussion with students.

9. Develop an activity for engaging children from grade 4 in mapping some spatial area within their immediate environment. Field-test the activity with a group of five students for whom it is appropriate. Indicate the school and grade level of the students, provide copies of their maps, and describe and evaluate the results.

10. Locate from newspapers or magazines instances of bias or distortion in reporting an event. Explain how such materials might be analyzed in a social studies class.

11. Identify in any source examples of logically invalid arguments. For each argument, use the circle technique illustrated in the chapter to show that the arguments are invalid.

REFERENCES

Anderson, J. L., & Henner, M. (1972). *Focus on self-development: Involvement*. Chicago: Science Research Associates.

Bartz, B. (1971). Maps in the classroom. In J. M. Ball, J. E. Steinbrink, & J. P. Stoltman (Eds.), *The social sciences and geographic education: A reader*. New York: John Wiley.

Brophy, J. (1992). Probing the subtleties of subject-matter teaching. *Educational Leadership, 49,* 4–8.

Byrnes, D. (1987). *Teacher, they called me a ____!* New York: Anti-Defamation League of B'nai B'rith.

Cole, M., & Cole, S. R. (1989). *The development of children*. New York: Scientific American.

Collins, H. T. (no date). What's in a name? *Resource pack: Project LINKS*. Unpublished manuscript, George Washington University, Washington, DC.

Hawking, S. W. (1988). *A brief history of time: From the big bang to black holes*. New York: Bantam.

Institute for the Advancement of Philosophy for Children. (1987). *Philosophy for children*. Upper Montclair, NJ: Montclair State College, Institute for the Advancement of Philosophy for Children.

Jarolimek, J., & Parker, W. C. (1993). *Social studies in elementary education* (9th ed.). New York: Macmillan.

Louie, B. Y. (1993). Using literature to teach location. *Social Studies and the Young Learner, 5,* 17–18, 22.

Muir, S. P. (1985). Understanding and improving students' map reading skills. *Elementary School Journal, 86,* 207–215.

Scherer, M. (1992). Solving conflicts—Not just for children. *Educational Leadership, 50,* 14–15, 17–18.

Seefeldt, C. (1989). *Social studies for the preschool-primary child* (3rd ed.). New York: Merrill/Macmillan.

Somer, R. (1978). *The mind's eye*. New York: Dell.

Task Force on Scope and Sequence. (1989). In search of a scope and sequence for social studies. *Social Education, 53,* 376–387.

Wilson, S. (1990). *Mastodons, maps, and Michigan: Exploring uncharted territory while teaching elementary school social studies*. East Lansing: Michigan State University, Center for the Learning and Teaching of Elementary Subjects, Institute for Research on Teaching. (ERIC Document Reproduction Service No. ED 328 470)

Wittrock, M. C. (1986). Students' thought processes. In M. C. Wittrock (Ed.), *Handbook of research on teaching* (3rd ed.), pp. 297–314. New York: Macmillan.

Wittrock, M. C., & Goldberg, S. G. (1975). Imagery and meaningfulness in free recall: Word attributes and instructional sets. *Journal of General Psychology, 92,* 137–151.

SUGGESTED READINGS

Anderson, C. C., & Winston, B. J. (1977). Acquiring information by asking questions, using maps and graphs, and making direct observations. In D. G. Kurfman (Ed.), *Developing decision-making skills.* 47th Yearbook. Washington, DC: National Council for the Social Studies.

Auth, T. (1977). *Behind the lines.* Boston: Houghton Mifflin.

Bacon, P. (Ed.). (1970). *Focus on geography: Key concepts and strategies.* 40th Yearbook. Washington, DC: National Council for the Social Studies.

Carpenter, H. M. (Ed.). (1963). *Skill development in social studies.* 33rd Yearbook. Washington, DC: National Council for the Social Studies.

Chapin, J. R., & Gross, R. E. (1973). *Teaching social studies skills.* Boston: Little, Brown.

Cleary, F. D. (1977). *Discovering books and libraries: A handbook for students in the middle and upper grades* (2nd ed.). New York: H. W. Wilson.

Cole, M., & Cole, S. R. (1989). *The development of children.* New York: Scientific American Books.

Downey, M. T., & Levstik, L. (1991). Teaching and learning history. In J. P. Shaver (Ed.), *Handbook of research on social studies teaching and learning* (pp. 400–410). New York: Macmillan.

Education Development Center. (1968). *Man: A course of study (MACOS).* Cambridge, MA: Author.

Elkind, D. (1978). *A sympathetic understanding of the child: Birth to sixteen* (2nd ed.). Boston: Allyn & Bacon.

Grun, B. (1979). *The timetables of history.* New York: Simon & Schuster.

Kenworthy, L. S. (1977). *Reach for a picture.* How To Do It Series. Washington, DC: National Council for the Social Studies.

Kreidler, W. J. (1990). Beyond "He started it!" Empowering elementary children through conflict resolution. *Forum: The Newsletter of Educators for Social Responsibility, 90,* 3, 5.

Manson, G. A., & Ridd, M. K. (Eds.). (1977). *New perspectives on geographic education.* Dubuque, IA: Kendall/Hunt.

Martorella, P. H., Martelli, L., & Graham, A. (1983). *Looking at me: Webstermaster activity sheets.* New York: McGraw-Hill.

Muir, S. P. (1990). Time concepts of elementary school children. *Social Education, 54,* 215–218.

National Geographic Society. (1988). *Teaching geography: A model for action.* Washington, DC: National Geographic Society.

Philosophy for children. (1987). Upper Montclair, NJ: Institute for the Advancement of Philosophy for Children, Montclair State College.

Remy, R. C. (1979). *Handbook of basic citizenship competencies.* Alexandria, VA: Association for Supervision and Curriculum Development.

Rice, M. J., & Cobb, R. L. (1978). *What can children learn in geography?: A review of research.* Boulder, CO: ERIC Clearing House for Social Studies/Social Sciences.

Schreiber, J., et al. (1983a). *City, town and country: Teacher's edition—Workbook.* Glenview, IL: Scott, Foresman.

Schreiber, J., et al. (1983b). *Neighbors near and far: Teacher's edition—Workbook.* Glenview, IL: Scott, Foresman.

Spradley, J. P., & McCurdy, D. W. (1972). *The cultural experience: Ethnography in complex society.* Chicago: SRA.

Steinbrink, J. E., & Bliss, D. (1988). Using political cartoons to teach thinking skills. *The Social Studies, 79,* 217–220.

Tar Heel Junior Historian Association. (1989). *Teacher's supplement: North Carolina's coastal plain—Tar Heel Junior Historian.* Raleigh, NC: Author.

Task Force on Scope and Sequence. (1984). In search of a scope and sequence for social studies. *Social Education, 48,* 249–262.

U.S. Department of Commerce, Bureau of the Census. (1991, June). *1990 census profile.* Washington, DC: Author.

Vukelich, R., & Thornton, S. J. (1990). Children's understanding of historical time: Implications for instruction. *Childhood Education, 67,* 22–25.

Wynar, C. L. (1986). *Guide to reference books for school media centers.* Littleton, CO: Libraries Unlimited.

Promoting Reflective Inquiry: Developing and Applying Concepts, Generalizations, and Hypotheses

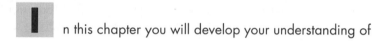 n this chapter you will develop your understanding of

1. The role of concepts in the social studies curriculum.
2. Instructional strategies for concept learning.
3. The role of facts, generalizations, and hypotheses in the social studies curriculum.
4. Instructional strategies for developing generalizations.
5. The use of the term *problem* in social studies instruction and of instructional strategies for problem solving.

What are concepts, facts, and generalizations? What role do they play in the development of the reflective, competent, and concerned citizen?

To function effectively and to advance, a democratic society requires reflective citizens who have a well-grounded body of concepts, facts, and generalizations concerning human behavior, their nation, and the world. In applying such knowledge to civic affairs, citizens must be able to develop and test hypotheses and to engage in problem solving by using factual data and well-formed concepts. These reflective abilities are acquired cumulatively; they begin early in the home, become more formalized with the onset of kindergarten and schooling, and may develop throughout life.

In Chapters 1 and 12, it was noted that individuals organize knowledge into structures known as *schemata*. The elements of these schemata include a complex, interrelated web or network of concepts, facts, generalizations, and hypotheses. We now consider teaching strategies and learning environments designed to provide students with subject matter and experiences that stimulate the development of such knowledge structures.

A. CONCEPTS IN THE SOCIAL STUDIES CURRICULUM

All learning, thinking, and action involve concepts. They broaden and enrich our lives and make it possible for us to communicate easily with others. Because individuals share many similar concepts, they can exchange information rapidly and efficiently without any need for explaining in detail each item discussed. Similarly, when a communication breakdown occurs, it often is because one of the parties lacks the necessary concepts embedded in the conversation. Not infrequently, this breakdown happens in social studies textbooks when the author assumes certain knowledge that the student does not actually have.

As we learned in Chapter 1, concepts are hooks on which we can hang new information. When we encounter new subject matter that does not appear to fit on any existing conceptual hook, we may broaden our idea of what some existing hook can hold or may create a new one. These conceptual hangers allow us to tidy up our knowledge structure. They also make it easier to learn and remember information.

In their simplest form, concepts may be regarded as categories into which we group phenomena within our experience. Concepts allow us to sort out large numbers of people, objects, and events into categories such as cars, plants, nations, and heroes. As phenomena are sorted into concept categories, we discern their basic or distinguishing characteristics. We may check these characteristics against our memories of past examples or prototypes that represent our notion of a typical case of the concept.

Personal and Public Dimensions of Concepts

Concepts, however, are more than just categories. They also have personal and public dimensions because the categories into which we sort our experiences contain all of the personal associations we have accumulated in relation to the concept. As an illustration, an individual's concept of *money* encompasses more than a mental file drawer that includes checks, bank drafts, currency, and credit cards. The concept also is attached to our economic goals, our perceptions of financial issues, and many other personal associations with money that make our concept unique.

Considerable evidence demonstrates that culture generally plays a large role in shaping this personal pattern of associations (see, e.g., Cole & Scribner, 1974; Hunt & Banaji, 1988; Whorf, 1956). Some investigators also have argued that language, specifically, is an important influence.

In contrast to the set of unique personal associations that each of our concepts incorporates, some defining properties are shared in common: the public aspects of concepts. They are the characteristics that distinguish one concept from another and permit easy exchanges of information and experiences. These shared features of concepts mean that although a professional banker and I, for example, have had different levels of experiences with *money*, we can communicate easily with one another concerning the fundamental aspects of the concept.

Misconceptions and Stereotypes

Much of the formal learning of concepts in schools often consists of correcting misconceptions—incorrect or incomplete concepts—as well as forming new ones. Many students, for example, have the misconception that all deserts are hot places. When students focus on the *non*critical properties of concepts and assume they appear in all examples of the concept, they often develop *stereotypes*. As an illustration, on the basis of a limited range of experiences with Americans classified as *Italians,* a little boy may have developed the stereotype that Italians are "people who have dark hair, use their hands when talking, and like spaghetti." From his limited and isolated experiences with some members of the ethnic group, the child has overgeneralized to all Italians.

Concepts in Social Studies Texts and Materials

By the time they finish school, students will have encountered the names of thousands of concepts in their social studies classes and textbooks and their daily life experiences. A sample list of some that are found commonly in intermediate and middle school social studies programs, materials, and texts are shown here. Only a fraction of items such as these actually will be learned as concepts and become more than a familiar word (Martorella, 1971).

allies	conflict	freedom	ocean	scarcity
altitude	culture	holiday	peace	self
assembly line	custom	island	poverty	shelter
atlas	democracy	map	power	suburbs
boundary	desert	money	prejudice	supply
causality	discrimination	nation	progress	tariffs
city	Earth	nationality	refugee	transportation
colony	equator	neighborhood	revolution	war
community	family	North	river	waste

The typical basal text includes a great many concepts; some it attempts to teach the students, and many it assumes they already know. If the concepts in texts and instructional materials are to be more than words for students, they must be taught prior to or concurrently with lessons that assume their understanding.

Often texts and reading materials for young children are heavily loaded with abstract concepts, which then are explained with other abstract concepts. Consider the concepts in an example from a basal social studies text for the second grade. Alongside a picture of a globe with an equator drawn around it, this statement appears: "The globe also shows the equator. The equator is an imaginary line. It goes all around the globe."

The Process of Learning a New Concept

It would be difficult for you to recall vividly the processes that were involved in learning many of the concepts you already possess. To recapture this sensation, I will ask you to learn two new concepts. In doing so, I will be placing you in the shoes of a student who frequently is confronted with the same type of cognitive task in social studies classes. As you engage in the learning process, reflect on your strategies, successes, mistakes, and feelings about the process.

Consider the two concept instruction frames in Figure 15.1 and Figure 15.2 and then answer the questions they pose. When you think you have learned the concept, compare your responses with the Answer Key at the end of the chapter.

FIGURE 15.1
The Concept of *Squarp*

All of these are squarps.

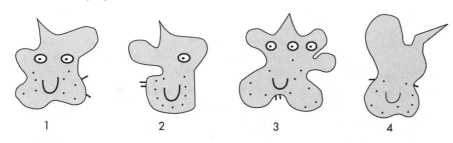

None of these are squarps.

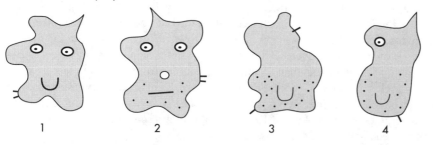

Which of these are squarps? What is a squarp?

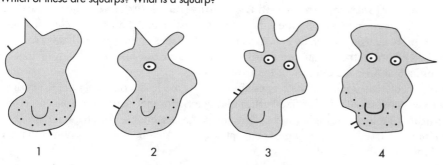

FIGURE 15.2
The Concept of *Zrapple*

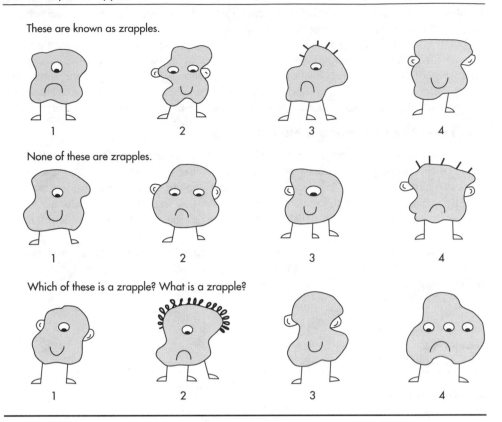

The experiences associated with attempting to learn these new concepts should have sensitized you to some of the problems that students experience. Difficulties often begin with trying to remember (and spell correctly) what appear as strange names. Your experience also may suggest how students sometimes have thoughtful reasons for wrong answers. Most importantly, the exercise should have revealed how *learner problems are often due to the nature of the instruction provided, rather than to student inadequacies.*

Sources of Difficulty in Concept Learning

The exercise also should have confirmed that different levels of difficulty are associated with demonstrating learning of a concept. Recall that I asked you to *state* the concept rule (or definition) for each of the two concepts, as well as to *identify* examples. Stating the concept rule in your own words or even selecting a correct definition among incorrect ones is a different and more difficult task than identifying examples from nonexamples.

The two examples in the exercise were designed to represent different types of problems associated with concept learning. Two types of concepts, *disjunctive* and *conjunctive,* were included (Bruner, Goodnow, & Austin, 1962). Zrapples represented disjunctive concepts; squarps represented conjunctive concepts.

Disjunctive, conjunctive, and relational concepts. Disjunctive concepts such as zrapples have *two or more* sets of alternative characteristics that define them, rather than a single one. In social studies, *citizen* is such a concept. Citizens of the United States are those who *either* are born in the country *or* fulfill some test of citizenship *or* are born in another country of parents who are citizens of the United States.

The other concept, *squarp,* which is conjunctive, is the least complex type to learn. A conjunctive concept has a single, fixed set of characteristics that define the concept. All of the many different examples of squarps share the same essential set of characteristics. An example of a conjunctive social studies concept is *globe.* A globe is a round object that has a map of the Earth drawn on it.

You were not asked to learn the most complex type, a relational concept. Unlike the other two types, relational concepts have no single fixed set of characteristics. Rather, they can be defined *only by comparison to or in relationship with other objects or events. Justice, far, prosperous, greed, fair,* and *near* are examples of relational concepts in social studies. One cannot tell, for instance, whether a person, place, or thing is "near," only whether it is near something else, and then only by using some criterion to make a judgment of nearness. Philadelphia may or may not be considered to be near Baltimore. It depends on whether the context of analysis deals with city blocks or planets.

Concrete and abstract concepts. A further source of difficulty associated with learning concepts is their degree of concreteness or abstractness. *Concreteness* refers to what we can perceive directly through one of the five senses. *Abstractness* refers to what we cannot directly perceive through our senses.

In practice, the line between what is concrete and what is abstract seldom is drawn so clearly. Consider the list of social studies concepts presented earlier. Some clearly cannot be directly perceived, such as *freedom;* others clearly can, such as *map.* However, many concepts—community and family, for example—lie somewhere between being concrete or being abstract. Aspects of community and family, such as people, are visible, but other important characteristics, the relationships of individuals to one another, for example, are abstract. So too with many other concepts similar to zrapple and squarp.

B. INSTRUCTIONAL STRATEGIES FOR CONCEPT LEARNING

Among all of the concepts that we learn, only some are appropriate to teach formally in schools. Many concepts, such as *pencil, flag,* and hundreds of other common ones generally are learned informally by students. Others are too complex to teach directly.

Teaching concepts begins with a teacher's identification of a list of significant concepts appropriate for teaching in the social studies program. A simple rule of thumb might be to teach at least one new important concept each time a unit is introduced. After identifying the concepts, the teacher then can analyze each one in preparation for selecting materials and teaching strategies.

Concept Analyses

A concept analysis involves identifying (a) the *name* most commonly associated with the concept, (b) a simplified *rule* or definition that specifies clearly what the concept is, (c) the criterial attributes that make up the defining characteristics of the concept, and (d) some noncriterial attributes that are characteristics often associated with the concept but nevertheless nonessential.

An analysis also involves selecting or creating some different examples of the concept, including a best example or clearest case of the concept, and some related nonexamples of the concept. These provide contrast by showing what the concept is not.

Statements of the criterial attributes and definitions of concepts can be found in general dictionaries, specialized dictionaries such as the *Dictionary of Political Science,* and textbooks. Identifying the noncriterial attributes of concepts requires some reflection because they take many forms. As noted in the example of the little boy and Italians, noncriterial attributes appear in examples of virtually any concept. As a result, their presence often misleads students into believing they are essential features of the concept.

Because of the diversity of concepts, no specific number of examples is required to teach a concept. The set of examples provided, however, should represent adequately the range of cases that appear in common usage. For example, in teaching the concept of *transportation,* the set of examples should include land, sea, and air, motorized and nonmotorized, and large-scale and small-scale cases, as shown later in this chapter.

Nonexamples are most helpful to a learner if they are related closely to the concept being learned in one or more respects. For example, in teaching the concept of *island,* it is helpful to use nonexamples such as isthmus and peninsula and then to point out how they differ from island.

Consider how a typical concept analysis might proceed by using the concept of *island:*

- **Concept name.** Which name is associated most commonly with the concept? (Illustration: island)
- **Concept definition.** What is a clear and simplified definition that describes the essence of the concept? (Illustration: An island is a body of land surrounded by water.)
- **Criterial attributes.** What are the distinct, essential characteristics that make up the concept? (Illustration: land, water, surrounding)
- **Sample noncriterial attributes.** What are some nonessential characteristics that often are present in cases of the concept? (Illustration: habitation, tropical climate, vegetation)
- **Best example.** What is a best or clearest example of the concept? (Illustration: aerial photo of a body of land showing vegetation and water surrounding the land)
- **Other concept examples.** What are some other interesting, different, and learner-relevant examples of the concept? (Illustration: islands with people, islands with no vegetation, islands in different bodies of water, islands in very cold climates)
- **Concept nonexamples.** What are some contrasting cases of what the concept is *not* that will help highlight its significant features? (Illustration: peninsula—a body of land that has water on only three sides)

Assessing Concept Learning

Concept learning can be assessed at several levels. The most basic level requires students to select an example of the concept from a set of cases that includes nonexamples. For example, a teacher asks a student to identify an example of an *atlas* from a collection of different types of reference books or to point to an instance of an island on a map. Further levels of testing include

1. Identifying the criterial attributes of the concept (Illustration: from a list of characteristics, select water, land, and surrounding as those criterial for island)
2. Identifying the noncriterial attributes of the island (Illustration: from a list of characteristics, select climate, size, and vegetation as those noncriterial for island)
3. Identifying the concept rule (Illustration: from a list of choices, select the correct definition of island)
4. Stating the concept rule (Illustration: correctly answer the question, What is an island?)
5. Relating the concepts to other concepts (Illustration: correctly answer the question, How are islands and peninsulas similar and different?)
6. Locating or creating new examples of the concept (Illustration: using an atlas, locate five new instances of island)

Instructional Model for Teaching Concepts

Research concerning how individuals learn concepts has provided a sophisticated, empirically based set of instructional guidelines for aiding students in learning concepts (Howard, 1987; Martorella, 1991; Tennyson & Cocchiarella, 1986). From the extensive body of research on concept learning, we can abstract a basic instructional model that consists of eight steps as follows:

1. Identify the set of examples and nonexamples you plan to use and place them in some logical order for presentation. Include at least one example that best or most clearly illustrates an ideal type of the concept.
2. Include in the materials or oral instructions a set of cues, directions, questions, and student activities that draws students' attention to the criterial attributes and to the similarities and differences in the examples and nonexamples used.
3. Direct students to compare all illustrations with the best example and provide feedback on the adequacy of their comparisons.
4. If criterial attributes cannot be identified clearly or are ambiguous, focus attention on the salient features of the best example.
5. Where a clear definition of a concept exists, elicit or state it at some point in the instruction in terms that are meaningful to the students.

6. Through discussion, place the concept in context with other related concepts that are part of the students' prior knowledge.
7. Assess concept mastery at a minimal level—namely, whether students can discriminate correctly between new examples and nonexamples.
8. Assess concept mastery at a more advanced level; for example, ask students to generate new exemplars or to apply the concept to new situations.

Discovery and Expository Approaches in Teaching Concepts

In implementing the instructional model for teaching concepts, teachers may elect to use a discovery instructional strategy. Students engaging in learning concepts through discovery approaches try to determine which attributes are criterial to the concept and to infer its rule. The teacher in discovery approaches serves as a resource and a guide.

An alternative is to use an expository instructional strategy, wherein the teacher makes explicit the defining elements of the concept, including the criterial attributes and the concept rule. With expository approaches, the teacher provides relevant data to students in the most direct way possible (Borich, 1992).

Effective discovery and expository teaching strategies both try to stimulate student curiosity and involvement. They both also use thought-provoking questions and are sensitive to the individual differences among students.

Discovery approach. To illustrate, a teacher using a discovery approach with the concept *refugee* might first provide students with cases characterized as examples of refugees, along with some appropriately labeled nonexamples. The cases would be related to students' prior knowledge of Middle Eastern issues that were studied earlier in the year.

The best example of the concept would be clearly labeled and used as a point of reference throughout the discussion. The teacher would provide feedback and information as requested and needed by students regarding critical and noncritical attributes and the concept rule. Reference materials might be available, as would access to the school library.

As a next step, through a series of questions the students could be guided into a comparison of the cases in order to discover the common characteristics of the concept. The inferred characteristics would be listed on the chalkboard as hypotheses. After further discussion and clarification of refugee cases, the teacher could ask the class to correctly identify new examples of refugees from a set of cases that contain nonexamples such as *alien* and *immigrant.*

At this point, students also could be asked to offer a definition of the concept. Their definition then could be checked against those offered in specialized reference works or texts treating refugee issues. Based on comparisons with the texts, the class would arrive at a tentative working definition of *refugee.* This then might be modified in the future as students encounter new information or issues that suggest that a broadening or qualifying of the definition is appropriate.

As a culminating assignment, the class might be asked to test its understanding of the concept further by locating incidences of refugees across the world over the past three years. In completing the assignment, the students would be asked to specify attributes—that is, the victim, the nature of political violence, an indication that the victim sought refuge, and a sign that the refuge was in another country.

Expository approach. An expository approach to teaching the concept *refugee* would proceed in much the same way, except that the teacher would inform the students of the lesson objective in a more explicit and straightforward fashion. The teacher also would exercise more control over the direction of the lesson. For example, at the outset the teacher might alert the class to the objective and identify the concept to be learned by writing this information on the chalkboard. The teacher also would relate the concept to the students' prior knowledge of related Middle Eastern issues.

As the lesson developed, the teacher would point out the criterial attributes and note their common occurrence among all examples, rather than depend on students themselves to infer these conclusions. The best example would be analyzed in terms of the criterial attributes identified. Other examples and nonexamples would be compared to the best example and the differences and similarities highlighted and summarized.

At some point in the lesson, the teacher might write the concept rule on the chalkboard or direct students to a functional definition in text or reference material. The teacher would make certain through feedback and practice opportunities that all students demonstrated an understanding of the critical attributes and rule of the concept. Assessment of concept learning would proceed in the same fashion as with a discovery approach.

Concept Hierarchies

Often it is helpful for both the teaching and learning of concepts to order a series of concepts into a *hierarchy*. Even when concepts are not learned in a hierarchical fashion, ordering them in this way at some point often makes remembering them and their relationship to one another much easier.

The work of Novak and Gowin (1984) with what they identify as *concept mapping* illustrates the application of hierarchies. Developing hierarchies of concepts initially involves placing them in context in an organized way through identifying the most all-encompassing of the concepts in a set. Then the concepts are related to one another in a logical sequence or diagram, along with brief phrases that link them.

Consider the set of concepts as follows: *sea level, rivers, transportation, mountains, oceans, islands, lakes, Earth, land areas, continents, water bodies.* The example in Figure 15.3 depicts a concept map that organizes the concepts in some logical sequence according to their relationship to one another. Kleg's (1986, 1987) instructional materials for teaching the concepts of terrorism and genocide also offer two clear and detailed examples of how concept mapping can be applied to social studies instruction.

Concept maps and teaching coordinate concepts. Concept maps also afford the teacher a useful indicator of which concepts may be taught concurrently, such as *river, lake,* and *ocean,* shown in Figure 15.3. Each of these types of concepts, known as *coordinate* concepts because they are on the same level in the concept hierarchy, can be used effectively as contrasting nonexamples to help teach the others. That is, not only can examples of *lake* be used to teach that concept, but the same materials function as nonexamples of *ocean.*

FIGURE 15.3
Concept Map
SOURCE: From P. H. Martorella, "Teaching Concepts." In James M. Cooper (Ed.), *Classroom Teaching Skills* (4th ed.). Lexington, Massachusetts: D.C. Heath, 1990. Reprinted with permission.

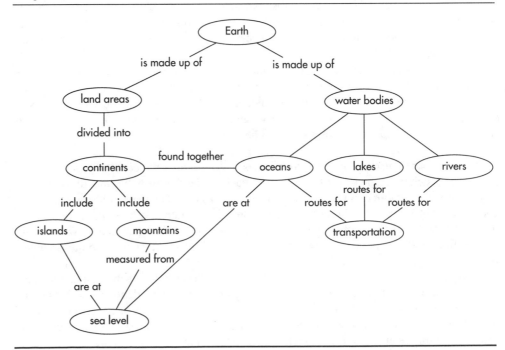

Concept Teaching Materials and Activities

In a number of ways, teachers can create special materials or activities related to concept development. These include *concept minitexts, student concept folders,* and *concept bulletin boards.*

Concept minitexts. A *minitext* is a short, self-instructional text designed by a teacher to teach a single concept to a specified student group. It may be used at any grade level where children are able to read. Minitexts include *all* of the instruction a child will require to learn a new concept, including an assessment at the end.

They may use pictures from magazines, photos, drawings, and the like, as well as narrative material, integrated into an interesting format. For interest appeal and durability, they also usually have an attractive cover and are sturdily constructed.

To construct a minitext requires the completion of a concept analysis and the application of the eight-step instructional model for teaching concepts. Unlike informational texts and other books, the purpose of a minitext is to teach *one* important concept effectively. The criterion for a successful minitext is whether a student for whom it is designed is able to learn the target concept as a result of using the minitext.

Concept folders. An ongoing activity in which both the teacher and the students can participate is the creation of classroom *concept folders.* One concept (e.g., *family, map, pollution, prejudice, poverty*) is identified for each folder. The number of concept folders to be created for a classroom is flexible. Concept folders may be tied into units and used to provide in-depth information on key subjects. They also may be included in learning centers.

The teacher and the students first identify and clarify the criterial attributes and the rule of the concept for each folder and examine some examples and nonexamples. Then they begin to collect data related to the concepts in the folders, which are kept in the classroom. A time limit is set for collecting items.

Data may be in the form of pictures, cases, articles, photographs, slides, or observations. For primary children, the teacher needs to provide examples of the types of materials they may collect in the folders. Containers such as file folders, shoe boxes, and large envelopes can be used to store the data. All items the children contribute to the folders should include their names for returns.

After the stated period of time, students in small groups can examine and discuss the contents of each folder. They also may create a display. The teacher may wish to add more structure to the activity by providing a set of discussion questions or, alternatively, to lead the discussions.

Concept bulletin boards. A bulletin board, prepared either by the teacher or the students, can be used to highlight examples and nonexamples of a concept. As with concept folders, bulletin boards can contain pictorial or written materials.

Examples and nonexamples of concepts should be placed close to each other and labeled appropriately. After the initial bulletin board is developed, students can be encouraged to look for further examples and similar nonexamples and add to the display.

C. FACTS, GENERALIZATIONS, AND HYPOTHESES IN THE SOCIAL STUDIES CURRICULUM

In what ways are facts, generalizations, and hypotheses distinguished from concepts? As we have seen, concepts are the building blocks of knowledge. They are part of every fact and generalization that we know. If our concepts are ill formed or incomplete, so will the ideas we build from them be improperly shaped. When we think, make a decision, or act, we draw on a network of schemata that includes interwoven concepts, facts, generalizations, and hypotheses—the major elements of reflection.

The Nature of Facts

Citizens are bombarded daily with facts and assertions that appear to be facts. Facts appear in many forms and relate to trivial, as well as significant, matters. A fact is a statement about concepts that is *true* or verifiable for a particular case on the basis of the best evidence available. From a concept cluster that includes *island, ocean, group,* and *state,* the fact statement arises: "A group of islands located in the Pacific Ocean makes up one of our states." Other examples of facts are:

- Our Congress consists of the House of Representatives and the Senate.
- Franklin Roosevelt served more terms than any other president.
- The state with the largest population is California.
- Tallahassee is south of Peoria.
- When our Constitution was adopted, women were denied the right to vote.
- In our country, Christmas is celebrated on December 25.

Often an assertion is accepted as a fact by an individual even though it may not be supported by evidence or may be considered by most people to be false. Many people accept as a fact, for example, that Columbus was the first European to reach America, even though considerable evidence to the contrary exists. Other assertions are accepted as facts on the basis of the best evidence available at one point, only to be proven false later. The *fact* that the sun revolved about the Earth was only grudgingly discarded by the world as false in favor of the newly verified *fact* that the moving body was actually the Earth.

In our society facts are valued. Individuals often go to great lengths, spending much time and even money to get them. People who have knowledge of facts or have access to such knowledge often have considerable power and status; witness heads of countries, inventors, and columnists.

Learning facts in meaningful contexts. All students need to have experiences in locating, identifying, organizing, and verifying significant facts. The facts they are asked to remember also should have functional meaning. A student can learn two lists of 50 pairs of names—one with capitals and states and the other with nonsense words—in the same way. Neither list has any real immediate functional value beyond gaining recognition or success, unless some meaningful context is provided.

Facts learned outside of some meaningful context are often quickly forgotten, long before they can be put to any functional use. More importantly, they are not integrated into students' schemata of previously acquired knowledge. This last point is illustrated by the child who had memorized all of the names of American presidents in the correct order but who cannot give the names of any three presidents who had served during the last half of the twentieth century.

Teaching students techniques for more efficiently retrieving meaningful facts from memory is a worthy instructional objective. Citizens frequently need to remember a great number of names, places, events, dates, and general descriptive information in order to clarify and link new knowledge in functionally meaningful ways.

The Nature of Generalizations

From an instructional perspective, a generalization is a statement about concepts that is true or verified for all cases on the basis of the best evidence available. Generalizations are similar to facts in that they also are true statements about relationships between or among concepts. Generalizations, however, summarize and organize a great deal of information obtained from analyses of many sets of facts. The summary results in a single, wide-reaching assertion that applies to the past, present, and even future. In contrast, facts assert claims about specific instances.

To illustrate, compare the following fact and related generalization.

Fact
- New Orleans typically is warmer in the winter than Milwaukee.

Generalization
- Climate varies from place to place.

Unlike facts, generalizations also have the capacity to *predict* when they appear in the form of "If . . . then" statements. For example: "*If* there is a national election, *then* the turnout of white-collar, professional, and business people likely will be greater than that of semiskilled and unskilled workers." The statement makes a prediction that "If one set of conditions is present (national election), a second set of consequences will follow (a pattern of voter turnout)."

As students engage in examining and analyzing data for patterns and then summarizing their conclusions, they progress toward deriving generalizations. For instance, after children have examined and compared pictures of various families from many countries, socioeconomic settings, and racial groups, they have an information base for developing a generalization. They now can be guided to find an organizing principle for bringing order to their experiences under a generalization such as, families everywhere take many different forms.

Other examples of social studies generalizations that children could formulate after analyzing and summarizing data are as follows (adapted from Harcourt Brace Jovanovich, 1990):

- Events happen in sequence.
- A community's activities are unique and are affected by natural resources, landforms, and climate.
- Communities change over time.
- Each person is a member of different groups.
- All places have a past: neighborhoods, communities, and countries all have histories.
- The environment can affect how people live.
- As a society becomes more complex, so does its government.

The Nature of Hypotheses

Unlike a fact or a generalization, which is a verified truth statement, a hypothesis is an untested idea or guess that seeks to explain some phenomenon. The process of forming a hypothesis begins when we make some attempt to resolve or answer questions, such as, Why do people in different places often wear different types of clothes? Why do we say the Pledge of Allegiance every day in school? What are the causes of poverty? Why does the government subsidize the tobacco industry at the same time that it requires health warnings on cigarette packs?

The hypotheses we propose in order to answer questions such as these may be sophisticated and informed, or they may be naive and poorly grounded. In either case, hypotheses, once formed, then are *tested* through the gathering and comparing of evidence that supports or refutes them. When a hypothesis appears to "hold up," or to be true after extensive evidence has been gathered, it can be regarded tentatively as either a fact or a generalization. Which of these two it will be depends on whether it applies to a *particular* case (fact) or to *all* cases (generalization) within some universe. Not infrequently in the social sciences, as a result of future tests in the context of new evidence, an original hypothesis may be revised or even discarded. Figure 15.4 is a summary of the differences among concepts, facts, generalizations, and hypotheses.

FIGURE 15.4
The Nature of Concepts, Facts, Generalizations, and Hypotheses

Concepts	Categories into which we group people, objects, and events
Facts	Statements about concepts that are true or verified for a particular case on the basis of the best evidence available
Generalizations	Statements about concepts that are true or verified for all cases on the basis of the best evidence available.
Hypotheses	Untested ideas or guesses that seek to explain some phenomena

Some hypotheses can never be verified or refuted because all of the necessary evidence is impossible to obtain. Speculations about "what might have happened" had certain events in history been altered fall into this category—for example, the hypothesis: The United States would not be a major world power if Jefferson had not approved the Louisiana Purchase.

Students engaged in the development and testing of hypotheses need practice and assistance at each grade level, including help with generating plausible hypotheses to explain and answer simple but interesting problems and questions. They also need assistance with gathering and comparing data to test them.

Children in the primary grades can begin their experiences through practice in developing basic hypotheses for fundamental issues such as: Why do people around the world have different houses? Students in the intermediate and middle grades can go beyond the school into the community to do fieldwork that tests their hypotheses. For example, intermediate and middle-grade students might develop and conduct a survey to test the hypothesis: People in our neighborhood will recycle trash if encouraged to do so.

As they progress in developing and testing hypotheses, children can be introduced gradually to the concept of *multiple causality,* which is crucial to analysis of many issues in the social studies. Understanding multiple causality requires that students recognize and accept that more than one hypothesis may be correct; often several causes explain or account for an event. This last statement relates to events rooted in history (e.g., What caused the Civil War?), as well as to everyday social phenomena (e.g., What causes conflicts in families?).

D. INSTRUCTIONAL STRATEGIES FOR DEVELOPING GENERALIZATIONS

As in teaching concepts, strategies for aiding students in the development and testing of generalizations may employ either *expository* or *discovery* approaches. The two approaches differ chiefly in the degree to which they place the responsibility on students to identify relationships among cases and to derive the actual generalization. Both approaches involve students in thinking, doing, and learning. Both also guide students in understanding the necessary relationships among items. To provide variety, instruction should include some mix of both approaches.

Expository and Discovery Approaches for Teaching Generalizations

Expository approaches may take many forms. These range from simply calling attention to statements in texts and helping students find supporting evidence, to having students themselves offer generalizations that the class tests.

The basic steps in an expository approach might be summarized as follows:

1. State, write, or call attention to some generalization that is the learning objective for the lesson.
2. Review major concepts that are part of the generalization.
3. Provide instructions, questions, cases, relevant materials, and assistance to illustrate and verify the generalization.
4. Have students identify, find, or create new cases of the generalization.

As an example, consider a fourth-grade class in which the objective is to have the students understand the generalization: The environment influences the type of shelter that people have. Ms. Olski, the teacher, begins the lesson by first writing the generalization on the chalkboard.

Next she reviews the major concepts in the generalization: *environment, influences,* and *shelter.* This is done by asking the class to refer to the text glossary. She then summarizes the meanings on the board.

Once the concepts have been clarified, the class is divided into five groups, each of which is given one of the following questions to answer.

- What are the parts of your home?
- What are the different types of shelters that people in this area have?
- How are these different shelters constructed?
- What different kinds of weather conditions do we have in this area?
- What are some things that all shelters in this area have?

After discussion, each group shares its conclusions with the class. Then Ms. Olski outlines their major points on the board, under the headings: *Area, Type of Shelter,* and *Type of Environment.*

At this point the teacher introduces pictures of many types of shelters in use around the world, including boat houses, caves, tree houses, yurts, thatched huts, stilt houses over water, and solar houses. Along with each type, she provides a short explanation concerning their construction and the environments in which the shelters are found. Each example of shelter also is summarized under the three headings on the board.

The class is redirected to the generalization written on the board at the outset of the class. The teacher then leads a brief question-and-answer session covering the relationship of the various examples to the generalization.

As a following step, Ms. Olski asks each of the five groups to identify some new cases of shelters. She also asks each group to consider how the environment in which the various shelters are found has influenced the design.

The children are encouraged to use the library, as well as to consult the trade books available in the classroom. At the conclusion of its research, each group shares its findings with the entire class, adding its information to the three categories on the board. Ms. Olski then summarizes the findings and relates them to the generalization.

Had Ms. Olski used a discovery approach, the procedures would have contained many of the same elements. The chief difference would have been that she initially would not have revealed the generalization. As we saw in the example of the discovery approach used to teach a concept, the role of the teacher is to structure the introduction and analysis of materials and procedures in such a way that students themselves will infer or discover a generalization from their investigations.

Instead of stating the generalization at the outset by writing it on the board, Ms. Olski would begin by reviewing the significant concepts embedded in the generalization. Most of the remainder of the session would proceed as in the expository approach.

Toward the end of this discussion, the students would be asked to sum up what they had learned about shelters and environment. After raising some focused questions about the reasons for similarities and differences in the shelters the class had examined, Ms. Olski might ask: "How could we put in one sentence what we have learned about the relationship of environment to people's shelters all over the world?"

Using Data Retrieval Charts

In using either discovery or expository strategies to teach generalizations, data retrieval (or data) charts, accompanied by focus questions to process the data, are useful media. Such charts consist of rows and columns of categories and cells of related data. Data charts are particularly appropriate for group projects. Tasks can be divided easily, with each member taking responsibility for providing either a row or a column of data.

To provide the structure for the chart, a teacher first needs to identify the generalization to be taught. From this come the categories of items that will be used for the rows and columns of the chart.

Let us examine an example of how a basic generalization can serve to shape the structure of a chart that primary children will use. The generalization to be developed with the chart is, life-styles change over time. The cells of information in the chart will contain a mixture of pictures and written data.

In addition to determining the generalization to be developed to construct the shell of the chart, we need to identify what the two sets of categories, our row and column indicators, will be. In examining the generalization, we can see that we will require data on some *representative life-styles* and some *time periods.* Let us say that we assign the data on life-styles to columns and that we pick five aspects of life-styles: clothing, automobiles, houses, toys, and children's entertainment.

To the rows we assign three indicators of time periods: today, when our parents were children, and when our grandparents were children. Our chart shell, as shown in Figure 15.5 is now complete. It remains for the teacher and the students to fill in the cells with pictures, drawings, and narrative. The teacher, for example, could begin by partially completing a chart to model for students how data are to be recorded in the cells.

FIGURE 15.5
Data Retrieval Chart Shell

Life-Styles Change over Time					
Time Periods	**Style of Clothing**	**Types of Automobiles**	**Style of Houses**	**Children's Toys**	**Children's Entertainment**
Today					
When Parents Were Children					
When Grandparents Were Children					

After the cells have been filled with information, some further structure is required to analyze, compare, and summarize the material. One procedure for systematically processing the data obtained for each family is to begin by comparing the information by rows (e.g., What was life like when your grandparents were children?) or by focusing on contrasts (e.g., How did life when your grandparents were children differ from life today?).

If a discovery approach were used, the teacher would have students complete the chart and process the questions. Then students would be encouraged to try to summarize all of the data in a single sentence, as a way to infer the generalization concerning life-styles.

With an expository approach, the teacher would begin by stating the generalization or by writing it on the chalkboard. After the cells were filled with information and the data were analyzed, the teacher would direct the students' attention to how they supported the generalization.

E. THE REFLECTIVE CITIZEN AND PROBLEM SOLVING

The terms *inquiry, critical thinking, the scientific method, reflective thinking,* and *problem solving* all have been used at one time or another to refer to the process by which individuals find solutions to problems through reflection. In the process of problem solving, students engage in activating prior schemata that include related concepts, facts, generalizations, and hypotheses. They also integrate new subject matter into meaningful knowledge structures.

Problem solving thus is a way to better organize and interrelate existing knowledge, as well as to acquire new information. The elements of reflection are not learned as isolated bits of information but as part of a pattern of psychologically meaningful knowledge. Students do not first learn facts, for example, and *then* engage in problem solving. They use knowledge already acquired and add new elements, such as facts, concepts, and generalizations, *as* they engage in problem solving.

Most discussions of reflective thinking or problem solving derive from the work and writings of the American philosopher and educator John Dewey. His ideas on reflective thinking are laid out in detail in two books, *How We Think* (Dewey, 1933) and *Democracy and Education* (Dewey, 1916). In these works, especially the first, Dewey developed clearly the nature of a problem and its relationship to reflective thinking. His ideas have been applied to the teaching of social studies by a number of prominent social studies educators, including Engle (1976), Griffin (1992), and Hunt and Metcalf (1968).

Uses of the Term *Problem* in Instruction

The term *problem,* as it occurs in discussions of problem solving, generally is used in three ways. It refers to *personal* problems that individuals experience, such as how to become

FIGURE 15.6
General Problem-Solving Instructional Model
SOURCE: Adapted from *How We Think* by J. Dewey (Boston: D. C. Heath, 1933). Reprinted with permission.

1. Structure some aspect of the subject matter students are to learn to create a puzzle, dilemma, discrepancy, or doubt.
2. Have the students internalize the problem by asking them to verbalize it. Clarify the problem if necessary.
3. Solicit some hypotheses from the students that might explain or account for the problem. Clarify terminology where necessary, and allow sufficient time for a student reflection.
4. Assist students in testing the validity of the hypotheses generated and in examining the implications of the results. Where necessary, assist in providing reference materials, background information relevant to the subject matter, and keeping students on the topic.
5. Aid students in deciding on a tentative conclusion that seems to be the most plausible explanation for the problem, based on the best evidence available at the time. Stress the tentative nature of the conclusion, because future studies and further evidence may lead to a different conclusion.

more popular, get along with others, or cope when you lose your job. The term also is used to refer to significant *social* problems faced by our society or the world. These might be such issues as poverty, inequality of opportunity, crime, and unemployment. A third usage relates to the condition wherein individuals find a new situation problematical or experience a *psychological* state of doubt. The classic example of this usage was provided by Dewey, who cited the case of an individual who comes to a fork in a road and has no sign to serve as a guide concerning how to proceed.

Instructional Strategies for Problem Solving

Problem-solving instructional approaches may be based on one or more meanings of the term *problem*. The broadest application of problem solving, however, involves the third meaning of problem, creating a state of psychological doubt. It allows the teacher to use any subject matter in a problem-solving approach.

A psychological problem is created when the teacher succeeds in structuring, displaying, and sequencing subject matter in a special way. It is not the subject matter itself, but the way it is presented that makes it psychologically problematical. The power of the approach derives from the natural tendency of individuals to be highly motivated to relieve the cognitive discomfort they experience. They attempt to do this either by solving the problem or by finding explanations to account for it.

Any subject matter can be used for problem solving in this sense. The only requirement is that a teacher be able to frame it so as to pose and then help resolve an interesting and intriguing question. Not every topic, however, lends itself easily to the development of problem-solving strategies, because it is often difficult to create a sharp, relevant problem focus for all students. Given individual differences among students, all members of a class may not experience the problem with the same level of intensity or even perceive that a problem exists.

Problem-solving strategies require that teachers create cognitive disequilibrium in students. This is a state wherein a student perceives that something is peculiar, frustrating, irritating, puzzling, disturbing, contrary to what is expected, or incongruous. Disequilibrium is induced to cause students to attend to the subject matter being taught, regardless of its topical content or their relative degree of interest in it. Students are asked to resolve the basic issue that puzzles them: Why is this so? or How can this be? or What is the cause of this?

A basic five-step model for this type of problem solving, adapted from Dewey (1933), is presented in Figure 15.6. It outlines the basic sequence of activities that a teacher should follow in engaging students in problem solving.

An example of how the problem-solving model actually operates, with movement back and forth between the steps, is given in Figure 15.7. It presents a teacher's summary of a class session involving a group of 10- and 11-year-old children that lasted 90 minutes. The general subject matter under consideration was political elections and political institutions.

FIGURE 15.7

Summary of a Problem-Solving Activity Involving a Class of Fifth- and Sixth-Grade Students

[a]Quoted in Richard Hofstadter, *The American Political Tradition* (New York: Alfred A. Knopf, 1948), p. 116.
[b]*Ibid.*

Initially the students were asked to respond to the question, "What comes to mind when you think of Abraham Lincoln?" The function of this question was to settle the class, review their prior associations with Lincoln, and alert them to the problematic episode that was forthcoming. After approximately 10 minutes of free exploration without challenges, the class was told that the teacher wished to share a problem with them.

"Listen to these two statements made by Abraham Lincoln, and then tell me if you can see what my problem is. The first statement, let's call it A, is taken from the works of Abraham Lincoln":

Statement A

Let us discard all this quibbling about this man and the other man, this race, and that race and the other race being inferior, and therefore they must be placed in an inferior position. Let us discard all these things, and unite as one people throughout this land, until we shall once more stand up declaring that all men are created equal.[a]

"Is there anything in this statement that seems odd or out of order?" The students thought not, and so we proceeded to the second statement, B. "Listen to this second statement, let's call it B, also taken from the works of Lincoln":

Statement B

I will say, then, that I am not, nor ever have been, in favor of bringing about in any way the social and political equality of the white and black races: that I am not, nor ever have been, in favor of making voters or jurors of negroes, nor of qualifying them to hold office, nor to intermarry with white people....

And inasmuch as they cannot so live, while they do remain together there must be the position of superior and inferior, and I as much as any other man am in favor of having the superior position assigned to the white race.[b]

"Do you notice anything wrong now? What is the problem here?" At this point, students were given some time to reflect upon the statements, verbalize the discrepancy in various ways, and generally to clarify the specific problematic issue. After the problem was restated in several ways, the statements were both repeated to the class.

To implement the third step of the model, the question was raised, "How do you account for these two statements, both made by Lincoln?" The students had many immediate hypotheses, which were clarified and recorded on the board. Four basic hypotheses were suggested as follows:

1. He changed his mind.
2. He was speaking to different groups with each of the statements, and he told each group what he thought they wanted to hear.
3. One statement was what he thought to himself (e.g., as in a diary), and the other one was the one he told people.
4. He was misunderstood (i.e., his words were taken out of context).

After exhausting the many responses, some of which were simply variations on the same theme, the point was emphasized that several possibilities existed concerning our guesses (hypotheses). Only *one* might be correct, *several* answers might be true, or *none* of our explanations might be correct.

"What kind of information," the students were asked, "would we need to have in order to check out our guesses and see if they might be correct?" Responses were clarified and listed on the board under the label "Initial Facts Needed." They fell into four categories: (1) when the statements were made, (2) to whom they were made, (3) what the rest of the statements (context) were like, and (4) where they were made.

At this point several possibilities were open to the teacher: (1) have the students themselves initiate a search for relevant facts, either individually or in groups; (2) ask certain students to volunteer or appoint volunteers to research the facts; or (3) provide certain facts for the students to test the hypotheses. The third option was exercised due to time and other constraints and to focus attention on the testing rather than on the data-gathering process. In effect the teacher acted as a research resource for the students. Such a role is both legitimate and often efficient, depending on the objectives of a lesson. The amount and sequencing of factual information provided by the teacher, however, are important variables.

Consider the procedures employed by the teacher. With respect to the first fact needed, the students were informed that statement A was made on July 10, 1858, and that statement B was made on September 18, 1858. These dates were read aloud and then written on the board. The class expressed surprise.

FIGURE 15.7 cont'd

"What do these facts do to any of our guesses?" the class was asked. The students suggested that the facts eliminated the first hypothesis. After soliciting their rationale, the teacher qualified their conclusion with the observation that "Lincoln *might* have changed his mind on this point in just two months, but it was a short period of time for such an important issue."

As to the second fact required, the students were briefly instructed on how the quotes and their sources could be authenticated. "In this case," they were told, "we are placing some faith in the reliability of the historian who gave us the information that it is correct." It was noted that we often have to do this but that sometimes the historian proves to be in error, as later research reveals. In indicating that our best immediate evidence was that the statements were *not* taken out of context, it was also indicated that the statements were parts of speeches.

While the teacher had no information concerning to whom the speeches were made, the class was told that statement A was made in Chicago while statement B was given in Charleston. These facts were written on the board alongside the respective dates:

Statement A: July 10, 1858, Chicago.
Statement B: September 18, 1858, Charleston.

These new facts were greeted with "oohs" and "aahs."

Again the question was raised, "What do these facts do to our guesses?" The students suggested that the third and fourth hypotheses were rejected and the second was strengthened. When pressed for an explanation of how hypothesis 2 was strengthened by the facts, they indicated that the audience for statement A was Northern while that for B was Southern. When pressed for further clarification of this point, they indicated that the Chicago group, being Northern, would be *against* slavery while the Charleston group, being Southern, would favor it.

Psychologically speaking the class was ready to stop at this point. It had struggled with a problem and had reached what appeared to be an obvious conclusion supported by facts. Many of the children were smiling with some satisfaction, and all the hands had gone down.

The problem was regenerated quickly, however, with the following sequence of instructions: "By the way, what was Lincoln's purpose in making speeches in 1858?" Some were not sure; most said he was running for president. In a 2- to 3-minute lecture, the group was briefed concerning Lincoln's remote presidential possibilities in 1858, the conditions that made his nomination actually possible, and how presidents campaigned and were elected in that period. This new information clearly presented some confusion within the class.

Someone then contributed a vague recollection of the Lincoln-Douglas debates and suggested that the statements might have been part of them. No one knew the context of the debates. This information was provided for the class and followed by the question, "In what state did Lincoln's Senate campaign take place?" After some discussion this question was resolved in favor of Illinois.

Then the students were asked, "What would Lincoln be doing campaigning in the *South* for a Senate seat in Illinois?" This question caused considerable consternation and generated a great deal of discussion but was never answered to anyone's satisfaction. I then added two bits of new information to the facts already listed on the board:

Statement A: July 10, 1858, Chicago, *Illinois*
Statement B: September 18, 1858, Charleston, *Illinois*

Amid the noisy reactions, the teacher raised in succession the issues of why the class had seemed so sure of its earlier conclusion, how the new facts affected their list of hypotheses, and how Lincoln could make such contradictory public statements in the same state. They acknowledged that their stereotypes of Northern and Southern behavior colored their interpretation of the earlier facts, that they now required more facts, and that communication systems in 1858 were much different than those we have today.

A wall map of the United States was used to illustrate the next set of facts. Chicago was located and the general characteristics of its population in 1858 noted. Similarly the city of Charleston, in the southern part of Illinois, was identified on the map. From this discussion it emerged that Illinois in Lincoln's day, much like today, represented sharp divisions in political opinion in the northern and southern sections. The location of Charleston, Illinois, suggested the possible kinship with the proslavery stands of the bordering Southern states as well as physical separation from Chicago.

The students had renewed confidence in hypothesis 2, after their momentary loss of faith. The final challenge to their tentative conclusion took the form of the question, "How did senators get elected in those days?" No one knew. It was explained that people didn't get to vote for senators until the twentieth century, about the same time that women were given the right to vote. This explanation was followed by the question, "What would Lincoln be doing *campaigning* for the Senate?" A final brief explanation sufficed: Lincoln campaigned for state legislators pledged to vote for him as senator if they were elected to the state legislature.

Because the lesson occurred in February a few days before Abraham Lincoln's birthday, the teacher used Lincoln as the springboard for developing the initial problem focus.

Problem Springboards

In the lesson just analyzed, two brief quotations from the same individual served as the problem springboard. A *problem springboard* is an initial activity in a lesson that presents puzzling or intriguing data. Springboards can take many forms: charts, tables, graphs, pictures, cartoons, drawings, maps, recordings, films, videotapes, field trips, observations, as well as different types of print materials.

One of the teacher's major roles in creating problem-solving activities is to ascertain what is likely to appear problematical to students in the context of the subject matter to be studied. Unless a teacher has organized material in a way that arouses students' initial curiosity concerning the problem, they are not likely to attend to the problem. If students do not perceive any psychological problem that requires a solution, no real problem solving will occur.

The general problem-solving instructional model outlined in Figure 15.6 provides only a basic road map. Dewey himself suggested that problem solving, as it occurs in natural settings, does not always follow through steps in a set order. In solving problems, individuals often "jump ahead," temporarily skipping steps, and at other times they return to a step already passed. He cautioned:

> The five phases . . . of thought that we have noted do not follow one another in a set order. On the contrary, each step in genuine thinking does something to perfect the formation of a suggestion and promote its change into a leading idea or directive hypothesis. It does something to promote the location and definition of the problem. Each improvement in the idea leads to new observations that yield facts or data and help the mind judge more accurately the relevancy of facts already at hand. The elaboration of the hypothesis does not wait until the problem has been defined and an adequate hypothesis has been arrived at; it may come at any intermediate time. (Dewey, 1933, p. 115)

More than the form of the subject matter, it is how and when the teacher introduces it, as well as the questions, comments, and cues he or she uses, that determine whether a psychological problem is created for students. As students express surprise or disbelief, look perplexed, or shake their heads, for example, they offer signs that a teacher has succeeded.

Case studies as problem springboards. Case studies are brief sets of data that present a single idea, issue, or event in some detail. Case studies attempt to present in-depth coverage of a narrow topic. Further, through concrete materials, they seek to make vivid some general or abstract issue in the context of a problem.

Case studies may be presented through many media: transparencies, teacher-made sheets, records, video- and audiocassettes, films, and various print materials. Four basic types of case studies are (Newmann with Oliver, 1970)

1. *Stories and Vignettes.* These are dramatized accounts of either authentic or fictitious events.
2. *Journalistic Historical Events.* These include original newspaper accounts, recordings, or video records of historical events, eyewitness accounts, and the like.
3. *Research Reports.* These include materials such as the results of studies, statistical tables, and census reports that have been organized and summarized.
4. *Documents.* This category includes a range of items such as speeches, diaries, laws, and records.

For the intermediate and middle grades, a case might be constructed around a taped interview with a logger and a set of photos showing the effects of deforestation. This case could be used to launch a unit on how to manage our natural resources.

Answer Key: Concept Learning Exercise

In Figure 15.1, numbers 1 and 4 are *squarps*. Squarps are figures that have a smile (upturned mouth), freckles, two extended whiskers, and a point on the head.

In Figure 15.2, numbers 2 and 3 are *zrapples*. Zrapples are figures that have *either* one eye and a frown (downturned mouth) *or* two ears and a smile (upturned mouth).

SUMMARY

This chapter has helped develop your understanding of the role of concepts in the social studies curriculum; of instructional strategies for concept learning; of the role of facts, generalizations, and hypotheses in the social studies curriculum; and of instructional strategies for developing generalizations. In addition, you learned about the use of the term *problem* in social studies instruction and of instructional strategies for helping students develop their problem-solving skills in social studies.

Chapters that follow will provide further detailed understanding of how to integrate social studies into the curriculum.

QUESTIONS AND ACTIVITIES FOR DISCUSSION

1. Select a basal social studies textbook for any grade 4–9. Identify the text title, the grade level, the author and publisher, and the copyright date. List all of the concepts that are included in ten pages of the text, beginning with the first page of a chapter. For this exercise include only those concepts that are nouns or adjectives. After you have collected the data, discuss these questions: Which concepts appear with the most frequency? Which do you consider to be the most difficult? The least difficult?

2. Select a social studies concept that typically is taught in grades 4–9. Using the information in this text, create a minitext to teach the concept. After the minitext has been revised and completed, field-test it with a student for whom it was designed and who has not yet learned the concept. Compare your minitexts and your field-test results. What changes would you make on the basis of your experiences?

3. Identify two generalizations from each of the social sciences, other than those found in this textbook. As references you may wish to consult introductory textbooks and specialized reference works. Select only generalizations suitable for developing social studies lessons. Compare your lists and discuss any problems you had in identifying appropriate generalizations.

4. Select one of the types of case studies described in the text. Identify a class or group, grades 4–9, with whom you would use the material, and develop a case study on any subject appropriate for that audience. Discuss specifically how you would use the case as a springboard to a problem-solving activity.

5. Develop a strategy to teach a social studies concept to a fourth-grade student. Use the eight-step instructional model and the concept analysis form provided in the chapter. You may use either a discovery or an expository approach.

6. Repeat the procedures from the previous activity, except substitute a sixth-grade student.

7. Select one of the generalizations identified in the previous activity and a grade level 4–9. Develop a lesson plan to teach the generalization by using either a basic expository or discovery strategy.

REFERENCES

Borich, G. (1992). *Effective teaching methods* (2nd ed.). Columbus, OH: Charles E. Merrill.

Bruner, J. S., Goodnow, J., & Austin, G. A. (1962). *A study of thinking.* New York: Science Editions.

Cole, M., & Scribner, S. (1974). *Culture and thought.* New York: John Wiley.

Dewey, J. (1916). *Democracy and education.* New York: Macmillan.

Dewey, J. (1933). *How we think.* Boston: D. C. Heath.

Engle, S. H. (1976). Exploring the meaning of the social studies. In P. H. Martorella (Ed.), *Social studies strategies: Theory into practice* (pp. 232–245). New York: Harper & Row.

Griffin, A. F. (1992). *A philosophical approach to the subject matter preparation of teachers of history.* Dubuque, IA: Kendall/Hunt.

Harcourt Brace Jovanovich. (1990). *Harcourt Brace Jovanovich social studies scope and sequence.* Orlando, FL: Author.

Howard, R. W. (1987). *Concepts and schemata: An introduction.* Philadelphia: Cassell.

Hunt, E. B., & Banaji, M. R. (1988). The Whorfian hypothesis revisited: A cognitive science view of linguistic and cultural effects on thought. In J. W. Berry, S. H. Irvine, & E. B. Hunt (Eds.), *Indigenous cognition: Functioning in context* (pp. 57–84). Boston: Martinus Nijhoff.

Hunt, E. B., & Metcalf, L. E. (1968). *Teaching high school social studies: Problems in reflective thinking and social understanding* (2nd ed.). New York: Harper & Row.

Kleg, M. (1986). Teaching about terrorism: A conceptual approach. *Social Science Record, 24,* 31–39.

Kleg, M. (1987). Genocide: A concept action model. *Social Science Record, 24,* 68–73.

Martorella, P. H. (1971). *Concept learning in the social studies: Models for structuring curriculum.* Scranton, PA: INTEXT.

Martorella, P. H. (1991). Knowledge and concept development in social studies. In J. B. Shaver (Ed.), *Handbook of research on social studies teaching and learning* (pp. 370–384). New York: Macmillan.

Newmann, F. M., with Oliver, D. W. (1970). *Clarifying public controversy: An approach to teaching social studies.* Boston: Little, Brown.

Novak, J., & Gowin, D. B. (1984). *Learning how to learn.* Cambridge, UK: Cambridge University Press.

Tennyson, R. D., & Cocchiarella, M. J. (1986). An empirically based instructional design theory for teaching concepts. *Review of Educational Research, 56,* 40–71.

Whorf, B. (1956). *Language, thought and reality.* Cambridge, UK: Cambridge University Press.

SUGGESTED READINGS

Hofstadter, R. (1948). *The American political tradition.* New York: Knopf.

Husik, R. (no date). *Family minitext.* Philadelphia: Temple University, Department of Elementary Education.

Martorella, P. H. (1994). Concept learning and higher-order thinking. In J. M. Cooper (Ed.), *Classroom teaching skills* (5th ed.). Lexington, MA: D. C. Heath.

Wittgenstein, L. (1953). *Philosophical investigations.* New York: Macmillan.

CHAPTER 16

Social Studies as the Integrating Core: Literacy, Literature, and Culture

magine that five fifth-grade teachers at a nearby school decide to plan two interdisciplinary units together over the course of the year, one in the winter and one in the spring. They are making a commitment not only to meet regularly in the fall for planning, but also to gear their planning toward units that would bring together subjects and skills they normally teach separately, subjects and skills such as reading, writing, and social studies. Their rationale is that valuable instructional time is lost when reading lessons and writing lessons do not overlap one another and when, together, they do not overlap social studies lessons.

Children cannot simply read *reading* or write *writing*, these teachers reason, so why not direct their reading and writing toward the content they need also to learn? This is, after all, precisely the content to which children should be learning to apply their developing reading and writing skills. In this way, two things are accomplished. Skills are used to help achieve valued content goals, and the skills themselves are strengthened by being engaged with content. This reasoning stands on firm ground: As research on reading and writing makes abundantly clear, rather than simply to learn to read and write, a learner learns to read and write about specific things in particular ways (Langer & Applebee, 1986).

As most teachers will attest, interdisciplinary education and collaborative unit planning are two of the most popular trends in elementary and middle school education. But no clear pattern for either has emerged yet. Some teachers, such as the five mentioned, are concerned mainly to combine reading and writing instruction with subject matter instruction. Others are interested primarily in integrating social studies with science, mathematics, and the arts. Still others are eager to find powerful themes around which all curricular areas, from reading to math and music appreciation, can be brought together. In this chapter, we present ways the teacher can begin to build experience and a repetoire of strategies for integrated education.

Specifically, in this chapter you will

1. Examine sample exemplary integrated units for teachers who want to integrate social studies education with other disciplines.
2. Examine sample units and their lessons that integrate social studies education with reading, writing, and other skills.
3. Learn more about the meaning of integrated education.
4. Learn about the potential pitfalls when integrating student learning.
5. Develop your understanding of the changing concept of literacy.

6. Develop your understanding of the importance of blending literacy education and social studies education.
7. Learn about the power of and procedures for student writing of original biographies.
8. Explore the importance of culture as a component in integrated education.

A. EXEMPLARY INTEGRATED UNITS

We begin with some examples, a gallery of exhibits drawn from actual classroom life. These examples are based on program descriptions that appeared in Walter C. Parker's "Social Studies Trends" column in *Educational Leadership* in March 1987, November 1987, and October 1989. We invite readers, in the spirit of concept formation, to use them to develop a concept of interdisciplinary education.

EXHIBIT A	IN THE YEAR OF THE IMMIGRANT

Three fifth-grade teachers at an urban elementary school joined together to plan an integrated unit on the theme, *immigration*. The gathering of diverse peoples on the North American continent, they believe, is one of the most important ideas treated in the social studies curriculum. Could their 11-year-old students grapple with the idea in a way that was both engaging and rigorous? These teachers decided they could.

"We tried to give the kids a real feeling for what immigration is like," one teacher said. They provided students with lots of information, some drawn from textbooks and films, and some from literature, helping them all the while to connect that information to personal experiences and prior knowledge. Moreover, the teachers built into the unit plan ample opportunities for children to apply historical information to current immigration events and controversies.

IMMIGRATION UNIT RESOURCES

Films: *Golden Mountain on Mott Street*
The Girl Who Spelled Freedom

Trade books: *Immigrant Kids*, Russell Freedman (Dutton, 1980)
Journey Home, Yoshiko Uchida (Macmillan, 1978)
In the Year of the Boar and Jackie Robinson, Bette Bao Lord
(Harper & Row, 1986)

As students read and dramatized the books and watched the films, they used the information they were gathering to write in their journals about leaving a beloved homeland, anticipating a new life, being welcomed, being turned away, and feeling one's ethnic identity for the first time because one is for the first time *different*. The teachers especially had them write on the themes *coming* (immigration) and *going* (emigration). Several children wrote the following:

Coming to a new language

Away from a place where snow is deep

Coming to weather that can't make up its mind

Away from soldiers in uniform with tanks and guns

Coming to streets paved with gold

Away from where the rivers flow

Coming to cement streets

Away from the people who love me

Coming to dangerous people.

As well, they wrote advice to children who might immigrate. Some children warned of "really bad gangs like Crips and Bloods." Others told how to find one's way around the local airport. One student was concerned that immigrants from agrarian cultures

Continued

would not know what to do with a toilet. "In America, there are things that are different," she wrote.

> There are toilets that you sit on. You do not have to squat down and get your legs sore. I'll teach you how to flush it. *Flush* means to push a button or handle and the water goes down and clean water comes up.

Working with the school's reading and music specialists, the fifth-grade teachers invited from the community a young composer, actors, and mime artists to help draw all this together into a fifth-grade big event that would culminate the learning. All the writing and reading and discussing would be pulled together in a script, featuring movement, dance, mime, and song. All 75 fifth-grade children, they agreed, would have a part. Together they produced a musical drama, "In the Year of the Immigrant." The chorus to the title song went as follows:

> Away, away, to have a better home,
> for better education,
> for better occupations,
> together in a nation we shall call home.
>
> Immigrants bring us new perspectives,
> moving our world in new directions,
> bringing together different ways of life.
>
> Welcome the changing forms of culture,
> welcome the changing forms of fashion,
> moving in the hope of finding a better way.

The school has one of the most diverse populations in the district, with Asian Americans and South Pacific Islanders, African Americans, and European Americans in roughly equal number. One-third of them were classified "at risk." Some spend up to two hours on a bus each day. Not one of the 75 children missed any of the daytime or evening performances of "In the Year of the Immigrant."

EXHIBIT B	AN INTERGALACTIC BILL OF RIGHTS

Fifth-grade teacher Tarry Lindquist believes that one of the most powerful ways to plan units is to engage children in meaningful projects. As they participate in a project's tasks—reading, writing, debating, constructing, simulating, dramatizing, and so on—students are required to learn many skills and much content. This is knowledge that a less capable teacher might try to teach outside of such a meaningful project. But incorporated within project activities, the knowledge is more likely to be learned in a way that the learner will remember and later be able to use. Higher-order thinking and the acquisition of knowledge become two sides of one coin.

Mrs. Lindquist received the Teacher of the Year award from the National Council for the Social Studies. In the integrated unit we describe here, one of many extraordinary units she has designed, Mrs. Lindquist practices two powerful principles: First, rather than trying to teach the necessary facts, ideas, and skills before beginning a project, *start* with the project and incorporate the facts, ideas, and skills learning as they are needed. Second, be sure this knowledge is important. Design projects around the knowledge students should be learning, not the other way around.

The Museum of Flight in Seattle, Washington, was about to unveil its new gallery—a huge, glass structure with airplanes on display in every direction. Mrs. Lindquist wanted her students to learn facts about the United States Constitution, but she also want them to grapple with the *concept* of constitution. She also wanted them to develop citizenship skills, especially the sort needed to work with other citizens on difficult public policy issues. Furthermore, she wanted them to learn more about space, extending the astronomy studies they already had begun and building on their fascination with the idea of living beyond our solar system. She embedded this learning in her project.

The year before, with funding provided by a bicentennial celebration organization, Mrs. Lindquist had gathered elementary teachers from around the state at a weekend retreat. The teachers' goal was to create a lesson plan that would have students simulate

Continued

the decision making that occurred at the Constitutional Convention of 1787, and to sit-uate this learning in a genuine challenge that paralleled the challenge the framers faced in 1787. For the challenge, the teachers decided on the likelihood of space colonization in these students' lifetime, and made the following four assumptions as the project's initial provisions:

High-density population centers will be common because permanent colonies in space will be tremendously expensive.

The trend toward multiethnic crews of both sexes will continue, and probably predicts future populations of space colonies.

As a consequence of prolonged breathing of pure oxygen in controlled environments, humans likely will evolve into a different species. (Mrs. Lindquist called it *homo spatialis*.)

The present system of jurisprudence practiced in the United States may not transfer to civic life in space. For example, light bends differently in space. Eyewitness accounts, taken for granted on Earth, could be worth much more, or much less.

Mrs. Lindquist arranged to have 50 fourth-, fifth-, and sixth-grade students from as many classrooms move into the museum's new gallery for an overnight stay before it was opened to the public. Like astronauts, the children were exploring unknown space. And, like the framers of the U.S. Constitution who ventured to Philadelphia in 1787, each student came to this convention as a representative of his or her class. Their job, like that of the framers 200 years before, was to create a new document, one that did not exist anywhere: an intergalactic bill of rights.

Each of the 50 classrooms that eventually sent representatives to the intergalactic convention first developed a space colony. Students identified its physical size; location (some were on moons, some on space stations); optimal population size, density, and ethnic and gender composition; climate (both controlled and uncontrolled); and natural resources and related products. They also wrestled with space colony culture, making decisions about political life, economy, food, costume, and holidays and traditions.

Shortly after forming their colonies, the children learned that their colony's government had signed an intergalactic constitution with the others that would regulate relations among the 50 colonies. However, signing had been contingent on the framing of a bill of rights. The colonies were afraid that their rights would be lost to an authoritarian central galactic government, or to an overbearing majority that might gain control. The students' task, then, was to frame a draft bill of rights and elect a representative to take it to the intergalactic convention, to be held at the Museum of Flight.

At the convention, representatives were in a bind. They had to balance the wishes of their constituents back home with a healthy concern for the intergalactic *common good*. To do their work, representatives were assigned to "pods" of five, with a high school student who served as senior counselor. Eventually, two pods merged to form a group of ten; these reformed into other groups of ten, and so on—each time encountering different representatives with sometimes unique ideas and arguments, everyone presenting, defending, and rethinking their positions. Finally, agreements were struck and the Bill of Rights signed.

EXHIBIT C   EXPLORE

Explore is an integrated social studies/science curriculum developed by teachers and curriculum specialists in a Colorado school district together with the renowned concept learning and thinking skills expert, Sydelle Seiger-Ehrenberg. (The *Explore Curriculum* was developed and written jointly by Sydelle Seiger-Ehrenberg and School District no. 12, Adams County, Northglenn, Colorado, 1990. All material in this section is quoted or adapted from *Explore* curriculum documents.) This is a K–6 program.

Pat Willsey, like Tarry Lindquist, believes deeply in the blending of thinking skills instruction with concept learning. Willsey, a key player in the development of *Explore* and now an elementary school principal in the district, took seriously the admonition of researchers to integrate thinking and knowledge instruction: "There is no choice to be made between a content emphasis and a thinking skills emphasis. No depth in either is

Continued

possible without the other" (Resnick & Klopfer, 1989, p. 6). Note this blend in *Explore's* outcome statement: "As a result of using thinking strategies and other relevant skills, K–6 students will develop an understanding of the orderliness, diversity, relationships, and changes that exist/occur and are created in the natural world and in human experience. Further, they will learn to make intelligent, responsible decisions/choices/judgments/plans in light of each understanding."

The curriculum for grades 3 and 4 concentrates on the first two conceptual themes, respectively. Students are to become proficient in the use of thinking strategies for developing deep and flexible understandings of *orderliness* (consistency, pattern) and *diversity* (variety, uniqueness) that exist or are created:

- in living things
- in the natural environment
- in communities of people and other living things.

Further, these third- and fourth-grade children are not expected to develop these understandings only to have them lie dormant in their minds. Rather, they are to learn to *use* them and, through usage, further develop them by making reasoned judgments and plans in light of their understanding. This activity is built directly into the unit plans. Note how this curriculum design, like Mrs. Lindquist's, emphasizes the interdependence of thinking (judging, planning) and knowing (understanding orderliness and diversity in living things, nature, and human communities).

Rounding out the third- and fourth-grade *Explore* curriculum is the study of occupations and avocations in which people use and develop greater understanding of living things, nature, and human communities. Following are four lessons in the first of twelve units. Because our space is limited, we present abridged and slightly revised versions. We begin with the introductory lesson to the grade 3 curriculum.

Introductory Lesson

Intended Learning Outcome: Students will be aware of the general procedures they will be following this year to study science and social studies topics.

Students are told that this year they will be studying science and social studies "as if all of you were scientists." They are then placed in pairs to discuss the question, "From what you know, what does it mean to be a 'scientist'? What does a scientist do?"

As students share their responses, the teacher often asks *verification* questions, especially the central question of science, *How do you know that's true?* This becomes a common question in *Explore* classrooms. Eventually, the teacher presents the following four-step procedure on a chart:

The scientific way of learning
Step 1—Question

Step 2—Hypothesize, Predict

Step 3—Investigate

Step 4—Analyze/Evaluate Data, Conclude

The teacher then puts the following list on the board:

Some things scientists investigate
What plants need to grow

What the stars and planets are made of

How people in communities get along with each other

What the dinosaurs looked like

How people lived long ago

How people live now

Continued

What happens when you mix certain chemicals

How we know about weather and climate

After making sure that the class understands each item on the list, the teacher asks students what they know about each topic *as a result of scientists investigating it.*

The teacher then asks the students to go back over the list and name the kind of scientist that investigates some of these things. For example, "What do people call a scientist who investigates stars and planets? life in human communities? how people lived long ago? dinosaurs?" It is not important that students learn all the names of scientists, but that they realize, first, that there are different types of scientists and, second, that social studies stems from the work of *social* scientists.

To review, the teacher then says, "As you study science and social studies this year, you will be working just like the scientists we have been talking about. What does that mean? What will you be doing? What are the four things we said all scientists do?"

Assessment 1. The teacher displays a list of activities related to airplanes and says to students: "Suppose we were going to study airplanes and how they fly, and I told you that you would be working like real scientists. Which of the things on this list would you expect to be doing?"

a. Make up a story about airplanes.
b. Find some facts about airplanes and how they fly.
c. Ask questions about airplanes and how they fly.
d. Draw a picture of an airplane.
e. Describe a trip you took on an airplane.
f. Try to think of possible answers to your questions about airplanes and how they fly.
g. Build a model of an airport.
h. Keep looking for more facts about airplanes to see if the answers to your questions are right.

Assessment 2/homework. The teacher reviews the four-step procedure, then shows students a rock, leaf, shell, or similar item, giving them this task: "Suppose you were a scientist and had never seen anything like this before. What would you do to investigate it? Be prepared to tell us what you would do, how, and why."

Unit 1, Lesson 1

Focus Question: (Each lesson begins with a focus question to direct student/teacher attention.) What is true of all living things that distinguishes them from nonliving things?

Intended Learning Outcome: Students will develop a concept of living things in terms of both the characteristics common to all living things and those that distinguish living things from nonliving things.

Question. The teacher introduces the lesson: "First we are going to study living things and how they are *alike.* Since we're going to work as *scientists,* what is the first thing we need to do to study living things?" The teacher then reviews the chart, The Scientific Way of Learning, now focusing on the topic, Living Things and How They Are Alike.

Hypothesis. Student attention is focused on the question, "How do we know whether something is or is not alive?" The teacher points to the second step in the four-step procedure and asks students what they need to do after they have asked a question: come up with possible answers. Then the teacher repeats the question, and students hypothesize. The teacher elicits responses, helping students to explain what they mean, and writes them on a chart:

We *think* something is alive if it has these characteristics:

_____

_____

_____

Continued

_____

_____

_____

The teacher emphasizes that students should give the information they *think* is true. Later they will investigate to find out which of their present ideas are correct. After a few characteristics are placed on the chart, students work in pairs to come up with additional responses.

Investigation. The teacher helps children to move into step 3 of the scientific procedure: "As scientists, what is our next step?" Students should respond that they need to *investigate,* that is, find new information to check the accuracy of what they have put on the chart, and find out what else belongs on it. They may ask, "How can we find the kind of information we need?" At this point *Explore* takes students through a detailed introduction to their textbooks and other references where relevant information might be found. This amounts to teaching students how to *use* their textbooks as an information source.

Once students are familiar with information sources, they are ready to investigate, to test the characteristics they have listed on their charts. *Explore* uses the concept formation strategy. The teacher says, "To test our ideas, let's investigate several living things and find out whether the things we have listed are true of all of them." Each child is given a data-retrieval chart (see Figure 16.1).

In pairs, using the reference books they just studied, students gather the information each question requires for each living thing on the chart. Pairs then report their work to the whole class, and the teachers uses a class-size retrieval chart to record their work. A transparency of the student chart placed on an overhead projector works well.

Analyzing data/concluding. The teacher guides students through the concept-formation strategy as a way of making sense of all the data by drawing it together into a concept. "Let's see what all this information tells us about all living things. First, what do you see is true of some living things but not of others?" Here the teacher is eliciting

FIGURE 16.1
Data-Retrieval Chart

Retrieval Chart Living Things					
List from chart	bird	tree	fish	cactus	person
Moves? How?					
Grows? For how long?					
Changes? In what ways?					
Reproduces others like self?					
Needs food? What kind? From where?					
Needs air?					
Needs water?					

Continued

differences among the examples. Then students are directed to focus on *similarities.* "What do you find is true of *all* living things, regardless of what kind?" After this, students are asked to compose a conclusion, or *summary:*

We know something is a living thing if it

_____

_____

Writing a conclusion. Students write an informational (expository) paragraph explaining what living things are, giving examples, and telling how they differ from non-living things.

Classifying. Continuing the fourth step in "The Scientific Way of Learning," students are helped to push their understanding of the concept still further. The teacher has them test their conclusion and at the same time identify the characteristics that distinguish living from nonliving things by having students inspect a nonliving thing—a cloud, an airplane, popcorn, fire, or a balloon.

The teacher says, "Let's consider something nonliving, like a cloud. What answers do we get to each of the questions on our chart when we ask it about a cloud?" Later, "Based on the information we now have about a cloud, what about it could make it *seem* like a living thing?" and, "What is true of all living things that is not true of a cloud and proves it is not a living thing even if it moves?"

Labeling. Students should be introduced to the term scientists use as a synonym for a living thing: *organism.*

Review. Students are helped to review *how* they learned what distinguishes living from nonliving things.

Assessment. The teacher prepares a bulletin board with two sections, one marked LIVING THINGS, the other NONLIVING THINGS. Students are directed to bring in a magazine picture or drawing of something that belongs in each section. Each student should be prepared to tell the class the characteristics that make each item belong in one category or another.

Unit 1, Lessons 2 and 3

We briefly sketch here the other two lessons in the first unit of the third-grade *Explore* curriculum. The focus question of Lesson 2 is this: What do all living things need to survive and develop as they should? Here the intended learning outcome is that students develop a concept of the *needs* of all organisms. The concept they develop, again using a data-retrieval chart and the concept-formation strategy, will include these characteristics:

- clean air and water
- nutrition
- sufficient light and warmth
- protection from enemies and disease
- opportunity for the organism to reach its potential.

The focus question of Lesson 3 is this: What decisions, choices, judgments, plans, and so on, do people have to make to see to it that living things have what they need to survive and develop? The intended learning outcome is that students develop awareness of and commitment to individual and group *action,* which ensures that living things can meet their needs for survival and development.

This lesson moves children from conceptualizing what living things are, and what they need to thrive, to perceiving reasons for human action on behalf of living things.

living things: attributes → **needs** → **action**

In this way, this first unit of *Explore* goes to the heart of the most important of the five themes of geography: human-environment interaction.

Continued

There are two main learning activities in Lesson 3. The first has students consider cases where threatening conditions are putting living things at risk by making it difficult or impossible for them to get what they need. Students are then helped to suggest courses of action that might improve the situation.

Sample situations:

1. There has been a very heavy snowfall. All the food and water for birds and deer has been covered with snow for several days and the animals can't get to any.
2. It has not rained for weeks. The farmers are worried because their crops are not getting enough water.
3. People who picnic near the lake have been throwing junk into it for years. Much of this junk is harmful to the fish, insects, birds, and plants that live in or near the lake.

Students discuss these situations in small groups (three or so) and recommend courses of action. Two focus questions guide their work on each case:

1. Which living things would have trouble surviving if no one did anything to change the situation? Explain why they would have trouble surviving.
2. What could people like you and me do so that the living things in this situation could survive? Explain how each suggestion would help the living things survive.

The second learning activity has children gather data on situations in which the needs of living things are threatened *and* in which people took specific actions that helped living things meet their needs. The teacher assembles reading materials about such people and/or invites them to class from the community. After gathering and recording data about them, students use the concept-formation strategy to compare and contrast these people and their specific actions. Finally, they return to the courses of action they suggested in the first part of the lesson, revising and adding ideas for action based on the information they gathered about real situations.

B. MAKING SENSE OF INTEGRATED EDUCATION

The exhibits described suggest just a few of the possibilities available to teachers wanting to integrate social studies education with other disciplines and with instruction on reading, writing, and other skills. These are ambitious projects that may be difficult for the student teacher or beginning teacher to undertake. The first two probably cannot be done by a teacher working alone, at least not in the forms presented here. *Explore* is feasible for a beginning teacher, but it assumes the teacher has a well-developed understanding of the concept-formation strategy and considerable experience with blending instruction on content and thinking. There may be simpler ways for a teacher to begin to develop integrated courses of study, and we look at one of these, learning with biographies, in the next section. First, however, we shall define some terms and anticipate some of the pitfalls of planning interdisciplinary units.

Definitions

To understand integrated or interdisciplinary education, one must first understand the idea of academic disciplines. These are fairly distinct bodies of knowledge, each with its own preferred method of study. Anthropology, for example, is concerned with accumulating a body of knowledge (facts, concepts, generalizations, questions) about culture and customs; anthropologists' preferred method of accumulating this knowledge is ethnographic fieldwork. Biology, sociology, political science, literature, history, and archaeology are other distinct bodies of knowledge and method. The school subject called "social studies" is itself an interdisciplinary field. It draws on history and the social sciences—geography, political science, economics, anthropology, sociology, and psychology. The school subject called "science" is also interdisciplinary, drawing on biology, chemistry, physics, physiology, and other natural sciences. "Art," too, is interdisciplinary, combining drawing, painting, sculpting, writing, and other skills.

Interdisciplinary education, however, usually refers not to integrated work *within* these school subjects but *between* and *among* them—between and among social studies, science, literature, art, music, math, and so on. As well, it refers to the development of literacy—reading and writing competence—within these school subjects. Compare these definitions.

Discipline: A specific body of teachable knowledge with its own key concepts and generalizations, methods of inquiry, and special interests.

Interdisciplinary: A knowledge view and curriculum approach that purposefully draws knowledge, perspectives, and methods of inquiry from more than one discipline together to examine a central theme, problem, person, or event. (adapted from Jacobs, 1989; see also Gehrke, 1991)

Under this definition, interdisciplinary education brings several categories of knowledge together for the purpose of helping children more fully understand the object of study. Note that the purpose is not to eliminate the individual disciplines but to use them as tools or resources. Wise teachers do not hide the disciplines from children; instead, they call the disciplines by their proper names and help children to examine them. Recall that the *Explore* curriculum teaches children about the different kinds of science and scientists in its introductory lesson. This is to help children develop a more mature understanding of inquiry itself and an appreciation for diverse *ways* of knowing. Anthropology brings a cultural perspective to a topic, while political science brings questions about power and freedom. Biology brings still different concepts, interests, and questions.

Interdisciplinary education's singular strength, then, is its potential for helping children to get beyond superficial knowledge. It can enable them to develop in-depth, multidimensional understandings on topics that are worth the time and effort. There is little sense in the traditional practice of separating American history and American literature, which in some ways are two dimensions of the same topic. The integration will enrich students' knowledge of each and strengthen their grasp of the whole. Reading, discussing, and dramatizing Esther Forbes's *Johnny Tremain* and Patrick Henry's "Give Me Liberty or Give Me Death" speech—both integral to the study of the American Revolution—deepens the understanding that will come.

Pitfalls

Skillful teachers manage to avoid most of the pitfalls that inevitably accompany innovations in curriculum and instruction. Interdisciplinary education has its own set of pitfalls and conceptual errors.

Either/or thinking ("putting all the eggs in one basket"). This error involves the assumption that either a discipline-based curriculum or an interdisciplinary curriculum is always the right thing to do. As discussed in the opening of Part I, neither is true. Both are needed at different times and for different purposes. It is important to exercise professional judgment, using each when appropriate. This is the eclectic approach, and for thoughtful teachers, it is usually the best course.

Trivializing learning. While discipline-based education sometimes fragments knowledge, thoughtful teachers recognize that interdisciplinary education can create its own problems. It is particularly susceptible to trivializing the curriculum. This occurs when unimportant content is selected for instruction simply because it easily can be integrated with other content. Meanwhile, important content goes untaught. Just because a learning activity crosses disciplinary boundaries does not make it worthwhile. What makes an activity worthwhile is that students are forming or extending a powerful understanding or skill. (Recall Mrs. Lindquist's second principle.) As psychologist Jerome Bruner put it years ago, "The first object of any act of learning, over and beyond the pleasure it may give, is that it should serve us in the future. Learning should not only take us somewhere; it should allow us later to go further more easily" (Bruner, 1960, p. 17). Here is the point: Teachers need to be sure that learning activities are significant and that they contribute to the accomplishment of major curriculum goals (Brophy & Alleman, 1991, p. 66).

Confusion. Interdisciplinary education needlessly confuses learners when teachers require them to study simultaneously topics that more fruitfully could be examined separately. Imagine students trying to study three cultures' customs, literature, art, and scientific achievements all at the same time. The loss in analytic clarity and the increased difficulty would not justify the gains hoped for by integrating social studies, literature, art, and science. Experts in any field do not attempt to tackle a problem by focusing their attention on all its parts at once. John Dewey advised, wisely, that we limit a topic for study in such a way as to avoid what he called "the great bad." This is "the mixing of things which need to be kept distinct" (Dewey, 1927). Experts limit the problem they are working on; they analyze it, break it into its component parts. They do this to understand the big picture better and, therefore, to know where they most profitably might begin chipping away at the problem.

We should not train students to study a topic by making a jumbled mess of it. Readers may remember the helpful clear plastic illustrations often found in a biology textbook. These made it possible to achieve a sort of layered understanding of the human body. Readers are permitted to focus only on the skeletal system, or only on muscle tissue or major organs, and then to lay these systems on top of one another to examine the whole picture and the interaction of parts.

*Dis*integration, then, can be helpful. It also can be needlessly fragmenting. Knowing how and when to separate topics to discern them and make them meaningful and knowing, on the other hand, when to integrate them is a major achievement of skillful teaching.

Confusion also can result when so-called integrated activities require students to do things they are not prepared to do, such as role-playing scenes from Mexico when they have learned nothing about Mexico except its location on a map (Brophy & Alleman, 1991, p. 66). Whether in interdisciplinary or disciplinary contexts, instruction should always build carefully on knowledge children already possess, develop in them an awareness of the knowledge they lack, and strategically introduce them to new knowledge.

A little of this, a little of that. Closely related to the pitfall of trivializing learning is what one expert calls "the potpourri problem" (Jacobs, 1989, p. 2). This occurs when a unit is composed of bits of information from each discipline. If the subject is the Mayan Civilization, for example, we will find a bit of history, a bit of art, a bit of science, and a bit of math, but not *enough* of any to integrate into a meaningful whole.

Pet solutions. The fifth pitfall—the rush to pet solutions—occurs when a potential solution is embraced before alternatives have been carefully considered (Roby, 1985). Fads often become pet solutions, but so do old habits, as with the teacher who for 20 years has had children choose their own writing topics rather than narrowing their choice for them. Currently a popular pet solution is the idea of "themes" (or phonics or the whole language approach) as the cure-all for elementary school curriculum planning. The essence of any pet solution is that critical thinking is sacrificed to a dearly held belief; professional judgment is replaced with a new habit. There is no substitute for good judgment in teaching. Avoiding each of these pitfalls is a matter of exercising judgment.

C. WHERE TO BEGIN? THE LITERACY CONNECTION

Thoughtful teachers continually experiment with new approaches to curriculum planning and instruction, trying something different, observing its effects, revising the plan based on these observations, and trying again. Teachers' time and energy are limited, however, so it is best to have a rationale for beginning with this experiment rather than some other one, for beginning here rather than there. Bruner's advice is perhaps the best: Begin with learning that not only takes students somewhere important, but that allows them later to go further more easily.

Recalling this advice, the most significant place to begin interdisciplinary unit planning probably is with the blending of literacy education and social studies education. Both are strengthened as a consequence of being combined, and the combination permits students later to go further more easily with each. By literacy education we mean reading and writing treated as a common enterprise. Integrating literacy education with social studies education, returning to the idea with which this chapter began, gives literacy education the kind of context it needs. Strong literacy education cannot take place in a vacuum; it is most successful when situated in the collaborative pursuit of content goals. Likewise, it is through reading and writing that children are engaged with the social studies topics.

An example: Fourth-grade children are developing their reading ability as they are helped to read short stories, newspaper accounts, and expository (textbook) material about two remarkable American reformers, Sojourner Truth and Susan B. Anthony. They are developing their writing ability as they write original biographies of these women in cooperative groups. Moreover, they write the script for a winter play called "Profiles of Great Americans," and read and write poetry on the theme *courage*. The principles realized in this example are simple but powerful:

1. Literacy instruction should overlap instruction on important content. The overlap generally robs neither and it strengthens both. As a rule of thumb, the more overlap, the better.
2. Literacy instruction should be embedded in a rich social environment where high expectations are combined with lots of support, coaching, practice, and feedback. In other words, children need to be *apprenticed* into literacy (Resnick, 1990). Cooperative learning can be a good vehicle for such interaction, as we will see in this chapter.

With these two principles in hand, we can now present the idea of learning through biography. Drawing on the work of Myra Zarnowski (1990), we detail a strategy for bringing literacy and social studies together in a powerful and exciting way: students writing original biographies of important historical figures.

D. PRODUCING ORIGINAL BIOGRAPHIES

Sojourner Truth was first "sold" when she was 9 years old, probably in the year 1807. She was born a slave in New York State to a Dutch man named Hardenbergh, so that was her name, too—Belle Hardenbergh. When she was 9, John Neely became Belle's new owner. He paid $50 and got both the Dutch-speaking African girl and 100 sheep. Two years later, after learning some English and suffering beatings at the hands of the Neely family, she was sold again, this time for $105 to Martin Schryver, who had a farm near the Hudson River. In 1810, Belle was sold yet again. Her new master, Mr. Dumont, wrote in his ledger, "For $300, Belle, about 13 years old, six feet tall." Years later, with the help of Quakers, Belle won her freedom and took the name Sojourner Truth. It was a good handle for the life she was about to live: a seeker and speaker of truth.

Her speeches attracted great crowds and are today among schoolchildren's favorites. For example, in May of 1851, she addressed a women's rights convention in Akron, Ohio. Before she or any of the other women could speak, Protestant ministers—all male—dominated the proceedings, deriding the women who wanted social reform. Francis Gage later wrote what happened after the ministers were through:

> Then, slowly from her seat in the corner rose Sojourner Truth, who, till now, had scarcely lifted her head. She moved solemnly to the front, laid her old bonnet at her feet, and turned her great speaking eyes on me.
>
> There was a hissing sound of disapprobation above and below. I rose and announced, "Sojourner Truth," and begged the audience keep silence for a few moments.
>
> The tumult subsided at once, and every eye was fixed on this almost Amazon form, which stood nearly six feet high, head erect and eyes piercing the upper air like one in a dream. At her first word there was a profound hush. She spoke in deep tones, which, though not loud, reached every ear in the house and away through the doors and windows:
>
> "Well, children, where there is so much racket, there must be something out of kilter. That man over there says women need to be helped into carriages and lifted over ditches—and to have the best place everywhere. Nobody ever helps me into carriages or over mud-puddles—or gives me the best place at the table!"

Raising herself to her full height, and lifting her voice to a pitch like rolling thunder, Sojourner asked, "And ain't I a woman? Look at me! Look at my arm!" She bared her right arm to the shoulder, showing her tremendous muscular power. "I have ploughed and planted and gathered into barns, and no man could get ahead of me! And ain't I a woman?

"I could work as much and eat as much as a man—when I could get it—and bear the lash as well! And ain't I a woman?

"My mother bore ten children and saw them sold off to slavery, and when I cried with my mother's grief, none but Jesus heard me! And ain't I a woman?

"Then that little man in black says women can't have as many rights as men. If the first woman God ever made was strong enough to turn the world upside down all alone, these women together" (and she glanced over the platform) "ought to be able to turn it back and get it right side up again! And now that the women are asking to do it, the men better let 'em."

Long cheering greeted this. "I'm obliged to you for hearing me," she concluded, "and now old Sojourner hasn't got nothing more to say." (Francis Gage's account was published in an antislavery journal and reproduced in Claflin, 1987, pp. 81–82.)

Sojourner had much more to say. When she wasn't speaking for women's rights, she was speaking against slavery. And after President Lincoln ended slavery, Sojourner worked in Washington DC—"Mr. Lincoln's city"—to overcome the remnants of slavery: racism and deeply entrenched prejudice. She tried to help freed Africans find work and homes, and she worked for a time as a nurse in Freedman's Hospital. These were chaotic, heartbreaking times. The Civil War, in which her son fought in the famous 54th Massachusetts Regiment, became a slaughter on both sides. And just as it ended, Lincoln, whom she had met and much admired, was killed by an assassin.

Still, she was not defeated. Another biographer, Jeri Ferris, writes of yet another of Sojourner's efforts to right wrongs:

One afternoon as Sojourner walked back to the hospital with an armful of blankets, she was so tired she just couldn't walk any more. Horsedrawn streetcars clanged up and down the road, filled with white folks. Sojourner waited for a car to stop, but none did. Finally, as yet another car passed her, she called out, "I want to ride!" People crowded around, the horses stopped, and Sojourner got on. The conductor was furious and demanded she get off. Sojourner settled back in her seat. "I'm not from the South," she said firmly, "I'm from the Empire State of New York, and I know the law as well as you do."

The next day she tried to ride another streetcar. Again the conductor would not stop. Sojourner ran after the car and caught up with it. When the horses stopped, she jumped on. "What a shame," she panted, "to make a lady run so." The conductor threatened to throw her off. "If you try," she said, "it will cost you more than your car and horses are worth." He didn't.

The third time Sojourner tried to ride a streetcar, she was with a white friend. "Stand back," shouted the conductor to Sojourner, "and let that lady on."

"*I* am a lady too," said Sojourner, and she stepped aboard with her friend. (Ferris, 1988, pp. 53, 55)

We provide this sketch of the life and times of Sojourner Truth to introduce a strategy for helping children to produce original biographies. The creation of an original biography is a splendid way to invite children to read, write, and discuss their way to an in-depth understanding of great citizens such as Sojourner Truth. The names in the following list are a small sample of other persons whose life and times warrant in-depth study by elementary school children. In the spirit of concept formation, teachers can select three or four people who *together* would help children to form the concept of *democratic citizen*. Thus the class could write three or four biographies during a school year, all the while keeping track of the similarities among these people—similarities that make them all examples of democratic citizens:

- They knew that popular sovereignty is the bedrock of democracy, and that this means taking personal responsibility for the health of civic life.
- They took time from their private lives to be active in civic life.
- They understood the difference between complaining and proposing solutions.
- They understood, within the constraints of their times, that democracy means majority rule *and* minority rights.
- They exhibited courage on behalf of these principles.

Biographies of democratic citizens

James Madison	Abraham Lincoln
Susan B. Anthony	Jane Adams
Thomas Jefferson	Mary McLeod Bethune
Benjamin Franklin	Gordon Hirabayashi
Eleanor Roosevelt	Patrick Henry
George Washington	Martin Luther King, Jr.

Democratic citizen, of course, is not the only concept around which subjects can be selected for biographies, though it is one of the most important. Other central ideas are *explorers, inventors and scientists, champions of the poor, friends of nature, leaders, dictators, revolutionaries,* and *heroes.* Recall that the discussion of concept learning emphasized multiple examples. Here this means that a teacher might orchestrate children's biographical studies around one of these themes, having them produce over the year three or four biographies on that theme rather than one each on different themes. This approach should help children to build an in-depth understanding of that theme. On the other hand, teachers might, to cover more ground, mix the kinds of subjects about whom their children write, for example, choosing a hero (Crazy Horse or Harriet Tubman), an inventor (Benjamin Franklin or Eli Whitney), a scientist (Galileo or Newton), and a great citizen (Sojourner Truth or James Madison). Figure 16.2 suggests several themes and related subjects.

FIGURE 16.2

Examples of Thematic Clusters of Persons of Prominence Suitable for Biographical Study

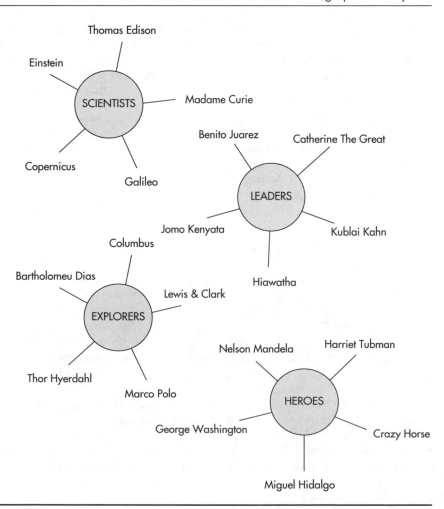

Procedure for Writing Biographies

The teacher will need to (a) select the person about whom children will write their biographies, (b) help the children learn about the person and keep track of what they are learning, (c) help children reflect on the person's life and identify key events, (d) orchestrate the co-operative production of biographies in small groups.

Selecting a subject. Several criteria guide the selection of subjects for children's biographies. Most important is that the person chosen bring children into contact with powerful ideas of history, government, geography, economics, and/or other social studies disciplines. Individuals who can help children build understandings of one or more of the following seven themes will not only bring children to the heart of social studies but also build firm foundations for further learning:

1. The multicultural nature of societies. North American society, for example, is composed of many ethnicities, all races, men and women, rich and poor.
2. The nature of democracies, the conditions that sustain them, and the conditions that undermine them.
3. Human-environment interaction.
4. Great economic transformations—nomadic to agrarian to industrial economies, for example, with the nearly complete cultural change that results.
5. The international system—world geography, area studies, hunger, economic interdependence, development.
6. Participatory citizenship—social responsibility, participation in public problem solving.
7. The enrichment of human life—arts, entertainment, religion.

Another criterion for subject selection is the likelihood that children will be captivated by this life. It may help some children become more interested in the person if information is available on his or her childhood. Ben Franklin's early troubles with his brother James, for example, James Madison's illnesses as a child, and Sojourner Truth's harrowing childhood all seem to fascinate children, broadening them by giving them access to *other* children's lives—lives that are different but reassuringly similar, too. Learning a great deal about a person can itself make that person captivating to the younger biographer. As this student quite wisely reported, one cannot know for certain what makes a subject interesting. He seems to conclude, however, that familiarity breeds interest, not contempt:

> Everyone else was real interested in Hiawatha but I wasn't because, well, the things I knew about him just were boring. But the more I found out, the way they learned to hunt and stuff in the long house, and all the magic, well it got real interesting. Now I know him a lot.

A third key criterion is the availability of materials. The "snapshot biography" method we outline here requires students to learn a great deal about the subject (Zarnowsky, Chap. 4). If the subject is obscure, chances are good that neither the textbook nor the school library will have ample books, primary documents, narrative biographies, or other materials.

Consider how Mr. Brem, a fourth-grade teacher, selects biographical subjects. He has decided to weave a yearlong study of *leadership* through the state history curriculum his school district requires in that grade. He wants his pupils to study and eventually write biographies of three state leaders. He wants the leaders to be culturally diverse, and he wants them to expose students to different historical periods and geographical areas of the state. Now Mr. Brem begins his materials search. A booklet he received last year from the state arm of the League of Women Voters provides information on several civic leaders, and he asks a committee of students to select one of these for the class to study. The social studies education office at the state capital publishes material on the state's governors; Mr. Brem selects the state's first governor. Now he has selected two of the three subjects he needs. Since they are both European Americans, Mr. Brem wants the third leader to belong to an ethnic minority.

Unaware of who this might be or where materials can be obtained, he appoints another committee of students to go to the school librarian for help. The librarian refers them to information on a civic leader who helped to organize the early Chinese-American community in the state. Now the class has a set of three leaders and is ready for the reading-and-writing approach to biographical study.

Learning about the subject of a biography. Before children can begin to write about a biographical subject, they need to learn something about him or her. Let us be clear, however, that the learning sequence is not read, then write. Rather, it is write a little, drawing on prior experience, then find out a little. Write some, learn a little more, write some more, and so on. One of the major advances in the science of instruction in the past ten years is that teachers do not have to provide all of the facts before asking students to think. The advice instead is to integrate data gathering and reflection. The teacher should concentrate student attention on the higher-order task, in this case production of the biography, which in turn motivates gathering facts about the subject and interpreting his or her life.

So, students begin learning about the subject, let us say Sojourner Truth, by finding out a little something about her. Perhaps the teacher begins by reading aloud for just 20 minutes from Jeri Ferris's book, concentrating on the beginning of the story when Sojourner is taken from her mother and sold to Mr. Neely at the age of 9. Then the teacher asks the children to discuss this passage—the idea of buying and selling persons, in this case a child. She asks them to imagine the feelings of Belle on the auction block and the feelings of her mother and father. She may ask them what they have learned elsewhere about the enslavement of people. Perhaps some of them will talk about the Jews in Egypt in biblical times, maybe some have seen the restored version of the old movie about Spartacus, perhaps some will talk about the Holocaust. Some children may know quite a bit about the capture and subsequent ownership of Africans through books they have read or lessons they have had in prior grades or in church. The discussion will provide the teacher with diagnostic information about children's current knowledge of slavery while activating the students' prior knowledge.

Now the teacher can ask students to bring out their journals and begin to write. She may ask them to write about the same things she previously asked them to talk about, which should be the easiest for them. Then she might ask them to predict what will happen to Sojourner in her new master's home. This should make them want to gather more information. Where will they get it?

The teacher knows that Sojourner's life with Mr. Neely is documented in the textbook. So, the next day she has children take out their journals to remind themselves of the predictions they wrote yesterday. Then, they are given 20 minutes to read the pertinent section in the text and return to their journal to write what really happened. Next, the teacher turns student attention to the map of the Northeast in the textbook and, based on clues given in the passage read aloud yesterday and the text passage today, helps them to find the state where Sojourner first was bought and sold (New York). In their journals, she has them enter the date and sketch a map of New York under the title, Where Sojourner Truth's Story Begins.

Now that they know where the story began (the geographic theme, *location*), students are helped to get a feel for New York (the geographic theme, *place*). Their teacher has them go to their cooperative teams and, working with the textbook, answer these questions:

1. What states, countries, and bodies of water border New York?
2. Is the geography of New York all the same, or are there different landforms? If so, what are they?
3. If Sojourner was able to fly away from the Neely farm, which route would have the fewest mountains to fly over?

The teacher then tells students to sketch all of this on a blank handout map of New York, including a legend so readers can understand their symbols.

The next day, the teacher reads aloud Virginia Hamilton's retelling of the folk tale, *The People Could Fly*. A wonderfully hopeful tale, though at the same time tragic, it tells of African slaves literally flying from bondage to freedom.

But when the people were captured for slavery, we learn in the tale, they shed their wings. The slave ships were too crowded for wings. A few, however, kept the power. Toby did, and he used it to help the others to escape. One day Sarah was hoeing and chopping as fast as she could, a hungry baby on her back, but the baby "started up bawling too loud." The Overseer hollered at Sarah to keep the baby quiet, but Sarah fell under the babe's weight and her own weakness. The Overseer began to whip her. "Get up, you black cow," he called. Sarah looked to Toby: "Now, before it's too late," she panted. "Now." Toby raised his arms and whispered the magic words to her. "Kum . . . yali, kum buba tambe."

> Sarah lifted one foot on the air. Then the other. She flew clumsily at first, with the child now held tightly in her arms. Then she felt the magic, the African mystery. Say she rose just as free as a bird. As light as a feather (Hamilton, 1988).

Afterward, students return to their journals to reflect on this new material. The teacher now could highlight the themes *freedom, suffering,* and *survival,* and children could be directed to compare this tale to others they have heard on these themes.

The teacher continues over the next two or three weeks to read aloud from biographies and other accounts of Sojourner Truth, as well as from related stories and reference material. Student committees are sent to the library to gather data on people, places, events, and issues raised in the teacher's readings that students want to find out more about. As well, the teacher assembles some material for the students to read themselves—material in the textbook on Lincoln's decision to free the slaves and material on influential abolitionists: Frederick Douglass, who escaped from slavery in the South; William Lloyd Garrison, who published *The Liberator,* an abolitionist newspaper; and the Grimké sisters, Angelina and Sarah, who moved north after having been raised with captive Africans on a South Carolina plantation. This information helps to elaborate the children's understanding of Sojourner's life, as well as her civic missions, and should lead to their producing much stronger, richer biographies.

For this reason, information on the women's movement of the 1800s needs also to be gathered, such as the Seneca Falls Convention convened by Lucretia Mott and Elizabeth Cady Stanton in 1848. This is the same movement Sojourner jolted with her "Ain't I a Woman" speech, delivered three years later at a second women's rights convention.

The setting for all this information needs also to be grasped; consequently, students should study the geography of New York, Ohio, and Michigan—the three states where Sojourner spent much time working, speaking, and living. In this way, students learn about the subject of their biography and gradually piece together in their minds a model of Sojourner's life and times.

Reflection and setting priorities. After several weeks of reading, writing, and mapping their biographical subject's life, children are ready to reflect on this life and its times and places, and to select key events. A few of these events will become the focal points of the chapters in the book students will write together. The following procedure is recommended (Zarnowski, 1990, Chap. 4. Reprinted with permission from the National Council for the Social Studies):

1. *Opening.* The teacher announces that today is the day the class begins to pull together all that has been learned about the subject, and informs students of what is to come.
2. *Brainstorming.* The teacher asks students to brainstorm all the events in the subject's life that they found interesting, all the events they believe were pivotal in the subject's life, all the events they figure made the subject the most and least proud, and so on. The point here is to get a long list of varied events in the subject's life. Here are just a few of the events in Sojourner's life that students have suggested:
   - the time she was separated from her mother
   - the second time she was sold
   - the third time she was sold
   - confronting Mr. Dumont
   - rescued by Quakers
   - names herself Sojourner Truth

- "Ain't I a Woman?" speech
- meeting President Lincoln
- working as a nurse in Washington, DC
- confronting the trolley conductor
- meetings with Garrison and Douglass.

When the brainstorming slows, the teacher has students take a break—go to recess, clean the room, do something physically active. When they return, they open their journals and search for other events to add to the list. They come up with more:

- being born in captivity
- speaking out for women's rights
- becoming an abolitionist
- living in New York
- traveling by buggy in Ohio.

3. *Selecting.* Students now are asked to move into cooperative groups of four or five children each. Their first task as a group is to select four or five of the key events brainstormed by the whole class. These might be the four events that interested students the most, or the teacher might direct them to use other criteria. For example, if the teacher previously has worked with children on the meaning of time lines, she or he might have them divide Sojourner's life into four equal segments and choose one event from each segment. Or, the teacher might have them choose one event in each of four categories: meetings with remarkable people, life as a slave, speeches, life as an abolitionist.

Once the key events have been selected, the children in each cooperative group divide the events among themselves, each choosing one event. Dividing the events—and thus the labor—is crucial to the coming task: producing an original biography.

Writing and illustrating. The students are now ready to write and illustrate a biography of their subject. Each cooperative group will produce a biography on the same subject, in this case Sojourner Truth. Some teachers have each group use the same biography title, *The Life and Times of (Sojourner Truth).* Others let each group create its own variation on this title.

Each person on the team is responsible for one chapter. The chapter's topic is the key event selected before. Groups will have different chapters in their books because each group will choose a different set of four key events. However, if the teacher wishes, he or she can use the cooperative groupwork technique called Jigsaw (Aronson, 1978). In this technique, one member of each small group is working on the same key event as one child on each of the other groups; consequently, these children can meet together to work on their chapter.

The teacher achieves this by *not* allowing groups to select their own four events. Rather, after the large-group brainstorming of key events, the *large group* also selects four events that will become the chapters in the groups' biographies. Thus, the book may shape up like this:

Title: THE COURAGE AND CONVICTION OF SOJOURNER TRUTH

Chapter 1: "Sold for 50 Dollars!"

Chapter 2: "New Name, New Life"

Chapter 3: "Ain't I a Woman?"

Chapter 4: "The Trolley Incident"

The child on the team who is responsible for Chapter 1 joins with other children from other teams also working on "Sold for 50 Dollars!" Meanwhile, the child on each team responsible for Chapter 2 joins with the other "2s," and so on. These are called *expert groups.* Together they discuss what they will write and draw, read one another's drafts, and provide feedback. This is advisable with younger children who are just beginning to write early versions of paragraphs; the group support is helpful, and the teacher can more easily monitor and coach her four expert groups than if every child in the room were writing on a different topic.

Whether the teacher uses the Jigsaw technique or not, the children's work has two parts: They have to write a description of the key event for which they are responsible, and they must draw an accompanying illustration. The least experienced writers may produce only a one- or two-paragraph description, and may fit their illustration on the same page. The teacher may press more experienced writers, however, to produce a two- or three-page description. The illustration is embedded in the text somewhere as in "real" biographies. Skillful teachers are able to boost their children's confidence about both the writing and the drawing by encouraging them to "just get started, get something on paper, pull something together from your journal, whatever; we'll go back and polish it later." (Teachers and children who play the board game, *Pictionary,* understand that illustrating is very different from producing realistic drawings. Virtually anyone can illustrate.)

Each team thus produces the rudiments of a biography: a title page and four chapters. But real biographies have more, and so should these. The following parts of a book make a more complete biography, and they generally can all be done even by the youngest children:

Title page. Title plus complete publication information, for example: The Life and Times of Sojourner Truth (see Figure 16.3).

Foreword. Written by someone other than the four authors, for example, a parent, another teacher, the mayor, a school board member, a bus driver. Instruct the Foreword writer to write no more than one page and to address two matters:

1. Tell readers some ways you feel you can relate personally to the person about whom the biography was written.
2. Tell readers something about the book.

Introduction with time line and map. The introduction should contain a brief message to readers telling them the subject of the book: Who is its subject? Where and when did he or she live? What, in a nutshell, did he or she do? Why? It is also considerate to tell readers the topic of each chapter. A helpful way to portray the *when* is to sketch a time line of the subject's life. The *where* statement should be illustrated with a map, either physical or political, or both, with a legend to help readers understand the symbols.

Chapters 1–4. Each chapter needs a title and author name. Its body is a written description of a key event in the subject's life with an illustration that captures the key event.

FIGURE 16.3
An Example of a Biography Written by Students as a Cooperative Learning Project

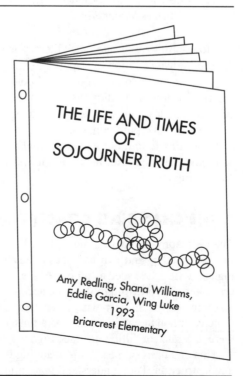

About the authors page. Ask each child to write a sentence or paragraph about her- or himself. The teacher might ask each group to decide how long the author statement should be. Children can be prompted to tell readers their full name, the name of the city or town where they live, their age, and something they like to do:

> Wing Luke lives in Denver, Colorado, with his family. He is 9 years old and loves to play soccer. He wrote Chapter 4, "The Trolley Incident."

Summing Up: The Biography Approach

The biographical approach we have discussed has four parts. Here we summarize each. We then give some concluding remarks on the literacy revolution.

1. *Selecting the subject.* Generally this is done by the teacher since he or she knows better than students which historical figures are worth studying—which subjects not only will engage children today but prepare them to go further later.
2. *Learning about the subject.* Writing a biography with one's peers requires much learning about the subject's life and times. In the method outlined above, the learning happens through reading from the textbook and other reference books, reading trade books and folk tales, hearing the teacher and others read aloud, library research, film, interviews, recordings, map study, discussion, and so on. Children need to be apprenticed into the use of a wide variety of information sources to build in-depth understandings. As well, the learning happens though writing itself. Consequently, the writing does not come after all the learning about the subject but is woven into the reading and discussion with the help of journals.
3. *Reflection and setting priorities.* Students reflect back on the life they have been studying and brainstorm key events. Eventually, a handful of events are selected that become the chapters of the biographies.
4. *Writing and illustrating.* Working together and dividing the labor, children write and illustrate a biography of their subject. All groups in the class may be producing biographies of the same subject. The chapters of each of these biographies may be the same, permitting Jigsaw cooperation among children from different groups who are assigned to the same key event, or the chapters may vary from group to group. Another variation has different groups produce different biographies related to a common conceptual theme, such as *leadership*.

Biography writing integrates literacy learning with social studies learning. By embedding literacy instruction in important social studies content *and* collaborative group work, the teacher creates the kind of social context that can support in-depth learning. Reading comprehension and writing instruction become much more than plodding through new vocabulary and learning sentences and paragraphs in a vacuum; literacy comes to mean problem solving, interpretation, competing interpretations, conversation, provocation, writing and rewriting to find out what one thinks is true and what one believes ought to be done, and experimenting with new possibilities that exist now only in the imagination. This is "high" literacy.

E. THE CHANGING CONCEPT OF LITERACY

The biography-production method we have been discussing is embedded in a conception that sees reading and writing not as fixed abilities that one either has or lacks. Rather, reading and writing are seen as processes—more precisely, as *crafts*—that evolve through trial, error, and support from those more accomplished. This process-oriented notion of literacy learning is different from what research told us only 20 years ago (Hull, 1989). Then, it was quite common to define literacy as a finished product: You either had it or you didn't; you were "literate" or "illiterate" (see Figure 16.4).

This emphasis on process is changing the way highly skilled teachers orchestrate literacy instruction. They understand that an individual's reading and writing skills grow and change over time. One's literacy is not static; it evolves, and its evolution depends on the

FIGURE 16.4

Literacy Research Emphases

EARLY RESEARCH EMPHASIS	CURRENT RESEARCH EMPHASIS
Reading and writing instruction are separated. Both are separated from content learning. Reading and writing are fixed abilities that, like muscles, are the same everywhere. Reading and writing are finished products.	Reading and writing instruction are integrated. Both are developed within content learning. Reading and writing ability evolves like a craft and mirrors the local literacy community. Reading and writing are complex processes.

individual's social context, that is, his or her "literacy community." All of us belong to one sort of discourse community or another, and that membership functions to socialize us into one or more patterns of using our minds—of reading, writing, and talking. We might be socialized into a literacy community that expects and rewards no more than minimal language use—say, for reading street signs, a ballot, and directions on a medicine label; for "filling out" job applications, "filling out" worksheets, and "completing" credit card applications. This is the vocabulary of low literacy.

It is low because the tasks lack challenge and intellectual rigor. They signal low expectations for students. On the other hand, we might be socialized into a literacy community that has a higher vision of literacy and, consequently, expects and encourages something quite different (see Bereiter & Scardamalia, 1987). Here, language is used in the service of higher-order, important tasks, for example, to plan research on civic problems with an eye toward improving social life, as an avenue to satisfying aesthetic experiences in literature and the arts, and as a means of lively conversation and, hence, conflict resolution and mutual understanding.

When literacy is defined in this more empowering way, literacy instruction cannot remain the same. It, too, needs to change. Now practice and coaching, focused on the *processes* of reading and writing, become the centerpieces of instruction. Learning by doing is the path, and the doing overlaps important content goals. This is the essence of *whole-language learning.* Content, whether the parts of the United States Constitution or the cultures of Asia and Africa, is the landscape on which the path is laid. Continuous feedback and guidance, both from the teacher and from more accomplished peers, makes success possible.

Now, the children do not read a story about rainbows in the morning, then try to write three complete sentences about a story on penguins from the basal reader, and in the afternoon fill in a worksheet on yet another topic, this time from social studies. Instead, students spend a good part of the day integrating reading, writing, and social studies, and other subjects as well. They do this by working on biographies of someone whose life and times carry them imaginatively and deeply into essential content. The biographical approach is, of course, only one vehicle, but it is a powerful and feasible one. The noted biographer Milton Meltzer observed that the biography approach is

> a vehicle for developing children's natural curiosity about people and the world around them to the point where they themselves investigate a particular life and, through the artful use of language, tell that human story to others. (Meltzer, Foreward to Zarnowski, 1990)

F. THE CULTURAL CONNECTION

We have seen that learning to read and write is best thought of as an apprenticeship, and that this apprenticeship inevitably occurs within a set of expectations. The classrooms of our best teachers are "high" literacy communities: Children are expected to do more than "fill out" this or "complete" that; they are expected instead to develop the crafts of reading and writing and, as they do so, to bring them to the service of important social studies (and science and mathematics) understandings. We now take these notions of high literacy and integrated education one step further by considering the importance of *culture.* (See Figure 16.5.)

FIGURE 16.5
Schematic Representation
of Integrated Education

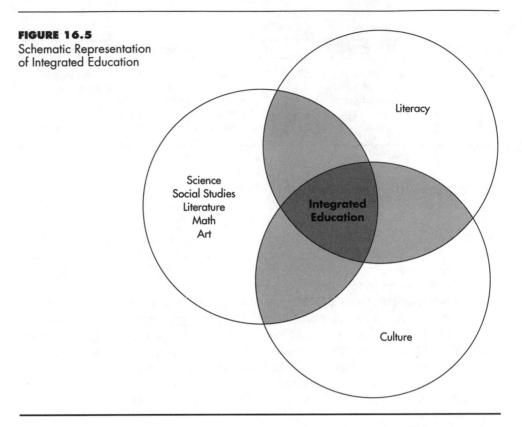

Teachers committed to high literacy appreciate two facts. First, classrooms are multi-cultural places. Students differ from one another and the teacher in one or more of these categories of culture: ethnicity, race, gender, and social class. Second, topics often need to be studied from more than one cultural perspective. Together, these add up to what is called *multicultural education.* We will examine each in turn.

Hospitable Learning Climate

As for the first, skillful teachers create learning communities that genuinely welcome cultural differences among the children gathered there. These teachers are as eager to find out about the cultural backgrounds of their children as they are to discover any other diagnostic information that will help them to individualize learning. Differences are not treated as disadvantages; they are not even perceived that way. Rather, they are perceived and treated as part of the child's experience—his or her prior knowledge—that must be integrated into teaching and learning if desired outcomes are to be reached. This is a tall order. How do these teachers do it?

Perhaps the most helpful thing they do is not implementing a set of techniques but cultivating in themselves an *attitude.* They cultivate in their own professional behavior an anthropologist's perspective on their own cultural roots and those of the children. They recognize that they themselves have been socialized into one or more cultures—that they are not culturally neutral, suspended above ethnicity, race, class, gender, and particular linguistic traditions. Quite the opposite, teachers are thoroughly immersed. Every teacher speaks one or more language and dialect; every teacher belongs to one racial group or another and to one ethnic group, gender, and social class or another.

Skillful teachers do not make much of this fact in overt ways, they don't "advertise" their culture, but they are keenly aware of it and appreciate how profoundly culture influences their point of view and what they do with students. Fundamentally, *this cultural knowledge helps them more clearly to see the cultural tapestry of the classroom—themselves included.* Perceiving clearly the cultural roots of their own speaking, thinking, and behaving helps them to not ignore the classroom tapestry but instead to pay attention to it, study it, develop expertise on it, and use it. This makes it possible for them to provide what we might call "a hospitable learning climate" for all their students, whatever their cultural backgrounds. It is a learning community that honors diversity. Consider the following case.

Mrs. Carey teaches in the third grade, where the social studies theme is "Communities Now and Then." She has always prided herself on being able to tell both short and long versions of America's story. The long version is the one she tells in her third-grade class, and it takes a whole school year. Her children study European and Asian immigrant communities, both now and long ago. They build replicas of the Plymouth and Jamestown colonies but also St. Augustine, Florida, and Santa Fe, New Mexico. And they study the Chinese men who immigrated to work the railroads, reading Lawrence Yep's *Dragonwings*. Her short version reduces the nine months to a phrase, "We are a nation of immigrants."

This short version, really a title for the yearlong study, indicates the main idea around which Mrs. Carey orchestrates content and instruction. It is the *storyline,* to use a metaphor from literature, and functions powerfully to fashion teaching and learning.

After years of telling this story, Mrs. Carey realized that her own immigrant experience, several generations before, along with her own studies in school of the great European immigration around the year 1900, had unknowingly shaped the storyline. She looked at her Hispanic and African American students and realized they were not part of the "nation of immigrants" storyline. Most of her Hispanic students did not immigrate; rather, the land of their ancestors, once in Mexico, was annexed to the United States after the Mexican-American War. And the ancestors of her black students hardly immigrated; they were forcibly removed from Africa.

She began an effort to change her story. She wanted to do this for the sake of accuracy, but she also felt that the old storyline may have kept some of her students from really going after this material. Maybe they felt that the story, like somebody else's shoes, didn't fit them. For the moment, Mrs. Carey is experimenting with two story lines, "We are a nation of many cultures" and "*E pluribus unum*—out of many, one."

Multiple Perspectives

The second aspect of multicultural education emphasizes a compare-and-contrast approach to the content children are to learn. Teachers make it a point to plan units so that a topic is studied from more than one perspective, and the children must wrestle with their similarities and differences. This strategy has important advantages over the single-perspective approach.

First, any one perspective is prevented from being put forward as neutral (as one teacher put it, "This isn't a perspective, this is the truth!"). Second, children are introduced to the heart of historical thinking: making sense of competing accounts. Third, children are provided learning opportunities that involve comparison across multiple cases. This is strong pedagogy. Research suggests that it increases retention and facilitates students' later *use* of this material when they are working on other things.

An example of the multiple-perspective approach is provided in Figure 16.6. It uses children's literature and should help a beginning teacher to build a lasting habit.

With this example of the multiple-perspective approach to integrated unit planning, we close this chapter with the emphasis on culture. This is as it should be. Literacy education and interdisciplinary education both are steeped in culture. Both depend on apprenticeships in learning communities that expect great things of all children: high literacy and in-depth knowledge.

FIGURE 16.6
A Multicultural Perspective

Materials:

Historical fiction. The Collier brothers' *My Brother Sam is Dead* and *War Comes to Willy Freeman.*

Cultural Perspectives:

These two pieces of historical fiction present very different perspectives on the American Revolution. Sam's story is told by his brother Tim. Both Sam and Tim as European American males. Their father is against Sam joining with the American rebels to drive out the British. Younger Tim is torn between his father and Sam. Willy, on the other hand, is a young female who has to disguise herself as a male because she is alone and separated from her family. Soldiers are everywhere. Also, she is African American. It doesn't make much difference to her which side wins. Both enslave Africans. Her father, unlike Tim's, joins with the rebels and, before many pages are turned, is killed defending a rebel fort.

Activity:

Children write in their journals while reading these books. The culminating activity is to write a new story in which Tim and Willy meet and learn of one another's experiences and perspectives on this war.

Note:

These stories should be combined with data gathered from the textbook, maps, and other informational sources so that students are not left only with narrative, fictionalized treatments of the war for independence.

SUMMARY

This chapter has helped you build experience with and a repertoire of strategies for integrated education. Chapters that follow will provide further detailed understanding of how to integrate the curriculum.

QUESTIONS AND ACTIVITIES FOR DISCUSSION

1. Find instances of the phrases "fill out" and "complete" in curriculum plans and materials. These are presented here as typical examples of *low* literacy. But is this always true? Are the contexts within which you found the phrases typical of low literacy? Discuss with classmates and teachers what you found and what you mean by "low" and "high" literacy.

2. Rank order the three exhibits given in the beginning of the chapter according to the following criteria: (a) student interest, (b) focusing students on essential social studies content, (c) likelihood of producing "peak experiences" (experiences so vivid, exciting, and fulfilling that they stay with a person virtually for a lifetime). Compare your responses to others.

3. Of these three exhibits, the *Explore* curriculum was described in the greatest detail. Do you think it warranted such treatment? Share it with two or three other educators and ask them their opinion.

4. Review the *Explore* curriculum. Then add a fifth lesson to the four-lesson unit that was described. Select one of the following topics for its focus, then write a *focus question* and an *intended learning outcome* statement.
   - careers involving the study and/or protection of living things
   - international comparison of living things and their needs
   - an organism's "potential"
   - biographies of one or more people studied in Lesson 3
   - community service related to actions suggested in Lesson 3.

5. Ask the librarian in two different elementary/middle school libraries to give you a tour of the biography sections. Ask the librarian to identify several of the more popular biographies. As you examine them, consider these questions: (a) What conceptual themes are suggested by these subjects? (b) Could any three or four of them be woven through a school year, all related to a single theme (e.g., leadership)? (c) Which eras of American history are not represented by biographies in either library?

6. Design an array of biography "book" formats. What forms could fifth graders' books take?

7. In addition to "snapshot" biographies, to what other genres of writing might children be introduced? Plan the lessons that would introduce them to one of these other genres. For example, plan

an introduction to *historical fiction,* then plan the lessons for teaching them to write the sort of historical fiction suggested in the final examples—a story about the meeting of two people from different texts. Finally, sketch unit plans related to other genres (e.g., poetry; plays).

8. Select three eras of United States history and assemble multiple-perspectives curriculum materials for each.

9. Study the diverse cultural identities of a group of children. Use firsthand observation, interviews, and reference books (e.g., ethnic studies textbooks). Take field notes, as an anthropologist would. Pay special attention to the variation within groups. For example, children of European ancestry are not "all alike," nor are children of Asian or African ancestry. Similarly, children whose first language is Spanish differ widely from one another.

REFERENCES

Aronson, E. (1978). *The jigsaw classroom.* Beverly Hills, CA: Sage.

Bereiter, C., & Scardamalia, M. (1987). An attainable version of high literacy: Approaches to teaching higher-order skills in reading and writing. *Curriculum Inquiry, 17* (1), 9–30.

Brophy, J., & Alleman, J. (1991). A caveat: Curriculum integration isn't always a good idea. *Educational Leadership, 49* (2).

Bruner, J. (1960). *The process of education.* Cambridge, MA: Harvard University Press.

Claflin, E. B. (1987). *Sojourner Truth and the struggle for freedom.* New York: Barron.

Dewey, J. (1927). *The public and its problems.* Chicago: Swallow.

Ferris, J. (1988). *Walking the road to freedom: A story about Sojourner Truth.* Minneapolis: Carolrhoda Books.

Gehrke, N. J. (1991). Explorations of teachers' development of integrative curriculums. *Journal of Curriculum and Supervision, 6* (2), 107–117.

Hamilton, V. (1988). The people could fly. *Cricket, 15* (6), 21–26.

Hull, G. A. (1989). Building an understanding of composing. In L. B. Resnick & L. E. Klopfer (Eds.), *Toward the thinking curriculum: Current cognitive research,* ASCD Yearbook (pp. 104–128). Alexandria, VA: Association for Supervision and Curriculum Development.

Jacobs, H. H. (1989). The growing need for interdisciplinary curriculum content. In H. H. Jacobs (Ed.), *Interdisciplinary curriculum: Design and development* (pp. 1–12). Alexandria, VA: Association for Supervision and Curriculum Development.

Langer, J. A., & Applebee, A. N. (1986). Reading and writing instruction: Toward a theory of teaching and learning. In E. Z. Rothkopf (Ed.), *Review of research in education,* vol. 13 (pp. 171–194). Washington, DC: American Educational Research Association.

Resnick, L. B. (1990). Literacy in school and out. *Daedalus, 119* (2), 169–185.

Resnick, L. B., & Klopfer, L. E. (Eds.). (1989). *Toward the thinking curriculum: Current cognitive research.* Alexandria, VA: Association for Supervision and Curriculum Development.

Roby, T. (1985). Habits impeding deliberation. *Journal of Curriculum Studies, 17* (1), 17–35.

Zarnowski, M. (1990). *Learning with biographies: A reading and writing approach.* Washington, DC: National Council for the Social Studies and National Council for Teachers of English, published jointly. © National Council for the Social Studies. Reprinted with permission.

SUGGESTED READINGS

Aoki, E. M. (in press). Turning the page: Asian Pacific American children's literature. In V. J. Harris (Ed.), *Using multicultural literature in the classroom.* Norwood, MA: Christopher-Gordon.

Banks, J. A., & Banks, C. A. (1989). *Multicultural education: Issues and perspectives.* Needham Heights, MA: Allyn & Bacon.

Brown, R. (1991). *Schools of thought.* San Francisco: Jossey-Bass.

Graves, D. H. (1983). *Writing: Teachers and children at work.* Portsmouth, NH: Heineman.

Heath, S. B. (1983). *Ways with words.* New York: Cambridge University Press.

Paley, V. G. (1981). *Wally's stories.* Cambridge, MA: Harvard University Press.

Rutherford, F. J., & Ahlgren, A. (1990). *Science for all Americans.* New York: Oxford University Press.

CHAPTER 17

Learner Involvement through Activities

I t is a common assumption that when learners are involved in creative activities, less in the way of "real" learning takes place. Traditional attitudes toward learning suggest that it must be accompanied by a hard-nosed, joyless discipline. The feeling is widespread that if children enjoy what they are doing in school, the program is not intellectually rigorous. The following narrative describes a parent's attitude on just this point:

> At first we were quite concerned when we found out that Lori was to be placed in Mr. Allison's room the next year. His room had such a relaxed atmosphere about it, and he was very popular with the kids. We just assumed, I guess, that a teacher who was so well liked by all the children could not be very effective in maintaining a disciplined environment for learning. I must say this assumption was wholly unfounded.
>
> Mr. Allison was clearly the most creative, imaginative, and overall the most effective teacher Lori had during the seven years she attended that school. He always had the most unusual things going on in that room that would so hook the kids that they spent hours of unsupervised study on what they were doing. Schoolwork seemed to be a sheer delight, strange as that may seem. They analyzed advertising techniques in a unit on consumerism; they simulated law and justice procedures; they studied the effects of immigrant groups on American life and culture; there were art, poetry, music, and dramatic activities galore. Once they constructed a whole set of authentic models of Indian villages representing various tribes that inhabited this part of North America in pre-Columbian times. This involved the children in an incredible amount of research and information gathering in order to do the constructions. There were always games, puzzles, inquiries—tremendous interest grabbers. It was the only time I can recall that children had literally to be told to go home after school. If not, they would stay until dinnertime.
>
> Mr. Allison convinced my husband and me that disciplined learning did not have to give the appearance of rigidity and drudgery. He seemed to embrace the philosophy that a teacher should obtain "maximum learning with minimum effort." But the "minimum effort" only seemed that way because of the tremendous motivating power of the creative activities he used. Actually, I have not seen children work any harder nor be more productive in their efforts than their year with Mr. Allison. (an actual case from Minneapolis, Minnesota, reported to one of the authors)

How does a teacher develop this type of stimulating program for students in social studies? In part, this comes from an imaginative teacher who is able to capitalize on the natural interests and curiosities of children. The teacher encourages them to raise questions and to suggest ways of working. These, then, are converted into interesting study activities. In this chapter we will discuss ways that creative and expressive activities can be used in social studies for any or all of the following purposes:

1. to stimulate children's interest
2. to develop various aspects of thinking
3. to give direction and purpose to learning
4. to encourage initiative, exploration, and research
5. to aid in applying factual information obtained through research to concrete situations
6. to provide a setting in which to use socialization and human relations skills
7. to clarify complex procedures
8. to aid in developing an understanding of concepts and generalizations
9. to relate various components of the school program to one another
10. to provide opportunities for thinking, planning, sharing, doing, and evaluating
11. to provide an outlet for creative abilities
12. to provide an opportunity for recognition for the nonverbal, nonacademic child.

The shortage of funds has forced cutbacks in the services of special teachers for art, music, drama, and even physical education in many schools. This means that the regular classroom teacher has to assume more responsibility for these subjects if anything at all is to be done with them. This set of circumstances provides the regular teacher with the opportunity to do a considerable amount of meaningful teaching of these subjects and skills within the framework of the social studies curriculum. In those districts where special teachers *are* available in these fields, it is to the regular classroom teacher's advantage to work closely with them in integrating these subjects and skills in the classroom curriculum in social studies.

A. CONSTRUCTION AND PROCESSING ACTIVITIES

Most children love to make things. They build villages and castles in the sand at the beach; they build boats to float in a nearby pond; they construct birdhouses, model airplanes and cars, and wigwams. These natural sensory-motor play and creative-building activities are valuable for children in and of themselves. They give countless opportunities for thinking and planning as well as for creative expression, use of tools, physical activity, and the development of coordination. Children need many experiences of this type. In social studies, however, these values are only incidental to the chief purpose, which is *to extend and enrich meaning of some aspect of the topic being studied.* The excellence of the final product is, likewise, not a major concern. What is important is the learning that has occurred as a result of the construction activity. This being true, authenticity, genuineness, and truthfulness in the representations are important considerations in conducting construction activities. If constructions are inaccurate, contrary to truth and reality, they may be detrimental to learning because they reinforce incorrect concepts.

It is possible to use construction activities to motivate children's work and to establish more clearly children's purposes for doing things. For example, the teacher of a primary grade conducting a study of the dairy farm might suggest that the class construct a model farm in the classroom. Naturally, the children will want to make their model as authentic as possible; therefore, a considerable amount of research will be necessary as they proceed with the building of the farm. In fact, they cannot even begin unless they know what it is they want to do. This gives them a genuine need for information. The children's purpose in this case may be to learn about the dairy farm to be able to build a classroom model of it. The teacher's purpose, however, is to have children form accurate concepts and understandings of a dairy farm; the construction activity is being used as a vehicle to achieve that goal. Under this arrangement, both learner objectives and teacher objectives will have been achieved.

Selecting Activities

In selecting a construction activity for social studies, the teacher should consider the following criteria:

1. The activity is useful in achieving a definite objective related to social studies.
2. It clarifies, enriches, or extends the meaning of some important concept.
3. It requires children to do careful thinking and planning.
4. It is an accurate and truthful representation.
5. It is within the capabilities of the children.
6. The time and effort expended can be justified by the learnings that occur.
7. It is reasonable in terms of space and expense.
8. The needed materials are available.

There is no limit to the items that children can make in projects related to the social studies. The following have been used successfully by many teachers:

Model furniture
Books
Musical instruments
Simple trucks, airplanes, boats
Puppets and marionettes
Paper bag dolls
"Television" set with paper-roll programs
Looms for weaving
Animal cages
Animals of art materials
Maps (pictorial, product, relief, floor)
Candles
Soap
Baskets, trays, bowls
Foods (making cookies, jelly, butter, ice cream)
Ships, harbor, cargo
Retail food market and equipment
Scenery and properties for stage, dioramas, panoramas
Holiday decorations
Jewelry
Pottery, vases, dishes, cups
Covered wagons, churns, butter paddles, wooden spoons, and other pioneer gear
Post office
Bakery
Fire station
Dairy farm and buildings
Oxcarts
Circus accessories
Playhouses
Model Indian villages
Purses, hot pads, table mats, small rugs
Birdhouses and feeding stations
Seedboxes, planters
Tie-dyeing
Production of visual material needed in the unit, such as pictorial graphs, charts,
  posters, displays, bulletin boards
Block printing

The following suggestions are offered to help the teacher use construction activities in teaching social studies.

Discuss the purposes of the activity with the children. The practice of having children make stores, build boats and covered wagons, or do Indian crafts without knowing why they are performing these activities is open to serious question. Children may not have any idea of the real purpose or significance of the construction. It is suggested, therefore, that at the beginning of such an activity, the reasons for planning it should be discussed and understood by all. The purposes for the construction should be reviewed from time to time during the activity.

Plan the method of procedure with the children. The initial planning will take a considerable amount of time if every detail is to be taken into account. Such extensive planning is not necessary or entirely desirable, for it tends to make children impatient. Decisions must be made, however, as to the basic materials needed, the major responsibilities and who will assume them, the committees needed and who will be on them, where the construction will take place, where needed information may be obtained, and a general overall plan. After the construction project is under way, there will be time each day to do additional specific planning. It is best to plan in a general way and get started and leave the details to be worked out at a later time.

Plan methods of work with the children. Construction activities involve working in groups, using tools, perhaps hammering and sawing or other noisy activities, and somewhat more disorder than is usually found in regular classroom work. This means that unless rules and standards concerning the methods of work are established and understood, there is likely to be much noise, commotion, and general confusion. Therefore, it is recommended that the teacher and the children discuss and decide what the rules of work are to be. These might include

1. How to get and return tools and construction materials.
2. Use of tools and equipment, including safe handling.
3. Things to remember during the work period: talking in a conversational voice, good use of materials to avoid waste, sharing tools and materials with others, consideration for others, doing one's share of work, asking for help when needed, and giving everyone a chance to present ideas.
4. Procedures for cleanup time. It is well to establish a "listen" signal to get the attention of the class. It can be playing a chord on the piano, turning off the lights or ringing a small bell. When the listen signal is given, children should learn to stop whatever they are doing, cease talking, and listen to whatever announcement is to be made. In this way, the teacher can stop the work of the class at any time to call students' attention to some detail or get them started at cleanup. Cleanup is one procedure that can be done in a routine way. When the signal is given, all work stops, and the children listen for directions, restore the room to its prior condition, and assemble at the circle or go to their desks.

Provide plenty of time each day for planning, working, cleaning up, and evaluating. Before work on the construction activity is begun each day, time should be spent in making specific plans. This is to ensure that everyone will have an important job to do and that the children will know their responsibilities. It also is a time when the teacher can go over some of the points the class talked about during its previous day's evaluation. "You remember yesterday we had some problem about which group was to use the tools. Which group has the tools today?" Or "Yesterday our voices became a little loud at times. Perhaps we can be more careful about that today."

During the work period the teacher will want to move from group to group observing, assisting, suggesting new approaches, helping groups in difficulty, clarifying ideas, helping children find materials, and supervising and guiding the work of the class. Children will be identified who need help in getting started, those who are not working well together, those who seem not to be doing anything, or others who may be having difficulty. The teacher will keep an eye on the time and stop the work of the class in time to ensure a thorough cleanup.

An important part of each period is the evaluation that occurs after the work and cleanup. During these times, the teacher will want the class to evaluate the progress it is making on the construction as well as the way children are working with each other.

"Were we able to make progress in building our store today?"
"How do you think we might change the color to make it look more real?"

"Does anyone have any ideas how Steven's group could show more action in its mural?"

"Did anyone see signs of unsafe handling of tools today?"

"I wonder if the mountains aren't too high on Julie's group's map? Did you check that against the picture in your book?"

The precise points discussed in such an evaluation will depend on the class and its work. In any case, some attention should be given to (1) progress on the construction, (2) methods of working together, and (3) problems that need attention the next day.

Make use of the construction in some way, relating it to the unit under study.
When constructed objects are completed, they should be put to good use. In the primary grades such a project may serve well for dramatic play activities. A market in the classroom, for example, gives the children an opportunity to play customer, grocer, checkout person, or other personnel associated with a market. They read labels and prices, rearrange the material on the shelves, keep the store clean, and so on. In the middle and upper grades, objects made can be examined, discussed, and displayed. A mural can be used for study purposes. A child can explain the way some object is constructed, its main features, how it was used, its history, why it is no longer used, and similar information. In some instances, children can share the information learned and the object they have constructed with other classes in the school. Constructions are of value only insofar as they relate to the work of the class; when they have served this purpose, they should be removed.

Closely related to construction activities are those that help the child understand the various steps or stages in the production of some material item. They deal with the *process* of changing raw materials into finished, usable items and, hence, involve *processing of materials*. These activities help children understand and appreciate the complexities of produc-

---

Examples of Construction Activities

Communities

After a study of both urban and rural communities, the class was divided in half. One group was assigned the project of constructing a rural community; the other, an urban community.

Ms. Stillwater planned with each group separately, starting with the development of a list of services and facilities needed in each community. Each child was responsible for constructing at least one part of the community.

For several days before construction was to begin, the children brought in cartons, shoe boxes, and other "building materials" that were to become their communities.

Using paint, construction paper, shellac, and team effort, the children transformed the cartons into urban and rural communities and placed them on butcher paper streets on the floor around the classroom.

Relief Maps

Mr. Russo's class had been studying the state's history, and he believed that there was a need for the children to understand better the role that geographical differences had played in the state's development. He thought that the construction of relief maps might be a good method for the children to achieve this understanding.

Because such a construction was too large a project for individual children, he asked them to organize themselves in groups of two or three with whomever they could work best.

Mr. Russo provided the children with a papier-mâché recipe and the necessary construction materials. He encouraged them to be innovative in adding things to their maps that would highlight the significance of relief features.

After he was satisfied that the children understood what they were to do, he had the groups begin planning their maps. He provided a regularly scheduled work period each day and supervised and assisted the groups as needed. The completed relief maps were displayed and discussed in terms of the role of geographic features in the development of the state.

ing some of the basic material items that most persons use in everyday living. They are commonly used to illustrate the hardships, labor, skill, and ingenuity required of pioneers and early people in a time when it was necessary for them to produce basic materials for themselves. The most common processes used for this purpose are making butter, candles, paper, sugar, salt, bricks, natural dyes, jelly, ink, books, ice cream, soap, and weaving and dyeing cloth.

There are some instructional problems, however, in processing materials in the classroom. For example, is it appropriate to demonstrate the hardships experienced by pioneers in making candles by dipping, by using such modern-day conveniences as an electric hot plate as a source of heat and an aluminum container for the wax? In most classrooms it is, in fact, impossible to duplicate conditions under which candles were made in the seventeenth century. Almost any raw material the class uses in its processing will in all likelihood *already* be semiprocessed. The child may, therefore, leave such an experience with a lack of appreciation of the complexities involved in the process—a misfire of the precise learning the teacher had hoped to put across.

Some processes require extremely careful supervision by the teacher because of physical danger to the children. Candlemaking means heating tallow, wax, or paraffin that can ignite if allowed to become too hot and cause severe burns if dropped accidentally on one's person. Soapmaking calls for the use of lye, always potentially dangerous. These points are mentioned not to discourage the use of construction and processing but to alert the beginner to the real need for careful supervision while such activity is taking place.

B. MUSIC ACTIVITIES

Music activities make an important contribution to social studies instruction. Through the universal language of music, the child may extend communication to other peoples, races, and cultures, both past and present. Various songs and music forms are associated with periods in our national history, and many songs relate directly to heroes or great historical events. Musical expression is an emotional experience, piercing through everyday inhibitions and extending into the inner reaches of one's personality. Music inspires patriotism, love of country, loyalty, and fidelty. It is for this reason that marching bands are used in holiday parades and between halves at football games. Nation-states have used music effectively in building a feeling of national solidarity. Music has a profound effect on individuals as well as on groups.

Integrating Music in the Classroom

Music educators have worked diligently to break the shackles of the "music period" concept of music education and have consistently recommended a greater integration of music in the total life of the classroom. Music activities, therefore, not only contribute to social studies instruction but support the music program itself. The material that follows suggests some possibilities for the use of singing, rhythmic expression, listening, and creative music activities in social studies units.

Singing. For almost any social studies unit, the teacher will find appropriate and related songs for children to sing. One of the chief values of singing is its affective quality; it gives the child a *feeling* for the material not likely to be obtained in any other way. Through singing, the child senses the loneliness of the voyageur, the gaiety of a frontier housewarming, or the sadness of a displaced people longing for their homeland. Folk songs can be springboards to the study of a period in history, to the contributions of ethnic groups, to the life-styles of a group, and to many social studies topics. Singing is an experience that can broaden children's appreciation of people everywhere. In the study of communities around the world, the teacher will want to use the songs of various national groups. This provides opportunities to learn more about a culture through the language of music.

Some educators have recognized the rich learning resource folk music provides, and they have promoted the use of folk songs in social studies classrooms. (Laurence I. Seidman, C.W. Post College, and John Anthony Scott, Rutgers University, have made several presentations at NCSS annual meetings.) Contemporary folk songs such as "Little

Boxes," "We Shall Overcome," "Detroit City," and "Sittin' on the Dock of the Bay" convey powerful social messages. Cowboy songs such as "I Ride an Old Paint," "Colorado Trail," "The Night Herding Song," and "Git Along Little Dogie" have both lyrics and melodies that are hauntingly reminiscent of the lonely life of this American folk group. "The Yellow Rose of Texas," "When Johnny Comes Marching Home Again," and "Over There" are associated with significant conflicts of this nation (Texas Independence, Civil War, and World War I, respectively). Teachers interested in learning more about the use of folk songs in the classroom should write to John W. Scott, P.O. Box 264, Holyoke, MA 01041, or to Diana Palmer, 433 Leadmine Rd., Fiskdale, MA 01518, for information about the newsletter entitled *Folksong in the Classroom.*

Rhythmic expression. Rhythmic and bodily expression tend to release one from the crust of convention and formality of everyday life and provide a means of self-expression. Through rhythms, bodily expression, and folk dances, the child develops grace and poise and learns the amenities that are characteristic of such social activities. Folk dancing and folk games in themselves are pleasurable and legitimate social activities for children. They provide for teamwork and allow the child to participate in the activity with several other boys and girls. Folk dancing and folk games usually involve eight or more children with a continual shifting of partners. For this reason, folk dancing is well suited for children in the elementary and middle schools.

In social studies, the teacher will want to use the various folk dances and rhythmic activities that are characteristic of many countries, as well as those associated with various periods of our national history. Because ethnic heritage studies have become popular in schools, activities of this type can be particularly meaningful. Far from being solely a recreational activity, rhythmic expression provides a wide range of possibilities for social learnings in general and especially for the social studies.

Creating. Social studies topics provide many opportunities for the child to create musically. This can be done on an individual basis or as a class project and with almost any topic by any age group. Perhaps creating music is not used more frequently by teachers because they feel that a considerable amount of technical knowledge is necessary. The need for the technical skills of music is greatly overestimated, but if the teacher feels insecure, there will ordinarily be someone available who does have such skills and can be of assistance. This person might be a music supervisor or teacher, the high school music director, another classroom teacher, or a parent volunteer.

In its simplest form, creative music is a melody or sounds children learn to associate with the topic being studied. For example, the children may make sounds that remind them of a factory, a circus, or a train. Later these sounds can be used in the development of an actual melody. Children commonly produce creative verse to which they may add an appropriate melody. In the middle and upper grades such creative music activities may include the development of words and music for pageants, plays, puppet shows, or simple musicals. These original numbers are frequently of good quality musically and are favorites of the children for years afterward—an indication of the satisfying and long-lasting quality of creative music.

Children can also be encouraged to create their own lyrics for melodies with which they are familiar. Such an activity is especially appropriate when the class is preparing an original play or pageant associated with a topic in social studies. Or, children may find the writing of lyrics to be worthwhile simply as a creative experience. Children can be encouraged to develop lyrics that convey a funny message, or that tell a story about the topic (a ballad), or that speak to the qualities of some person or character, or that use language associated with a particular place or historical period, or for other interesting purposes.

Listening. Although singing, creating, and rhythmic expression involve *performing* or *doing* aspects of music, listening places the child in the role of a consumer of music. This role deserves more attention than is usually given it because it is the type of musical experience that continues throughout life. Long after most persons stop performing musically, they enjoy listening to music. Relating music listening to the affairs of life and living is, therefore, essential.

Examples of Music Activities

Spanish Song

During a unit on the children of Mexico, Ms. Juarez shared some of her own ethnic background with her class. She was able to teach them a few simple folk dances and folk songs she had learned as a child in Mexico.

After learning the words to the songs in Spanish, the children asked her to teach them other words and expressions in Spanish. By the end of the year, many children had developed a fair speaking vocabulary of greetings and commonly used expressions in Spanish.

Period Music

Mr. Cole's fifth graders were studying the development of the United States. He thought it was important for them to learn how music reflects the mood of the nation at a particular time. He was also able to get examples of popular music from the middle of the nineteenth century to the present time. The lyrics of these songs were analyzed in terms of national events and concerns of the time. Mr. Cole was also able to get recordings of some of these songs and, without telling the class the period from which the song came, asked them to try to determine when the selection was popular.

Listening to music should be an imaginative experience for children. The teacher can help them learn of mood in music and contrast what is bright, happy, and lively with music that is quiet and restful. Through listening the child learns to identify the use of music by different groups throughout the world—it provides for another direct cultural contact with people of many lands. The teacher will have no difficulty obtaining recordings for the purposes described.

C. CREATIVE ART ACTIVITIES

Creative art is widely used in social studies instruction because many topics and activities inspire creative expression. A trip to a farm, airport, zoo, post office, or fire station all give impetus to the desire to create. Observing bulldozers, cranes, demolition crews, as well as going on a hike to a nearby park or stream, are the types of experiences from which come the creative artwork of children. Through an art medium the child may be able to symbolize experiences, express thoughts, or communicate feelings that cannot be conveyed through the use of conventional language.

Many parallels could be drawn between art experiences and music experiences in social studies. Like music, art provides a cultural link with the many peoples of the world, past and present. It also places the child in the roles of creator and consumer as does music. It deals directly with feelings, emotions, appreciations, and creative abilities of children. In addition to the many desirable outcomes associated with any creative endeavor, creative art experiences have much to offer in stimulating and strengthening learning in the social studies.

In the course of the social studies unit, the teacher might use any of the following art activities:

Preparing murals	Poster making
Free painting	Making models
Making illustrations	Making cartoons
Weaving	Making booklets and books
Block printing	Crafts related to some locality or country
Clay modeling	Constructing dioramas to illustrate scenes
Potato or stick printing	Planning and preparing exhibits
Chalk, charcoal, and crayon drawing	Sewing
Pencil sketching	Making properties for plays, pageants
Making designs and costumes	Wood carving
Making puppets and marionettes	Toy making

Examples of Creative Art Activities

Apple Dolls

Fourth graders peeled and dried apples to make apple-head dolls. They added yarn hair and formed bodies of wire. Each doll was dressed to resemble some well-known historical figure.

Puppets

In a study of India, fourth graders constructed movable rod puppets. They used the puppets to dramatize folktales from India.

Soap carving   Finger painting
Basket making   Indian sand painting
Indian beadwork

Creative art expression as used in social studies may take two forms. The first of these might be described as *personal* and is performed by the children because it expresses an idea or gives personal satisfaction. Having the experience is its own reward, and the child need not share such a piece of art with anyone although children often want to. Artwork of this type is not evaluated in terms of the product produced but in terms of the satisfactions the experience itself gives the learner. Any of the art media can be used for personal expression.

A second type of creative art expression can be thought of as *functional* in that the product is used in connection with some other activity. It might be a mural to be used as the background for a dramatic activity. It might be a model of something that will be used to illustrate an explanation. It could be a visual aid the child plans to use in making a report to the class. In artwork of this type, the representation has to be reasonably accurate and authentic; consequently, the teacher will need to guard against having the children copy exactly the illustrations they find in reference materials.

The poorest of all art experiences are those that are patterned rather than creative. The teacher might, for example, ditto a diagram of a turkey and have children color certain feathers red, others brown, and others black. Children who follow the directions precisely and who can color within the lines are highly rewarded with teacher praise. Then the 25 turkeys, all alike, are posted on the bulletin board under the caption "We Do Creative Work." Such conspicuous misuse of art may also take the form of silhouette profiles of Lincoln, hatchets and cherries, covered wagons, or Christmas trees. Teaching of this type tends to depress any creative art ability or interest in art expression that an imaginative child may have, and should be avoided.

D. DRAMATIC ACTIVITIES

Dramatic representation in any one of its many forms is a popular activity with children—one in which they have all engaged during their early years. What child has not "been" a firefighter, a cowhand, a jet pilot, or a doctor during the fanciful and imaginative play of early childhood? Dramatic activities have great value in promoting social studies learnings by helping sharpen the child's power of observation; giving purpose to research activities; giving insight into another's feelings; providing experiences in democratic living; helping create and maintain interest, thereby motivating learning; and affording an excellent opportunity for the teacher to observe the behavior of children.

The most structured dramatic activity is the *dramatization,* which requires a script, staging, rehearsal, and an audience. It may be used to show some historical event, to represent the growth of a movement or idea, to represent life in another period, or to demonstrate some problem of living. Children are usually involved in a considerable amount of creative work in productions of this type. They may plan and prepare costumes, do the artwork necessary for staging and properties, plan a program, send invitations, and make all arrangements attendant to the project. This requires that the children do a great deal of planning, working together, evaluating, and participating.

The least structured dramatic activity is the spontaneous acting out or reliving of situations from the child's world. It is called *dramatic play*. As this activity is used in social studies, the term *dramatic play* is an unfortunate one because it suggests entertainment. Perhaps the terms *creative dramatic representation* or *representative living* would describe more accurately what is involved in the activity. When kindergartners and first graders are playing various roles of mother, father, sister, brother, doctor, and nurse in a corner of the classroom, they are engaging in dramatic play. Free dramatic play is a natural activity for young children, and they participate in it with little or no stimulation from adults. During the periods of free dramatic play, the teacher can learn much about the personalities of individual children—who they identify with, their attitudes toward others, their willingness to share, and their emotional maturity.

As children move into the second and third grades, there is less evidence of spontaneous dramatic play. At this stage of growth, dramatic play usually requires more suggestion and stimulation from the teacher and may be used profitably to help the child understand or appreciate some phase of human relationships. These slightly more structured dramatic activities are referred to as *role playing, sociodrama,* or *creative dramatics.*

Role playing, sociodrama, or creative dramatics is used to present a specific situation for study and discussion. There is no prepared script, it is unrehearsed, speaking parts are not memorized, and properties, if used at all, are held to a minimum. Some small amount of properties may be used simply to help children remain in role. These activities are used to teach or clarify social values, to focus attention on a central idea, to help children organize ideas, to extend vocabulary, and to promote a greater insight into the problems of others by casting children in another's role. Because they portray problems in human relationships, they provide an excellent basis for discussion and evaluation. They should be followed by a discussion of questions of this type: "Which character did you like best? Why?" "Which one did you like least? Why?" "How do you suppose the person *felt?*" "If you had been in the wagon master's place, what would you have done?" "Have you ever known anyone like that?"

This final discussion and analysis requires that the situation be cut before the problem has been solved and before the outcome is a certainty. Otherwise, there would be little room left for thoughtful consideration of the problem.

Closely related to creative dramatics is the use of *reaction stories.* Reaction stories are brief narrative accounts dealing with human relations that are used to uncover various attitudes and emotions. They may be written by the teacher or may be passages selected from published works. They deal with a variety of topics such as sharing, teasing, responsibility, peer pressures, respect for property, and intercultural relations. The story is read to the children, and they are asked to tell their feelings about characters, situations, what they would do under similar circumstances, what alternatives were available to the characters, and

---

Examples of Dramatic Activities

Shopping

Ms. Beatty wanted the children to be able to cope with situations that might arise while they were shopping. She listed situations that could present a problem, such as returning faulty merchandise, knocking over displays, becoming separated from their parent, or inquiring about the location of the restroom. The children added other situations to the list.

Ms. Beatty asked the children to role-play the situations. These were discussed in terms of possible and responsible actions in such situations.

Signing the Declaration of Independence

Ms. Hall's class had been doing research on the signers of the Declaration of Independence. Each child had been responsible for finding out about at least one of these historical figures.

Ms. Hall then asked various groups of children to reenact the signing of the document. She encouraged them to react as the person they represented might have done.

other comparable reactions. This critique is similar to the one held at the conclusion of a creative dramatics activity.

E. SIMULATIONS AND INSTRUCTIONAL GAMES

A fifth-grade class was studying the concept of *assembly-line production* in its unit on the growth of industry in the United States. In the discussion, the children contrasted assembly-line production with custom-made, individually built products. The class listed the strengths and limitations of each method of production:

Assembly line
Strengths

1. It is faster.

2. Every product is the same.

3. Can be produced at low cost.

4. Because of low production cost, more people can afford to buy the product.

Weaknesses

1. Sameness makes for an uninteresting product.
2. Production can be slipshod because no one person is responsible for it.
3. The sameness of the work makes for a boring job.
4. A poor worker or a breakdown can stop the whole production.

Custom built

1. "One-of-a-kind" product.
2. Higher quality because an individual worker is responsible for it.
3. Product can be made to fit the desires of the buyer
4. Work is less boring to the workers.

1. Products are more expensive.
2. Buyers cannot be sure of the product's quality because each is different.
3. Fewer people can afford to buy the product.
4. It takes longer for workers to become skillful in doing all the tasks needed to make the product.

The teacher pointed out to the class that each of the items they listed could serve as a hypothesis that they might be able to test. "Is it really true," she asked, "that assembly-line production is faster? Do workers on an assembly line become bored more quickly than those who make the whole product themselves? Do workers take greater pride in their product if they do it all themselves and sign their name to it? How could we test the truth of the statements?" The teacher and the children decided they could test their hypotheses by using a simple simulation involving the manufacture of envelopes.

The class was divided into two groups: One would be assembly-line workers; the other groups would be custom workers. The teacher provided cardboard templates, or patterns, of an outline of an envelope, scissors, paste, and used ditto paper that would be needed to manufacture envelopes. After the pattern was placed on a piece of paper, its outline could be traced and could then be cut, folded, and pasted to make the finished product. The assembly line was arranged according to a division of labor as follows:

ASSEMBLY LINE

Pattern tracer	Cutters	Folders	Paster	Stacker
Number of workers: 1	Number of workers: 2	Number of workers: 2	Number of workers: 1	Number of workers: 1
Equipment: pattern pencil paper	Equipment: scissors	Equipment: none	Equipment: paste	Equipment: none

Total workers: 7
Supervisor: 1

SUPERVISOR

The custom workers consisted of seven individuals (the same number as on the assembly line) and a supervisor. Each of the seven workers had his or her own pattern, paper, pencil, scissors, and paste and was required to do all the steps necessary to make an envelope. These children would be required to put their own name on each envelope they produced and were encouraged to personalize their own product.

All children in both groups took turns, and all participated in the activity. The supervisor from each group could make changes and substitutions as needed. Three children served

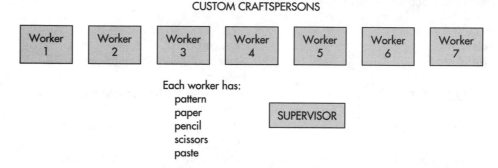

CUSTOM CRAFTSPERSONS

as a quality-control panel that would accept or reject finished products in terms of quality of workmanship.

When all preparations were completed, the teacher gave the signal to start, and both groups began manufacturing envelopes. After a half hour, the production was stopped, and the debriefing took place. Children were able to test their hypotheses in terms of the data they generated through the simulation.

We have here an example of a simple simulation. It is a strategy designed to reconstruct as closely as possible some of the essential characteristics of the real thing. Simulations and gaming strategies are enthusiastically accepted by those teachers who pursue innovative approaches to social studies teaching. The simulation may be a simple one devised by the teacher, as described here, or it may be one of the growing number of commercially prepared simulations and games now available.

The Nature of Simulations and Games

A *game* may be defined as an activity that involves rules, competition, and players who become winners and losers. The outcome of some games depends entirely on chance, as in the case of tossing dice. In other games, the outcome is determined less by chance and more by the decisions made by the players, as in chess or checkers. Most games involve both elements of chance and skill. It is significant that persons who are involved in a game are called "players." This suggests that games are associated with amusement—they are intended to be enjoyed. When games are used for educational purposes, they are often referred to as *instructional games* in order to avoid creating the impression that they are used only for entertainment. For this reason, too, instructional games frequently are called *simulations*. Instructional games tend to minimize chance and enjoyment aspects, although most contain some elements of chance and most are enjoyed by the participants.

A simulation gives the illusion of reality but removes most of the elements that are irrelevant and those that would be dangerous to the participants. In the use of simulators in pilot training or driver training, wrong moves by the trainee do not result in disastrous crashes or collisions. Likewise, in educational simulations, errors of judgment or unwise decisions do not produce disastrous social consequences.

Experts do not agree about the distinction between games and simulations. Not all games are simulations—note, for example, such games as hopscotch, jacks, or jump rope. Similarly, not all simulations are games, as in the case of astronauts working in a simulated weightless environment. However, in education these activities often take on characteristics of both games and simulations. Consequently, they are popularly, although perhaps not altogether precisely, called *simulation games*.

Values of Simulations and Instructional Games

The values of simulations and instructional games for use with intermediate- and middle school–age children are not firmly established. Research evidence concerning the effects of simulations and games at the intermediate and middle school levels is sparse. Nonetheless, the following points seem to be well grounded on the basis of research and practice.

1. Simulations and games are highly motivating. Children enjoy participating in these activities and do so without much urging from the teacher. The fact that learners show increased interest in the subject when they are involved in simulation games is well documented. One can assume that part of this interest is generated by the reality created by the simulation, by the competitive, gaming aspects of it, and by the fact that there are clearly defined goals to be achieved. Because of their motivating power, it is easy to get children involved in simulation games. Even children who are typically on the fringes of most class activities often become enthusiastically engaged in instructional games and simulations. These activities seem to appeal to the natural inclinations of children to be involved in imaginative play, make believe, and role playing.

2. Simulations and games have been used successfully for instructional purposes outside of school. They have been used in teaching military operations for many years. They are used in training programs in business and industry, in teaching management skills, in the space program, in medicine, law, political science, and many other fields. Computer science has made it possible to develop these simulations and games at a sophisticated level. Because they have proved their usefulness in instructional settings outside of school, it is fair to assume they would have value for in-school instruction as well.

3. There seems to be evidence that simulations and games are effective in dealing with learner attitudes. Wentworth and Lewis (1973, pp. 437–438) cite several studies that report positive learner response after participating in a simulation or game. Many of these studies have been criticized on technical grounds, making it difficult to generalize their findings. Nevertheless, the impact of games and simulations on learner attitudes is widely reported.

4. There seems to be considerable doubt about the effects of simulations and games on cognitive gain. The research to date does not show that simulations have a clear advantage over other learning resources and procedures in promoting cognitive learning. Perhaps this is because the learners must have the prerequisite skills and must understand the basic concepts before the game is played. That is, the simulation game provides opportunities for the *application of knowledge and skills* rather than breaking new cognitive ground. This might explain, also, why researchers rather consistently report gains in the affective but not the cognitive area.

5. Almost without exception authors and researchers speak to the importance of the postgame or "debriefing" session. It is in these critiques that the major learnings can be identified and discussed. These sessions allow the participants to explore in some detail what choices were available to the players, what decisions were made, and how those decisions contributed to the outcome. In this way, the simulation or game provides the group with a common and shared experience that can be used to extend and enrich learning. From an instructional point of view, the debriefing session must be considered integral to the game itself.

Using Commercially Prepared Simulation Games

Presently there are many commercially prepared simulation games available for use for the intermediate and middle school grades. In the January 1980 issue of *Social Education,* Sharon Pray Muir provides an annotated list of 88 simulation games for elementary school social studies. In preparing this list, she made a thorough search of the field and included only those that are appropriate for use in grades K–6 and that deal directly with social studies concepts and processes. The list includes the title, recommended grade levels, amount

---

Selected Simulation Games

Economics

IMPORT, grades 4–5, 2–4 weeks, 18–35 players, $10. Simulates activities of six importing firms in various parts of the world. Each firm buys from several countries. To win, a firm must buy eight products from three countries and sell them at a profit. Simile II; SSSS; EMI.

Economics/History

ROARING CAMP, grades 4–7, five 10-minute periods, 18–35 players, $10. Players are given a $600 grubstake with which to file a mining claim and try their luck as prospectors. Each person pays $400 for initial tools, supplies, and equipment and $200 a year thereafter to keep him or her going. Chance selection of plots on which to file claims controls those who hit pay dirt and those who "lose their shirts." Simile II; EMI.[a]

[a]From S. P. Muir, "Simulation Games for Elementary Social Studies," *Social Education, 44,* pp. 37, 38.

---

of time needed to play the game, number of players, and the cost. She also indicates the social science discipline with which the simulation is associated.

A teacher may use a simulation game strictly in accordance with the instructions provided or may adapt it to suit local needs, learner abilities and interests, and instructional objectives. The teacher must be thoroughly familiar with the game before introducing it to the class. It is advisable for the teacher to play the game with friends or fellow teachers before using it as an instructional tool.

Computer Simulations

The computer can organize and manipulate data with amazing speed, and therefore it is an ideal tool for use for simulations. Once a simulation has been played, students can formulate their own hypothetical propositions in the form of "What if" questions and have the computer respond to them. This kind of creative question asking and decision making is useful in developing thinking skills.

Perhaps the best known of the commercially prepared social studies simulations for the elementary and middle school grades is *The Oregon Trail,* developed by the Minnesota Educational Computing Consortium (MECC), 3490 Lexington Avenue North, St. Paul, MN 55126. The story line is that of a wagon train party moving Westward in the 1800s. Along the way the wagon train has to deal with a number of contingencies such as foul weather, sickness, hostile Indians, and dangerous animals. As each is encountered, a decision has to be made, and a poor decision can have disastrous consequences for the entire party. The object is to get the wagon train to Oregon. This is an interesting simulation and one that is well suited for elementary and middle school children.

Popular simulations involving citizenship education are *Decisions, Decisions* (for grades 5 and above), *Choices, Choices* (K–6), and *Our Town Meeting* (5–8), all from Tom Snyder Productions (123 Mt. Auburn St., Cambridge, MA 02138). The first two can be used with an entire classroom and only one computer; the third is designed for use with up to 15 students and one computer. All promote group interaction and community decision making. Another software developer, Focus Media, produces *And If Reelected,* a presidential simulation for grades 7 and up. Students grapple with numerous public policy controversies, such as nuclear waste and budget deficits.

Emphasizing geography is the very popular *Where in the World Is Carmen Sandiego?* Produced by Broderbund Software (17 Paul Dr., San Rafael, CA 94903), this exciting game has students play detective as they use geography clues and a reference book (*The World Almanac and Book of Facts*) to solve a crime. Also available are *Where in the U.S.A. Is Carmen Sandiego?* and *Where in Europe Is Carmen Sandiego?*

Other commercially prepared simulations that have been used with success in intermediate and middle school grades are (1) *The Market Place* (grades 3–6), produced by MECC, designed to develop economic concepts and relationships as the player is placed in the role of an entrepreneur; (2) *President-Elect* (grades 8 and above), produced by Learning Arts, P.O. Box 179, Wichita, KS 67201, which has to do with variables associated with the election of a president of the United States; (3) *Agent USA,* produced by Scholastic, 730 Broadway, New York, NY 10003, which simulates a secret agent traveling around the United States in search of a bomb as students assist in selecting best routes; it is intended to develop map-reading and geography-related skills; and (4) *Stock Market* (grades 4–6) and *Millionaire, The Stock Market Simulation,* both produced by Learning Arts, designed to teach principles of the stock market. These examples illustrate the range of subject matter included in a growing list of simulations and games available for social studies education. The National Council for the Social Studies journal, *Social Education,* provides an update on new simulations and other resources for computer applications to social studies.

Preparing Your Own Game

After some knowledge of, and experience with, simulation games, some teachers have been encouraged to prepare their own games with or without a computer. This is a formidable task, and the teacher may wish to collaborate in such an effort with a colleague. Also, children themselves in the middle and upper grades can assist in creating a simulation game. In any case, the teacher may find the following questions to be of help in constructing a simulation game.

1. What instructional purpose is to be served by the game? That is, what objective or objectives are to be achieved through the use of the simulation game?
2. What real-life situations can be used to illustrate or dramatize the objectives? In most cases, this will call for the preparation of a narrative (referred to as a *scenario*) that establishes the situation and makes explicit the problem, conflict, issue, or process to be simulated.
3. What is to be the sequence of events, and how much time will be required or allowed for each?
4. What players will be involved? How many are there to be? How are they to be grouped?
5. What are the specific objectives of individual or group players? How are success or failure experiences to be recognized and recorded? What resources (votes, play money, political support, food, and so forth) will players have for tradeoffs and bargaining?
6. How do individuals or groups interact to register wins or losses?
7. What is the role of the teacher to be?

F. SOCIAL PARTICIPATION

The real test of a social studies program comes in the out-of-school lives of children. If the school has provided them with new insights, improved skills, or increased awareness and sensitivity to social affairs, such learning should be apparent in their out-of-school behavior as children and later as adults. The objectives of social studies education, in other words, are tested in the way that learners apply them to social reality in and out of school. In its statement of curriculum guidelines, the National Council for the Social Studies speaks of *social participation* as one of the four essential components of social studies education (1979, p. 266). (The other three components are *knowledge, abilities* (skills), and *valuing.*)

To be socially active does not mean that young children have to be concerned with the great social issues of our time. But they can and should be involved in experiences that bridge the gap between what is learned in school and the world in which they live. They can and should practice skills and apply knowledge that prepares them for intelligent and responsible involvement in social affairs of the society of which they are a part.

Of course, children are not going to be able to be socially active without some help and encouragement from their teacher. The following are a few examples of activities that teachers have used successfully with elementary- and middle school–age children.

1. Middle graders formed a volunteer Good Neighbor Club to help elderly residents in the neighborhood with yard work, errands, and other assistance as needed.

2. A class interviewed parents, school personnel, and adult friends and neighbors to determine the ethnic background of people living in the area. They used the data to prepare an exhibit entitled "Living and Working Together—Our Ethnic Heritages" to be displayed in a local store window. This included maps, photographs, and artifacts secured from the neighborhood.

3. A group organized a food gathering campaign for the Neighbors in Need Program.

4. On a walk around the school neighborhood, a class noticed that a main sidewalk was so badly damaged that children on their way to and from school had to walk into the street to avoid it. The class wrote a letter to the city council asking that the sidewalk be repaired. They received a letter from the president of the city council thanking them for their concern and assuring them that it would be repaired. He also commended them for their display of civic responsibility. The sidewalk was repaired.

5. A class developed a working relationship with a nearby retirement home. Residents who were able to were invited and came to school activities. The children also put on programs for the retirees at the home. As the project developed, parents of the children also became involved. Some of the parents invited residents to their homes for dinner and took them to church and for Sunday drives. The senior citizens had skills and hobbies that they shared with the children.

6. Students made tray favors for a local convalescent home for each of the major holidays during the school year.

7. Sixth graders collected and refurbished used toys and donated them to Goodwill Industries for redistribution.

8. Ninth-grade students collected books in the neighborhood for the local library's used-book sale.

9. A class made a survey of their homes to look for safety hazards or fire dangers and corrected them.

10. A social studies class sponsored a bicycle safety program in the school.

11. Eighth graders volunteered to do free babysitting for mothers on Election Day.

SUMMARY

In this chapter you have reviewed a variety of ways that creative and expressive activities can be used in social studies to integrate learning of the subjects and skills of the school curriculum.

QUESTIONS AND ACTIVITIES FOR DISCUSSION

1. Select a unit topic for a grade in which you have a special interest. Suggest ways that the activities discussed in this chapter could be incorporated in such a unit.

2. Criticize or defend the following statement: Social studies for intermediate and middle school children should be more activity oriented than subject-matter centered.

3. When you visit a school classroom, observe the type of construction activities under way. Are they accurate and authentic representations? What purposes was the teacher hoping to accomplish through the use of construction?

4. Demonstrate to your peers how you would proceed with a processing activity of some type (i.e., making butter, dipping candles, weaving a basket, and so forth). Indicate the concepts being developed in the activity.

5. Obtain or write an unfinished, open-ended story that could be used as a role-playing activity for children. Put the characters in a social problem situation. What alternatives are open to the major characters in the story?

6. Suggest situations that might be developed into a simulation game. With the help of two or three peers, develop a simple simulation game.

7. Develop plans for a social participation project for a grade of your choice. Have your plans critiqued by your peers.

8. The use of song lyrics was discussed in the text. What possibilities can you suggest for the use of song lyrics in learning about the period in which a song was written?

REFERENCES

Muir, S. P. (1980). Simulation games for elementary social studies. *Social Education, 44,* 35–39, 76.

National Council for the Social Studies. (1979). Revision of the social studies curriculum guidelines. *Social Education, 43,* 266.

Wentworth, D. R., & Lewis, D. R. (1973). A review of research on instructional games and simulations in social studies education. *Social Education, 37,* 437–438.

SUGGESTED READINGS

Akenson, J. E. (1991). Linkages of art and social studies: Focus upon modern dance/movement. *Theory and Research in Social Education, 19,* 95–108.

Association for Supervision and Curriculum Development. (1990). *Educational Leadership, 48.* This issue is devoted to the theme "social responsibility."

Braun, J. A. (1986). *Microcomputers and the social studies: A resource guide for the middle and secondary grades.* New York: Garland.

Fowler, C. (1989). The arts are essential to education. *Educational Leadership, 47,* 60–63.

Katz, L. G., & Chard, S. C. (1991). *Engaging children's minds: The project approach.* Norwood, NJ: Ablex.

Lewis, B. A. (1991). Today's kids care about social action. *Educational Leadership, 49,* 47–49.

McClure, A. A., & Zitlow, C. S. (1991). Not just the facts: Aesthetic response in elementary content area studies. *Language Arts, 68,* 27–33.

Nelli, E. (1980). Mirror of a people: Folktales and social studies. *Social Education, 49,* 155–158.

Singer, D. G., & Singer, J. L. (1985). *Make believe: Games and activities to foster imaginative play in young children.* Glenview, IL: Scott, Foresman.

Sunal, C. S. (1988). Studying another culture through children's games. *The Social Studies, 79,* 232–238.

Turner, T. N. (1988). "And what do you think he saw?" Using chain songs and rounds. *Social Studies and the Young Learner, 1,* 22–24.

Wentzel, K. R. (1991). Social competence at school: Relation between social responsibility and academic achievement. *Review of Educational Research, 61,* 1–24.

Wharton-Boyd, L. F. (1983). The significance of Black American children's singing games in an educational setting. *Journal of Negro Education, 52,* 46–56.

IV

Selected Integrated Activities for Language Arts and Social Studies

As has been discussed throughout this book, for higher levels of thinking and for learning that is most meaningful and longest lasting for children, it is absolutely necessary to use instructional techniques that encourage interaction and cooperation among all students, that depend upon collaborative learning between the students and the teachers, and that integrate the disciplines.

Further, as we have emphasized throughout, as a classroom teacher and member of a community of learners, your instructional task is to (1) plan for and provide developmentally appropriate hands-on experiences and to (2) facilitate the most meaningful and longest lasting learning possible once the children's minds have been activated by those experiences. Part IV presents activities designed to do just that.

As we stated at the beginning of this book, the term *integrated curriculum* (or any of its synonyms) refers to both a way of teaching and a way of planning and organizing the instructional program so the discrete disciplines of subject matter are related to one another in a design that matches the developmental needs of the learners and that helps to connect their learning in ways that are meaningful to their current and past experiences. In that respect, integrated curriculum is the antithesis of traditional, disparate, subject-matter-oriented teaching and curriculum designations.

Today's interest in the development and implementation of integrated curriculum and instruction has arisen almost simultaneously from a number of sources: (1) the successful curriculum integration enjoyed by exemplary middle-level schools, (2) the literature-based movement in reading and language arts, and (3) recent research in cognitive science and neuroscience about how children learn.

As is true for traditional curriculum and instruction, an integrated curriculum approach is not without critics. An integrated curriculum approach may not necessarily be the best approach for every school or for all learning for every child, nor is it necessarily the manner by which teachers should or must always plan and teach. Attempts to connect children's learning with their experiences fall at various places on a spectrum or continuum of sophistication and complexity.

The activities presented in this final part and chapter are designed to encourage interaction and cooperation among students, to encourage collaborative learning between students and their teachers, and to integrate in interesting and meaningful ways the disciplines of language arts and social studies, and sometimes other disciplines as well. Where the use of each falls on the spectrum of integrated learning is up to you. In addition to the wisdom and guidance offered by authors John Jarolimek and Walter C. Parker as to the pros and cons of using integrated instruction (see Chapter 16, section B), when selecting activities for children's active learning, you should ask yourself

- Does the activity involve more than one subject area?
- Does the activity involve the children in exploring a topic in depth and over an extended period of time?
- Does the activity provide interesting, meaningful, and accurate learning that relates to children's daily lives?

CHAPTER 18
Activities for Integrated Language Arts and Social Studies
Activities 1, 2, 7, 12–16, 19, and 20 are from John Jarolimek and Walter C. Parker, Social Studies in Elementary Education, *9th ed. (New York: Macmillan, 1993); Activities 3, 5, 6, 10, and 11 are from Peter H. Martorella,* Social Studies for Elementary School Children: Developing Young Citizens *(New York: Macmillan, 1994); Activities 17, 18, and 21 are from Joseph O'Beirne Milner and Lucy Floyd Morcock Milner,* Bridging English *(New York: Macmillan, 1993), by permission of Macmillan Publishing Company.*

ANCIENT GREECE: THE DAWN OF A NEW AGE AN INTERDISCIPLINARY THEMATIC UNIT (GRADE 6)
This unit is contributed by Nancy Mortham, Courtesy of Nancy Mortham.

- Does the activity provide opportunity for the children to work collaboratively and cooperatively while making and recording observations and gathering and defending their own evidence and to express their results in a variety of ways?
- Does the activity accomplish the objective(s) for which it is intended?
- Is the activity within the ability and developmental level of the students?
- Is the activity worth the time and cost it requires?
- Within reasonable limits, is the activity safe for children to do?

The activities selected for Chapter 18, and in the thematic unit that follows, are likely to meet these guidelines. ■

CHAPTER 18

Activities for Integrated Language Arts and Social Studies

In this chapter we present a collection of activities that encourage inter-action and cooperation among students, that depend upon collaborative learning between the students and the teachers, and that in interesting ways integrate the disciplines of language arts and social studies and, in some instances, other disciplines as well.

Each integrated activity is presented in a way that should make it immediately usable to you. Some take more class time to do than do others. While some are grade-level specific, others are not. Before selecting those best suited for use with your own distinctive group of students, you are advised to study each one.

The title of the activities, their order of presentation, and their designated grade level are as follows. (Note that those without a grade-level designation are appropriate for any grade in the intermediate and middle school. Activities that are grade-specific might also be adaptable for use in other grades.)

ACTIVITY 1:   Thank-You Letters to Members of Our Community (Grade 4)
ACTIVITY 2:   Place Names: Where Did They Come From? (Grade 4)
ACTIVITY 3:   Creating a Data Base
ACTIVITY 4:   Packing Your Suitcase
ACTIVITY 5:   Reducing Crime
ACTIVITY 6:   Teaching about Native Americans (Grade 4)
ACTIVITY 7:   People of Prominence (Grade 5)
ACTIVITY 8:   Take Refuge: A Board Game
ACTIVITY 9:   Women's History in the "Attic Trunk"
ACTIVITY 10:   Building a New City
ACTIVITY 11:   Women of the American Revolution
ACTIVITY 12:   China Today (Grades 6–7)
ACTIVITY 13:   Bias in News Articles (Grades 6–8)
ACTIVITY 14:   Cultural Borrowing (Grade 6)
ACTIVITY 15:   Futuring (Grade 6)
ACTIVITY 16:   Symbolic Messages (Grade 6)
ACTIVITY 17:   The Prospector and the Kid (Grade 9)
ACTIVITY 18:   Survival Dilemma (Grade 9)
ACTIVITY 19:   Teaching Social Studies through News Stories
ACTIVITY 20:   Local Controversy
ACTIVITY 21:   Letter Writing (Grade 9)

| ACTIVITY 1 | **Thank-You Letters to Members of Our Community (Grade 4)** |

Time: Two class periods

Objectives: To reinforce the value of consideration for others.
To learn how to write thank-you letters.

Interest Building: The class was invited to and visited a senior center for the purpose of seeing a display of crafts prepared by the members. The experience was a positive one for the children, and the teacher has suggested that they prepare and send thank-you letters.

Lesson Development: Ask children to brainstorm what they *liked* about their visit and what they *learned* from their experience. List these, in separate columns, on the chalkboard and save.

- Explain that thank-you letters are an appropriate way to express gratitude for visits, hospitality, and so on, and that is how each member of the class will thank the senior citizens.
- Review letter format.
- Distribute the assignment sheet in the form of a letter for the class to use as a reference. (The body of *your* letter could be the following: "Your assignment is to write a thank-you letter to our friends at the Forest Park Center. Remember to include one thing you liked about the visit and one thing you learned. Your paragraph should be at least five sentences long. Please hand in your rough draft by Friday.")
- Review your letter directions with them.
- Children write first draft of individual letters.
- Make corrections as needed.
- Children write final drafts of letters.
- Send letters.

| ACTIVITY 2 | **Place Names: Where Did They Come From? (Grade 4)** |

Time: One class period and followup

Objective: To explore the origin of names within a specific geographical area.

Interest Building: Brainstorm a list of names of places with which you are familiar within a geographical area. After brainstorming, compile an additional list from maps that have been distributed (example: a map of the home state or local county). Perhaps a total of 50 or 60 names would be a good stopping point.

Lesson Development: Categorize the names as to their origin: Indian names, names of explorers, famous people, early settlers, ethnic names, and so forth.

Have the children decide on the fairest way of distributing the names so that each has two or three place names to research.

Each child will then research the names, using resource books, interviews, and letters to various city or community information sources to determine the origin of the name. This is done over an extended period of time.

Summary: As each child obtains the information, display it on a bulletin board, attaching it with yarn to the particular geographical location on a map. Relate this information to the history and settlement pattern of the area.

Materials: Maps of the area under study.

| ACTIVITY 3 | **Creating a Data Base** |

CREATING A DATA BASE

Some data-base software programs, such as AppleWorks and Bank Street Filer, are generic; that is, they contain no data and are "shells" that will organize and synthesize any type of data. They allow students to create their own information systems on any topic with any categories of information.

FIGURE 18.1

Categories to Include in the Sample Data Base

Name of state (abbr): _____ Total population of state: _____
Estimated number of homeless: _____
Homeless as % of total population: _____
Percentage of homeless who are males: _____ Females: _____
Percentage of homeless who are children (17 yrs. or less): _____
Annual state and local governmental expenditures for the homeless: _____
Types of shelters provided (select type from the list): _____
_____

For example, suppose a class research project involves collecting some basic data concerning the nature, scope, and seriousness of the problem of the homeless in America. The teacher has divided the class into ten groups, each responsible for five states. After some discussion, the teacher and the groups identify the basic questions they want to have answered from the research:

- Who are the homeless (e.g., gender, number of children)?
- How extensive is the problem of the homeless (e.g., number)?
- Where is the problem of the homeless the greatest in the United States (e.g., states with highest percentage)?
- How much are local and state governments doing to solve the problem of the homeless (e.g., state expenditures, type of shelters provided)?

One group lists on a large sheet of paper the categories of data that it recommends the class collect and enter into the data base according to the procedures specified in the software manual. The categories that the students initially include in the data base are shown in Figure 18.1.

Other groups make further recommendations, and the teacher points out some changes in the categories that are required by the protocols of the data base—for example, not using commas in recording numerical data. The class as a whole then finally adopts a common list of categories.

As a next step, students proceed to do research and mathematical calculations to identify the required information. Then they enter the data under each category. Once this is accomplished, students can use the data base to answer their questions.

Packing Your Suitcase*   ACTIVITY 4

PART 1

Read children this version of the scenario, which simplifies the details and stresses the perspective of a refugee child:

> A war is going on in your country. Your parents feel your family is in danger living at home. They decide to escape to another country where you could be safer. At supper one night they tell you that your whole family will leave first thing in the morning. After supper you are to pack the things you will take with you in a backpack or suitcase that you will carry yourself. You can only take five kinds of things. Pack your bag with the things you would want to take with you.

*From *Uprooted: Refugees and the United States* by D. M. Donahue and N. Flowers, in press, Palo Alto, CA: Educators' Network, Amnesty International USA.

Ask the children to go home and actually pack a little bag with the things they would want to take or to make a list of those things.

PART 2

Have the children share their lists or bags and discuss how they made their choices.

a. What did they take and why?
b. What did they have to leave behind and why?
c. What was the hardest thing to leave behind?

PART 3

Encourage the children to express how they might feel if they really had to pack and leave home. Explain the purpose of this experience to the children: to help them understand the feelings of refugees who must really face this experience.

ACTIVITY 5   **Reducing Crime**

The system of decision making by ratings can be used with intermediate and middle school students. It requires that various choices of individuals within a group be weighted and averaged through ratings. The technique commits a group to accept the decision that receives the best average rating from all members. It is an especially appropriate technique for resolving issues for which several attractive alternative actions exist, none of which have attracted support of a majority.

Consider the situation in which a group of seven students in a fifth-grade class are trying to decide which various actions their local government should take to reduce crime. Through research, the students identify and list five major types of actions the government may take. Then they individually rate each of the five actions in order of their first through fifth choices (see Figure 18.2).

Each student's first choice is given a 1, the second a 2, and so on, to the last choice. The individual ratings then are totaled; the action with the *lowest* total score becomes the group's choice. An optional final step in the rating technique is to permit the members to discuss their ratings further and then to conduct a second round of ratings to arrive at the final decision.

The figure also indicates how the rating technique can produce a *group* position that represents some compromise for everyone. In Figure 18.2 the group's selection through rating (Community Citizen Watch Groups) was *not* the first choice of any single member. Further, it was only the third choice of a majority of the members.

FIGURE 18.2
Example of Decision Making by Ratings (Issue: How Our Local Government Can Help Reduce Crime)

POSSIBLE ACTIONS IDENTIFIED FROM RESEARCH	INDIVIDUAL RATINGS OF GROUP MEMBERS							
	TOM	**TAMMY**	**ANN**	**BILL**	**SAM**	**LEA**	**RON**	**TOTALS**
Hire More Police	4	1	2	5	1	5	2	20
Put Police on Foot Patrols	1	5	1	4	3	2	5	21
Ban Handguns	2	4	4	3	5	3	1	22
Community Citizen Watch Groups	3	3	3	2	2	2	3	18
Longer Jail Terms for Criminals	5	2	5	1	4	4	4	25

Teaching about Native Americans (Grade 4)*

Culture and diversity
An individual's culture strongly influences his or her behavior and values.
Southwest region
Post–European contact to 1990
In the study of the Navajo, students have learned about such things as traditional hogans, sheepherding, and artwork, including weaving. They have also studied the physical beliefs of the Navajo. The wonderful story of *Annie and the Old One* (Miles, 1971) will help link these cultural elements to the real world of the Navajo children and Navajo values, behavior, and way of life.

Basic Concepts:
Organizing Generalization:
Culture Area:
Time Period:
Background:

Objectives:

Knowledge (content): students will

1. state in their own words why they believe Annie acted as she did. Their discussion should reflect an awareness of her love for her grandmother, her reluctance to face her grandmother's impending death, her developing understanding of the Navajo belief in the circle of life, and her subsequent change in behavior;
2. relate Annie's family and feelings for them to their own families and experiences; and
3. discuss the relationship between values and behavior, and give some examples from their own lives.

Skills: students will

1. practice making inferences—"Why was the weaving stick important to Annie and her grandmother?"

Values (organic): students will

1. gain understanding and appreciation of another culture's beliefs regarding death; and
2. begin to understand that behavior, including their own, is related to values and that their way of life (culture) helps to determine their values and their behavior.

Activities:

1. Read aloud *Annie and the Old One* (Miles, 1971).
2. Class discussion:
   a. "Annie's Navajo world was good." What do we already know about Annie's Navajo world? Answers are likely to be related to environment, family, and ways of life. Illustrations in the book are excellent and will help students understand the relationship between the environment and way of life. Solicit ideas about what Navajo people believe is important. The story gives examples of the importance of some items. (weaving stick, sheep, etc.), people, and basic belief systems.
   b. Give some examples of how Annie was trying to keep her mother from finishing the rug.
   c. Why was Annie trying to keep her mother from finishing the rug? Discuss the following statements:
      • "My children, when the new rug is taken from the loom, I will go to Mother Earth."
      • "Your grandmother is one of those who lives in harmony with all nature—with earth, coyote, birds in the sky. They know more than many will ever learn. Those Old Ones know."
   d. Navajo people believe in the circle of life. Discuss the following statements:
      • "The sun comes up from the edge of earth in the morning. It returns to the edge of earth in the evening. Earth, from which good things come for the living creatures on it. Earth, to which all creatures finally go."

*From "Teaching About Native Americans: A Sample Lesson" by K. D. Harvey, L. D. Harjo, and J. K. Jackson, 1990, Teaching About Native Americans (Bulletin 84), p. 7. Washington, DC: National Council for the Social Sciences. © 1990 National Council for the Social Sciences. Reprinted with permission.

- "The sun rose but it also set." "The cactus did not bloom forever." "She would always be a part of the earth, just as her grandmother had always been, just as her grandmother would always be, always and forever."
    e. What does this mean, ". . . Annie was breathless with the wonder of it"?
    f. How did Annie's behavior change? Why?
    g. Can you think of any beliefs that you and your family have that help you decide how to act? The teacher should record these ideas on a chart or chalkboard.
    h. Encourage students to summarize, in their own words, the relationship between culture, values, and behavior.

Extension:	Depending on the focus and length of the unit of study, the teacher might want to extend this lesson to help students understand the behavior of Native American people in other historical periods.
Evaluation:	Students will be able to state the generalization in their own words.
Materials and Resources:	Miles, M. (1971). *Annie and the old one*. Boston, MA: Little, Brown and Company. Navajo rug, model of a Navajo loom, and weaving stick, if possible.

ACTIVITY 7	**People of Prominence (Grade 5)**
Time:	Variable—three to five class periods
Objective:	Children will develop an awareness of the qualities and traits that characterize persons of prominence.
Interest Building:	Have children list as many names of "famous people"—living or dead—as they can think of in five minutes. Then have them discuss their lists in terms of what the individuals did to make them famous. Do a quick check on the number that were political figures, war heroes, sports figures, etc. Have children speculate on why these particular individuals became well known, whereas most of their contemporaries did not. Tell the class that over the next few days they will study the qualities and traits of famous people more carefully.
Lesson Development:	Have a wide selection of biographies of prominent people available for children. Ask each child to choose one biography to read. The books are to be read in the next week, and children are to answer the following three questions:.

1. What did you admire about the person?
2. What qualities did the person have that made him/her come to the attention of others who knew him/her?
3. What did the person do that made him/her famous?

	At the completion of the assignment, have children discuss their ideas with classmates in groups of four. Have them try to find qualities or traits that were common to each of the persons about whom they read. Have each group report findings to entire class and discuss.
Summary:	Generate a list of qualities that (1) applied to all, (2) applied to some, (3) applied to a few, (4) applied to none. Discuss reasons for differences. Solicit individual reactions in terms of how they might apply some of these qualities to their own lives.
Materials:	Biographies of prominent persons at a reading level suitable for the class, to be secured from the school library.

Ideas for additional lessons:
1. Familiarize children with several well-known fables. In groups of four or five, have children dramatize the fable as it was originally written. Then have the children develop another skit illustrating an application of the message of the fable to some aspects of modern life. Discuss.

2. Have children develop a running list of proverbs. Place each proverb on an index card and post on the bulletin board. (*Example:* "The nail that sticks out gets hammered," "A rolling stone gathers no moss," "Where there's smoke, there's fire," "When pulling weeds, be sure to get rid of the roots.") Have children discuss those they find especially interesting and have them generate examples of applications in ordinary living. Relate the discussion to specific values or moral messages being conveyed in the proverbs.

Take Refuge: A Board Game*   ACTIVITY 8

Take Refuge!

Materials: A die
Gameboard
Rules of the game
2 to 4 players

Cut out the playing pieces along the dotted lines. Fold each along the solid line; glue the bottom to a square of lightweight cardboard to form a stand.

To make the gameboard and parts more durable, mount them with rubber cement on cardboard, then cover each with clear plastic adhesive paper. Before you cover them, add color with felt tip markers.

After you play the game, answer these questions:

1. How many good things happened to you as you played this game?

2. Did you find this game frustrating? Why or why not?

3. How would you feel if the things that happened in this game happened to you in real life?

Rules of the Game ———————————————

Each player chooses a token and throws the die. The highest number starts by putting his or her token on square 1. Other players follow accordingly. Whenever a player lands on a shaded square, he or she must follow the instructions for that square.

The first player to reach square 58 is the winner. But to reach that square, you must throw the exact number needed to land on 58. If you throw a number higher than what you need, move to 58 and continue the count by moving backwards. When you reach 58, you have become accepted as a refugee.

---

3. You forgot your passport! Return to 1.
6. Miss a turn while you look for food.
9. You sprain your ankle on a rugged path. Wait here until all the others have passed you.
11. A fallen tree blocks your path. Miss a turn while you go around it.
14. A wild animal chases you back to 12.
16. You discover a shortcut. Go to 20.
19. You're lost. Return to 17.
22. A scary noise awakens you. Run to safety at 21.
26. Your brother has fallen behind. Find him at 23.
28. A border patrol is looking for you. Hide in 27.
32. You're stuck in a barbed wire fence. Miss one turn.

34. The police arrest you and send you back to your country. Return to 1.
38. You are placed in a transit camp. Miss 2 turns.
40. You are so hungry, you take corn from a field. The farmer chases you back to 39.
44. A heavy storm comes. Take shelter in 42.
48. Miss a turn waiting for a boat to take you across the river.
51. Bad winds slow you down. On your next turn, move forward only 1 space.
53. You left your passport on the other side of the river. Go back to 50.
57. You get a fever. Miss 2 turns.

This game was inspired by the real-life drama of millions of men, women and children. They are refugees: people who must abandon everything—home, friends, sometimes family—in order to save their own lives or their freedom.

As they run for safety, refugees face hunger, sickness, even death. When they finally reach a country that lets them stay, they have new problems: learning a new language, adjusting to a new culture, finding jobs, houses, school, medical care.

As you play this game, try to imagine what it must be like to leave behind everything you own, to run for your life, and to become a refugee in a strange new country. It happens to millions of people every year—and for them, it isn't a game.

---

*From *Take Refuge!* by Holy Childhood Association, (no date), Washington, DC: Reprinted with the permission of the Holy Childhood Association, Washington, D.C.

Women's History in the "Attic Trunk"*   ACTIVITY 9

The old attic trunk has always been a source of fascination to those who discover it and the treasures it holds. The attic trunk can be explored in the classroom, too. It is a particularly useful method to introduce students to women's history of a particular era. An attic trunk from the decade of the twenties, for example, can be easily assembled to form hypotheses about the changing status of women in that decade.

The "attic trunk" for the twenties that I have constructed is a sturdy cardboard box with a hinged top covered with woodgrain-design contact paper. Although some items that I included are of general interest about the era, others relate specifically to women. The trunk is recognizable as a woman's possession. It contains original artifacts, women's accessories, and photocopies of other items, including historical documents that pertain to issues directly affecting women of the decade. Among the items and documents that I have been able to find or borrow are the following:

* High school and college yearbooks, 1923–1929
* Photocopics of John Held "flapper" drawings
* A fringed, satin flapper dress (a costume that I had made)
* Actual photographs from the era (my family's, which included family scenes, such as my grandparents and their three small children posed by the family car)
* Photocopies of magazine advertising, with emphasis on those ads directed toward women, from Blue Moon silk stockings to electrical appliances to automobiles to cigarettes and cosmetics
* An actual dress, purse, and other accessories from the period, borrowed from another teacher
* *Good Housekeeping,* April 1920, article supporting the Sheppard Towner Maternity Bill
* Principles of the National Birth Control League
* Editorial cartoons protesting restrictions on birth control
* Declaration of Principles of the National Women's Party, 1922
* Copy of the 1922 proposed ERA
* *Good Housekeeping,* September 1925, containing articles debating labor laws for women
* Any popular magazine article debating ERA in the twenties.

Other teachers need not limit themselves to these examples.

Building a New City   ACTIVITY 10

A new community is being planned. Everything in the community is new. All of the decisions about how the community will be built must be planned carefully: where the people will live, where they will shop, work, go to school, practice their religion, and have fun.

Below are some things the planners will have to think about. Put a 1 in front of the thing that you believe is the most important one for the planners to think about. Put a 2 in front of the next most important thing. Continue until you have numbered all of the items from 1 to 7.

_____   People should be free to buy or build a house any place they like.

_____   Lots of churches and temples should be built.

_____   There should be plenty of schools, libraries, and colleges so that everyone can learn.

_____   There should be a large police department.

_____   People should have lots of things to do that they really enjoy.

_____   All people should be treated equally.

_____   There should be jobs for everyone who wants them.

*From "Women's History in the 'Attic Trunk' " by L. J. Barnes, 1988, in *Teaching American History: New Directions,* edited by M. T. Downey, p. 18. © National Council for the Social Studies. Reprinted with permission.

ACTIVITY 11   **Women of the American Revolution***

"Women of the American Revolution" is an example of a unit that is available from a professional organization, the National Center for History in the Schools (Pearson, 1991). The basic goal of the unit is to introduce students to the American Revolution by focusing on the conflict through the perspective of women. The unit consists of four lessons of varying length, with corresponding objectives as follows:

Lesson one objectives:
1. To learn the role colonial women played in the turmoil that preceded the Revolution.
2. To understand some of the causes that led to the Revolution.
3. To practice interpreting documents that reflect various points of view.

Lesson 2 objectives:
1. To understand that war affects whole societies, not just soldiers.
2. To consider some of the ways women participated in the war.
3. To experience how history is written.

Lesson 3 objectives:
1. To learn the sense in which the Revolution was truly revolutionary and to understand its limitations.
2. To understand that many eighteenth-century women recognized and resented their lack of legal and political autonomy.
3. To consider why, despite women's contributions, they failed to achieve legal and political rights.

Lesson 4 objectives:
1. To understand the effect of the Revolution on women's lives.
2. To consider the way that human events can have unintended consequences.

A portion of the text of Lesson 2 from the unit is shown in Figure 18.3

Social studies textbooks also are organized into units. For example, one third-grade text was divided into five units that normally would be spread over the 36 weeks of the school year. The subject matter of each unit was organized into three to five subtopics or chapters. Each chapter, in turn, was organized into three to six related lessons. Resource materials, follow-up activities, and evaluation measures were provided in each unit.

FIGURE 18.3
Lesson 2 Activities

---

1. Ask students what men did during the Revolution. If students know that many men were soldiers, ask them to speculate about who was doing the work normally done by men. Tell them they are going to read a document that will help confirm their suspicions.
2. Have students read **DOCUMENT D,** an excerpt from Sarah Frazier's *A Reminiscence,* a description of her grandmother's part in the war.
   a. Discuss the document's reliability and representativeness. The document was written long after the events described, raising doubts about its accuracy. Moreover, the existence of an iron works suggests that these were people of greater wealth than was typical for yeoman farmers.
   b. Besides taking over men's occupations this document suggests women were busy with a variety of other activities. Have students list the responsibilities women assumed during the Revolution. They should begin with information obtained in this document, but also have them brainstorm about the kind of support armies require.
   c. Remind them that this was a war fought on home soil. When armies moved into a region, homes became hospitals, barracks for soldiers, and warehouses for supplies and ammunition.
   d. The constant interaction between soldiers and civilians allowed many women to become spies.

(Continued)

---

*From *Women in the American Revolution.* Copyright ©1991 by Jim Pearson, University of California, Los Angeles. Reprinted with the permission of National Center for History in the Schools, University of California, Los Angeles.

FIGURE 18.3 cont'd

e. Women also provided moral support; they often travelled with armies, sharing in soldiers' hardships even as they cooked, cleaned, nursed, and comforted the men.

f. Sometimes wives accompanied their husbands into battle, loading guns and attending the wounded. Even in regions free of combat, women improvised the scarce staples and manufactured goods no longer being brought from England.

g. Remind students of the story that began this unit; women organized and acted when hoarding was suspected. Have them consider the accuracy of this account. Reading it to them again may be useful.

- *If the dialogue is invented, how can they be sure the whole story is not made up?*
- *When historians write, where does the record of the past end and the story of the past begin?*
- *Another way to put this question is to ask them how free should historians be to interpret the past?*

The issue is extremely complex and students cannot be expected to do more than discuss the question. One of the reasons for raising the issue at all is for them to understand how, until quite recently, women could be almost completely excluded from accounts of the Revolution.

h. After students have finished this list, ask them to speculate about the patriots' chances for victory without women supplying the resources and support to continue the struggle.

HISTORICAL RESOURCE: DOCUMENT D

Sarah Frazier's *A Reminiscence,* an Account of Her Grandmother's Behavior during the Revolution

Mary Frazier did much to help Washington's army at Valley Forge. Sarah Frazier wrote the following account about her grandmother's actions during the winter of 1777–1778.

. . day after day collecting from neighbors and friends far and near, whatever they could spare for the comfort of the destitute soldiers, the blankets, and yarn, and half worn clothing thus obtained she brought to her own house, where they would be patched, and darned, and made wearable and comfortable, the stockings newly footed, or open ones knit, adding what clothing she could give of her own. She often sat up half the night, sometimes all, to get clothing ready. Then with it, and whatever could be obtained for food, she would have packed on her horse and set out on her cold lonely journey to the camp—which she went to repeatedly during the winter . . .

All the cloth and linen that my Grandfather wore during the war were spun at home, most of it by [my grandmother's] own hands. All the clothing except weaving. All the business of every kind, she attended to Farm, Iron Works, and domestic matters. In Summer as soon as it was light she had her horse saddled, rode over the farm and directed the men about their work, often rode down to the creek, where Sharpless' Iron Works are now, and was back at breakfast time to give her attention and toil to the children, servants, & household affairs. (reprinted from *Pennsylvania Magazine of History and Biography, XLVI* (1922), pp. 55–56.)

China Today (Grades 6–7)   ACTIVITY 12

Time: Ten class periods

Objectives: Students will learn basic information about the People's Republic of China. Students will refine research and small-group skills.

Interest Building: For several days as the class is reading the text's overview of China, invite students to bring to school other recently published materials about China (books, magazines, travel brochures). Display these in a learning center.

Preview the resources.

Lesson Development:

- Using the text and resources for inspiration, brainstorm a list of topics that would be suitable for small-group information-gathering projects.
- Have a member of the class list the topics on a chart in the learning center (see Sample Chart).
- Divide the class into study groups of five children each.
- Study group assignment: Elect a leader. Meet, discuss, and agree on and sign up for a topic.

- Decide on subtopics to study.
- Use outline format for taking notes.
- Organize report into an introduction, main body, and conclusion.
- Prepare visuals. Some ideas include charts, graphs, time lines, and illustrations from resources.
- Practice giving the oral report.
- Assign report dates.
- Give students a copy of each evaluation form. Discuss expectations (see sample evaluation forms).

Summary: Groups give their oral reports, with each member contributing to the presentation. They field questions and comments from their audience.

Sample Chart: China Today Reports

Topics	Names of Group Members	Report Date
Family life and education Geography and natural resources Economy: Agriculture and industry Political system: Leaders and history Holidays and festivals Cities Tourism and transportation Arts and athletics Science and technology		

China Today Report: Sample Teacher Evaluation

	Yes	No	Comments
Was an introduction used? Were the main ideas presented? Were supporting details given? Was there a clear conclusion? Were visuals used? Was teamwork evident? Group Grade: _____			

China Today Report: Sample Group Evaluation

Topic: _____

_____

What did you do well?
How could you have improved your report?
List the resources that you used.

Evaluation: Complete the evaluation forms. Base the group's grade on a consideration of both evaluations.
Collect each student's notes. Evaluate these on an individual basis.

Resources: Text: *World Regions,* Macmillan/McGraw-Hill
Recommended trade books:
China, Here We Come! Tang Yungmei
Two Chinese Families, Catherine Edwards Sadler
Red Star & Green Dragon: Looking at New China, Lila Perl
The People's Republic of China: Red Star of the East, Jane Werner Watson
Dragonwings, Lawrence Yep

Bias in News Articles (Grades 6–8)

One class period
To learn to detect bias in news accounts.
Secure two accounts of the same news story, such as those in the following example. Make copies and distribute one of each to members of the class.

Opposition to Gun Control Remains Strong

Legislation pending in Congress would ban possession of the kind of handgun used in the attempted assassination of President Reagan in Washington, DC, in March, 1981. But opposition remains strong, especially in the House.

The present law banning imports of manufactured cheap handguns was passed in 1968 after the killings of Senator Robert F. Kennedy and Rev. Dr. Martin Luther King, civil rights leader. The law permits importing parts that can be assembled and sold in the United States.

A much tougher bill was approved by the Senate in 1972 after the shooting of Governor George C. Wallace, but the House never acted on it. Senate sources said that the members have shown a willingness to pass tough gun control laws but are waiting for some sign that the House is ready to do so, too.

Meanwhile, the lobbyists opposing gun control continue their efforts to stop such legislation. They remain consistent in their view that there is not necessarily a correlation between gun control and the actions of fanatics.

Little Hope Seen for Gun Control Legislation

Long overdue legislation pending in the foot-dragging Congress would ban possession of the kind of vicious handgun used in the nearly successful assassination attempt on President Reagan in Washington, DC, in March 1981. But the carefully coordinated opposition to tough gun control remains strong, especially in the politically sensitive House.

The present mild law banning imports of manufactured cheap handguns was reluctantly passed in 1968 after the ruthless murders of the popular and respected Senator Robert F. Kennedy and Rev. Dr. Martin Luther King, Nobel Prize–winning civil rights leader. The so-called gun control law permits importing parts that can be easily assembled and freely sold to fanatics in the crime-ridden United States.

A much tougher bill was approved by the Senate in 1972 after the brutal shooting of Governor George C. Wallace, but, as usual, the conservative House never acted on it. Senate sources said that enlightened members have shown a willingness to pass much-needed tough gun-control laws but are waiting patiently for some hopeful sign that the House is ready to do so, too, however belatedly.

Meanwhile, the lobbyists opposing reasonable gun controls continue their clandestine efforts to sabotage such legislation. They remain consistent in their warped view that there is no correlation between gun control and the actions of fanatics.

Have the children underline the *facts* in each story.
Using a chart, analyze the stories separately according to FACTS and NONFACTS. Compare the facts in each account to determine if there are any discrepancies.

Analyze the two accounts sentence by sentence by having students identify all nouns and the words that describe them (adjectives). List these on the chalkboard or a chart as follows:

Account No. 1		Account No. 2	
Nouns	Adjectives	Nouns	Adjectives
opposition	strong	opposition	carefully coordinated strong
		gun control	tough
House		House	politically sensitive

Have children search newspapers and listen to news programs on television and radio on their own and bring to class examples of stories that contain elements of bias in the way they were reported.

Discuss with the class the conditions under which it is appropriate for news media to express opinions on issues.

ACTIVITY 14	**Cultural Borrowing (Grade 6)**

Time: | Two class periods
Objective: | To learn how contact with another culture changes ways of living.
Interest Building: | Begin the presentation by discussing with the class changes in ways of living with which they are familiar. This should lead to the idea that the ways of living of people all over the world are changing.

Display a photograph of the tundra region showing a sled being drawn by a snowmobile with sled dogs and a tent in the background. Ask students whether they think the photograph is one that was taken a long time ago or in recent years and why they think as they do. This should lead to a discussion of the presence of the snowmobile, which means that the group has had contact with the industrial world.

Lesson Development: | Divide the class into groups of three, and using the resources available have students make an inquiry into the specific changes that have taken place in Eskimo life as a result of contact with the outside world and the impact of those changes on traditional Eskimo life. Their findings should be recorded on a chart as follows:

Change	Result
Motorboats	
Snowmobiles	
Guns and steel traps	
Canvas tents	
Sewing machines	
Schools	
Others (specify)	

Provide sufficient time for the groups to do their research, then reassemble as a whole group. Summarize the findings of all groups on a master chart on the chalkboard. Discuss the findings along these lines: How have these changes been helpful to Eskimo life? How have these changes been harmful to Eskimo life? Is it important to keep Eskimo traditions and skills alive? How might this be done?

Lead the discussion toward the more general problem of what happens when people of one culture have contact with another culture. This deals with the concept of cultural borrowing, although the term need not be introduced to the children at this time.

Summary/Follow up: | Have the children, again in groups of three, find other examples of cultural borrowing in back issues of *National Geographic* magazines you have provided. Have them explain how their examples illustrate cultural borrowing.

Materials: | Large photos of traditional Eskimo life.
Texts, supplementary books, and references on Eskimo culture.
Several back copies of *National Geographic* magazine.

Futuring (Grade 6)   ACTIVITY 15

Three class periods	Time:
Learners will be able to identify present trends and to project the consequence of a specific trend.	Objective:
Suggest that the class has gathered together in the year 2025 for a reunion. Have them speculate on what their lives will be like then. Define *trends,* and have the students list current trends such as more mechanization in our daily lives or the increased use of computers.	Interest Building:
With the students working in groups of three, have them choose one of the current trends and brainstorm all of the consequences of that trend, such as more leisure time in the case of the mechanization trend, which leads to more recreation needs, which means an increase in the use of state parks and the like. Ask the students to organize their ideas for sharing with their classmates.	Lesson Development:
In the next class period have each group identify consequences that seem to be negative. Ask them to develop an ideal plan that could make this consequence beneficial to people in the future.	Summary:
None necessary, but outside sources have commercial materials on this topic. Two possible references are these:	Materials:

The Center for Curriculum Design
823 Foster Street
Evanston, Illinois 60204

Science Fiction Research Association
Box 3186
The College of Wooster
Wooster, Ohio 44691

Symbolic Messages (Grade 6)   ACTIVITY 16

One class period	Time:
Children will deduce certain information about a country from symbols placed on its coins. Children will relate the symbols to basic values of that country.	Objectives:
At least one coin for each child, preferably coins or facsimiles of coins, from several different nations.	Resources:

Teacher:	Boys and girls, for the past few days we have been studying the use of signs and symbols. At the close of our discussion yesterday we came to an important conclusion. What was it?	Lesson Development:
Child:	We said that we could tell what people considered to be important to them by the symbols and signs they use on their buildings.	
Teacher:	Yes. Now today you will have a chance to test that idea in a slightly different way. Each of you will be given a coin to use. Study the coin carefully and see how many things you can tell about the country just from what you see on the coin.	

Coins are distributed to the class. After they have had time to make their observations, ask the children what they have concluded. As these are presented, write them on the chalkboard. Have each child tell *why* the conclusion was made. Pass the coins about for other children to inspect. Items such as the following may surface in this discussion:

> These people believe in God.
>
> They want (or believe in) liberty.
>
> They are able to read their language.
>
> Men must be more important than women in this country.
>
> They construct large buildings.
>
> They speak more than one language.
>
> It is an old country.
>
> They have a queen (or king).
>
> They are a peace-loving people.
>
> They are proud of their wars and war heroes.
>
> They want people to be courageous.

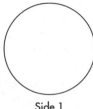

Side 1

Follow up: Imagine that the United States is planning to issue a new coin and there is a contest to get the best design. You decide to enter the contest. The rules are these:

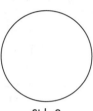

Side 2

1. Write down two ideas that best describe what people in our country think are important to them.
2. Think of and draw symbols that could be used on a coin to show these two qualities.

ACTIVITY 17   ## The Prospector and the Kid (Grade 9)

Each student is given a photo of an old prospector and a sad kid (or any other dissimilar and provocative pair). Each writes a monologue as if he/she were the prospector or the kid saying what would be on his/her mind. Students are paired as prospectors and kids and read their monologues to each other. They talk about how they see the characters in the monologues. Then as a team they write a dialogue where they find a common ground and speak to each other. After they read the dialogue, they plan a story line for a vignette in which the two talk in the context of the events of a story. Finally the students read the story and discuss their sense of what it is about. They explore ideas, the characters, and the tone. Then each student writes an essay which locates something universal or public in the relationship of the pair: loneliness, differing views of time among the very old and young, healing grief. Thus, students move from monologue to dialogue to story to essay.

REMEMBERING A TEACHER

This activity moves students from conceptualization to talking to writing. Group students in pairs. Have each partner in turn follow the steps given here.

STEP 1: Make a list of six of your elementary school teachers. Think of each of them, their habits, favorite phrases/sayings, special clothing, unique gestures, and other things that made them special people, jotting down notes beside each name. Then select your best-remembered teacher and tell a partner about him or her.

STEP 2: As you describe your special teacher, do more memories awaken than when you originally made notes? (Full stories often emerge. Questions evoke new memories and the explanations draw out other new information.)

STEP 3: After you have described this teacher to your partner, retrieve as much new information as possible in note form. Draw lines indicating any relationships you see (webbing). Do these relationships suggest a strategy for writing? Draft a story now at great speed, capturing all of the details from your notes. Read your story. Do you discover in it any organic unity? Do you make any unexpected discoveries about your former teacher or yourself?

STEP 4 (optional): Rewrite your story in a more finished form.

Survival Dilemma (Grade 9)   ACTIVITY 18

A sophisticated and challenging way to promote students' work at a high level of abstraction is contained in a simple lifeboat scenario. The question posed in this exercise, introduced by E. A. Kahn in 1984*, is what *things,* not people, do we select to jettison? The old values clarification exercises forced students to toss overboard least favored companions, but this task requires individuals to look at the context and decide which items are most valuable for the task of survival.

SURVIVAL DILEMMA

A ship is sinking and you have managed to board a lifeboat with 12 other people. Most of the people were not able to reach the cabins to get warm clothing, so they are in street clothes. One woman is in a bathing suit. The ship is in the North Atlantic, and the temperature is near freezing, with strong winds and high waves. The lifeboat is an open wooden craft with no motor, so it must be rowed. You may have to spend several days at sea depending on when the boat is spotted. The ocean is very foggy with low, heavy clouds. The boat is dangerously overloaded, and in order to keep safely afloat you *must* remove 60 pounds of weight. You must decide which items you will remove. For safety reasons, you cannot suspend any items from the lifeboat. You cannot remove any of the people. You must choose from among these items:

- 3 skin-diving wet suits, each 5 lbs.
- a 2-gallon container full of water, 15 lbs.
- 4 wool blankets, each 2 lbs.
- a large S.O.S. flag, 3 lbs.
- 30 cans of tuna fish (flip tops), each 1 lb.
- 8 oars, each 5 lbs.
- first aid kit, 10 lbs.
- 5 slicker raincoats with hoods, each 2 lbs.
- battery operated signal light, 8 lbs.
- 2 buckets for bailing, each 3 lbs.
  TOTAL—145 lbs.

We ask students to make thoughtful individual decisions about which 60 pounds are to be tossed overboard, before we ask groups of five to agree on the best solution to the problem. Each student writes a paragraph listing and justifying his or her choices; each group selects the best and combines them into a single document. When all groups have had enough time to collaborate, we call on one group to list the items selected to be jettisoned and their reasons for tossing those. We then invite other groups to challenge this group's selections and to offer better lists. These exchanges usually lead us to question what these expendable items represent beyond themselves. Categories of items begin to emerge: oars and flag, as a sail, represent movement or mobility; tuna and water represent sustenance; signal and flag represent communication; oars, wet suit, and blanket represent protection.

---

*From Kahn, E. A. (1984, June). Lecture to the National Humanities Faculty, Summer Institute, Grand Rapids, MI.

ACTIVITY 19   **Teaching Social Studies through News Stories**

This activity involves a created news story (Figure 18.4) that is a typical example of the type of controversial issue that can be useful in teaching social studies concepts and skills. As you read this story, based on an actual incident in the Puget Sound area, think of (1) the issues it presents and (2) what possibilities it holds as a teaching vehicle in the middle and upper grades.

How can a news story of this type be used for social studies instruction? Here are a few suggestions:

1. Use the procedure learned for making an analysis of this situation—that is (a) have students identify the *facts* of the case, (b) have students identify the *issues* in the case, and (c) have students identify *alternative solutions* to the problem and list the consequences of each alternative.

FIGURE 18.4

WHALE CAPTURE CREATES WAIL

Six killer whales are being held inside the Aqua Life, Inc. nets at Cook Inlet while Bill Holberg decides which ones, if any, will be kept for aquarium exhibits. Hundreds of people watched the capture from boats and shore yesterday afternoon.

The huge mammals swam slowly round and round inside two purse seine nets today, surfacing to "blow" for only moments. They stayed under for five minutes at a time. A large bull whale and a small calf that escaped the capture were nowhere to be found.

Governor Reconsidering

Meanwhile, a political storm was gathering over the capture operation. The governor today interrupted his skiing vacation long enough to say that he was "reconsidering" the state's position on making the inlet a sanctuary for killer whales. The state's senior senator in Washington said that a declaration of support for the governor for a whale sanctuary would clear the way for protection of the sea animals. Earlier efforts to get support from state officials for the idea were unsuccessful. The senator also said, "Apparently this man [Holberg] had a valid permit. But there aren't going to be any more. This is the end!"

Depth Charges Used

An assistant to the State Game and Fisheries director, Jack Binns, watched the capture from about fifty feet away. Binns said Aqua Life, Inc. boats used "sonar, radar, and 'depth' charges" to drive the whales into smaller and smaller coves and finally into the nets. He said he watched three men in power boats racing across the water atop the whale school, "dropping 'depth charges' as fast as they could light them. I've never seen anything so disgusting in all my life," he said today. "This ought to be stopped right now."

A federal enforcement officer who supervised yesterday's operation said, "there is nothing in the permit that prohibits the use of such explosives."

Use of Charges Denied

Many citizens complained about the capture operation. An automobile dealer from South Harbor said he saw an airplane dropping "tomato can"–size cannisters that apparently exploded as the plane herded the whales. Bill Moss, veterinarian for Aqua Life, Inc., said no such charges were used. He said the whale chasers used "firecracker"-type explosives thrown from boats to herd the whales. Holberg himself was aboard the Aqua Life, Inc. boat, *KANDU,* and was unavailable for comment.

Court Action Threatened

Environmentalists and others bitterly opposed the capture of the whales. Fred Russell, president of the state's largest environmental protection group, PROTEX, demanded that the whales be released. He said his group was prepared to take the matter to court if necessary to prevent Aqua Life, Inc. from keeping the creatures. "This is an outrage," he said, "and we are not going to sit by and let it happen."

Russell cited a Canadian biologist who found that only about sixty-five killer whales remain in the Straits of Georgia and Juan de Fuca and in Puget Sound. Earlier data had placed the number of whales at about three hundred.

Overlapping Jurisdiction

The power to create a whale sanctuary rests with the federal government, but federal law says the governor of a state that contains the sanctuary may veto its creation. This overlapping of jurisdiction sometimes creates confusion or results in no action being taken.

Until today, federal officials thought the governor opposed creation of a killer whale sanctuary in this area. The governor's staff said that no record could be found of the governor's ever having opposed such a proposal.

The senior senator renewed his call for a sanctuary, something he has advocated since 1974. There is no reason to believe that the governor will oppose the creation of the killer whale sanctuary.

2. Use this story as a springboard for an in-depth study of endangered species. More than 500 kinds of animals are listed as rare or in danger of extinction, including blue whales, Indian and Siberian tigers, Asiatic lions, snow leopards, eagles, condors, grizzly bears, alligators, and whooping cranes. Students should get into the values question of whether or not an animal has to be "useful" in order to be protected.

3. Have children study the roles of federal, state, local, and volunteer groups in decision making regarding issues of the type presented in this story. This should get them into local and state regulations concerning the conservation of natural resources and environmental contamination. It should also confront the matter of what individual citizens or groups of citizens can do when they see something happening that they believe to be unconscionable, even if legal.

4. This story provides an excellent setting for the study of the issue of capture of wild animals for use in circuses and zoos. Should zoos be allowed at all? Do animals benefit from zoos?

5. This story can provide the basis for the study of the web-of-life food chains—that is, how changes in the population of one animal change the number of another animal on which it feeds. This can be coupled with a study of wildlife management, hunting and fishing regulations, and the concept of *open season.*

6. Study the lives of individuals who have dedicated themselves to the preservation of wildlife and other natural resources: John Muir, Jack Miner, Rachel Carson, Gifford Pinchot, and local environmentalists.

7. Develop this news story into a role-playing activity in which the issues are highlighted and satisfactory resolutions played out.

8. Have children in committees develop "position statements" to represent the point of view of the various principals in this controversy: the whale hunter, the governor, the president of the environmentalist group, an irate citizen, the director of Aqua Life, Inc. (who would receive the captured whales), and so on.

9. Use the story to build interest in developing a social-action project dealing with ecology or conservation. A second-grade teacher in Wisconsin reports the following activities that were developed in such a project:

   a. The children helped others become aware of the problems faced by endangered wildlife by sharing their research findings with their family, friends, schoolmates, clergy, and neighbors.

   b. They wrote letters to state and federal officials to urge their support of legislation designed to protect wildlife.

   c. They presented programs that dealt with the potential threats to wildlife by land developers, trappers, poachers, snowmobilers, hunters, pesticide programs, campers, and so on.

   d. They compiled a list of guidelines and distributed them to each child in the school, explaining ways individuals can help. These are some of the guidelines:

      (1) Refuse to shoot birds and other wild creatures "just for the fun of it."

      (2) Refuse to participate in cruel and senseless "chases" of wild animals on snowmobiles, in cars, on bikes, on foot, or in boats or planes.

      (3) Refuse to destroy animal homes.

      (4) Refuse to disturb baby birds and animal babies in their nests. (Marsha Gravitz, "You and Me in the Classroom," *Instructor,* 82(8), (April 1973), 43)

10. Find out about the purposes and activities of organizations concerned about protecting the environment such as the Sierra Club, the National Wildlife Federation, Nature Conservancy, and Greenpeace.

These suggestions provide interesting extensions of a news story. Of course, no one class would engage in all of them; indeed, it is unlikely that more than one would be used. Perhaps the teacher could create others even more suitable than those provided here. The point of this list is simply to illustrate the wide range of possibilities that inhere in well-selected current news stories. They provide the excitement of controversy, they are relevant to the current stream of human events, they deal with public policy issues, and they lend themselves exceedingly well to social participation projects.

ACTIVITY 20   **Local Controversy**

The news story shown in Figure 18.5 is a good example of the types of controversial issues that can be found in nearly all communities, large or small. Here are a few other examples:
Whether to

- Allow an area to be rezoned for a shopping center.
- Permit freeway construction through a residential or farming area.
- Close an elementary school.
- Build an athletic stadium.
- Allow a golf course to be built.
- Pass a dog leash ordinance.
- Allow animals to be used for medical research.
- Allow certain forms of gambling.
- Restrict trash burning.
- Construct a new hospital.

These issues present good opportunities for teaching how to deal with controversy. A teacher might proceed as follows:

FIGURE 18.5

COURT STOPS FURTHER TREE REMOVAL

Orders Environmental Impact Statement

Opponents to the clearing of land on the Richards's property succeeded in getting a court order to stop the tree removal until a study is done to determine the environmental impact of such cutting.

The owner, Charles Richards, has insisted that he has a legal right to harvest the timber on his property. The local…

1. Have the children identify the facts of the case. In an examination of the airport news story (Figure 18.6), some of the facts are these:
   a. Jet aircraft produce objectionable noise.
   b. A sizable number of homeowners are disturbed over the noise level.
   c. The homeowners are insisting that the Airport Commission do something about the problem.
   d. The homeowners have engaged an attorney to represent them.
   e. The noise problem reduces the possibility of sale of the homes in the affected area.
   f. Money for the purchase of the homes by the Airport Commission is not now available.
   g. Modern urban areas must have conveniently located jet plane air service.

   In identifying facts, it is important not to confuse them with opinions or with issues. For example, one would need further documentation that the noise "is endangering the health of residents" as is claimed in the story. Also, it is *not* a fact that the only solution to the problem is the purchase of the homes by the commission.

2. Have students identify the *issues* in the case. In looking for issues, one is seeking to find out why there is a problem. Usually, this involves conflicts of values. In the airport case, for example, the following are some of the issues:
   a. Is it possible to locate metropolitan airports completely away from residential areas?
   b. Have the dollar values of these homes been reduced because of the airport location?
   c. Should the homes of those residents who moved into the area *after* the airport was in operation be purchased?
   d. How can the residents insist on the commission's purchasing their homes when there is no money available?
   e. Who should bear the cost of the purchase of the homes? The local taxpayers? Travelers who use the airport? The airline companies whose planes make the noise? The federal government?
   f. Does a public facility that results in a nuisance to nearby residents require that the homeowners be paid for damages?
   g. How severe must the nuisance be before a claim can be justified?

3. Have students identify alternative solutions to the problem and list the consequences of each alternative. In this type of analysis it is not necessary to come to consensus as to the best solution. In the airport case, these alternatives might be proposed:

FIGURE 18.6

HOMEOWNERS PROTEST AIRCRAFT NOISE

More than two hundred irate homeowners jammed the chambers of the Metropolitan Airport Commission last evening to protest noise from jets at the International Airport. Property owners are demanding that the commission secure funds to purchase homes immediately adjacent to the airport. They insist that the noise has reached a level that is intolerable and that it is endangering the health of residents.

"When a plane flies over our home, all conversation must stop," claimed one resident. Similar complaints were made by other homeowners. "It is impossible for us to conduct instruction when planes fly overhead," said Brian Sorokin, a teacher at Stevens School, located near the airport.

Marvin Sherwin, attorney for the homeowners, said his group would resort to legal action if appropriate measures are not taken immediately by the Airport Commission. He could foresee no satisfactory solution to the problem short of clearing the area of homes. "These families bought their homes without knowing that an international airport was to be placed next door to them," he said. "They cannot sell their homes and they cannot live with the present noise level. The commission must deal with this problem," he added.

Members of the Airport Commission refused comment except to say that the problem is a serious one and that funds were not presently available for the mass evacuation being proposed by the residents. Robert Randall, chairman of the commission, said he did not know whether federal monies are available for such removals, but that "all possibilities would be explored."

Proposals	*Consequences*
a. Reduce jet noise by reducing landing and takeoff speeds.	a. May not be safe; would not solve the problem completely.
b. Develop less noisy jet engines.	b. Would take too long to develop quieter engines. May not be possible to develop such engines.
c. Relocate the airport.	c. Would be very costly. Would simply move the problem somewhere else.
d. Purchase homes and relocate only those residents who owned their property before the airport location was established.	d. Does not solve the problem for the remaining residents. It is unfair and probably not legal.
e. Purchase all homes in the affected area.	e. Would require huge sums of money not now available. Would establish a precedent for other cases of a public facility creating a nuisance.
f. Do nothing.	f. Commission would be subject to legal action and would eventually have to do what the court directs rather than making the decision itself. Would generate additional public ill will.

Cases such as this lend themselves well to role playing and simulation. For example, some children could play the parts of the commission members, the homeowners, the attorney, the teacher, and others. The information could be secured by the students from the point of view of the role they are playing. If a local issue is the focus of the study, children can get information from the community by interviewing individuals, researching background information on the problem, and through local news stories. If the airport case were used, the teacher would need to provide data for the various roles. For example, each player or group of players would receive information prepared by the teacher such as:

> *Homeowner.* You have owned your home ten years. The airport planning began three years after you made the purchase. You and your wife have three children, ages eight, six, and two. You are worried that your children's hearing will be damaged by the noise. You have had your home for sale for a year. Three buyers looked at it, but decided not to buy when they found out about the jet noise problem.

Similar instructions would need to be prepared for all other players in the simulation.

Situations such as this also can be used to have students speculate about the future. For example, how might we deal with the problem of jet aircraft noise (or any of several other issues) in a futuristic setting? Here the children do not need to be constrained by what is practicable and feasible—or even possible. They simply let their creative minds imagine what might possibly become alternatives at some future time.

ACTIVITY 21 ·   **Letter Writing (Grade 9)**

This teaching activity is the most elaborated activity in our book. It is one we have used successfully with high school students of all ages and abilities. You will observe that it teaches more than insight into letters by linking letter writing to the private writing of students as well as to the literary letters of others. We begin our lesson with caution. We are aware of the danger of drawing attention to something that is so personal and, hopefully, spontaneous. We don't want to spoil the natural and introduce self-consciousness and contrivance. But we try to demonstrate to students that the promise outweighs the danger.

Begin instruction with the following survey. Ask students to commit their responses to paper, but also use it for discussion if the class is open to self-disclosure.

Letter writing survey

1. Do you ever write notes in class to other classmates?
2. Why do you do that? If you will see the person later, why take the risk? What drives you to write notes?
3. How many letters have you received in the last month? From whom have you heard?
4. How many letters have you written? Are you writing to anyone out of town or do you write letters to those you could just as easily call?
5. What prompts you to write letters? Is the motive like your motive for writing notes? Do you see them as anything more than the occasion to pass along information?
6. What other kinds of writing do you do that is not assigned by a teacher?
7. Which is more important to you, a letter written to you from someone you know and value? A well-written story by an accomplished writer?
8. What do you think is the most common form of writing (involving verbal communication with another) for the average adult?
9. Think for a moment about any of your adult friends or family, those who are not professional writers. What occasions prompt them to put a pen or pencil to paper?
10. Have you ever seen sections of your English textbooks devoted to the writing of letters?
11. Do teachers ever discuss letters as an important form of writing?
12. What does your work in class lead you to conclude is the premier genre of writing? The novel? The short story? The poem? Personal memoirs? Diaries? Journals? Letters?

We discuss the written answers to these personal questions with the whole group. With the class sensitized and conscious of letter writing, we move to the students' own writing. Here is the sequence of our in-class assignments and our instructions.

1. **Note to a Classmate**
   a. Begin by writing a note to a partner, a note about anything that's on your mind at this moment, the kind of note you might write in any given school day. Be candid. (Any public reading of your note will be undertaken only with your approval.)
   b. Now send your note, read your correspondent's note, and respond on the back. Return the note to its origin.
   c. Talk as a class about what just happened.
      • If I were to spy on your note writing and say "All right, Leah, is that something you'd like to share with the class?" would you be embarrassed? Is the communication that confidential?
      • What delights you in writing the note? In receiving it?
      • What kind of message does it contain?
      • What was the best note you can ever remember receiving in a class?
      • If you are not a note-passer, have you ever envied those who are?
2. **Postcard to Your Family**
   a. Shift your location from the classroom to home. Imagine that your family is away for two weeks and you find a postcard from them in the mailbox. Here is what it says:

   Everything is going well. The food is good. The company is enjoyable. I wish you were here. I want to hear from you. Please write.

   b. Write a postcard back to them responding to their request.
   c. Exchange cards with another student and talk together about what you've each written to your family.
   d. How do these cards differ from the notes written to a classmate? Which interested you most? In which was the writer the most spontaneous? Which had the greater specificity? substance? imagination?
   e. Would any of you read your postcards to the class? If you were the family hearing this account, would you have additional questions you'd like to ask of the writer?

f. Cartoonist Gary Larson senses the common event of letters from family or close friends. (We distribute several *Far Side* cartoons featuring letter writing between animal families and friends.) Do you notice anything in these cartoons that reminds you of your experiences with letters?

3. **Letters to a Friend**
    a. Imagine now that a friend, rather than your family, is away. Write a letter or postcard back to that friend.
    b. Don't share this correspondence. Is there any difference between it and what you wrote to your family? What?
    c. Consider this observation:

    If you want to discover your true opinion of anybody, observe the impression made on you by the first sight of a letter from him.

    Arthur Schopenhauer

4. **Published Letters**
    Read the following excerpt from a seventeenth-century letter of Madame de Sévigné (1626–1696) about a royal house party during which a disconsolate cook took surprising action. (Many other letters, of course, would serve for this activity.)

    PARIS, Sunday, April 26, 1671.
    This is Sunday, April 26th, and this letter will not go out till Wednesday; but it is not so much a letter as a narrative that I have just learned from Moreuil, of what passed at Chantilly with regard to poor Vatel. I wrote to you last Friday that he had stabbed himself—these are the particulars of the affair: The king arrived there on Thursday night; the walk, and the collation, which was served in a place set apart for the purpose, and strewed with jonquils, were just as they should be. Supper was served, but there was no roast meat at one or two of the tables, on account of Vatel's having been obliged to provide several dinners more than were expected. This affected his spirits, and he was heard to say, several times: "I have lost my honor! I can not bear this disgrace!" "My head is quite bewildered," said he to Gourville. "I have not had a wink of sleep these twelve nights; I wish you would assist me in giving orders." Gourville did all he could to comfort and assist him; but the failure of the roast meat (which, however, did not happen at the king's table, but at some of the other twenty-five), was always uppermost with him. Gourville mentioned it to the prince, who went directly to Vatel's apartment, and said to him: "Every thing is extremely well conducted, Vatel; nothing could be more admirable than his majesty's supper." "Your highness's goodness," replied he, "overwhelms me; I am sensible that there was a deficiency of roast meat at two tables." "Not at all," said the prince; "do not perplex yourself, and all will go well." Midnight came: the fireworks did not succeed, they were covered with a thick cloud; they cost sixteen thousand francs. At four o'clock in the morning Vatel went round and found every body asleep; he met one of the under-purveyors, who was just come in with only two loads of fish. "What!" said he, "is this all?" "Yes, sir," said the man, not knowing that Vatel had dispatched other people to all the sea-ports around. Vatel waited for some time; the other purveyors did not arrive; his head grew distracted; he thought there was no more fish to be had. He flew to Gourville: "Sir," said he, "I can not outlive this disgrace." Gourville laughed at him. Vatel, however, went to his apartment, and setting the hilt of his sword against the door, after two ineffectual attempts, succeeded in the third, in forcing his sword through his heart. At that instant the carriers arrived with the fish; Vatel was inquired after to distribute it. They ran to his apartment, knocked at the door, but received no answer, upon which they broke it open, and found him weltering in his blood. A messenger was immediately dispatched to acquaint the prince with what had happened, who was like a man in despair. The duke wept, for his Burgundy journey depended upon Vatel. The prince related the whole affair to his majesty with an expression of great concern; it was considered as the consequence of too nice a sense of honor; some blamed, others praised him for his courage. The king said he had put off this excursion for more than five years, because he was aware that it would be attended with infinite trouble, and told the prince that he ought to have had but two tables, and not have been at the expense of so many, and declared he would never suffer him to do so again; but all this was too late for poor Vatel. However, Gourville attempted to supply the loss of Vatel, which he did in great measure. The dinner was elegant, the collation was the same. They supped, they walked, they hunted; all was perfumed with jonquils, all was enchantment. Yesterday, which was Saturday, the same entertainments were renewed, and in the evening the king set out for Liancourt, where he had ordered a *medianoche;* he is to stay there three days. This is what Moreuil has told me, hoping I should acquaint you with it. I wash my hands of the rest, for I know nothing about it. M. D'Hacqueville, who was present at the scene,

will, no doubt, give you a faithful account of all that passed; but, because his hand-writing is not quite so legible as mine, I write too; if I am circumstantial, it is because, on such an occasion, I should like circumstantiality myself.

a. Does this letter interest you? Do you think it provides any insight of value to you? What impresses you about it?

b. A contemporary of Madame de Sévigné once said, "When you have read one of Madame de Sévigné's letters you feel a slight pang, because you have one less to read." Can you see in this excerpt why she was valued by her contemporaries?

c. Model Madame de Sévigné by describing an event or situation in your recent life. Can you imagine what someone in 300 years might make of what you are describing?

We go on to read and discuss a variety of published letters. They include a range of writers—Lord Chesterfield, Abraham Lincoln, Emily Dickinson, George Eliot, Rainer Maria Rilke, Anne Morrow Lindbergh, H. L. Mencken, Etty Hillesum, Flannery O'Connor, Leslie Marmon Silko—and of letter types—anecdotal, reflective, satiric, humorous, literary. Our approach to these letters varies. Often we give groups a number of letters and ask them to select ones they want to share with the whole class. Discussion easily follows the groups' oral reading. Questions that readily open discussion include the following:

• Had you received this letter, how would you have responded?

• Have you ever gotten such a letter?

• Does it make you want to write back?

The published exchange of letters between correspondents adds the dimension of a dialogue. Reading the give and take between two minds resembles eavesdropping (which may account for the power of these collections). For instance, some of our students have been entranced by a slim volume of letters between the poets Leslie Marmon Silko and James Wright, *The Strength and Delicacy of Lace* (1986). Our students have also been intrigued with fictional letters. C. S. Lewis writes a robust batch, *The Screwtape Letters* (1959), between an older devil, Screwtape, and his apprentice nephew, a fledgling devil, Wormwood, to present a theological argument about the nature of the human struggle between good and evil.

5. **Letters to the Teacher**

The unit concludes with student letters to the teacher in which they explore their reaction to the unit.

Ancient Greece: The Dawn of a New Age
An Interdisciplinary Thematic Unit
(Grade 6)

The teacher of a self-contained sixth-grade class designed this unit around a number of disciplines—geography, science, mathematics, physical education, literature—to help the children learn about ancient Greece and to make comparisons between life today and life 2,000 years ago in Greece.

UNIT OVERVIEW

This sixth-grade ITU includes a wide variety of multisensory activities involving language arts, mathematics, science, art, drama, social studies, health, and physical education. Each lesson requires 45 to 75 minutes, with lessons 1 and 11 each requiring two consecutive days. This unit will take about three weeks. There are several extension activities in addition to the 11 detailed lesson plans.

This unit is planned for a class of 34 students but would be suitable for a class of any size. Since most classrooms contain students with diverse abilities and backgrounds, this unit is sensitive to that fact. Only minor accommodations will be necessary for children that are mainstreamed.

There are several cooperative learning group activities which assume that the students have had prior experience working effectively in cooperative groups. If children have not had prior experience in cooperative learning groups, then these lessons should be preceded by a discussion of the expected behaviors and responsibilities when working cooperatively with others. Further, it is recommended that students be in teams of four or five at the start of the unit, as this facilitates easy transition into group work and allows for a team-based behavior management system if desired.

To support this three-week theme, an arranged environment should be created in the classroom which can include posters, artifacts, Greek music, trade and resource books, and simple toga costumes that can be worn during specific activities. Bulletin boards can be created utilizing the students' myths from Lesson 4 and the vase art extension activity.

GENERAL GOALS OF THE UNIT

This unit is designed to explore

- The major changes in Greek society from 2000 B.C. to 400 B.C.
- Greek mythology.

- The effects of Greece's geography on its people and their way of life.
- How the early Olympic games differed from those held today.
- The class structure in early Athenian society.
- Greek architecture.
- Two very different city-states: Sparta and Athens.

This unit is designed to include these goals of the California History/Social Studies Framework:

- Knowledge and cultural understanding
- Democratic understanding and civic values
- Skills attainment and social participation.

UNIT ASSESSMENT

There are three components for assessment of student learning: the students' unit folders, the unit test, and anecdotal notes. Additionally, students are encouraged to assess their own performances through self-and group assessments.

LESSON 1   **Introduction to Ancient Greece**

OBJECTIVE

After reading assigned text material and utilizing resource books and posters around the room, students will create small-group presentations that will be performed for the class.

MATERIALS

Resource books, posters, artifacts, student text.

ANTICIPATORY SET

Today we are beginning an exciting unit on ancient Greece. We will participate in a wide variety of activities and will have many opportunities to work in cooperative groups on special presentations and projects. Today, we are going to form groups that will be in place for the remainder of the unit.

PROCEDURES

1. Put students in teams of four or five students per team.
2. Assign each team a topic to research from one of the following:

The Minoan Age	The First Use of Coins
The Mycenaean Age	The Final Battles
The First Olympics	The Dark Ages
The Age of Expansion	

3. Student teams create presentations that will be performed in front of the class the next day. This may be done in the form of a play, newscast, report, discussion, and so forth.
4. The following day, students present to the class.
5. After each presentation, team members will prepare an outline on the board to include who, what, when, where, and why or how.
6. The presenters will respond to questions as the class takes notes on the information presented.
7. After the presentations, the students will evaluate their own listening behavior using the assigned rubric.

CLOSURE

What is something interesting that you learned today and that you didn't know before? Did your group have any problems while researching information or putting together your presentations? (Discuss cooperation when working in groups and the importance of giving each member of the group a chance to contribute ideas.)

EVALUATION

Group presentations will be teacher evaluated as to content. Students will self-assess their listening behavior using the assigned rubric.

Timelines   LESSON 2

OBJECTIVE

After a review of the major events in early Greece and the creation of a people time line, students will draw their own time lines documenting significant events of this period.

MATERIALS

Text as a resource; white, unlined paper; rulers; masking tape time line on the classroom floor.

ANTICIPATORY SET

Yesterday, your groups presented information based on what was read about different events in early Greece. Today we are going to create a time line so that we can see the progression of events over time as they occurred in Greece.

PROCEDURES

1. Discuss the purpose of the time line, how to read it, and the meaning of B.C. and A.D.
2. Create a sample time line on the board using important personal dates offered by members of the class.
3. Point out the masking tape time line on the floor and ask each group to select one person to stand at the correct spot on the time line that represents the event it presented yesterday.
4. After students are in place, they will give a brief recap of the information they presented yesterday. Stress the very long span of time covered as compared to the history of the United States.
5. Students will create their own time lines on paper that include all of the dates represented by the students on the people time line.

The Minoan Age	The First Use of Coins
The Mycenaean Age	The Final Battles
The First Olympics	The Dark Ages
The Age of Expansion	

CLOSURE

We have been talking about events in Greece dating back to 2000 B.C.
Raise your hand if you can tell me how many years ago that was. If a time line was written the same way as the number lines we see in math, how would we write the numbers that we refer to as B.C.? (They would be negative numbers.)

EVALUATION

Observe students as they form the people time line and as they create their own time lines with the given information.

LESSON 3   Vocabulary

OBJECTIVE

After completing a vocabulary scribble, students will define and illustrate the vocabulary words.

MATERIALS

Vocabulary scribble; textbook as resource.

ANTICIPATORY SET

Early Greeks stored grain in large vases—examples of these are displayed around the room. Today you are going to color a vase based on the vocabulary from our Greece unit.

PROCEDURES

1. Describe how the students are to color the vase. (The word and its definition must be colored the same color.)
2. Students should use their texts as a resource.
3. Allow students time to complete the activity (about 15 minutes).
4. As students complete their scribble, they may begin writing definitions and creating illustrations for each word. After starting this in class under the teacher's guidance, this will be completed as homework.

ANSWERS TO VOCABULARY SCRIBBLE

barter—to exchange one product for another
tragedy—sad story of a flawed hero
monarchy—rule by a king
democracy—government by the people
comedy—funny play with a happy ending
sanctuary—a sacred place to honor gods
helot—state slave
city-state—independent self-governing units
tyrant—leader who seized power by force
oligarchy—rule by a few people
ephor—government leader

CLOSURE

Which of these words define a form of government? Which of these words are nouns that describe a person in ancient Greece? There are two words that we still use today to describe entertainment genre. Which are they?

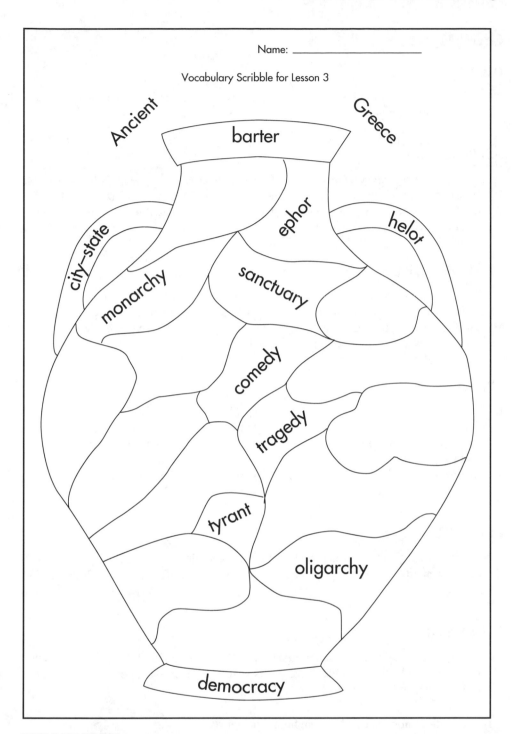

Name: _____

Vocabulary Scribble for Lesson 3

EVALUATION

The vocabulary scribble and the definitions and illustrations will be included in the student's Greece folder.

LESSON 4   Greek Myths

OBJECTIVE

After listening to/reading Greek myths and discussing what constitutes a myth, students will write their own myths.

MATERIALS

Prometheus and the Story of Fire by I. M. Richardson (New Jersey, Troll Associates, 1983), overhead transparency of "Perseus Meets the Medusa" (adapted by Lanette Whitnell from *D'Aulaires' Book of Greek Myths*); visual display that illustrates the components of a myth.

ANTICIPATORY SET

I'd like to share with you a poster that will help you remember the major components of a myth. (Present and discuss the poster depicting a large black cauldron entitled "Brew Up a Myth." On the cauldron are cards that read "Imagination," "Mystery," "Pre-Science Explanation of Nature," and "Belief in Supernatural Powers.")

PROCEDURES

1. Teacher read aloud *Prometheus and the Story of Fire.*
2. While brainstorming with students, compare/contrast myths and legends. (Teacher records student ideas on the board.) Encourage students to add to the descriptions on the myth cauldron.
3. Students participate in a choral reading of "Perseus Meets the Medusa."
4. Students write their own myths.

CLOSURE

Raise your hand if you think you can explain why the stories we heard and read today are classified as myths rather than as legends. (Students may refer to the myth poster for assistance.)

EVALUATION

After students complete their rough drafts, they will receive feedback from their peers using the Myth Checklist as a guide. Final drafts will be teacher evaluated using the established rubric, which is

The myth demonstrates a belief in higher powers (gods).	12.5 points
The myth explains something in nature.	12.5 points
Writing skill	75.0 points

Myth Checklist

1. Does this myth demonstrate a belief in higher powers (gods)?   yes   no
2. Does this myth try to explain something in nature?   yes   no
3. In this myth I like _____.
4. Suggestions: _____
_____

Author of the myth: _____
Peer reviewer: _____

Mapping   **LESSON 5**

OBJECTIVE

After creating a puzzle map of Greece and discussing how geography played an important role in the development of Greek society, students will complete information retrieval charts.

MATERIALS

One map per cooperative learning group (CLG), which is cut into the same number of pieces as there are members of the group; retrieval charts; 8.5″ × 11″ white unlined paper; glue.

ANTICIPATORY SET

Today, in your cooperative learning groups, you are going to put together puzzles of Greece. Each of you has one piece to a puzzle, and I would like you to fit your piece into the puzzle. When the puzzle is complete, glue it to the plain white paper.

PROCEDURES

1. Groups complete their puzzle.
2. In their groups, students read the section of the text that deals with the geography of Greece.
3. As a class, brainstorm how the geography affected:
   a. the development of city-states: isolated, close-knit communities due to mountains and sea.
   b. trade: by sea; must trade for goods they could not grow or make.
   c. farming: only one-fourth of the land was suitable for growing grain; grew grapes and olives.
   d. culture: trade led to extensive contact with people from other cultures, leading to the spread of products and ideas.
4. Students will complete their individual retrieval charts.

CLOSURE

Let's share some of our ideas from the retrieval charts. (Students will volunteer to share their responses.) Although the geographic terrain and climate affect a culture, it takes people working together to build a community. The people who successfully settled in the Aegean region formed tightly knit communities to build and shape their civilization.

EVALUATION

The geography retrieval chart will be added to the Greece folder. Students' responses will be evaluated during the discussion.

Ancient Greece Retrieval Chart for Lesson 5 _____

How did geography and climate influence ancient Greece in the following areas?
Farming: _____
_____

Trade: _____
_____

The development of city-states: _____
_____

Culture: _____
_____

Use this space to record any important ideas you discover during this discussion.
_____
_____

LESSON 6   **The Olympic Games**

OBJECTIVE

After comparing and contrasting the early Olympic games with the present-day games and watching a video of Olympic heroes from the past, students will brainstorm what qualities are important in an Olympic athlete.

MATERIALS

The Olympic Challenge video

ANTICIPATORY SET

Did anyone watch the Olympic games that were recently on television? Raise your hand if you can tell me something about the attitudes of the athletes you watched.

PROCEDURES

1. Discuss the early Olympic games:
   a. The purpose was to honor the gods.
   b. War ceased while games were played.
   c. Only men participated.
   d. Games were held every four years.
   e. The games began with just a 200-yard foot race and later included other races, boxing, wrestling, discus throwing, horse racing, and chariot races.
2. Compare and contrast this to the games of today.
3. Write the following question on the board, which students are to think about as they view the video:

   What personal qualities are often found in Olympic athletes?

4. View video.
5. Make a list on the board as students share the qualities that make an Olympic athlete (perseverance, talent, pride, dedication, determination, courage, endurance, fortitude to set goals and work to fulfill those goals).

CLOSURE

Many of the qualities that make a successful Olympic athlete are also the qualities of any successful person. What do you think this means? (Discuss goal setting, dreams, etc.)

EVALUATION

The quantity of student contributions and the level of student thinking can be recorded and/or evaluated during class discussions.

LESSON 7   **Discus-Throwing Records**

OBJECTIVE

After observing the teacher create a bar graph on the board while he/she thinks aloud, students will design a bar graph that graphically displays the given Olympic discus records.

MATERIALS

Graph paper, overhead transparency, Olympic records.

ANTICIPATORY SET

Let's take a vote and find out which fruit is the favorite of most class members. Raise your hand if apples are your favorite. Oranges? Bananas? (Teacher writes information on the board and then creates a bar graph to display the results, thinking aloud while creating the graph.) The neat thing about a bar graph is that we don't have to look at the actual numbers to know at a glance which fruit is the favorite. We need only to compare heights on the bar graph.

PROCEDURE

1. Students work individually to create a bar graph of the Olympic discus records.
2. Students make a prediction for the next summer Olympic games based on previous years and graph their prediction.
3. Students write a short paragraph explaining the reasons for their predictions.
4. Allow time during closure to let the students discuss if they would like to make further predictions by collecting data and making bar graphs.

CLOSURE

When we create/read bar graphs, we are more interested in making comparisons and observing for trends than in knowing the exact numbers that are graphed. How do the previous discus records help us in predicting what will happen in the next summer games in 1996? (Note: The number of years between each discus record fluctuates. So, in predicting for 1996, we should take into account that there is only a difference of 8 years from the previous entry.) What else would you like to predict on the basis of your collection of data and the creation of a bar graph?

EVALUATION

Students will include their bar graphs in their folder. They will also respond to the following open-ended question: Can these discus records continue to climb indefinitely?

Olympic Discus Records

YEAR	DISTANCE IN FEET
1896	96
1912	148
1932	162
1956	185
1972	211
1988	226
1996	?

Let the Games Begin   **LESSON 8**

OBJECTIVE

After discussing proper exercise procedures, computing target aerobic heart rates, and creating pulse rate graphs, students will monitor and record their pulse rates while participating in movement activities.

MATERIALS

16 Frisbees; straws; participation awards; graph paper; target heart rate bulletin board; watch with a second hand; blue, red, and green crayons.

ANTICIPATORY SET

When is the last time you participated in a physical activity for at least 15 minutes that made your heart beat faster and your body sweat? Today we are going to learn how to exercise safely and effectively so that we can be physically fit.

PROCEDURE

1. Brainstorm why it is important to exercise regularly.
2. Introduce the physical activity sequence: warm up, stretch, aerobic activity, and cool down.
3. Explain how maximum heart rates and target heart rates are calculated: maximum = 220 − age; target = 60%–80% of maximum rate.
4. Students calculate their target heart rates, and then teacher introduces the Target Heart Rate bulletin board.
5. Students create line graphs to record the following color-coded data:
   Resting pulse rate in blue.
   Aerobic pulse rate in red.
   Recovery pulse rate in green.
6. Teach students proper procedure for taking and recording a ten-second pulse and record resting pulse rates.
7. Students participate in the following activities:
   warm up: fast walk around $\frac{1}{10}$-of-a-mile course
   stretch: stretch legs, arms, back
   aerobic activity: modified kickball, in which one entire team runs the bases while the outfield passes the ball and runs to form a circle at a designated place.
8. During activity, students take their aerobic pulse rates.

Bulletin Board Display for Lesson 8

Age

Target Heart Rate

	5	6	7	8	9	10	11	12
90%	194							
		193						
80%	172		192					
		171		191				
60%	129		170		190			
		128		170		189		
50%	108		128		169		188	
		107		127		168		187
40%	86		107		127		167	
		86		106		126		166
			85		106		125	
				85		105		125

Slow Down

Right
On
Target!

Work Harder

9. After a cool-down walk of several minutes, students take their recovery pulse rates.
10. Both pulse rates are recorded on students' graphs.
11. Students participate in a fun Olympic activity as a tie-in to the ancient Greece unit:
    Javelin throw using straws
    Discuss throw using Frisbees

CLOSURE

Raise your hand if you can tell me the proper physical activity sequence. Why is it important to warm up and stretch before an aerobic activity? Who can explain how we calculate our target heart rates? We will be keeping track of our pulse rates for the rest of this month as we participate in physical education activities. As you begin to exercise regularly, you will find that your resting pulse rate will become lower and your recovery rate will be quicker.

EVALUATION

Pulse rate graphs will be added to the ancient Greece folder. Students will be encouraged to monitor their own improvement. Only those students who participate in the movement activities will receive an award for participation, which is also worth points at the end of the unit.

Pulse Rate Graph Sample for Lesson 8

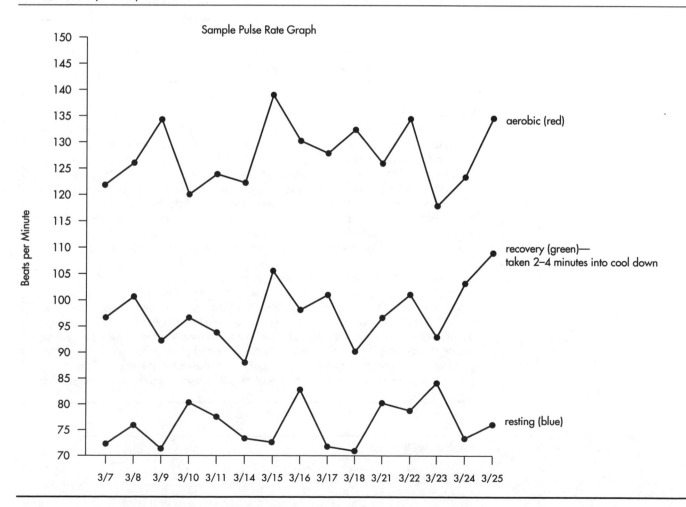

Sample Participation Award for Lesson 8

ANCIENT GREECE
GAMES DAY

PARTICIPATION AWARD

PRESENTED TO

_____

Simulated Role Play for Lesson 9

Set up: Place eight chairs in the front of the room for the key characters in this simulated town meeting: 5 citizens, 1 metic, 1 wife of citizen, and 1 slave. Arrange the other chairs in rows for those members of the town not allowed to speak in the meeting. The other three metics should sit closest to the key characters in case they wish to speak.

   Scenario: While at the busy town center where metics were selling their wares earlier in the day, turmoil erupted. A slave, who was accompanying the family members of a citizen, was accused of stealing food from one of the metics. No one actually saw this happen except the metic, who is accusing the slave of stealing, and the wife of the slave owner, who claims it was not the slave but another thief who is at fault. Since slaves have no legal rights and are not citizens, a crime such as stealing can result in severe fines for the slave owner and possible banishment or even death for the accused slave.

   The slave owner is called to a town meeting accompanied by the rest of his family. All other citizens and people of the town are present at this meeting and are listening to arguments from the metic's point of view and from the slave owner's point of view. The slave owner's wife quietly supplies her husband with information but is not allowed to speak to the assembly. The accused slave is not allowed to speak. The slave owner, since he is a citizen, is the only one who can speak on behalf of the slave. The metics may speak, but they cannot vote as to the guilt or innocence of the accused slave.

   After all arguments have been heard, the citizens take a vote and determine the verdict.

LESSON 9   **Greek Society**

OBJECTIVE

After discussing the four classes in Athenian society, students will participate in a simulation of a town meeting and will complete their retrieval charts.

Information Retrieval Chart for Lesson 9

Greek Society

LEVEL	DESCRIPTION	RIGHTS	RESPONSIBILITIES
Citizens			
Family of Citizens			
Metics			
Slaves			

Compare democracy in the United States today with the democracy of ancient Greek society. List the similarities and differences.

SIMILARITIES	DIFFERENCES

MATERIALS

Retrieval charts; simulated role-play description sheet; game cards: Citizen, Family of Citizen, Metic, Slave; identification necklaces for children, accused slave, accusing metic, and wife of citizen.

ANTICIPATORY SET

As students enter the room, hand each student a game card that identifies his or her role in the role-play simulation. Explain briefly that they will be participating in a simulation and that they are to stay in character until the town meeting is finished. (Note: for a class of 34, cards should be divided proportionately as follows: 15% citizens = 5; 48% family of citizens = 16; 12% metics = 4; and 25% slaves = 8.)

PROCEDURES

1. Arrange the classroom for the town meeting scene.
2. Discuss the four levels of ancient Greek society:

    Citizens: Men over 18 may vote, hold office, speak at town meetings, own slaves, and are protected by laws.

    Family of citizens: Wives and children, who may not vote or speak at town meetings and have no rights, privileges, or protection under law.

    Metics: Foreigners, tradesmen, shopkeepers, and craftsmen. They may not vote or hold office, but they may speak at town meetings and are protected under law.

    Slaves: Whether POWs or sold through the slave trade, slaves may not vote or hold office. They have no protection under the law, no job choice, and may have a family only with their master's permission.
3. Read the scenario from the simulated role-play sheet.
4. Reiterate the roles and powers.
5. Students hold the town meeting.
6. Students form groups of three or four and complete the information retrieval chart.

CLOSURE

Ask students to differentiate between the roles of citizens, family of citizens, metics, and slaves. Ask them which they would prefer to be. Compare and contrast democracy today with that of ancient Greece.

EVALUATION

The retrieval chart is a required element for the student folder. Students will also be assessed according to participation in the simulation.

LESSON 10   ## Column Experiment

OBJECTIVE

After discussing early Greek architecture and the scientific method, students will experiment to find which of the given column designs will support the most weight.

MATERIALS

Data collection form; 9 × 12-inch construction paper; tape; rulers; supplemental teaching information form; pictures illustrating the three architectural styles.

ANTICIPATORY SET

Let's take a minute to look around the room at the pictures of early Greece which show us examples of their architecture. Raise your hand if you think you can tell me something about how the early Greeks built structures.

PROCEDURES

1. Encourage students to share what they already know or think they know about architectural design.
2. Using the supplemental teaching information as a resource, discuss the three orders of Greek architecture: Doric, Ionic, and Corinthian. Show examples of each.
3. Discuss the steps of the so-called scientific method and why we should think of it as a cyclic rather than linear process. (As new data come in, an earlier conclusion may be thrown out, and the process repeats all over again.)

Paper Column Experiment for Lesson 10

Focus question: Will a single sheet of paper support a heavy book? Try this experiment to find out.

Purpose: What do I want to find out?

Which of the tested columns will support the most weight?

Hypothesis: What do I think?

Experiment:

1. Roll a 9 × 12 piece of construction paper so that it is 9 inches long and has a diameter of 1 inch.
2. Stand the paper on end to form a 9-inch-high column.
3. Add math books to the column until the column collapses.
4. Repeat with the following column specifications: 9 inches long with a 2-inch diameter; 6 inches long (folded in half) with a 1-inch diameter; and 6 inches long with a 2-inch diameter.

Analysis: Collect and interpret data

Relative Strengths of Various Columns

NUMBER OF MATH BOOKS			
12			
11			
10			
9			
8			
7			
6			
5			
4			
3			
2			
1			
0			
Column	9 × 1	9 × 2	6 × 1 (doubled)	6 × 2 (doubled)

Conclusions: What did I learn?
What questions do I now have? (This will lead to a new purpose, perhaps a new experiment.) _____

_____

4. Describe the experiment they will conduct and clarify any questions they may have about it.
5. Put students in their CLGs and assign the following roles: recorder, runner, gatekeeper, thinker.
6. Allow students enough time to conduct their testing and to record their results.

CLOSURE

Ask groups to share their results and write them on the board. Discuss the need to make multiple trial tests when conducting an experiment. Have students calculate the average result for each tested column using the data collected from the board.

EVALUATION

Each student will include the completed experiment form in his or her ancient Greece folder. Each student's level of understanding can be assessed by reviewing the student's conclusions and by further questioning.

Supplemental Teaching Information Sheet for Lesson 10: Classical Greek Architecture

(adapted from *The Book of Buildings: A Traveler's Guide*, by Richard Reid (Michael Joseph Limited, 1980)

General Information: The earliest buildings of Greece were of sun-dried bricks, timber, and decorative terra-cotta. Later, stone and marble became the chief materials. Mortar was rarely used, the finely cut blocks being held by metal dowels and clamps. Although the Greek architects were aware of the arch and vault, their approach was relatively conservative. The megaron, with its portico entrance and low-pitched roof, was the model for Greek temples. The earliest temples were timber, their forms later translated into mud/brick, and finally stone. The two basic elements of timber structures, vertical supports (columns) and horizontal members (entablatures), were transformed into the three carefully proportioned orders, or styles, of Greek architecture: the Doric, Ionic, and Corinthian.

The Doric: The earliest and simplest of the classical orders. The fluted columns stand firmly on their platform without intermediate bases. The abacus is deep and plain.

The Ionic: This elegant order is recognized by the capital of spiral-shaped scrolls called volutes.

The Corinthian: The last and most elaborate order. The tall, fluted column was capped by an elaborate stylized carving of acanthus plants. The decorative character of this order made it popular with the Romans.

Doric   Ionic   Corinthian

LESSON 11   Sparta/Athens

OBJECTIVE

After discussing selected terms, students will research an assigned topic and report on it to the class.

MATERIALS

Text, resources already available in classroom.

ANTICIPATORY SET

When we discussed the geography of Greece we talked about the development of city-states. What is a city-state? Are there any in existence today? (Yes, Singapore.)

PROCEDURES

1. Discuss these terms: government, economy, life-style, monarchy, oligarchy, and democracy.
2. Have students count off by four, creating eight random groups of four each.
3. Assign the following topics, one to each of the eight groups.

Government/Athens	Government/Sparta
Education/Athens	Education/Sparta
Economy/Athens	Economy/Sparta
Life-style/Athens	Life-style/Sparta

4. Student teams research their topics, focusing on comparing and contrasting Athens and Sparta.
5. Groups present their information to the class and create an outline on the board.
6. Students ask questions of the presenters and take notes on the information given.
7. As Extension Activity #1, students can create murals based on their research on their topic.

CLOSURE

What were some ways that Sparta and Athens differed? How might we account for these differences? Where would you rather live, Sparta or Athens?

EVALUATION

Students will be completing self- and group assessments on their presentations. Teacher will evaluate the presentations with respect to content accuracy and completeness.

EXTENSION ACTIVITY #2

Students can hold a debate based on the final question: Where would you rather live, Athens or Sparta?